Margaret Mitchell & John Marsh
The
Love Story Behind
GONE WITH THE WIND

Margaret Mitchell & John Marsh

The Love Story Behind
GONE WITH THE WIND

Marianne Walker

PEACHTREE PUBLISHERS, LTD.
Atlanta

ℚ

Published by
PEACHTREE PUBLISHERS, LTD.
494 Armour Circle, NE
Atlanta, Georgia 30324

Manufactured in the United States of America.

First paperback edition, 1995

10 9 8 7 6 5 4 3 2 1

Cover and book design by Candace Magee
Composition by Ann Walker Pruitt

Library of Congress Cataloging-in-Publication Data

Walker, Marianne, 1933—
            Margaret Mitchell & John Marsh : the love story behind
Gone with the wind / Marianne Walker.
                    p.   cm.
            Includes bibliographical reference and index.
            ISBN 1-56145-082-0 Hardcover
            ISBN 1-56145-104-5 Paperback
                    1. Mitchell, Margaret, 1900-1949—Marriage.
2. Mitchell, Margaret, 1900-1949—Correspondence. 3. Marsh,
John R. (John Robert), 1895-1952—Marriage. 4. Marsh, John R. (John
Robert), 1895-1952—Correspondence. 5. Women novelists, American—
20th century—Correspondence. 6. Women novelists, American—20th
century—Biography. 7. Authorship—Collaboration—History—20th
century. 8. Love-letters. I. Title. II. Title: Margaret Mitchell and
John Marsh.
PS3525.I972Z94   1993
813'.52—dc20
[B]

93-26481
CIP

For the man in my life,
Ulvester Walker

And in loving memory of my parents,
Joseph D. and Rose Spatafora Cascio

Contents

Preface

Although I did not realize it at the time, the genesis of this book occurred in early 1985 when I reluctantly agreed to give a talk about *Gone With the Wind* for a Kentucky Humanities Council program. Like millions of others, I had seen the film made from the novel but had never read the novel itself or anything about its author.

When I got a copy of the book to read, the first thing I noticed was that the dedication page simply says, "To J.R.M." I remember wondering then, "Who is J.R.M. ?" A few days later I learned that Margaret Mitchell dedicated her novel to her husband, John Robert Marsh, who was born and reared in Maysville, Kentucky. Since Maysville is not too far from where I live, I decided to go looking for traces of him and his famous wife.

After needling my husband into going along with me, I set out with him early one chilly Saturday morning in October 1985 on what he called "an authentic wild goose chase." A sports addict who would have preferred to watch a televised ball game, he told me outright that he thought the expedition would be a waste of time and that I would ultimately be disappointed. And as the day worn on, it looked as if his predictions were correct. Our search first led us to Maysville, then back down to the Blue Grass region around Lexington, and then, finally, with some instructions from a rural postal clerk, to a remote community called Clays Ferry. Much to our surprise, we ended up that afternoon in a three-room log cabin built on a woodsy, steep bank near the Kentucky River. This cabin was the home of Francesca Renick Marsh, the widow of John Marsh's youngest brother, Ben Gordon Marsh. An avid bird watcher and watercolorist who had been an art teacher at the Sayre School on North Limestone Street in Lexington, Francesca belied her eighty-three years. She drove her red Chevrolet sedan wherever she wanted to go; attended church every Sunday; read several books every week; hiked daily in the woods; and swam in the Kentucky River two miles a day, eight months out of the year, right up to a few months before her death in 1987. Self-reliant, she lived alone in this charming cabin she and her husband had bought in 1952, only two years before he died.

In looking back, I know now that we were lucky on two accounts that day: first, because I appeared on her doorstep as a teacher preparing to make a talk about her sister-in-law's novel, not as a writer seeking information for a book; and second, because her son, Renny, a geologist from Texas, was visiting her. As I learned later, Francesca had been so disappointed with the manner in which her famous relatives had been characterized in print that she adamantly refused to have anything to do with writers. Then, too, her home had been burglarized earlier that year, and she had adopted a guarded manner toward strangers. Had Renny not been there, I doubt if she would have let us in that day. But apparently she was satisfied with my reasons for presenting myself to her, and she invited us into her parlor filled with lovely old furniture, paintings, family mementos, and books—many of them foreign editions of *Gone With the Wind*. The moment I stepped into that room, I knew I was onto an adventure. And I was right.

It was inevitable that Francesca Marsh and I became friends. Like Margaret Mitchell, I have always enjoyed listening to old people, hearing about the past and the lives of others. Biography is my favorite type of book. So my interest in her and in the author of *Gone With the Wind* did not end a few days later with my lecture at the public library, and I visited her as often as I could.

As I look back now, I realize how favored I have been to have known Francesca, for she, and the others I met through my friendship with her, gave me an authentic, not merely a nostalgic, connection with the past. I learned about John Marsh and Margaret Mitchell, who was called Peggy, just the way one gradually learns about her ancestors—from listening to relatives and friends talk about them. Hearing Francesca and the others talk about people and days long "gone with the wind" intrigued me in a way that nothing else ever had and made me want to know more.

However, the idea of writing this book did not occur to me until the rainy, winter afternoon in 1985 when Francesca dragged out an old cardboard box filled with stuff that she had been saving for over a half-century. I will never forget the excitement I felt when I saw that old box filled with yellowed, fragile newspaper clippings, snapshots, postcards, telegrams, old *Atlanta Magazines,* and a small, tied bundle of unpublished letters that John and Peggy had written to his family. These letters are a part of the Round Robins that circulated for nearly twenty-five years among John and Peggy, his two brothers and two sisters, and their spouses. Aside from those letters, the first thing that caught my attention was a picture of John in an *Atlanta Sunday Magazine* interview dated December 1949, only four months after Peggy's unexpected death. His answer to the question, "How would you describe your wife?" startled me.

> "Well," he began, "first of all, she was a lot of fun. . . ." He spread his hands helplessly. "How can you sum up a personality like her in a few words? My starting point is she was a lot of fun. Maybe someday I can succeed in putting the rest into words. But not now."

Because it is so unusual for anyone to describe an individual with whom he has lived for nearly a quarter-century as being "a lot of fun," I immediately thought that their relationship must have been a very special one. But neither of the two Mitchell biographies available at that time had given me that impression.[1]

That evening at Francesca's, I sat for hours on the floor near the fireplace going through the materials in that box, reading those letters aloud, and listening to Francesca flesh out accounts of events that were mentioned in the letters. When she began to describe her first visit, as a shy young bride, with the Atlanta Marshes, newlyweds themselves in 1927, I felt as if I had actually been transported to the Marshes' Crescent Avenue apartment. She had a clear memory of events that had occurred over fifty years earlier, and as she spoke John and Peggy came alive for me. The kind of exceptionally personal detail and first-hand knowledge I was getting from the letters and from Francesca indicated that the Marshes had a remarkable and unique relationship. By the time I rose to leave that evening, I had gained a much clearer understanding of this man who, mysteriously enough, has been largely ignored or inaccurately portrayed, and yet played such a vital role in Mitchell's life and work. I knew that the full story of Margaret Mitchell had not yet been told. As my husband and I drove home that night, I was fascinated with what I had discovered and frustrated by what I did not know.

On my next visit, I asked Francesca if there were other family members who had letters and recollections that they would share. With a resounding "Yes," she introduced us, through letters and long-distance calls, to Rollin Zane, the widower of Frances Marsh Zane (John's youngest sister) and to his son Craig Zane. More important, she also introduced us to Mary Marsh Davis and her husband Edmund, nicknamed Jim.

The Davises, gracious and friendly, opened their home to my husband and me in 1987, and I am eternally grateful to them. Mary Davis is the daughter of Henry Marsh, John's oldest brother. After her parents divorced in 1919 when she was only three years old, her father's mother gave up her position as the principal of a grammar school in Maysville, Kentucky, sold her home, and moved into Henry's home in Wilmington, Delaware, where she looked after Mary until Henry remarried in 1927. Thus, Mary was reared primarily by her grandmother Mary Marsh, after whom she was named. While she was growing up, she and her grandmother visited her uncle John and aunt Peggy in Atlanta, and she also saw them on the many occasions when John and Peggy attended Marsh family reunions and when they visited her father and grandmother in Wilmington, Delaware.

After Mary and Jim married, in their teens, the two of them continued to exchange visits with the Atlanta Marshes throughout the years. As a result of this close association, the Davises were able to give me information and valuable insight into the Atlanta Marshes' personalities. In his modest but firm manner, Jim quickly shattered many popular misconceptions about the Marshes.[2] He also gave me a copy of the extensive Marsh genealogy that took him years to research and complete.

Most important of all, Mary Davis gave me access to 184 personal letters. This collection includes 43 letters Peggy wrote to Mary, her grandmother, and her father; and 141 letters John wrote to his mother, Henry, and Jim Davis. Not one of Peggy's 43 letters has been published before, and only portions of two of John's 141 have been published previously. This treasure, which spans over thirty years, had never been shown to anyone else outside the family.[3] It was a thrilling experience for me to read these letters for the first time. What I found so compelling was those first-person voices emanating from the letters, voices that give John Marsh and Margaret Mitchell a real presence, a physical reality, a flesh-and-blood humanness.

Because of their mother-daughter-like relationship, her grandmother gave her letters from John and Peggy to Mary. Because of her closeness to John and Peggy, her father also gave Mary some of his letters. Peggy's letters to Mary's father are most revealing because Henry and Peggy were close and, too, she felt she could trust him. These letters were written long before she became famous, and thus long before either she or John had become inhibited in their correspondence. They provide fascinating insight into the Marshes' relationship, the times in which they lived, and the passion Mitchell inspired.

The information I gained from all these letters and from members of the Marsh family allowed me to look closer at Margaret Mitchell and John Marsh than any other writer has ever been able to look, and what I saw confirmed my initial impression that the true story of this marriage had not yet been told. By the time we left the Davises, I could clearly see that John Marsh had not only been an exceptionally devoted husband but had also played a vital role in the making of his wife's great novel. The evidence I was accumulating demonstrated that John Marsh had not only nurtured Margaret Mitchell's imagination by providing a constant environment of creative stimulus, but he had also given her precisely the kind of help she needed to do what she had always wanted to do—write a blockbuster of a book. Not just an extraordinarily supportive husband, he was an editor who lovingly provided the kind of editorial expertise Mitchell needed throughout the entire time she worked on the novel. An excellent writer and editor, John offered her ideas and advice, and at night and on weekends he patiently read and edited every line of her manuscript as she produced it. As John himself explained in his December 18, 1949, interview with Medora Field Perkerson for the *Atlanta Magazine:*

> I started reading right from the time she started writing and we would talk about it. As you know, talking things over sometimes

makes an idea come clearer. In trying to write it out beforehand, the mechanical labor may get between the writer and the idea. I was always more confident than she was that she could write a good book. She didn't have enough confidence in her own ability.

In the ordinary sequence of publishing, an editor comes on board after a manuscript has been completed and helps improve the finished product; editors are not involved in the creative process, are not around when the writer sits staring at that blank page. Thus, Margaret Mitchell enjoyed a unique advantage—she was married to her editor, who also adored her. With this new understanding of the Marshes' relationship, I felt obliged to write this book.

From the Davises' home we went to Washington, D.C., to visit Craig Zane and his father Rollin Zane, the widower of John's youngest sister. Rollin Zane permitted me to use his wife's collection of forty-six letters; of these, Peggy wrote twenty-nine, and John wrote seventeen.[4] We then drove from Washington, D.C., to Atlanta, where we met our next major source of information—Joe Kling. An Atlantan, Joe worked as a reporter with Peggy and John at the *Journal* from 1925 to 1926. Although he was a few years younger than they, he socialized with them and their newspaper crowd. After John left journalism and went to work in the public relations department at the Georgia Power Company in 1926, Joe Kling followed him there in 1928. The two men worked side by side from 1928 to 1945, and when John retired in 1945 after having a major heart attack, Joe took his place as the chief of the public relations department.

A few years after the death in 1938 of his first wife, Evelyn Lovett, Joe married Rhoda Williams, who was John's personal secretary for many years, including those critical years before, during, and just after the publication of *Gone With the Wind*. Rhoda helped John prepare the *Gone With the Wind* manuscript and proof sheets for Macmillan, and she typed numerous letters that John wrote in the process of managing the book's business. No one—except Peggy, her father, and her brother, Stephens— was closer to John or knew more about his private business than Rhoda Kling. Joe and Rhoda talked to John almost daily for over twenty years, and they associated with him and Peggy on a very personal level as well as on a professional one. They all remained friends until death separated them. A quiet-spoken, learned man, Joe showed infinite patience in answering all of my many questions and in helping me clarify my perceptions. He was an invaluable source of information.

Our next trip took us to the far northeast mountainous corner of Georgia, to Dillard, where we talked with Mary Singleton, the first female editor of Georgia Power's magazine. John appointed her editor at a time when it was unheard of to place women in such executive positions, and she worked with him for many years. Like the Klings, Mary Singleton associated with John and Peggy socially as well as professionally. They were all friends who had much in common. After Peggy's death, John often went out to dinner and to the opera with Mary and Susan Myrick, another old friend who had served as an arbiter of southern manners and speech for the *Gone With the Wind* film.

An excellent writer herself, Mary had a remarkable memory for the kinds of details biographers need and love to hear. Fascinating to listen to, she recalled some of her conversations not only with John and Peggy but also with her coworkers Rhoda Kling and Grace Alderman, another Georgia Power employee who typed almost all of Peggy's manuscript to send to Macmillan. As a result, Mary was able to recreate for me some memorable scenes from those harried *Gone With the Wind* years, and she also gave me first-hand information about the premiere, John's major heart attack, and Peggy's fatal accident and funeral. She contributed significantly to my understanding of the Marshes' relationship as she talked about the intensity of the love John had for Peggy; the sympathetic understanding he had for women's issues; the exactness he as an editor demanded from himself and from others; and the dedication he had to upholding moral principles without ever appearing self-righteous.

On another trip to Atlanta in the late summer of 1987, I talked with Deon Rutledge, a pleasant, attractive woman who worked along with her mother cooking and cleaning for the Marshes. Her mother, Bessie Berry Jordan, started working for the Marshes shortly after their marriage, and because she was their full-time housekeeper and cook for years, her daughter Deon practically grew up in the Marshes' apartment.

As Deon and I sat in the lobby of a downtown Atlanta hotel, I was impressed by her modesty and affection for both Marshes. She showed me the big brown scrapbook on *Gone With the Wind* that her mother had started over fifty years ago and kept adding to until her death. With great pride, she pointed out the *Sunday Magazine* article that her mother had written as a tribute to Peggy shortly after Peggy's death. As Deon fondly turned the pages of the scrapbook and reminisced, she thrilled me with some glimpses of the past and made me feel as if I were actually back there in the Marshes' apartment. When she came to a picture of John, whom she obviously respected and loved, she laughingly told me how frightened of him she was at first because, she said, "He was so tall and big and had such a deep, low voice." Shaking her head, she exclaimed, "He was so different from Miss Peggy." When we both suddenly realized how late in the afternoon it was, we laughed about how quickly our time together had flown by. Just as she rose to leave and was gathering her things, she looked at me and said matter-of-factly, "Folks don't know it, but he helped her write that book!"

Over the following years, I talked to a number of other people who gave me insight into the Mitchell-Marsh relationship and the times in which the Marshes lived. These included Sam Tupper, the Marshes' neighbor and friend; Richard Harwell, the University of Georgia archivist who was the first to work with the collection of Mitchell-Marsh letters that Stephens Mitchell donated to the University of Georgia Library in the late 1960s; and Franklin Garrett, Atlanta's foremost historian.

Like Margaret Mitchell, I have a special affection for librarians and a reverence for libraries. Five major archives opened their doors to me and gave me access to letters and information. For three summers, my husband and I made trips to the University of Georgia in Athens, where he and I spent all day every day for weeks examining the Margaret Mitchell Marsh Papers, well over fifty-seven thousand items, as well as numerous papers in the other related files. In addition, we researched all the Mitchell papers and interrelated files in the Atlanta History Center Library Archives. I found information about John's college and journalistic careers in the Margaret I. King Special Collections Library at the University of Kentucky, where John earned his bachelor's degree in 1916, and we visited Maysville, Kentucky, where the Mason County Museum provided information about the town as it was when John grew up there. While in Maysville, we talked to Martha Comer, a local newspaperwoman, who told us about her interview with Peggy at Traxel's Confectionery in November 1940, when John brought his wife to Kentucky for the first time. From the Robert W. Woodruff Library at Emory University, I obtained copies of fourteen letters that Peggy wrote to Harvey Smith from 1927 to 1944. I spent most of one summer reading over twelve thousand frames of microfilm from the *Gone With the Wind*—Margaret Mitchell—Macmillan File at the New York Public Library.

By 1991, I had finished all of my research and completed my manuscript, which I was in the process of revising and editing, when Oxford University Press published Darden Asbury Pyron's *Southern Daughter*. This Mitchell biography contains far more information than its two predecessors do, and I read it with great interest. However, my sources had given me a new and different view of John Marsh and his role in his wife's life and career, a fresh understanding of the Marshes' relationship and of them as individuals. My exclusive access to the Davises' letters and my long talks with the most reliable witnesses—the family, the close friends, and the coworkers who knew the Marshes well throughout their marriage— enable me to provide new and important insight into a marriage that has never before been accurately described.

Thus, in writing this book, my first objective is to focus on Mitchell's private life in order to provide the reader with new information. In doing so, I want to make Margaret Mitchell and John Marsh come alive. Both were complicated, talented, warm-blooded human beings who had strengths and weaknesses like all of the rest of us, but who experienced a rare relationship full of astonishing success and heart-wrenching tragedy. In a world where ephemeral or traitorous relationships abound, a long union filled with loyalty, love, trust, and humor deserves a comprehensive reexamination.

My second objective is to show that John Marsh's deep attachment to Margaret Mitchell was pivotal to her work and to her life. Without a doubt, she had all the fiery imagination, all the hardy attachment to her environment, and all the raw material that a writer needs to create an epic like hers. But she did not have the technical skills, the self-discipline, or the confidence to transform her ideas into a completed manuscript of the quality of *Gone With the Wind;* her deep-seated insecurities hampered her in many ways. With his intellectual depth, maturity, education, and writing ability, John provided whatever she lacked. Her dedication of *Gone With the Wind* "To J.R.M." is only a hint of the significance of their relationship and the influence it had on the origin and fruition of her great Civil War novel.

I have tried to be as objective as possible, not glossing over her weaknesses or overemphasizing her strengths—or his either, for that matter. The conversations I quote are not fictionalized, but are transcribed as they were related to me by the participants.

Emerging now from my long study, I must confess that I feel conflicting emotions. I am happy to complete my work on this book but am also a little sad to part from my subjects, for I agree with John Marsh: Margaret Mitchell was a lot of fun for me, too. But then, so was he.

Notes about the Letters

In typing her letters, Margaret Mitchell, a poor typist, rarely hit the apostrophe key; she generally either omitted the apostrophe or hit the "8" key instead. For the sake of clarity, I have replaced "8's" with apostrophes. I have also added some punctuation. Otherwise, I have not edited any of these original letters. The letters reproduced here are, with the aforementioned exceptions, as they appear in the original sources. In a few instances where quoting an oddity in the original letters appears to be an overlooked printer's mistake, I have used "[sic]" to make clear to the reader that the mistake is in the original material. Some of these letters were typed; others, handwritten. Some had envelopes, others did not.

Before she became famous, Mitchell rarely dated her letters to the family; she usually scribbled only something like "Sunday afternoon" or "Monday night." Because she wrote many of her early letters while she was at work at the *Sunday Magazine* from 1922 to 1926, but did not want her editor to know that she was using his time for her personal business, most of these letters do not bear the name of the recipient or the date; they have only "slug heads," newspaper jargon for instructions temporarily inserted at the top of copy. I have been able to assign dates to these letters, sometimes a day, month, and year, sometimes only a season and a year.

I have gathered a total of 230 personal letters that John and Peggy Marsh wrote to members of the Marsh family. I have quoted major portions of 80 of the 184 letters from the Davises' collection, and have used information from the remaining 104. I have also quoted several passages that have never been quoted before from Margaret Mitchell's 46 letters to Frances Marsh Zane. In addition, I used information from two of John Marsh's unpublished handwritten letters that Joe Kling gave me.

All other letters quoted here are originals or carbon copies of originals housed in the Margaret Mitchell Papers in the University of Georgia's Hargrett Rare Book and Manuscript Library; in the New York Public Library's Rare Books and Manuscripts Division; in the Robert W. Woodruff Library at Emory University; and in the Atlanta History Center Library Archives.

Some information and a few of the quotations are from letters to which I had no access to the original. These are from Finis Farr's *Margaret Mitchell of Atlanta* (Morrow, 1965), the first Margaret Mitchell biography, which was authorized by Stephens Mitchell; and Jane Bonner Peacock's *Margaret Mitchell—A Dynamo Going to Waste: Letters to Allen Edee 1919-1921* (Peachtree Publishers, 1985), a valuable collection of twenty letters Mitchell wrote to a beau from 1919 to 1921. Mrs. Peacock edited these letters and researched this period of Mitchell's life. Also extremely useful were Richard Harwell's *"Gone With the Wind" as Book and Film;* Richard Harwell's *White Columns in Hollywood: Reports from the GWTW Set by Susan Myrick;* and E.I. (Buddy) Thompson's *Madame Belle Brezing.*

Acknowledgments

In writing this book, I consider myself blessed with the privilege of drawing from primary material unavailable to others, and for that privilege I am indebted to the Marsh family, particularly to Francesca Marsh and her son Renick Marsh; Mary Marsh Davis and her husband Edmund "Jim" Davis; and Rollin Zane and his son Craig Zane. I am equally grateful to Joseph and Eugene Mitchell, the Mitchell heirs, and the Trust Company Bank as Executor and Trustee Under Trusts created by Stephens Mitchell, who gave me permission to quote from the Mitchell letters. I thank Paul Anderson, the Mitchells' attorney, who has been most helpful and kind. I also thank the Macmillan Company for allowing me to quote and use information from the *Gone With the Wind* Macmillan file.

My warm thanks go to Joe Kling, who was a valuable source of information. Through the long process of my writing this book, my husband and I have grown close to Joe, and we value his friendship and his patience with my endless questions. My special appreciation goes to Deon Rutledge and Mary Singleton, who also furnished important information.

I have been fortunate in other ways, for the University of Kentucky Community College System granted me a sabbatical leave from Henderson Community College for the academic year 1988-89, enabling me to devote myself full-time to research and writing. During the course of that year, my husband and I traveled several thousand miles collecting material.

Librarians have been most helpful to me. Laura O'Keefe, Melanie Yolles, and Francesca Pitaro at the New York Public Library's Rare Books and Manuscripts Division responded quickly and pleasantly to my urgent requests. Others just as courteous and efficient were Thomas Camden and Mary Ellen Brooks and their staff at the University of Georgia's Hargrett Library; Anne Salter at the Atlanta History Center; Beverly Allen and Linda Matthews at the Emory University Robert W. Woodruff Rare Book and Manuscript Library; Dr. Frank Stanger and B. J. Gooch at the University of Kentucky Margaret I. King Library Division of Special Collections and Archives; Pearl Allen Posey, Donald Wathen, and the staff at the Henderson County Public Library; and Mike Walters and the staff at Henderson Community College Library.

Others who have helped me are Mary Rose Taylor and Thomas Weesner, who gave me information about the Marshes' residences and other places in Atlanta; Dr. Virginia Grabil, professor emeritus of English at the University of Evansville, who read portions of my manuscript in 1991; and Dr. Marshall Arnold, who secured for me a copy of John Marsh's academic transcript from the University of Kentucky and information about the university as it was when John was there.

For their help in gathering photographs, I would like to thank especially Ted Ryan of the Atlanta History Center, Janice Sikes of the Atlanta-Fulton Public Library, and Peter Roberts of Georgia State University's Pullen Library.

The contribution made by Betty Koerber, my friend and my husband's secretary, is immeasurable. Supportive and encouraging, Betty organized and reorganized my hefty collection of letters and notes into folders, worked on the genealogy charts, typed the endnotes in proper form, and printed my numerous revisions of the manuscript—more revisions, in fact, than I care to admit.

My wholehearted appreciation goes to Julie Bookman for her initial and continued enthusiasm for this biography and for all her hard work; and to Margaret Quinlin and her staff at Peachtree, especially Jennifer Knight, Candy Magee, Jill Lambert, Kathy Landwehr, Laurie Warlick, Ann Pruitt, and Jill Conversano.

For Emily Wright, my editor and mainstay throughout, I have great appreciation, respect, and admiration. Emily is an expert editor, and her intelligent advice helped me to improve many oversized chapters.

Deserving to be mentioned here too are my children—Chris, Beth, Trish, Amy, and my son-in-law, Scott—who helped in various ways. And my special love goes to little William and Elizabeth for their patience with their grandmother while she did her "scribbling."

And, finally, my greatest gratitude is for my husband, to whom this book is dedicated. He helped me every step of the way.

A MAN OF CHARACTER

All my life I have been beset with Mitchells. My college sweetheart was named Mitchell; my new sweetheart, wife and eventually my widow is named Mitchell; my washerwoman for the past twenty-five years, who regards us as her children and during the period of the war scarcities, gives us presents of kleenex and other rare items, is a Mitchell; the company where I work has at least a dozen Mitchells in prominent positions; the firm of accountants who handle Peggy's bookkeeping is Peat, Marwick, Mitchell and Co., and the man in their organization who works on her books is a Mitchell, but not related to their Peat, Marwick, Mitchell. And now my new boss is a Mitchell who was born in Maine almost on the Canadian line, moved to South America in his young manhood, but was inevitably and unerringly drawn to Atlanta by the destiny which surrounds me with Mitchells. I might add that most of them are pretty fine folks. I'm just curious as to why I should collide with them at every turn of my life.

—John Marsh to his mother, spring 1945

1

IN ATLANTA'S OLD OAKLAND CEMETERY, after the funeral service for Margaret Mitchell on August 18, 1949, family members urged her husband to go home and rest. But John Marsh, frail from a major heart attack three years earlier, insisted on staying until his wife's body had been lowered into its final resting place. Calm but pale, he sat leaning forward, head bowed, arms outstretched with his elbows resting on his knees. His fingers restlessly reached out and tapped the support of the canopy over the grave as he stared at the freshly dug mound of red Georgia clay. In a low voice full of emotional resonance, he said to a friend: "When you think of all the serious illnesses I have survived, I guess you can say there's a reason I outlived her. So I could do a few things for her."[1]

Those last few things John Marsh did for Margaret Mitchell were a measure of his dedication to her. Performing what he knew to be her wishes, he burned nearly all of the original manuscript of *Gone With the Wind* along with its corrected proofs and related papers.[2] In the backyard of the Marshes' apartment, at the corner of South Prado and Piedmont avenues in Atlanta, he set the priceless pages afire in a tall wire basket, the one the janitor used for burning leaves.[3] Except for Bessie Jordan, who had been the Marshes' faithful housekeeper since they were newlyweds, and Eugene Carr, the janitor, who stood back and watched, John was alone.[4] "I didn't want to see him working at it," said Stephens Mitchell about the destruction of his sister's papers. "The job made John feel sad, and me too. And I was glad he had to do it instead of me."[5]

After watching his employer sit staring for a long time at the contents of three cardboard boxes that he had emptied into the wire basket, Eugene Carr handed him a box of kitchen matches and asked softly, "Mr. Marsh, don't you want me to do this for you?" Without looking up, John sadly shook his head no, rose from his chair, and began his mission. As the papers burned and quickly turned into ashes, he became overwhelmed with sorrow, and he wept. Alarmed at seeing him so distressed, Bessie, watching from the kitchen window, telephoned Margaret Baugh, the Marshes' secretary, who lived nearby. When Miss Baugh arrived, John asked her to finish destroying the papers. "The janitor offered to do it for me," she recalled, "but John said 'This is a trust,' and I stayed there until every scrap was consumed."[6]

Later, in her notes, Margaret Baugh explained:

> You see it was this way: Margaret wanted her papers destroyed, manuscripts, and letters. After her death he [John] took on the job—destroyed the clothes she had on at the time of the accident, the manuscript of *GWTW*, maybe *'Ropa*, and maybe the novel of the 1920s. This was such a distressing experience that he turned over to me the destroying of the correspondence. After we had burned a lot of letters, we found some of them would have been useful in carrying on. So the burning stopped. (To my relief, for it was distressing to me too.) Then, after John's death Steve had the responsibility, and he had me burn the remaining manuscripts and some more letters.[7]

Fortunately, Stephens did not have Margaret Baugh destroy all of Peggy's material; thousands of letters and papers were spared. In the late 1960s, after publication of the Margaret Mitchell biography that Stephens had authorized Finis Farr to write, Stephens donated to the University of Georgia Hargrett Library the bulk of his sister's papers—over fifty-seven thousand items—which include not only her and John's letters and papers but also some of Stephens's, along with his extensive family genealogy, portions of his memoir, and many letters written by his parents and grandparents. Margaret Baugh's notes are also in this valuable collection.

It is not difficult to imagine the sadness John Marsh felt as he destroyed the papers that represented his life with Margaret Mitchell. The Marshes' entire domestic life—twenty-four years—centered on *Gone With the Wind*. During the first and happiest decade of their marriage, a lot of their lovemaking went on while they were working on the manuscript.[8] Perhaps *Gone With the Wind* is not the only novel that resulted from the link between creativity and sexuality, but it is one novel that did. And after the book was published, something that neither of them ever expected, the remainder of their lives was spent in taking care of the complex international business that emerged from its phenomenal success. The book was their only child, and it was one that needed constant supervision. It had consumed their lives just as the fire consumed the papers.

Margaret Mitchell loved her manuscript, which she often spoke of as her "first baby."[9] She could not destroy it, nor would she sell it or give it away to a library. When the Hollywood producers David O. Selznick and Jock Whitney asked her in 1937 if they could borrow or buy the manuscript for film advertisement purposes, she declined, saying she thought she had destroyed the manuscript, knowing full well she had not. Her feelings about having others see the manuscript are emphatically expressed in a letter she wrote Selznick's assistant Katharine Brown, who also attempted to purchase the manuscript on Selznick's behalf: "The whole truth of the matter is that I do not care where my book, as a book, goes, but I do not want even one sheet of manuscript or one line of notes to survive."[10]

In late 1948, she began to put her house in order, and on several occasions she discussed with John and her brother what was to be done if she died before Stephens and if John were unable to carry out her wishes, or if she and John died at the same time. She made it clear then, as she had done many times before, that she wanted her manuscripts, her notes related to them, and her personal papers destroyed; she was also adamant about not wanting sequels, comic strips, and abridgements.[11] Then, too, she wanted the Mitchell family home on Peachtree Street torn down if neither she nor Stephens lived in it. In her five-page will, which she wrote in her big, scrawling handwriting on Sunday afternoon, November 21, 1948, only nine months before she died, she left the manuscript, all rights and royalties, all of her papers, letters, childhood writings, and, with a few minor exceptions, all of her possessions to John.[12] But she wrote nothing in her will about wanting anything destroyed because she did not need to do so. John and Stephens not only knew her wishes but also felt as she did about them. Stephens said, "Margaret once told me, 'If John and I die together'— and that almost happened in her accident—'you see that my papers are torn up.'"[13]

The fact that she felt so strongly about wanting her material destroyed and yet did not destroy it herself but left the job for John to do was characteristic of Peggy; it followed her pattern. She was not subordinate to him, but she was dependent upon him to take care of everything for her. And he did. As one of their journalist-friends put it, John was everything to Peggy—"husband, father, business manager, friend and watchdog."[14]

In his own will, written only eleven days after Peggy died, John left portions of the manuscript that he had decided to keep, the copyrights, royalties, and all the other materials related to *Gone With the Wind* to Stephens Mitchell.[15] Then, in July 1951, he wrote a codicil to his will. The first line of the codicil states:

> My wife, Margaret Mitchell Marsh, wanted her private papers destroyed. She did not wish them to fall into the hands of strangers. She believed that an author should stand or fall before

the public on the basis of the author's *published* work. She believed that little was ever gained from studying an author's manuscript and private papers, and that, more often than not, this led to false and misleading conclusions. Knowing the uncertainties of life, she placed upon me the duty of destroying the papers if she should die without having done it. She did so die, and I have tried to fulfill the obligation. As a part of the painful job, I have destroyed the original manuscript of her novel *Gone With the Wind* and all related papers, proof sheets, notebooks, notes, et cetera, except as described below.

He then lists what he had saved of the *Gone With the Wind* papers "as a means of authenticating her authorship of the novel." He explained, "If some schemer were to rise up with the claim that her novel was written by another person, it would be tragic if we had no documentary evidence and therefore were unable to beat down the false claim. So I am saving these original *Gone With the Wind* papers for use in proving, if the need arises, that Peggy and no one else was the author of her novel."[16]

He included two or three drafts of chapters; several proof sheets that he described as "carrying her handwriting and mine"; samples of other related papers such as chronologies, lists, and notes she made in collecting information; and a few of the large manila envelopes in which she kept the chapters. He concluded: "With this material, I am confident it can be proved not only that my wife Margaret Mitchell wrote *Gone With the Wind*, but that she alone could have written it."[17] Without showing the material to anyone, not even Stephens Mitchell or Margaret Baugh, he sealed it in a large manila envelope that he marked in his bold hand, "Do not open."[18] On July 26, 1951, he locked the envelope in his safety deposit box in the vault of the Citizens and Southern National Bank on Marietta Street in Atlanta.[19] He ordered that the papers were to remain sealed "unless a real and actual need for them arises for the purpose stated. If such a need never arises, the envelope and contents are eventually to be destroyed unopened."[20] In the early 1960s Stephens wrote in his memoir, "Those things are still sealed in the envelope, the ones John selected and put there. The rest are burned."[21]

Peggy's desire to have the original manuscript destroyed and John's codicil raise many questions. What—if anything—would the contents of that envelope prove? How did he go about deciding which manuscript pages to burn and which to save?[22] Why did she want the manuscript destroyed? It is difficult to understand why he—a prudent man with intellectual depth and maturity—did not simply leave all of the material of incalculable literary and monetary value to one of the many universities or libraries that sought it so that scholars and lay people alike could examine it. Only if he had done so could there be no question of Margaret Mitchell's authorship. So why did he burn the entire proof? Or, did he carefully burn all that which he thought may have suggested something other than proof?

The question of her authorship was just one of the many tales that snaked out soon after *Gone With the Wind* became an unexpected sensation.[23] But of all the many rumors, the "most persistent," Stephens said, "were the stories that Margaret had not written the book at all." Stephens explained, "Many fool people claim that John Marsh wrote the book. . . . John and I decided that we were going to save enough of the notes and the manuscript to prove that Margaret wrote this book."[24] A sensitive person who had great pride but little confidence in her own ability, she was devastated by this one rumor that John had written the novel or had helped her write it.[25]

Ironically, Peggy had unwittingly given rise to this rumor herself. When her popularity was at its height, immediately after *Gone With the Wind* was published in 1936, she allowed the Atlanta Public Library to exhibit two pages of the original manuscript in an enclosed cabinet with a glass top. This exhibition, shown for several weeks in the library, was viewed by thousands. The notes and liberal editing on the pages were in John's handwriting, which was easily recognizable to anybody who had seen it.[26] Some of the people who knew the Marshes well had taken for granted that John, an established journalist and an editor, had contributed significantly to his wife's work. And they were convinced after glancing at the pages that he indeed had helped her because the pages appeared in the book exactly as John had edited them in the manuscript.[27] When rumors about his collaboration emerged, Peggy realized what a mistake she had made in letting manuscript sheets go. In December 1936, she wrote her friend Herschel Brickell, a reviewer for the *New York Post:* "I want my manuscript and do not want it floating around for I intend to burn it just as soon as I get those leaves back which the MacM co. inveigled out of me when I was too exhausted to argue. . . . The proof sheets are going to be burned, too. . . . I don't want anyone to see them just as I did not want anyone to see the ms pages but couldn't help myself. Don't ask why. I dont know."[28]

Exquisitely sensitive to criticism, Peggy could never ignore gossip and lies. She spent an inordinate amount of time tracking down misstatements and rumors and writing long responses to them, as well as to questions and to praise. But this questioning of her very authorship seared her soul; she was never able to dismiss it privately or to confront it publicly, as she had done with other rumors. The codicil to John's will proves that he, too, took it seriously and did not consider it mere local gossip. More important, it underscores his enduring effort to protect her, even in death.

Just three years after her death, the respected southern journalist Ralph McGill wrote an article based on his friendship with Peggy and John and on the knowledge of fellow journalists who knew her in her early years. Although the article compliments Peggy, McGill explains that all her friends were surprised by her achievement.

> Not one of the merest handful of persons who knew she had written a book had seen it or had the faintest idea of what it was about. Candor compels one to say that the most loyal friend would not have believed that even by rubbing an Aladdin's lamp she could have written the book. She hid herself completely, inwardly, and in many things, from her best friends.[29]

Margaret Mitchell did not need an Aladdin's lamp; she had John Marsh. And it is no exaggeration to say that just as she dedicated *Gone With the Wind* to him, so he dedicated his life to her. His burning their beloved manuscript was a fitting end to a relationship marked by his burning devotion to her. Without that devotion, it is unlikely that *Gone With the Wind* would ever have been written. If love is defined as an intrinsic good, full of mutual pleasure—physical and intellectual—friendship, loyalty, trust, humor, and, as Aristotle writes in his *Rhetoric,* "as wishing for someone what you believe to be good things—wishing this not for your own sake but for his—and acting so far as you can to bring them about," then *Gone With the Wind* is not a love story; it is a novel of failed romances. Ironically, the true love story lies behind *Gone With the Wind,* in the lives of the author and her husband.

2

Their first meeting in late September 1921 was the result, like nearly all things in life, of a circumstance of fate. Ironically, it occurred just a few days after John had written to his mother on September 18, 1921, that he was thinking about making some changes in his life. He assured her: "Don't feel that I am going to do anything wild and daring. I wish to goodness I had in my past record just one thing wild and daring. I haven't and I don't suppose I ever will." Little did he know then that the most wild and daring person that he would ever know was about to enter his life and change it forever.

John met Peggy one night at the March Hare Tea Shop, better known by its frequenters as "the Rabbit Hole." A popular downtown Atlanta gathering place, this "tearoom" was located in the basement of the Haynes Building at 2 1/2 Auburn Avenue, just a block from Peachtree Street but in a shabby neighborhood.[30] Just getting over the flu, John had almost not gone there that night. He went only because he was pressed to go by his best friend, O. B. Keeler, a sportswriter at the *Daily Georgian* where John worked as a reporter.[31]

With its bohemian atmosphere, the Rabbit Hole was the favorite gathering place for aspiring, out-of-work writers, a few college students, charming young women known as flappers, and young newspapermen who would drop in between assignments or after deadlines. In the dim candlelight they would dance or sit around the red-checkered, oilcloth-covered tables, talking and sipping their drinks (bootleg gin or corn whiskey mixed with Coca-Cola). This was an era when cynicism spread like prairie fire across the country, when many lost their faith in traditional values that had long been taken for granted. Then, too, the Nineteenth Amendment granting women full suffrage had just been passed in 1920 and had brought with it a cascade of changes in the roles of women. Known as "the intelligentsia," coveys of young people, like the Rabbit Hole crowd, disillusioned with traditional values and materialism, gathered in Green-wich Village-like places across the nation to discuss the problems the older generation had left for them to straighten out. The young people who met at the Rabbit Hole had high ideals and expectations and great books in their heads. In a letter to his mother in the late fall of 1921, John described them as "a sort of almost-intellectual society set, young revolutionaries after a fashion who actually have ideas, though some of them are far from certain as to what those ideas are."[32] He had been to the Rabbit Hole only one time before that fateful night, for it was not the type of place or group that attracted him. Individualistic and disdainful of trivial social pursuits, he was self-made, having earned his present position by hard work and self-denial. Busy making a living, he had no time to sit around being disillusioned and, besides that, he upheld the traditional values scorned by the Rabbit Hole group.

Margaret Mitchell, then twenty-one years old, not only fit right into the Rabbit Hole crowd but was the leader of the pack. More than anything else in the world, she wanted to be a writer. Although nothing she had written had been published, she nevertheless thought of writing as her profession, so on the evenings when she was not dancing with her fraternity boyfriends at such elegant places as the Georgian Terrace, she sought the company of other aspiring writers in the charged atmosphere of the Rabbit Hole. On the night when John walked into the place, Margaret Mitchell was already there, and she captured his attention instantly. She was the loveliest thing he had ever seen.[33]

She was sitting, like a fragile centerpiece, on top of one of the tables, her back held straight and her legs daintily crossed at the ankles. She looked strikingly beautiful, young, and small. She was wearing a dark green woolen dress with a cream lace collar that circled high around her slender neck. With its long, straight skirt and tight-fitting bodice, the dress emphasized her tiny waist and shapely little body. Her long, auburn-tinged dark hair, piled high on the back of her head, made her creamy complexion look luminous. Her green eyes sparkled with merriment as the young men, circled about her, listening to her tell an anecdote, burst into laughter.[34] In many ways, she was not different in personality or appearance from her heroine Scarlett O'Hara, although she violently objected to such a comparison.[35] But her friends said that reading the description of Scarlett on the first page of *Gone With the Wind* is reading a description of Peggy herself.[36]

> Scarlett O'Hara was not beautiful, but men seldom realized it when caught by her charm. . . . In her face were too sharply blended the delicate features of her mother, a Coast aristocrat of French descent, and the heavy ones of her florid Irish father. But it was an arresting face, pointed of chin, square of jaw. Her eyes were pale green without a touch of hazel, starred with bristly black lashes and slightly tilted at the ends. Above them, her thick black brows slanted upward, cutting a startling oblique line in her magnolia-white skin.

As John was soon to learn, she was a master storyteller, noted for her extraordinary ability to dramatize and embellish ordinary events. When he asked someone who she was, he was told that she was a rich debutante and the most popular girl in town. To get a date with her, he was advised, "Get in line!" He did not reply to that remark, but he was challenged by it.

Although Peggy looked demure during this high-flying period that John later named her "flapperoty era," there was nothing demure about her.[37] She even categorized herself as the "Vamp de Luxe."[38] In responding to an old beau's remark about her being "a devil and a flirt" and not playing "square with men," she answered saucily, "When a girl knows the male psychology as thoroughly as I do—when she knows the thousand and one small tricks by which a girl can 'innocently' run a man wild or sweep him off his feet—when she knows these things and is small and helpless looking, to boot, and she doesn't use these aforementioned tricks—well, I'd say she played fair!"[39] But Peggy did not always play fair.

Before she became aware of his presence, she had already swept John right off his feet. As he stood in the background, watching and listening, he found her irresistible. His interest in Ruth Gimbel, an Ohio girl whom he had been dating steadily for a year, vanished.[40] Within a few days of his meeting Peggy, he wrote his sister Frances about what he called "an ardent young revolutionary with a helluva lot of common sense as well.

You'll like her, I'm sure." Then he added, "If you don't, I promise to choke you on the spot."[41]

3

At that time Peggy was attracted, much to her father's regret, to rebels, gamblers, and dashing playboys who flaunted their reckless and arrogant attitudes. John Marsh fit into none of these categories. Twenty-six years old, he was an old young man, conservative and quiet. There was nothing daring about him; his thoughts and behavior were deeply conventional. He was highly principled, but not self-righteous, and he cared nothing for organized religion, a view appreciated by Peggy's father, Eugene Mitchell, who shared the sentiment. John had supported himself since his early teens, paying for his own college education by writing for the *Herald* and the *Leader,* newspapers in Lexington, Kentucky. And he, along with his oldest brother, was helping to support his mother and his youngest sister, who at that time was in college. Born and reared in a small town in northern Kentucky, he graduated with a degree in English from the University of Kentucky in 1916. While on a fellowship doing graduate studies at the university, he taught two classes of English composition and continued to write for the newspapers until World War I broke out. Then he joined the service. After his two-year stint in the army, he returned to newspaper work in Lexington for a few months and then moved to Atlanta, where he landed a job as a reporter for the *Georgian.* About returning home to Kentucky, he wrote his mother, "I may move back there when I become a famous writer."[42] By the time he met Peggy, he had been working in Atlanta on some interesting assignments for over a year. He was an established journalist with an excellent professional reputation.

Despite, or perhaps because of, the fact that he was different from all the other men that she found attractive, Peggy was drawn to John. She found his blond, patrician handsomeness appealing, and his maturity comforting. Because he was more intellectual than any other man she had ever known, she felt reassured by his attention to her. Because she was the prettiest, the friendliest, and the most sought-after girl he had known, he took pride in her interest in him. They became immediate friends. The chemistry between them, from the start, was profoundly reciprocal, but perhaps not identical. Like all those other young men, John was enchanted with her beauty, warmth, and personality. And just like all those others, he was stimulated by her sexuality. He fell in love with Peggy at first sight and claimed that his falling into such a love was "a soul-shaking, terrifying experience."[43] He wanted physical intimacy but was too shy, too much of a gentleman to act on his desire. He was afraid he would lose her. Just the reverse may have been true of Peggy who, in searching for psychological intimacy, wanted John as an intellectual companion, as a protector and a teacher. At that time, she desperately needed approval from someone she regarded as wise and sensible, someone she trusted. As he began to fulfill all those roles so admirably and generously, she became attracted to him sexually. Soon, each became irreplaceable to the other.

In the beginning of their friendship, she took the initiative by inviting him to escort her to several debutante balls during the Christmas holidays. Having grown up in a small town in a large family dependent upon the limited income of a school-teaching, widowed mother, John had no experience attending such social functions. Although he was older than she, more educated and experienced in many ways, he was also conspicuously more naive about romance. His mother and his sisters were models of virtuous womanhood, and all the girls John had dated were more of the conventional type, not like the tantalizing little chameleon Peggy was at that time. John had had no experiences with a woman like her. One of her friends, William Howland, described her best when he wrote, "At times, she looked like a very good little girl—which she was. At other times, she looked like a very bad little girl; which she could be. But never a dull little girl. Or a mean little girl."[44]

Just a few days after meeting this woman who would dominate the rest of his life, he wrote his sister Frances:

> An Atlanta girl is the only girl who interests me. She is one of last season's debutantes, lives in a beautiful house way out on Peachtree Street, is very small and is named Mitchell. She has a beautiful long name, Margaret, which has been shortened to a pert "Peggy." To counteract the effect of that word "debutante," I have been to see her twice and both times have spent the entire evening in conversation, without any stimulation, erotic or otherwise. She is the first girl I have met in Atlanta with whom I have been able to enjoy sensible conversation.[45]

By Thanksgiving, anyone with half an eye could tell at a glance that the tall, quiet newspaperman from Kentucky was deeply in love with the quirky little debutante. At times, she appeared to be in love with him. But no one could be sure because she continued to go out with other men and to play—to the hilt—her role as southern belle.

What soon separated John from her other admirers and made him the object of her serious attention was his recognition of her burning desire to be a writer. He listened to her and validated her intellectually. No one else, except her mother, had ever done that. She had not excelled in her schoolwork or in any other area and had the reputation of being a party girl, one who was lively, unconventional, sexy, and funny. No one appreciated or even saw the serious side of her. Even though her own life thus far had no direction, was unproductive, wasted in social trivia, and dependent upon her father's income, Peggy admired people who were independent, who worked hard and who had, as she put it, "the courage to take it on the chin" as John was doing.[46] From the time she first met him, she knew intuitively that he was "buckwheat," a term she always used to describe people who had integrity and character. This metaphor came from her childhood when she often heard her grandmother and great-aunts, who were farmers, say that there were just two kinds of people: wheat people and buckwheat people. One day not long after she met him, Peggy nicknamed John "Buckwheat."[47] She then explained the analogy to him, as she did to many others later: "Take wheat, when it's ripe and a strong wind comes along, it's laid flat on the ground and it never rises again. But buckwheat yields to the wind, is flattened and when the wind passes, it rises up just as straight as ever. Wheat people can't stand a wind. Buckwheat people can."[48]

Because of her sense of adventure—her favorite books were boys' adventure stories and mysteries—she loved John's work. She envied his trek with revenuers into the Georgia mountains on a stormy day to chase bootleggers and the shiny little pistol he had been given to keep as a souvenir of the trip. She was more than impressed with the national attention he received just about the time they met for his controversial interview with the new leader of the Ku Klux Klan. His long interview with Imperial Kleagle Clarke won him praise from the *Georgian* and also from the *New York World,* who called John "one of the most capable and painstaking journalists in Atlanta."[49]

His life was different from that of her fraternity boyfriends. She admired not only his work but also his education. Because of his use of the language and his vocabulary, anyone who listened to him for a few moments knew that he was intelligent and well educated. In contrast to her southern drawl and lapses of grammar, his clear diction made every syllable distinct. Her voice had a lilting, soft but high pitch to it; his was deep and low. Although he had a keen sense of humor, which delighted her, he also had a kind of no-nonsense air. From the beginning of their friendship, she looked upon him as almost an authority figure. She respected and valued his judgment.[50]

4

Before John met Peggy, his letters to his mother are all about his work. But after November 21, 1921, when he announced that he had just met the "introducingest person" he had ever known, his letters are all about Peggy and their social life. He wrote enthusiastically about the formal balls that he and his "new Sweetie" had been attending at the Georgian Terrace and the fun they had been having. His happiness is evident in this letter to his mother:

> I suppose right at the start you want to hear a report on the present condition of my health. It's great—I'm fat and getting fatter. I am beginning to fear double chins. . . . The day before I went to bed with the flu, my doctor stuck me on the scales and weighed me in at 134 pounds. A couple of days ago I was in his office, got on the same scales and I weighed 145 pounds. I can cheerfully say that I have become much better satisfied with Atlanta and with life in general during the month past. I honestly feel great, physically and mentally. [51]

Perhaps the most obvious sign of his involvement with Peggy was the change in his workaholic habits. "I am by a great effort of will power not working so hard at the office that I am too tired to go out in the evenings occasionally," he told his mother. Also, he said he was trying to cure some of his other bad habits; he had stopped "drinking coffee and coca cola" and had become a "sweet milk fiend." He added: "I don't stay up late *every* night, stopped drinking cocktails, using cocaine, heroin and opium, dipping snuff, chewing tobacco, bootlegging whiskey and chewing my fingernails, etc." A chain smoker since he was sixteen, he wrote: "Of course, I am still smoking cigarettes, *of course*. 'They never stop,' . . . but if some one will invent a substitute for that I promise to give it a trial."[52]

By mid-December, he and Peggy were seeing each other nightly. Having looked forward to spending all of his Christmas vacation with her, he was furious when, two days before Christmas, the *Georgian* sent him, its star reporter, to cover Eugene Debs's release from the U.S. Penitentiary in Atlanta. A colorful Socialist who ran for the presidency five times, Debs was always making national news, first for organizing a union for railroad workers who went on strike the following year, then for making an antiwar speech during World War I. He was convicted under the Espionage Act for his speech and given a ten-year sentence in the Atlanta federal prison, but his sentence was commuted on Christmas Day 1921. Because none of the newspapermen knew exactly when Debs would be released, John angrily spent Christmas Eve "sitting in a hard chair in the prison front parlor wishing Debs was in the bottom of the Atlantic Ocean."[53] Christmas Day he described as "darn cold . . . and the warden wouldn't even let us inside the gate, so we marched up and down outside, about 40 of us, including the motion picture men and Socialist delegation" until late Christmas afternoon when Debs was finally released. John got his interview with Debs, hurriedly wrote his story and lined up photographs to go with it, and then tried to reach Peggy. But she had already gone with another date on a round of holiday parties. So he sadly returned to his room in Mrs. Prim's boarding house on Peachtree Street and sat alone in his rocking chair in front of the fire with nothing more entertaining to do than play with the family's new kitten. By eight o'clock, he was in bed, exhausted and disappointed, wondering where Peggy was and missing her badly.[54]

In late 1921, the editor of Kentucky's *Lexington Leader* wrote John asking, for the second time, if he would return to work on its staff and be its highest-paid reporter at thirty-five dollars a week—a high salary in the newspaper world in those days.[55] Although he was proud of the invitation, he declined. He wanted to stay in Atlanta to be near Peggy, who had changed his life in wonderful ways—at first.

C H A P T E R **2**

*O*PPOSITES ATTRACT

I spent the Sunday afternoons of my childhood sitting on the bony knees of Confederate Veterans and the fat slick laps of old ladies who survived the war and reconstruction.
> —Margaret Mitchell to Julia Collier Harris,
> 28 April 1936

As I get older and see other people who have grown up in other families, I come more and more to appreciate my own.
> —John Marsh to his mother,
> Thanksgiving Day 1923

1

BY EARLY 1922, JOHN AND PEGGY WERE DEEPLY INVOLVED, seeing each other daily. But no pair ever looked more mismatched. Although she was exquisitely built, she was barely five feet tall and weighed scarcely ninety pounds. She looked even smaller standing next to John, who was slightly over six feet tall. She held herself erect and walked energetically, with quickness and grace. He was lean, nonathletic-looking, and slightly stoop-shouldered. He had the habit of walking slowly, head down, vest buttoned, suit coat opened, hands thrust into his trouser pockets. His round, metal-rimmed glasses made him look scholarly. Handsome with classical features, he had an oval face with a high, wide brow, a straight nose, pale blue eyes, and a fair complexion. His blond hair was thick and straight; he wore it without a part, brushed straight back from his forehead. He was always dressed in dark, three-piece suits, plain ties, and starched, white, high-collared shirts. She dressed expensively in the latest fashions and favored greens, aquas, and blues, which brought out the color of her eyes, the feature that first attracted people's attention.[1]

Her friendliness and warmth won her an impressive following of friends, mostly male. His reticence and self-reliance did not win many close friends.[2] However, as she would soon learn, he was fiercely loyal to the few he had. Both had keen senses of humor, but his was subtle and whimsical; hers, garrulous and ribald. She frankly enjoyed not only hearing but also telling shocking stories. Good at uttering one-liners unexpectedly, he was not a joke teller but was a great audience for one. He was the one who laughed loudest at Peggy's stories and always egged her on to tell them. He was quiet and mannerly; she was noisy, usually creating a lot of laughter around her. He was prudent; she was daring. He spoke carefully; she said whatever popped into her mind. Her whole person seemed to shout, "Hey! Everybody! Look at me!" He did not care whether anyone noticed him or not and preferred that no one did.[3] While she loved to shock the older generation, he went out of his way to be respectful. Like a mischievous child, she frequently used obscenities; he used them sparingly, but more effectively. Most comfortable around men, she worked at being "one of the guys."[4] Because he was such a good listener, women liked to talk to him.[5] Other, more subtle differences were also noticeable. Observant and appreciative of beauty, he was sensuous; but she was sensual. He was noted for his veracity; she, for her verisimilitude.[6]

Although she was twenty-one when they met, she was still immature and irresponsible in some ways. Not having a real sense of herself, she played various roles as if she were continually searching for an identity. At times, she would be the rowdy, fun-loving flapper who took enormous pleasure in shocking Victorian dowagers—the joke-telling gin-drinker who could hold her "likker," dance all night, and still be able to see to it that all the drunks got home safely. Sometimes, she played the dedicated, social-conscious reformer; at other times, she was a nonconformist without a clue as to her cause. Her personae included a vampy seductress; a modest, quiet southern lady; a fervent feminist protesting male power; a devoted daughter nursing her aging father; an amateur author writing only for her own amusement; a serious writer of serious fiction. One other role she consistently played, or maybe actually endured, was that of a sick person who suffered from mysterious illnesses that baffled her physicians.

In contrast, John's ego was always in place. Having defined his values in early childhood, he behaved in a consistent manner throughout his entire life. He had a staunch sense of responsibility and personal deportment; he embodied the noblest characteristics of chivalry and was self-reliant—almost to a fault. In spite of his calm exterior, he exhibited some compulsive behaviors. For example, he was fiercely competitive, determined to excel at whatever he undertook; he was rarely without a cigarette either in his hand or drooping in the corner of his mouth; he was excessively hard working and impatient with those who were not; he did a job himself rather than asking someone else to do it, particularly whenever he believed that the job had to be done right. He did not always trust his employees to do certain things correctly, and this habit did not endear him to some of his colleagues. Not a sportsman, not a card player, not an athlete, he was never one of the good old boys. Working among men who loved to fish and hunt, he was outspoken about his belief that it is wrong to kill animals.[7] Although he despised incompetence, he overlooked weaknesses in people and often went out of his way to help those who lacked confidence and strength. He had genuine concern for his colleagues and subordinates.[8] John was the type that people would go to when they were in trouble or needed advice. He was the type of person who needs to be needed, and Peggy leaned deeply into this need.[9]

She was the type people wanted at their parties. Three traits made her the center of attention at any gathering she attended: first, her perceptive ability to find something remarkable about each individual, particularly anyone who was shy or young, and to make that person feel special; second, her humor, which she was careful never to use at the expense of another's feelings; and third, her ability to tell anecdotes, oftentimes rowdy or scary ones.[10] Stephens, her brother, said that she demonstrated this talent for storytelling even when she was a small child. Before she learned to read for herself, Stephens read fairy tales, mysteries, and adventure stories to her. With her incredible memory and imagination, she could, at an early age, enthrall her playmates by dramatically retelling these stories. According to Stephens, one little boy was afraid to walk home alone after an evening of Peggy's spine-tingling tales.[11] As a grownup, she could embellish any ordinary event, tell anything in such a funny way that her companions would break up in laughter. Annie Couper, one of her friends from childhood, explained how Peggy could take the most minor incident and retell it in such a way that the participant in the incident could hardly recognize herself. "You can meet Peggy in Rich's basement when both of you are dog tired and feeling mean and scuffed and later that same evening hear Peggy tell of the encounter and not even recognize yourself in the two happy, carefree and glamorous witty people she describes."[12]

Peggy radiated spontaneity and enthusiasm, the qualities that John found most appealing, probably because he lacked them. Realizing that he was too cautious, he told his mother shortly before he met Peggy: "Unfortunately, I always think about things too long to do anything unusual."[13] His self-effacing modesty was not a sign of insecurity; his self-confidence was evident too. Having earned his own way since he was about twelve years old, he knew that he had control over his circumstances, and he knew how to weigh his options and estimate the consequences of his decisions. He was also more realistic and confident about what he could achieve. And he was always more optimistic than Peggy. He approached projects and problems far more reasonably than she did. Just like her father, she had an excitable, nervous temperament and, early on, she looked to John to shoulder some responsibilities for her. Reared with the notion that any sign of negative emotions, such as fear, jealousy, or disappointment, was unmanly, John concealed his anxieties and always appeared outwardly calm, self-assured, and unflappable. After their marriage, he was always in charge of their domestic and business matters.

Despite all their differences, the Marshes were compatible. Everyone who knew them well said that they were. Even George Cukor, the first director of the *Gone With the Wind* film, remarked after meeting them in 1939 that John Marsh was "the ideal husband for Margaret Mitchell."[14] And indeed he was. It was evident to all who knew them that John always wanted what was best for Peggy and did all in his power to bring about the best for her. She knew that too. Margaret Mitchell could have married any man she wanted, but she chose to spend her life with John Marsh because she loved and respected him. Had he fallen in love with a less spectacular woman, perhaps he would not have paled, so to speak, in the minds of others looking back across the years and writing about Margaret Mitchell. Almost any man would probably appear nondescript in the company of a woman who, like the brightest star in the evening sky, dominated every scene in which she appeared.

Perhaps what made their companionship ideal was the confluence of their differences, for each supplied what the other lacked. They were bound by their mutual dependence and desire to please each other. They were of equal rank in their relationship, and until their deaths, they were faithful to each other and to the roles they tacitly understood each was to play in their union: she, the writer; he, the editor. Except for the facts that they had both been influenced at a critical age by the death of a parent and that both had been profoundly influenced by their mothers, everything else about their childhoods, families, and hometowns was different. The distinct differences in their upbringing had everything to do with their personalities as adults and with the way they interacted with each other.

2

To begin with, Peggy came from the womb of the deep South Confederate establishment. All of her ancestors were prosperous landowners with fervent sentiments for the South. She was of the fifth generation of her family to live in Atlanta, and she was enormously proud of the fact. Her great-great-great-grandfather, Thomas Mitchell, was the first Mitchell to come to Georgia in the mid-1700s. As a lieutenant in the Georgia Brigade in the Revolutionary War, he was granted land in Georgia.[15] Nearly all of his descendants remained and prospered in Georgia. Her father's father grew up on a farm at Flat Shoals, about fifteen miles from Atlanta. Her mother's people—the Fitzgeralds and Stephenses—came from Ireland in the early 1800s and settled around Fayetteville, Georgia, in what is now known as Clayton County. In that beautiful county, far out on the old Jonesboro Road, her great-grandfather Fitzgerald established a huge cotton farm and peach and apple orchards, and he built a large, rambling farmhouse that Peggy loved and idealized as Tara in her novel. This Fitzgerald land, stained with the blood of Confederate and Union soldiers, was precious to her.

Peggy was profoundly affected by her mother and her mother's people. Although she was more like her father and his people in her looks and temperament, she was more influenced by the Fitzgeralds. Born on January 13, 1872, in her parents' large Jackson Street home, Maybelle was the first of the eleven children of John and Annie Elizabeth Fitzgerald Stephens. She was christened Mary Isabelle but was never called that. A lovely woman, small with delicate features, Maybelle had red, curly hair, fair skin, and purplish blue eyes. Until she was thirteen, she and her two younger sisters, Annie and Estora, were taught by their mother's spinster sister, "Aunt Sis," how to write and to read the classics. Aunt Sis also taught them music and painting, "gentleness of demeanor, dignity of carriage, kindness of heart and gaiety of temperament," wrote Stephens in his memoir. He added, "Their mother, having twelve children, was a little too busy to bother about such fine points."[16]

Unlike her own mother, who cared nothing for literature, religion, and social issues, Maybelle inherited her love for those things from her father and her maternal grandfather, Philip Fitzgerald, and also from her mother's sisters, Mamie and Sis. In her early teens, Maybelle attended the Bellevue Convent school in Quebec, where she learned to speak French fluently. But at her own insistence, she returned to Atlanta to finish her studies at a secular school. Intelligent, serious minded, and studious, she graduated with honors from the Atlanta Female Institute. In 1892, when she was twenty, she married Eugene Muse Mitchell.

3

Peggy's father was born on October 13, 1866, in Atlanta. He was the first of Russell Crawford and Deborah Margaret Sweet Mitchell's eleven children. Because his mother was pregnant every other year for twenty years, Eugene learned to be self-reliant at an early age, and he helped his mother by looking after his younger siblings. When his mother died, he was only twenty, about the same age Peggy was when her mother died. A perfectionist, he was highly disciplined, well organized, and studious. He was also inflexible in his views and sensitive about his short stature, which he inherited from his mother's people—the Sweets. Like all the other Mitchells when they were young, he was scrappy; at Means High School in Atlanta, he was always getting into fights. Stephens described his father as "intensely reserved, with a great deal of pride. . . . He did not like to fight, but fought because pride drove him to it."[17] In this respect, Peggy was exactly like her father; she had great pride. But unlike him, and much to his regret, she did not excel in school. In 1885, Eugene graduated from the University of Georgia, receiving both the A.B. and the B.S. degrees. A member of Phi Beta Kappa, he was honored for earning the highest grade point average ever earned by a student at the university—99.6.[18] In 1886, he received his law degree, also with honors, from the University of Georgia.

Although his nickname at the university was "the long-haired, short-legged genius," he modestly wrote, "I never had any genius unless an unlimited capacity for work be such."[19] If he had been left to choose his career, he would have been a historian, an author and a teacher of history. He knew the history of the Civil War and of Atlanta thoroughly, and he was an excellent writer. But, instead of doing what he wanted, he studied law at his father's insistence. Other lawyers said that Eugene Mitchell's legal papers were models of clearness and conciseness and that it was impossible to misinterpret a will that Eugene Mitchell had drawn. In discussing this phase of the practice of law, Eugene instructed his son, "In drawing a Will, just look after the grammar, and the law will look after itself."[20]

In 1893, a year after he married Maybelle Stephens, he established a law firm with his brother, Gordon Forrest Mitchell. Twenty-six years later, after his son Stephens graduated from the University of Georgia Law School and joined him in practice, he renamed the firm Mitchell & Mitchell.[21]

Eugene and Maybelle's first child, Russell Stephens Mitchell, died in infancy in 1893; their second child, also christened Stephens, was born in 1895; their last child—Margaret Munnerlyn Mitchell—was born on November 8, 1900, on their eighth wedding anniversary. All three children were born in a two-story, six-room frame cottage, 296 Cain Street, which was on the north side of Cain Street between North Boulevard and East Jackson Street. Their home was in a pleasant part of town, in a neighborhood of well-off families who had known each other for generations.[22]

4

Maybelle's mother, Annie Elizabeth Fitzgerald Stephens, lived a few doors away in a big, rambling house full of kinfolks. Her house was headquarters for the entire family.[23] Preceded in death by her husband, John Stephens, Annie inherited from him a whole block on Jackson Street. John Stephens had given all eight of his children property on this block, and they built homes and raised their families there. Thus, Peggy grew up literally surrounded by grandparents and relatives of every degree and age, as well as swarms of visiting kin, spanning three generations.[24] All were steeped in the history of the South and the Civil War, and all were great talkers—especially the Fitzgeralds and the Stephenses, who were gifted storytellers.[25] None was a more powerful storyteller than Grandmother Annie, who told Peggy endless tales about the Civil War, bloodthirsty Yankees, freed slaves, scoundrelly scalawags, cheating carpetbaggers, and the importance of behaving well in the face of either defeat or prosperity.

Every Sunday afternoon the Mitchell family would visit with the older generation of relatives. "I spent the Sunday afternoons of my childhood sitting on the bony knees of Confederate Veterans and the fat slick laps of old ladies who survived the war and reconstruction," Peggy wrote in a letter in 1936.[26] "And I heard them talk about friends who came through it all and friends who went under. They were a pretty outspoken, forthright, tough bunch of old timers and the things they said stuck in my mind much longer than the things the people of my parents' generation told me."

One Sunday they would visit her father's people, who all gathered at the home of Russell Crawford Mitchell, her paternal grandfather, who lived in town on Ivy Street. The next week they would go out to the country to visit her mother's folks—aunts, uncles, and cousins who lived on her maternal great-grandfather's farm on the old Jonesboro Road, near Orrs Crossing. Peggy loved this farmplace, and she loved her grandmother's saintly spinster sisters, Mary (called Mamie) and Sarah (nicknamed Sis or Sadie), who lived there and ran the cotton farm and the fruit orchards until they died in the 1930s. At all these family gatherings, the two favorite topics for discussion were the Civil War and the family history. Years later, Peggy described the old folks' genealogical sessions as "climbing up and down the family tree and venturing out onto limbs and twigs which will hardly bear any weight."[27]

Grandpa Russell Crawford Mitchell left a strong impression on Peggy, although she was only five years old when he died. She remembered him well, with his jet-black eyes and his great swooping side whiskers shaped like porkchops. A colorful personality—wiry, tough, and shrewd—he had a stockpile of Civil War stories, for he had fought in eleven battles, including the ones at Seven Pines and Bull Run. In the bloody Antietam campaign, near Sharpsburg, Maryland, he was severely wounded when he was struck twice across the head with a couple of minié balls; the bullets tore through his skull, making two long grooves in it but not destroying any part of his brain. He was left for dead on the battlefield until a soldier picking up rifles noticed his faint breathing and loaded him onto one of the wagons. Several days later, after a long, bumpy journey to south Georgia, he was taken to an army hospital.[28] He fully recovered, and in the process fell in love with one of the volunteer nurses, Deborah Margaret Sweet. After the war, they married and moved to Atlanta, which was emerging from Sherman's ashes.[29] A shrewd realist just like Rhett Butler, he went into the lumber and real estate business and quickly amassed a fortune.[30] After his wife died when she was only forty, he remarried and had two more daughters.[31]

In writing her novel, Peggy wove some of her Grandpa Russell's experiences and features into her characterization of Rhett Butler. As Stephens pointed out, no child could forget being raised onto that old cavalryman's bony knees and told to put her fingers into the grooves in her grandfather's skull while the old man's trembling hand guided the fearful child's fingers to the spot. "Feel it, child? Do ye feel it?" the old man would ask.[32] One summer when Peggy was seven or eight, her father, who had heard his father's "grooves story" hundreds of times, drove his family to Sharpsburg. They walked all over that field, once soaked with blood, trying to determine where the batteries had been captured and where Grandpa Russell had been wounded.[33] From that time on, Peggy enjoyed exploring Civil War battlefields in her area and learning about their history.

As an imaginative, curious child with an eye for detail and a keen memory, she listened intently to the telling and retelling of these stories, which shaped her world and presented her ancestors as epic heroes. She grew up with an abiding sense of Georgia's history. Years later, in explaining how she got the idea for *Gone With the Wind,* she said that she supposed she got it "in the cradle." She had heard so much when she was very young about the battles and the hard times after the war that for years, she said, she believed her parents had been through it all.[34] "In fact I was about ten years old," she wrote, "before I learned the war hadn't ended shortly before I was born."[35]

After describing her ancestors as "a remarkably tough bunch of people," she explained, "I don't mean tough in the modern slang meaning of the word. But tough in its older meaning, hard, resistant, strong."[36] Each of the old men had fought in the Confederate Army and continued to fight the war in their memories whenever two or three of them got together. Each of the old ladies had nursed the wounded and the dying in hospitals and struggled to manage the farms while their menfolk were away.[37]

5

Unlike John Marsh, whose childhood was filled early with responsibilities and marred by the death of his father, Peggy had an idyllic childhood. Her brother Stephens described it as "serene and happy in a way that was possible only in a world where one felt absolutely secure."[38] Everything about her childhood and her environment—house, neighborhood, relatives, playmates, parents—nurtured her imagination and later emerged in one way or another in her novel.

As they were growing up, neither she nor Stephens had responsibilities or any kind of work to do around their house or yard. The Mitchells had plenty of servants, although none of them appears to have been the prototype for Scarlett's outspoken Mammy. The large vacant lot next to their house was Peggy and Stephens's playground, an ideal place to fly kites, play ball, race ponies. And it was here that Peggy, dressed like a little boy, romped and played with her brother and the neighborhood children from daylight to dark.[39] Her mother dressed her in boy's pants and shirts after an accident occurred when Peggy was only three. Her leg was burned when her light, ruffled dress caught on fire as it brushed against the opened coal-burning grates used to heat the house. Although the injury was not serious, Maybelle feared that such an incident might recur in a more serious manner, and that same afternoon she put all of her daughter's pretty dresses away except for special occasions. When Peggy went out to play, she wore boy's clothes and a tweed cap under which her long blond hair was tucked. (She was light-haired until her teens.) Though very small and delicately built, she was really a sturdy child, and very active. The boy's clothes suited her. Neighbors took to calling her "Jimmy" from a fancied resemblance to a small boy who figured in a comic strip that ran in the *Journal*. Throughout her life, she preferred loose, comfortable clothes and often wore overalls, shorts, or slacks. In a letter to Henry and Mary Marsh on July 3, 1933, Peggy congratulated them on the birth of their second daughter Jane. Recalling her childhood, she wrote,

> I had no sister and yearned for one to the extent of telling the family doctor that I was sure that Mother would just as soon have a little negro daughter as a white one if he really was out of little white girls, as he solemnly told me. (I got soundly tanned for that remark, by the way.) Other little girls had sisters and it was so convenient! They always had some one to play with. They were not obliged to control their tempers and stay on good terms with neighboring little girls in order to have companions. They could stick out their tongues, pack up their doll rags and walk off switching their small behinds and refuse to play with me, secure in the knowledge that they had sister for company. And when they grew older, they could and did wear each others clothes and have each other to confide in about "what-I-said-to-him-and-what-he-said-to-me." And it seemed to me that sisters near in age always lured more beaux into a house than a lone girl could do single handed and, at sixteen, that was a very serious matter. . . . I used to ask for a sister on Christmases and birthdays and Mother was quite willing to oblige me but had terrible luck in the matter so I had to grow up with the none too tender companionship of Stephens who felt that girls were, at best, a care and that if I wished to play with him, I would have to be a boy named Jimmy. And so I was a boy named Jimmy till I was fourteen.[41]

When Peggy was two years old, her father moved their family into a larger house, No. 187, on the southeast corner of Jackson Street and Highland Avenue. In 1903, as his law practice prospered, he moved his family again, this time into a twelve-room, two-story, Victorian brick house at No. 179 Jackson Street. This was the house that Peggy loved the most. Her favorite private place to read and write was on the wide, front porch overlooking Jackson Street. Shaded with honeysuckle vines during the hot part of the summer day, it was the coolest spot after sundown, when there was usually a little breeze. Large, old trees shaded the house, and May-belle's flower gardens decorated it. Directly behind the house was a stable for the cow and the small Texas plains pony that her father bought Peggy when she was about three years old. By the time she was five, she had taken many falls but she, no sissy, learned to ride well. When she and Stephens were older, their father purchased a horse for them. Unfortunately, the horse was not surefooted and, in 1911, he fell on his side while Peggy was riding him, injuring her leg. Her father sold that horse and never bought another one.[42] However, she continued to love horseback riding and went every chance she got.

Although Maybelle indulged her daughter, she disciplined her too. Stephens wrote, "Mother used her slipper on Margaret," particularly when she acted self-conscious, stand-offish, and silent when she was very young.[43] Whenever she would hide behind her mother's skirt and refuse to speak to strangers, friends, or even relatives, her mother would take her upstairs to her parents' bedroom and swat her little seat with a house slipper, telling her sternly that she must talk to people who were polite enough to notice and speak to her. "You must always respond to people! Not to do so is rude," Maybelle exclaimed, "and rudeness ranks with sins which cry to heaven for vengeance."[44] By the time Peggy started school, she no longer suffered from shyness. She was never pushy or arrogant, but she could always hold her own in any company. No one who knew her well as an adult ever suspected that she had been a diffident child.

In a letter that Maybelle wrote to Peggy, who was no older than four or five at the time, we get some idea of Peggy's precocity and penchant for mischief. Vacationing in White Springs, Florida, Maybelle wrote her daughter: "I received your letter today and it was a fine one. I never saw better writing and it was so easy to read. I am having a nice time down here but am lonesome for my little ones. . . . I am glad you and your father and Stephens are having a good time. Be sure and be good to your father and dont tease Stephens too much."[45]

Peggy was also a tomboy with a strong sense of adventure. She loved playing baseball, engaging in mud-ball battles, climbing trees, playing war, playing cowboy and Indians—but never dolls. Stephens said he never once saw his sister playing with dolls although she, like her mother, loved cats and kittens and had lots of them.[46]

In summertime, the children played outside nearly every day all day long, until dark. In the wintertime, they were allowed to play only for a couple of hours after school, and then they had to study their lessons. Both parents expected their children to excel in schoolwork. Stephens did. But Peggy was often mischievous, talkative in the classroom, and slipshod about her lessons although she managed to maintain average grades. To the end of her life, she preferred learning what she wanted to learn and not what someone else tried to drum into her head. Just like her Scarlett, she had to see the immediate, practical value of acquiring information before it interested her.

One of her earliest memories of schoolwork had to do with her mother. As a grownup, Peggy frequently told this story because she said the genesis of her novel lay in it.[47] When she was not quite six, she told her mother she could not do arithmetic, did not want to go to school, and saw "no value at all in an education." Her mother angrily snatched her up in her arms, plopped her in the buggy wagon, and took her, on what Peggy said was one of the hottest September afternoons she ever saw, for a fast, bumpy drive on the old country road that led to Jonesboro. As she pointed out the crumbling plantation mansions in their sad disarray, Maybelle told Peggy about the wealthy people who had once lived in these fine houses, about how secure their world had been, and about how suddenly "their world exploded beneath them." Peggy explained, "Some of the ruins dated from Sherman's visit, some had fallen to pieces when the families in them fell to pieces. And she showed me plenty of houses still standing staunchly. . . . And she told me that my own world was going to explode under me, some day, and God help me if I didn't have some weapon to meet the new world." Describing her parent as "an idealist with a very wide streak of common sense," Peggy said her mother exclaimed, "What you could do with your hands and what you had in your head is all anyone has left after her world has exploded. So, for God's sake, go to school and learn something that will stay with you. The strength of a woman's hands isn't worth anything but what they've got in their heads will carry them as far as they need to go."[48]

6

Much has been made of Peggy's thrift, of what one of her biographers calls her "stinginess."[49] Harvey Smith, one of her friends, wrote that Peggy was so scrupulously careful to pay every penny she owed that it was sometimes embarrassing, and that she was just as exacting in requiring that every penny owed her be repaid. "Certainly her fear of poverty," he added, "was one of the motivating characteristics of her life just as the strange compulsion to have people (or was it herself) believe her to be ill and suffering."[50]

Here again, opinions of those who knew her well differ. Jim and Mary Davis pointed out several examples of times when they, as a struggling young couple with three small children, benefited greatly from Peggy's and John's generosity, which included paying for the Davises' stay in the Biltmore whenever they visited Atlanta. And, Jim pointed out, it was Peggy who insisted on paying for braces to straighten the teeth of all the Davises' children. Deon Rutledge, who worked for the Marshes, also spoke of Peggy's generosity to her and to her mother Bessie. Deon explained that once, when she went through a difficult period, Peggy sent her on a week's vacation to New York City. When Deon decided to remain in the city for a year, Peggy sent her a weekly paycheck, which she called "stand-by pay," every week throughout that entire year.

While Smith exaggerates Peggy's obsession with money, it is true that she had acquired from her family an insecurity about financial matters. Her father was never a risk taker, and after he and Maybelle, as newlyweds, endured the panic of 1893, he became even more conservative than ever. Years later, he told Stephens that the financial depression of 1893 had "taken out of him all daring, and put in its place a desire to have a competence assured to him."[51] In addition to her father's influence was her mother's reminder to her at an impressionable age that she had better be prepared for changes and adversity or else she would be defeated by them. Then, too, there were all those tragic stories her grandparents and relatives told her in her childhood about how the family had lost everything in the Civil War. As she said many times, her family lived to incredible ages and had incredible memories, and she was brought up on stories of the hard times after the American Revolution, after the Seminole War, in the panic during Andrew Jackson's regime, and after the Civil War. She heard over and over how bad things were in the panics of 1873, 1893, and 1907. She later explained that these influences kept her constantly aware of the possibility that, as her mother had told her, the world could "explode" at any time: "I suppose that explains why I wrote a book about hard times when the country was enjoying its biggest boom."[52] In view of her background, it seems she was conditioned from infancy to be concerned about her financial security.

7

Eugene Mitchell adored Maybelle to the end of his life, and the letters he wrote to her during their courtship are as beautiful as any in literature. A bountiful provider, he generously gave her and the children everything they ever wanted. But he was, without a doubt, a bit overbearing. He had a strong, dominating personality; he was argumentative, excitable, and forceful about expressing his opinion. Even though he agreed to have his children baptized and reared as Catholics, his disdain for the Catholic Church worried Maybelle. Early in her marriage, Maybelle learned how to protect herself from the difficulties of living with Eugene by having episodes of undiagnosed maladies. During the first decade of their marriage especially, she had many vague health problems that permitted her to "rest" with out-of-town relatives and to take "cures" in resort areas with mineral springs.[53]

During their mother's frequent absences, the young children, left in the care of their father and servants, entertained themselves with play and books. Peggy's love for reading and writing manifested itself very early. Stephens said that his sister began "to write stories just as soon as her fingers could guide a pencil and join letters into words. She did not wait to be able to spell. The stories were forming too fast in her. As soon as she finished one, she started another. Her main diversion seemed to be to write, not to talk."[54]

Reading and writing were two activities her mother encouraged. The Mitchells were a reading family, and their home was filled with many books and periodicals. Maybelle started reading to the children when they were infants and taught both to read and write before they entered the first grade at the Forrest Avenue School. One of Maybelle's classmates, Mary Johnston, was the author of two well-researched novels about the Civil War. Maybelle read and reread these books to Peggy, and each time she read certain sections, she and her child would break into tears. After her own book became famous, Peggy explained that in the process of checking the section of her novel about the campaign from the Tennessee line to Atlanta, she wanted to be certain that she had described the weather correctly. An old veteran told her that it had rained for twenty-five days at Kennesaw Mountain, that the rain came "up to the seat of my pants!" But she wanted to know for sure. When reference books did not supply the answer, she turned to Johnston's *Cease Firing* because she knew it was the best-documented novel ever written about the Civil War.[55]

Stephens recalled, "When I think of Margaret back in those days on Jackson Hill, I usually see her in a starched dress, her short blonde hair brushed back from her face, sitting on the top step of the porch, deep in Grimm's Fairy Tales."[56] Her reading stirred her imagination and inspired her to write plays and stories in little school tablets that her mother bought for her. Her earliest stories are written in pencil in a bold, clear print; the later ones, in ink. The covers of some of these little books, which were no bigger than four by five inches, were bound with string and illustrated with charming crayon drawings also done by the author.[57] These little books are precious evidence of a writer in progress.

Her childhood writings reflected her favorite books: *Treasure Seekers, The Story of the Amulet,* and "The Psammead." She loved the stories by E. Nesbit, and *Five Children and It* and *The Phoenix and the Carpet* were her most treasured volumes. When she was grown, she gave copies of these two books to all of her nieces and nephews and her friends' children. Long after she became famous, she kept her own two, well-worn copies of the little books in her bookcase. She liked to read boys' stories, particularly those by George Alfred Henty. Stephens remembered that during one period she collected series, such as *The Rover Boys.* When he criticized her for doing so, telling her that the plots were always the same and the style always terrible, she said that a good plot would stand retelling and style did not matter "so long as you can understand what the characters are doing."[58] She also loved the romantic adventures of George Barr McCutcheon and Richard Harding Davis, and her early writings, which bore such titles as "The Fall of Ralph the Rover," "In My Harem," "The Cow Puncher," "A Darktown Tragedy," "The Little Pioneers," and "Phil Kelly, Detective," reflect the influence of those two writers.

Through the years, Maybelle encouraged Peggy to write and lavished praise on her works. Her writings were not shown to anyone except her mother and occasionally her father, but no one else, not even her brother. The family, Stephens said, did not treat her as if she were "a genius" though her mother, no doubt, thought Peggy was one.[59] Maybelle saved every one of her daughter's stories, storing them in white enamel bread boxes that she called "safes."[60] Stephens wrote: "I don't know how soon the first bread box was filled up, but several of them went along with us when we moved from Jackson Hill to Peachtree Street. By the time Margaret went off to college, there was an imposing row of breadboxes on a shelf in the storeroom. She never stopped writing."[61]

When she was about ten or twelve years old, she evaluated her own talent by writing in the front of one of the copybooks: "There are authors and authors but a *true* author is born and not made. Born writers make their characters real, living people, while the 'made' writers have merely stuffed figures who dance when the string is pulled—That's how I know that I'm a 'made' writer."[62]

When Peggy became a teenager, her mother took her on short summer vacations to resorts like Wrightsville Beach in Wilmington, North Carolina, and Atlantic Beach at Jacksonville, Florida, where she got to meet other young people her own age. Once a year, Eugene Mitchell took the family on long vacations to Boston or New York, and they took several trips on ocean liners up the Hudson River to Albany, New York. Peggy excitedly looked forward to the melodramas her parents took her to see whenever they visited New York. Once back home, she used the ideas she got from them in her own writings. The early plays that she wrote, directed, and starred in, using neighborhood children to fill minor roles, were full of action and what she called "cold, unscrupulous, revengeful" villains, children hiding between the walls of frontier forts, Indian attacks, and brave defenders.[63]

8

More philosophical and attuned to her children's psyches than her husband ever was, Maybelle had a calming influence on him. For example, when seventeen-year-old Peggy, who had been in and out of love dozens of times, became engaged to Clifford Henry, a young lieutenant in France during World War I, her father became furious thinking about the possibility of his only daughter marrying some man about whom he knew nothing. While Peggy and her mother were on a trip to New York, where they met the young man's parents, Maybelle wrote reassuringly to her husband, "Dear, you must have had no youth or forgotten it if you attach so much importance to the affections of seventeen years. . . . Why worry over what can't happen for four or five years and 99 to 100 will not happen at all. . . . So put *your* mind at rest about this affair, as there can come no harm of it."[64] Maybelle always deflected Eugene's temper away from Peggy.

Maybelle was also more sensitive about everything than Eugene was. She was concerned about the poor and the injustices heaped upon women and blacks—injustices that do not seem to have bothered Eugene at all.[65] Although Stephens wrote that his father "never hesitated to take unpopular stands on public issues, nor to place himself in danger of violence, at a time when Atlanta had dangerous mobs, and when rioting and lynching were common," Stephens provided no examples of his father's stands.[66] However, we do have evidence of Maybelle's sensitivity to the suffering of others. In one of his letters written while she was away resting with her relatives, Eugene admonished her: "You injure yourself by troubling over other people's misfortunes."[67]

Peggy and Stephens loved their father but they adored their mother. Long after she was grown, Peggy described her mother in a letter to Harvey Smith:

> No, I'm not what mother was as she was the smartest and the kindest and the most attractive woman I ever saw. She was a real aristocrat if ever I saw one and carried no side at all. She was passionately interested in every thing that drew breath, and being an aristocrat it never once occurred to her that she could be demeaned by associating with anyone, even the lowliest. She was constantly taking up with strange people on street cars and trains

and having exciting and animated arguments with them. She stopped the car at Five Points, if necessary, to call to old negroes who had worked for her or her family and held long, public conversations with them on their love lives and their miseries. She never turned any hungry or needy person from her door and I've seen her peel off her gloves on cold days to put on the blue hands of poor children and only restrained [her] by my wails from giving my muff too. And lots of times, we walked home from town because she'd given her last cent and car fare to someone who needed it. I don't believe she ever consciously gave a thought to social position as social position. She simply took it as naturally as the air she breathed that she was "good folks" and would have thought it very ill bred to ever admit that she thought it.[68]

Fans of *Gone With the Wind* may see the resemblance between Maybelle and Scarlett's mother, Ellen, and even between Maybelle and Melanie. Also, the kind of relationship that Ellen and Gerald O'Hara have in the novel is similar to the relationship that Peggy's parents had.

As her husband's business steadily prospered and he became more and more involved in civic activities, Maybelle pursued her own intellectual interests in religion and social issues. She studied her Catholicism thoroughly and was prominent in the affairs of the Sacred Heart Church. She advanced the modern but unpopular notion that women, as well as men, should have an active role in the leadership of the church. Much to the clergy's dismay, she spoke often and openly about this role and was one of the founders of the Catholic Laymen's Association.[69] She was also one of the founders of the women's suffrage movement in Atlanta. Basing her argument on the principle of justice, she objected to paying taxes on the property and the money she had inherited from her father without the privilege of voting on how the money should be spent.[70]

In 1909, Eugene Mitchell was able to purchase a large lot on Peachtree Street and build a two-story, classical colonial-style house with terraces, the kind that many Georgians were building after the turn of the century as a reaction to the ornate architecture of the Victorian age.[71] The family moved into 1149 (later numbered 1401) Peachtree Street in the fall of 1912, when Peggy was twelve. Stephens wrote that this house was "exactly the house Mother had wanted to live in. It was in every detail the complete fulfillment of her dreams and I believe she was completely happy here though the time was shorter than any of us could have foreseen."[72] It is no exaggeration to describe this residence as a mansion. The ground floor spread for seventy feet; it had a parlor, a sitting room, a music room, a dining room, a large kitchen, a pantry, and a huge front entrance hall. Upstairs were spacious bedrooms that opened onto porches. The front rooms were usually kept open but could be closed off by tall folding doors.

Inspired by the children in this new neighborhood, who liked to act, Peggy began writing plays. "Her taste and style were melodramatic," Stephens said. "Action was the big thing. And lots of it from the opening line."[73] With Maybelle's encouragement Peggy recruited children to act in her plays, and the performances were conducted in the great front rooms of the Peachtree mansion. Peggy and the neighborhood children, dressed in homemade costumes, delighted the audience of mothers, grandmothers, and whomever else they could find to support their theatrical endeavors. Maybelle made these occasions special by serving desserts. These performances created many happy times for mother and daughter, but this house would never have the happy memories for Peggy that the Jackson Street house had. The Peachtree house was always too large, too formal, and too cold to suit her; and it was associated with sadness because it was there that her mother died in 1919.

9

In 1914, Maybelle enrolled Peggy in a fashionable private finishing school—Washington Seminary, which was in walking distance of their home. Originally named the "North Avenue Presbyterian School for Women," it had, by this time, moved to Peachtree Street and changed its name.[74] Peggy usually walked to and from school with the neighborhood children. In her first years at Washington Seminary, she was chubby and still much the tomboy. Her nickname, which she bitterly resented, was "piano legs."[75] She was not studious, and one of her report cards shows her barely passing geometry and Latin, making *C*'s in French and in English, but *B*'s in history and in mythology, suggesting that she did well in subjects that interested her. Mrs. Eva Wilson Paisley, an English teacher, took a special interest in her but was unable to convince her to study hard.

Not all the girls in this school liked Peggy, who ran around with a small group called the "Happy Gang." After her best friend, Courtenay Ross, was accepted into the Pi Phi Sorority (Courtenay's older sister was already a member), Courtenay nominated Peggy. But Peggy was blackballed. It was a shocking rejection, one that neither she nor her family ever forgot. In writing about this period in his sister's life, Stephens recorded in his memoir, "Margaret did not like Washington Seminary. She did not get an invitation to join any of the school sororities, but she had begun to meet people outside of school circles and she never lacked for men friends." Although Stephens never explained the reason for her being blackballed— he may not have known the reason—he did write that "at school she had

~ 35 ~

made enemies as well as friends. The judgment of adolescents was wrong, but it led to much bitterness. There are people in Atlanta who have always disliked Margaret Mitchell and will always dislike her. Margaret never forgot who were her enemies."[76]

According to *Facts and Fancies,* the senior yearbook, Peggy did achieve some successes. She belonged to the Senior Round Table, a five-member honorary group of class leaders, and she was the secretary and president of the Washington Literary Society and of the Dramatic Club. She was also the literary editor of the yearbook during her senior year. [77] In concluding his assessment of this period in his sister's life, Stephens wrote, "At the end of her school days, we find a girl who had not made a social success at her school, though she came of an old family who had sufficient means to provide her with the proper things for a young girl entering on her social life in the city." The rejection she felt at Washington Seminary fed into her natural inclination toward rebelliousness, which manifested itself a little later in behavior that worried her father and grandmother.

By the time she had turned seventeen, she had slimmed down to less than ninety pounds. She dressed in stylish, feminine fashions, and usually wore long skirts because she thought her legs were ugly. Without any effort on her part, she attracted boys who began to look upon her as something other than a good shortstop. She and Courtenay were popular with boys, and they went to many parties at the Piedmont Driving Club and the Capital City Club. With the help of their parents, they also hosted many beautiful parties, some for the soldiers at Fort McPherson and at Camp Gordon. Their first formal dance was on November 24, 1916, when Courtenay's parents gave a dance for her at the Piedmont Driving Club. Another dance, given by Courtenay's parents at their home on 47 The Prado, on June 28, 1917, was reported in the society section of one of the Atlanta newspapers. The names "Margaret Mitchell" and "Berrien Upshaw" were included in the guest list.[78] At that time, Upshaw was one of Courtenay's dates, but later he would play an important role in Peggy's and John's lives.

The Washington Seminary did not prepare Peggy for Smith College, where her mother sent her after her graduation. One of the pioneers in the promotion of higher education for women, Smith College was somewhat beyond the norm for most of Atlanta's debutantes. But Maybelle believed that Peggy would be better off going far away to college, meeting new people, getting a fresh start.[79] Her reasons for selecting Smith are evidence of her concern that Peggy achieve social as well as academic success. Two weeks prior to the day she had to attend registration at Smith, Peggy left Atlanta with her mother for a vacation in New York City, where they shopped, visited museums, saw Broadway plays, dined in the finest restaurants, and stayed in the Waldorf-Astoria, the city's best hotel. Their letters to Eugene and Stephens are full of excitement and news; and the old, faded snapshots of this trip, their last time together, show their smiling faces radiant with happiness.

10

After her mother's sudden, unexpected death in the flu epidemic in January 1919, Peggy came home, of course, for the funeral, but at her father's insistence returned to Northampton to complete her freshman year. She had been a great social success at Smith; she made many friends, particularly with the Amherst College boys nearby, who were enthralled with her southern style of femininity. But she was not academically successful, and her vivid memories of her mother's expectations made her even more aware that she was not. Shortly after receiving her midterm grades, she wrote her brother on March 17, 1919:

> Steve, sometimes I get so discouraged I feel that there is no use keeping on here. It isn't in studies, for I'm about a "C" student— but I haven't done a thing up here. I haven't shone in any line— academic, athletic, literary, musical or anything. . . . In a college of 2500 there are so many cleverer and more talented girls than I. If I can't be first, I'd rather be nothing.[80]

At the end of the term, her father asked that she return to Atlanta to keep house for him and her brother. At eighteen, unhappy and uncertain about her future, Peggy returned home.

11

Like Peggy, John came from a sturdy stock of hard-working men and women who had courage and endurance. His ancestors knew neither great wealth nor extreme poverty. Modest, self-reliant, and intelligent, they were self-contained and quiet people, unlike the great talkers in Peggy's family. They were what is called in northern Kentucky "backbone people," what Peggy referred to as "buckwheat people."[81]

John's family took pride in having been among the early settlers of Kentucky, the birthplace of Abraham Lincoln and Jefferson Davis, the opposing presidents in the Civil War. His ancestors fought in the Revolutionary War, in the War of 1812, and in many Indian battles. Before settling in Kentucky, his mother's people had been well-to-do tidewater Virginians of English and French Huguenot ancestry.[82] His maternal great-great-great-grandfather, Thomas Berry, served as a captain in the

Continental Army and was General George Washington's bodyguard at Valley Forge for three years. In Clarke County, Virginia, Berry's Ferry is named after Thomas, and Berryville, Virginia, for Thomas's brother, Benjamin.

In 1776, when Kentucky became a county of Virginia, John's maternal ancestors, along with many other Virginians, moved into the frontier wilderness that the Cherokee Indians named "Kentucky," their word for "Dark and Bloody Ground."[83] The land was given that name because of the many bloody battles the early settlers fought with the Indians there. In fact, William Kennan, his mother's great-grandfather, was a famous strong and swift runner in his youth and is recognized in Collins's *History of Kentucky* as a "brave Indian fighter."[84] Also recognized in that book is John's maternal great-great-grandfather, John Kercheval of Huguenot ancestry, who was a representative in the Kentucky legislature for many years.

John's people on his father's side were all frontiersmen who in the early eighteenth century hacked their way across the mountains in Pennsylvania to Kentucky or came down the Ohio River in flatboats. One group floated down the river with a piano strapped to their flatboat. They endured many hardships before they carved out a place for themselves in northern Kentucky, in what is now known as Maysville.[85]

Before and for a long time after the Civil War, Maysville was a prosperous community, established as a town by the legislature of Virginia on December 11, 1787. Stretched out narrowly on one of the highest banks of the Ohio River in northern Kentucky, Maysville is located at the mouth of Limestone Creek and was called Limestone until about 1793. Built on what was known as Limestone Landing, it was a bustling port of entry used by pioneers, traders, hunters, and adventurers, floating down the Ohio River in their crude wooden flatboats, canoes, and rafts in the late eighteenth century. While John was growing up there, it had a population of eight thousand.

Because of its great salt licks south of the Ohio River, Maysville attracted buffalo for over ten thousand years. The wide, winding path that the buffalo stomped out from the banks of the river down the hill into the valley and on to Blue Licks is still known as the Old Buffalo Trace.[86] The first settlers used this path as a gateway to the West as early as 1751.[87]

So it was that while Peggy as a child explored old entrenchments and Civil War battlegrounds and listened to endless tales about bloodthirsty Yankees, John and his brothers explored the Old Buffalo Trace, searched for arrowheads on the banks of the Ohio River, and listened to old-timers talk about the fierce skirmishes they had had with Tecumseh and his allies.

His father's parents were Abi Neal and Jacob Marsh, a farmer who moved from his birthplace in West Union, Ohio, to Mason County in 1856, shortly after he and Abi were wed. For many years, they lived at the mouth of Lawrence Creek. They were married for fifty-five years and had seven sons and two daughters. Their third son was John's father, who was born on October 23, 1855, in South Ripley, Ohio, less than ten miles from Maysville. He was named Millard Fillmore Marsh after the president who had gone out of office in 1853, the president who loved the Union more than he hated slavery and thus enforced the Compromise of 1850. When Millard Marsh was only a year old, his parents moved to Charleston Bottoms, three miles west of Maysville, and there he grew to manhood, working on his father's farm in the summer and attending public school in the winter. When he was twenty-one, he accepted a teaching position at the Maysville Seminary, but he resigned after a brief time to take charge of a private school at Brooksville, about eighteen miles away, in Bracken County. While teaching at Brooksville, he studied law in nearby Cincinnati, Ohio, and the following spring was admitted to the Maysville bar. For several years he practiced law in Maysville, where he also had a real estate and insurance business. In 1885, he became the editor of the *Maysville Daily Bulletin* and held that position until his death, nearly twenty years later.[88] Well liked in the community, he was nicknamed "The Squire" because of his gentlemanly manner.

On December 23, 1889, Millard married the blue-eyed, blond-haired Mary Douglas Toup, eleven years younger than he. Born in October 1866, Mary was the daughter of Sara Jane Kercheval Kennan and Robert A. Toup, both of whose parents were born in Virginia and came to Fleming County, Kentucky, as young adults.[89]

Millard and Mary's third child, John was born at eleven o'clock Sunday morning on October 6, 1895, in his parents' plain, two-story, white-frame house on Forest Avenue, in Maysville. Blue-eyed and towheaded, he was christened John Robert after his mother's father, her brother, and her great-grandfather Kercheval. The least robust of the Marshes' five children, John was remembered as the child who did not join in outdoor games with other children, but stayed on the sidelines and watched. Also, perhaps because of his frailness, he developed early a reputation for stoicism, independence, and scholarship. His quietness was made more noticeable by the easy gregariousness of his older brother Henry.

Nicknamed "Little Squire" because he resembled his father, John was the only one of the children who liked to visit his father's newspaper office. Many of the townspeople even figured that he would grow up to be a newspaperman like his dad.[90] Forty-five years later and close to death, John wrote about his memories of the *Bulletin* one afternoon after he had toured the splendid new offices of the *Atlanta Journal*. Wondering if the filthy, noisy, bustling old offices did not produce far better newspaper writers than the sophisticated new ones did, he thought about his father's office and wrote that it was "crowded, cluttered, and dirty enough to produce genius, if my theory is correct. Among my outstanding memories of going there to see Father is the pot of flour paste on his desk, how messy it was and how bad it smelled."[91]

In 1904, after suffering from what appeared to be a mild attack of typhoid fever, from which he seemed to recover, John's father became very ill on the day after Christmas. In the early morning hours of December 30, he died, apparently of a heart attack, in much the same manner as John would die years later. He died in the same bed and in the same upstairs bedroom where all of his children had been born. He was only forty-nine years old; John, a spindly-legged little boy, was only eight. In Maysville, where Millard had lived all his life, he was admired for his intelligence, modesty, and unselfishness. So many people attended his funeral service at the Christian Church on the bitter-cold Sunday afternoon of January 1, 1905, that some had to stand in the Sunday School room at the rear of the pulpit. In his eulogy, the minister compared him to the biblical character Barnabas, whom Millard apparently tried to emulate, having marked the passages describing Barnabas in his own Bible. The *Evening Bulletin* announcing his sudden death described him as "a good, kind, gentle, Christian man, generous to a fault and greatly beloved by his colleagues." Years later, John said that he never forgot the chill he felt in his veins on that cold, windy day as he stood alongside his young mother, brothers, and sisters as they silently watched their loved one's pine-wood coffin lowered into the hard ground.[92]

12

His father's death had a profound influence on John. It not only robbed him of a beloved parent and changed his family's household drastically, but it forced his mother to go to work, and it robbed him of his childhood. Katharine, the oldest child at fourteen, was sent away to a nearby boarding academy for a while, and Henry, the next-oldest at eleven, took various jobs after school to bring in some extra income. Only eight years old, John was given the responsibility of helping his grandmother look after five-year-old Ben Gordon and three-year-old Frances.[93] Even though he was just a child himself, he nurtured and protected his siblings as if he were an adult. Unable to remember their father because they were so young when he died, Ben Gordon and Frances grew up thinking of John as their protector. To the end of his life, they went to him for advice. In fact, long after Frances was a grown, married woman with sons of her own, Henry thought that John continued "to baby" her, just as John had done while they were all growing up.[94] Years later, Frances hinted at the slight conflicts she occasionally had with Henry when she said: "John always had a feeling for people. My oldest brother always had a career in ballistics and chemistry. He was a scientist. He did not have that feeling for people or understanding of them. And my younger brother loved farm things, and he ended up working in the agricultural department. But John and I were the closest of all the children—we were both interested in people."[95]

As a middle child will often do, John learned to serve as a link between the older and the younger children and between the children and the grownups. His skill at mediation became a hallmark trait that benefited him as an adult. Systematic about everything, when he was around ten years old he adopted what was to become a lifelong habit—keeping meticulous records of nearly everything in his small, neat handwriting. Because of his ability to record and to write, as a teenager he worked placing orders and keeping record books for Miss Anna Frank and her brother George in their retail men's clothing store on Main Street. They were so fond of him that they helped pay his expenses when he moved to Lexington to attend the University of Kentucky.

Some people in Maysville credited John's inner strength and sensitivity to the close relationship he had with his mother during his early illnesses. When he was only three, he came down with scarlet fever. Fearing that the other children would become infected also, his mother sent them to stay with her widowed mother, Sara Jane Kercheval Kennan Toup, who lived in the white house next door with her unmarried sister, Molly Kennan, and Mary's bachelor brother, Bob. During this separation period while little John, his dad, and his mother were confined to their house, she read to him and played games with him. She also made little puppets out of old socks and rags for each of her children. Every morning and evening, she would stand at the window that faced the house next door and look across the lawn at the window that framed her little loved ones' faces. Holding her son in one arm and a puppet in the other, she would amuse all the children with her pantomimes.[96]

Although John slowly recovered from the fever, he was left extremely thin and frail, with a weakened heart and damaged hearing—conditions that contributed to his lifelong reticence and also made him subject to continual illnesses. Because he was so often sick in bed or convalescing in the house, he turned to books for his entertainment. A little later on, he took to teaching reading and writing to his younger brother and sister.

13

With the untimely death of her husband, Mary was left with enormous responsibilities. Never having worked outside her home, she now had to find a way to support herself and her five young children. She also had to look after her aging mother, aunt, and her bachelor brother. For women, opportunities for jobs were limited in those days, and Mary took the first job she was offered. She became a teacher at the First Ward School on West Second Street, down at the far end of Maysville. She had a three-mile walk there and back each day, for although Maysville had a streetcar line, in those days carfare would have been an extravagance for her.[97]

Because of her own plight, Mary was sensitive to the suffering of others. Across the street from her school was the January and Woods Cotton Mill. Many of the poor people who worked long hours for a pittance in the mill sent their children to the First Ward School. When Mary realized that nearly every one of these children went all day without having anything to eat, she recruited some volunteer carpenters to build a makeshift kitchen in the basement of the school. Then she organized a group of women to come in every morning to prepare hot meals for the children. This act alone endeared her to many people, and her open and honest affection for children also made her admired and respected. After several years, she was promoted to principal of the Forest Avenue Fifth Ward School, only a short walk from her home.[98] She was best remembered as a woman not given to engaging in trivial conversations, complaints, or gossip, and was described as hard-working, soft-spoken, and modest. Dedicated to her family, she never remarried.

Her belief in God sustained her and made her fearless, optimistic, and resilient. She read her Bible daily, and for many years she taught Sunday school classes for young people. She had an indomitable quality—that born fighter's spirit to keep going on no matter how difficult life got.[99]

Remembering her childhood and her mother's cheerfulness, Frances said later, "I never felt poor. I know people sometimes depress their children, but our mother never did that. She would stay up late at night making and embroidering many dresses for us, and I'd be the prettiest girl at the party. She was that kind of a mother. And she never talked 'You can't do this because we haven't got the money.' We just knew we didn't have the money. But we never felt poor."[100]

Eager to foster in her children a love of nature and of books, she taught them all to read before they went to school and to value books as a great source of information. To her credit, all five of her children went on to earn college degrees. When they all were small, she read passages from the Bible to them daily, and she also read Aesop's fables and other didactic literature.

As they grew up, she had them take turns reading aloud from Homer and the Greek tragedians, from Goldsmith, Shakespeare, Gray, Dickens, Austen, and the Brontës.[101] She took them to church and to Sunday school every Sunday; and on holidays and birthdays, she took them to visit their father's grave. She often gathered them together for picnics and long walks, teaching them the names of wildflowers, trees, and birds, and how to note changes in the seasons and weather. For many years, she was Maysville's official weather observer, an unusual responsibility for a woman in the early 1900s. Her weather reports were published in the local newspaper.[102]

Her love for books and music and her reverence for the English language influenced John and Frances; her love for wildlife and nature influenced Henry, Ben Gordon, and Katharine. To all of her children, she passed on her strong sense of independence, loyalty, and responsibility. Despite the loss of their father, the Marsh children grew up loving and being loved, with the warmth and security of a happy childhood. As adults, they remained close to each other.[103] Once they began to move away from home, John's mother started what she called Round Robin letters. She wrote a letter to the oldest child, who in turn wrote a letter and mailed it along with Mrs. Marsh's to the next child, who would do the same. The "Robins" formed a perpetual network of communication among the family for over two decades—until Mary Marsh's death in 1950.

A poignant letter that John wrote to his mother on Thanksgiving Day 1923, when he was twenty-eight years old, indicates that Mary Marsh must have been a remarkable parent. Lonely and sad, missing Peggy, who at that time had left town because she had created more problems for herself, her family, and for him than he thought could ever be solved, he wrote:

> I do have you to be thankful for and there's no harm in telling. As I get older and see other families and other young people who have grown up in other families, I come more and more to appreciate my own. Looking at it scientifically, and not sentimentally, I can thank you for a home environment which has given me a body that remains healthy in spite of my neglect and abuse and for a mind that is free of so many of the obsessions and unpleasant complexes that so many people acquire in their childhood. I haven't the bitterness in me that I find in other people because I never experienced neglect or thoughtlessness from you and the unreasoning fears that lurk in the background of so many minds because of forgotten childhood unpleasantness are not lurking in my mind. I appreciate these things and I am thankful for them.

John had been profoundly influenced in a positive manner by the women in his family. He had grown up watching his mother, grandmother, and aunt struggle to keep their family together. They did it without complaining, blaming, or succumbing to their emotions. He remembered how hard they worked to keep up their homes, doing many of the needed repairs themselves, and how they sewed, gardened, and stored vegetables for the winter. Except for his uncle Bob, a harness maker, and brief memories he had of his grandfather and his father, he had no adult male in his family to learn from. The strong role models in his childhood were all good women, and thus he grew up with a sympathetic understanding of and concern for women. He was sensitive to their needs. Too, he had grown up not only looking after himself but also looking after his younger brother and sister. His natural inclination was to be protective and caring and, of course, that suited Peggy's dependent personality perfectly.

C H A P T E R **3**

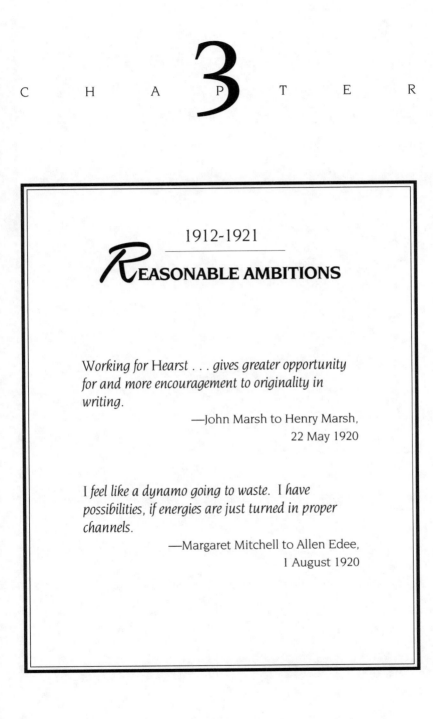

1912-1921

*R*EASONABLE AMBITIONS

*Working for Hearst . . . gives greater opportunity
for and more encouragement to originality in
writing.*

—John Marsh to Henry Marsh,
22 May 1920

*I feel like a dynamo going to waste. I have
possibilities, if energies are just turned in proper
channels.*

—Margaret Mitchell to Allen Edee,
1 August 1920

1

IN THE FALL OF 1912, while Peggy was still a chubby adolescent attending Washington Seminary, John moved to Lexington to enroll in the College of Arts and Sciences at the University of Kentucky, where his older brother Henry was already working toward his degree. At that time all residents of Kentucky who met the enrollment requirements were admitted into the university free of tuition.[1] But many, like Henry and John, had to work to pay for their books and living expenses.

Because he was the oldest son, Henry assumed a leadership role with the rest of the children, whom he tried to look after as his father would have wanted him to do. In order for John to room with him and share expenses, Henry moved from Mrs. Frazer's boarding house, where he had been living, into an apartment on 120 East Maxwell Street, a convenient location halfway between the university and the town. Later, Henry was to say that he saw very little of John except at mealtimes and in the evenings. Once at college, John lost much of his shyness, becoming involved in numerous activities and making many friends. But Henry said later: "We had different sets of friends." Indicating that John behaved in a typical younger-brother fashion, he added: "He resented help I tried to give and referred to me as his private conscience. We got along all right, but we didn't have too much to do with one another at school."[2] They never had any classes or campus activities together because John's studies were in humanities and journalism, while Henry's were in the sciences.[3] During his college years, John courted a classmate, the pretty, red-haired Kitty Mitchell from Bowling Green, Kentucky.[4]

He applied for a degree in English, a rigorous program that, at that time, required its majors to read some world literature in its original language. During his freshman year he studied Greek, advanced Latin (concentrating on the study of Livy and Horace), German (which included intensive study of Schiller and modern dramatists), and English composition (which, according to the university bulletin, stressed "accuracy of expression rather than proficiency in style"). He also took physical education and the required military science. His favorite upper-level courses included those in British Romanticism, which focused on Wordsworth, Byron, Shelley, and Keats; and Victorian Authors, which examined the works of Thackeray, Tennyson, the two Brownings, and Swinburne.[5] He studied Shakespeare, the history of the English language, principles of literary criticism, Old English, Middle English, Anglo-Saxon studies, ancient history, and something called "pro-seminary," a senior course designed to train students in the principles of form and method. It was a required course for all English majors, and the subject of study varied from year to year; John's class examined the lives and works of Milton and Browning. In addition, he took classes in logic, chemistry, physiology, geology, trigonometry, advanced German, and three courses in journalism. His graduate work included two semesters of advanced composition and two semesters of Principles of English Criticism.

In addition to his coursework, he participated fully in all the literary and academic clubs. A sign of having reached the pinnacle of social success and intellectual achievement at the University of Kentucky was membership in the Canterbury Club. Only those persons who showed a marked interest in and talent for story writing, poetry, criticism, and drama were eligible, and no student was admitted who was not unanimously elected. John was a member all four years. He was the associate editor of *The Kentuckian,* the college yearbook; one of the editors of *The Kentucky Kernel,* the college newspaper; and a member of the Strollers, a dramatic organization that brought much favorable attention to the university. Also, he belonged to Alpha Delta Sigma, a fraternity for journalists. Although he enjoyed swimming, he was not athletic, nor was he particularly interested in attending athletic events. Because both of his brothers were sports enthusiasts (Ben Gordon played basketball for the University of Kentucky), John went to ball games with them occasionally, but his primary interests were literature and music. Like his mother, he loved the opera.

2

Having to support himself, he took a part-time job immediately after he settled in Lexington. He started out as a proofreader for the *Lexington Herald,* a morning paper; soon he was promoted to reporter. A little later on, he wrote for the *Lexington Leader,* the evening paper. In those days, the Lexington newspapers started its cub reporters on police beats, for police reporting required the cub to achieve accuracy in securing details, and forced the cub to learn every section of the town and country.[6] Back then, newspapers did not highlight news about unsavory characters and deeds as they do now; that kind of information and identification was relegated to columns labeled "Police Report," and this was John's beat.

By covering the police beat, which involved becoming friends with policemen and accompanying them on their night walks and calls, young reporters got to know all the law enforcement people and all the county's interesting, though shady, underworld figures. And that is how John got to know Belle Brezing, who operated "a gilded mansion for men," perhaps the "most elegant" and "most orderly of the disorderly houses" in the nation, according to a *Time Magazine* article noting Belle's death in 1940. The cub reporters and the policemen covering "the tenderloin section," so called because of its bribes and handouts, viewed their duty as a choice assignment. Belle's kitchen always cordially beckoned them in for a delicious meal, quite a treat for a poor college student. In exchange for her culinary offerings, she could depend on the policemen to restore order in case there were fights, or to dispatch drunks, and she could count on the newspapermen to keep silent about certain reports and the names of certain clients.[7] It is not unreasonable to think that on many nights young John Marsh sat right alongside a policeman in Belle's kitchen, enjoyed a fine meal, met many interesting people, and heard many colorful stories—stories that he could not write about in his letters to his mother and sisters. However, he did discuss such matters with his brothers, and later with his wife, who had no knowledge of such places but great curiosity about them.[8]

In the 1916 University of Kentucky yearbook, the statement next to John's senior class picture describes him as follows: "Only a few men on the campus know John's real worth. He has worked silently and calmly regardless of any immediate reward. We who know him know only that when John promises you to do anything, you can just as well forget it, knowing it will be *done.*"

And interesting too, in that same yearbook, is the class prophecy predicting that in ten years John Marsh would be a proofreader for the "Bowling Green Suffrage Journal." His classmates made this statement because John was proofreading the articles written by Kitty Mitchell, his college sweetheart, a suffragette who planned to return to her hometown of Bowling Green, Kentucky, to write articles about women's issues.[9] The prophecy is important to note because it suggests that even at this early stage John was influencing the writing of others.

In 1916, he graduated with a bachelor of arts degree, with a major in English. He was then accepted into graduate school and hired as a part-time English instructor. He taught two sections of English composition at the University of Kentucky while he was doing his graduate work and at the same time still writing for the *Lexington Leader;* his articles now carried his byline.

In September 1917, he enlisted in the Barrow Unit of the Armed Services at Lexington. According to a Frankfort, Kentucky, newspaper clipping datelined February 26, 1917, John was paid the highest compliment by a rising vote of the Kentucky legislature commending him for patriotism in joining the army.[10] Although many others in that area volunteered to go into the service, John was the only young man who received a standing ovation from the legislators, indicating how much he was admired and respected, both professionally and personally. He enlisted in a hospital unit organized by Dr. David Barrow of Lexington; his unit was called to duty in February 1918. He was first sent to England to work in the office of a hospital for seven months, and then to France. While away, John frequently wrote long, descriptive letters to his family and also many articles that the *Leader* published. In 1918, the editor of that newspaper wrote to Corporal John Marsh asking him to return to the staff: "Personally I consider you a young newspaper man of unusual promise and I believe you have the personal character back of your talent to support any reasonable ambition which you may have in connection with your literary work."[11]

3

Just about the same time that Peggy, after her mother's death, was returning to Northampton in early 1919 to complete her spring semester at Smith, John was on his way to France. He was stationed at a hospital in Savenay, which he described as "an insignificant little French village located on the Loire river not far from the Coast, but the Americans have made it hum."[12] In a letter to his mother on March 15, he described his surroundings, saying that from the third floor of the main building, where he worked, he could see the village of St. Nazaire and beyond that the sea. "The Loire river valley is just to the southwest of us, a beautiful wide plain cut into tiny fields by hedges and dotted here and there by small villages or farm buildings huddled together. The river becomes an arm of the sea and widens out into the proportions of a bay before it finally loses its identity in the Bay of Biscay."

Stationed in an area where there were eight base hospitals within a radius of a few miles and several thousand patients, John wrote that the most serious patients were taken to his hospital—Base Hospital 69, "located in a French school building, an 'Ecole Normale,' built of irregular blocks, with almost a stucco effect." He explained, "Some of the buildings of the school just across the road are still used by the French and are filled with students, young men, who wear dark blue uniforms and little smashed down soldiers' caps like we see in pictures of the Blue and the Gray." Not wanting to worry his mother with detailed accounts of the suffering that he saw in the hospital, he simply said: "There is scarcely a day when from one to three hospital trains do not leave from here with patients for the States or arrive with new cases from the interior. I have seen more men short a leg or so here than I ever saw in one place before."

In addition to the hospitals, he said there was a large detachment of marines, military police, and several hundred prisoners of war:

> This is my first experience with captured Germans and Austrians, and I find it interesting to study them. All the types can be seen, the extremely youthful, rosy-cheeked lad, the angular be-spectacled professor type, the heavy brutal Hun (occasionally), but most often the stolid, slow, submissive type that doesn't look any different from the Germans in the States. They are "well-nourished," warmly clothed and apparently not at all rebellious against their condition. The guards who take the P.W.'s out to work on the roads say that it is impossible to lose them. Occasionally one gets separated from the others but he is always sure to come back as soon as he can find the way.

One weekend in May, he visited Dijon and wrote descriptions of the magnificent museums that he visited there. However, he thought that the most interesting place to visit was the Rue de Forges, a street where the Huguenots' quarters used to be located and where, he said, "I conjectured that our Kercheval ancestors might have lived." Giving a little history of the place, he wrote: "It was here that the Huguenots were assembled one day back in 1500, several thousands of them, and it was planned to massacre them all, but someone intervened and, instead, they were driven out of the city. It sounds very much like the story of our ancestors, and I am trying to find some history here that will tell me more about it. I haven't met anyone over here by the name of Kercheval yet but stranger things have happened."

In one of his letters to his mother, he enclosed a book of Keats's poems that he had purchased in England and said he wanted back when he got home. He also enclosed a little present for his sister Frances. He called it a "golliwog" and said that he had gotten it in England, where these items were considered "lucky charms and worn for protection against air-raids."

In describing his location, he wrote that Savenay had narrow, dirty streets, but good cafés where "one can buy eggs and French fries, occasionally steak and a few others things that taste like a million dollars." Apparently his favorite café was the Café des Allies, a tiny place that he said was "presided over by Susanne, who does not look like a mademoiselle, with her yellow hair, rosy cheeks, and bovinely pretty face. I found out that she is a Belgian, and for the Americans she is the *belle* (no pun intended) of the village, characteristically vivacious and with enough English to 'carry on.' . . . My French is progressing slowly."

Like thousands of other soldiers' mothers, his mother worried, among other things, about John's falling in love with some girl overseas. She must have mentioned something to him about being careful in his associations with the French women, because John reassured her: "Don't worry about me and the mademoiselles francais. . . . I haven't even seen a goodlooking one since I left Paris. Incidentally . . . it is well to remember that just at present I am too much interested in at least one Kentucky girl to be able to realize that there are any others in the world."

Not long after he made that comment, he received word that Kitty Mitchell, that Kentucky girl he was so interested in, had met and married a wealthy, older Cuban businessman and gone to live in Santiago. This news devastated John. Yet, painful as it was at first, he was willing to maintain the friendship that she wanted to keep with him. A few years later, Kitty visited him in Atlanta on two occasions, and they corresponded with each other throughout the remainder of their lives.

Just a few weeks before he was to return home to the States, John became seriously ill with ptomaine poisoning after he, along with at least three other soldiers, consumed some contaminated food. He remarked to his brothers later that he felt "pretty ridiculous going through the war without getting a scratch and then damned-near getting killed from eating supper in the army mess hall."[13] In 1927, the government sent him financial compensation for this illness.

4

On June 9, 1919, he wrote his mother that he was headed home to the States and expected to be in Kentucky by the middle of July. "When we came over here all of us were thoroughly confident that we would be coming back to see our families and friends some day, but when we leave our French friends and our friends in the Army and among the 'Y' girls, it is with certainty that we will never seem them again. C'est la guerre!" His troop left Beaune for Marseilles on Wednesday morning, June 11, at six o'clock. On June 30, while still on board the U.S.S. *Belvedere* about three hundred miles from New York, John wrote about what a great experience his trip through the Mediterranean was and how much he enjoyed his visit to Gibraltar, where he was permitted to go ashore one morning to see the "quaint old Spanish town that apparently pays little attention to the mighty fortress above it and is still so thoroughly Spanish that the English names to the streets and other English features seem incongruous." Crossing the Atlantic was uneventful, he told his mother, "until a storm raised merry

H——— Up to this time, I had sometimes regretted that I had crossed the ocean and back without seeing a storm, now I am satisfied. . . . Best get the fatted veal up in the barn lot because I am coming for it with my teeth sharpened up on 16 months of corned willy, goldfish, plum and boiled potatoes. You don't know how much it will mean to me to be home again."

Discharged as a sergeant, he returned to the United States on June 30, 1919. After a visit with his family in Maysville, he went back to work in Lexington, Kentucky, at the *Leader*.[14] But, within a few months, he decided not to stay in Lexington. In late March 1920, when he was twenty-five years old, he moved to Atlanta, an exciting newspaper town where he got a job as a reporter for the *Daily Georgian,* one of the chain of papers owned by William Randolph Hearst.

When he first arrived in Atlanta, he rented a room in a boarding house on Currier Street, saying, "It was in a rather a run-down neighborhood with a family easiest described as 'poor but honest,' but with somewhat inconvenient ideas concerning 'bath nights.' I couldn't quite get accustomed to that flaming lithograph of 'Paul and Virginia Fleeing before the Storm' which adorned my bedroom wall."[15] Soon Ed Danforth, a classmate of Henry's at the University of Kentucky and also a writer for the *Georgian,* told him about a vacancy in the place where he was boarding. John moved into this house, which had an excellent location, just a block from the Georgian Terrace Hotel, on 305 West Peachtree Street. The landlady was a Mrs. Prim, a widow with a daughter in grammar school. John described Mrs. Prim as congenial, and as "a motherly sort of woman of 'the quality,' who keeps every thing perfectly clean."[16]

After a month in Atlanta, he wrote his brother Henry that he was beginning to feel at home as a Georgian, though he missed his family and friends in Kentucky. "The Kid Sister [Frances] and I had become great buddies and if I could afford it or could find work for her here wherever I go I would 'carry' her about with me. That word 'carry' appears in every sentence uttered by a Georgian. They 'carry' their girls out to dinner, and 'tote' a box of candy out when they go to see her."[17] He went on to relate an experience that he recently had when he became "a revenooer and went into the Georgia moonshine section to raid some stills and capture a good feature story" for his paper. Because he covered the Federal Building, he said,

> I got wise to a big raid which was to be pulled off in North Georgia, a section where there are more stills to the square foot than there are to the square mile in Kentucky. A party of about ten of us, officers, and a moving picture photographer, went up in automobiles and stayed three days, knocking down the stills in quick

order and traveling over some of the poorest excuses for roads I ever thought possible. A big rain forced us to come back and I wasn't at all sorry as my bones had begun to work loose and wobble about in my skin as a result of the jolting.[18]

As a souvenir of the trip, one of the officers gave him a black Smith and Wesson .32 revolver that the officer had taken off a moonshiner. "It is the long size and will kill at 75 yards I am told. I didn't try it out." This was the pistol that he later gave to Peggy when she felt as if she needed one.[19]

5

With its great railroads, hotels, and fine restaurants, Atlanta was a popular convention city in the 1920s, just as it still is now. Well-known personalities in sports, theater, politics, business, and opera were steadily passing through and, in those days before television, they were all too willing to get good press coverage through interviews and statements. The three big newspapers were the *Atlanta Journal,* the *Atlanta Constitution,* and the *Georgian,* two of them built facing each other across the street and the other right around the corner. Each day, they raced to get editions on the street and tried to out-muscle each other in news coverage, features, sensations, reforms, and blazing headlines. With radio in its infancy, newspapermen were constantly struggling to get any important news out first in "extra" editions. The *Georgian* was the *Journal's* most formidable competitor because the *Constitution* was only a morning paper.[20] Although it had never been as financially or politically successful as the *Journal,* the *Georgian* was relentlessly competitive. For thirty years, the two papers battled furiously. In December 1939, the *Journal* bought out the *Georgian.*

The newspaper world that John fit right into was a rugged, masculine world in the 1920s. William S. Howland, a reporter for the *Atlanta Journal* at that time, said that reporters—he, John, and others—"wrote hard, factual news stories—often of crime and punishment—but with an almost fanatical zeal for factual accuracy and with a politeness, strange in today's news writing, when dealing with unfortunates."[21]

About his new job, John told his brother Henry:

Working for Hearst is no different from other newspaper work, except that it gives greater opportunities for and more encouragement to originality in writing. I don't know what effect it will have on my reputation in the future when I try to join up with some other paper, but there is nothing in the way the *Georgian's* office is run to give any grounds for condemnation. Of course, I frequently disagree with the editorials, but that has been my experience with every paper on which I have worked.[22]

By late 1921, when he met Peggy, John had led an interesting, hard-working, successful, and relatively happy life. He had great confidence in himself and was optimistic about his future. Just the opposite was true of Peggy; she felt decidedly unhappy, shamefully unsuccessful, and woefully uncertain about her future.

6

After Peggy's return to Atlanta from Smith College, at her father's request, she launched her career as a socialite by entering the Debutante Club for the winter season of 1920-1921. Her picture, along with Courtenay Ross's, appears in the *Atlanta Constitution* on September 26, 1920, above an article titled "A Debutante Group for the Social Season of 1920 and 1921."[23] The sole purpose of the organization was formally to introduce the young girls from old, aristocratic Atlanta families to others from the same social sphere. Expectations were that all the debs would marry well.

Taking her new role seriously, she began to study fashions. "When a girl is making a social career, clothes are a uniform to be worn like a soldier's—always well done—never sloppy."[24] Although she was never the least bit neat about keeping her room or even her house tidy, she was fastidious about her person and dress. She carefully selected a wardrobe that not only complemented her beauty and size but also suited the various roles she wanted to enact. Photographs of her during this period show her demurely dressed in dark, tailored suits and t-strapped heels, or with bulky sweaters worn over long skirts together with crisp, white, tailored blouses, low-heeled shoes, and cloches jauntily pulled down on one side of her head. Other, more glamorous pictures show her seductively staring into the camera, dressed in bare-shouldered, diaphanous evening gowns and with ribbons in her dark hair. At this stage of her life, she was very pretty.

Adjusting to being home again was difficult, especially without her mother to deflect her father's criticisms of nearly everything she did. Since Maybelle's death, Eugene had become overly protective and crankier than ever. He had always had difficulty understanding his daughter once she became a teenager, but now he did not understand her at all. After having had a taste of freedom that she could not give up, Peggy began asserting her independence by smoking cigarettes, using profanity, staying out late at night, insisting on being called "Peggy" rather than "Margaret," and seeing other young people of whom her father and grandmother disapproved. She and Peggy Porter (Margaret Lowry Porter), who lived in the house directly behind the Mitchells', ran around with what one of her friends described as "renegades of various types, divorcees, girls with reputations and often with more uninhibited wit and joy of life than the usual girls of this age."[25] Her unconventional ways and her dating every night of the week were the subjects of much delicious gossip that worried her father and outraged her grandmother.[26] In no time, her relationship with her father began to deteriorate because of what he thought of as her rebelliousness and unseemly decorum.

Barely four months after her return, she wrote to her friend Allen Edee that she was now letting three men court her at the same time.

> Just at present, my irate Pa is wildly desirous of sending me to a convent or feeding me Paris Green or presenting me a silk-lined padded cell. . . . You see, Al, every time a man comes to our house twice, Dad has spasms if he hasn't known said victim's family all his life and the victim's family tree back to the days when our family hung by their tails (pardon me) to the tree next to them. . . . I had absolutely no matrimonial designs on any of the three, but when Dad and Grandma kept nagging me about "ruining my social career," I arose and registered an oath in Heaven that if they didn't let me see my friends in peace, I'd elope with the first man who would have me. . . . Father thought a convent would be just my speed, but Steve (bless him!) remarked that I was such a perverse creature that, once away from the family's eagle eye, I would elope with a garbage man, just to be annoying. Dad chose the lesser and more certain of two evils, so here I am.[27]

The "here I am" meant that she was suffocating in a stifling household with her father, the model of conservatism and respectability; her brother, a young lawyer who loved her but did not always understand her; and her grandmother, a strong-willed 75-year-old, known for speaking her mind, particularly when some moral issue conflicted with her principles—which was often. Grandmother Stephens moved into the Mitchells' home shortly before Peggy returned from Smith because she thought that it was improper for a young unmarried girl to live alone in a house with two men, even though the men were her father and brother.[28] This garrulous woman, who lived to be ninety, survived her husband by thirty-eight years and outlived four of their eleven children. The self-appointed head of the Mitchell-Fitzgerald clan, she meddled in everyone's business and she was, at times, mean. She annoyed many people but none more than Peggy, who, a few years later, told Henry Marsh that the most unhappy period of her life was from 1919 to 1922.[29]

7

Throughout these years, Peggy's letters to Allen Edee, her "best gempmum frien'" from Amherst, reveal her frustration and uncertainty. While John's letters to his family during this same period were full of the excitement of challenge and discovery, Peggy's letters to Edee frankly describe the difficulties of her life at this time.

For one thing, housekeeping for her father had become anathema to her. Even though the ten-room Mitchell house was always staffed with at least three black servants—Susie, the cook and housekeeper; Charlie, the gardener, who also drove Grandmother Stephens around the city; and Lula Tolbert, who cooked the evening meals and cleaned up afterward—Peggy found overseeing the residence sheer drudgery. "Life is rather full now, for housekeeping is rather strenuous till one gets accustomed to it," she wrote Edee. "The servants nearly drive me mad as they steal stockings and collars, spill the beans (both literally and figuratively!) when company is here, and if not continually urged on to nobler efforts would 'draw their breath and their pay!'"[30] Later on she complained about the butler, "who thought he was merely for ornamental purposes."[31]

Much to her further annoyance, her father insisted on keeping the house much too cold in his attempt to reduce his fuel bill. His business had slacked off dramatically in the early 1920s because of the boll weevil depression. The boll weevil had played economic havoc in destroying cotton crops all over the South, and as a result, hundreds of banks closed. There was little work for a real-estate law firm, and Eugene Mitchell's income was greatly diminished.[32] With inflation, high food costs, and a reduction in household funds during this postwar era, Peggy had to manage all the household accounts carefully, and managing household accounts was not one of her talents.

Thus, as conditions in the Peachtree mansion became more and more unbearable for her, she turned to using illness as a protective device, a technique that she may have observed her mother using. Her letters to Allen Edee from July 1919 to December 1921 are noticeably full of talk about her sieges with flu, colds, sprains, bone injuries, back pain, an inordinate number of accidents, and emotional depression. Peggy consistently capitalized on her small size and frailty, saying such things as, "It's hell to be small."[33] Another time she wrote, "I go to pieces under a heavy nervous strain. That, of course, reacts on me physically and I go under."[34]

Although she did not say why, she thought Atlanta was "the swiftest, hardest town in the world to stay good in, particularly," she pointed out, "when one is cursed by a restless, emotional nature and intermittent moods of black depression and reckless diablerie."[35] Her negative emotions manifested themselves in physical problems that allowed her to avoid unpleasant activities. For example, when the body of Clifford Henry, the young soldier with whom she was briefly engaged before she left for Smith, was brought home for burial sometime in the early spring of 1921, Peggy was "too ill" to attend the funeral services in Connecticut. A few weeks later, in May, after she had agreed to visit Smith and Annapolis with Dot Bates, her debutante friend, she again complained of illness, saying, "I've been damn sick." She added, "It will be hell if I'm not strong enough to do all this, won't it?"[36] However, her illnesses did not curtail any of her social activities at home.

Because her medical records are not available, we have no way of knowing whether she was genuinely sick that often or merely indulging herself, using illness as a way of getting attention and avoiding responsibilities. But it does indeed appear that she enjoyed playing the role of a languishing Camille, and it is interesting to note that she was never ill while she was away at Smith. She did not even get the flu, as many of her classmates did, during the flu epidemic in Northampton in 1918.

One thing is clear: her preoccupation with her health did not start until after she came home to Atlanta. Even then, she managed to stay well while she was relatively content and busy doing things she enjoyed. In August 1919, as a result of her complaints about the pains in her side, she had surgery for appendicitis. A year later she had surgery for adhesions. She sprang back quickly from her appendicitis operation because she wanted to participate in Atlanta's biggest celebration—a week-long commemoration of the War between the States. This fall festival honoring the United Confederate Veterans flooded Atlanta with distinguished visitors, politicians, aged veterans, and their families. It was an exhilarating time for her. The city bustled with picnics, bands, parades, speeches on the courthouse steps, box lunch auctions, and grand balls in the Municipal Auditorium. Fascinated with anything concerning the Civil War, Peggy enjoyed serving as one of the Georgia Maids of Honor and chauffeuring the old veterans around town. She loved talking to old people who had lived through the war.[37]

After the celebration was over and things quickly settled down, her turmoil about going back to school began. "More than ever is the call for more schooling, more than ever the desire to know if I'm worth anything strong," she wrote Edee. "It's heart rending to see the days slip and the girls go back to school."[38] Yet she did not want to return to Smith because her class had moved on, and she did not like the idea of going to Wellesley

(Smith's rival) or to nearby Agnes Scott College, as her father had suggested. "I can't figure it out, and I'm all at sea. I really want to go to college, yet I believe I could do more good specializing in designing or short stories. Oh! I don't know."

As the leaves turned and fell and the weather grew chillier, she grew more melancholy and restless. Writing letters became her favorite pastime because of the favorable and immediate response they brought her. Oftentimes she would answer letters moments after she received them, letting her other work go undone. In one long, rambling reply, she told Edee that she had just received his letter and that she "ought to be seeing to the housecleaning and the garden-planting or even to straightening up this room—but I ain't; this room is a wreck. It reminds me of Room 23 at 10 Hen [her room at Smith], so complete is the chaos."[39] Indeed, all her life her room was generally a wreck, littered with ashtrays, clothes, shoes, hose, books, magazines, and paper—lots of paper.[40]

In writing these early letters to Edee, she did a lot of soul-searching. In this revealing one, written only eleven days after her nineteenth birthday, she confessed:

> I am as acutely unhappy as it is humanly possible to be and remain sane.
>
> You ask why, I suppose—and that's the trouble; I don't know why. Allen, I've got things that many a girl has sold her soul to get—social position, money enough to buy what I want, looks and brains sufficient to get by, a family who loves me, friends who care for me, and a few men who would marry me if I loved them. A girl is a fool, a damn fool, not to be happy with all that, wouldn't you think? Well, I'm not and I don't know why. I keep life filled and speeded up so that I can cheat myself into believing that I am happy and contented, but oh! Al, when night comes and I go to bed and turn out the lights, I lie there in the dark, I realize the absolute futility of trying to kid myself. No, my dear, this depression is nothing new! . . . There is something missing in my life. For a year now I have been trying to figure out what it is, for it is vital to happiness—but I can't find out. . . . If you have any idea what's wrong with me, for God's sake tell me![41]

8

As time went on, her depression was worsened by her grandmother's implacable insistence that she defer to her elders. One night in early 1920, she and her grandmother had such a violent quarrel that the old woman called a taxicab and moved her belongings into the Georgian Terrace Hotel, even though it was nearly midnight. Her relationship with her grandmother was never good after that argument, and the unpleasantness between them spread to other members of the family and developed into a bitter argument over property that Peggy's mother had held as trustee. Although Stephens and Peggy waived the claims that they had inherited from their mother's estate, some of their mother's people held such an animosity toward Peggy, because of what her grandmother had told them about her, that they asked her not to claim kin with the Stephens family.[42]

Indisputable evidence of the seriousness of this estrangement—which lasted until Peggy's death—is found in a letter that Peggy wrote on June 4, 1947. In answering her cousin, Alix Stephens Gress, who had requested information about their forebears, Peggy wrote: "I realize that the bitter persecution visited on the Atlanta branches of the family by my mother's people was not your fault, for you were a child at the time. But the memory of it is still so vivid to those of us who went through the lawsuits brought against us, the attempt on my father's life and on mine, the scandalous and humiliating scenes made at funerals of those we held dear, that I really find it difficult to write to you at all."[43] In this six-page, single-spaced letter, Peggy asked that Alix keep the letter secret between the two of them because she had "promised to never again assert any relationship" with the Stephens family. Nothing in her or her brother's papers explains her intriguing comments about the attempts that were made on her and her father's life, or by whom they were made.

9

With all their underlying sadness, those riotously personal letters Peggy wrote to Allen Edee between 1919 and December 1921 are important because they provide the key to understanding the person she was when she met John Marsh in November 1921. Showing that her head was full of girlish romantic nonsense as she struggled to attain authority in her relationships with men, they provide insight into the problems John faced loving a woman who used her sexuality as a weapon.[44] Also, they leave no doubt as to where Scarlett O'Hara came from, for the similarities between Peggy and her heroine are too numerous and obvious to ignore. Sometimes it is difficult to distinguish her voice in these letters from Scarlett's in the novel, as when she boasts to Edee about her ability to make any man feel that he is the only one to whom she can "take every sorrow and joy . . . and be sure of sympathy and understanding."[45] When it came to securing favors, she was just as charming as Scarlett ever was: at one point she implored Edee, "I'll love you forever and be meek and submissive and won't pick on you or bawl you out or anything—Please!"[46] In giving men compliments, she was skillful: "I appreciated the letter, the advice and the dissertation, even tho I made no comment on them at the time," she flattered Edee. "It is seldom that a girl gets a man's opinion of love, marriage, passion, etc., and *this* girl, for one, appreciates all such information, for insight and knowledge of a man's feelings on such subjects have helped her in a few tight places."[47]

She described her flirting tactics to Edee while at the same time denying that she was a flirt. Telling him about a man who was trying to make a good impression on her and "keep his black past dark," she wrote, "here's where I lay low, look wide-eyed innocence and see what happens."[48] In trying to sound worldly, she saucily bragged about having "something of a reputation here for being able to size men up quickly and accurately."[49] However, her brother said the truth was that she "did not have good judgement in men," and that led her to make some embarrassing mistakes.[50]

Part of her charm for John was her ambiguity and her immaturity. Like many modern young women, she was confused by social forces that encouraged women to reject the Victorian standards of their mother's day and to be independent and autonomous, but at the same time also encouraged them to be mere beguiling ornaments attracting men into marriage so that they could fulfill their biological function of maternity. Without her wise mother to guide her and to depend upon, she was confused about her role as a young, single woman.

Tradition, in her day, held that girls were divided into two major classes: the nice girls who saved sex for marriage; and the trashy girls who did not. This last category actually led to a third class, which included unmarried girls who became pregnant and had to disappear for several months under the pretense of visiting relatives afar. Some of these unfortunates returned empty-handed but with a sad glint in their eyes; others had fatherless babies in their arms. In Peggy's mind, the unfortunates were truly unfortunate in the worst kind of way, since pregnancy was abhorrent to her under any circumstances. As for the nice girls—well, they were awfully boring. However, at a tender age, she had been too greatly influenced by her parents and by the Catholic Church, which emphasized celibacy and chastity above all else, to throw all caution aside. And she remembered well her grandmother's description of what happened to "fallen women"—namely, nice men did not marry them. Still, she curled her long, sooty-black eyelashes, rouged her cheeks, kept her hair and body squeaky clean, and wore perfume and sexy little dresses. She did her best to play the dual role: nice and trashy.

In writing to Frances, John's youngest sister, who was unmarried at the time, Peggy later wrote candidly about her views on premarital sex and virginity.

> Virtue for virtue's sake. Only—well virginity—or what passes as virginity—is as saleable a thing on the marriage market today as it was in Babylon although it doesn't bring such a good price, people not being so interested in it now. But it is a fairly good thing to have around, for after all, one does get married.
>
> I hope you wont think I'm too brutally frank about the matter of seduction . . . but training is so strong in girls, that a lot of them cant help reverting to the early idea about being "ruined" even though their educated brains say, "Boo" to the idea. But the idea will persist and it does a lot of damage, mentally, particularly, unless the man is a very good sort and an understanding sort, too. I'm sure I don't know why women put such a value on the first man, but lots of them do—and the mental affect [sic] of being ruined is some times catastrophic. And then again, the bad affect [sic] is usually heightened by the unfortunate fact that the first time one is seduced, it is all so very disappointing. It isnt at all the glamorous affair that the Michael Arlens of this world are going to be sent to Hell for writing about. All poetry and literature and art seem to be in a conspiracy to make it seem that there was some thing tremendous about the whole affair when there really isn't, when you get down to brass tacks. It's pleasant enough and all of that when you happen to know some thing about it and have experience and the rare luck to strike up with some one whose temperament is like your own. But, it's my humble opinion that, except in a few cases, the first time and the first dozen times of being "deceived" are disappointing. I am up, on the subject, at present for two of my young friends have but recently parted with their virtue and two others are seriously meditating it. Despite the outward appearance of cynicism and sophistication of the two latter, I'm awfully afraid that they are the kind of girls who would ruin very easily. And after they had wept about their sin it would be useless to argue with them to effect that if they *were* ruined, it was only their own beastly training that ruined them and not the physical entry of the young gentlemen concerned.[51]

Despite her cynical view of virginity, Peggy recognized all the social and emotional dangers of premarital sex. However, while she was away at Smith and after, she appears not to have seen too much harm in petting and necking. Like many others, she believed that as long as she did not go "all the way" and, particularly, as long as she—"pretty soft and helpless looking"—put up a good struggle against the young man's advances, she was chaste. Her compulsion to deny any responsibility for sexual encounters made her relate to Allen Edee several amusing experiences she had with some of her more ardent young admirers. In one of her long accounts of such an evening, she wrote this scenario:

> "Please go home," I pleaded. "Well, kiss me goodnight and I'll
> go." "Kiss you, hell! Go home." He moved over and perched on
> the arm of the sofa. "I love to hear you say naughty words," he
> grinned. "When you try to be rough, you are so feminine!" Then
> he put his arm around me. I didn't want to yell for Steve. I was
> too weak to fight but I knew I'd go wild if he tried to man-
> handle me.[52]

Her frequent claims of being just "too weak and too tired" to defend herself against a brutish man are shallow but downright funny. One evening after a dance, she invited her escort into her father's home to say their goodbyes. Although she rebuffed his advances, she says she was "so tired and weak" that she was "dizzy." And because she was such "a fwagile li'l fing," the man lost control of himself, picked her up in his arms, and, she said, "proceeded to caveman me in the old and approved style."[53]

> Well, I was so sickened and helpless that I began to cry and begged
> him to put me down, but he wouldn't . . . I couldn't yell because
> there was no one in the house but Grandma, and she would never
> have recovered had she entered upon such a scene. I was pretty
> unnerved by that time, and moreover, I had a particularly feminine
> curiosity to see what would happen if I did promise [to marry
> him]. So I said I'd marry him if he would only put me down and
> not kiss me.[54]

To Allen Edee, she clearly exonerated herself in all sexual matters: "Since I left Hamp [Northampton], if ever a man has kissed me or held me in his arms, it has been because he was stronger than I and I had too much pride (or discretion!) to call for aid. Since I left Hamp, no man has been able to penetrate the wall separating superficiality from real feeling."[55] Refusing to take any responsibility for her "carnal sins," she told him that she had done all she could; she had "drawn a line that men can't pass except by force."[56] According to her own letters, she had necked with Edee on Sugar Loaf Mountain on several occasions and had had such a good time she missed her curfew, but she reprimanded him for not trusting her or believing her when she told him about how "good" she really was. "I suppose you think I 'neck' with every man who takes my fancy. You think that because I liked you and showed that it is impossible for me to pursue successfully my 'conservative' career. I'm sorry to disappoint you, honey, but I *am* doing it—and successfully."[57] Then, just a little later, she wrote Courtenay Ross, "I'm a soulless wretch, and I'm mixed up with five men already."[58]

10

No matter what she said or wrote about playing fair with men, she often acted thoughtlessly, provoking young men's interest and then tormenting them with her games of teasing and denying. Behaving in such a way created an imbalance of power in the relationship, giving her the upper hand she needed to feel successful. In 1920, she wrote to Courtenay Ross about going to a fraternity dance with a date who adored her: "I was wearing that 'lo and behold!' black evening dress, and I looked better than I ever have. (Pardon conceit, bum, but I did. You see, I gained weight during flu, and black straps look well on good shoulders.)"[59] The evening ended with her usual behavior; she righteously defended her honor by saying to her escort: "'Take your hands off me. I'm not going to marry you. You are too damn sensual.' Ye gods! I didn't intend to let that part slip out, for A.B. thinks I am the soul of innocence—and then the fun began!"

> Court, when you've liked and trusted a man, it is no pleasant sight to see him lose his head and go wild. It was the evening dress, I guess, and the fact that both straps slipped down at this inopportune time. Anyway, I never had such a hectic time in my life before I got him out. . . . I felt absolutely dirtied up everywhere he touched me. When I at last went up to my room and looked in the mirror, I nearly fainted! One strap had let the dress drop horridly low, giving a wickedly rakish air. My hair was completely down, and I looked for all the world like "Act I, Scene II. Why Girls Leave Home!" I hate men. No, I don't, there are some decent, clean, self-controlled men.

Although she dressed beautifully, with her off-the-shoulder gowns, she behaved as if she were annoyed when men "stared lustfully" at her. "Ever know a man who makes you acutely conscious that your dress is too low?" she asked Courtenay. "That's A.B. I suddenly began to loath [sic] him. I took sidelong glances at him, noting his sensual mouth and closely cropped moustache and meeting his assured, faintly sneering eyes. I hated him. His very nearness made my flesh crawl."[60]

Years after *Gone With the Wind* was published, Charles E. Wells, a psychiatrist who at that time was associated with the Vanderbilt School of Medicine, wrote an interesting essay on "The Hysterical Personality and the Feminine Character: A Study of Scarlett O'Hara." Dr. Wells points out that even though "Scarlett sexualized all relationships. . . . it appears likely that she remained sexually frigid throughout her first two marriages, but since she married each of these men with full awareness that she felt no sexual attraction for them, this might be expected. She clearly was not frigid in her sexual relationship with Rhett Butler, her third husband."[61]

Perhaps Peggy was like her Scarlett. Before she fell in love with John, she, too, appears to have enjoyed the adventure of eliciting intimacy more than engaging in physical intimacy itself.[62]

11

In none of her letters in late 1921 does she mention meeting John, but she does mention Red Upshaw, a disreputable, troubled young man who was soon to play an important but brief role in her and John's life. "I inherited him [from Courtenay Ross] a year and a half ago," she wrote Allen Edee.[63] Not one of her contemporaries could see what she saw in Red, who was described by Helen Turman as "dull and on the gauche side."[64] A college dropout, an alcoholic, and a floater who never held down an honest job or accepted any kind of responsibility, Red had a sociopathic personality that Peggy found strangely attractive. Stephens said that at first none of them, himself included, realized that Red was "dangerously unstable."[65]

Her first date with Red was in the spring of 1920 when he invited her to a Sigma Nu house party at the University of Georgia, where he was a student. Peggy rode the train to Athens to meet him. During this trip, they had a good time until she injured her leg while horseback riding with him and a group of friends.[66] After that weekend, they dated frequently until he left Athens for the Annapolis Naval Academy, where he had been readmitted. In June, while he was on his way to Honolulu for the navy's summer camp, he came to Atlanta to offer her his opal-jeweled Sigma Nu pin. Although she was reluctant to accept it, which indicates that she was not that interested in him at that time, she wrote, "I'm wary of pins entailing obligations," and she took it on the condition that she could return it when he got home.[67] She added, "He objected to this but I was firm. . . . Then I lost the damn thing." Describing how she ran around to pawn shops frantically looking for a pin to replace the one she had lost, she wrote, "He's the nicest boy ever and the loss really wouldn't matter so much to him, but things are so that I can't tell him." Apparently, Red did not show up that summer to reclaim his pin or Peggy. She did not hear from him again until the late spring of 1922, after she had struck up a serious romance with John.

In December 1921, in the midst of all the debutante activities and not long after she had met John and was going to parties with him, she claimed to have cracked some ribs in October, to have rebroken them on Thanksgiving Day, and yet to feel "perfectly all right" physically. "It's my 'morale' that's the question," she wrote Edee, describing her black mood. "Just let me get upset or mad or cry or be happy—and bingo! Every muscle seems to go slack and the jolly old pep goes and in the reaction that comes on I'm too exhausted to give a damn.... Right now I can step off ten miles and never raise a sweat, but just let Dad begin to fuss at me about something or let me forget and go on one of my old swearing rages and then it's goodbye for awhile for me! Do you get what I mean?"[68]

In this last letter to Edee, she spoke of having two personalities: "Mine was never a tranquil temperament, and to lead a stolid, unemotional existence is no easy task for me!" After she went on some kind of "emotional spree and hated somebody gloriously for a couple hours," she wrote, "the reaction hits me—it's like another Margaret coming to the surface. I just don't care—nothing seems to matter. My reason can plead with my lethargic second self that I'm a damned fool, that I have everything that matters.... I have work enough to keep me busy, play enough to amuse me, and more love than the law ought to allow one girl. And yet, old dear, when the gloom descends, all that isn't any consolation."[69]

This passage describes her state of mind at the time she met John and as she was dating him. And it helps us understand why she behaved toward him as she did a few months later. Defining her problem herself, she wrote, "I want to love one man and be loved by him above all other women. I want to marry and help my man and raise healthy, honest children. My only trouble is that I can't love any man enough. I've tried—oh, so very hard, but it's no go."[70]

Oppressed by her domestic responsibilities, sad about her estrangement from her mother's people, bored with her social obligations, and resentful of always being identified as "Eugene Mitchell's daughter" or as "Stephens Mitchell's little sister," Peggy was restless and unhappy as the fall of 1921 approached. She was not doing anything constructive. She had a date every night and something going on all day, but she was accomplishing nothing. "I feel like a dynamo going to waste," she wrote Edee. "I have possibilities, if energies are just turned in the proper channels."[71]

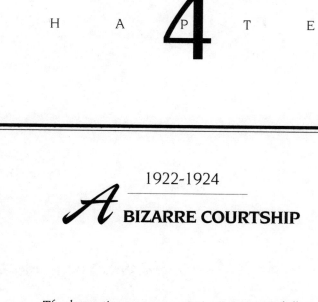

1922-1924

A BIZARRE COURTSHIP

The dramatis personae are Miss Peggy Mitchell, Mr. Red Upshaw, *one of her lovers and my room mate, and* Mr. Marsh.

—John Marsh to Frances Marsh,
27 March 1922

1
———————

IN THE BEGINNING OF THEIR FRIENDSHIP, John and Peggy spent many quiet hours together just talking. After parties, they would return to the Mitchell house, where they would sit together on the sofa in the cold front parlor, often talking until dawn.[1] Like Scarlett, who knew "she could tell Rhett anything,"[2] Peggy knew, early on, that she could tell John anything and he would not make judgments of her. He cared in such a pleasant manner about everything she thought and did that she loved being in his presence. In some ways, he was like an adoring father. Certainly, he was a new breed of admirer for Peggy: self-reliant, intelligent, and understanding. And she marveled at his ability to stay calm during stressful situations. Because she and all her family had such excitable temperaments, she wrote Frances, "I like your family. They don't get hysterical or emotional."[3]

Unlike her other admirers, he did not put pressure on her to have sex with him. She thought their conversations were stimulating, and she did not behave as coquettishly as she did with others. "John never tried to rape me," she wrote later. "In fact, he was the only one of my gentlemen friends who didn't apparently have any dishonorable designs upon me. It used to worry me an awful lot and I wept many tears for fear that I was losing my sex appeal. He confesses at this late date that he desisted only because every one else was doing it and he blandly hoped to shine by contrast."[4]

None of her other suitors valued her in the manner that John did, nor were any of them serious about books or ideas. Not a one of them had his classical education. His knowledge of literature and of other subjects overwhelmed her, and with the responsive curiosity of a bright child who was eager to please, she became his student. Her vocabulary increased and she began to adopt many of his views, particularly his passion for writing with factual and grammatical accuracy.[5]

Even though she felt comfortable telling him about her aspirations for literary achievement, she did not let him read any of her manuscripts—at first. But in a short time she grew to trust him and showed him, first, the copybooks that she had filled as a child and kept hidden from everyone except her mother, and then, a little later, her short stories. The fact that she let him read her work indicates her trust in him because not even Stephens, with whom she was close, was ever privy to her writing. Stephens said that she never permitted him to read anything she wrote and that he never read any of *Gone With the Wind* until it was in typescript.[6] The rejection that she had received from the editors to whom she had sent her short stories had devastated her and had made her uneasy about showing them to anyone.[7] But John was different. With his education, teaching experience, and background as a reporter, she knew that he was someone who could advise her appropriately. When he praised her work, told her that she had talent, and said that someday she would be famous, she glowed with delight. She began to look to him regularly for approval, which he abundantly provided.

Their common interest in books and writing gave them much to talk about even though their literary tastes differed. He admired biographies and the classics and preferred nonfiction to fiction.[8] She liked popular romances, mysteries, adventure stories, and poetry. "Her taste and style were melodramatic," wrote Stephens in remembering their childhood. "Action was the big thing for her. And lots of it from the opening lines."[9] Like her father and brother, she regularly read the Atlanta newspapers and the *New York Sun;* but unlike them, she concentrated on the features section. Until she was grown, she read three youths' magazines: *The Youth's Companion, Saint Nicholas,* and *The Chatterbox.*[10] Her parents had to bribe her, when she was a child, with little monetary rewards to read Shakespeare and some of the other notables. Shortly after she became famous, she confessed:

> Most of my "classical" reading was done before I was twelve, aided by five, ten and fifteen cents a copy bribes from my father and abetted by the hair brush or mother's number three slipper. She just about beat the hide off me for not reading Tolstoy or Thackeray or Jane Austen but I preferred to be beaten. Since growing up, I've tried again to read *War and Peace* and couldn't.[11]

She thought it was an absurd waste of time struggling to read things that had to be analyzed or explained. Her untutored taste, as she grew up, leaned toward mysteries and verse, which she copied in her scrapbooks, memorized, and recited. Until she went to Smith, her writing, full of dialogue and fast action, was imitative of popular contemporary novels.[12]

Early in their relationship, John suggested some books for her to read. But she quickly let him know that she liked to discover books for herself and did not like being told to read something because it was literature. Since one of her attractions, for him, was that she was always herself, he did not try to change her even though he was amused by some of her childish views.

Over time, however, John did have an effect on her literary values, primarily by giving her books, reading them aloud with her, and talking to her about them—all activities they enjoyed doing to the end of their life together.[13] After dating John steadily for awhile, she became more sensitive about her passion for popular literature. In a letter to Julia Collier Harris on April 28, 1936, Peggy described the literary insecurity she had felt in the early 1920s.

> I used to ride the car to town with your husband quite frequently. And I always had about ten books in my arms. I was dreadfully anxious to impress him with my erudition but it never failed that when he sat down beside me and took a peek at my arm load the titles of my books were *The Corpse in Cold Storage, A Scream in the Night, The Clutching Claw.* Sometimes I ardently wished I could have swallowed them. When I was laden down with *Records of the War of Rebellion* (each book weighed three pounds) did he come and sit by me? Never. But just let me have a cargo of mystery murder stories and up he popped and grinned and said "Aha! Ruining your mind again with cheap mysteries."

Peggy never left the library with just one book. She always had an armload. She read, not just skimmed, very quickly and throughout most of her adult life, finished a couple of books nearly every day. In addition to light fiction, histories of the South fascinated her. By the time John had met her, she, at twenty-one, had read every book on southern history in the Atlanta Public Library.[14]

2

The flurry of parties and dances did not end with the holidays, and John and Peggy continued to see each other almost daily. Even though she seems to have had many minor illnesses during this period, she did not let her ill health interfere with her hectic social life. Nearly all of her friends were getting married, and she not only attended bridal parties but also hosted many. Her days and nights were packed with bridge luncheons, club meetings, rehearsal parties and weddings, teas, and dinner dances. Her life was not like the lives led by the women in John's family, nor was it the life that he wanted for himself and for her. But he did not complain.

Within only three months, they had moved into a passionate attachment for each other. "My new Sweetie may be the reason why I haven't written to you any sooner," John wrote Frances in late January 1922, "though that isn't a good reason. It is a fact though that I have spent about as much time with her as the law allows . . . and I have been reveling in the sensation. Peggy and I have reached the stage where we are swapping favorite books and treasured souvenirs of the past having completed the period of exchanging philosophies of life and conversationally turning the pages of family picture albums."[15] Sitting up talking all night until each was "deaf, dumb, and blind!" was her favorite thing to do on dates.[16] Unlike many men, who are unable to talk in the sense that most women mean "talk," John talked—and listened, too. He fulfilled her need for a relationship that centered on something more than sex, although the erotic component of his attachment to her was compelling for him. As he told his brother Henry, it was "clearly a case of love at first sight" for him, but he was too afraid to jeopardize the relationship by forcing his appetites on her. John believed Peggy returned his love, but during all the time that she was seeing him, sharing her innermost secrets, watching him fall deeply in love with her, she was seeing other men.[17]

3

John knew all along that he was just one of the many men who had fallen for Peggy; but because she had led him to believe that she preferred him to all the others, he did not worry—too much. Also, the fact that Stephens and Mr. Mitchell admired him made him feel confident. But his love for Peggy made him vulnerable, especially since he did not want to play romantic games and did not even know how to play them. If she were trying, as she had often done with others, to rile him with her flirtations—trying to elicit jealousy as a sign of his devotion—it did not work. What she did not understand at that time was that in John's view an excessive display of emotions of any kind was inappropriate behavior and unmanly. Unable to manipulate him as she did the others, she may have resorted to drastic measures to stir up his sense of competition. A few years later in writing to Frances, a more mature Peggy admitted candidly what a tease she had been:

> I used to have an elegant time in my early youth (for which John says I should have been shot) by giving a life-like imitation of a modern young woman whose blistering passions were only held in check by an iron control. It frequently succeeded.[18]

Although John exhibited no jealousy, he was bothered by the fact that his competitors were, or appeared to be, better off financially than he was. They all had their own automobiles and, as college students from well-to-do families, they had much more free time than he did. Trying to improve his station in life and thinking about marriage in the future, he had been looking around for a better job, for his was becoming more demanding. He regularly worked eight to ten hours six days a week, usually had assignments two nights a week, and on Saturdays he often worked late into the night. On the evenings when he had to work late, Peggy went out with others, and he had no choice but to accept that. He may have figured that if he waited patiently she would finally grow up and realize that he was the best man for her. However, the following passage, which he wrote to his sister Frances, suggests that he feared Peggy might not change:

> I am not contemplating matrimony, as much as I would enjoy it. Peg and I are indulging in a form of liberal platonism that would require a detailed and elaborate explanation that I don't propose to go into here. Enough to say that we have made a solemn promise not to fall in love with each other. Peg has made a success at that sort of relationship as she has the largest and oddest collection of men friends, real friends, pals, of any girl of twenty I have ever encountered. I am proud to join the circle. And I suppose eventually like the others I will be secretly in love with her, covering up an apparently hopeless passion.[19]

His use of the phrase "a form of liberal platonism" is puzzling. One of the meanings of the word "liberal" is loose or approximate, or morally unrestrained.[20] Given her attitudes about sex and about how a girl could stay virtuous while still having fun, John's phrase could very well mean that he and Peggy were not always able to transcend their physical desires and maintain a purely spiritual relationship—that they took liberty with the philosophy of platonic friendships. To get some insight into Peggy's coquetting, we can turn to her novel, where she incorporated her own attitudes into Scarlett's. When Scarlett is reflecting on her mother's and Mammy's training, on the rules that they have said all "ladies" must observe, Scarlett thinks that she has obeyed those rules except in her dealings with bachelors, with whom she worked out her own code of ethics:

> But with young bachelors—ah, that was a different matter! You could laugh softly at them and when they came flying to see why you laughed, you could refuse to tell them and laugh harder and keep them around indefinitely trying to find out. You could promise, with your eyes, any number of exciting things that would make a man maneuver to get you alone. And, having gotten you alone, you could be very, very hurt or very, very angry when he tried to kiss you. You could make him apologize for being a cur and forgive him so sweetly that he would hang around trying to

kiss you a second time. Sometimes, but not often, you did let him kiss you. (Ellen and Mammy had not taught her that but she learned it was effective.) Then you cried and declared you didn't know what had come over you and that he couldn't ever respect you again. Then he had to dry your eyes and usually he proposed, to show just how much he did respect you. And then there were— Oh, there were so many things to do to bachelors and she knew them all, the nuance of the sidelong glance, the half-smile behind the fan, the swaying of the hips so that skirts swung like a bell, the tears, the laughter, the flattery, the sweet sympathy.[21]

Peggy was indeed an expert in the use of feminine wiles, and little did John realize the extent to which she used them.

4

Despite uncertainties in his relationship with Peggy, John entered the new year in high spirits. In early April 1922, he gave up his job at the *Georgian* and went to work as the assistant manager in the public relations department at the Georgia Railway and Power Company (later known as the Georgia Power Company). He was appointed editor of the company's magazine. The pay was much better and, as Joe Kling said, "the work was much more respectable." Working for a newspaper in those days, Joe said, was "a raffish job," and most of the staff were heavy smokers and drinkers; the soot covered the office buildings inside and out. "The place was grimy, stale-smelling, and freckled with dead roaches. The power company was different; all the men were always clean shaven, dressed neatly in suits, white shirts, ties, and the offices and the building itself were clean and very nice. Getting that job was a step up for John, and for me, too, because I went to work for him there in 1928."

On March 9, 1922, John wrote his mother,

Naturally I am just bound to write to you all since the new station-ery with my name on it has just come up from the printer. . . . Having been a newspaper man for a few years I believe I am inoculated against any high and mighty airs in my present exalted position, but I shan't deny my childish pleasure in seeing my name on the letter-head of a responsible business organization.

Enclosing copies of the magazine he put out, he added: "Being editor is interesting work. I can turn myself loose and write anything I want to write. That's fun, after being under a city editor for many years, and it's still more fun when I ride downtown on our street cars in the morning and see the people laughing at the jokes in my paper and sometimes reading the more serious and weighty articles."

In earlier letters, he had talked about helping Frances find work in Atlanta, and in this letter, he spoke of wanting to bring her to Atlanta in April if he could manage it financially. "About a job for her this summer—that's one of the reasons I wanted her to come down. If she can talk to some of the newspaper people down here, and they can have the chance of looking her over she has a much better chance than if it had to be handled indirectly. I am hoping that I can get her in with me. We are going to have to enlarge the department, and I would prefer to have her if it can be arranged." He mentioned another reason he wanted his sister to visit: "I want Frances to meet my new sweetie." The opera season was to begin the last week of April, and he wanted to take her and Peggy to some performances. Peggy was visiting Augusta Dearborn, her best friend, who lived in Birmingham, Alabama. Pursuing a career in opera herself, Augusta was planning to return with Peggy to spend a week in Atlanta during the opera season. John went on to say, "Peg will have a visitor at that time and has asked to entertain Frances also." Wanting others in his family to meet Peggy, he said he wished his mother and Henry would also arrange a visit to Atlanta soon. Sounding happy and optimistic, he closed saying that he was planning a few trips to get acquainted with the company property. Obviously, he was looking forward to enjoying his new job and his life with Peggy.

What started out as a wonderful spring turned into a troubling time for John, and, for different reasons, it was no easier for Peggy.

5

All the young, well-to-do girls who had attended Washington Seminary were trained for nothing more serious than making their debuts and getting married. After graduation, they automatically became members of the Debutante Club. During this period the Atlanta debs received a great deal of newspaper publicity, which at that time was a very modern notion; as Peggy pointed out, according to "the old Southern way. . . a lady's name appears in print only when she's born and buried."[22] The *Journal*'s Sunday rotogravure section regularly printed pictures of the debs, and Peggy's pictures were often included. One Sunday a photograph of her seated on the cowcatcher of a locomotive and waving a trainman's hat was featured with the caption: "Miss Margaret Mitchell believes that driving a locomotive would be next to skimming the clouds in an aeroplane."[23]

The debs were usually accepted, later, into the Junior League, the highest-ranking women's social organization in the South. But for some reason that is not clear, Peggy was not invited to join the Junior League; this omission was made more noticeable by the fact that many of her relatives and friends were members. That she was not invited to join shocked and infuriated her family and generated gossip in her social set. However, at this time, Peggy never seemed to care what people said about her, and she viewed affectation and smugness as challenges that only spurred her to see how far she could go in shocking and annoying her elders. Some rumored that her unconventional behavior and her noticeable popularity with men created her poor image with the senior League members.

Others claimed that their disapproval stemmed from the scandal she created at the benefit ball sponsored by the Daughters of the American Revolution on March 13, 1921. At this ball, she and A. Sigmund Weil, her partner, who was a student at the Georgia Institute of Technology, performed their sensual l'Apache dance—a dance they learned, after much hard practice, from watching it in the film *The Four Horsemen of the Apocalypse*. Peggy loved to dance and was a very good dancer. She put her heart and soul into this dramatic performance. The dance itself was daring enough for its day, and the newspapers had a good time reporting it and carrying photographs of it. The *Constitution* pointed out: "One other debutante offering herself and all she was on the altar of charity was constantly *hors de combat* because of the strenuosity of the Apache dance—Margaret Mitchell, you know."[24] The *Journal* stated that the most striking feature of the ball was "the Apache dance by Miss Margaret Mitchell, one of the prettiest of the debutantes." However, some of the older ladies present at the ball expected to see an Indian dance, not a Parisian hoodlum spectacle, and they considered the dance obscene. As if her swiveling hips, seductive glances, and thrashing about on the floor were not enough to send the elders' blood pressure soaring, there were those tiny, tinkling brass bells Peggy wore on her red and black garters, under her short, skimpy costume. But it was that long, lewd kiss her partner gave her at the end of their sensational performance that really sent the ladies' heads reeling. Gasping, they asked each other, "Did you see how he *kissed* her?" and "What can Eugene Mitchell be thinking of to allow it?"[25] The Debutante Club was shocked that one of its new members had offended the older members' sense of propriety.

Then, the club was further annoyed when Peggy led a small group of girls in arguing that the Junior League ought not to say where the money earned from the charity ball was to be given. The League won, and the five hundred dollars the ball produced was donated to the Home for Incurables. According to Farr, who heard Stephens Mitchell's first-hand account of this event, "Without question, at this time Margaret fell from favor with many of the city's ruling dowagers."[26] Her grandmother was furious with Peggy, and their differences now were irreconcilable. Eugene Mitchell was gravely disturbed but, without Maybelle, he did not know how to handle his wayward daughter.

Whatever the reasons, Peggy's name was not included in the December 1921 Junior League roster, something she and her father were to resent for the rest of their lives. "In my gone and forgotten deb days," she wrote Frances in 1926, "I was a probationer of the League, did a year's work in the hospital among what is laughingly referred to as Social Diseases and never made the League because I was a wild woman."[27] The truth is she wanted to belong to the high-society set, but she did not want to conform to its standards. Peggy nursed a grudge against the League for eighteen years. When the premiere of the film based on her novel was celebrated in Atlanta, the Junior League sponsored a big, fancy *Gone With the Wind* ball for the Hollywood producers, directors, stars, and Atlanta's most elite society. Of course, Peggy was invited to attend as the guest of honor. But, to show that she still remembered, she refused their invitation, feigning illness, and did not attend the ball given in her honor.

6

Around the end of March 1922, Red Upshaw returned to Atlanta and joined the debutante crowd's scene. From the moment he watched Red slide onto the cushioned seat next to Peggy in the corner booth where they were sitting at the Rabbit Hole, John knew things were going to be different. And they were.

Red was everything that John was not. Sexy and self-indulgent, he was as unruly and undependable as John was mild-mannered and dependable. At twenty-two, four months younger than Peggy, Red had never completed anything he had started. After an unsuccessful year at the University of Georgia, he dropped out. Then, through his father's good connections, he was awarded admission to the United States Naval Academy, but he flunked out in short order. He returned to the University of Georgia for one semester and failed again. Somehow he managed to get readmitted to Annapolis, where he barely lasted a term. The University of Georgia allowed him to reenroll, but he never completed his work there.

Tall and handsome with red, wavy hair and blue eyes, he had a rawboned look and a dissolute air. He came from a well-to-do family in Raleigh, North Carolina, where his father, William Upshaw, had a successful insurance business. In fact, for many people, his family background was the only point in his favor. Although he had no steady employment—he was bootlegging when John met him—he had a new car and money that he was always ready to spend. John did not own a car; he did not even know how to drive one, nor did he have the free time that Red had. By the time he got around to seeing Peggy in the evenings, he had put in a full day as a reporter and was often tired. He had to be conservative with his money because he was helping Henry support Frances, their youngest sister, until she got established and also their mother, a retired elementary school principal relying largely on what her sons gave her."[28]

When Red came on the scene, Peggy was particularly vulnerable to making mistakes. Her extended adolescent streak of rebellion was at its peak. She had created the Junior League Charity Ball fiasco and the enormous rift with her mother's family; now she seemed bent on creating another disaster for herself and those who loved her. Later, she drew from her own painful experiences when she wrote about Scarlett, who created a mess for herself too: "Scarlett had made too many enemies to have many champions now. Her words and her actions rankled in too many hearts for many people to care whether. . . scandal hurt her or not."[29]

And so it was with Peggy. Her friends' sympathies lay with John and her father and brother. Mr. Mitchell and Stephens knew that if they protested her relationship with Red, they would only propel her more directly to him, for she resented their criticism and rejected their advice with such vigor that she always did the direct opposite of whatever they wanted her to do.[30] As an almost maliciously staggering blow to John, she suggested that Red, who was looking for an apartment, room with John. Always more than willing to do whatever she asked, John permitted his competitor to share his room—an uncomfortable arrangement to which he sorely regretted consenting.[31] Much to John's further discomfort, Red told others that John Marsh was his best friend in Atlanta.[32]

Among the papers that Frances saved is an undated, yellowed newsclipping that John sent her from the *Atlanta Journal* sometime during the summer of 1922. It confirms the gossip about the trio: "Inseparable friends for a long period and equally under the spell of a certain charming Atlantan, they have served her hand and foot for many months, have continued in their friendly appreciation of each other and successfully hidden every trace, if trace there be, of any small pangs of jealousy which her smiling too often in first one direction or the other might have occasioned."[33]

For John, loving Peggy meant living on an emotional roller coaster. Even though she had talked about cherishing "the childish ideal that somewhere there is a man who will love and respect me far more because I have kept above the cheapness of passing passion," she rejected such a man when she found him. And her words about playing "square . . . and being faithful and conservative" and wearing a "Reserved" sign around her neck when she became involved in a serious relationship were empty words.[34] She did not play fair. She saw nothing wrong in letting both John and Red court her. They were her most devoted escorts; she had no time for others now. They took her out separately or together, whichever way she preferred. Their friends observed the steady trio and thought it was a "crazy arrangement."[35] Those closest to her, like Stephens and Aggie Dearborn, knew that she loved John, not Red, even though she did not seem to know it. Although he played the role of the nonchalant romancer and behaved as if he were confident that she was merely going through a phase, John suffered silently. It was against his nature to show any weakness such as jealousy, anger, or disappointment. Perhaps he was afraid to let her know how much he loved her; perhaps he thought as Rhett did when he told Scarlett just before his last departure, "I loved you but I couldn't let you know it. You're so brutal to those who love you, Scarlett. You take their love and hold it over their heads like a whip."[36]

The first mention of Upshaw in any of John's letters comes in late March 1922, when John introduced his rival to Frances by sending her a photograph of Peggy and writing:

> I am enclosing a picture or two which may be of interest. The dramatis personae are Miss Peggy Mitchell, Mr. Red Upshaw, one of her lovers and my roommate, and Mr. Marsh. Scene—The Mitchell front porch. Time—any Sunday morning or afternoon and any other afternoon or evening. Theme—I could love the one or the other if either dear charmer were gone. Moral—Don't weaken.[37]

This photograph of Peggy's smiling profile, with her dark, glossy hair piled on the back of her head and her sweater collar rolled up around her neck, was John's favorite picture of her even though the person she is smiling at is Red Upshaw.

It would be difficult to overstate John's patience with Peggy during their courtship. The strength of his love and of his desire to be loved made him willing to accept whatever part of the relationship she was willing to give him—even if it meant sharing her, for a while at least, with Upshaw.

7

During this period, when she was secretly leading each man to think she loved him more than the other, Peggy displayed a feature of Scarlett's exploitative personality. At twenty-two, Peggy had mastered the art of flirting, and lacking any other focus for her energies, she needed the attention of men—the serious attention of several men at the same time—

to bolster her self-confidence. Always candid about how she viewed romantic relationships, she wrote Frances, "Really there's nothing in the world to boost a girl's morale like the knowledge that there's a gempmum fren' all ready to seduce her if she gives him one half the chance. This knowledge was all that kept me going lots of times when I wanted to slump. . . . I think a man who makes improper proposals is a positive necessity in a girl's life—just as much of a necessity as a man whose intentions are honorable and who believes you the personification of ignorance and innocence."[38] With this attitude, she enjoyed the best of both worlds with John, the gentleman, and Red, the rascal.

But by now, John was deeply in love with her. "Peggy has become a habit with me by this time," he wrote his mother in April 20, 1922:

> Red Upshaw, my roommate, and I are the most consistent rushers of the young lady and between the two of us we scarcely let a day get by without seeing her. The other night between 5 and 7 o'clock neither one of us knew where she was and as this was an unprecedented situation we did some tall scrambling about until we found her. It happened that she had been trying to locate one of us so she could report. . . . She is an odd type but has lots of remarkably fine qualities. . . . She has [a] . . . boyish expression and whimsical twist to her mind. I am making no plans to marry her but if things continue to develop satisfactorily it is a possibility to be considered at some time in the future when both of us get in the proper frame of mind. I believe I am the favored suitor, but it hasn't reached the point where it is worrying either of us yet.

Immediately after she arrived in Atlanta and met the cast of characters, Frances worried. During this first visit with her brother in Atlanta in April 1922, Frances was Peggy's guest in the Mitchells' home. Although she was far more conservative than Peggy in every way, Frances liked her well enough and easily understood why her brother found her so captivating— but she did not approve of Peggy's behavior. She did not at all like the manner in which Peggy was treating John. After Frances returned to her own home, she told her mother about what she had learned and said that she was afraid their John was headed for a big fall. She explained that this triangular courtship Peggy was promoting was destined to break John's heart, and he did not seem to realize it. When Frances met Red at one of the parties they all attended, he told her outright, "John thinks he is going to win but I'm pulling the big guns." Frances assumed that he meant he was using his sex appeal, which she admitted "he had lots of."[39] She described the following incident: John brought Peggy home from a date about 10:00 P.M.

Red was already at the Mitchells' house waiting for his turn. John bent over Peggy's hand, kissed it, and said, "Red, I now surrender to you the woman we both love." Frances added, "Being John, this mock gallantry became him, but I was afraid that Peggy would laugh with John and marry Red."[40] And that's exactly what she did.

While John was naively thinking he had the edge in Peggy's affections and was, in his characteristically thoughtful manner, working up the nerve to ask her to risk his uncertain future in advertising, the impulsive Peggy decided to marry Red. Playing a variety of games was her technique, and perhaps she thought that such an announcement would force John into a commitment, make him realize that he had to speak out for her if he wanted to win her. Her decision shocked her family and friends—and it devastated John.

Instead of showing his emotions, he acquiesced quietly and retreated. Concealing what he described as his "shattered nerves," he behaved like a gentleman and even agreed, after she asked, to serve as Red's best man.[41] But he was so distraught that he resigned from his good job at Georgia Power so that he could get out of town fast. After calling Henry to tell him what had happened and what he had done, Henry immediately traveled to Atlanta to be with him and to lend him some money.[42] Having gone through a painful divorce that he had not sought, Henry understood something about John's loss, and he knew that John was handling his grief the only way he knew how—by quickly leaving the Atlanta scene. John wanted to avoid all the prenuptial parties because he could not bear to see Peggy clinging to Red the way she had once done with him. The fact that he quit his new job at Georgia Power and took a lesser, more unstable one with Legare Davis, a freelance publicity agent, is significant proof of his grief. John was far too conservative and responsible a person to do such a thing under normal circumstances.

Davis sent him to Tuscaloosa, Alabama, to head the University of Alabama's campaign to raise funds for its new building project. This fundraiser was an enormous undertaking that John organized and directed successfully; it turned out to be a healthy distraction for him because it demanded all of his energy and attention. On July 30, 1922, the day when his first story on the campaign appeared in all the big Alabama papers, John wrote a long, wistful letter to his mother telling her, "Your wandering boy is farther away from home than he has been for a long time." Easing his way into talking about what was uppermost in his mind and also trying to reassure his mother that he was all right, he wrote that he was living in an old southern home about half a mile from the university and within walking distance of town.

It is owned by a Mrs. A. F. Buck, a charming little woman with snow white hair, who has little to do but dig around her flowers as a corps of negro servants handles the work under the supervision of a fat, very black 'mammy. . . .' I get my meals here, and for the first time since childhood, and very early childhood, I am eating dinner at noon and supper at night. Everything is very leisurely and quiet and peaceful. The folks take their time, and an hour and a half for lunch seems to be the usual rule. Some of the stores close up entirely at noon. But it wouldn't be possible to hurry, as the weather is so warm. Tuscaloosa is in the Alabama plains and some days the air scarcely stirs.

His letter is a long, informative one—two full, single-spaced pages. But the most important item he saved for the very last paragraph.

You may be interested in knowing that Peggy's engagement to Red was announced in today's papers in Atlanta. It wasn't a surprise to me, as the three of us have known about it for some time. I naturally regret that I couldn't get her myself, but it didn't work out that way and the three of us are still good friends. They are to be married in September and I am to be the best man.

Please don't write that I am better off for not getting her. . . . That's a blunt statement for a man to make to his mother, and I don't suppose you would make it. But it wouldn't be pleasant for me to be given that sort of consolation, so I am making the blunt statement to prevent it. You'll pardon me and take into consideration that I have a few sore spots today.

To have been cast aside for a man as irresponsible and unstable as Red Upshaw made John's disappointment and loneliness all the more painful. None of Peggy's close friends liked Red and said they could not understand what she saw in him. Feeling sorry for John, they had been on his side all along. Stephens said one of his sister's friends told him: "I saw the announcement of Margaret's engagement. It's a great mistake. She's in love with John Marsh and doesn't know it."[43] Augusta Dearborn, Peggy's closest friend and John's, too, later tried to explain Peggy's decision by saying that Peggy had a need "to mother people" and had even tried to mother her at times. Augusta thought that with his selfish and wild behavior, Red stirred Peggy's immature mothering instincts in a way that John did not. Peggy may have believed that she could change some of Red's bad habits after they married, an explanation that is supported by passages in some of her letters to Allen Edee, where she mentions helping her boyfriends give up bad habits such as "likker and wild women."[44]   Augusta also believed that Peggy may have been vulnerable to Red's sensuality.[45]

Francesca gave another and even more plausible explanation. She thought that Peggy wanted to see how far she could go before John did something to stop her.[46] Without doubt, it was always the chase, not the catch, that stimulated her. She had acknowledged earlier to Allen Edee that leading "a stolid, unemotional existence" was no easy task for her, that sometimes she just did not care about anything and did whatever she felt like doing with no thought for the consequences. When John failed to display any anger or jealousy upon learning of her decision to marry Red, she had to go through with the plans that she had put in place. John did not rescue her at the last minute as she expected he would. Incapable of creating the kinds of emotional scenes that she was accustomed to and found exciting, he just turned and walked away—even though he adored her. Joe Kling said, "John always kept himself under tight control regardless of circumstances or provocations. You got the impression of iron self-restraint. He never shouted or ranted; neither did he seem indifferent to stressful situations. He was simply a person on a strong leash."[47]

8

This temporary triangular relationship was the inspiration for the fictional one that Rhett endured with Scarlett and Ashley. Many of those who have tried to identify the real-life models for the characters in *Gone With the Wind* have suggested that Rhett Butler was drawn from Red Upshaw.[48] However, with the exception of Belle Watling, Peggy based none of her characters on specific real-life models. Instead, she scrambled appearances and personalities, taking bits and pieces from various real people to draw her characters. For example, she made Ashley's fondness for books and music and his blond countenance resemble John's; and she made Rhett's appearance like that of her black-haired, black-eyed, dark-skinned, handsome grandfather—Russell Mitchell. And although she gave Rhett Butler some of Red Upshaw's characteristics, in developing Rhett and his relationship with Scarlett, she endowed him with many of John's personality traits.

Rhett has John's self-control, confidence, and independence. Like John, Rhett is a loner; he functions independently of the other southerners. He has John's disdain for "imitation gentility and shoddy manners and cheap emotions."[49] He has John's cool-headedness and ability to take charge and deal with any situation. Rhett has a red-haired female friend who runs a fancy bordello in Atlanta; John knew the red-haired Belle Brezing, who ran a fancy bordello in Lexington. And Rhett's loyalty to, love for, and patience with the vain, selfish Scarlett, while she frittered her time away waiting for the idealistic Ashley, strongly resemble characteristics in John's personality and behavior, not Red Upshaw's by any stretch of the imagination.

But the most striking similarity between John and Rhett lies in their fatherly attitudes toward the women they loved. Rhett wants to do everything for Scarlett, and he always treats and speaks of her as if she were a child to be "petted and spoiled." John was extremely protective of Peggy, and he treated her as if she were his child; he took care of everything for her, and she had no responsibilities except those she elected to assume. His nickname for her was "Baby," and in conversations with close friends and family and in his letters to his family, he often referred to Peggy as "that child." In *Gone With the Wind,* Rhett often treats and speaks of Scarlett as if she were a child. After they marry, Rhett gives her many extravagant gifts and Scarlett thinks, "Yes, as Rhett had prophesied, marriage could be a lot of fun. . . . Now she felt like a child, every day on the brink of a new discovery."[50] While on their honeymoon in New Orleans, Rhett dismisses the maid and brings Scarlett her breakfast tray himself, and he "fed her as though she were a child, took the hairbrush from her hand and brushed her long dark hair until it snapped and crackled."[51] At another point in the novel, Rhett picks her up in his arms "like a child and held her close."[52]

The experiences that Red, Peggy, and John had are recreated in the drama of the Scarlett-Ashley-Rhett romance. The words that Rhett speaks to Scarlett here are words that John may have spoken to Peggy after she made her fateful decision:

> Did it ever occur to you that I loved you as much as a man can love a woman? Loved you for years before I finally got you. . . . I wanted to take care of you, to pet you, to give you everything you wanted. I wanted to marry you and protect you and give you a free rein in anything that would make you happy. . . . No one knew better than I what you'd gone through and I wanted you to stop fighting and let me fight for you. I wanted you to play, like a child—for you were a child, a brave, frightened, bullheaded child. I think you are still a child. No one but a child could be so headstrong and so insensitive.[53]

Near the end of the novel, when Rhett is getting ready to leave for the last time, he tells Scarlett what John may well have thought about Peggy as she prepared to marry Red: "You're such a child, Scarlett. A child crying for the moon. What would a child do with the moon if it got it? And what would you do with Ashley? Yes, I'm sorry for you—sorry to see you throwing away happiness with both hands and reaching out for something that would never make you happy. I'm sorry because you are such a fool because you don't know there can never be happiness except where like mates like."[54] John makes a similar point in a letter to his sister written shortly after Peggy's marriage to Red. He wrote: "It is my observation that it takes more than love to make a successful marriage."

The only real difference between Rhett Butler's devotion to Scarlett O'Hara and John Marsh's to Margaret Mitchell is that Rhett got tired of waiting for Scarlett to grow up.

9

Less than a month before Peggy was to marry Red, John, in Tuscaloosa, wrote the following letter to his sister Frances:

> Your first letter in reply to mine telling of the Peggy misfortune pleased me no end. It made me proud of you when you stood up and talked back to me. After trying a year or so to train you to do your own thinking, it is gratifying to me that the training has been so completely successful. After your lecture I shall continue to hold on to my Third Person Impersonal attitude and may you do the same. I admire the success of people who are of the Red type (well characterized by you, by the way), but I prefer myself. I have found my attitude brings a certain amount of success also.[55]

What he meant by those last two lines is not clear, but he may have thought he would eventually win Peggy if he waited. Perhaps he felt, as her family and so many of her friends did, that her marriage was destined to fail. In this same letter, he added the following cryptic lines, which reveal that Peggy was no more ready to give John up entirely than he was willing to give her up, even though she had decided to marry someone else.

> Peggy and I are quite romantic these days. Friends though divided and all that. Write to each other frequently and interestingly. While I write this letter I am waiting on a long distance call to her. She has been sick again and I have decided she has lived long enough without me. I am going to run over to Atlanta Sunday and be the Kind Doctor if she will let me. We are a funny couple. Sometime within the next five years I may tell you the full account of the affair. It is intriguing and in spots dramatic.

John went on to convey Peggy's advice to Frances about Frances's current romance and her invitation to visit Peggy in Atlanta, thus indicating that Peggy planned to remain on intimate terms not only with John but also with his family.

10

Despite John's disappointment and her family's opposition—her grandmother, father, and brother could not stand the sight of Upshaw—Peggy married him at 8:30 on Saturday evening, September 2, 1922, in a formal wedding at her father's house. Atlanta's "best and truest society were present," John reported to his mother four days later.[56] Peggy made all the arrangements herself. Other than taking a hiatus from their hostilities to attend a bridal tea on September 1, then the wedding itself, Annie Fitzgerald Stephens refused to have anything to do with helping her granddaughter prepare for the event.[57] Peggy's aunts on her father's side assisted her. They also stood in the receiving line, but none of the Stephenses did, except two aunts and their daughters and, of course, her grandmother, who did it for appearances only.

With a heavy heart, John arrived in Atlanta on Thursday morning. Taking a cab out to the Mitchells' house, he found Peggy, dressed in overalls, looking prettier than ever with her hair pulled back and tied with a pink ribbon. After nervously chattering on about how the three extra servants she had hired failed to show up, she put John to work within half an hour after he arrived. He wrote that he moved furniture, buffed the waxed hardwood floors and woodwork, arranged some presents in the display room, and "wrote the stuff for the newspapers."[58] After a couple of hours, she sent him around to Red's apartment, where he said he found Red "as wild and nervous and helpless as a bridegroom is expected to be." In checking Red's "clothes and equipment," John discovered that the groom did not have a dress suit to wear after the ceremony. John wrote, "I stuck him into his car and we spent a hectic two hours shopping before I turned him loose, and then I had to dress him, and push him up into the line at the altar when it came time for him to say 'I do.'" He added, "I was by the house for a few minutes two hours before the wedding and she was still in her overalls. Went from them to her bridal gown."

The wedding took place in front of an altar, constructed in the large front hall and covered with palms, ferns, and lilies. The altar faced the stairs so that the guests watched the ceremony from the parlor and from the library on either side of the hall. The reception was held in the dining room, where the receiving line was formed. She had the entire house bedecked with baskets of pink and white roses, gladioli, lilies, and ferns; garlands of smilax embroidered the chandeliers and doorways and were entwined on the wide stairway down which she and her father walked to the altar. So many white candles in silver candelabra glowed profusely throughout the house that night that her father worried during the entire ceremony that the house was going to burn down.[59]

Her bridesmaids and flower girls wore lavender tulle and silver satin and carried bouquets of orchids and pink roses. Peggy wore a long, traditional, white satin bridal gown, seeded with tiny pearls, and a long veil that cascaded from a pearl-seeded headband, a style popular during the flapper period. John said that he had never seen her look more beautiful.[60]

However, in the midst of this elegant, traditional southern wedding, she surprised her guests when she—always a show-stopper—appeared at the top of the stairs carrying one dozen long-stemmed, scarlet roses, not the traditional white bouquet. When her father saw those red roses, he glared and whispered loudly, "What the hell are those doing here?" She shushed him, smiled, took his arm, and started walking down the steps.[61] As an outward symbol of her separation from the Catholic Church, she had the ceremony performed by Reverend Douglas, pastor of St. Luke's Episcopal Church. The groom, the red roses, and the Protestant minister were more than her grandmother and her Fitzgerald relatives could stand. They had nothing to do with her after this wedding.

Two preteenage first cousins on her mother's side were her flower girls, and her bridesmaids were Dorothy Bates Kelly and Martha Bratton Stevens. Augusta Dearborn was the maid of honor. Courtenay Ross, who had married Lt. Bernice M. McFayden a year earlier, could not attend because she was with her husband, stationed in the Philippines, but her mother served the punch at the reception. The groomsmen were Stephens and Winston Withers, one of her old boyfriends. The best man, standing straight and tall and handsome next to the bridegroom at the foot of the stairs, was John Marsh. Later, Peggy told Francesca that the moment she saw John and Red standing side by side that night, she knew she had made a dreadful mistake.[62] In 1924, she told Courtenay Ross the same thing, that she knew almost immediately that she had married the wrong man.[63]

Peggy and Red spent the first night of their married life in an Atlanta hotel. They did not leave town until the next night when, according to John, "The wedding gang, three of us who were in the procession [Augusta, Winston, and John], carried them down and put them on the train."[64] While they spent their honeymoon in Wrightsville Beach and at the Grove Park Inn in Asheville, John, lonely and depressed, went back to work in Tuscaloosa. What he did not know until later was that on her wedding night and during the honeymoon, Peggy was lonely and depressed too.

In writing to his mother on September 6 about the wedding, which he called "a grand and glorious affair," he tried to conceal his sadness, but it is present in his first paragraph:

> I didn't realize how very long it had been since I wrote to you until I began checking up on myself today as part of the process of beating back to normalcy. I don't suppose you mind—I hope you will understand what I mean and for that reason will forgive me for saying—I haven't had much time to think of my family for some time. That isn't a nice thing to say and I don't mean it literally—only—that the jolly old brain has been whirling a bit rapidly for some time and such things as concentrating on letter writing would have been difficult.

All the sympathy he had received at the wedding made him acutely aware that his behavior was unusual for a jilted lover. Thus, he went on to say, "Don't think the two were imposing on me. It was a pleasure for me to have even that sort of a part in the wedding and an abundance of energetic hard work prevents thinking. . . . The fact that I, Red's chief rival, was his best man caused a good deal of comment, and I found myself before I left Atlanta completely surrounded by a halo of romance because I had done the thing." Then, he confessed something that worried his mother terribly:

> It's an odd sort of situation. Peggy and I are very close to each other, closer than any other man has been to her with the exception of Red. I love her more than I did Kitty, which is saying a lot, and she cares for me very deeply. If one or two things could have been arranged, the positions at the altar might have been reversed. However, it's all over now and I am beating back to normalcy. . . .

His mother feared that it was not over, and Frances knew for certain that it was not, and that her brother would not get back to normalcy for a long time.

By this time, Frances had graduated from college and had moved to New York in the summer of 1922 to seek her career in writing. John scribbled her a note indicating that he was not able to keep his staunch attitude after his "halo of romance" vanished. His tone in this undated note is unlike that in any of his other letters:

> Brava! Viva! New York, ho! and to hell with the commonplace! Adventur-r-r-re, R-r-romance! I always wanted to do that sort of thing but never had the courage to make the plunge. It will make me proud if a sister of mine has the courage to do

something I thought over too long.

I am glad you are getting rejection slips. I never even got *that far*. We are going to make a success of you yet. You are at least two years ahead of me when I graduated.

Write to Peggy, but don't bear down *too* heavy on the congrats. Tell her you hate her for not marrying me, but wish her good luck anyhow. Ask her for some inside dope on how a girl tosses a lover into the ash can, and that lover still remains her devoted slave. That's what I am, hers and yours.

But his loneliness and sadness are even more evident in the following poignant passage he wrote to his mother:

I said I hadn't had time to write to you. Dearest Mother, there were many times when I wanted you terribly. No one else could have taken your place. But I am the sort that doesn't like to put out much in the way of admitting things I feel, and since you weren't here and no one else could take your place I went through it with my head up and barrels of cheerio for the entertainment of the mob. We're all children even when we grow up, I suppose, and we don't want nobody else but our mothers some times.[65]

1922-1925

*L*OVE REGAINED

I *have fallen, and I am glad of it. I have been in love with Peggy for a long time, as I said, but it wasn't nothing like this here.*
— John Marsh to his mother,
20 January 1925

1

—————

AFTER THEIR BRIEF HONEYMOON, Red and Peggy returned to Atlanta to live in the Mitchells' home, a big mistake considering how Mr. Mitchell and Stephens felt about the marriage. But they had no place else to go. Red had no job and, much to Peggy's dismay, no money. Their arguments began on their honeymoon, when she discovered that he did not have enough money to pay for the cottage they had rented. Although he was estranged from his family, he took her to Raleigh so that she could meet his parents and he could borrow some money from his father before they returned to Atlanta.[1] Peggy was unhappy and depressed from the moment she said "I do."

Living with his father-in-law put a terrible strain on Red; and his unpredictable, slightly ominous personality butted head on with Peggy's bull-headedness. He expected to be waited on, and he often came home drunk late at night. They began to have violent arguments that sometimes included her father.[2] This situation bred such a strained atmosphere that Mr. Mitchell took to his bed.[3] By the end of September, Peggy wrote John in Tuscaloosa, telling him about her troubles. The first chance he had to take two vacation days, he headed back to Atlanta, where he found her despondent. Married less than a month, she told him she wanted to divorce Red. Emotionally committed to her as much as he had ever been, he promised that as soon as his role in the fundraising campaign for the University of Alabama was over, he would move back to Atlanta to find work.[4]

In a letter to Frances, he explained that the marriage was

> tragic from the start as it was fated to be a failure. The two of them love each other very much, but they are as dissimilar as it is possible for two people to be, with virtually nothing in common in temperament, viewpoint on life, likes or dislikes. It is my observation that it takes more than love to make a successful marriage. Everyone recognized the big chance they were taking when they married, and things have worked out as we feared they

~ 93 ~

would. Their total lack of congeniality caused constant small clashes that threw Red off his stride . . . and were threatening Peggy with a nervous breakdown.[5]

Keeping his bootlegging activities a secret, Red would leave the house, be gone for two or three days, and then return, refusing to give any explanation. But shortly before Thanksgiving, he disappeared. Fearing his return to harm her or, perhaps, just fearing harm in general, Peggy started sleeping with a pistol near her bed.[6] Because her family and friends had advised her not to marry, she felt embarrassed and depressed. Although she had always appeared to be indifferent to public opinion, she was now keenly sensitive to what others thought of her and would remain so for the rest of her life. During this period, her relationship with some of her mother's family became even worse than it had been before. She believed that every relative disapproved of her, and she was nearly right. Some despised her for creating one scandal after another and for besmirching the family name with talk of divorce immediately after her elegant wedding. She grew listless, declined to supervise the servants, and stayed in her room all day sleeping or reading. Knowing the critical situation in the Mitchells' house, her friends left her alone. No longer a debutante, she went to no parties. Miserable at home, she longed to get away, to be independent, but wondered what kind of job she could get. The southern culture of that period frowned on women who worked outside the home. No women in her family earned their own way, for nice girls did not work—they married. Teaching was perhaps the only completely acceptable career for gentlewomen, but only if they remained unmarried.

Her predicament was torturous. She was married, but without a husband to support her, she still lived in her father's house. She had rejected her Catholic religion, yet she was still influenced by its teachings against divorce and remarriage. She had no job skills, and she had thrown away her opportunity to get an education. She had been brought up in wealth, but now she had little money. She was totally dependent upon her father, whose law practice, like many other businesses during the boll weevil depression, had fallen on hard times.[7] The expense of her wedding placed a burden on her father that he did not need or deserve at that time, particularly considering the circumstances of her marriage. She hated being dependent on him, so she turned to John for advice and for financial help.[8]

2

Although the kind of social prejudice that her father subscribed to placed journalism and acting in the same low-life category, John encouraged her to apply for a writing position at the *Journal* for two major reasons: she wanted to be a writer, and he had friends in journalism. Because the *Constitution* was a morning paper and the staff had to labor throughout the night to get the paper out, he did not want her to work there. Even though the *Georgian* was an afternoon paper, he did not want her working there, either, because of the stressful working conditions. The only other afternoon paper was the *Journal* and it, like the *Constitution*, was locally owned and staffed mainly by Atlantans. It was also the most profitable paper, strongly supported by Atlanta and its environs.[9]

In his earlier letters, John had invited Frances to come to Atlanta so that he could help her get a job at a newspaper. "The job I would like to get for you in Atlanta," he wrote her around the end of March 1922, "would be as a writer on the Sunday magazine of the Atlanta Journal, feature story work which now employs several very gifted young writers. Failing in that I hope to land you in work of somewhat similar nature." But after Peggy's separation from Red and the difficult circumstances in which it placed her, he never mentioned such an offer again and even discouraged his sister from seeking newspaper work in general, particularly in Atlanta. He encouraged her to go on with her writing, but not newspaper writing.[10] At first, Frances was a little miffed. Francesca Renick Marsh believed that his main reason for discouraging Frances from coming to Atlanta was that his sympathy lay with Peggy; he believed that Peggy needed his help more than his sister did. As a college graduate with an excellent academic record and a few short published pieces as well, Frances had marketable writing skills. Peggy had less to offer an employer and was in a difficult situation at the time.

Because there were no vacancies in the magazine staff then, John made arrangements for Peggy to have her first job interview, sometime during that late fall, with Harlee Branch, the city editor at the *Journal*.[11] Even though John knew Peggy's prospects of getting a job as a reporter were virtually nonexistent, he believed that the experience of having an interview would be good for her. Branch was impressed by her earnestness and the way she went about asking him for a job. "I wanted to give her a job," he said. But, as he explained, the *Journal* did not feel the time was right to hire women except on the magazine and society sections, which were both well staffed then.[12] Always more optimistic than she, John saw something positive even in the rejection; at least now the city editor knew her and perhaps would call her when he got ready to hire a female reporter or when a position opened up in the magazine or society sections.

In the early 1900s, Sunday magazines, intended to entertain, were introduced by newspapers competing with the powerful Hearst papers; which were intended, as owner William Randolph Hearst said, "to engage brains." Filled with photographs, interviews, feature articles (often on fashions, socialites, and women's issues), these magazines were enormously popular and their growth opened up opportunities for women who wanted to be writers.[13]

The editor of the *Journal*'s popular *Sunday Magazine,* a 32-page illustrated publication, was the sandy-haired, tight-fisted Scotchman, Angus Perkerson. Although John did not know him well, he had a good friend who did—O. B. Keeler, at that time the golf editor at the *Journal.* In mid-December 1922, when Keeler learned that a young woman was quitting the magazine staff before Christmas to get married, he promptly told John that he would speak to the editor on Peggy's behalf.[14] Perkerson agreed to hire Peggy, but only on a temporary basis because he was skeptical about any debutante's ability to get to work on time, much less hold down the job. "We handle a great deal of copy and I don't go in for extensive alteration—haven't time to," he told her. "What we are looking for is straightforward writing without self-conscious tricks, and it's surprising how few people can do it. You either can or you can't. I'll try you out, and we'll see if you are one of the people who can."[15] Years later, Perkerson recalled: "I remember very distinctly how Peggy came down to see me one day.... She looked very tiny. She was wearing a suit and a beret. We talked for a while in the sort of file room which adjoined that room where we all worked—all five of us.... Anyhow, she got the job—and kept it."[16]

In recounting her version, Peggy wrote,

> I made my debut and then went onto the Magazine Section of the *Journal* somewhat to the consternation of my father. I had no newspaper experience and had never had my hands on a typewriter but by telling poor Angus Perkerson outrageous lies about how I had worked on the Springfield Republican (How could I? And all my people good Democrats?) and swearing I was a speed demon on a Remington, I got the job.[17]

Thus, with no training and no education, Peggy was hired as a feature writer to fill the place left by Mrs. Roy Flannagan. Her first work day started at 8:00 A.M., and her first day on the job was probably December 22, 1922, because her first story with the byline "Peggy Upshaw" appeared in the December 31, 1922, issue. However, her name does not appear on the payroll roster until the week of January 22, 1923. Her salary was twenty-five dollars a week, the going pay for female writers in those days.[18]

Peggy surprised Perkerson. She was conscientious about getting to work early and enthusiastic about accepting her assignments. Later, he admitted:

I was a little worried about putting her on the staff, because she was a society girl, and I said . . . "Medora, I reckon we'll always be waiting for her to get to work." But I was wrong there—she was always waiting for us when we got there in the morning, because she came to town on the street car and had to leave home before the cook got there. So she ate her breakfast in the little cafe in the building—the *Journal* folks called it "The Roachery"—and then she sort of opened up the office.[19]

And, as John had suspected, in no time at all nearly all of the young men in the building were infatuated with her. Medora Field Perkerson, the editor's wife and a staff writer, took an instant liking to her and the two enjoyed a close friendship that lasted the rest of their lives. Peggy got around to warming the heart of Harlee Branch, the shouting city-news editor who was said to spit nails at reporters, particularly the cubs. Even Walter Sparks, the straitlaced *Journal* photographer, noted for sternly lecturing the female staff on their demeanor and dress, fell under her magnetism. They became great friends, and he went with her on many of her assignments. When he died years later, Peggy wept openly at his funeral service.[20]

Another old curmudgeon who appreciated her youthful gaiety and interest in him was the composing room foreman, who was so cranky that even Perkerson avoided him. The staff marveled at her ability to get the foreman to hold the forms open for late copy. Little did they know that she had sensed the old man's loneliness when she first met him and had secured a place in his heart by going to him with her first problem. Terrified when she was handed her first job of reading proof, she went sweet-talking to the foreman in his grimy quarters, which reeked with the odor of hot lead and rang with the cacophony of linotypes. Starved for a little attention and appreciation, he was delighted to help her and promised no one else would know that she could not read proof. He would do it for her, he said, until she got "the hang of it." When he died not too long after that incident, Peggy asked Medora to attend his funeral service with her at Clarkdale, about thirty miles outside of Atlanta.[21] After seeing her there, the workers in the composing room would do anything for her.[22]

Bill Howland, who was writing for the *Journal* at that time, recorded his first impression of Peggy:

It was in May, 1924, when I had just come to the *Journal*'s busy but dingy city room as a very wet-behind-the-ears cub, slightly exposed to professional newspapering for a few months in Nashville. Along with other cubs I was being put through a pretty rough course of sprouts by City Editor Branch, a super trainer of reporters. While we went through the often dreary daily grind of writing—and re-writing again and again and again—obituary notices, civic club reports, police items—all the minor bits of news that fall to the lot of the cub reporters—a tiny, reddish-haired, electric-eyed sprite from the *Sunday Mag* department from time to time would come in to look up words in the big dictionary beside the city desk. She was so small that she would have to stand on tiptoe and lean over the big book, often exposing an inch or so of white skin above the tops of her rolled stockings. When that happened, in those days when legs were not the public ocular property they are today, there would be considerable mis-typing and slowing down in production on the part of young reporters. This soon caught Mr. Branch's alert eye. He stopped it by calling our visitor to his desk, and saying, in the most fatherly fashion: "Miss Peggy, I'll have to ask you to stop using the dictionary— you're upsetting my young men."[23]

3

Her first assignment was an easy one, having to do with whether skirts were going to be shorter. In 1922, women still wore rather long skirts although World War I had introduced the raised hemlines. Perkerson sent her to interview the socialite Mary Hines Gunsaulas, who had just returned from Europe with her new Parisian wardrobe. During the course of the interview Mrs. Gunsaulas, who posed for photographs in her Paris dresses, casually mentioned that she had been in Rome the day that Mussolini and his black-shirted Fascisti marched into Vatican City and took over the government. Not abreast of world events, Peggy said:

Mussolini was not even a name to me then, but it sounded interesting and I listened and asked questions while Mrs. Gunsaulas told more. I came back and wrote my story about skirts and tacked all this other incident onto the end. Mr. Perkerson—I did not call him Angus then—turned the story hindside before, and started it off with the eye-witness account of Mussolini taking over the Italian government.[24]

Although her first story, "Atlanta Girl Sees Italian Revolution," is easy to read, it is amateurish. It is mostly a series of direct quotations strung together, and on the whole it is a little disconnected and unorganized. Also, it noticeably fails to describe what Mrs. Gunsaulas looked like or even what she wore.[25] However, her second article shows marked improvement. By the time it was written, John had finished his fundraising drive for the University of Alabama and had moved back to Atlanta to be near her and to begin another big campaign for Legare Davis.

In the first week of February 1923, Atlanta had a bit of winter; sleet and ice were frozen on the trees and wires, and a raw wind and freezing temperatures made going outside uncomfortable. John had been working night and day helping Davis inaugurate a national campaign named "Save the South," a movement to fight the boll weevil. In a letter to his mother on February 5, 1923, he talked about his work and Peggy's; he also enclosed one of Peggy's stories, titled "Graveyard Dirt Is Newest Conjur Charm." Indicating that even in those years he was not only lending his editing skills but also giving her ideas about characterizations, he told his mother: "You may recognize an old friend (the name at least) when you read Peggy's story in this week's *Journal Magazine* which I have mailed to Frances." He explained that Peggy was assigned to get a feature story on blacks who did voodoo magic. However, after an extensive search through Atlanta's "Darktown," she and John failed to find one, and so he told her about Omie, an interesting old black woman he and his family admired in his hometown. After listening to his description of this old woman, Peggy used her imagination, he said, and gave the name of Omie to the woman in her story. He thought his mother would enjoy reading the piece for that reason.[26]

Not wanting to remain a full-time freelance publicity agent for Legare Davis because that job required him to travel, John started looking for work in Atlanta now that Peggy needed him there. In April 1923, he went to work for the *Journal*, not as a reporter but as a copyeditor, so that he could remain in the building, be near her, and be available to help her with her work. He had an excellent reputation as a reporter, and as a copyeditor he became known as "a stickler for correctness."[27]

It was common knowledge at the *Journal* that John helped Peggy in every way he could, including proofing her drafts whenever he got the opportunity. Helping her with her work gave John a valid reason for spending time with Peggy. Although Red had disappeared, she was still married to him, so she and John, well aware of the gossip about her, tried to keep their courtship a very quiet one.[28]

The original drafts of Peggy's articles have long since disappeared, so there is no way of knowing how much work John did on them. However, his handwriting is on some of the galley proofs of her articles saved in the Hargrett Library. Then, too, it is possible to distinguish two different styles in Peggy's articles for the *Magazine:* an informal, energetic, loose style that sounds like Peggy's speaking voice; and an objective, factual, straightfor-ward style that suggests John's editing. Having made his living for five years doing hard-news reporting, John had a clear, smooth, logical, and effective style of writing. Some of his articles are available also, and it is noticeable that some of Peggy's early pieces have the more professional tone and style of John's articles. For example, the contrast between her first and her second article, "Plant Wizard Does Miracle Here," which appeared on January 7, 1923, demonstrates obvious improvement. This second piece gets to the point much more quickly than her first article, and it closely follows the fundamental principles of good newspaper writing. For another example, her article "Police Station 31 Years Old and Shows It," in the August 12, 1923, issue of the *Magazine*, is more objective, direct, noticeably less turgid than some of her other pieces. Years later, Angus Perkerson remarked that Peggy "wrote like a man."[29] Surely, John's influence and his editing to some extent account for the direct, "masculine" style of some of her articles.

In the margins of some of Peggy's galleys, John wrote comments about avoiding shifts and spelling inconsistencies; in one place, he had marked three different usages—"going," "gwine," and "goin'" in her quoting of the same speaker.[30] He struck out adjectives, which she tended to overuse, replaced words, and reconstructed phrases or sentences. His corrections did indeed improve her writing by making it fluent and clear. For one example, her article "Atlanta Subdebs Pass Up Tutankhamen," published March 11, 1923, is about a group of Atlanta girls who had just returned from visiting Egypt, where the excavations of the mummified remains of Tutankhamen were creating world news but little interest for the Atlanta debs. On this one-page galley proof, John made five corrections.

His reactions to her writing were by no means always critical and correcting. When she scribbled, "This here is mine—and its rotten!" on her article "When Mrs. Bell Ruled the 'Bell House Boys'" (June 24, 1923), he scribbled back: "I can't see what makes this story eat on you. It shows good reporting in the historical data collected and the number of prominent men interviewed. I also like it because it does not rave, but gives the facts and lets them sell themselves." Another time he wrote, "You have an ability to make your people lifelike which is seldom an accomplishment of newspaper reporters. *This is very well done.*"[31] Although he helped her with organization and development and corrected her grammar and punctuation, John recognized that she was excellent at writing descriptions and dialects, and he told her so. In the margin near her description of One-Eyed Connelly, a person who managed to attend many public events without ever buying admission tickets, John wrote *"Good!"* next to this passage: "Connelly is a thickset, short man, with a bullet head set on a short, thick neck. His eagle nose is crisscrossed with scars, his face full and placid, and his one green eye shines with the quiet confidence acquired only by one who is convinced in his own soul of the laudability of his life work."[32]

When she and John were together going over her mistakes, he would often gently rub the back of her neck and softly insist that she be accurate not only in gathering her facts but also in writing them down.[33] Always trying to dismiss her fears, he regularly praised her work. On one occasion, he wrote, "I hope my pleasure over your ability to write so much more smoothly than you used to won't have the effect of making you 'flowery.' That would be too bad. Oh my yes!"[34] Through her relationship with John, she learned her trade rapidly, and her self-esteem grew immeasurably.

In a letter on June 11, 1923, he wrote his mother about his "two pupils," one of whom was his sister Frances, who was sending him copies of her manuscripts for advice. "My other 'pupil,' Peggy," he wrote, "is making good progress, and now in addition to her newspaper work she is writing 'the Great American Novel.' Knocks off a page or two at a time when she has a few minutes to spare." Then he added this eerie prediction: "There are places in it which show signs of being good stuff. We may have a famous friend some of these days."

All the virtues of a lover, a friend, and a doting father were combined in John. He offered Peggy adoration, protection, and all the help she needed to do what she wanted to do—write. He nurtured her creative imagination and gave her the confidence she lacked, asking nothing in return. By early 1923, her dependence upon him was fixed permanently.

Although she never learned enough about grammar, punctuation, spelling, and trimming to read copy well, she made herself useful as a member of the magazine staff in other ways. Because she was charming and pretty, she was often sent as a representative to welcome visiting celebrities and to act as their Atlanta tour guide. Also, Perkerson gave her the special task of returning to disappointed mothers all of the rejected baby pictures sent in for the newspaper's frequent pretty baby contests. In addition to getting out the magazine, the staff was responsible for the Sunday rotogravure picture section, known as "the Brown Section." She helped with selecting pictures and writing captions for them, a task she enjoyed.

Working for the *Sunday Magazine* gave Peggy a sense of independence, confidence, and purpose that she had never known. It gave her self-respect. By the end of February, she looked prettier and healthier than she had looked in several months. Although she was still married to Red, whose whereabouts were still unknown, she and John were seeing each other as often as they could. Everyone who knew them could tell that they loved each other very much.[35] Gradually, she resumed her social life, but now her new friends were mainly John's newspaper friends at the *Journal:* O. B. Keeler, Allan Taylor (who had an obvious crush on Peggy), Bill Howland, Frank Daniel (who dated the much older Frances Newman), Joe Kling (who was then courting Evelyn Lovett, whom he later married), and Roy Flannagan and his wife, whose place Peggy had filled at the magazine. The only friend from her old crowd whom Peggy still cared to see was Augusta "Aggie" Dearborn, who by this time had married the Georgia artist Lee Edwards.

This group, along with a few others like Anne Couper, Peggy Porter, Frank Stanton, and Kelly Starr (the head of the publicity department at Georgia Power), made up what was known as the Peachtree Yacht Club, although yachting had nothing to do with their friendship activities. (There are no yachts in Atlanta, and even if there had been, the group collectively could not have afforded one.) Howland remembered a hilarious party one night at the Mitchells' Peachtree home when the group suddenly decided they wanted to have a costume party. Searching the house for whatever they could find, they decked themselves out in ridiculous-looking outfits, went downtown, found two strangers, and brought them back to the house to judge which costume was the best.[36] Indeed, they were a rowdy group of practical jokers who knew how to have a good time.

4

When Peggy entered the newspaper world, it was a rugged environment. "The staff was composed entirely of men—most of them about equally proud of their ability to drink hard as to work hard," wrote Howland.[37] Riding the streetcar every morning, she had to cross town to get to the *Journal*, an old, dingy, five-story, red-brick building alongside the railroad tracks. Its entrance was on the Forsythe Street viaduct, in a run-down section of Atlanta. A young copyeditor at the *Journal* while Peggy was there, Joe Kling described the *Journal* building as "hopelessly dirty inside and out, partly from breathing train smoke day and night and partly from benign neglect." On the first floor was a small café where, Kling said, "You could get a glass of milk and two slices of bread (no butter) for a dime. But you had to keep a sharp eye out for cockroaches. This spartan diet suited the copyreaders (of whom I was one) partly because we were under strain to get back from lunch in fifteen or twenty minutes and partly because we all had some form of stomach trouble from the working conditions." He added, "The cockroaches did not confine themselves to their natural habitat, the café, but made themselves at home wherever their fancy led them. They were more than ordinarily fond of the glue pots (actually mucilage which was used for pasting up copy)."

Because the locomotives back then burned soft coal and belched thick, black smoke, the side of the *Journal* building facing the tracks was continually enveloped with dark, smelly clouds of smoke from the puffing engines. Howland said that when the windows were kept closed during the winter, breathing got to be a problem for everyone inside. During the summer, when the windows were kept open, he claimed it was not unusual "for a red cinder to fall on one's desk. And it required iron concentration to take news over the phone or to write news, with locomotive whistles bellowing, engine bells clanging, just outside the window."[38]

In spite of their poor working environment, long hours, and low wages, the staff believed that they put out the best paper in the nation, and they had an esprit de corps that is rarely found in any workplace. Everyone, from the elevator man to the editor in chief, knew each other by name.

> At lunchtime, reporters, editors, top executives, pressroom men in overalls and sweaty shirts, and every other variety of *Journal* worker, crowded into the little café on the first floor, sat at rickety tables or milled about at the counter, shouted back and forth, told jokes, ate the rugged fare. . . . If you were ever accepted as one of them, you became part of a hard working, hard hitting team. Not everyone made it; simply being hired was no guarantee of your acceptance into the *Journal* fellowship. Peggy Mitchell did make the team.[39]

When Peggy joined the staff, the *Magazine* was only ten years old. Its office, which she nicknamed "The Black Hole of Calcutta," was on the third floor, along with most of the executive offices, the society department, and the stereotyping equipment.[40] Describing the layout of the building, Kling explained that on the first floor, all the principal business (bookkeeping, advertising, subscription, accounting, etc.) was conducted. On the second floor were the photographic departments, morgue (or files), and more offices. On the fourth floor were the linotype machines; and on the fifth and top floor were the news departments, local and wire (telegraph) news, sports, and also the Associated Press, which occupied leased space. He pointed out,

> Because women worked on the third floor, their offices, although still gloomy, looked a little better. The magazine offices had curtains on the windows, but just as in all the other areas which were disorderly and dirty, anything that could be in a state of disrepair was. Cockroaches scampered around as much at home as reporters, and crusty brass spittoons and dirty ashtrays were everywhere. Soot-dust covered everything. Furnished with only one telephone with one extension, beat-up looking, old wooden desks, a couple of tables laden with newspapers, and several old typewriters, the magazine office was cluttered.[41]

Peggy was given a desk right across from Medora's, and she was also given a straight wooden chair that was much too high for her short legs to touch the floor when she sat down. The janitor trimmed the legs off the chair until he got them even and short enough for her to sit in the chair comfortably. Her typewriter was old and did not have a backspacer, but that did not matter. She made so many mistakes, using the two-finger-hunt-and-peck system, that a backspacer would have slowed her down. Even when she was given a new typewriter, she never used the backspacer.[42] Her typing never improved. To the end of her life, she rarely hit the apostrophe key; her apostrophes consistently appear as "8's."

She worked for the *Sunday Magazine* for nearly four years, and she wrote one signed article, and maybe one unsigned one, nearly every week except during her two three-month leaves of absence. The articles were approximately twelve to fifteen hundred words each. She also wrote some book reviews and while on leave wrote the "Elizabeth Bennet's Gossip" column. She wrote on a variety of topics. Some of the titles of her stories were "Laundry List Sung by Atlanta Sub-Deb," "Through the Cave of Lost Indians," "No Dumbbells Wanted, Say Atlanta Debs," "Atlanta Man Just Missed Tutankhamen," "Bridesmaid of '87 Recalls Mittie Roosevelt's Wedding," and "Valentino Declares He Isn't a Sheik." Two of her favorite pieces were interviews: one with the movie idol Rudolph Valentino and the other with Tiger Flowers, the great black prize fighter. Always a good sport and a daredevil, she agreed on one occasion to be photographed in a rather dangerous stunt. While she was getting the story on sculptor Gutzon Borglum, who attempted to carve a Confederate memorial on one side of Stone Mountain, she was placed into a sling that swung out of a window on the top floor of a tall downtown office building.

The editor of the *Journal* was Major John S. Cohen, who had as his managing editor John Paschall. Both were excellent newspapermen. Howland described Harlee Branch, the hawk-eyed city editor, as a man who was able "to spot a tipsy reporter or an error in a story seemingly a block away, and who could think of night assignments with almost demoniacal perception for a reporter who had a date. He kept his staffers on their toes by continually bellowing at the top of his very adequate voice."[43] Hedley B. Wilcox was the business manager who first entered Peggy's name and salary in his ledger for the week of January 22, 1923.[44] These men and all the others on the *Journal* staff were John and Peggy's loyal friends. They were highly protective of the Marshes after Peggy became famous. In fact, in Atlanta and in other places in the South, nothing was printed about her that she did not want printed.

Prior to and during the time Peggy wrote for the *Magazine*, the *Journal* had a cadre of good writers who all went on to make names for themselves:

Erskine Caldwell, Don Marquis, Laurence Stallings, Ward Morehouse, Ward Greene, Grantland Rice, Morris Markey, Roark Bradford, W. B. Seabrook, and O. B. Keeler, who wrote a biography of the golfer Bobby Jones. Also, there were Frances Newman, who stunned Atlanta in 1926 with her novel *The Hard-Boiled Virgin;* and Medora Field Perkerson, who wrote two successful mystery novels, one of which was made into a film. Medora's best-known book was *White Columns of Georgia.* It was about the state's antebellum homes and was reprinted several times.[45] As Peggy boasted to a friend in 1938, "We sho' Gawd got a flourishing crop of authors in Georgia now! Not long ago we could only point to Frances Newman and then hastily brag about Uncle Remus. But Now! It looks to me like Georgia's got another money crop and it's writers."[46] Not a one of those writers achieved the success that Margaret Mitchell did.

5

In early March 1923, when a remorseful Red returned to Atlanta, John greeted him with tension and a sense of doom. Just as he had feared, Red tried to woo Peggy back to him. John was distraught. When she allowed Red to move back into the house with her, her father was so upset he became ill, and John began to suffer physically, too. The strain of having to repress his feelings for Peggy once again made him look older and tired. And although he never talked about his feelings, he had the look of a man who was holding hurt deep inside himself. That look made him seem even more vulnerable.

In June, he wrote his mother that he was thinking about taking "a cheap and sensible vacation" that he thought would be "wonderful for his health and his disposition."[47] He wanted "a week of unadulterated loafing in the Georgia mountains" because he felt "the need of getting away from people and getting out into the open spaces." But such a trip was not possible, as he explained in his next letter just a month later:

> I suppose I may as well tell you the unpleasant news now as later on. . . . Peggy is planning to get a divorce. The thing has been on the way for some weeks and the actual break came two weeks ago.
>
> The thing has been quite wearing on everybody concerned, especially the three of us. . . . My position has been a very difficult one, as you can understand . . . with both of them calling on me constantly, it wasn't possible for me to cut loose from them entirely, as I wanted to do many times. It would have saved me a lot of worry, perhaps. On the other hand, my "soothing

influence" may have been a factor in preventing a more tragic break.[48]

Although he could not tell his family what he meant by "preventing a more tragic break," he meant that statement literally. Red had become so unstable that he could not control his anger and began to abuse Peggy physically. After each of these encounters, he would run away for a while, and then return, begging her to forgive him. At that time, she weighed less than ninety pounds and was defenseless against such a muscular man, well over six feet tall. The first time John saw Peggy's arm and face swollen and bruised from a beating Red had given her, he was devastated.[49]

In her divorce testimony before a jury the following July, she stated that Red had beaten her with his fist so brutally on July 10, 1923, that she required medical attention. On one occasion, he jerked and shook her against a bed, causing her to be bruised all over her body. During another argument a few days later, she testified that he hit her in the eye, causing it to swell and remain closed for several days. At yet another time, he pounded her arm with his fist so hard that her arm became swollen, discolored, and painful.[50]

In a strange sense, Peggy bore these bruises proudly, for they were outward signs—proof—that she had indeed tried to sustain her marriage and that the divorce was not her fault. In those days when battered wives were not topics of public discussion, John did not feel comfortable writing to his family about the abuse Peggy had suffered. In his June letter to his mother he wrote only, "Living in an atmosphere of this kind as I have since the first of the year has not been the most pleasant thing one could imagine." The fact that he mentioned Peggy's problems at all indicated his need to confide in someone.

Not only did the Mitchells want to keep secret Red's physical abuse of Peggy, but they also tried to hide what John called "the last straw."

Red's love of adventure and excitement and his desire to clean up some easy money caused him to embark on a career of "rum-running." He had been running whiskey into Atlanta from the Georgia mountains for about a week before Peggy found out about it, telling her he was traveling for his company. I was the only one who knew about it, and I wasn't able to dissuade him he is such a headstrong character when he gets one of his wild ideas in his head.

The same day Peggy told Red that she could not stand his conduct any longer, the professional bootlegger he was working with double-crossed him and got away with two hundred dollars, his entire capital stock. At that point, Red finally agreed with her that the only hope for either of them was a divorce. As John said, "If they had tried to stick it out together it would have been ruinous for both of them, the ruin possibly taking a tragic form."[51]

On November 14, 1923, she filed for divorce, the first divorce in either the Mitchell or the Fitzgerald family. The staunch Catholics on her mother's side considered this divorce a public mortal sin. Thoughts of the disappointment her mother would have felt tormented Peggy. No more flippant attitudes from her now; she yearned for approval and protection. The pain she had caused her family, herself, and John by marrying Red enabled her a few years later to write about Scarlett's being haunted by the thought of her mother's disappointment in her. Scarlett says to Rhett,

> "Mother was—Oh Rhett, for the first time I'm glad she's dead, so she can't see me. She didn't raise me to be mean. She was so kind to everybody, so good. She'd rather I'd have starved than done this. And I so wanted to be just like her in every way and I'm not like her one bit. I hadn't thought of that—there's been so much else to think about—but I wanted to be like her. I didn't want to be like Pa. I loved him but he was—so—so thoughtless."[52]

Peggy could only write this passage once she had realized her own propensity to thoughtlessness and had experienced the damage it caused herself and others. As she grew to have a better understanding of herself, she was able to transfer her disapproval of her own behavior to Scarlett.

After her novel became a success, Peggy received letters from psychiatrists praising her for developing such a fascinating study of "a partial psychopath"—Scarlett. In thanking Dr. Hervey Cleckley, a psychiatrist in Augusta, Georgia, for his opinions about Scarlett, whom he described as "a very convincing figure" who had an "inward hollowness and a serious lack of insight," Peggy wrote: "Such words, coming from a doctor like you, are very flattering to me. Perhaps most authors would not take it kindly that a psychiatrist spoke of one of their characters as a 'partial-psychopath,' but I feel distinctly pleased." She went on to say,

> I have thought it looked bad for the moral and mental attitude of a nation that the nation could applaud and take to its heart a woman who conducted herself in such manner. I have been bewildered and amused, too, when my book has been attacked because I pictured in detail a "passionate and wanton woman." I thought it would be obvious to anyone that Scarlett was a frigid woman, loving attention and adulation for their own sake but having little

MARGARET MITCHELL & JOHN MARSH

or no comprehension of actual deep feelings and no reactions to the love and the attention of others.

6

Unable to eat or sleep, Peggy went into a deep depression. On Thanksgiving Day, 1923, John described her condition in a poignant letter to his mother:

> Peggy finally cracked under the strain and had to stop work. The unpleasant experiences she has had the past year wore her down until she was ordered by her physician to knock off and rest for a while. She was rather sick for a while, very close to a nervous breakdown, but she got better and is now in Florida enjoying the warm weather and sunshine. She plans to travel for a while and may go on to Cuba. If she does, she has promised to call on Kitty.

Enclosing some money to help his mother with her Christmas shopping, he apologized for not being able to send more, saying that he was disappointed in collecting some money that he had earned outside office hours. "My remittances are coming in very slowly," he wrote, but confidentially explained to Henry later that he had given what little he had to Peggy.

Sad and lonesome, he had dinner alone at the Winecoff Hotel Restaurant, his favorite downtown eating place, where the waitresses, "all middle-aged white women," thoughtfully looked after him without "unpleasant familiarity." His meal reminded him of the ones his mother prepared on Thanksgiving when he was a child, and so he wrote his mother:

> I am writing to tell you that I am thankful that I was permitted to be born into your family and for having had a few very happy years as an immediate and actively-participating member of that family, and also for turkey that was cooked just right as a memory I can look back on and be thankful for when the turkey I eat in restaurants and hotels is merely turkey and not an annual event that one looks forward to for days and looks backward to for years.

Peggy returned to Atlanta from Florida just before Christmas of 1923, and much to everyone's disappointment she started seeing Red again. For a while it looked as if they were going to get back together. In retrospect, Francesca explained: "She just was not a stable person. It was not that she loved Red or even believed that their marriage would work out eventually. It was that she wanted the world to know that she had tried to save her marriage, that the divorce, which was scandalous in those days, was the last resort. I think she was just trying to make everything look right though she may not have even understood that then. But she kept John torn-up all that time."[54] As before, John handled his pain the only way he knew how—by leaving Atlanta again. After working only eight months at the *Journal*, he moved to Washington, D.C., to work for the Associated Press. On December 15, 1923, just before he left Atlanta, he wrote to Frances, who was appalled at his switching jobs again. Knowing that she and his mother would be upset with him, he tried to sound as if he were moving to D.C. to advance his career. Faking a jovial mood, he asked her:

> Are you pleased with my becoming an A.P. man? And with my getting all this varied experience? My experience when I have been with the A.P. for a while will fit me to take almost any sort of newspaper job that comes my way. I have been eligible to a city editorship for some time, and when I have added the A.P. experience I will feel qualified for a managing editorship some where.

Because all of John's rapid job changes during the years prior to his marriage to Peggy correspond to changes in his relationship with her, there can be no doubt that his move to D.C. was an escape from the pain of seeing Peggy back with Red. At least, that's what his mother, Frances, and the rest of his family believed.

In this same letter, dated December 15, he explained that Peggy was back in Atlanta but only to visit her father, brother, and him. Embarrassed and depressed, she thought she could never again live in Atlanta, where she believed she had "ruined" her reputation. Even though she still had a claim on her job and her leave of absence was about to expire, he wrote that he had the "idea that she is going to be compelled to give up the work altogether." Her mental state must have been gravely impaired at that time because John was never one to exaggerate about anything. He was desperately unhappy during this period because it looked as if he had lost her forever, either eventually to Red or to something else he could not control.

He explained that she had left Atlanta "with very indefinite plans and a vague idea of going to Cuba," but had only gotten as far as Daytona, Florida, where she had gotten off the train because she was feeling too bad to go any further. She had stayed there a week and gone on to Miami for two weeks, then come home. Her visit to Miami, he said, "did her lots of good and convinced her that her only hope of getting back her health and strength is to get in a warm climate and stay there six months or a year." He added, "She is back now, chiefly for the purpose of getting things in shape and working out some plan." According to a later letter John sent his mother, Peggy never went to Cuba. She never cut herself away from him entirely for very long.

His letters to his family during this terrible period in his and Peggy's lives show that she wrote him and called him regularly. She continually poured out her unhappiness to him, refusing to let him get on with his own life and constantly keeping him mixed in her turmoil. She told his brother Henry that John was the only person who loved her "without any if's, and's, or but's." Once he had moved to Washington, she realized how dependent upon him she had become, and she could not bear his being away from her. She wrote to him often.

Meanwhile, Mrs. Marsh was having a difficult time understanding her son's relationship with this married woman, whose behavior she did not approve. Just a month before Peggy was to testify for the first time before a jury deciding her divorce, John wrote his mother,

> I am leading a very retired life these days. I have decided this is the first time in my life when I am permitted to be a gentleman of leisure and I propose to enjoy it. Sleeping until noon and loafing all afternoon has a certain attraction to it, even if one has to work all night in order to make up for it. For the first time in my life also, I am not the least worried by the fact that I know no one here and talk to no one except the men at the office. I don't seem the least worried about it, and I have actually enjoyed doing nothing but stay at home in the afternoons, reading part of the time, writing occasionally, and sleeping frequently. I sleep until noon and take a nap from three o'clock to five, which ought to be ideal for a lazy man. You see, I have never been lazy, though most of my life ineffectual. I am now striving to become lazy, in the hope that it will be excellent for my shattered nerves and my emaciated physique. I can't see that I have become any more fatter, though the nerves are better as evidenced by the fact that one day I didn't smoke but 25 cigarettes.[55]

A day or so after writing that letter, he decided to visit his mother, who was now living with Henry and his young daughter Mary in Wilmington, Delaware. Making a valiant effort to be cheerful, he told his mother, "I'm coming a running with my head stuck out in front for some of your strawberry shortcake. I haven't tasted any in the past two thousand years made the way you can make it." But he wanted Frances not to make plans for him to go to any dances because "when evening comes I shall probably be too tired to wish to have the responsibility of being interesting to a strange girl.... Dances are something I always preferred to train for, and I shall have to start this one tired." He wanted his mother and sister to know that his plans could change abruptly because he might have to return to Atlanta on short notice. Speaking paternalistically of Peggy and Red, he explained:

> My two children have been going round and round again the past two or three weeks and they have about reached the stage where they either cut each other's throats or peaceably agree never to see each other again. If things don't clear up right quick, I may be compelled to make a brief trip to Atlanta to straighten them out. I don't expect it, and I don't care to make the trip as I would have only a few hours there, but it may be necessary.[56]

John went to Delaware the following weekend. On this visit, he talked more freely to his family than he felt comfortable doing in a letter. He told them about Red's emotional and physical abuse of Peggy, and what it was doing to all three of them. After listening to him and seeing him so sad, thin, and pale, his mother and sister became even more worried; it was plain to them then that he was so emotionally involved with this woman, who seemed bent on destroying him, that his physical and emotional state was being injured. They tried to reason with him and urged him to break away entirely from Peggy before it was too late. But Mrs. Marsh and Frances knew that their advice had fallen on deaf ears. After he returned to Washington, they decided to visit him there in a few days. But, on June 22, just a week after Peggy appeared before the jury, he sent his mother an unusually brief but polite letter clearly discouraging her and Frances from making their trip to Washington. What had happened was that Peggy had unexpectedly come to spend the weekend with him. During this visit she told him that she loved him and wanted to be with him always.[57]

7

John stayed in Washington until the end of August, when it was clear to him at last that Peggy had made a clean break with Red, and then he returned to Atlanta. Upon his arrival, he went straight to the Georgia Railway and Power Company and asked for his old job back.[58] Then he went to the Mitchells' house where he found Peggy looking frail, but happy to see him. Although she was much improved, he wrote that she was still not as strong as she should have been and her nerves still were not in the best condition. He wrote his mother, "Apparently she has escaped the internal injuries I was afraid of and should get better steadily."[59]

His mother and sisters did not know what to think about John's obsession for this young woman who treated him so badly. Peggy was not the kind of girl Mrs. Marsh had expected her son to love and to marry; yet he so obviously adored her.[60] They simply could not understand his behavior or Peggy's.

On September 7, 1924, he wrote his first letter in two years that reflects any true happiness and also a little abandonment of his conservative manner. He had always wanted an apartment instead of a boarding room, but never could afford one. Now he "took the fatal step" and leased a small apartment (one room, plus a kitchen and a bath) because he and Peggy needed more privacy than boarding houses provided. This apartment was Number A-3 of the Langdon Court Apartments, 111 East Tenth Street, between Peachtree and Juniper streets. He wrote that in helping him move, Peggy had been"invaluable," for she added a "note of refined elegance to my bachelor quarters." She made curtains and brought over a bridge lamp and a couple of pictures from her father's house. John added that she was also "active as my field representative in the arrangements for the surprise [housewarming] shower."

> As a result I am a changed man. Life has disclosed new aspects to me, I am interested in things that formerly I scorned. I read advertisements of the department stores avidly and rush down to join bargain sale crushes, by chance an old Ladies Home Journal fell into my hands and I carried it away to study surreptitiously its hints to the home-maker, and when I have dates with my lady friends, no longer do I play the sheik—I am too much interested in getting their advice on such weighty matters as draperies, furniture arrangements and household economy.
>
> You have no idea how many things I have learned about Atlanta in these two weeks. I have lived here nearly five years now but when I started out to furnish my apartment I didn't know where people bought things, except men's clothing, cigarettes, and corn whiskey. Now I can discuss learnedly which of the department stores have good furniture, which of the furniture stores charge too much, where one goes for draperies of the right sort, and where one can pick up perfectly good pieces in second-hand stores for next to nothing. When I was here before once or twice, I was dragged into the department store section by girl friends who had bits of shopping to do in the course of dates with me. Always I entered these feminine establishments blushingly, felt like taking my hat off as soon as I entered the door and was in a fever of embarrassment unless some of my friends should see me there. Now, after these two weeks, I feel perfectly at home

in any store in Whitehall street, feel no embarrassment in walking right up to a girl clerk and saying brazenly, "I want to look at some SHEETS AND PILLOW CASES!" (Fancy that!), and regard the discovery of a bargain as a distinguished achievement. It has been quite an education for me.

He and Peggy celebrated his twenty-ninth birthday on October 6 by having dinner in his new apartment. His next letter, dated October 15, 1924, the day before Peggy's divorce was granted and her maiden name officially restored, is more candid about his love life.

> I hope you haven't disowned me, though I am fully aware I have given you legal grounds for checking me off the books as a prodigal son who has expired under the statute of limitations. I've not really forgotten you, and I hope you remember me as a member of the family. . . .
>
> I believe in course of time I will settle back to a somewhat normal existence. For the past month and fifteen days I have been on a spree, and such things, of course, can't continue forever. Eventually they wear themselves out. After trying three or four times to get this one under control by the use of will power, I decided the common sense course was to let it run wild until it ran down. Meanwhile my correspondence and other things have suffered, but all things have an end and until then I crave your indulgence.
>
> The new regime, in fact, has already been ushered in. Peggy has agreed to give me two nights a week off. Witness this letter on the first one. I haven't had dates with her, I might say, every night since I reached Atlanta, but one has to sleep occasionally, has not one?
>
> Being a trifle more serious—I'm awfully sorry I have been so slow in writing to my family, but I have let my work and Peggy completely occupy my time. Both are highly interesting and each of them deserves and rewards attention. With Peggy, six months' absence may or may not have made our hearts grow fonder, but it certainly did stack up an awful stack of things that have had to be said and done since I got back. We aren't caught up yet, but I think we are making progress.

Then, in answer to his mother's question, "What is a Murphy bed?" he explained:

A Murphy bed, My Dear Mother, is a door-bed. You open an innocent looking door, and in a'trice transform your staid and sober library into a scandalous bed room. It is the Jazz Age descendent of the Mid-Victorian folding bed, and has the advantage that it doesn't fold up on one's self in the middle of the night.

News Item—Peggy is in much better health now than any time since I have known her. Except for a sprained ankle, she hasn't been sick at all. She is even gaining weight. I think my being here is good for her.

8

On January 20, 1925, John announced to his mother that he was going to marry Peggy. The previous night, he had gotten Mr. Mitchell's approval and now was writing for his mother's. He was especially relieved by Mr. Mitchell's reception of the idea, for "the old man" not only consented but also seemed pleased; he opposed only one thing, and that was their intention to live in their own apartment. Grown accustomed to having Peggy home and John frequently around the house, Mr. Mitchell felt as if John was taking Peggy away from him and he wanted them to stay. But John insisted that they start their married life in privacy. "It would be nice to live at the Mitchell home, but I would rather live in a one room apartment with Peggy than in a big house on Peachtree Road with in-laws."

All the anguish that he had been through in the previous years had vanished. Relaxed and happy at last, he wrote:

Having lost her once and now regained her, she is doubly attractive, and the troubles we have been through have given me an insight into her character which makes me respect and admire, as well as love, her more than any woman who has come into my life since I grew up. . . . I have been in love with Peggy for a long time, as I said, but it wasn't nothing like this here.

So, we have decided to toss our several distastes for matrimony into the lake, and give the ancient and honorable institution a trial. We are even going to live in my little one room bachelor apartment exclamation point. I am sure I must be in love with her, to be willing to give her half of my already limited quarters or to feel any confidence that the close confinement won't have us snapping at each other's throats within a week. She's a very thoughtful, considerate, unselfish, sensible sort of person, and I shall try to be the same, and I believe we will be able to make a go of it. . . . We haven't had time yet to talk about definite plans.

Personally, I can't see any good reason for waiting any great length of time. If we had married today, it couldn't be called hasty, because we have known each other so long and so well. . . .

We may even elope. It would certainly save a lot of trouble and fuss and unnecessary excitement that seems to be preliminary to most weddings. Peggy doesn't want the unnecessary preliminaries, and I am opposed to her being subjected to that unnecessary strain, now that she is at last in good health and building up, after years of almost constant sickness. Have I told you how well she is doing? For the past several weeks, she has been getting better and better, putting on weight until she now weighs 115 pounds and is positively beautiful. . . . I don't want her to lose what she has gained by having to go through the usual wedding preliminaries.

So here beginneth a new chapter. It looks interesting at the start and I believe I shall like it. She is a daughter I am proud to bring to you, and I hope all of you will love her as much as I do.

9

The "new chapter," which promised such long-awaited happiness, was delayed by a dramatic turn of events on January 21, 1925. It was a turn that prompted Peggy to admit, "John has been so very good to me that it's a by word among our friends—they all say that 'turn about is fair play' now that I'm the one who sits by and holds the hand."[61] What ended up as a life-threatening condition began benignly enough one afternoon shortly before Christmas when John started having the hiccoughs. At first, Peggy and friends at work laughed and teased him. They offered all kinds of home remedies, but nothing worked. In an effort to help him, Peggy researched and wrote her article "What Causes Hiccoughs" for the *Magazine*, December 28, 1924.[62]

The hiccoughs did stop for a couple of weeks but then suddenly started up again in a more forceful form. As the days passed and he continued to hiccough with every breath he drew, the situation was no longer funny to anyone. Peggy was terrified. John could not eat or sleep, and after having these spasms intermittently for two weeks, he was exhausted, unable to go to work or even to leave his room. Because she could not leave her job until four in the afternoon, she made the janitor in John's apartment building promise that he would check on her patient regularly and get him coffee and soup from the corner restaurant.[63]

By early February, she felt unable to handle the situation alone any longer. She had Kelly Starr, their friend and John's boss, help her take John to St. Joseph's Infirmary. While at work Monday morning, she realized that she had to let the Marsh family know what was going on. "Please excuse this slug head," she wrote Frances, "but I am at the office and Angus thinks that there is no crime so black as to use office hours for letter writing. But if I dont write you now, I dont know when I'll get a chance."[64] She explained that immediately after John had obtained her father's consent to the nuptials, he got sick with the flu, "a bran new type, the 'hiccoughing flu'.... He hasnt been seriously or painfully ill—I dont want you to be worried—but as it has interfered with his eating and sleeping and he has become very weak. His doctor pumps out his stomach every day and that seems to help some."[65]

Relieved to have him in the hospital, Peggy went on to say, "He was pretty apathetic when we got him there Saturday night but I noted with pleasure when I called Sunday morning that he seemed interested in life and even confided to me that he had circumvented my schemes to give him a shiny-nosed day nurse and a billowy Jewish night nurse and had lured in from the hall a pretty nurse who was 'Sex Conscious!' By this I knew he was getting better."[66]

They had been planning to be married on Valentine's Day, "the only date on the whole calendar," she said, "for which I unashamedly cherish a sentimental weakness (Probably because John has always sent me violets with long purple streamers on that day!)."[67] Now those plans, she moaned to Frances, had been "knocked galley west" by his present illness.

> How ever, I do know that we'll just have a little wedding with a few of the gang present. There are quite a few of our friends who have committed the unpardonable sin of marrying people who either didnt like me or didnt like John. And John and I have decided that we wont have any one at our wedding who doesnt like both of us. Of course if we can induce the very proper Courtenay Ross MacFayden to leave her prissyfied husband (who disapproves of me) at home and come with the rowdy Frank Stanton—and Kelly Starr to leave his wife at home and bring the equally rowdy Anne Couper, we will have a wedding to our taste. But I'm afraid such a wedding would cause a scandal as the folks that dont like us would be madder at not being invited than the ones who do like us.[68]

On February 14, John showed no improvement. Annoyed because the doctor handling the case for three weeks had not been doing much other than letting nature take its course, Peggy and Kelly Starr called in another physician, Dr. Arch Elkin, who, she assured Mrs. Marsh, had already been able to diminish the violence and the frequency of John's hiccoughs.

Continuing to make her wedding plans, Peggy explained that she and John were planning a very small, quiet wedding—"not more than a half dozen or dozen at the most"—and they wanted her and Frances to come to Atlanta for it. Suspecting how uneasy Mrs. Marsh must have felt about her, she searched for the right words. Her sincerity rings through here:

> Frankly, I'm not bothered so much about the wedding or trousseau or parties as I am about marrying John. I want to marry him so I can look after him as he has looked after me for the last three years. He's worked and worried himself thin and sick and now that the happy ending has come he's in the hospital! So I want to get him out and marry him and make him rest up and get fat.
>
> You and Frances were so sweet in your letters to me, welcoming me into your clan. . . . I appreciated your letter so very much, especially when I know that most mothers have violent misgivings at hearing that their sons are going to marry women who are divorced. How ever, I can only say that I love John most sincerely, first as a friend who I had learned to trust and lean on because of his honor and his strength and next, as a sweet heart because he was ever so considerate and loyal. I don't think I can say more for a man, even to his mother! I know pretty well, I'm not all the wonders he thinks I am but to date I have succeeded pretty well in keeping him fooled and if I can just keep him that way the rest of our lives, I think we will be very happy.[69]

On Friday, February 26, Peggy was encouraged because John was, at last, showing little signs of improvement. "I go down and fill him full of gossip and scandal (I'm a regular receiving station when it comes to picking up both of those) and jokes and it seems to help him—if he doesn't laugh too much for that always starts him off again. He's discovered a way of inhaling cigarette smoke that effectually stops the hiccoughs as soon as they begin."[70] When one of his elderly lady friends called offering to take care of him while he recuperated at her home, Peggy wrote Frances, "I am going to have to marry him to protect him. . . . There's various and sundry ladies, both married, single and divorced, who cherish sentimental feelings and yearnings about John, mainly because he has such lovely manners, knows how to appreciate a misunderstood wife in a well nigh Jurgenesque manner, to make discreet love with his eyes and to kiss hands with just the proper degree of restrained emotion."[71]

10

Every time it looked as if he were getting well, John would get sick again with high fever, abdominal pain, sore throat, and the hiccoughs. It was the unpredictability of his condition that frightened Peggy most of all and made her obsessively concerned with anything that remotely resembled a symptom in him or her. On the day of one of John's setbacks, she wrote that he "looked like Hell and that simply broke my heart as I had thought he was on the way back to being well. . . . I so hated to see it happen. Seems to me that the road back from 119 pounds to 160 is going to be endless and I only wish I had John's guts so I wouldnt get tired or discouraged."[72] Beginning to fear that the spasms would never stop, Peggy thought that he had the perfect right to develop a fear complex about recurrences; she admitted that she had one. But he had not been afraid "and he isnt afraid of them," she wrote Frances. "He has been remarkably patient through out all this. I know I would have worn out myself, two doctors and three nurses cursing and howling."[73]

Although his medical records are not available and, unlike Peggy, he did not record his every illness, ache, and pain, John apparently had had an ulcer and a bad gallbladder for some time before the spasms began. Never one to talk about his health, much less complain about it, he worked hard and long hours no matter how bad he felt. When Dr. Misel, whom Peggy identified as "a stomach specialist," finally discovered that part of John's problems stemmed from "a cardiac ulcer," she informed Henry: "He [Misel] says from all indications that this one has been there since 1917. . . . John has been in the reportorial habit of eating all hours in weird places. Greek joints and the like, so dear to journalists that the ulcer had no chance to heal. I dont know if thats all that is causing the hicking but it no doubt has much to do with the aggravation of it."[74] But because Dr. Misel failed to diagnose the diseased gallbladder until later, John's condition continued to worsen. The letters Peggy wrote to the Marshes at the beginning of his long illness show that some of the medical treatments administered at first, such as emptying his stomach daily and feeding him rich foods that he could not digest, were unfortunately as damaging to his health as the mysterious spasms were.[75]

Peggy wrote Frances, "Seems that Johns stomach was inflamed clear through the walls before they finally found out what ailed him and changed his diet. Seems as if some of the many doctors who tramped in and out, pulling their whiskers and uttering wise saws during those terrible two days might have figured out what was wrong but they didnt."[76]

When the specialist recommended neurological testing, which also failed to show the cause of the hiccoughs, Peggy began to wonder if John were not experiencing some psychogenic problems. Even though she never attributed any of her own ailments to psychogenic reasons, she was beginning to wonder, as John's condition continued for so long, if there really were not some underlying psychological cause. After the medical tests failed to show any organic disturbances in his nervous system, she confided to Henry: "The idea had been formulating in my mind that a large part of John's trouble must be psychic. . . . I've seen lots of women turn to sick head aches and hysterics in a perfectly unconscious effort at mechanical protection—or in subconscious protest against some thing that was offensive to them—I know I'm too bitten on the psychoanalytical stuff. . . . Isn't it a funny mess?" she asked Henry.

Although Frances and Mrs. Marsh never gave an indication that they disapproved of her, she suspected that they did. So she never mentioned to Frances or to Mrs. Marsh any of her beliefs about John's subconscious mind causing his problems, fearing such remarks might irritate them. In her letter to Frances, she said she took "an instant dislike" to one consulting physician, who was "not worth a hoot in Hades." She explained,

> I suppose I took a dislike to him when after poor John had been sick as a dog for a week and unable to eat or digest anything this poor ass of a medico remarked to Kelly Starr that there really wasn't anything wrong with John except a "A touch of the nerves." . . . I yearned to swat him for his diagnosis. How ever there is no use criticising a doctor to a patient's face as it dont do much good and only makes them feel uneasy.[77]

On March 7, he suffered yet another serious setback, and the underlying sadness in Peggy's letter to Frances four days later is evident:

> Yesterday when I tiptoed into the hospital room, John was sleeping—and hicking right along. He continued to do so all during my visit which was rather short yesterday. He had been doing it since the night before. He said that Miss Tuggle [a nurse] had objected to his stopping the attacks by inhaling his cigarettes so deeply that his lungs absorbed all the smoke—It was beginning to irritate his throat. So he stopped doing it and the hiccoughs kept up intermittently. . . .
> I had so set my heart on seeing him step right along the uphill road that it rather knocked the pins from under me to see him at it again yesterday. . . . I havent been sleeping at all well lately or eating any too much. . . . I look a wreck.[78]

The next day, his fever soared and could not be brought down; the physicians advised her to notify his family. Frantic with worry, Mrs. Marsh asked Henry to go to Atlanta and, if possible, to bring John home to her. Later, Henry said his greatest fear was that he would have to bring his brother's body home for, at that time, the only patient on record for having hiccoughed as long as John had died. That evening in early March, when Dr. Elkins told Peggy that John might not survive the night, she broke down sobbing.[79]

Not knowing how to treat his condition, the physicians, as a last-minute effort, decided to sedate him to the point of unconsciousness. They figured that if they could halt the spasms long enough to give him several hours of peaceful sleep, he might regain his strength. At that point, nothing could be lost. After he was asleep, Peggy went into his darkened room to see him. As she stood quietly by his bed, staring sadly at him, she thought how serene and handsome he looked and what a good and brave man he was. Without disturbing him, she lightly kissed him and slipped out of the room. She walked downtown, went to a movie alone, and was home by eight, frightened and sad.[80]

Henry Marsh arrived in Atlanta on the ninth of March, but because the doctors stood firm about John's having no visitors during this critical period, he did not see his brother until three days later. Nervous and angry because even she had not been allowed to see John, Peggy wrote thanking Frances for having not only one brother with whom she could fall in love, but two. "I never felt so relieved in my life as when I saw Henry coming up the steps—he looked so much like John that I knew every thing was going to be alright." Standing in the "etheriodiform atmosphere" of the hallway, listening to Johnny, as she called him, tell the nurse "plainly what a damned ass she was and how much he wanted me," she fumed as she nervously waited for Henry to finish talking to the physicians.

> Oh, I was in a bad way by the time Henry blew in. He cocked an attentive ear to my vituperative remarks about the doctors and life in general, sucked on his pipe and said, 'Well, lets eat.' I think hes an infinitely sensible person! . . . I like your family. They don't get hysterical or emotional.[81]

Feeling an immense sense of relief when Henry took charge of the situation and insisted that she rest, she grabbed a taxi and arrived home before her father and Stephens had come in from work. She went straight upstairs to her room, fell across her bed fully clothed, and cried herself to sleep. Around two, she woke up enough to remove her shoes, but not her clothes, stockings, or hair pins, and crawled under the covers. She slept from 5 P.M. to 6 A.M., when sunlight streaming through her bedroom window woke her up. That day she "felt like million" for the first time in a long time; she knew everything was going to be all right. When she went downstairs that morning, she found the lights on. "Poor father and Steve must think I stayed out all night . . . probably they sat up wondering whether I had been kidnapped or was just being modern and leading my own life, like the girls in the magazines that father condemns but reads religiously. I'll have to do some tall explaining tonight."[82] Her contribution to the *Magazine* that Sunday, March 15, 1925, reflects what must have been uppermost in her mind. Her article is titled "Marriage Licenses That Are Never Used."

The enforced sleep helped John, and by the end of the next day he looked better. Peggy remarked that she had never realized the value of sleep:

> If he can just grab off ten hours sleep he looks as if nothing had ever happened to him and if he misses it, he looks like a fatal accident looking for an unhealthy place to happen. Yesterday, his unfeeling nurse pulled down the covers and insisted on displaying John's "shameful condition" as he called it— histhinness—and I was stunned. He doesnt look so thin in the face but he looks like a famine victim in the body. I could have wept over it but he seemed very chipper.[83]

11

The only interesting distraction Peggy had during John's long ordeal came one day in a letter addressed to John and postmarked Cuba. It was from Kitty Mitchell, his college sweetheart, who had disappointed him by not responding to the letter he had sent her before Christmas, announcing his engagement. Peggy thought the reason for Kitty's silence was that he had gone overboard about "his over weening passion for me and his desire to make me his'n."[84] Always thinking that she was expert in matters of romance, she wrote Frances,

> I rated him for telling her how much he cared about me, as there are few women who can bear with equanimity the spectacle of a lover they have turned down, finding solace and happiness with another woman. John was rather hurt about it all, saying that he thought it was rather small of her because the poor darling didnt know that it's only one woman in a thousand who is generous enough to be sincerely glad in the happiness of her old flame.[85]

In Peggy's view, the letter from Kitty was "a peach," and she said it made him very happy. Actually, it was only a moment's distraction for him, but a delightful one for her, giving her something to think about for days and to write at length about to John's sister. "Kitty is a sort of beloved legend to him and men have so few really beautiful legends that I hated to see it ruined in any way by a touch of reality and human nature creeping in."[86]

By the end of March, signs of spring were beginning to peep out of the earth and appear in the bright blueness of the sky. Life was a little less strenuous now. She took the time to have her tonsils "painted with silver nitrate,—they were choking me to death—and also time to hang out in a beauty parlor for three hours (and $5) as John had peered at me worriedly and said I looked like an advance agent for a famine."[87] Starting to get back into her old routine, she ended a letter to Frances by describing herself, not as "a wild woman," as she had done earlier, but as "an old and decrepit lady, past my hot-blooded youth and all that jolly sort of rot and so thankful to the bon Dieu that I have the One Man that I'm willing to fore swear all most all the others."[88]

She added that John has "roses on his cheeks that put to shame the ones in my little brass box and a vast eagerness to talk and hear news but those damnable hiccoughs keep on just the same."[89] He had the honor, she recorded, of being the only case on record where a patient hicked thirty-one consecutive days and did not die, and she wished he had not picked such an exclusive disease that doctors knew nothing about. "It would have been so much easier to treat if he had gotten delirium tremens or some thing fashionable."[90]

John spent nearly three months in the hospital before the hiccoughs stopped completely. The source of his spasms was never discovered; they went away just as mysteriously as they had come. One cannot help wondering whether the ultimate source of his condition in early 1925 was the release of the emotional pain that he had suppressed up to that point, all that disappointment and grief that he had stored tightly inward.

Once the physicians were certain that the hiccoughs had stopped—this was in May—they removed his diseased gallbladder. After the surgery, he began to improve rapidly as he recuperated in the Mitchells' home, where Mr. Mitchell and Stephens welcomed him. During his convalescence, Peggy and John started a pattern that they were to follow for the next decade. After their supper, they talked and worked on her assignments and on a story that she had begun earlier. This work was probably her novella "'Ropa Carmagin." According to Stephens Mitchell, "[John] would read Margaret's articles and take them to her with suggestions for improvement in usage and style pencilled in the margins. And he was always right."[91] During this period, they established their roles: he the editor, she the writer. They also established the basis for a mature and loving relationship.

John's steadfast devotion and his illness changed Peggy in significant ways; they matured her. If she did not know in the beginning of their relationship that she loved him, she knew now. Indeed, she had become as devoted to him as he had always been to her. Although they were of equal rank in their relationship, it was always she who, in talking or in writing letters, quoted John, not the reverse. She was forever saying or writing: "John says. . . ." or "John thinks. . . ." or "John did. . . ." or "I'll let John read this. . . ." or "I'll ask John what he wants to do about. . . ." Joe Kling said that there was never any question about John's being the "boss in the Marshes' household." Their friends and family described her as "hero-worshipping John," and with her tendency to exaggerate, they added that she "sometimes made him larger in life than he really was."[92] If this was the case, perhaps it was because she had once come so close to losing him.

12

In June 1925, thinking their troubles were over, they planned their wedding. Then, one pleasant evening while they sat talking and looking at one of her drafts, John suddenly became quiet. She looked up at him and gasped. His head had fallen back slightly; his eyes remained opened but rolled back so that only the whites showed. He was motionless except that his left hand, which held the cigarette he had been smoking, was trembling vigorously. Although he somehow managed to hold the cigarette, it slipped down behind his fingers and burned them, though he appeared not to be aware of the burning. Terrified, she thought he was dying, and she screamed for Steve and her father. Suddenly, John was back to normal again. He appeared not to know what had happened to him or even to be aware that anything had happened. He stared perplexed at his burned fingers. He had completely lost consciousness for a few seconds, and then regained it without ever realizing he had lost it.[93]

For the rest of his life, John periodically suffered from these seizures, a mild form of epilepsy that may have been a residual effect of the more serious spasms and the high fever that had nearly killed him earlier.[94] Whatever their cause, they were a source of concern and embarrassment to him. Because they came without warning and for no apparent reason, day or night, he never drove an automobile. Peggy always drove their car, and she did not like for him to be alone. She feared that someday the seizures would intensify and render him helpless. Friends and coworkers got used to seeing them, and merely did their best to remove that ever-present cigarette from his hand.[95] Mary Singleton remembered the little burn spots on his fingers. She and Joe Kling said that John's spells came more often when he was under severe stress.

After he returned to work in early summer, he made a heroic effort to give up cigarettes entirely, but it was not an easy matter for him as the office in which he worked was nearly a madhouse, and the nervous strain was often heavy. Kelly Starr, a likeable, charming man but a known alcoholic, unloaded his responsibilities as head of the department on John. Thinking about Kelly's problems, Peggy wrote,

> If ever I needed any thing to make me thankful that J isn't a drinking man, it's the spectacle Kelly Starr has been making of himself for the last six months. Every morning he's "never going to touch another drop," he tells the assembled staff, meanwhile thanking them for their touching loyalty to him during sprees. And by ten o'clock in the morning he's kite high. Some times he's away from the office for a day or two—during which time the office gets some work done. When he returns, approximately sober for a hour, he insists on upsetting and changing all the work in his absence and then totters off again before deciding what ought to be done about it all. He's certainly in awful shape and if he belonged to me I'd shoot him and put him and his office force out of their misery. Naturally, this state of affairs, coupled with the heat, doesn't make John feel any too good at times and the added strain of cutting down cigarettes is very uncomfortable.[96]

13

On June 15, 1925, Peggy and John used their lunch hour to run to the courthouse to get their marriage license. He gave his correct age, twenty-nine, but she, who was twenty-five, gave her age as twenty-two. It is highly probable that at that time even John did not know exactly how old Peggy was. Always reluctant about telling her age, she either shaved off a few years or refused to give it at all.

At five o'clock on the evening of July 4, 1925, at the Unitarian-Universalist Church on West Peachtree Street, they were married. Augusta was the bridesmaid and Medora, the matron of honor. The best man was Frank L. Stanton, Jr., son of the Georgia poet who wrote "Mighty Lak a Rose," "Jes a Wearying for You," and other lyrics. Medora recalled that it was a traditionally hot July 4. In a cool, high-ceilinged, upstairs bedroom of the Mitchells' white-columned house, she helped Peggy dress in a knee-length, pansy-purple georgette gown, a high style in 1925. "That afternoon she had the glow that makes all brides beautiful. Hers was a beauty with an elfin touch, a Puckish smile and that incalculable quality called charm. She was very happy and very gay." Medora added, "Peggy didn't want a slow-drag wedding and we stepped lively down the aisle to a speeded-up Loehengrin. . . . We practically fox-trotted down the aisle. Afterwards we all raced to their small apartment."[97]

That night, their friends catered the simple wedding reception in John and Peggy's apartment on Crescent Avenue. All had a happy time. The next day the newlyweds boarded a train that took them to the north Georgia mountain region, to the lovely but isolated Linger Longer Lodge, a cabin owned and used by Georgia Power's publicity department to entertain executives and editors.

From that time on, nothing and no one ever came between Peggy and John or ever threatened the deep bond between them. They would have no children and virtually no social life or interests away from each other, nor any separate aspirations.[98]

C H A P T E R

6

1925-1926

A WRITER IN PROGRESS

*I won't ever believe [Frances Newman's] novel is a
failure, because it has had the good effect of getting
Peggy roused up again over her novel, and we are
at work on it again. I might write more except that
I am going to take a stab again at the opening
chapter of the fifteenth revision of the Adventures of
Pansy. Peggy has promised to work on it if I'll help
her get started again, so here goes.*

—John Marsh to Frances Marsh,
8 December 1926

1

THE MARSHES STARTED THEIR LIFE TOGETHER in a midtown apartment so tiny, unattractive, and dark that they nicknamed it "El Dumpo." Joe Kling, who visited them there often, recalled, "That place was a dump!"

The Dump was located in a neighborhood that had been labeled "Tight Squeeze" after the Civil War, when the road was very narrow and crooked and inhabited by a rough lot of criminals. That name was abandoned in 1887, when the road was straightened, but Eugene Mitchell appears to have revived the term, at least among the family. In 1931 he wrote an article for the *Atlanta Historical Bulletin* that included information on the history of the "Tight Squeeze" area, and he found it amusing to use the old name to describe John and Peggy's new neighborhood. According to Peggy, holdups and purse snatchings were still common, and Tight Squeeze was certainly an appropriate name for an area inhabited by many struggling young couples like John and Peggy. It may be, too, that the name fit the appearance of the neighborhood, which was made up of a section of Peachtree Street extending about three blocks from Peachtree Place to Eleventh Street. Tenth Street was the principal cross street, and at its intersection with Peachtree a fair amount of commercial development had taken place. The office buildings and stores were built as close to the street as it was possible to put them, in contrast to the original residences, with their yards, lawns, trees, and shrubbery in front. According to one source, the general appearance must have made Peachtree seem narrower than it in fact was and suggested a tight squeeze. The greater-than-normal amount of traffic at that time, created by the Tenth Street shopping area, may have added to the optical illusion.[1] The Marshes thought that the neighborhood was convenient, for the post office on Tenth Street was only two blocks away and the grocery store only a block away.

Their apartment, Number 1, was on the ground level on the northwest side of what was known as the Crescent Avenue Apartments. A three-story, dark red-brick building with a steep, green, sloping roof, 17 Crescent Avenue (now 979 Crescent Avenue) was located at the corner of Crescent

Avenue and Tenth. It was originally a single-family home built in 1899 on Peachtree Street by the Cornelius Sheehans. Then, in 1913, it changed hands and its new owners pushed it further back on its deep, sloping lot toward Crescent Avenue and remodeled it into a ten-unit apartment. The Marshes' apartment, only two rooms plus a kitchen and a bath, had dark woodwork, dark, faded wallpaper, dark hardwood floors, and an unpleasant, musty odor.[2]

They had no money for wallpaper, but they did paint some of the woodwork white.[3] The only attractive feature in the entire place was a triple set of tall, leaded, beveled-glass windows with beveled mirrors on each side in an alcove of the front room. It was into this alcove, about a year after their wedding, that John—in an effort to lift the depressed spirits of his bride—brought home a second-hand Remington typewriter and a very wobbly, golden oak table, just large enough to hold the typewriter and a stack of paper.[4] In this alcove and on this typewriter, nearly all of *Gone With the Wind* would be written.

Because he had to borrow money to pay all of his medical expenses, John was deeply in debt when they married. Shortly after their marriage, Peggy had trouble with her left ankle, and her visits to specialists added to their debt. Even though he was making more—seventy-five dollars a week—at the Georgia Power Company than he had made at the *Journal*, which paid him only forty dollars, he could not get all of his bills paid, and he loathed being in debt. He was used to being poor but not to being in debt. Mr. Mitchell offered to lend him some money, but John refused his help. Angus Perkerson gave Peggy a couple of raises so that her salary was now thirty dollars a week, the maximum amount paid to female newspaper writers.[5] By 1925, she had agreed to write, in addition to her regular features, the *Journal*'s "Elizabeth Bennet's Gossip," a column that Frances Newman, a librarian and book reviewer, had created in 1921 and written for four years until she launched her career as a novelist. The column contained no gossip, just breezy little anecdotes about Atlantans, and it was easy to do, though gathering the material was time consuming. Peggy wrote Frances, her sister-in-law: "I once told John that the Elizabeth Bennet Colymn [sic] was going to keep the wolf away from the door, and he brutally asked if I was going to read it to the wolf."[6]

Knowing that the next five or six years would be lean ones did not bother Peggy. She told Frances, "I hope you get tied up some day to a man who means so much to you that you dont give three whoops about money as long as you have enough to eat, a last years over coat and money enough to see Harry Langdon and Ben Turpin [actors] . . . and if I can just keep John fascinated by my brightly colored beauty, my brilliant wit, and my otherwise charming personality, all will be well."[7] A year later, her attitude had not changed. When Henry, whose first marriage had failed, was hesitating to remarry a young woman with whom he had fallen in love, Peggy advised him:

> If its just a matter of money, I'd say, go ahead and point with pride at myself and J. J is paying one third of his money to the Company, and one third to doctors. I regularly pay out all but five a week of my monumental salary on doctors bills and last years clothes. (Yes, five a week is what I wrote. I have a credit account at the quick and dirty here where I breakfast and lunch.) We are poorer than Hell ever was and yet we make out very well . . . and are visited by all timorous couples contemplating matrimony who want their morale boosted by the sight of two poor but happy people.
>
> Really, it is possible to get by on an amazingly small amount providing you have some affection for your poverty partner—and some hope of things picking up some time or other. I know I sound Pollyannaish but I dont mean it that way. I was poor with one man and it was unmitigated Hell because he was a poor sport and bellyached eternally and wasnt willing to put out to better himself financially.
>
> I guess it would have been a mess even if we'd have had a million. But in this, my latest matrimonial venture! I am as happy as if I had five pairs of silk stockings and a couple of new dresses— which is my idea of wealth. As Mary Hunter seems to be a very sensible girl I imagine she could be pretty happy with out having a million—as long as you ladled out soft soap as tirelessly as J does.[8]

2

The Marshes' early life was sweet, serene, and filled, Peggy told Henry, with much "thoroughly improper lovemaking."[9] With no money for theaters, dining out, or travel, they entertained themselves by working on Peggy's writing projects, reading aloud to each other, and doing crossword and jigsaw puzzles.[10] About those "nerve-wracking" puzzles, she wrote her mother-in-law, "John and I go at them like we were paid to do it and sit up past midnight on some of them, sweating and wailing aloud."[11] In an almost childlike manner, she enjoyed being read to. One night after finishing James Branch Cabell's latest story in the *American Mercury*, John read to her the Book of Revelations from the Bible. When she told him she had never heard of Revelations before, he said that was doubtlessly because of her Catholic upbringing. The next day she was still thinking about what John had read when she wrote Frances:

> I had read all the Bible, I thought, including the Begats, but I never had heard about the beasts with eyes in their behinds who guarded the throne of the God of Israel nor of the Heavenly horses who toted their tails in their mouths. I was fascinated by it all because it was so much like the hallucinations of acute alcoholism and paresis.[12]

Although she was now more sedate than she had ever been, she still loved to shock. The first thing she did in their apartment was to tack on the front door two calling cards: one read "Miss Margaret Munnerlyn Mitchell" and the other, "Mr. John R. Marsh." A day or so later, a masculine caller, who was brought along by some friends for a visit, read the cards on the door and misunderstood the marital status of his hosts. When he tried to outsit John that evening, Peggy decided that the joke was on her and the cards came down that night. The new card read "Mr. and Mrs. John R. Marsh."[13]

A few months after their marriage, she reported to her mother-in-law:"John and I are making out very well in our new roles and havent had but one row yet and that was over whether lima beans and butter beans were one and the same. Having spent my summers on a plantation, I knew they were different and he, with his superiority said they were the same, only one was the debutante and the other was the dowager. But that's our only trouble so far—unless you take into consideration the herds of visitors who plague our lives."[14] Their unmarried friends, who all worked within walking distance of The Dump, as they called it, ignored the fact that the newlyweds needed a lot of privacy, and in those early days made the Marshes' apartment their meeting place.[15]

> They generally come between 6 p.m. and 10 p.m. and those are sacred hours devoted to the preparing of supper. Once, John got supper in an hour and forry five [sic] minutes but the strain nearly killed him. But when five or six people blow in at 8 and find us in the throes of supper, its very inconvenient. . . . Its also inconvenient when Frances Newman calls on us at early dawn (12:45) on Sunday mornings and expects us to receive in bed. We have a sign on the door now with visiting hours on it. Maybe that will stymie them.[16]

Young reporters and impoverished writers enamored with her would stop by in the afternoons, sometimes before John came home. But he never seemed to mind that she had more male friends than he did or that they visited her during his absence. He was never jealous; she gave him no reason to be. Every one of them knew that she was committed to her marriage and completely loyal to John. She was warm, friendly, and fun; according to Medora, she was "such good company, that the Marshes' apartment was a pleasant place to visit."[17] During these visits, she and her guests would often read aloud to each other from the works of southern writers such as James Branch Cabell, whom they all greatly admired for his interest in preserving the aristocratic ideals of the conservative South. When Stephen Vincent Benét's long poem *John Brown's Body* came out, Allan Taylor, one of the Marshes' friends, rushed over to the Marshes' apartment with a copy that he had purchased.[18] As he read parts of it aloud to her, Peggy said she wept because it was the most beautiful thing she had ever heard. In 1936, she wrote to Benét telling him, "I never had anything in the world take hold of me more swiftly, more absolutely. He [Taylor] read all afternoon and when he went home that night he went without the book for I bought it from him and sent him home protesting. And I sat up all night to finish it. And then it was months before I could bear to try to write again. After reading what you'd done nothing I wrote sounded above the 'Rover Boys' or perhaps, to be kinder, 'The Little Colonel.'"[19] She memorized most of Benét's poem and would recite passages from it when she and John took long Sunday-afternoon drives on the backroads around Atlanta.[20]

John good naturedly went along with whatever plans she made. She and the others frequently organized potluck suppers where everyone would chip in, supplying whatever was needed. After these suppers, the group would often sit around until the early morning hours having serious conversations or, depending on their mood, playing charades or writing dirty limericks. According to Mary Singleton, Peggy was by far the best at pantomimes and imitations, but John was the best at writing limericks. Penciled on bits of paper, some of his limericks are in the Margaret Mitchell Marsh Papers in the Hargrett Library. One reads, "A shapely fan dancer from Wheeling / Performed with remarkable feeling / Not a murmur was heard / Not a sound, not a word / But fly buttons hitting the ceiling!" He also enjoyed writing absurd mixed-up maxims like "Don't hide your wolf under a bushel of sheep's clothing."[21]

3

The group that gathered at the Dump in 1925, 1926, and 1927 was much like the earlier Rabbit Hole crowd. These young intellectual men and women saw themselves as the vanguard of the social revolution later called the Roaring Twenties, an era right after World War I when Americans, weary of reforms and crusades, renounced puritanism and busily engaged themselves in having fun and making money. Automobiles, electricity, radios, "talking" motion pictures, neon lights, Coca-Colas, dances like the Charleston, and orchestras like Duke Ellington's and Paul Whiteman's— all popular items on the American scene—gave great pleasure. Although religious fundamentalism took an aggressive form, most Americans re- sisted Prohibition and any infringements on their personal liberties. This was a period characterized by nonsense, light-heartedness, and a revolt from the Victorian principles of sexual morality. Freed from the constraints of social disapproval, the gang that gathered at the Dump reveled in their new-found freedom to discuss sexual matters. And they discussed every- thing from Freudian case studies to erotic literature to dirty jokes and limericks. However, it would be wrong to say that Peggy, John, or any of the others had a morbid interest in nudity or sexuality or the kind of pornography available today that depicts explicit injury or violation. In the aftermath of the sexual revolution of the 1960s and 1970s, pornography has become vastly different from the erotica of Peggy's generation, which, by comparison, seems harmlessly mild now. After all, in her day, "pornog- raphy" was the label given to the works of such writers as Lawrence, Balzac, Flaubert, Havelock Ellis, Freud, and Aristophanes. All forms of sexual expression were open territory for discussion in 1925 among the Marshes' flamboyant group—and Peggy, who had been a rebel since childhood, was perhaps the most flamboyant of all.

The Dump was furnished with some fine Victorian pieces from her father's house and with some treasured mahogany pieces from her grand- parents' farmhouse, but much of John's "mission" furniture remained, including a bed from what Peggy called "the early Rutherford B. Hayes era."[22] Peggy hoped eventually to replace this "plain" bed, she said, with "a walnut one that towers up with carved acorns, squirrels, obese cupids and perhaps an angel with a flaming sword on it."[23] Meanwhile, to make the bed more interesting looking, she cut the most titillating picture from an elaborate brochure advertising an expensive set of books on the adventures of Casanova, placed it in a dimestore frame, and hung it above the bed. Surprising her husband when he came home one afternoon, she pointed to the illustration. Later, Peggy wrote to Henry about the Casanova set, explaining that it was a collection she coveted but could not afford, and boasting to him about the picture snipped from the brochure:

> It now hangs on one side of our bed—one of our most obscene and highly prized possessions. The back ground is black—there's a

medieval looking bed, a lady in it so nude as to make the word nude seem pale, and in a position which defies description. Then there is Cassy himself, minus clothing standing beside her with an expression on his face that also defies description. It horrifies all our purer friends but they dont dare mention it. However they cant seem to keep their eyes off of it.[24]

For their Christmas present that year, Henry sent John and Peggy that $150 set of *The Adventures of Casanova.*

Peggy had a number of close men friends, but none were as close as her brother-in-law Henry, for whom she felt special affection. Henry saw in her what had attracted his brother: the delicate quality of her physical beauty combined with her earthiness of spirit. In addition to exchanging "forbidden" books, such as Havelock Ellis's seven-volume *Studies in the Psychology of Sex*, Shiek Nafzouia's *The Perfumed Garden,* and the Casanova set, they wrote each other letters, and whenever she and Henry were together, they talked and laughed like intimates.[25]

After she let Harvey Smith, her youngest, most ardent admirer, borrow one of those "censored" books Henry sent her occasionally, she related the following incident:

> Henry, some thing dreadful has happened. My priceless "Perfumed Garden" is in the hands of the Philistines! Like an idiot I lent it to an intelligent young man who is interested in things erotic, as are all young men intelligent or other wise. I shouldn't have done it, of course. I've never let anyone but you get hold of it. This young college lad hid it in an old hat box and as luck would have it his mother did spring cleaning and found it. Poor Lady. I hate to think what she went thru when she read it. And my name in the front and her darling in the habit of spending four afternoons a week at our apt! "What huzzies these young married women are!"
>
> She still has the book. Harvey is still in disgrace and I still have jitters for fear she'll burn it—after she's memorized it![26]

In connection with Peggy's enthusiasm for erotica, it has been alleged that John lacked libido, that Peggy was disinterested in sexual intercourse, was perhaps even frigid, and that she channeled her sexual energies into an obsession with pornography.[27] However, individuals who knew the Marshes well disagree with this assessment. When confronted with the notion that Peggy and John had a sexless, platonic marriage, Joe Kling, among others, laughed and said, "I doubt that!" Mary Marsh Davis,

Henry's daughter, and her husband Jim Davis, who also knew the Marshes well, consider the allegations false and irresponsible. Jim Davis explained:

> Peggy and John appeared to have a normal husband and wife relationship—sexually and every which way, and maybe, better than most. How would anyone possibly know about the most intimate aspects—the sexual life—of anyone else, and at this late date? There was never any question in any of our minds about Peggy's and John's enjoying their connubial bliss. But, about the pornography business, I do know for sure. Henry had a small collection of books which he found artistically amusing. They were not especially erotic, certainly not what we now call "porno," but books such as *The Decameron, Jurgen, Lady Chatterly's Lover,* some stories by Balzac, and other such tripe. He would send them to Peggy now and then for her amusement; she was a daredevil and, I suppose, wanted to be "one of the boys." I think this doesn't tell us much about either one of them. This was the "flapper" period, remember, and drinking and smoking and reading erotica and wild dancing and driving fast were all a part of the times.[28]

4

As part of her effort to be "one of the boys," Peggy liked to give the impression that she could "hold her likker." As Harvey Smith said, "She was so true a product of the prohibition days that she dearly loved the idea of being a great drunk (not a habitual one but a bender type) but didn't actually like the experience of feeling drunk, drank seldom and little but got quite unheard of reactions to a given amount of alcohol."[29] Even during her debutante days, when she attended lots of gin-drinking parties, she was the one who stayed sober to drive the others home and to nurse their hangovers. She liked to give the impression she was more daring and tough, in every respect, than she actually was.[30] Smith explained, "She dearly loved to tell of the great drunks she had been on some years before we knew her. John was usually spared these accounts but would have backed her up if she had said she swallowed the Titanic with nothing but a lemon for a chaser."[31]

Her flair for dramatically calling attention to herself and her need to be provocative and entertaining made her claim to be a big drinker. But there is no evidence to support that she ever had "a drinking problem," as one biographer has stated.[32] In fact, she was very critical of those who had drinking problems. When she and John went out for dinner or to parties, they would have a couple of drinks, but they never kept alcohol in their home until years later, after John had his first major heart attack and his physician prescribed a drink of whiskey in the evening. No one saw them more often over a long period of years than Joe Kling, and he said, "The Marshes were abstemious."[33]

In thinking about the sprees John's boss, Kelly Starr, indulged in, Peggy wrote Frances in 1926, "Thank the Lord, John doesn't drink. I dont see how he escaped it as every reporter I have ever known, except one, drank like a fish. That one had a weakness for cocain."[34] It is doubtful that Peggy ever tried cocaine, though John, when he first moved to Atlanta, may have done so. However, she loathed the idea of being denied the freedom to choose whether to drink or not, and she was as strongly opposed to Prohibition as she was to censorship. She went on to tell Frances:

> All this Prohibition stuff makes me sick and I'm organizing my little playmates to admit they are twenty-one so that Atlanta can poll a big drinking vote when the likker question comes up to the people's vote again. I feel very strongly upon this subject because every one in this office drinks bootleg corn and the smell in a close steam heated office is beyond description. Lets all get together, girls, and bring back the good stuff!

On this account, she enjoyed writing Henry about the night she "blanked out" from having too much to drink on an empty stomach. When Augusta Dearborn, who lived in Birmingham, came to spend the Christmas holidays with them, they all decided to go out on the town. Because Peggy and John had not been out socially since they married, they were looking forward to this outing with friends. Afterwards Peggy described the night to Henry in a cocky manner:

> Aggie cares naught for likker. John cant and dont drink and I've been doing precious little this last year. How ever most of my little playmates are accomplished rum hounds and the parties they gave Aggie were wet. I had not been drinking at all until New Years night when I gave a party at the nigger theatre down in our slum district. Rye was up to 18 a quart and corn to 20 a gallon. I refused to let John pay so much for it—no use spending that much on people who dont care whether they drink rat poison or picric [sic] acid was the way I felt. So John finally got some for 10 a gallon.
> As ill luck would have it, I felt very low that night. Wasnt used to staying up so late and all the parties and funny food had worn me out so I decided to brace with one drink before going to

the show. The gang welcomed me back to the fold with cheers and I had had three before we started. Alas. I had been pure for so long—and the stuff was this here mean stock yard likker and before we even reached the theater, I had started leading the gang in my exceptionally tuneless contralto in "The Bastard King of England" which some how seemed the very thing to sing. John evidently thought so too for he abetted me.

She did not remember much about the show "except that it was punk" and that at intervals in the Charleston she stood up and shouted "'Gal, shake that thing!' which was the only thing John made objections to." Apparently, she got too loud, and John asked her to sit down and be quiet for awhile. Once seated, she blanked out. The next thing she knew it was morning. John and Augusta were pouring black coffee into her and horrifying her with their description of her behavior the previous night at a new hotel "whose interior," she said, "I have no memory of ever seeing." Here's her account:

I found a blue paper cap, danced the Charleston (and I havent been able to dance in a year on account of my bum ankle) sang "Two Little Girls in Blue" with truly telling affect and showed my new garters amid plaudits of the audience. Well, John didnt know I was out as he knew in ye olden days that I always carried alcohol like a lady and he thought I knew what I was doing. Well, I didnt and I suppose I'll never get through hearing about other things I did. I hate to think that I ever drew a blank—it seems that I was an animated and perambulating vaudeville and that the gang enjoyed me to a marked degree. I'm off for another year. The smell makes me ill. It certainly doesnt pay to drink if you are out of training.[35]

5

Those first few months of her marriage, Peggy continued to work hard on her assignments, which mainly dealt with superficial topics. Describing her writing as "rotten," she was never satisfied with her work. Then, in the late fall, she received a special assignment that delighted her.

Throughout the late summer and fall of 1925, a group of Georgians made plans to have five Civil War generals from each southern state represented in the memorial to be carved by Gutzon Borglum on Stone Mountain. Although the ambitious plan failed, Angus Perkerson decided to let Peggy, because of her interest in the Civil War period, write two articles on two of Georgia's generals. As it turned out, her first article, which appeared on December 6, 1925, was so successful that the editor and the readers wanted more. She ended up writing four articles about five generals: John B. Gordon, Pierce M. Butler Young, Thomas R. R. Cobb, Henry Lewis Benning, and Ambrose Ransom Wright.[36] These articles are her best and, by far, they were the most satisfying for her to research and write. This project prepared her for what she wanted to write about later, although neither she nor John knew that at the time.

She was pleased with herself as the holidays approached. And in spite of their poverty, Peggy described her and John's first Christmas together in 1925 as the "loveliest Christmas of my whole life."[37] Still basking in the praise she had received for her articles on the Georgia generals, she got back to work on her own book. The only blot on her entire holiday period occurred when her father fell down the cellar stairs in his home and had to be hospitalized. Then, later, in helping him turn in his bed, she sprained a muscle and for several weeks complained about her "bum shoulder" and her inability to write.[38]

Healthier and happier than he had ever been, John wrote his mother that he was "inordinately proud of himself" because he had finally gained weight. "He weighs 153 now," wrote Peggy. "A month ago, he began to slyly loosen his belt, when ever he sat down. Then he began unbuttoning the top button. Now he is in anguish if the second one isnt open when he sits down. I've drawn the line at the second button for I cant have him arrested and so we've compromised by his promising to buy a new suit. He said if I'd been a good wife I could have put a godet or a gore in the back of his trousers!"[39]

John asked that his mother and the others not send Christmas presents because he could not handle the additional expense of buying them presents. So rather than send presents, the Marshes sent Peggy and John a barrel of delicacies, which they received a few days before Christmas. "When your barrel arrived," she wrote the family, "my first horrified thought was that you had run amuck and broken all prohibition laws and sent us a gallon of shine or home made wine. The truckman who unloaded it gave me a comradely nudge and said, 'Here's your Christmas likker, lady.' He evidently expected to be asked in by the way he hung around."[40] As John pried open the barrel, Peggy's friends Peggy Porter and Annie Couper watched. Peggy went on to say that "the two of them have a sweet tooth the size of the Woolworth building" and to describe how they squealed with delight when they saw that the barrel was filled with homemade breads, cakes, jams, jellies, preserves, summer sausage, cheese, and nuts. Seeing this bounty prompted John and Peggy to make their first and sudden plunge into social life since their marriage. They had open house on New Year's Day, inviting fifteen guests; forty came. "Every thing was so jammed,"

Peggy wrote in this same letter, "that it reminded me of that verse of Horatius about 'Those behind cried "Forward!" And those in front, cried "Back!"'"

Since the apartment was so small they used every bit of space. They served tea, coffee, cakes, nuts, and four kinds of sandwiches that Peggy herself made early that morning. They decorated with white candles, red velvet ribbons, magnolia leaves, and branches of pine, holly, and mistletoe that they gathered from the countryside. All of their wedding presents, she told Mother Marsh, were displayed, except Henry's books (this was the year Henry sent them the *Casanova* set). "Henry's books I locked up, as I did my other valuable books for I never trust literary people alone with our collection. They have no souls where it comes to lifting books and I've lost too many at parties."[41] On the coffee table in the front room, she placed the hammered silver tray that John's oldest sister Katharine had sent them, and the silver tea spoons that came from his Uncle Bob. She put the lovely lace scarf that Mother Marsh had given them on their bedroom dresser, which she said "must needs be a buffet in times of stress." The dainty boudoir pillow that Gordon and Francesca had sent was placed on their blue silk and lace bedspread. Above the handmade guest towels with the filet inlets that Katharine had made for them, Peggy said she tacked "a warning" saying "just for ornament." In the candle glow, the place looked lovely.

A few days later, in thanking Henry for his gift, Peggy explained that she and John liked to give each other books for Christmas and that they had "made it a practise of giving each other low, vile or suppressed books on holidays and on other sech occasions," but that year she and John could not give each other anything if they wanted to entertain their friends during the holiday and pay the rent too. Therefore, Henry's gift was especially appreciated.[42]

6

Starting in January 1926, John received a raise, making his salary as assistant to Kelly Starr one hundred dollars a week, good money in those days.[43] "We are still in debt over our heads," he wrote his mother, "and this won't do any more than take the chill off the water, but that's something, and maybe we will really get paid up on our doctor's bills some day. It doesn't seem hardly possible, but it may actually happen in the course of time."[44]

Running the public relations department in an unofficial capacity because of Kelly Starr's disruptive problems and absenteeism, John was earning recognition and respect. With pride, Peggy sent Henry and Mrs. Marsh samples of his work, saying they were "departures from the Power

Co styles of advertising. . . . They seem to have gotten results. More over they've been picked up by the Ry [railway] and Electric magazines and given favorable comment—and John's received nice letters from other companies about them. I'm real proud of him and of them."[45]

In the short time he had been managing the publicity, John had successfully managed to improve the public's attitude toward the company. With his friends in the press, he was able to get newspapers to adopt an attitude of friendliness in handling news about the company. For example, the *Georgian,* his first employer in Atlanta, had in previous years been the Georgia Power Company's bitterest foe. But after John took charge of publicity in 1926, the *Georgian* presented Mr. Atkinson, the president of the company, the silver cup given annually by that paper to Atlanta's first citizen.[46] "I have never had a job which was more interesting and it becomes more interesting every day," John told his mother. "I am becoming as solicitous about this big, sprawling, awkward Company and its standing in the community as if it were my own child, and the other day when our big boss was selected for the annual award as Atlanta's most valuable citizen in 1926 I was as happy about it as if the award had been given to me."[47]

While John's professional life was productive, interesting, and satisfying, Peggy's was not. Even though she realized the *Journal* was giving her a liberal education that she could never get any place else and was forcing her to learn some things about writing, she was bored churning out weekly articles on banal topics. She was too intelligent to enjoy writing about such questions as "Could a girl be virtuous and bob her hair?" "Could a woman have a home and husband and children and a job, too?" "Should a woman roll her stockings, park her corsets, be allowed a latch key?" "What made girls pretty?" "Do working girls make the best wives?"[48] Occasionally, she would have an exciting assignment, like the articles on the Civil War generals and her interview with Harry K. Thaw, who in 1906 at Madison Square Garden shot and killed the well-known architect Stanford White for having an affair with his wife. And nothing, she thought, was more fun than her visit on a "wild and rainy day" with Mrs. W. E. Baker, the last surviving bridesmaid of Mittie Bulloch, mother of Theodore Roosevelt.[49] But then there were a few other assignments that frightened her, although she told no one but John. Neither he nor she liked the idea of her being sent, along with a group of geologists, into Salt Peter Cave near Kingston.[50]

Now that John was making more money, she began to chafe at the restraints of her job. She began to complain to his family, and no doubt to everyone else who would listen, that writing for the *Magazine,* meeting "one god-damn deadline after another," was putting too much pressure on her.[51] Nervous strain, she kept telling them all, was never anything she handled well. In what appears to have been her only piece published outside the

Magazine, she hinted at her weariness with her job. Her article "Matrimonial Bonds" appeared in the March 1926 issue of the *Open Door,* an Atlanta publication put out by the downtown Hart Building. She wrote about a young couple, Nancy and Bill. Like herself, her fictional character Nancy is a smart young working woman who will make a good wife.

> Nancy has been through it all—been through the long hours of office work when employers were grouchy and she was tired, been through the long strap hangings on smelly homebound cars. She's learned how much a dollar means. A dollar is not just a shining silver disk or a crackling bit of paper. It's so many hours wait when you want to be out swimming, so many hours of making tired fingers fly. And she won't be quite so eager to say airily, "Charge it!" After she is married, she'll think three times about buying chiffon stockings by the dozen. For if she loves Bill she can't help thinking how much of his sweat went into those dollars.

After her experiences with Red and with that brief period when the bottom fell out of her father's business, Peggy feared financial insecurity. She equated money with freedom and by now had learned to manage money wisely. No matter how much she and John made, she never felt financially secure. Despite his salary increase in 1926, John still could not whittle their medical debts down to a comfortable figure, and her concern for money kept her at her job for a while longer. In fact, by this time, she began to see herself as a veteran journalist capable of tutoring others as John had once tutored her.

In one of her letters to Frances in early 1926, Peggy marveled at the incompetence of the newly hired female writers, whom she described as "Little Elsie Dinsmores." According to Peggy, every time the son or daughter of one of the *Journal*'s advertisers or political allies appeared in the city room looking for work on the newspaper, the city editor sent them upstairs to the magazine department. She complained that all of her spare time at work was taken up

> trying to whip cubs into shape; rewriting their hashed up stuff, gently, oh, so gently explaining the elements of grammar and rhetoric and harshly, oh, so harshly cursing when they turn in "I" stories.
>
> And just when I've taught one the rudiments of proofreading (oh, yes, we have to read 39 pages of proof) and explained about pasting up copy and how it cost five dollars every time they cut the

copyright line off Milt Gross or Will Rogers, they commit some dreadful sin against journalism and get the gate. Then another, equally dumb, equally excited about the romance of being a girl reporter, equally certain she's going to scoop the world, and equally ignorant of how leads should be written, is thrust upon us.

And so my days are taken up with teaching and with trying to find a moment to write my own stories and my nights with trying to get out the line of chatter that pays enough to cover the rent. Then, ever and anon, I get a chance to earn a dishonest penny by writing articles for poor woiking girls magazines at ten bucks a throw, which buys supper on Sunday nights, at horsey hostelries which we could not other wise afford. But, after all this is done there aint much time for nothing else.

She supposed that this kind of work was good training, but it was "certainly wearing." In this five-page typed letter, she complained to Frances that she never had any time or energy to write anything for herself or hardly to see John. "If it wasnt for Saturday afternoons off I wouldnt even know I was married."

7

In January 1926, in another long letter, Peggy related to Frances an incident that she described "as one of the most interesting things I've run across in a long time." One of the *Journal*'s newest cubs, whom she designated as "one of those pretty short haired children just out of Journalism class," was sent out to get a story about a woman who had left her money to have her ashes scattered over the deep blue sea "instead of being buried or parked on someone's mantel." To Peggy's dismay, the cub ambled back somewhat aghast by the fact that the lady who now owned the ashes, "a sturdy Methodist, had told her that the ashes were those of a woman who had lived high, kept an assignation house in the days when Atlanta was 'open,' drunk her fill of champagne, lent and borrowed money from Atlanta's most prominent and finally cashed her checks at the ripe age of sixty." Apparently, the Methodist lady had taken her in when she was sick, not knowing who she was, and did not learn her identity until after "the rowdy soul's departure, when a diary had been unearthed." Peggy wrote:

Of course, the cub hadn't gotten the diary. I shrieked at the lost opportunity. Ever since reading "Madeline" which I believe to be one of the most moral and helpful books ever suppressed, I've wanted to locate a real one. And right here is one, covereing [sic] the years between her coming to Atlanta from Australia, how she got her house started, who came, how she barred much drinking and kept it respectable—in other words, one of those honest to God "human documents." If I had been on the story I'd have been carried out dead before I'd have left without it. But the cub murmured that the Methodist lady was intending to burn it. Oh, the mental processes of the godly![52]

As she thought about trying to persuade the Methodist lady that publishing the diary, "minus names," would keep the "faltering footsteps of many a pure girl from etc. etc.," she continued:

And I really mean it. I'm not moral, myself, thank the Lord, but I do think a few more books published about the sordidness and lack of romance in prostitution would do a lot for the counter jumpers who fancy it an improvement on their honest professions. So I'm working the Methodist thru the moral end of it and she's conferring with her husband. Even if they didn't give me the right to publish it, I'd like to read it over the week end. I imagine it involves nearly every well known person in Atlanta. John and I could enjoy a quiet Sunday at home with Blanche Betterouse's diary![53]

Later, Peggy wrote of Scarlett, "Like most innocent and well-bred young women, she had a devouring curiosity about prostitutes."[54] Peggy seems to have had a similar curiosity, and it must have been around this time that John told her about Belle Brezing, the famous madam of Lexington, Kentucky, whose resemblance to Belle Watling in *Gone With the Wind* is too extraordinary to be coincidental.

In this same letter, which is dated "Saturday, Jan the some thing, [1926]," Peggy explained that John was trying to get compensation from the government for the ptomaine poisoning he and three other soldiers had gotten from eating contaminated army food while they were in Beaune, France, during the war. She wrote, "It would be great if the benificent Govt would put out a little on the Mitchells and the Marshes." She also talked to Frances about the problems John was having at work. "The office he works in is such a mess. The boss is a good egg but goes on periodical sprees (the period being every four days) and insists on taking the other boys with him—then it takes them two days to get over it and two days to be remorseful. And during that time they dont do any work and John does most of his [Starr's] jobs and his, too." Given his arduous working conditions, John was often tired, as Peggy points out: "John can use more sleep than any white boy I ever saw. . . . As I try to turn him in by eleven every night, we don't go many places and all that Sunday means is a chance to sleep till three o'clock in the afternoon and eat breakfast at four."[55]

8

If Scarlett's favorite method of repression was procrastination, Peggy's may well have been illness. When her whole life is spread out like a cloth, a pattern of illnesses emerges. These illnesses appear whenever she felt the pressure of having to meet deadlines or experienced a period of tranquility. Her life had to be filled up, or she suffered from boredom. Hers was never "a tranquil temperament," and as she had admitted earlier, "to lead a stolid, unemotional existence is no easy task for me!"[56] All during John's nearly five-month ordeal before their marriage, she managed remarkably well. She held down her job, ran the house for her father, dealt with hospital staff and physicians, and cared for John. That kind of tumultuous experience gave her an exhilarating, emotional edge; it was boredom she could not tolerate.

Just as soon as their married life settled down, John became healthier and happier than he had ever been. He adored his wife and loved his job. But he was busy making a living for them and was not as available to her as he had once been. As Peggy's letters during 1926 show, her health did not improve in view of her happiness in her new married life and protective environment. Once locked into a tranquil routine, she began to complain, first to Henry, but then to the others in John's family.

In early spring 1926, she wrote Henry about not having had anything to eat in eight days except lettuce, tea, dry toast, and a few strips of bacon. She spoke of having nothing but "an increased feeling of irritability and lassitude," which she blamed on her ankle. "My ankle . . . went bad again for no apparent reason, swelled up and all of that. It was really serious because it was supposed to be well and a recurrence in a spot where you've got arthritis isnt so good. The doc slipped me the pleasant news that I'd probably get a permanently stiff ankle out of it and set about finding what caused it all." She had the notion that something within her system was poisoning her ankle.

Teeth tonsils etc have been played with and finally they tracked the trouble to my digestion. Said I'd been injudicious in my diet which is a polite way of telling me that I ate two pounds of rare beef a day and nothing else but lettuce. Also, my gin drinkers liver showed up although my life has been comparatively pure during the last year. Any way, my digestion is poisoning my

~ 145 ~

system and ankle is getting it all. So I'm not eating any thing at all these days . . . I feel so light its a wonder I stay on the ground.[57]

In April, she had her tonsils removed, following what she claimed was the advice of her specialist, who thought her "dreadful" tonsils were the source of the infection in her ankle.[58] "Don't you let any one ever tell you," she wrote Frances, "that its 'a slight operation, no pain at all and you're up in three days.' It's been ten days now and I am just getting to where I can eat and still can't swallow with out pain." Almost sounding like a crank, she complained, "Appendicitis was nothing compared with it. I'm waiting patiently to see if it will have any effect on my foot. Seems that I have to watch diet, teeth, tonsils, sinuses, etc. to make sure there's no poison being put out by any of them and if I still don't improve, I guess they'll have to operate on my foot." She continued,

I'm on crutches and haven't touched the floor in three weeks except on the one glorious day the doc told me he might have to fuse two ankle joints together and make it solid for life. I felt somewhat depressed, came home, bought a quart of rye, and took three drinks, threw away my crutches and getting a taxi went calling on all my friends. I had a lovely five hours. I didn't even know I had a bad foot until I sobered up when John came home and he, poor angel, kindly sat up all night rubbing the blamed thing.[59]

Although her ankle was the chief source of her discomfort, it was only one of her many disabilities. If her numerous letters mentioning her many ailments are any indication of the frequency of her speaking about them, we can assume that she talked often about "feeling po'ly."[60] Any man less understanding than John would have been annoyed with such complaints. However, he was so patient and understanding that he may even have reinforced her behavior. She indicated her need for his sympathetic understanding when she thanked his sister for sending her a novel by Storm Jameson.

I sat up all of one night to read it. The only thing I couldnt understand about it all was Laurence's relations with her husband for she obviously didn't love him nor he her. She had no conception of passion nor he of consideration. I can't imagine anything more distasteful than living with a man who became bored every time you had a pain—but I thank you for comparing me to her—even if I havent her singleness of purpose or her courage.[61]

Baffled by her mysterious ankle problem, the specialist who had treated Peggy for several weeks with no success ordered her to stay at home and rest—just the prescription that she wanted. Around the middle of April, she took her second sick leave. Having barely started work on a novel a year or so earlier, she wrote her mother-in-law: "One good thing that this rest will do me—I can do some work on my much neglected novel which has gathered dust for the last year during John and Dad's death beds [sic] and my getting settled down here. The doctor said I'd be out of work three months in all and I ought to be able to write three novels in that time."[62]

However, settling down to writing was more difficult to do than she had imagined, and she ended up spending more time reading popular fiction than writing. In a letter thanking Frances for sending her books, Peggy shows the kind of light reading material she was consuming: "And have you read 'Microbe Hunters?' We liked it so much. And I know, being an ex-young intellectual, that I shouldn't have liked 'Show Boat' but I read it in the magazine installments with my tongue hanging out."[63]

No longer the compulsive writer she had been as a child, she now saw nothing magical or pleasurable about writing. Over and over again she talked about how hard writing was for her. It seems that the more she learned about writing, the more defeated she felt. The more works by good writers she read, the more reluctant she was to write. Years later, in a letter to her friend Clifford Dowdey, also a writer, she explained how she suffered from reading good novels while she was developing her own.

> I am singularly a prey to a disease known in this family as "the humbles." Everybody's stuff looks better than mine and a depressing humility falls upon me whenever I read stuff that I wish I could have written. Temporarily the humbles kept me from doing any writing at all.[64]

All the reading that she had done for her series on the Civil War generals and for her own pleasure made her feel so intimidated that writing became impossible for her. Even though John praised her work, his high standards for writing had made her more aware of her inadequacies or, at least, what she considered her inadequacies. As an editor, he described himself as "a master flawfinder and a picayunish-emphasizer," but as his own writing demostrates, he was much more than a mere grammarian.[65]

In addition to copyediting her work, John also helped Peggy to formulate her ideas and consistently gave her moral support.[66] When she paused in a sentence, he could finish it, and she would say to him, "Yes, that's what I mean."[67] In her letters and conversations, particularly after she became famous, she said repeatedly that if John had not prodded her to write, she would have been content not to write. In the following passage from a letter to Frances, probably written sometime in late 1925 or early 1926, she shows how John not only prodded her to write but also collaborated with her:

> Among other literary things we've been trying to do is a one act skit, to be used by New Wayburn, who is producing the Junior League Follies. Even if he buys it and gives us $500 a piece in hot or cold cash, it won't be worth the agony I've gone thru on the matter. Its all Johns fault, of course, I'd never have taken the matter if he hadn't insisted.

The producer of the follies called her one day saying that they needed a skit and asking her to write it. She seemed like the ideal person to do the work because she covered the follies every year for the *Magazine* even though she had never made the League. Peggy told Frances,

> And I said, no-can-do, immediately. A while later, I recounted to John my refusal and with out further ado, he called up and told them that Miss Mitchell would be overjoyed (*i* here quote his exact words) to write the skit and would have it in two days. Since then life has not been worth living. I'd rather die than to have to hand stuff in at a certain set time. Of course, I didn't have any idea of what to write and neither did John.

A compulsive worker, John made his point clear.

> He said he wasnt going to see me get fat and lazy and turn down work I could do for no other reason than that I didnt have the energy to do it. So between us we wrote it and its every bit as wretched as it sounds. John is going to take it around to Wayburn this afternoon. I havent the heart to be with John when the axe falls and he's told its awful. John has such beautiful hopes about my eventually proving a genius. How such hopes persist after we've been married so long is beyond my comprehension.[68]

After they attended the follies, she added this postscript: "The Junior League Follies was a flop from start to finish. All wet if ever I saw a wet play."

10

By this time Peggy had finished "'Ropa Carmagin," the novel she had worked on with John while he was convalescing from his attack of hiccoughs and gallbladder surgery, and she had started working on a Jazz Age novel about the adventures of a teenager named Pansy. However, during the remainder of her leave, instead of working on her manuscript, she wrote long letters to Henry, to Frances, and to Mrs. Marsh. Now that John was so wrapped up in his work, the immediate response and approval these letters brought her was more satisfying than ever. Because she had never succeeded in selling any of her short stories, she found letter writing a much more congenial expression of her creativity than trying to attract publishers with her short stories. She adorned many of her letters with character sketches and scenes like this charming vignette she composed in a letter to Mrs. Marsh.

Madam, I take pleasure in announcing to you that your versatile and talented son has added fried chicken to his other culinary successes. Here to fore, he has contented himself with broiled steak and lamb chops but last night he got his blood up and did the best fried chicken I ever put in my mouth. Usually his cooking has been superintended by me by screaming directions from the bed to the kitchen such as "No, don't put milk in the okra—put it in the corn! Stir the tomatoe cream soup over a slow fire and pour the cream in *gently* so it won't curdle!"

But yesterday, I was trying out the new crutches which he has just bestowed on me and so I hopped into the kitchen to aid in the slaughter. Frankly, I had never fried a chicken in my life and I don't recall ever having seen one so cooked but I never believed in removing ones halo of omniscience before ones beloved, so I gave firm instructions about dismembering the fowl and rolling it in flour. I had an awful horror for fear it was meal you rolled the dinged thing in but stuck firmly to flour because it had been my first guess. I hopped nimbly out of the kitchen and back to bed before the actual cooking could begin so that my skirts should be free of the blame should catastrophe over take the unfortunate chicken—also free of spattering grease for John innocently stood on one side of the kitchen and hurled a drumstick into the pan of boiling grease, thereby causing a red hot shower that made him understand what the Christian martyrs went thru with boiling oil. But the chicken was noble and we were so immodestly proud of it that John is thinking of trying his hand at French pastries and layer cake.[69]

Clearly, she enjoyed the attention she received from her husband, who pampered her, not only cooking their meals but also carrying her around the apartment in his arms or on his back to keep her from using her crutches.[70] She wrote Mrs. Marsh:

If it hadn't been for John being John, I could never had endured this enforced rest with the slightest degree of cheerfulness. I should have chewed his ear off and wept on his neck whenever he came home at night. But he's such a good egg that its not so bad being laid up. I have felt very badly about putting extra work on him—the work of getting supper—for he's been working so very hard recently. We have been having record breaking heat—one day last week was the hottest in fifty years and there have been two men out at Johns office. That throws more work on him. He dont seem to gain weight but he doesnt lose any and I think if this terrible heat will only stop and another satisfactory man be secured for the office, he'll get fat. He ought to. He compliments his own cooking by eating prodigiously. It does me good to see it for for so many years he used to feed delicately off a lettuce leaf and a clear soup whenever we went out together.[71]

11

All through the early part of 1926, Peggy continually complained of "feeling fluey" or of having bronchitis, earaches, toothaches, infected sinuses, sore arms, sore breasts, sore eyes, sore shoulders, and long menstrual periods with painful cramps. These complaints may have been a manifestation of her depression, a plea for help or attention. With her life the envy of most of her friends, how could she openly admit she was depressed? Too occupied with problems at work, John did not recognize her state of mind; he just knew she whined a lot. In jest, he wrote Frances, "By now, Peggy has had everything except housemaid's knees and childbed fever."[72]

Raised with servants, Peggy had a keen aversion to housekeeping. No matter how messy the apartment got, or how dirty the ashtrays were, she never lifted her hand to tidy anything up. Eventually John grew weary of always coming home to find their apartment in a mess, and of having to cook their supper and shop for their groceries. So, in the spring of 1926 he hired old Lula Tolbert as their part-time housekeeper and cook. Knowing how

Peggy despised doing domestic work, he realized that sore ankle or no sore ankle, she was never going to keep house, certainly not the way his mother and grandmother had done, and there was no point in ever expecting her to do so.[73] Carrie Mitchell had been doing John's laundry for years, picking it up and delivering it at his apartment once a week, and after he married, she continued to do his and Peggy's laundry. Despite his financial bind, he considered Carrie and Lula necessities, not extravagances. But after a short time, Lula died, and Annie, a childhood nurse of Peggy's, took her place. Eventually her father sent Bessie Berry Jordon, his housekeeper and cook, around to the Marshes' apartment to help out. A loyal and devoted friend, Bessie remained with them for the rest of their lives.

In early spring 1926, in a letter to Frances, who by now had also decided to give up her newspaper job in Wilmington, Delaware, Peggy wrote, "I am of the opinion that I am through with my job at the *Journal*. . . . I have no business doing it. We need the money so badly—and this last doctor I've had on my foot is the most famous joint specialist on the east side of the Mississippi."[74] This physician told Peggy that she would eventually have to have surgery on the ankle, but until then she needed to keep her foot elevated and in a cast. His orders—"Give that ankle a rest and let's see if it doesn't improve!"—gave Peggy, at last, an authentic reason to quit her job. And she did quit. She received her last paycheck on May 3, 1926.[75] Confined to the apartment, hobbling around on crutches, she now had little else to do but read, write letters, and visit with Peggy Porter and Annie Couper, the only close friends she had who were still single. They stopped by the apartment nearly every afternoon. But she soon noted that even they had changed, and she became bored with their visits.

She may have felt some guilt, at first, about not working. But she brushed it aside quickly, particularly after she got angry with Angus Perkerson, probably because he did not want to pay her while she was taking her sick leave. She wrote Frances:

> I considered that Mr. Perk did me a dirty deal, while I was on sick [leave] and not being able to talk, I sent John down to tell him to shove my job up his—well, the place reserved for such things. Perk is a lousy little beast and I've gotten so tired working for him. However, he sent his wife Medora, out to patch up things and ask me to do Elizabeth Bennet while I was here at home. I don't know if I will. Lizzie is due tomorrow and I haven't written a line. I may keep up Lizzie for a while and then let it go but I dont think I'll go back on the mag. Unless the economic pressure becomes too hard to stand. For one thing, if I quit the dam job then I wont have any thing pulling me back to work and I'll stay at home long enough

to get my ankle well—instead of going back, half cured, because we need the money so dam bad. When I do get well, if I ever do, then I suppose there'll be time enough to look for another job. I suppose I'll land one on the "Georgian" tho I dont care for a Hearst paper. And then, again, I'm not so confident on writing for deadlines. I've always had a fair amount of time to turn out copy and deadlines rather frighten me. How ever, John wants me to stop work until I'm well, even if we starve and Steve and Father do, too. So I probably will. Dad, of course, wants to lend us some Jack, says he'll leave it to us when he dies, any way. But I think we'll try to buck through with out any borrowing for a while. As long as John keeps healthy, I'm not very bothered.[76]

12

Although she wanted to appear tough and independent, Peggy had the classic demanding-dependent personality, and John fitted her needs perfectly. Just a year before she met him, she had thought, "How nice it would be to just lie in someone's arms like a child, cuddled close against their shoulder, every aching muscle relaxed, every keyed-up nerve loosened, no worry, no responsibility—only peace—to drift and drift."[77] Now that she had that someone to look after her, she had no responsibilities or worries. And, at first, she was happy. She wrote Henry:

I have never been so happy since I got good sense. I've quit work (except for my rent paying colyum) and am freed of the nerve wracking tread mill and the slave driving editor which have been my lot for four years. I regret to say that my main occupation consists of sitting in a bright blue wicker chair, pillowed with scarlet cushions and looking out thru blue ruffled curtains at a tall lombardy poplar that quivers incessantly. I just set and don't even think. I aimlessly make lace pillows out of scraps and when the girls pile in every afternoon, Annie (my child hood nurse who is now cooking for us) serves tea.[78]

In this same letter, she explained how aware she was of her own changes in attitudes and lifestyle. She philosophized to Henry:

How have the mighty Fallen! It seems odd that I who loved action so much—who danced all night and rode all day and, of later years, considered the day wasted when I did not grind out thousands of words of "copy" should be content to sit and look at a waving tree! I suppose its the work of the Lord for I'd have to sit any way and it would be Hell if I were restless as of old. Of course, its largely due to John that things are as they are and he lays himself out to be nicer than usual with flowers and books and love making thoroughly improper in a couple married nearly a year.

During June, Henry came for a brief visit, and then her dearest friend, Augusta Dearborn, visited her again for a week. Her still-single standbys, Peggy Porter and Annie Couper, came over nearly every day. There were wedding parties to attend for her debutante chum, Libby Carroll, whom Peggy described as "one of those alleged wild young women, whose vocabulary is Rabelais out of Chaucer, conduct Scott Fitzgerald . . . and general outlook on life as sentimental as a prostitute." She wrote Henry, "She is getting married this week to the only boy she ever met who didnt try to feel her leg during the first five minutes of their acquaintance, so, of course, she is a changed woman."[79]

By the time hot, humid August rolled around, things had settled down again. John was spending long hours at the office working on an annual report and their friends were all going on with their own lives. After three months at home alone, Peggy became very bored. Her letters are no longer filled with funny anecdotes or character sketches. "As you gather, I do little else but read," she told Frances.

> By this time I've gotten fed up on fiction. John brings home large armfuls of books from the library and recently we've had every thing from Lombroso's "Female Offenders" to the "Casting Away of Mrs. Lecks and Mrs. Aleshine." Also the "Tertium Organum" and Frank Harris' "Confessions of Oscar Wilde." Did you ever read the "Organum?" You must, if you haven't. I must be ignorant, not to have read it long e'er this. Next to Ring Lardner's "I Gaspari" ("The Upholsterers") it is the most humorous (?) reference book on witch craft written in recent years.[80]

Because she was in a sour mood, she was not too happy when she learned that Mrs. Marsh and her young granddaughter Mary were coming to visit for a week in mid-August. For their guests, John rented an apartment nearby so that Peggy would not have to entertain them the entire day while he was at work. Even though her foot was in a cast, however, Peggy nobly insisted on giving them a grand sightseeing tour one afternoon. She borrowed her father's automobile and drove them, slowly and carefully, all around Atlanta. Because her mother's family still treated her as if she were a disgrace, she was surprised to find John's mother sympathetic and understanding. Unlike Grandmother Stephens, Mrs. Marsh never interfered with the lives of her children or their spouses. Also, Mrs. Marsh was never one to acknowledge her own illnesses, and she was appalled at the number of physical problems her young daughter-in-law professed to have. She enjoyed hearing about the novel her daughter-in-law had begun, and, thinking what a healthy distraction such work was for Peggy during her confinement, she encouraged her to work hard to finish it.[81]

Never one to offer to babysit with any of her friends' infants, Peggy cared little about having children around. But about John's niece, she told Frances, "Mary is certainly a well brought up child and I must hang laurels on your mother who not only has a way with her own children but even with her grandchildren. Mary seems to have none of the more heinous sins of childhood—interrupting, begging, whining, tattling and lying."[82]

After their visit, Peggy was exhausted and wanted no more guests for a while. When Frances wrote about coming to Atlanta, Peggy advised her to postpone the visit, not because she did not want to see her sister-in-law but because her nerves were frayed and her ankle was too sore. On August 23, she wrote,

> My disposition wears so thin that I even quarrelled with Aggie Dearborn and Peggy Porter—unheard of happenings and then John would become frightened lest I lure you South just when you were in your most loving and helpful mood, and sink my fangs in the fleshy part of your leg. And then you'd butt me over the head with a portable typewriter and go North to inform the family that I had an ingrowing disposition. Just at present I'm about as pleasant to live with as a porcupine or a snapping turtle.[83]

13

The letters Peggy wrote during the spring and summer of 1926 indicate that she was moody and cranky and that all she wanted to do was escape into fiction by reading, not by writing. She no longer mentioned working on her book. Instead, she talked about reading every new book that came out. She told Frances she liked Louis Bromfield's *Annie Spragg* and thought it seemed to be Norman Douglas out of Thornton Wilder. "Some day," she wrote, "I intend to commit the crime of visiting Italy and coming home and writing a story about the Younger Generation, instead of an expatriate colony of quaint and curious folks who have no connection with each other except the tenuous thread which is dragged in by the author."[84] She also liked Donn Byrne's *Destiny Bay,* "tho how in hell a north of Ireland man, Orange to the bone can write like a south of Ireland man is more than I can understand. As we are a family of long lived and long memoried folk, the battle of the Boyne seems no further in the past than Gettysburg and just as vivid. So naturally my ire rose occasionally at the casual references to the walloping my ancestors got for their genius at always picking the losing side."[85]

Although she was having trouble writing her novel about the adventures of Pansy, she had clear ideas about what constituted a good one. She despised "silly Englishwomen fiction writers ... with their sappy characters ... always having babies." She wrote Frances, "I've almost decided to lay off English fiction entirely." When Frances sent her the new novel *Three Kingdoms,* Peggy answered promptly, saying, "I reserve my thanks to you for likening me to Laurence Storm until I read it and if she is an ass who has no hot water in her house and a lot of children I'll make a special trip to Wilmington to brain you."[86] Her main objection was that no matter how wealthy or royal the English characters were, they were all too passive; and no matter how ancient and ancestral their manors were, they were all too gloomy and without household conveniences, like electric lights and indoor plumbing. Having strong views now about sex and marriage and an acute aversion toward the idea of childbirth, she added, "Worse luck, in an English novel, when a girl gets an 'offer' no matter how spavined and broken winded the offerer may be, she considers it very seriously and frequently marries him. It is depressing to read about places where men aren't cheap and where they dont know their proper place and dont ever send girls orchids and daily specials even if they are wild about them."[87]

Even though all her married friends either had babies or were expecting babies, she said repeatedly that she wanted none. After reading Silvia Thompson's *Hounds of Spring,* she told Frances she was "SO disappointed" because the character had

the usual baby. . . . English births are depressing. . . . They seem to be unattended by such refinements as scopalomine or ether and the husbands stand around the delivery room and mutter about cricket. Yes, I've said "depressing" six times so far. . . . And evidently birth control hasn't penetrated to England because the little garments always appear in the chapter directly following the wedding. I'm sure any manufacturer of well known birth control contrivances could start on a shoe string in England and clean up more than a realtor in Florida.

The lack of hot-blooded romance between the characters was another thing that rankled her. She raved on,

And English girls seem to be for ever marrying strong, silent, bird witted creatures about whose mental interiors they know nothing. And after fifteen or twenty years it is borne upon them that they know absolutely nothing about their husbands beyond the fact that he says "Hah" when he's rarely pleased. And English heroines seem to put up with so much more crap from their hubbies with out any back talk what so ever. An English husband says severely, "My deah, your conduct isn't cricket" and wife crawls off and dies instead of gulping a whiskey neat and roaring "Who gives a dam if it isn't, you S.O.B.?" Yes, I've found most of the English novels depressing.[88]

14

The depression Peggy experienced during her confinement was not new to her.[89] As she had done before, she wondered why she, who had so many good things that "many a girl has sold her soul to get," was not happy. That old feeling of being "a dynamo going to waste" plagued her.[90] Her life had changed drastically and its very serenity was unsettling. In this letter, dated Saturday, August 28, 1926, she wrote Frances:

Alas, all my wild little friends—who kicked the world in the teeth, were carried out of gentlemen's apartments feet first and considered underwear as unimportant as good manners. They are all falling in love with "nice boys," stopping drinking and smoking and hanging their legs out of taxi cab windows. Some of them are even wearing bloomers. And they are all as dull and stupid and hopelessly uninteresting and sentimental as prominent club women. I don't know how I'm going to be amused in the future if they all get pure. . . . At any rate, I resent their reformations because, as I'm pretty much tied to the house, I need their sprightly and unregenerate narratives of how they spent preceding evenings to lighten the burden of my enforced retirement. Peggy Porter is my only hope. I don't think she'll ever reform, thank the Lord, for her wildness is mental instead of physical. I suppose J and I unwittingly led the way to respectability. In days gone by, I always prided myself that I had never come home till there was nowhere else to go—and come home under my own power and prided myself, too, on the fact I'd never settle down. And now, the Lord has fixed it for me and settled me. Neither John nor I, for various physical reasons, will ever be able to drink—that is, unless we are fools. And I will never be able to dance any more—or John

~ 156 ~

stay up very late, as he needs all the sleep possible to keep him trim for his job. And we haven't any money to play poker or shoot craps, at least not enough to make either game interesting. And I haven't enough clothes to risk any of them playing strip. And any way strip is almost as old fashioned as fuzzy bobs. So, perforce, we've become respectable, willy-nilly. And these wild young things, seeing us happy and loving and penniless and respectable, think it must be wonderful. It's horrible to think that perhaps you've influenced young people into such a life. Instead of talking of their interesting shortcomings and their hangovers, they talk of things obstetrical, pink bed room furniture and how their Beloveds said that their love was pure and holy. I guess this is a moral universe after all and respectability is the punishment of the wild.

15

Now that reading was her chief diversion, Peggy read two or three books in a day, and John had difficulty keeping her supplied with reading material. On his way home from work every evening, he would stop by the library and, trying to remember what she had already read, get more books to take home. When he could not find any new mysteries or fiction, he brought home books on anthropology—her recent interest. The next morning he would lug back to the library the books she had devoured the day before, along with those he had to return because she had already read them. Because he rode the streetcar, this book exchange was an inconvenience, but he, the obliging husband, attended to it daily for months. He also borrowed from friends and urged Frances and Henry to keep sending Peggy books.

John kept telling her that the supply of reading material was going to give out and that instead of reading so much, she should write a book herself.[91] But telling her that was all he had done. He had not had the time to sit with her and talk about ideas. The Power Company had doubled in size since he had begun working for it, now employing some five thousand people, so he was busier than ever.[92] Peggy felt neglected and perhaps even unconsciously envious because he enjoyed his work. The job of enlarging his department threw such a heavy load on him that he wrote his mother, "I have heebie jeebies more or less regularly, but I never tackled a job that was more interesting. I feel like I have the biggest opportunity in my entire career and I am trying to make the most of it. I have already gotten another small raise, and I am hoping to get a Club membership out of the Company."[93]

His letters to his family became less frequent during this period, but the few he wrote continue to show his absorption in his work and his grave concern about Peggy's depressed spirits and illnesses. At a loss as to how to help her feel better, he became convinced at one point that she wanted to take some college courses that year, but that their poverty and her sore ankle kept her from doing so. He told his sister, "The fact that she didn't get to finish her college work at Smith has always been one of Peggy's secret sorrows, and I hope I can assist her in getting a college course some day." Sounding like a father, he added, "If our financial condition and her ankle show any improvement by the end of the first of next year, I may start her out at Oglethorpe at the beginning of the second semester."[94] Her talk about going to college was just that—talk; it was an indication that she was searching for something that would give her an identity, a sense of herself, a feeling of self-esteem. Now that she was no longer immersed in her job at the *Journal*, her sense of identity was dissolving.

As early as October 1926, John had taken a part-time job at night, "picking up a little extra money," he wrote his mother, "to keep the Marsh family in food and lodging and to keep our doctors supplied with closed cars." He had hoped to have some extra money for Christmas presents that year, but with all their doctors' bills, his financial condition looked grim. He wrote his mother that "the family wolf had become somewhat gaunt, what with the shortness of his rations, and I decided it was time to do something about it." He accepted an offer to assist the publicity man for the Atlanta Community Chest in preparing his newspaper stories for the annual campaign, a job that would last only a month. "I put in two or three hours a night down there, and as it pays $30 a week, it is considerable help. I wish it was to last indefinitely." When that job played out, he picked up another as a freelance publicity agent.

No one was to send them Christmas presents again this year. "It will make our poverty more unpleasant to have you send us presents when we can't reciprocate . . . financially we are even worse off than a year ago. Last year we had only debts, and this year we have both debts and expenses, so that we have to live on a basis of the strictest economy, with no margin for anything that isn't absolutely necessary."[95]

All during that summer and fall, he once again tried to cut down on his cigarette smoking. Trying to reduce his "daily quota of sixty cigarettes," he said he "frequently wondered if it wouldn't be better to go on and have tuberculosis of the throat or something instead of insanity, which seems to be threatening at times when I would rather have a cigarette than almost anything else in the world." Without the nicotine he said he did not maintain his normally high level of tension, was more relaxed and "let down and stupid and sleepy when the evening comes. So much so that I have been afraid on numerous occasions of losing the love and affection of my small wife, who is a human being and is naturally likely to become bored with a husband who nods over his paper within half an hour after supper is over."[96]

Thinking that a new hairdo would cheer her up, John suggested to Peggy that she get her hair bobbed in the popular new style. "If John had his way," she wrote Frances, "I wouldnt have a hair over an inch long as he likes it slicked down boyish." Proud of her obstinacy, she explained, "Never have bobbed because every one thought I'd be the first to do it. Never really wanted one till now and I'm not so rabid about it at present." The only advantage she saw to getting her hair cut was the time it would save her in the morning getting dressed. About her appearance, she added: "One thing that doesnt both [sic] me about our poverty—if I *had* million dollar clothes, I'd still look like a hat rack because I have to wear high laced shoes on account of my ankle and no matter what I wear it looks awful. I'm the modestest girl in five states—high shoes, long hair, horn rimmed specs and long skirts!"[97]

Actually, as Peggy matured she became more beautiful, and at twenty-six she was lovelier than she had ever been. Her complexion was flawless, her hair was darker and thicker, and her greenish-blue eyes still had that old power to mesmerize. The only difference—and that difference made her even more beautiful—was that her dreamy, lazy moods, her oppressive quietness, and her lassitude gave her countenance an aura of mystery.

16

Leaving his office in the evening, John would go directly to his second job and work another two or three hours. Not seeing him from early in the morning until late at night, Peggy found the days long and lonely. She always waited up for him, no matter how he late he was, and because she hated being alone in the dark, every light in the apartment would be on when he arrived. But one evening in the fall of 1926, John came home to find their apartment dark and Peggy lying on the couch weeping. As he gathered her into his arms, she explained that her cast was bothering her, but he sensed the trouble was more than that. "Well, let's just take that goddamn thing off!" he said as he went into the kitchen and returned with a hammer and a screwdriver. With dramatic chipping motions, he made her laugh and cry as he broke the cast off.[98]

That night was a turning point in their lives. John's moment of epiphany came when Peggy told him that she had heard that day that Frances Newman's novel was going to be published before Christmas. Looking at her intently and listening carefully, John came to the realization that his wife's problem was not her ankle, nor anything else physical. It was something spiritual.

She had adjusted well to their poverty and never complained about being confined in the apartment. What bothered her, she explained tearfully, was his talking all the time about his work, about loving his job, and his coming home so late and tired that he just went to sleep, sometimes without talking to her at all. Certainly she knew he was working hard for them, but that did not prevent her from feeling deserted. She had made no progress on her book because she missed having him to talk to and to confirm her ideas; he was the only person she trusted with her writing. She struggled to explain her ambivalent feelings, saying that she had in him everything she had ever wanted. She was happy, and yet she was unhappy; and that state of affairs did not make sense to her. Nearly twenty-six years old, she felt as if she had accomplished nothing.

As he listened to her words tumble out in a childlike voice full of pain, John realized that in a sense he had neglected her. Leaving her on her own to write was not working. She had no self-discipline; they both knew that. She could not impose deadlines on herself. She needed more direction than he had been giving her. With her excitable temperament and impatient nature, she needed his patience and assurance. She had ideas of her own, but she needed him to listen to her talk about them. After all, talking was something they always had done, as he had pointed out earlier:

> Both of us have an inordinate fondness for talking, and instead of clearing up one subject and getting on to the next, we spend hours arguing one small angle of one subject, all of which is highly unimportant but very interesting.[99]

That night John made a decision. He informed Peggy that he was not going to bring any more books home for her to read. She was going to write one of her own. He would see to it. And they were to begin that night.

Taking their sandwiches, drinks, and his cigarettes, they propped themselves up in their bed and talked for hours. They talked about the incomplete draft of her adventure story set in the Jazz Age, the one she had been working on off and on since before they married. Its main character was Pansy, a high-spirited, adventurous teenager, but the plot was an ordinary one—teenagers getting into trouble by drinking and driving. And, John pointed out, it was too much like all those boys' adventure stories she had consumed as a child and as an adult.[100] Although she saved the thirty or so pages of that manuscript, she apparently never worked on it again.[101] The other manuscript, the novella "'Ropa Carmagin," a tale of mystery, was better, but she had done all she needed to do with it, having completed it while John was recuperating in her father's home before they had married.[102] What she needed now was a new project with a new plot.

Doing all the things any good editor or teacher does in trying to draw a fearful writer into believing in herself, John convinced her that she should write what she knew best and cared about the most. Her writing had to reflect her own uniqueness, he insisted. He kept going back to her love for the old South and its traditions, to her hardy attachment to and reverence for Atlanta, to those stories she had told him about her grandparents and relatives, people, she said, who "could take it on the chin" and not only survive tragedy but grow stronger for going through it. Instead of trying to write adventure fiction, John urged her to write about people. He told her she should be writing an historical novel because she had a creative, historical imagination. Why not start, he asked her, by writing what she wrote best—descriptions of some characters, like those survivor types that she always had in her mind? John's advice was, "Create some great characters first and then let them generate the action for you."[103]

As she listened, she rummaged through the cardboard box of papers that she had saved when she moved from the *Magazine* office. She found her material on the Confederate generals. Having gathered much more information than she was able to use in those short articles, she had copious notes on General Benning's wife, with whom she had been so fascinated that she included a paragraph about her in the article. Those notes were a treasure trove.[104] A bountiful mother of ten children, Mrs. Benning not only looked after her own family, aging parents, and her brother's grieving widow and children but, with energy and competence, also managed the huge plantation and the slaves by herself while her husband was away fighting the Yankees. Mrs. Benning was only one example of many fine-mannered, soft-voiced, good women who survived after their luxurious homes and elegant manner of living had been completely destroyed. Many of those women survived in the face of terrible odds and rebuilt their new lives in their defeated South. The thought of these women inspired her, particularly when she added thoughts of her own grandparents and great-aunts Mamie and Sis. Then, too, as John pointed out, his own mother was an example of a survivor. Left suddenly alone after the unexpected death of her husband, Mary Marsh had had to figure out a way to support herself and five young children in addition to looking after her elderly mother, aunt, and brother.

"Why did some survive and others not?" Peggy asked John as she began to focus her attention on women survivors. Clearly, the excited discussion that she and John had that night directed her attention to a central idea at last and forged the way for Melanie Wilkes, Ellen O'Hara, and even Scarlett herself.[105] Little did John and Peggy know how far the results of their brainstorming session that night would take them, for they had discovered the essence of the novel that not only changed their lives forever but also the lives of many others.

The next evening John gave her a birthday present in advance. Smiling broadly, he appeared in their doorway with a stack of yellow copy paper and an oak typing table under one arm and a shiny but second-hand black Remington typewriter under his other arm. Peggy squealed with delight when she saw him.[106] Although he really could not afford the typewriter (the paper and table came from Georgia Power), he thought it was cheaper than paying for her visits to physicians. "Madam," he said as he set the typewriter on the little table in the alcove of the front room, "I greet you on the beginning of a great new career."[107]

17

Except for some penciled notes, every line of *Gone With the Wind* was typed on that typewriter and most of it done between 1926 and 1932. From that summer until her death, twenty-three years later, their domestic life centered around *Gone With the Wind*—first the writing of it and then the administration of the international copyright business and myriad other problems that resulted from the book's success.

In his long interview with Medora Field Perkerson in 1949 for the *Sunday Magazine,* John explained:

> She did not write it in longhand in bed as has sometimes been reported. She wrote every line of it on the typewriter, except for occasional pencilled notes. She wrote and rewrote. She was never satisfied with it. Even after it was published she always thought she should have done a better job. I started reading right from the time she started writing and we would talk about it. As you know, talking things over sometimes makes an idea come clearer. In trying to write it out before hand the mechanical labor may get between the writer and the idea. I was always more confident than she was that she could write a good book. She didn't have enough confidence in her own ability.[108]

18

The remainder of that year, 1926, John continued to hold down two jobs. Meanwhile, Peggy worked daily at her typewriter from early in the morning until John came home at night, when he would read what she had done. Following his advice, she framed her characters first, keeping Pansy

Hamilton, the young, strong-willed teenager as her protagonist. Actually, she said she wrote the ending of the novel first, and then worked her way backward.[109] With his keen sense of order, John kept working on the first chapter. During this period, Peggy hardly wrote any letters at all. She worked steadily although she kept no schedule, and interruptions did not seem to bother her. Clearly, the commotion over the publication of Frances Newman's novel was the impetus she needed to stop treading water, so to speak, on her own novel.

But then Frances Newman had always set Peggy's nerves on edge. A woman with prestige, Newman was the daughter of one of Atlanta's oldest families; her father, William T. Newman, was a federal judge. A brilliant person with an opinion about everything, she associated with an avant-garde group that included James Branch Cabell, one of Peggy's idols, and H. L. Mencken. Her relationship with the equally brilliant *Journal* writer Frank Daniel, nearly twenty years her junior, gave Atlanta's wagging tongues more to wag about. She was also a faddish woman who wore shades of purple almost exclusively. When her book appeared in the bookstores in early December, Atlantans were not surprised to see its cover done in vibrant shades of purple. But they were surprised when they saw the title—*The Hard-Boiled Virgin*—and shocked when they read the text, scandalous for its day. Newman's novel created an uproar in Atlanta.[110]

Perhaps only because she felt envious, Peggy was intimidated by the older, more successful woman, who was always pleasant with her but in a patronizing or condescending manner. Harvey Smith noted that *The Hard-Boiled Virgin* was a sort of challenge to Peggy, for with it Frances Newman obtained a bit of the very sort of renown that attracted Peggy so strongly. Others agreed with Smith's assessment here:

> Certainly Peggy had no real love for her and though she never said so I know there was a sort of feeling present that made Peggy flush, look down and almost visibly gnash her teeth at the mention of Frances' success. . . . I do not mean to say Peggy disliked Frances; merely that Frances' achievement made Peggy distinctly uneasy.[111]

John knew the effect that Newman had on Peggy. He asked his sister in a letter on December 8, 1926:

> Have you read *The Hard-Boiled Virgin,* yet? It's Frances Newman's first novel. . . . It is creating no end of a sensation here, with suggestions flying thick and fast that Frances should be tarred and feathered and run out of town. The town is

worse shocked than ever before in years. Frances has dared to trifle with things sacred to Atlanta, the Driving Club and old family names, in addition to writing in a book things most people "wouldn't think of," and admitting to adolescent thoughts "no normal child would ever have had." So Atlanta writhes and squirms, while sales of the book increase.

The thing most offensive to Atlanta is the fact that the book is obviously autobiographical, in large part at least, and Frances has seen fit to speak lightly, even scandalously, about her own family, which is one of the oldest and most conservative in town. I can't say that I approve her good taste in using her own family for copy, but I think she has written a very clever book.

We were around to see her Sunday afternoon and got our copy of the book autographed. Frances is all atwitter and screamed all over the place in her high pitched voice. She is a little bit taken aback to find the town snapping at her heels so unanimously, but I think she is really very proud of the sensation she is creating and is inwardly gloating over it.

I won't ever believe her novel is a failure, because it has had the good effect of getting Peggy roused up again over *her* novel, and we are at work on it again. I might write more except that I am going to take a stab again at the opening chapter of the fifteenth revision of the Adventures of Pansy. Peggy has promised to work on it if I'll help her get started again, so here goes.[112]

1927-1935

ℐN THE WAKE OF A MASTERPIECE

Peggy's eyes are better and she is beginning to commence to start work on the novel again which means that I am back at my problem of trying to figure out an opening chapter for the book. This time I am approaching the problem by studying the way other novelists get their books going. . . .
—John Marsh to his mother, December 1931

1

Once Peggy started work on her book about the Civil War and its aftermath, the whole atmosphere in the Marshes' apartment changed for the better. On the winter mornings when Bessie arrived for work before 7:00, she would find Peggy, usually a late sleeper, hammering away at the typewriter with papers scattered all over the floor. According to her brother Stephens, some days she typed nearly all day long, until John came home in the evening, and then, after they had their supper, she would type until midnight or so.[1] Later, Bessie was to claim that she had no idea at first that Peggy was writing a book; she thought she was merely writing letters.[2] Although Peggy did not discuss any of the details of her book with her father, she often asked him, an authority on Atlanta's history, questions about dates, events, places, and about some of her grandparents' experiences. Her father and brother knew only that she was writing a novel about a young girl in Atlanta during the Civil War; they never read a line of the manuscript. Her brother said that John was her only audience.[3] In fact, during the first few years of his daughter's marriage, Eugene Mitchell, a gracious host to all of the frequently visiting Marshes, would make a point of telling each one how marvelous he thought his son-in-law was, especially for the way he got his unpredictable, wayward daughter to settle down.[4] Secure in her married life, she was no longer defensive in dealing with her father, and their relationship became warm and loving as it had been when she was a child.[5]

In 1927, her friends had no idea what she was working on. Whenever they would drop in for an unannounced visit, they would find Peggy dressed in shorts and one of John's shirts, or in a loose housedress, and always wearing an eyeshade. There would be books scattered around her and a stack of yellow copy paper on the floor near the typing table. Peggy never looked annoyed when friends interrupted her work; they said she would merely remove the eyeshade and cover the typewriter and the manuscript with a towel she kept handy for this purpose.

Her brother Stephens was also fascinated by the history of the South, and he helped his father and others develop the Atlanta Historical Society in 1926. In that same year, Stephens was engrossed in research on the economic aspects of the Civil War for an essay published in the Historical Society *Bulletin*. On the evening when he brought his article to his sister to get her opinion, he observed her taking notes from an old volume of *The Medical and Surgical History of the War of the Rebellion*, published in 1879.[6] She told him she was studying the medical treatments used during the 1860s and was learning about uses of iodine and the treatment of dysentery. He in turn shared with her his discovery of some interesting but little-known information about what had happened to the Confederacy's store of bullion and into which northern and foreign bank accounts the profits of blockade running went. Praising his essay, she told him that the histories she had been reading mentioned precious little or nothing about the profiteers, and she was grateful to him for his research, which she incorporated into her manuscript.[7]

Although Stephens was never permitted to read a line of her manuscript, he understood how his sister worked and talked to Finis Farr about it:

Her philosophy was made up by the case system. That is a system of studying law where you get no rules and no text, but you study cases which have been tried and decided, and you find out how they turn out, and finally, after reading many cases and discussing them with your fellow students, you make up the rules yourself. Margaret's philosophy was a "case" philosophy. She did not try to make people fit a rule. She studied the people, and out of that came a rule. . . . She said that she practiced psychiatry on her friends and acquaintances. When she drew characters, it was from her observation of how people behave—it was not from any preconceived notion of how they *ought* to behave. She put them down as they were.[8]

2

Although John was more attentive to her needs now, he was still caught up in his own career, which continued to burgeon. He had begun to rise at Georgia Power, was working hard and long hours, and was making a name for himself. Temperamentally, he was not only more confident than she; he was also more confidently competitive. No better example of his competitiveness can be given than his determination to win the Coffin Award in 1927. Each year this award, originated by a vice-president of the General Electric Company, was given to the power company judged to have made the most outstanding contribution to the electric art and science of the time. Along with receipt of the award came prestige and national recognition. John had already won the first of the annual prizes for best advertisement in its field and now he wrote his mother, "I am more determined than ever that I must win my Coffin prize."[9]

To compete, the power companies submitted a journal of their achievement for that year. Sensitive to signs of imperfection, John could not always delegate responsibilities, particularly when he figured that a job had to be done absolutely right, so that year John single-handedly took over the entire job of publishing the Georgia Power's *Journal*. The job of winning was entering its last phase when he wrote his mother, "I hope all my life isn't going to be spent in frantic day and night work such as the past several months have required. Possibly working this way now will help me to arrive at easier circumstances in the future. But I would prefer not to have to be quite so industrious in this chapter of the life history." After a day's work in his office, he would go to the print shop and work several more hours on the presentation.[10] Some nights he did not come home until very late. Unable to fall asleep unless he was there, Peggy got annoyed. One night while she was waiting for John, she wrote his brother Henry, "You know this damn competition of John's—well tonight was the dead line." In this letter dated "Sunday night (or Monday morn 3 a.m.)," she explained,

> Oh, its been hectic. J has worked till 4 every morning for a week. He worked all last night, came home at 9 this a.m. Slept an hour and has been working since. He won't be home tonight either. I've been staying [up] till 2 a.m. but thats my limit. He goes into type tomorrow (if the bon dieu is willing) and then comes the mad week of proof reading (my job). Neither of us have good sense. John is able to type a little now but he is so far behind that he gets frenzies thinking about it. So by next week, he'll be dead.

John won the award that year. It was no secret that he also did the work that earned Kelly Starr the *Forbes* magazine's national award for the best publicity and advertising work done by a public utility company.[11] Another of his achievements around this time involved the new one-man streetcar, in which the operator who ran the vehicle also collected the fares. The public was accustomed to having two-man cars, run by a motorman and a conductor, and John was responsible for making the change acceptable to the public. When labor unions first heard about this new program, they rose up in wrath, and he had the first of one of his many union skirmishes. His skill as a mediator and his ability to appear calm under heated pressure enhanced his position in these frays, but did little for his ulcer.[12]

However, the busier he stayed, the more dejected Peggy became. Whenever she would get bogged down or frustrated with her writing and have no John around to talk to, she would turn to reading. The more reading she did, the more depressed she became. In the spring of 1927, after she read James Boyd's new Civil War novel, *Marching On,* she was convinced that her "life was ruin."[13] The reason why Boyd's novel devastated her so totally was that it was the first Civil War novel up to that time that dealt with romance, jealousy, and passion. It did almost exactly what she was trying to do—create a love story as well as a fictionalized account of the war's history.[14] As John had pointed out to her the night they had their long talk about the book she was going to write, she had to stop imitating the works of other writers. She had to develop her own strategies, and as he told her repeatedly, she was fully capable of doing that if she would just believe in herself. Proudly thinking that she had actually come up with a new strategy about a self-centered heroine full of human needs and passion, she felt defeated when she learned that someone else had already written something similar. She thought that her writing would never measure up to Boyd's— or to anyone else's, for that matter. She was wasting her time. She later wrote Clifford Dowdey, "My life was ruined for three months about 'Marching On.'"[15]

She actually got to the point where she and John believed she would be better off if she stopped reading entirely. But she could not do that and do her research too, because she secured much information from well-documented novels written about the war. In her letter to Dowdey, she went on to say,

My husband took me in hand brutally at that point and extracted from me a promise that I would not read any books on the subject except reference books. But in the course of my reference work it became necessary for me to discover on exactly what day of Johnston's retreat the rain began to fall. I knew where I could find it, although I had not read the book in twenty years. It was in Mary Johnston's *Cease Firing.* If I had contented myself with merely reading the item about the rain I would have escaped. But I am a weak vessel and before I knew it I had read the whole book and was down with another bad case of humbles. I could go on indefinitely about people who ruined my life.

When she finally turned back to her own novel, she swore she would never read another book on the Civil War until she had finished her own.

"Then," she said, "Mr. Stephen Vincent Benet struck me a body blow. . . . The result was that I wondered how anybody could have the courage to write about the War after Mr. Benet had done it so beautifully. Recovery was slow, and scarcely had I tottered to my desk when Mr. Stark Young arrived, terrible as an army with banners, and annihilated me with *So Red the Rose.*"[16]

The high spirits with which Peggy began 1927 certainly did not last. As her spirits fell, her health began to decline drastically again, and she stopped writing. The letters to John's family indicate that the spring and summer was a most difficult time in the Marshes' life because John's work load was so heavy, and he had to take frequent trips. However, he did not always leave Peggy home alone; he frequently took her with him even though she had to spend her days alone while he worked. In late July, on their return home from a brief business trip in New York, they went to Wilmington, Delaware, for an overnight visit with his family. Although he and Henry did not get enough private time to talk, Henry knew right away that John was troubled, especially after Henry had explained that he wanted to remarry and was hoping that John could increase the amount of money he was sending his mother, and thus leave Henry with more for his new household.

After their mother retired and moved to Wilmington, John and Henry supported her; and they also supported their youngest sister, Frances, until she married in 1927. (Ben Gordon, who was so much younger, could not help much; he was just out of college and getting started with his new married life in 1927 and needed help himself.) Because he was older, Henry considered himself the head of the family. Too, as a chemist he always had a better-paying job, and because his mother lived with him after his divorce and looked after his little daughter Mary, Henry contributed the most to their mother's income and had done so all along. Not as fortunate financially as his older brother, John had earned smaller salaries as a newspaperman and just about the time he was getting established at Georgia Power, he had become sick and been unable to work for nearly six months. In fact, he had to borrow money from Georgia Power to live on. Since his illness and marriage, he had reduced the amount that he sent his mother every month.

That August 1927, he felt so bad at being unable to contribute the increased amount that Henry had requested that he wrote his brother saying: "My failure to contribute to Mother's expenses has been bothering me for a long time and I would have been doing it all along if I hadn't had such a fight to make a go of things myself." He went on to explain that although the government had paid him a disability compensation for the ptomaine poisoning he contracted in the army, his financial situation was still very tight.

I wouldn't want to do anything to interfere with your plans. If my small contribution will be *too* small, so that you will have to delay the wedding, write me and tell me so frankly. I am writing to you with considerably more frankness than usual, and I would like for you to do the same.

The situation I am up against is this. Before the government came through we were in actual poverty. My very expensive illness was still unpaid for, and Peggy has been continuously under the care of doctors since we were married. We had been forced to reduce our expenditures to actual necessities, but in spite of everything, my debts were steadily increasing. Fortunately, the government came to the rescue and pulled us out of that hole. The compensation check enabled me to pay off all of the back debts, with the exception of the Power Company, which I still owe more than a thousand dollars. We are in considerably better shape than we were a few months ago, but doctor's bills are still taking a large share of my salary.

At his wit's end, John confided to Henry that Peggy was going to one doctor three times a week and had been doing so for months. Two other specialists had been called in for consultation twice and, he said, she had "to make several calls on the eye doctor, the ear doctor, the dentist, and others." About the only thing wrong with her that anyone had found was that she had two impacted wisdom teeth. "The expense of having them attended to won't be so very great," he wrote, "but this newest development is typical of what has been going on for months. As soon as one trouble was fairly well under control, another developed and so on."[17] John felt as if he were in a spiraling descent into debt. Distressed, he told Henry:

Peggy's condition is most discouraging. There is something wrong with the kid that the doctors haven't been able to find. That is my opinion, though I may be wrong. It may be that she is just damned unlucky and each of her various troubles is not connected with the others. . . . Until we can locate the trouble and eradicate it, she will probably keep on being sick more or less, with the possibility always that she may become seriously sick.[18]

It was some time during that terrible summer of 1927 that Peggy began complaining about soreness in her breasts; one side, especially, caused her much discomfort, she said, after she "carromed [sic] against the sharp point of the bed one evening."[19] She was in so much pain, in fact, that she said she could not type. Although her physician must not have thought that she had

A feminist in her day, Maybelle Stephens Mitchell nurtured her only daughter's love of southern history and her desire to write. This portrait was taken when Peggy was three and her brother, Stephens, was eight.

John Marsh inherited his literary talent from a father he had barely known. Newspaper editor Millard Fillmore Marsh died in 1904, when John, right at age three, and Henry, left, were still children.

In the fall of 1912, the Mitchells moved into this colonial-style mansion at what is now 1401 Peachtree Street. Eugene Mitchell had it built to fulfill his wife's dreams but unfortunately, Maybelle Mitchell di only seven years after moving into the stately home. Because Peggy Mitchell and her brother Stephens wanted only Mitchells to live there, Stephens had it demolished in 1952.

When John was born in 1895, the Marsh family lived in this house on Forest Avenue in Maysville, Kentuck

"She was a lot of fun," John Marsh said of his wife. In front of the Mitchell home, Peggy clowned around with her good friend, Augusta Dearborn Edwards.

In his youth, and as
a student at the
University of
Kentucky, John
Robert Marsh was a
confident and
easygoing fellow.

pposite page:
n her youth, Margaret Munnerlyn Mitchell was an athletic type, as revealed in this candid shot.

A portrait of youthful exuberance: Peggy Mitchell bound for home aboard a ship in July 1919, after her year at Smith College.

...ailing in another direction at about the same time: John Marsh enlisted in the Barrow Unit of the Armed ...ervices at Lexington, Kentucky. In 1918 he served for seven months in England, and later in France.

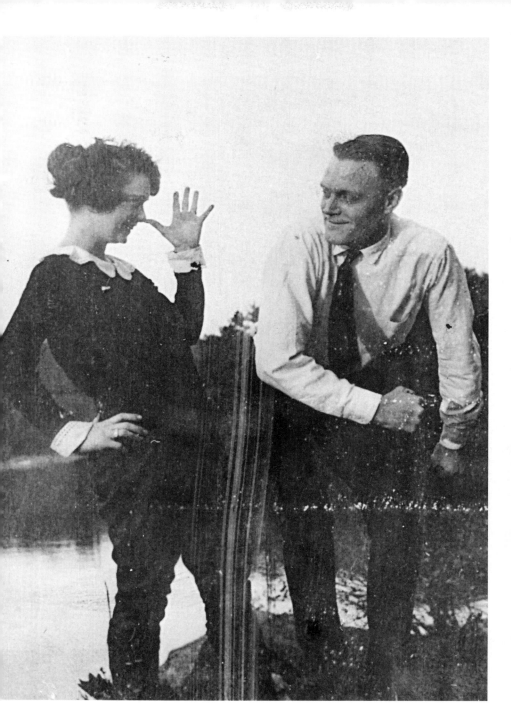

ɛgy hams it up with her suitor, Berrien "Red" Upshaw, who happened to be John's roommate.

posite page:

ll page) Peggy Mitchell on a camping trip, age twenty. Atlanta History Center.

set) Corporal John Marsh, probably on his way to France in 1919, where he was stationed at the ɛnch village of Savenay. Photograph courtesy of Gordon Renick Marsh.

This profile was John's favorite picture of Peggy, age twenty-two. Ironically, the picture originally included Red Upshaw, who became her first husband. Peggy also admired this image of herself, and upon her divorce found a way to get Red out of the picture: with a pair of scissors.

John was in love with Peggy from the moment he met her, but patiently waited in the wings until she realized she loved him, too.

Peggy Mitchell did not like to be reminded that on September 2, 1922, she married the wrong man: Berrien "Red" Upshaw. The wedding party included the bride's brother, Stephens, far right. Augusta Dearborn, third from left, was maid of honor; her hand is on the arm of John Marsh, who hardly looked his happiest as best man. Peggy's marriage to the bootlegger Red lasted 10 stormy months.

As her marriage to Red fell apart, Peggy threw herself into her job as a features reporter for *The Atlanta Journal.* She proved quite able to hold her own with Georgia Tech seniors who towered above her.

Peggy honed her storytelling skills writing for the *Journal's Sunday Magazine* in the early 1920s. Staffers include Medora Perkerson, seated, who became a lifelong friend. Peggy is third from right.

opposite page:
Silent screen idol Rudolph Valentino must have been charmed by the feisty reporter.

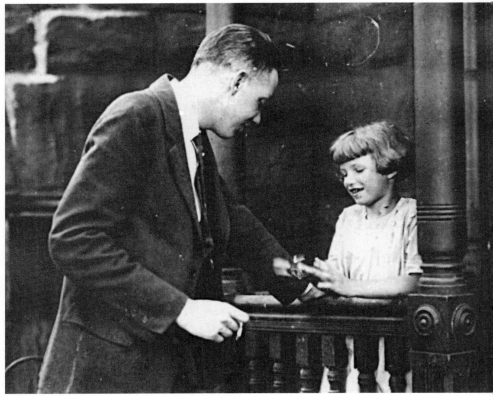

Mary Marsh Davis, daughter of John's brother, Henry, kept many letters the Atlanta couple wrote to members of the Marsh family. She has fond memories of visiting her Uncle John (shown here with young Mary) and Aunt Peggy in the early days of their marriage.

Peggy adored Henry Marsh, John's older brother, who was also the recipient of many spirited letters.

Throughout their marriage, both John and Peggy wrote affectionate letters to his mother, Mary, known to her brood as "Mother Marsh," shown here about 1925.

Peggy, "The Dump" (shown here in 1) was the only name for the first-floor, -corner apartment where she began and te most of her famous novel. Efforts now underway to save the crumbling town Atlanta building from the cking ball. Historical preservationists e renamed the site The Margaret chell House.

Inset: To be restored in time for the 1996 Olympic games, The Margaret Mitchell House with its museum dedicated to the author, is expected to be a popular Atlanta attraction.

owing page: Peggy called it "The Dump" because it was dark and dank. She worked on *Gone With Wind* at this window alcove, which provided the only good light in the apartment.

breast cancer (he did no breast biopsy), she was convinced that she had cancer or would have it, and she had John nearly convinced too. The possibility of serious surgery loomed before them always; if not the breast, as John wrote Henry, then perhaps an exploratory abdominal operation. "Due to her condition, however, we can't go into her for an exploratory operation, so that if the operation has to be performed, it may be an emergency operation." They seemed perpetually on the brink of disaster. "Peggy has been sick so much she has become very sensitive about it, and how she has stood up under all her pain and suffering and the even worse worry and suspense is more than I can understand." Concluding his letter, John wrote, "I might have written about other more pleasant things if it hadn't taken so long to recite my tale of woe. Let me hear from you, and I will try to write more entertainingly next time. Both of us are grateful to you for helping to make our visit pleasant. Come to see us some time."

As fall approached, things got a little better, perhaps because John was more sympathetic and did more to comfort her. He prodded her to write because he knew that writing—and especially doing research for her writing—was a wonderful diversion for her, particularly when it went along well. So now, when Peggy accompanied John on trips to north Georgia, where his company was building hydroelectric plants to furnish the impatient demand for more electricity, they took the typewriter and a part of the manuscript along, and she worked on the manuscript during the day in the hotel room while he went about his business. At night, they talked about it. Because of the Marshes' custom of "carrying" parts of the manuscript and the typewriter around with them, people who worked with John and went on those business trips with them knew that Peggy was "engaged on a piece of writing," but they did not know what it was and thought it might be a cookbook or an account of an historical incident about Atlanta. Then one day John admitted to coworkers that Peggy was working on a bit of fiction, and that was how the word first got out at Georgia Power that she was writing a novel.[20]

4

All during the winter and spring of 1928, the novel progressed rapidly. Peggy sank deeply into her private world, writing quickly and without any idea that she was in the wake of a masterpiece. According to her brother, when she worked, she worked furiously from early in the morning until John came home in the evening; then he would read what she had written.[21] But there were spells when she never touched the typewriter.[22] On those days, she would take the used car that John had purchased for her from an employee at Georgia Power in February 1928, and drive the backroads to small towns, where she unearthed treasures that she incorporated into her writing. In a letter to Frances in 1928, she said: "There seems to be such a wealth of characters quaint, curious, and interesting in smaller places that are not to be found in larger towns with out digging."[23] She loved doing this kind of research.[24] From her earliest days, she had been a rapt listener to stories, and the best storytellers, she knew, were the old people in small country places like Jonesboro and Fayetteville, where she has her Scarlett attend the Female Academy just as her Grandmother Stephens had done as a teenager. Peggy was always nostalgic for a way of life that had passed. "I have always loved old people," she wrote in a letter to a friend, "and from childhood listened eagerly to their stories—tucking away in my mind details of rickrack braid, shoes made of carpet, and bonnets trimmed with roosters' tails."[25]

5

The Marshes spent most of the summer of 1928 entertaining out-of-town visitors. In May, John heard from Kitty Mitchell again. She and her young son stopped for a three-day visit with John on her way to her parents' home in Bowling Green, Kentucky. It turned out that she had to stay for nearly a month after her son became ill and had to be hospitalized. Although the thought of seeing his college sweetheart after ten years did not appear to rekindle any romantic notions in John, the news jarred Peggy. Having led an inactive life for two years, she had gained a little weight, wore what she called ugly "Minnie Mouse" shoes, the orthopedic kind that supported her weak ankle, and dressed as plain as a Quaker. She was feeling a lot less like her previous "Vamp de Luxe" self. Kitty had been living in Latin America since her marriage to a wealthy businessman with whom she traveled around the world; she was coming from a far more prosperous and sophisticated environment than Peggy had ever known. This was during that period when the Marshes had no money for new clothes, so on the night they met their guest for dinner at her downtown hotel, Peggy wore a blue dress that John's sister Frances had sent her.[26]

The moment she saw Kitty—meticulously groomed, expensively dressed and jeweled—Peggy felt more than a little dowdy. A day or so later, she wrote Frances about this "legend's visit":

> She is a charming person—did you ever meet her—and I was so glad for the sake of both my sense of the fitness of romantic things, and John's memories and illusions that she returned to him, ten years after the conflagration, slimmer than ever—really a luscious figger, bobbed and sleek of head, unlined and piquant of

face and really not looking a day over twenty. Really, I gathered no end of excellent ideas as to conduct when visiting in the towns of ex fiances. We hit it off nobly after she once discovered that I regarded her as that unusual thing, a sequel to an interesting book that is better than the book was.[27]

Kitty's opinion of Peggy is not known, and although Kitty and John never saw each other again, they corresponded until his death twenty-four years later.

No sooner had Kitty left than John's mother and his nine-year-old niece Mary came to visit. Peggy wrote to Frances, praising Mary's good manners and adding, "And as for your mother—well, I'm proud to own her. Every one who met her told me afterward that it wasnt fair that I not only had a husband who was human but a mother in law who was wedded to the policy of non interference, sympathy, and understanding. In short, they finished, plaintively, it seemed as if Mrs. Marsh actually cared about me and that I returned the feeling."[28]

Also in 1928, John's youngest brother Ben Gordon, often called Gordon, and his bride Francesca made the first of their many visits to Atlanta. By this time, Peggy was a little weary of guests and told Frances in a letter a few months later:

But I didnt want to ask them to delay their trip for fear they might not find it convenient to visit, later. By "unfortunate" I mean they arrived when I had been menstruating for three weeks. (I hate folks who talk about their female troubles but there's no other explanation.) Ever so often that happens to me and I get where there's no putting up with me for my desires at such times are to sink my teeth into the combined calves of the world. But in spite of that I enjoyed them and the visit most thoroughly.[29]

As the newest addition to the family, Francesca, unlike Frances, knew little about Peggy's background with Red; and Peggy wanted to make a good impression on her. Fortunately, that was easy to do because they immediately liked each other. A tall, athletic-looking young girl with clear skin and light hair, Francesca was also a graduate of the University of Kentucky. She and Gordon had fallen in love while they were both students at the university and married after their graduation. A talented artist, she planned to be an art teacher. Feeling a slight sense of inferiority because she did not have a college education, Peggy lamented to John that now she was the only one in either of their families without a college degree.

Although three years younger than Peggy, Francesca had a kind of maturity that conveyed strength and competence, and she seemed older. With her preference for the outdoors and her love of children and animals, she and Gordon, the only sportsman among the Marsh men, were ideally suited. Having met Gordon before he married, Peggy noticed during this visit a striking difference in his personality—he was unusually talkative and obviously happy. Crediting Francesca with bringing him out remarkably, Peggy showed her more mature views about love when she wrote:

> Having someone wholeheartedly and obviously in love with him seems to be the best thing in the world for him. I liked Francesca so much because she didn't subscribe to the po' white notion so prevalent with most of my friends that the only way to keep a man in love with you is to "keep him guessing," play little tricks on him, to mystify him, get him jealous, etc. all in all, an adolescent notion, from my observation of the antics of my little playmates—and a notion which has resulted in a choice number of divorces which my brother is handling. She seems to have that sensible notion that a mature man and woman need have no hesitation in allowing each other to be absolutely sure of them. Perhaps I bear down on this point too much but, it seems to me such a simple thing but one that so few people follow out.

Then she explained that not only was she the only one in the gang she ran around with who was happily married but "I'm the only one who isn't afraid to let my husband know that he's the only one."[30] Showing that she retained some of her old vampy inclinations, she added:

> With the pleasant result that I have all the dates with ex flames that I want and have the house full of Tech boys, at tea time with out having scenes, passionate and recriminating with the man I live with. And also, the equally pleasant result that John is proud that I still have some sex appeal tho married. Gorden [sic] seemed to need just that sort of assurance and he really blossomed out. . . . Of course, being an utter egocentric, I always appreciate the qualities in other women which I fondly believe to be qualities of nobility as well as common sense, which I myself possess in large qualities.[31]

At that time, Francesca was nearly three months pregnant with what was to be her and Gordon's only child, their son Renny. She and Gordon were thrilled about the pregnancy, which prompted Peggy to express her own total lack of interest in having children.

Some have speculated that she and John did not have children because of her many illnesses. Others have suggested that she may have had endometriosis, which was not a medically recognized disease at that time. Still others have wondered if the long illness that John had just before their marriage made him unable to father children, and another theory holds that the Marshes were childless because of John's fear that his mild form of epilepsy (petit mal seizures) would be passed on in a more violent form. However, according to Francesca's first-hand knowledge of Peggy's views, they did not have children because they simply did not want any. They did not want to interrupt their lives by having children. In this same long letter to Frances about Gordon and Francesca's visit, Peggy commented on her views about maternity:

> Of course, I couldn't quite subscribe to Frank's [Francesca's nickname] outspoken desire for seven children and fourteen dogs. I've never owned more than seven dogs at once and cant help but feeling that the line should be drawn somewhere—It was a shock to me when I read in a delightful book on the ductless glands, last week that lack of secretion from the posterior pituitary gland causes a totally absence of the maternal instinct. I thought that the lack of mat and pat instincts in this family were due to mental and not glandular processes.[32]

The fact that practically every married woman in her circle was having babies or was interested in having babies did not change Peggy's mind about not wanting children. Francesca was due in February 1929; Frances was expecting her first child in November 1928; and Stephens and his wife Carrie Lou, who had been married about a year and a half, were sadly disappointed when Carrie Lou miscarried her first pregnancy. Peggy wrote Frances:

> They wanted babies like some people want millions of dollars.... I tell her not to be so blamed hasty that life is long and a baby will eventually show up. But to them its a tragedy. She's so interested in you and your baby—and envious too—if such unChristian emotion as envy ever could enter her mind. Personally, I am glad they havent had a baby yet as I think she ought to give herself a whole year, with no illness at all to give the baby a chance . . . but she don't see my view point.[33]

6

Recalling her first impression of the Atlanta Marshes, Francesca remembered her surprise at how openly affectionate and demonstrative they were. Whereas she and Gordon were modest and reserved, Francesca said it was not unusual to find Peggy sitting on John's lap, leaning back with her head tucked under his, dangling a house-slippered foot like a child. What struck Francesca as odd was what she called "his excessively protective attitude" toward Peggy, whom he called "Baby." Francesca said, "He delighted in having to take care of her. She was having trouble with her ankle at that time, and John would gather her up in his arms and carry her around the apartment. Sometimes she would climb onto his back, like a child, and be toted to her destination."

However, Francesca quickly pointed out that John's inclination to be protective was not reserved for his wife alone. For instance, when John learned that his young brother and wife were not taking the train to Atlanta but were instead driving from their home in Lexington, Kentucky, he instructed them not to drive directly into Atlanta's "dangerous traffic." He insisted they stop outside the city limits to telephone him so that he and Peggy could drive out to escort them into the city. Francesca said she would never forget how amused she and Gordon were by the way John ignored the fact that they were adults, and excellent, experienced drivers. Nevertheless, to please him, they did as he instructed.

7

It was during their first visit to Atlanta in the summer of 1928 that Francesca and Gordon heard and saw much evidence of a book in the making. Not knowing anyone who had even considered writing a novel, young Francesca was fascinated with her in-laws, whom she considered far more sophisticated than she and Gordon. Although neither John nor Peggy disclosed any details of the plot, he told them that the story was based on courageous women who found ways to survive after their worlds had been blown up under their feet. His face became animated when he told them about Peggy's knowledge of the Civil War and about the research she had been doing. Like an overly proud father, he boasted about her talent. He brought out her articles on the Georgia generals and talked about her discovery of the extraordinary life of Mrs. Benning, a prototype of the kind of woman Peggy admired. Because it was unusual in that day to hear any man talk about a woman's role in anything except domestic matters, Francesca recalled thinking then how much she admired John: "He was opposed to sexual stereotypes. He was very much an advocate for women's issues and rights, long before it was fashionable to be so, at least, in our crowd. He was a sensible and a very decent man, scrupulously honest, and modest. Never tried to put on airs." She added, "I never saw them that carefree and happy again. I just remember how happy they were then, but at that time we were all young and happy and yes, carefree."

Francesca said that Peggy enjoyed telling them about her visits with old veterans and her trips to abandoned churches, plantation houses, weed-covered cemeteries, and battlefields.

> She had been scouring the countryside, in that old car they had, for anything old, like diaries, albums, letters, surveys, clothes, and newspapers. It's hard telling how many hours she had spent in courthouses and libraries by the time I met her. I know she did much more research in the later years. I don't think most people realize the research that went into that novel!

From what Francesca saw and heard when she was there in 1928 and again later on other visits, and from what Peggy herself said and wrote in letters, the research was pure joy for her; it was the writing that was painful.

Because all the "Marshes were meticulous record-keepers," Francesca said that she was not surprised when John showed them a black leather, looseleaf notebook that he was filling with chronologies of Peggy's characters, who were "propagating like rabbits"; he also had begun a glossary of black and southern dialects. "Their excitement had to do with anticipation, like waiting for something to hatch. They looked forward to every day in much the same way that we looked forward to having our first baby." As Francesca pointed out, none of them had much money, but John was really strapped because he had those huge medical bills that worried him until he got them paid off. "Working on that book was their entertainment."

While he and his brother went for a walk that evening after dinner, leaving Francesca and the lame Peggy in the apartment, John spoke candidly. Because his people were the strong, quiet type who would never think of telling others how bad they felt, they had all wondered about Peggy's various recurring illnesses and were beginning to question the genuineness of her suffering. According to her letters to them, it seemed as if she were sick all the time. They felt sorry for John, who assured them, "Things are better now." He was convinced that his wife's continual physical problems were largely psychosomatic, a result of her depression, which in turn was the result of her feeling inferior. He explained that the writing project had clearly done more to improve her well-being than anything "any of the damn doctors had done and [was] a hellavuh-lot less expensive." He just hoped that he could keep her involved in it. It gave her something to think about other than herself.

8

By mid-1928, John's work had settled into a more pleasant routine, and he had received another raise, giving them a much more comfortable living. Although they were still not out of debt, they were happier than they ever would be and deeply engrossed in work on the book, which was progressing rapidly. Peggy was stuffing more and more manuscript pages into large manila envelopes to keep the chapters separated. The envelopes were stacked on the floor next to the typing table. Scattered on other tables and on the floor around the typing table were layers of other loose papers and many old history books and journals.

Because he had no outside interests, John always rode the streetcar directly home every evening. Unlike his contemporaries at the Power Company, he had no interest in athletics or outdoor activities. He did not fit into that male cadre that drank together, enthusiastically supported their old alma maters (usually either Auburn or Georgia Tech), and took frequent fishing and hunting trips together.[34] Instead of joining his cohorts for such activities in his off-duty hours, he looked forward to having dinner at home with Peggy and to reading what she had written that day and assessing what research remained to be done. Soon their small world was filled with fictional events and populated with characters that would eventually become known throughout the entire world.

As a child, Deon would go with her mother Bessie to the Marshes' apartment early every morning and catch the streetcar on the corner to ride to school. After school, she would return to the Marshes' apartment; she did this until she was old enough to stay at home alone. Deon said, "In those days, Mama did every thing—the cooking, the shopping, the cleaning. But, then, Miss Peggy would always say before we left for the grocery store, 'Now, Bessie, you get what y'all want to eat. You don't have to eat what we eat. You be sure and get what you feel like eating.' Miss Peggy was easy to please."

In a reflective mood, Deon provided an insider's view of the Marshes' home life. Since she grew up around the Marshes, she remembered well all those years that the Marshes spent working on what she called "those papers." Their routine was set, she said, and except for occasional visits with their families and a few close friends, they had no social life. Every evening after supper was the same; while Bessie cleaned the kitchen and Deon did her homework, the Marshes worked on "those papers," typing, reading, and talking.[35] "Of course," she added, "since we were servants, they didn't discuss what they were working on with us."

She said that John was the first one up and dressed in the mornings except on Sundays, when he would sleep till nearly noon. Because Peggy had trouble falling to sleep at night, she sometimes would sleep late, but not always. Sitting at the kitchen table in the mornings, as Bessie stirred around him, he read the paper and ate his breakfast alone. John and Peggy never ate breakfast together but always their supper and frequently their lunch, when he could get home. "He liked his eggs over-easy, and his coffee, hot with sugar and evaporated milk straight out of the can," Deon smiled, remembering. Just before he left for work every morning, he would bring Peggy a cup of coffee, "scalding hot and with the evaporated milk." An hour or so later, she would have her breakfast and then leave for town, dashing out of the house yelling, "Bessie, I'll be in the library!"

Leaving papers scattered all around the room in which she worked, Peggy instructed Bessie and Deon: "Don't move anything! I know just where everything is!'" As a little girl whose responsibility was to dust the Marshes' apartment, Deon found her job difficult because she was not permitted to move anything. Yet she knew that John expected her to do her task well. Until she got to know him better, she would cringe whenever she saw him running his finger over a piece of furniture, as he occasionally did, glancing down at her without saying a word. "But Miss Peggy never checked to see if I had done anything."

Laughing as she remembered how frightened of him she was at first, she said, "He towered over all of us. Not only was he tall, but his voice was so low and deep. If anything went wrong, Mr. Marsh took care of it for all of us." She, her mother, and Carrie Mitchell, the washerwoman, always called him "Mr. Marsh" to his face and behind his back, they called him "The Boss."[36]

Remembering fondly the moment she lost her fear of "The Boss," Deon described the morning when she boarded the streetcar to go to her segregated school several blocks away. As she got into the streetcar, she saw John seated in the front row next to the window, reading his newspaper. As she walked past him and some empty seats in the front of the car, he looked up at her and she mumbled, "Good morning, sir." She headed toward the back of the car where the blacks had to sit in those days. As she squeezed into a place in the back section, which was always crowded with school-age children and women going to work, she heard him call her name and looked up to see him beckoning to her to come sit next to him. Puzzled because she was not allowed to sit in the front with "the white folks," she looked at him quizzically, silently saying, "Me?" He nodded yes. She rose from her place and, with her little chin tucked down, quickly moved down the aisle and crouched breathlessly in the seat next to him. That was the first time she had ever sat in the front of a streetcar, and she was frightened. She felt as if everybody were staring at them. He nudged her arm and winked at her.

From that moment on, she thought of him as her friend. As she grew older, she not only respected but also admired him, and she claimed him as her favorite, putting him above "Mr. Stephens" and "Mr. Eugene Mitchell," whom she saw often. Deon stated matter-of-factly: "He sure did love Miss Peggy, he sure did love that woman."

9

For nearly three years, P. S. Arkwright, Georgia Power's president, had patiently contended with Kelly Starr's drinking problem and had tried to help Starr—likeable and capable, when sober—get his life straightened out. Arkwright knew well that John was keeping the publicity department afloat—that John was not only doing his own work but also all of Starr's and was doing it extremely well, without the appropriate recompense or recognition. And that worried him, for he admired John greatly. In the spring of 1930, while Arkwright was making a speech at one of the dams that the Georgia Power Company was just completing in northeast Georgia, Starr arrived noticeably late and drunk. When Starr created an embarrassing situation for his employer by asking him what he meant by a certain statement in his speech, Arkwright astonished everyone present when he fired Starr right on the spot.[37]

On May 9, 1930, Arkwright announced John's promotion to manager of the public relations department, one of the most important posts of its kind in the utility field. He called John "one of the ablest and youngest of the men engaged in this particular form of activity."[38]

In his new executive position, John had to travel more often, and he had to maintain a good relationship with reporters and editors all over the state, and also in the bordering states. Because they had many friends and acquaintances in the press, he and Peggy had been going to the annual Georgia Press Institute conferences ever since the first one was held in Macon in August 1928.[39] It was at that first convention that Peggy met Susan Myrick, the blond, husky-voiced farm editor of the *Macon Telegraph* and later the associate editor of that same paper.[40] Having much in common, the two women established a friendship that, nine years later, became valuable and fascinating to both of them. So for personal and for business reasons, the Marshes looked forward to these meetings. Peggy wrote, "Usually the Meet, held in the smallest towns in Georgia and during the hottest weather is a pleasant, somnolent affair, fish fries alternating with barbecues and, by night, editors and editresses sitting on beds, drinking corn and discussing job printing and the future of literature."[41]

In September 1931, just after they had returned from attending one of these gatherings of Georgia editors, John acknowledged his wife's contribution to his career. In a letter to Frances, he wrote:

> Being a power trust propagandist, it is part of my job to attend such gatherings, and the Company likewise pays Peggy's expenses for such trips, as she is a genuinely valuable helpmate on such occasions and has helped me in the ensnarement of several editors who might have been difficult if I had gone at them singlehanded. (Don't let this confession fall into the hands of the Federal Trade Commission.)[42]

Mary Singleton, who worked in the print shop at Georgia Power at that time, described John as "no glad-hander or back-slapper." Mary said, "He just could not mingle in a crowd, as Peggy could. With her ability to draw people to her and to be entertaining, she made an ideal corporate wife."[43] Her attendance was so vital to the success of these social gatherings that it got to the point where it really did not matter whether John, Joe Kling, or any other representative from Georgia Power was there at all. On occasions when he got tangled in business and could not attend, John asked Joe Kling to escort Peggy to the conferences to help Joe handle the press relations.[44] Kling said he felt superfluous with Peggy there.

These annual meetings were scheduled in different towns every summer, and visiting various places gave Peggy and John a chance to study different black dialects and southern colloquialisms. It also gave her ideas and raw material for her novel. For instance, in 1931, the conference met in Dalton, which is in the extreme northwest corner of the state, just a short distance from Tennessee and in the heart of the mountains. The town, completely surrounded by mountains, is in a valley with an altitude nearly three hundred feet less than that of Atlanta. That summer was a sweltering one, and nowhere was the heat felt more keenly than in Dalton. Hardly able to sleep because of the heat the entire time they were there, Peggy used her feelings of discomfort to imagine how the Confederate soldiers felt during their campaign there.[45] After they returned home, John wrote his mother:

> The most interesting detail of the convention was a trip to Chattanooga, thirty-five miles away, which included a tour of Chicamauga Park, Fort Oglethorpe and Lookout Mountain. The view from the latter was one of the most impressive I have ever seen. . . . Neither of us had ever been there and that tour, and the entire trip, was especially interesting because it was the scene of

big events in the Civil War—and in Peggy's novel.

The line extending northwest through Dalton to Chatta-nooga, at the southeast corner of Tennessee, was the line of Sherman's march on Atlanta. The railroad connecting the two places, Atlanta and Chattanooga, was one of the most important lines of communication for the Confederacy, and Sherman's advance was down this railroad line, a series of engagements being fought at various points through which we passed, as the Southern forces dropped back. Of course, his objective was Atlanta, and when he finally captured it, the South was doomed. Just seeing the places had its usual historical interest and seeing it in the heat of summer gave us a keen sympathy for the men who battled over the section and dragged cannons up the sides of those mountains in July and August.

Suggesting that he had read the entire manuscript as it was at that stage, he added, "One of the most interesting sections in Peggy's book tells of the approach of the northern army down the railroad line to Atlanta and the first awakenings of fear that the Confederacy might eventually be defeated, as the army fought and dropped back at Dalton, Resaca, Big Shanty, and then Kennesaw Mountain, which put them within 20 miles of Atlanta."[46]

After John began providing more and more details about the book, his mother wrote asking him if he realized that he had a great Civil War general in his family. Did he know, she asked, that his great-great-aunt Louisa Kennan was married to General A. P. Hill? In his response John wrote,

I don't know when I have been more embarrassed. . . . Peggy is threatening to turn me out without a shilling and my only reply is that in our family we had so many Confederate generals, I just couldn't keep track of all of them. Besides that, he meant more to us as Uncle Powell than as the great A. P. Hill, friend of Lee. (However, if we have any more family skeletons of this bright and shining character in our closets, please let me know about them right away. I may be able to handle the situation this time, but if it should come out on me later that Lee, Stonewall Jackson, or Albert Sidney Johnston was my grandpappy, and me unaware of it, I would never be able to appear in public again.)[47]

Three days later, Peggy wrote to her mother-in-law saying she had jokingly told John earlier it would matter little how great either of them ever became because they had no Confederate general in their background. Now they had one!

And every body who has any pretensions to being anybody in Georgia has a General just the same as they have bath tubs. I have always admired General Hill so much, since childhood when I heard that he always wore red flannel shirts on the battle field to give the Yankees a better target. And one of the family stories was that of my Grandfather Mitchell, who told how General Hill saved the day at Sharpsburg by riding his men on commandeered flat cars for seventy miles and then marching them at a run sixteen miles and reinforcing Lee just at sun down when the battle was apparently lost. So when the business of "Uncle Powell" was made apparent in your letter, I . . . told John that I was filing for a divorce on the ground of concealment of a Confederate General. I asked Father if that would be legal grounds and he, the cagy lawyer, said that he knew of one case where a woman in Georgia got a divorce because her husband had concealed from her, at the time of their marriage that he was a Republican . . . and that he would look up my case and let me know. However, he said, John was very culpable. Now my life is complete. I shall refer to Uncle Powell anytime any granddaughter of Gordon and Cobb throws her weight about.[48]

10

In 1931, Atlanta and its neighboring towns suffered the most prolonged drought since 1845. The resulting water shortage severely limited the output of the hydroelectric generating stations and forced the Georgia Power Company to buy power from other companies and to produce whatever it could by fuel generation. Georgia Power also had its first serious labor dispute when its electrical workers walked off their jobs in March 1931, in an effort to force Allied Engineers, a utility construction company doing some work for Georgia Power, to sign a union contract. Much public disfavor and ill will resulted from the strike, and a campaign was launched for municipal ownership of Atlanta's utilities. This effort stirred up a fury with citizens for a while and then faded out of sight when it was pointed out that if the city went into the utility business, it would lose about three hundred thousand dollars a year in taxes paid by Georgia Power. As a result of the strike, the city adopted an ordinance stopping Georgia Power from operating one-man streetcars in downtown Atlanta on the grounds that they created traffic jams and were a hazard. This ordinance was a setback for John, and so was the publicity about the strikers. As the public relations executive, he had to woo the public's favor all over again.[49]

This was a difficult period for John. As the economic depression deepened in the 1930s, its effects crept over the population, and Georgia Power also suffered. Thousands of good people lost their jobs through no fault of their own; their employers could not afford to keep them. Concerned about how he was going to keep all of his staff (about thirty people), John would remind them, in his staff meetings, of the hard times and the uncertainty of their jobs. The result was that he depressed everybody's spirits, thus accomplishing the opposite effect of what he intended. Sadly and reluctantly, he had to let some of his good workers go. Consequently, the morale at work was low, and this bothered him.[50] Like many other conservatives, he and Peggy had believed that if people would only be honest and persevere, work hard, and save, they could overcome any obstacles. But now, they were beginning to wonder if individual initiative was all that it took to succeed.

During this difficult time, Peggy spent much of her time nursing her father through illnesses and John, too, had to be hospitalized twice for his ulcer. She was still not well herself and was often confined to bed with back pain as a result of helping her father. She also complained about her eyes; she thought she had strained them from reading so many illegible old records, letters, and faded newsprint.

In spite of the Depression, John received another salary increase in 1932, indicating his value to the company and making him feel that his job was secure for as long as he wanted to keep it. He was finally able to pay all their old medical debts; buy Peggy a new car, a green four-door Chevrolet; move them into a better apartment; and increase the allotment he had been regularly sending his mother.

11

John told Medora Field Perkerson in an interview for the *Atlanta Journal's Sunday Magazine* in December 1949 that Peggy had written the greater part of her novel "between 1926 and 1930 . . . but it was not a completed book."[51] He said,

> Substantially the story was there in a lot of rough manuscript in so-called chapters, each in a big manila envelope. In these envelopes, along with the original version of a chapter, were many re-writes and notes. I say so-called chapters because, for example, one of the envelopes that she labeled "Road to Tara" contained material which later became four or five chapters of the book. All these many envelopes were stacked on the floor by the typewriter. Notes were scribbled on the outsides and as time went on the envelopes got pretty grubby looking.

The book had no title and the heroine's name was still Pansy. However, the story of the heroine was fairly well developed now, and even though the narrative had many gaps, the creative job was practically over. John went on to tell Medora,

> From 1930 to 1935 she worked on the book only now and then. She had reached the point where most of the creative job was done and there was nothing more to do except the drudgery of turning a rough manuscript into a finished one. If you think you have something good and intend to offer it to a publisher, you don't mind this hard work, but if you don't intend even to offer it, why bother?

As a specific example of what remained to be done, he referred to the chapter that summarizes the Reconstruction in Georgia and said that finishing this chapter "meant a lot of research had to be done and then boiled down. Why should she go to all that trouble when she probably would never send the manuscript to an editor?" As John's remarks to Medora reveal, Peggy had no intention of submitting her book for publication. Her novel was intended only for her and John's entertainment.

Except for chapters 2 and 3, which John had neatly typed on white paper, most of what she had was poorly typed on yellow paper and amply marked in pencil in her and John's handwriting. Because she did not work from the front of the story to the end, but wrote the ending first and then worked her way frontward in a haphazard fashion, many of the chapters were not numbered. Because she did not work steadily, she sometimes forgot what she had written earlier and produced additional versions of the same scene. Some sections of the manuscript were over six years old and soiled and torn in places. Some pages were crumpled because they had been thrown away and then retrieved. The large yellow envelopes into which literally thousands of pages had been crammed were in as poor shape as their contents.

Years later, Peggy said that the only times John ever got angry with her were the times she threatened to throw that "old stuff" away.[52] However, if she had been serious about throwing the manuscript away she would have done so by the fall of 1932 when they moved into a larger, much nicer apartment, one of the Russell Apartments, at 4 East 17th Street. But she did not throw any of it away.

Unlike their place on Crescent Avenue, this new apartment had large windows, letting in lots of light. And it had heat. "In La Dump," John wrote his mother, "we battened down all the windows in early fall and never opened them again until spring, preferring foul air to permitting any of our little supply of heat to escape. Here we are forced to throw open all of the windows at least once a day."[53] Peggy painted the dining room in her favorite color, watermelon pink; the living room, apple green; and all the woodwork, white. She used cream-colored lace curtains at the windows and bought an exquisite oriental rug for the living room floor. She wallpapered the bedroom and the bathroom in a floral pattern of bright pinks, creams, and greens.[54] From her father's house, she brought some lovely old pieces that dated to before the Civil War and had somehow survived it. She had some fine Victorian furniture from her Stephens grandparents' farmhouse, including a walnut wash stand with a marble top. Peggy was particularly fond of this piece and placed it in her living room. This apartment also had a special feature—a glassed-in porch, called a sun parlor in those days. It was furnished with white wicker furniture with colorful cushions in greens, yellows, and pinks. They used this porch, which was about eleven feet by twelve, as their office for the book work, thus keeping their formal living room and dining room neat.

Once settled in her pretty new home, Peggy turned the housekeeping over to Bessie and went right back to her fantasy world of Tara and its inhabitants, whom she loved, particularly the one whom she later sympa-thetically called "my poor Scarlett."[55] Soon, her new writing area was as untidy as the old one had been. On the floor next to her little typing table, the stack of envelopes containing the manuscript kept growing fuller and taller.

A letter from John to his mother in early December 1932 refers to Peggy's trouble with her eyes, and it shows that he was still working on the novel too, despite his demanding work schedule.

> Right now I am writing on our sun parlor with a window open, on the second of December. . . . Peggy's eyes are better and she is beginning to commence to start work on the novel again which means that I am back at my problem of trying to figure out an opening chapter for the book. This time I am approaching the problem by studying the way other novelists get their books going. And in the process am making at least a first chapter acquaintance with several good books I hadn't previously read.

12

Although they lived in different parts of the country now and all had their own families, the Marsh children were close and kept up with one another. John's brothers, Henry and Gordon, and their wives made frequent trips to Atlanta and to the Georgia Power cabin near Tallulah Falls, where they enjoyed long weekend vacations. And for years they never missed getting together with John and Peggy to see University of Kentucky-Georgia Tech ball games. While their mother was alive, all of the children circulated the Round Robin letters that they hated to write but loved to receive. Also, they all got together at least once a year for reunions. Every year Mrs. Marsh, who loved to travel, took turns visiting each of them. When they were all gathered together, they did as families do and talked about their children.[56] Because Peggy and John were the only childless couple in the large family, they were asked about "their book." John was always more enthusiastic in talking about it than Peggy. In reminiscing years later, Francesca said,

> Writing that book took years. It just sort of grew up and along with them. It was a wonderful pastime for her while she was having trouble with her foot and John wasn't making much money. And at first, we all believed that Peggy would really write a book. Though to be perfectly honest, after several years passed, not one of us expected a real book to materialize. Whenever we would ask about it, Peggy used to say, "Oh, it's awful, and I want to throw it away but John gets furious whenever I say that." Then she'd try to change the subject, and she would shush John from talking too much about it either. They were very close, you know, as childless couples often are. After a while, none of us ever asked them about the book for fear of offending them. Still, whenever we visited them in Atlanta, we saw those envelopes piled high.

One relative remembered seeing some envelopes stuffed into the bathroom towel cabinet and a few crammed under a fallen cushion on the sofa. Jim Davis said that for a while, in the Crescent Avenue apartment, Peggy used a stack of envelopes to prop up a corner of their old, green-velvet Victorian sofa until she got its broken leg repaired.[57]

John's family were not the only people who wondered what was going on with Peggy's novel. Friends, too, remembered seeing those mysterious, ubiquitous envelopes. At the Power Company socials, where she was popular, Peggy would often be laughingly hailed as the "great novelist" and asked, "How's that great American novel coming along?" She would either laugh frostily and shout something back, or purse her lips tightly and stare through narrow little slits of eyes that said, "Go to Hell!"[58] One of her friends said that Peggy reached the point where she took umbrage at any reference to her book. She thought that she and John had made a big mistake in ever mentioning the book, and as time passed and it became increasingly difficult to explain why no actual book had yet appeared, she grew to resent any comment or question about it. Sensitive to her feelings, John now had become noticeably quiet about it too, even with his family.

Not everyone liked or admired Peggy, partly because she was so open about her dislike for some people. Some women made catty remarks not only behind her back but also to her face about her pretending to be a writer.[59] Some gossips even poked fun at her for saying she was writing a book. Still others thought that if she could write the way she talked, she would have a bestseller.[60] Eight months after Macmillan bought the manuscript, Lois Cole said that one of her and Peggy's mutual friends had been "catty about Peggy's never-finished novel," until Lois startled her with the news about Peggy's contract.[61] The truth is that apparently no one—family, friend, or foe—believed that the ebullient little Peggy Mitchell Marsh was a serious writer capable of writing a novel, particularly one of the consequence and breadth of *Gone With the Wind*. Whatever the reason, the consensus was one of shock when her novel not only finally appeared, but became so gloriously successful.

13

In 1927, shortly after Peggy started working on her novel, Lois Dwight Cole, a Smith graduate from the Brahmin New England Dwight family, had been transferred from New York to Atlanta to run the southern branch of the Macmillan Company's trade department.[62] This was a fortuitous move for Lois Cole and for the Marshes.

To introduce Lois to Atlanta's female literary society, Medora, the grand dame of the Atlanta literati, gave a bridge luncheon at the Piedmont Driving Club. After lunch, when the ladies drew for bridge tables, Lois discovered her partner was Peggy Mitchell, whom she described as "a short, rather plump person with reddish brown hair, very blue eyes, and a few freckles across a slightly uptilted nose." After the cards were dealt, Lois asked,

> "Do you follow any particular conventions, partner?" Our opponents stared, and my partner said solemnly, "Conventions? I don't know any. I just lead from fright. What do you lead from?" "Necessity," I told her, at which she gave a sudden grin.[63]

Lois had a good mind, an excellent education, and an interesting job; she was the kind of woman that Peggy admired and wanted to be like. During refreshments, Peggy leaned close and whispered, "Can you come to supper Wednesday?" Accepting the invitation, Lois later wrote:

Over fried chicken and hot biscuits I discovered that evening that Peggy was one of the best conversationalists and storytellers one could find. Not that she monopolized the talk; she was, as she said, "a good ear," as genuinely interested in what other people had to say as she was in luring them to talk.[64]

Peggy did not offer the invitation with the idea of getting a Macmillan editor to read her manuscript. Strange as it may seem, she honestly had no intention of ever letting anyone, except John, read that manuscript, and certainly not a publisher. Her fear of rejection was so strong and her resentment of criticism so bitter that she was not about to provide an opportunity for either one. She invited Lois Cole to dinner only because she liked her and knew that John would too. Also, she was eager for Lois to meet Allan Taylor, their bachelor friend who worked for the *Journal*. From Tennessee originally, Allan was an old friend of John's; they had been roommates when John first arrived in Atlanta. For years, he had had such a serious infatuation with Peggy that he had reached the point where he annoyed her, much to John's and their friends' amusement.[65] Peggy had long wished that he would find someone else upon whom to heap his devotion, and now she believed she had found that person in Lois Cole.[66] Just as she had hoped, Allan was immediately attracted to the brainy, buxom, good-looking Yankee. The two of them started dating, and before long they married. Later, Peggy said she enjoyed being around Allan much more after he had fallen in love with Lois.[67]

The Macmillan branch office was not far from the Marshes' Crescent Avenue apartment, and Lois, on her way home from work, would frequently drop by in the afternoons to visit. "Once when I came in with a friend, Peggy, in shorts, blouse and eyeshade, was at the typewriter. She got up and threw a bath towel over the table. 'Well, Peggy,' said the friend, 'how's the great American novel coming along?' 'It stinks,' Peggy said with a half-laugh, 'and I don't know why I bother with it, but I've got to do something with my time.'"[68]

As an assistant editor always on the lookout for marketable manuscripts, Lois asked about the book. But Peggy would not discuss it. Intrigued by the envelopes and her friend's silence, Lois urged her to give her a glimpse of the manuscript. Peggy firmly refused. When Lois persisted and told her that "Macmillan would love to see it" when it was done, Peggy answered emphatically, "At this rate it won't ever get done, and no one's going to see it."[69]

In the late fall of 1930, while the nation was in the throes of an economic depression, Macmillan closed the branch offices of its trade department. Lois was transferred to New York, where she was promoted to associate editor. By this time, she and Allan were married and writing a series of juvenile stories under the pseudonym Allan Dwight. A year later, in her new role as an editor, she remembered her southern friend and wrote her a business letter on Macmillan stationery in December 1933. Lois asked Peggy if her novel were finished yet and, if it was, might Macmillan read it? In an equally businesslike fashion, Peggy answered that the novel was not completed and that she doubted it ever would be. But she promised that if she ever did finish it, she would let Macmillan have the first look.[70]

14

When her Grandmother Stephens died on February 17, 1934, Peggy was more profoundly affected than she had ever imagined she would be. She regretted all the arguments she had had with the old woman who had provided her with such a rich legacy of stories, and she regretted creating a break with her grandmother's family, who still had not forgiven her, although that break was by no means all her fault. When her dejection lasted well into the spring, John decided to boost her spirits by arranging a two-week vacation that would allow them to get away and perhaps to research and work on the book. His mother had just visited them, and listening to her talk about her extensive trip around the country got them excited about their plans. The Georgia Press Association conferences that they attended every year usually initiated their vacations. That year the conference was in Savannah.

No matter how far their destination, the Marshes never drove more than two hundred miles in one day.[71] When John worked, he worked hard and steadily, but when he vacationed, he rested. "Our plan is to dawdle along the way, going down one route and coming back another, visiting with folks in the various en route," John wrote his mother on June 16, 1934. In preparing for the trip, Peggy—now having problems with her feet—visited a Mr. Minor, who was making a pair of shoes for her. "Since the morning you left," she wrote Mother Marsh, "I have spent about half of each day at Mr. Minor's trying to get these blasted shoes in shape. At first, I asked for beauty and perfect comfort. Now, I would thank Heaven to be just able to walk in the things even if they did hurt. . . . I do so hate to wear my heavy black winter brogues with white dresses and almost wept at the thought of going to the editors' party where every one dresses fit to kill and having to wear my black gun boats."[72]

Around the end of June 1934, they began their trip, which John described as their "most ambitious" automobile vacation, and they brought sections of the manuscript and the typewriter along.[73] With Peggy chauffeuring, they did travel Georgia from one end to the other. They started out by going to the Press Association Conference in Savannah, one of their favorite places to study black dialect, which was interestingly not all the same. The only dialect spoken in Savannah and the Golden Islands was Geechee, a term derived from the Indian name of the Ogeechee River. The history of this dialect went back decades earlier to the time when shiploads of blacks were sold to the Golden Islands plantations. The slaves left on the islands were cut off from the mainland, and thus they kept their native language. As late as 1934 when the Marshes were visiting, the dialect still retained many African words and was difficult to understand by anyone except the natives of Savannah and the Golden Islands.[74] When she and John visited Savannah, they studied the dialect, took notes on it, and practiced speaking it with each other, and yet Peggy wrote as late as 1938 that she still had trouble understanding some of it.[75]

In addition to Geechee was another, somewhat similar dialect known as "Gullah," spoken only by the blacks around Charleston, South Carolina. Fascinated with the speech, John and Peggy took many notes on it. For instance, when they visited Magnolia Gardens in Charleston, they made notes on how their guides combined English with Gullah, recording "get" for "gate," "race" for "rice," and "ef" or "effen" for "if."[76]

Equally fascinated by speech variations, John and Peggy took many notes on all they heard as they visited various southern locales, and they became experts on all the southern dialects. In one area, they noted that "did" was used for "if," as in "did I pick up a snake I would be a fool."[77] They noted that "middle Georgia darkies (around Macon) have different constructions from the North Georgia ones. And those from the older sections of the state around Washington, Ga., have some pronunciations and constructions that are practically Elizabethan."[78] They also made careful distinctions between the dialects of field workers and house servants during the Civil War and Reconstruction eras.[79] His coworkers remembered how John delighted in listening to different dialects as he traveled around the state and said that he often made notes about the various ways words were pronounced.

Although most readers of *Gone With the Wind* do not realize it, the dialects in the novel are the result of much painstaking research and writing, and as such they preserve an interesting bit of history that otherwise may have been lost forever. For one of many examples, Peggy made her wonderful character Mammy a Savannah black who had lived in north Georgia for twenty years. If readers will notice in *Gone With the Wind,* Mammy's Geechee dialect is different from that used by the other blacks in the novel. Peggy and John were very proud of the dialect as it appears in the novel, and she bristled when anyone, not as enlightened as she about the subject, criticized her use of it.

Before going home that summer, they went to a cabin in a beautiful, secluded area near Tallulah Falls so that they could work on the manuscript without any interruptions and, no doubt, while the dialects were still fresh in their minds. In writing to his brother Henry about the place during this time, John showed that he had dialects on his mind because he spelled the names phonetically. He wrote "T'roar-ah" and "Tal-lu-lah," and referred to a "Mr. Meschine," who he said was the operator at the plant who looked after his affairs there.[80]

This cabin was owned by the Georgia Power Company and given to John to use for business as well as personal purposes. About two miles away, one of Georgia Power's hydroelectric plants and company villages was built near the Tallulah River Falls. The river meanders its way for about six miles around the stony shoulders of a mountain until it comes to a place so deep and narrow that the force of its descent against the rocks is so rapid and awe-inspiring that the Indians called the falls "Terrora," their word for "terrible." The Marshes loved this quiet place. It was where they had spent their honeymoon nearly a decade earlier and where Peggy often hid away from the public immediately after she became famous.[81]

After the long vacation, they returned to the cabin in late September when Henry and his new wife, Mary Hunter, joined them there, along with some of their newspaper friends, for a long weekend vacation.[82] On such weekends as this, John was the chef. He barbecued ribs, broiled steaks and potatoes, and cooked big pots of chili. In Peggy's old photograph album, there is a wonderful faded snapshot taken of her and the others sitting outside of this cabin. Dressed in a sleeveless shirt and shorts, sitting cross-legged in a lawn chair, she has her short hair tied back with a ribbon and an impish smile on her face. She looks beautiful and happy in this picture.

15

Shortly after midnight, on November 22, 1934, an accident involving the Marshes and a drunk driver occurred. With eerie foreshadowing, this accident took place in almost the exact location on Peachtree where Peggy later suffered her fatal accident. Rain had poured all day, and around midnight the Marshes were taking their dinner guest, *Journal* editor John S. Cohen, home. With Cohen in the front seat with her, Peggy was driving cautiously as she always did; the roads were wet and slick. When she started into the block between Peachtree Place and Eighth Street going south, getting ready to turn left, she asked John, who was sitting in the back seat, to see if any cars were coming. He said no. A few seconds later, they all saw the reflected headlights of an automobile coming fast from behind them. Peggy decided not to make the left turn, put out her hand to signal a stop, and slowed to a stop. There was no traffic on the street going in either direction, and they thought the car would pass them either on the left or the right. Instead, it slammed a solid blow into the center of the rear of the Marshes' car, knocking it some forty or fifty feet. Knocked unconscious momentarily, Peggy managed to jerk the wheel around so that the car did not hit the telephone pole at which it was headed. She suffered spinal injuries from the jerk when the other car hit them in the rear, and then again when she pulled the wheel around to prevent her car from crashing into the pole. Shouting to the other driver to stop, John ran over to him. The man, named Littlejohn, had a strong odor of whiskey on his breath, and he did not deny that he had run into them.

Neither Cohen nor John sustained any injuries, but for the remainder of that year Peggy wore a backbrace and was confined to bed because of back pain. For months she regularly visited Dr. Sandison, an Atlanta specialist who administered electric therapeutic treatments, and Dr. Mizell, the Marshes' family physician, who had been treating her for arthritis.

After the New Year's holidays, on January 20, 1935, John told his mother that his wife, "a real trouper," was feeling better and getting out a little. Both loved movies and had gone that day to see *The Lives of a Bengal Lancer*. He wrote, "She walks for exercise even if it does hurt her . . . life is beginning to get back to a somewhat more normal basis for us." But John told his mother that he had failed in his attempts to measure Peggy for a knitted dress Mrs. Marsh had offered to make for Peggy. He explained, "Her measurements, bust and waist, do vary enormously when she is practicing inflation and deflation and when sitting and standing, and I didn't consider myself a sufficiently competent architect to attempt to get her plans and specifications to you."[83]

16

That's how things stood, with nothing eventful happening, until April 1935 when Harold Latham, a vice-president of Macmillan Publishing Company, went on a scouting trip to the South. Having gone on scouting trips abroad, found good English authors unknown in the States, and successfully published their works, Latham thought he would roam around his own country looking for new books.

Caroline Miller, a Georgia writer, had won the Pulitzer Prize for 1934 with her novel *Lamb in His Bosom,* and perhaps for this reason Latham decided to tour the South in the spring of 1935.[84] When Lois heard about his tour, she said, "I told Mr. Latham about Peggy's book—that no one had read it except her husband John, but that if she wrote as she talks it would be a honey."[85] For that reason alone, Latham decided Atlanta would be his first stop.[86]

Lois told Latham how stubborn Peggy was about refusing to talk about her work, but she hoped that he, a mild-mannered, persuasive man, might be able to convince Peggy to let him see her manuscript. Lois also wrote to Peggy and to Medora asking them to make her boss's visit pleasant and productive. Thus, by working from both ends of the exchange, she hoped to accomplish her mission.[87]

Medora and Peggy took Latham to lunch at the Athletic Club and during their conversation, Medora told him that if he were looking for a novel about the South, "Peggy is your best bet." Latham turned to Peggy, asking her if she had a manuscript he could see. Leaving him the impression that she did not want to discuss her book, she answered emphatically, "No, I have no novel." Her reply demonstrates her lack of confidence in her manuscript, for most unpublished writers would have jumped at such an opportunity.

After lunch Medora, who had to go back to work at the *Magazine,* suggested that Peggy drive Latham out to Druid Hills to see the dogwood in bloom, and also show him Stone Mountain. During their drive, as they talked about southern literature, Latham asked Peggy again about her own work. Firmly but pleasantly, she told him again she was not ready to talk about it or to submit it.

The next day, Latham was the guest at a luncheon and tea given for Georgia writers by Rich's department store, which was exhibiting Georgia books and manuscripts. At this gathering, Latham approached Peggy more than once about her book and each time she replied, "I have no manuscript to show you." He was disappointed because his interest in her had been stimulated by his conversations with her and by the talk he had heard about her.[88]

In a letter to Lois Cole written several months later, Peggy described what had happened that day of the luncheon at Rich's.

> And that day he was here, I'd called up various and sundry hopeful young authors and would-be authors and jackassed them (that is a friend's phrase) about in the car and gotten them to the tea where they could actually meet a live publisher in the flesh.
>
> One of them was a child who had nearly driven me crazy about her book. I'd no more than get settled at my own work than here she was, bellowing that she couldnt write love scenes and couldn't I write them for her? Or she was on the phone picking my brains for historical facts that had taken me weeks to run down. As twilight eve was drawing on and I was riding her and some of

her adoring girl friends home from the teas, somebody asked me when I expected to get my book finished and why hadn't I given it to Mr. Latham.

Then this child cried, "Why, are you writing a book, Peggy? How strange you've never said anything about it. Why didn't you give it to Mr. Latham?" I said I hadn't because it was so lousy I was ashamed of it. To which she remarked—and did not mean it cattily—

"Well, I daresay. Really, I wouldn't take you for the type who would write a successful book. You know you don't take life seriously enough to be a novelist. . . . But, Peggy, I think you are wasting your time trying. You really aren't the type."[89]

With that remark, Peggy said, "I got so mad that I began to laugh, and I had to stop the car because I laughed so hard. And that confirmed their opinion of my lack of seriousness." Deciding then that she would give Latham the manuscript, she said, "My idea was that at least I could brag that I had been refused by the very best publisher."

After she delivered all the ladies to their own residences, she went directly home and called John at his office to tell him what had happened. She explained that Mr. Latham had asked her again about her manuscript and wanted to read it, and she asked him what he thought she ought to do.[90] John said, "Sure, let him have it. It can't do any harm and at least it will give us the opinion of somebody who would know whether it is worth the trouble of finishing or not."[91] Peggy, greatly agitated by now, was still not sure, and when John came home early from work, they talked some more. He convinced her that she ought to let the publisher have a look at it. Realizing that Latham was to leave by train at 7:30 P.M., they started rushing around the apartment gathering the envelopes and trying to get them into some kind of sensible order.

In a letter to Mother Marsh on April 17, 1936, Peggy described this important evening in her own comical manner:

It wasn't till I was in the lobby of his hotel that I realized what I looked like, hatless, hair flying, dust and dirt all over my face and arms and worse luck, my hastily rolled up stocking coming down about my ankles. As I progressed toward him in the lobby, I kept dropping envelopes and finally had three bell boys picking them up behind me. I only wish someone had picked up my stockings for I couldn't pull them up as my hands were occupied. Mr. Latham was a perfect gentleman and kept a straight face and acted as though all authors looked like me. I later heard in a round about way that he said that he never saw so small an author, so large a manuscript, and so dirty a face.[92]

According to Latham's own account, around six o'clock, shortly before he was to leave Atlanta, the telephone rang in his hotel room and "Miss Mitchell's voice came over it, informing me that she was downstairs in the lounge and would like to see me. I went down, and I shall never forget the mental picture that I have of her at that time—a tiny woman sitting on a divan, with the biggest manuscript beside her that I have ever seen, towering in two stacks almost to her shoulders."[93]

Talking very quickly lest she change her mind, Peggy explained that the manuscript was rough and incomplete and that some chapters had several versions. And adding that she had no first chapter, she told him, "I hadn't any idea of letting you or any publisher see it. I wrote it for my own entertainment. However, your comments about southern authors and southern books in our conversation yesterday have aroused my interest, and I am curious to know what you think of this one. You can't possibly be more surprised at being given it as I am at letting you take it."[94]

Excited about securing the manuscript, Latham asked her all sorts of questions, such as how she came to write it and what it was about. "Although many people in Atlanta knew that the book had been undertaken," he wrote, "no one seemed to have any facts on its theme." Peggy answered most of his questions, but she could not explain why she had been so secretive about it. Latham wrote:

> Why she had been hesitant about letting anyone see it—up to that time it had been shown to no one except her husband—is a question I cannot answer. . . . The book was very close to her. It represented hours of affectionate attention to details, and perhaps she did not wish to run the risk of rejection for publication, as that would have hurt. After all, how sure could she be of a friendly attitude from a northern publisher toward a book about the Civil War by a southerner?[95]

With limited luggage space, Latham had a bellboy rush out to purchase another suitcase into which he could pack the manuscript. On the train to New Orleans that night, he started reading, and the more he read, the more he realized that "here indeed was a significant novel of the South."[96] Although he read only a small portion, he modestly wrote later that he realized immediately that he was reading something of "tremendous importance. Any publisher would have recognized that fact. I was fortunate to have come along at the right moment."[97] He admitted that the physical condition of the manuscript itself was the worst he had ever seen. "But the mere untidiness of the script could not conceal the enchantment of the story."[98] Because he could not carry the voluminous manuscript around on his three-month tour, which was to end in California, he shipped it from New Orleans to Lois in New York.

Just a few days after he left Atlanta with her manuscript, Latham wrote Peggy a letter telling her how much he enjoyed meeting her. He said that although he had read only a small portion of her manuscript, "what I have read is very reassuring. So then, I shall take it or send it along and deal with it, when I get back, with the care which it deserves. I have the feeling that we are going to keep at this project until a novel is issued that is going to be regarded as a very significant publication."[99]

17

On April 16, 1935, the day after she received his letter, Peggy typed him a five-page letter. Trying not to sound too anxious, she dedicated the entire first page to their conversation about her offer to help him "unearth authors." On the second page, she got around to her real concern:

> I cannot tell you how pleased your words of commendation made me and how glad I am if the extracts you read interested you. If I had not met you and realized yours is an honest face, I'd be sure you were joking with me. I know the following confession sounds strange, coming from a would-be author, but you must take it at face value.... I am oppressed with the knowledge of the lousiness of what I write for even though I may not write well, I do know good writing.... I have felt that there was something lacking in me that other authors, real and fancied, possessed, that passionate belief in the good quality of their work. A belief so passionate that they have no qualms about gathering in groups and reading each others stuff. So far, no one but you and my excellent husband, who, after all, did promise "for better or worse" have been the only ones to see that five pound load of manuscript I foisted off on you. God knows, I am neither shy nor shamefaced for, as friends frequently point out, I have all the gentle and retiring qualities of a billy-goat but I do marvel that you thought there was anything at all in my stuff.[100]

In these early letters, Peggy had no qualms about mentioning John's reading her manuscript throughout the years she wrote it. Later, however, she would deny it.

In this long letter on April 16, 1935, she explained to Latham that she was "more than a little frightened" of his careful reading of her manuscript and proceeded to give him advance warning of its weaknesses. "The first chapter is missing. Second and third chapter are not even satisfactory first drafts. Brief, page and a half explanatory chapter at the end of part one missing (that shoots all of part one to hell and gone)." Parts two and three "stand up pretty well" but were not finished. She was conscious of "a terrible sag of interest and action somewhere between parts 3 and 4," and said that she had started to rewrite the entire five chapters but her injuries from a car wreck had prohibited her from doing so.

She informed him that there were two versions of part 4, "one having Frank Kennedy die in his bed, the second where he is killed in a brush between Federal troops and Ku Klux Klan. I had not finished this second version. I think this would be very confusing to any reader and I don't see how you made heads or tails of it."

A very important chapter, involving Melanie's extricating Pansy and Ashley from a scandal, was missing in part 4 because, she said, she "had not been strong enough to sit in Miss Jessie Hopkins library and hold ten pound files on my stomach." Also, a vast amount of political and social background of the early 1850s and the late 1860s was needed in part 4. "The story is appallingly thin on back ground towards the end," she warned him.

Another item she intended to change was "to right her wrong of making the Southern view appear to advance the notion that only the ladies were valiant" during the Reconstruction period.[101]

Referring to the fact that some envelopes included three or four versions of the same chapters, she explained, "They were put there for my husband's convenience in comparing and throwing away."[102] Earlier, she had told Henry that John could always tell her "what was crap," and that was why she saved all the versions.[103] She ended her letter to Latham by saying:

> So because of the above listed reasons, I fear that your Macm. readers may have a dreadfully difficult time making heads or tails of the stuff. What do you think? If, after you have read more you find that *you* get some continuity out of the story, then take it on to New York with my appreciation and thanks. But if on further reading, you find it too scrambled to be intelligible, send it back to me and I will remove the extra versions and where chapters are missing, put in a brief summary of what is contained in those missing chapters.
>
> I leave this in your hands. You decide whether to take it with you or send it back to me for straightening out. No, I do not mind if it is not returned until June. It will take until June for my back

to recover enough to sit for hours at a typewriter and perhaps not then, spinal injuries being slow at healing.[104]

In her closing, she is clear about wanting to get Latham's opinion, about trusting his judgment. She did not ask him, at this point, to return either of her manuscripts, for she had given him two: "'Ropa Carmagin" and *Gone With the Wind,* though the latter did not bear its title at that time.

Just as she was about to seal her letter, the morning mailman handed her another letter from Latham, telling her how wonderful he thought her manuscript was and thanking her for helping him in his search for authors. Exuberant about receiving two letters full of warm praise from the publisher, she added a postscript: "Thank you again for your encouraging words. I'm sure they'll have a more healing affect on my back than all the braces, electrical treatments, and operations the doctors devise.... We hope you unearth a Pulitzer prize winner here [in Atlanta] so it will be necessary for you to come back to Atlanta and stay awhile."

Little did she, or John, suspect at that moment that her book would win the Pulitzer Prize for being the finest American novel of 1936.

18

After those warmly enthusiastic letters from Latham in April, she expected to hear from him regularly. When the end of May rolled around without a word from him, she began to get anxious. By now, she thought, surely he had had time to read her manuscript. Why wasn't he writing to her? Hoping to jog his memory, she wrote him on May 30, 1935, describing her efforts to find promising authors for him. Not wanting to be pushy, she did not mention being concerned about her own manuscript although she was dying to know what was happening with it.

Her letter did indeed evoke a response, but not the kind she wanted. On June 10, Latham wrote saying that he had just returned to New York and had fallen into Macmillan's fall sales conference. Because his work had been delayed, he had not been able to read any manuscripts, but he said, "It was very nice of you to keep unearthing all these books for me, and I appreciate it very much." He did not mention a word about her manuscript.

Terribly disappointed, she imagined the worst possible scenario, the most humiliating kind of rejection. No amount of reassurance from John could calm her. She was utterly dejected. She was convinced that she had made a fool of herself letting the publisher have the manuscript in its poor shape. She knew that he thought she was an incompetent, and, being the nice man he was, he was trying to figure out a nice way to tell her. Ignoring John's advice to be patient, she decided she would rescue herself by asking

Latham to return the manuscript before he had a chance to send it back.

What she did not know was that Latham had sent the manuscript to Lois Cole so that she and his other advisors could read it. About that manuscript, Lois Cole later wrote:

> It was physically, one of the worst manuscripts I have ever seen. There was no first chapter, but Chapter Two was neatly typed on white paper. So was Chapter Three. Then came pages and pages of yellow paper, written over in pencil, and often three or four different versions of one scene. Then came more final chapters, then some would be missing entirely. There were two entirely different accounts of Frank's death. The last chapter was in its final form, for that, she told me later, was written first.
>
> In spite of the difficulties of reading the manuscript, I knew it was one of the most fascinating novels of all time.[105]

After Latham returned to New York in late May, he completed reading the manuscript himself and then quickly sent it to his friend Charles Everett, professor of English at Columbia University, whom Latham often asked for advice about manuscripts. Having no way of knowing what was going on, Peggy let her worst fears overcome her and, on July 9, she wrote Latham:

> I know that when a would-be author is lucky enough to have an editor looking over her stuff, she is a fool to write and ask to have her manuscript back. But that is just what I'm doing because I am very anxious to finish the thing and begin rewriting it. As to why I can't wait two or three months to start finishing it—that's a long story which I'll try to relate shortly. At present, I am out of my spinal brace and can sit up at the typewriter for an hour or so at a time for the first time in seven months. I am one of those clumsy or unlucky people who are always being run into by drunken autoists, sat on by horses, struck playfully with bottles by guests. Or I get influenza or a return of arthritis. Or some of my friends have babies and demand my presence at the birth. The last is far worse than the catastrophes listed before. At present, I am able to work and very anxious to work. However, knowing my past record, I realize that it is only a matter of time before I have an arm in a sling or my skull fractured again. With me, writing is sandwiched in between broken bones and x-rays and, as I am all in one piece at present it looks like flying in the face of Providence not to take advantage of it. So could I have my manuscript back, please?

When I look back on giving it to you I shudder at what I unloaded on you and marvel at my own gall—or thoughtlessness. In the shape it was in I dont see how you made heads or tails of it. Perhaps you didnt! If you have any suggestions and criticisms, I would be most humbly grateful for them if you have time to write me about it. And if you havent the time, I'll understand. I don't believe even you can see as many things wrong with it as I do or can think it as rotten as I think it. However, wrong or rotten, I want to finish it.

I have tried to work without the manuscript but have found it impossible as it has been so many months since I even reread it that I can't pick up the threads again. And besides I was just in the middle of cutting out about ten chapters at one place and putting in five chapters at another place. So I am all mixed up. . . .

I hope you do not mind my asking for my stuff and hope you understand. If you don't, ask Lois Cole. She saw me through innumerable broken bones, arthritis attacks, child births-of-friends and gall-stones-in-the-family.[106]

Her letter arrived before Latham had received his advisors' evaluations on the manuscript. Sensing her apprehension, he answered on July 15, "Of course, if you insist on having your manuscript back immediately I will get it from our reader, but I do hope you will not insist but will give me a week or so more."[107] He explained that he had given it to one of their "best and most trusted advisers, a man in whose judgment I have a good deal of confidence." Latham said that he had taken the liberty of removing from the envelopes what seemed to be duplicate sections or first versions and added, "I hope you don't mind." He was unable at that time to give her a final decision but told her, "I am very enthusiastic about the possibilities your book presents. I believe if it is finished properly, it will have every chance of a very considerable success, and for me you have created in Pansy a character who is vital and unforgettable."[108]

On the same day that she received Latham's letter, July 17, she answered it.

By all means keep "Pansy" longer if you feel it necessary. My sympathy goes out to the unfortunate reader who is trying to make heads and tails of it in its present disarranged form. As matters now stand, I am very glad you did not return the manuscript immediately for I would not have been able to resume work on it. Bessie, the black jewel of our kitchen, has meningitis and I have spent my time recently in the ward of our charity hospital savaging interns. Bessie seems to have a good chance for recovery now and, if I don't get meningitis, too, I should be free to work in a week or so. So keep "Pansy" a while longer if you like.[109]

19

When Professor Everett's rave comments and excellent summary of the novel reached him, Latham was convinced his first impression of the manuscript was correct and knew Macmillan had to buy it quickly. Everett's excitement, which remains evident throughout his writing, comes through clearly in his beginning. "There really are surprisingly few loose ends, and the number of times one's emotions are stirred one way or another is surprising. I am sure that it is not only a good book, but a best seller. It is much better than Stark Young's.[110] The literary device of using an unsympathetic character to arouse sympathetic emotions seems to me admirable. This is the story of the formation of a woman's character. In the peace and quiet of plantation life before the war, in the crisis of the Civil War, and in the privation of the Reconstruction period."

Everett concluded, "This book is really magnificent. Its human qualities would make it good against any background, and when they are shown on the stage of the Civil War and reconstruction the effect is breathtaking. Furthermore, it has a high degree of literary finish. . . . By all means take the book. It can't possibly turn out badly. With a clean copy made of what we have, a dozen lines could bridge the existing gaps."

Then he suggested two changes, both of which were bad pieces of advice, as it turned out. Interestingly enough, he did not like the ending, which he called "disappointing," and he wanted to use *Another Day* for the title. But without any equivocation, he instructed Latham, "Take the book at once. Tell the author not to do anything to it but bridge the few obvious gaps and strengthen the last page."[111]

Excited about this manuscript, Latham sent the following memorandum to his assistants: "It is a book of tremendous importance and significance, of that I have not the slightest doubt. We shall make a serious mistake if we do not immediately take it. . . . The manuscript is not in its final form but all that will be needed to put it into its final form will be the spur that will come with a contract. I feel more strongly about this proposition than I feel about any novel that has been in our hands for some time."[112] His enthusiasm, along with Lois Cole's and Everett's, swayed the editorial council, who agreed that Macmillan ought to take the manuscript.

On July 17, Latham sent the following telegram to Peggy: "My enthusiasm [for] your novel shared by our advisers. We would like to make immediate contract for its publication. Five hundred dollars advance. Half on signing. Balance on delivery manuscript. Account ten percent royalty first ten thousand then fifteen. My renewed congratulations and assurances. We undertake publication with tremendous enthusiasm and large hopes. Do wire your approval that I may contract immediately."[113]

Lois was so happily excited about her colleagues' and Everett's reactions to the manuscript that she sent Peggy a telegram saying: "Macmillan terribly excited about your book. I am most excited of all. Always knew you had a world beater even if no one could see it. Company planning great things for the book. How soon can you finish it?" Then she mailed a copy of Everett's evaluation to Peggy, who read it in amazement. For someone who had always been so sensitive about not having a college education, such praise from a professor of English at Columbia University made her dizzy, and it surely must have made John proud. Lois saved the response Peggy wired back to her:

Lois, your telegram just came and I am overwhelmed! It came at a grand time for I was just limping home from Grady hospital to lick my wounds, having been scragged by a young intern whom *I* have scragged several times in the course of Bessie's illness. Do you really mean they like it? You wouldn't fox an old friend, would you? I don't see how anyone made heads or tails of it. I am very twittery about your wire and, having phoned John and read it to him, he said, "You'd better sit down quietly so you'll have less distance to fall when the realization comes over you that someone besides me likes the damn thing." Well, John was right. I think I had better sit down quietly. I shall fall down in another minute. You are a lamb to send me such a swell telegram and I shall frame it.[114]

On July 27, 1935, a jubilant Peggy typed a four-page letter to Latham telling him that she certainly "had not expected so swell a report and it was only by bearing up sturdily that I kept from going to bed again with luminal and ice packs."[115]

About Professor Everett's suggestions, she said she only wished he had made more of them. He was absolutely right in saying that "the author should keep out her own feelings in one or two places where she talks about negro rule." She explained: "I hope I would have caught it in my rewrite—or that my husband would have done so but perhaps we wouldn't have. I have tried to keep out venom, bias, bitterness as much as possible. All the V, B & B in the book were to come through the eyes and head and tongues of the characters, as reactions from what they saw and heard and felt." About Everett's criticism of her describing Mammy's "ape face" and her "black paws," she said she did not remember exactly where those phrases were but she would track them down and change them. "I meant no disrespect to Mammy for I have heard so many negroes refer to their hands as 'black paws' and when an old and wrinkled negro woman is sad, there is nothing else in the world she looks like except a large ape. But I had not realized how differently this sounded in type."[116]

Professor Everett's criticism about the ending was, of course, wrong. He wrote, "There may be a bit too much finality in Rhett's refusal to go on. . . . And it might not hurt to hint as much a little more strongly than the last lines."[117] Peggy responded:

> I havent reread that part of the book in over two years. Due to my unfortunate habit of writing things backwards, last chapter first and first last, it's been a long time since I even looked at it and hardly recall what's in it. But he's probably right. My own intention when I wrote it was to leave the ending open to the reader (yes, I know that's not a satisfactory way to do!). My idea was that, through several million chapters, the reader will have learned that both Pansy and Rhett are tough characters, both accustomed to having their own way. And at the last, both are determined to have their own ways and those ways are very far apart. And the reader can either decide that she got him or she didnt. Could I ask you to with hold final criticism on this part until I have rewritten that and sent you the whole book to look over again? My vague memory tells me that I had done no more on that chapter than synopsize it. Perhaps a rewriting would bring it more closely to what the adviser wanted.[118]

About the two different versions of Frank Kennedy's death, the first by an illness and the second by the Ku Klux Klan, Everett said that he liked the death by illness because "K.K.K. material has been worked pretty hard by others." But Peggy justified her reason for preferring the second version. In rereading that part of the book, she had found "a very definite sag of interest over a range of six chapters. As 'Alice' would have said 'There was no conversation and absolutely no pictures' in that part. I was trying to build up that section in strength—and, by 'strength' I don't mean a lot of melodramatic incident." She asked if she could complete the book with the second, K.K.K. version, and if Latham and his advisors did not like it, she would change it to the first version. "God knows, I dont love that second version for its own sake. . . . The same applies to remarks written above about the ending. If you dont like the way it looks when you get the final copy, tell me so and I'll change it. I'll change it any way you want, except to make a happy ending."[119]

In this July 27 letter to Latham, she mentioned two other issues. The first had to do with the main character's name, which she was beginning to dislike.

> When I began this book and called the central character "Pansy," the unpleasant connotation of the word had barely reached the South. It is still not a popular term as I gather it is in other sections. Here, we refer to Pansies as Fairies or by another less euphemistic but far more descriptive term. However, if you think the name of Pansy should be changed please let me know and I will try to think of another name, equally inappropriate.[120]

In responding to Latham's two questions: "When is Ella born?" and "Where does Archie come into the story?" Peggy said that at the risk of further confusing him, she was sending him an incomplete draft of the chapters containing those two characters. She apologized for the chapters not having numbers and said, "The best way I can place them is to say that they come after the chapter on Gerald's death."

In a postscript, she asked for a little leeway on the title because her list of titles was missing. Bessie, her "black pearl," the only one who knew where everything was in the apartment, had been ill and she had to wait for her return before she would know where the list was. She added: "'Tomorrow is Another Day' was my first choice but someone's just used that. And 'Tote the Weary Load' came next though I think that's too colloquial."[121]

Concerned about her not mentioning the contract, Latham wrote her on July 30 saying he hoped that by now she had received it and had found it satisfactory. If it were not, he wanted to know how she wanted it changed: "I'll see what I can do about it. I shan't be entirely happy until the contract is an accomplished fact, you see." He liked her suggestion that they withhold the Pansy-Rhett outcome until the book was in its final form and wrote: "In fact, I think that's what we want to do with everything." He made it clear that Macmillan wanted to help her in every way. "We have large faith in this book—very large faith indeed—and we want it to be the best possible book that it can be." He assured her that they would spare no effort to bring that about, and once they published it they would spare no effort to make it the success that they were confident it would be. He added:

> And now I'll tell you a secret. I myself rather prefer the Ku Klux Klan ending to the other. I let Everett say his say on that

subject, but I don't altogether agree with him. I think your reason for the K.K.K. episode is a good one. I don't feel that the book sags anywhere—not for one chapter or one page—but I do think this K.K.K. material adds color and excitement, etc. So here, as in the case of other matters, follow your judgment. . . .

I do have the feeling that what you intimate might exist in some quarters in regard to the name "Pansy." The connotation of this name is not pleasant in certain circles, and, if you find another name that is as appropriately inappropriate, I should be in favor of making the change, I think.[122]

At that time the manuscript had no title; it was called simply "A Novel about the South." Wanting to give her as much leeway as she wished, Latham said he thought "Another Day" was a better title than "Tomorrow Is Another Day" but he was a bit afraid of using "Tote That Weary Load." "I wish I could make you understand just how I feel about this book," Latham wrote. "I think I am as happy over it as though I had written it myself."[123]

It would be impossible to overstate Latham's editorial role in finding the manuscript or his kind and gentle manner toward its author. His patience and his willingness to work with her and to go along with her instincts about all aspects of the novel were remarkable. Although others, including Lois Cole and Professor Everett, had reservations about certain aspects of the book and suggested changes, Latham never suggested that Peggy change anything except what she wanted to change. About his offer to send her suggestions from his other readers, she said she would welcome any suggestions that he sent her. She urged him not to feel hesitant about telling her what he thought about her "stuff,"

even if you say "this is lousy." All I ask is that you tell me *why* it's lousy. I am not a sensitive plant and can take criticism. Otherwise I should have died of mortification or been divorced long ago. You see, my husband is not only a boss advertisement writer but he was formerly that rare creature, a newspaper reporter who knew the difference between a "shambles" and a "holocaust." He also had a feeling for words and a feeling that there was an exact word for an exact meaning. And before that, he was professor of English at the University of Kentucky. I fear that nothing you or your advisers could say would be quite as hard boiled as what he has already said to me.[124]

C H A P T E R **8** P T E R R

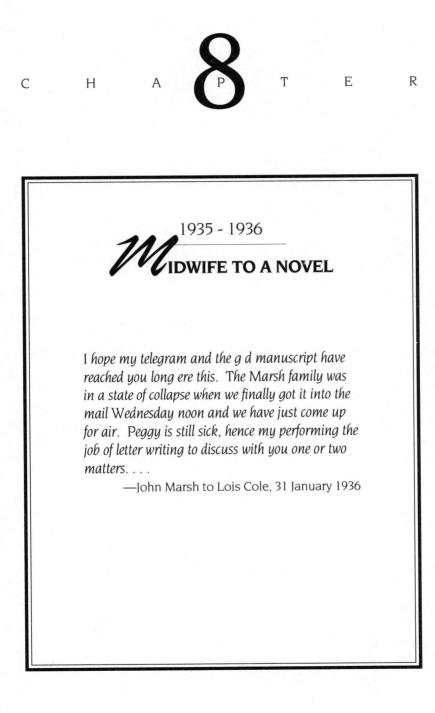

1935 ~ 1936

*M*IDWIFE TO A NOVEL

I *hope my telegram and the g d manuscript have reached you long ere this. The Marsh family was in a state of collapse when we finally got it into the mail Wednesday noon and we have just come up for air. Peggy is still sick, hence my performing the job of letter writing to discuss with you one or two matters. . . .*

—John Marsh to Lois Cole, 31 January 1936

1

ON THE WARM, HUMID MORNING OF AUGUST 1, 1935, when the two-thousand-word contract arrived in the Marshes' apartment, Peggy excitedly rushed to John's office, talking to herself as she drove hurriedly downtown. Once inside the building, she rushed past everyone, including John's secretary, without stopping to chat as she usually did. Waving an envelope in her hand, she strutted into his office, where he was working at his desk. The moment he looked up and saw the exuberant expression on her face, he knew she had the contract. As she plopped on his lap giggling, he opened the envelope and together they silently read it. Oblivious to the onlooking staff, they hugged each other tightly, kissed, and talked in whispers for a few minutes. Then they hurried out to her father's law office to show the contract to him.[1] A real estate attorney inexperienced in reading such contracts, he nevertheless selected some details that he thought Peggy ought to question. As he talked to them, he jotted down three questions he wanted her to ask Latham.

On that very afternoon, back in their apartment, she wrote Latham thanking him for taking a risk with her, an unknown author, and saying that the contract was "not only a fair but a very generous one."[2] Because the publisher had told her about the special promotional activity Macmillan had planned for her book, she told him: "I am very pleased that you think the book good enough to merit special attention. Only hope you do not lose money on me!" She stated that she was quite willing to sign up with Macmillan, but there were a few things about the contract that needed to be clarified. "I come from a legal family," she explained, "and, since childhood, have had it hammered into me never to sign *anything* without studious, even prayerful consideration of it. That is the reason, rather than any dissatisfaction with the general terms of the contract. . . . My father is a lawyer of the old school who can pursue a technicality to the bottom of the haystack—Lois can tell you about him!—and he suggested some of the questions I am asking."

Not wanting to appear "pickayunish," she wrote that she was not "a hard person to trade with," but her father insisted that the book be more clearly identified, "for failure to identify the property contracted for can render the entire contract invalid." She suggested that they identify the book as "a novel of the South (exact title to be determined)." Her second request had to do with wanting to see the cover design and the dust jacket before a final decision was made. Because she had seen so many books about the South that had jacket illustrations "of such un-Southern appearance as to arouse mirth and indignation," it was absolutely imperative that the cover be true to the South in every detail, just as the book itself was. Her third question had to do with the dramatic and motion picture rights, which the contract stated would remain with her prior to publication. "What happens to the dramatic and motion picture rights *after* book publication?" she wanted to know. She suggested that "a new clause be written stating the arrangement as regards dramatic and motion picture rights, separately from the matter of serial rights," which she said she did not understand either. Quoting the phrase "shall be apportioned as mutually arranged," she asked, "What would happen if they didn't mutually agree? Couldnt we arrange and agree now? I don't know what your usual agreements are with authors on this matter but I am confident that they would be acceptable to me." Her final question demonstrated her childlike simplicity and directness: she asked what would happen to her if Macmillan went bankrupt. "I havent a notion that you will but shouldnt there be something in the contract stating what my rights would be under such regrettable circumstances?"[3]

Peggy was also concerned about Latham's statement that he was eager to get the contract signed so that Macmillan could begin talking about the book. Afraid that he meant he wanted to start promoting the book right away, she wrote:

> As I told you I have been working on this book for several years and have never been able to finish it because of mine oft infirmities. My friends have continued inquiring about it, and, over a period of years the constantly repeated question of "Well, how's your book coming on?" has grown a bit wearing. Finally, last year, I answered all such questions by saying flatfootedly, "I have torn up the damned thing and I have no intention of finishing it and I hope to God you'll never mention the matter again." Besides, I hate to talk about anything I have written and would rather take a whipping any day than get cornered by even the best meaning of friends who think it only a courtesy to ask me questions.
>
> In fact, John and Lois are the only people I ever even discussed it with in any detail. I have avoided all conversations

about it when ever I could and my own preference would be to continue to avoid discussions of it with my friends until the job is actually done and the finished manuscript is in your hands. Only then, can I be *certain* that the work is actually completed.

My mind is made up to finish it, of course and in the shortest possible time. But with my habit of getting sick more or less frequently I do not know how long a time it will be before I can deliver it and it would be definitely embarrassing if anybody down here discovered that I signed a contract and then a period of months should drag on, during which my friends would be constantly asking me about the book and I would be able to make no answer except that I had gotten sick again and hadnt finished it.[4]

Peggy had been teased so much about the book that her feelings expressed here are understandable. Perhaps, too, she was afraid that she could not finish it—ever. At any rate, she said she had told no one about the contract except John and her father: "I wouldnt have even told Father except that he would have skinned me if he ever discovered I'd signed any contract without his first looking over it. And then, too, as he's the authority in these parts on Southern Civil War history, I'd have to confess eventually because I want him to check my material in every detail so the United Confederate Veterans and the embattled United Daughters of the Confederacy can't land on me like ducks on a June bug."[5] She did not mean to keep the publisher bound to secrecy until the manuscript was delivered, for she added: "The very minute when I feel that I have the job in hand and that the book *is* going to be finished, I will let you know and you can turn loose the dogs." She urged him to tell Lois, who had so many friends in Atlanta, not to let the word out just yet. "Then I'd have guests popping in at all hours to sit forever on the sofa and say 'Is it hard to write a book?' And there would be an influx of utter strangers with manuscripts which they'd want me to read and edit." Instead of ending her letter there, she wrote another half-page describing an incident involving a young woman who wanted her and John to edit her manuscript.

After typing six full pages, she closed, saying she was returning the contract and asking him to return her manuscript. "I am very anxious to work, as I have no carbon copy, I can't do a thing. I hate to see the days going by when I could be working. You see, I do not feel like a human being until the thermometer registers at least ninety. It's now at one hundred degrees and I feel fine and could probably work from cant-see till cant-see."

Expecting a signed contract so he could wrap things up before he left that weekend for his month-long vacation, Latham was taken back when he received her long letter full of questions. Disappointed, he showed the letter to Lois, who took a high hand in the matter, pointing out to Peggy that she was not dealing with some "fifth rate" publisher but one of the most esteemed establishments in the publishing world.

> The contract came from us and it was the regular printed form which some twelve thousand Macmillan authors have signed without a qualm—in fact I signed one myself. The additional clauses are worded in the same way that thousands of similar clauses and similar contracts have been worded.
>
> I do want to tell you, too, that if the Macmillan Company goes bankrupt you and no one else will be in any state to worry about what becomes of any novel. Gibraltar itself is no more firmly founded and we will go only with the last stage of the revolution.
>
> Mr. Latham and I are both somewhat exercised about the whole matter. We are both leaving for vacations on Friday and most anxious to have it settled before we go. Won't you put our minds at rest and say yes so that we hear by Friday morning?[6]

On the heels of that letter came Latham's reassuring one, answering all of Peggy's questions, he hoped, to her satisfaction. Because he would be vacationing for a month and his hopes were that she would accept the contract, he asked that she sign his letter signfying her approval of the contract and return the letter to him immediately. Later, at her convenience, she could mail the contract to Macmillan. At the moment he just needed to know if she approved the contract.

Reading Lois's letter and then Latham's, both of which arrived on August 6, Peggy was embarrassed and terrified that she had offended the Macmillan editors. She immediately wired Latham: "Please take this telegram as acceptance of contract signed contract in the mails today thanks for your courtesies and patience hope you have a nice vacation. Margaret Mitchell Marsh."[7] That same day, she wrote a letter apologizing for holding him up and for bothering him.

> After I got Lois' letter, I got the idea you all might think I suspected you and your company of bad faith or double dealing. That upset me for that idea hadn't occurred to me and I hasten to beg you to put such an idea out of your minds. I thought the contract ought to be binding on me as well as on you and there were three swell loop holes through which I could have crawled should I have lost my mind and taken such a notion.[8]

She concluded by saying: "You said in one of your letters you'd write me occasionally to prod me along. Please do it! Between your prodding and John's driving I ought to finish in a hurry."

Little did John know that morning of August 1, 1935, when he and Peggy sat huddled together in his office, happily and excitedly reading the Macmillan contract, how much law he would have to learn from that day on and how much law he and she would affect in the next twenty years. From that morning on, he managed every aspect of the book's business, even to the detriment of his own health.

But at the time of the contract they had not the faintest idea that they were embarking on a literary and financial adventure of *Gone With the Wind*'s magnitude, much less one that would still be thriving—on an international level—over a half-century later. All they could think as they read that contract was how wonderful it was to have such a prominent and respectable publishing house as Macmillan publishing Peggy's book. Although they did not know it, the contract was a standard one, with the author's royalty to be 10 percent of the retail price of the first ten thousand copies sold and 15 percent thereafter. Peggy was to receive a five-hundred-dollar advance against royalties, half on signing the contract, and half on receipt of the completed manuscript. Their main concern that day shows their sincerity and innocence. They hoped that the book would sell enough copies so that Macmillan would not lose money. At that point, the idea of their making money had not even occurred to them.

2

On August 13, Latham sent Peggy her manuscript, identified then only as "A MS of the Old South." Two days later, he sent back "'Ropa Carmagin" because he said it was too short for book publication. Suggesting that she hold it until after her novel was published, he thought she could then easily sell it to one of the better magazines. "It confirms my very high opinion of you as a writer . . . the novel is the big thing just now, so don't worry about this or any other short material you may have."[9] She was thrilled and grateful with such unexpected praise, and happy to see the envelopes again for the first time since they had left with Latham in April. The Marshes' 4 East 17th Street apartment looked like home again, for even Bessie had earlier commented about how different and empty the place looked without all the papers scattered about. When John came home that evening, Peggy shrieked with delight as she pointed to the stack of twenty-seven bloated envelopes piled on the dining room table and waved Latham's message in his face. John was to say later that he never forgot that moment or the positively euphoric look on Peggy's smiling face.[10]

Both sighed at the thought of the big job ahead of them, and then burst into laughter.

Several days later, as he was working in his office, John received a breathlessly excited call from Peggy saying that she had just received a duplicate copy of the signed contract and a check for $250.00 and that she was so nervous, she told him, "I'm going to take a luminal and put a cold towel to my head and go to bed." John replied, "Move over, baby, I'm coming home to get in bed with you!"[11] Somehow, that first check, even more than the contract, made the book a reality to them. For days, Peggy walked on air.

Anyone reading the letters in the Macmillan file and also the ones to the Marsh family during this period can tell that at this stage in the development of *Gone With the Wind,* John was in complete charge. Even though he and Peggy had to realize that the editing work would be a full-time job, and John already had a full-time job, they were not about to turn that manuscript over to some copyeditor in New York. Nor did Macmillan ever request that they do so. By now, Latham had to have been aware of the Marshes' unique relationship and of John's role as Peggy's editor. After all, she had mentioned his role in her letters to Latham and, no doubt, in conversations with him when he was in Atlanta, and his assistant, Lois Cole, knew the Marshes well and understood how they worked together. Joe Kling said emphatically that the Marshes' relationship was simply no secret: "Everyone knew that he helped her do everything. That was just their way of life. John would have been the only person she trusted with her work. That was just a given."

Some of his coworkers described John as "meticulous and exacting," and his close attention to detail became very useful at this stage of the book's life. Mary Singleton, who worked on the Georgia Power magazine with him, said outright, "He was the best editor I've ever seen. . . . I think his know-how was one reason *Gone With the Wind* was so good." Joe Kling agreed with her.[12] And she was right, for much of the success of *Gone With the Wind* is a result of John's keen intelligence, uncompromising standards, and careful scrutiny of the manuscript and the proofs. Important to remember too is that he was not only emotionally involved with Peggy, wanting her to be happy and successful, but he was also emotionally, intellectually, and creatively involved in producing the manuscript. He had a thorough understanding of the characters and of their story. After all, the book had been conceived in love and nurtured throughout the entire first decade of their married life.

The kind of urgency required at this point in the preparation of *Gone With the Wind* was exactly the kind that challenged John but devastated Peggy. Unlike her, he was a goal-oriented thinker; he liked to progress in an orderly fashion toward an end, and he had the discipline to stay with a task until it was finished to his satisfaction. Although it was to take them almost six months to complete the manuscript, John optimistically believed at that time, late August, that with both of them working together hard and steadily they could get the thing into a finished form and to a typist in less than six weeks. Although proofing the typist's copy would take careful scrutiny and yet more time, he still believed they could get the complete job done in six to eight weeks.[13] When Peggy told Latham that she expected to have the manuscript finished by Thanksgiving, he was delighted because that would mean publication in the spring.

John's first task was to find a typist. Although he and Peggy had decided not to mention the contract to anyone except her father and brother, they had to confide in Rhoda, John's secretary, because they needed her help now more than ever. Busy handling his Power Company business, Rhoda suggested Grace Alderman, a discreet young single girl who had just come to work as a stenographer for the company. Grace happily consented, and for the rest of her life, her claim to fame was typing the manuscript of *Gone With the Wind*.[14]

On September 3, Peggy wrote Latham:

> I am hard at work and, for the first time in my life, working is comparatively easy. Here to fore, it has been the most anguished of struggles to get anything at all on paper and rewriting, though I rewrite everything thirty times at least, has been a task too disagreeable to go into on paper. Things go more easily now, thank Heaven.
>
> As John says there's nothing like signing a contract, having a conscience about delivering the goods and burning your britches behind you.[15]

She wrote that there was "an awful lot to be done on grammatical errors alone." With honesty, she admitted, "Here to fore I've never bothered about grammar, punctuation, spelling, etc. as long as I was struggling merely to get things on paper. And there's an awful [lot] of loose ends to be hitched up and repetitions to be eliminated. And I'm trying to condense and to— well, it would take pages to tell you."[16] In this same letter she talked about her need to check some historical records. Because it had been two years since she took notes on the Dalton-to-Atlanta campaign, she was rereading the memoirs of Generals Johnston, Hood, and Sherman. "Although that campaign is only one chapter in the book I want it air tight so that no grey-bearded vet could rise up to shake his cane at me and say 'But I know better. I fit in that fight.'" She closed by saying that John, who was to get his two-week vacation at the end of September, had promised "to help me out with that damned first chapter and anything else I need." She said that if she did not come down with her "annual September 15th case of dengue fever," she expected to be finished in six weeks.[17]

3

"When the Macmillan Company bought my book my emotions were compounded of pleasure and horror, for I realized that I had not checked a single fact in that long manuscript," Peggy wrote in 1937 to a fan. Thus, her most compelling immediate concern was checking all the historical references. Because she had never intended to publish the manuscript, she said later that she had seen no reason "to plague" her brain studying military matters that she could not comprehend.[18] She had, of course, read reference books and used material from them but certainly not with the idea that anyone besides John would be reading her work. Lots of fact-checking needed to be done, for she had written all the military facts and phrases by relying on her memory of what the old veterans of the campaign had told her, not on any actual authoritative military records. Now, the thought of not having such documentation horrified her.

A year later, she wrote in regard to the military strategies and tactics: "Honesty forces me to admit that I do not know anything about them and have long been the despair of my military-minded friends. When they talked about 'enfilading' and being 'bracketed' . . . I can only suck my thumb."[19] The part of the novel that had to do with the military was the most arduous and time consuming for her to write and caused the most delay in getting the manuscript completed. As she explained later in a letter, she knew well the country between Atlanta and Dalton where the Sherman-Johnston campaign was waged. "Many of the old entrenchments are still there if you know where to find them, and to anyone interested in history the sad tale of that retreat is plain in these earthworks. . . . So I fought that campaign from memory and wrote it at far greater length than it appeared in print."[20]

The only way to make sure all the facts were correct was to check them off one by one, and that is exactly what John and Peggy did. They agreed they were not going to be embarrassed by errors they could avoid, for they already knew some people who would read the book only to search eagerly for errors. Too, it was vitally important to them that southerners like the book and find it to be true.[21] Peggy later wrote, "Before *Gone With the Wind* was published, I felt that I would curl up like a salted slug if the people in the South turned their faces from my book. Of course I wanted the

Northern reviewers to like it and humbly hoped that they would, but the good will of Southerners was what I prayed for."[22]

Later she explained that she had documented at least four sources for every historical event and for every nonfiction statement in the book, and that she had written an "hour-by-hour schedule of every recorded happening in Atlanta and around Atlanta for the last twenty-four hours of Sherman's campaign."[23] She studied Cox's Atlanta campaign harder, she boasted, than she had ever studied Caesar's Gallic Wars, and "if there was even a sergeant who wrote a book about that retreat, I read it. I know it sounds like bragging, but I do not mean it that way for the credit is only due an exceptionally good memory."[24]

A year after the novel was published, she acknowledged with great pride that there were only two errors in the entire novel, and only she and John knew what they were. "I placed the Battle of New Hope Church five miles too close to the railroad, and I had the final fortifications of Atlanta completed six weeks too soon."[25] In thanking Henry Steele Commager for writing a splendid review of *Gone With the Wind* for the *New York Herald Tribune Books*, she wrote, "You speak of my book not 'ruffling your historical feather.' Thanks for that. I positively cringed when I heard that you a historian were going to review me. I cringed even though I knew the history in my tale was as water proof and air tight as ten years of study and a lifetime of listening to participants would make it."[26]

In order to get that novel "air-tight," she and John began their editing process by working out a schedule that required Peggy to spend all of every weekday either in the library or in the courthouse records room or interviewing old veterans.[27] Her job was to find authorities for every factual statement in the novel. She spent countless hours checking references on such things as clothes, hats, hairstyles, flowers, crops, hymns, names, furniture, wallpaper, medical treatments, and literally thousands of other things. She knew the history of Georgia, the history of the Confederacy, the history of the southern blockade, and the history of the Reconstruction as well as any historian.[28]

While she was checking the section of the book that had to do with the campaign from the Tennessee line to Atlanta, she even tried to find out what the weather had been like at that time. Some of the old veterans had told her that it had rained for twenty days at Kennesaw, but she wanted to be certain. She turned to Mary Johnston's *Cease Firing*, that old book that her mother used to read to her when she was a child. "Mother was strong minded but she never failed to weep over *The Long Roll* and *Cease Firing* and I always bellowed too, but insisted on her not skipping sad parts. . . . I knew it to be the best documented novel ever written so I consulted it to see about the weather."[29]

Because she was confident about the correctness of her historical facts, she welcomed questions about the historical angle of the book. In 1936, when a fan asked her about the troop movement before the battle of Chickamauga, she answered, "I labored a long time over my background, and my bibliography runs into the thousands of volumes." That is probably no exaggeration. After the book came out, she complained about eye strain that was caused, she said, from reading so much of the "agate type in old time newspapers, which I read by the hundreds in checking the historical accuracy of my book."[30]

When Lois Cole wrote her on March 4, 1936, saying that someone who was reading the galleys "with excitement and enjoyment" believed he had found an anachronism and wanted to know if she were sure there were toothbrushes in 1868, Peggy proudly answered that she had three references in her notes on the toothbrush and one of her authorities was the *Oxford English Dictionary*.[31] She added: "I remember Grandma telling me how the blockade cut off whale bone stays and tooth brushes. They used split oak for the stays and for tooth brushes used a twig (willow twigs were popular) chewed till it frayed into fibers. Something like a present day snuff stick or did you ever see a snuff stick? Dearie, someday I must give you my imitation of a negro cook with a lip full of snuff and a snuff stick. It's my only parlor accomplishment."[32]

The task of checking facts and extensively revising sections of the manuscript for the sake of historical accuracy was arduous and time consuming. As John explained to Lois Cole, it was "one of the chief causes of the delay in delivering the final MS to you."[33] In this ten-page typed letter to Lois, dated February 9, 1936, John explained many interesting details about the editing of the manuscript and about how it achieved its final shape. Essentially, what they did was rewrite the whole book, as Peggy told Mother Marsh in January 1936. "Macmillan bought it [the manuscript] when it was in the rough draft stage and wanted to publish it practically 'as was' but it was written in so slovenly a manner that I felt I had to rewrite the whole book and in a very short time." About the sections requiring the most research, John wrote Lois on February 9:

> Originally, she had most of her Reconstruction background material concentrated into two other chapters. These were written before she had done all of her research work and when she was under the impression, as most people are, that Reconstruction arrived with a bang right after the war ended. Her further investigation showed that conditions were relatively pleasant in 1866, by comparison with the worse horror that developed over a period of years. This obviously made it necessary for her to split

up the background stuff and string it out through the chapters from 1866 to 1872.

His coworkers remembered well how distracted John was at his work during this period and how lenient Mr. Arkwright, the president of the company, was with him. Because it was impossible for Peggy to hunt for documentation, to write, and to revise, John helped her with the revision at night and every weekend.[34] According to his secretary and his typist, who dealt with him and with that manuscript on a daily basis, John spent hours working on it.[35] Every evening after he came home, he scoured the manuscript for errors in spelling and punctuation and for all items that needed documentation. He searched for inconsistencies, anachronisms, and repetitions, and shuffled the scenes into chronological order. Using his pen like a pocket knife, he whittled out whole chapters and carved out scenes within the chapters.[36] And all the long, detailed letters sent to Macmillan about preparing the manuscript for production as well as the ones regarding the proofs were from John, not Peggy.

One huge task alone involved checking the time frames to see if the characters developed correctly chronologically and if babies came at the right time and far enough apart. The fact that Peggy did not write the chapters consecutively made this search even more complicated. The notebooks that John had started keeping in 1927 on the characters' biographies now became a valuable source of material.[37] His notebook on the dialects was also extremely useful at this point in the manuscript's preparation, for he and Peggy had to be certain that the various dialects were appropriate and consistent throughout the novel. With his habitual tendency to record, John had kept careful track of their research in the matter of dialect, a subject that was so interesting and important to him and Peggy. In the early 1960s, when Stephens Mitchell authorized Finis Farr to write a biography of his sister, he showed Farr the notebook in which John had painstakingly recorded several varieties of regional speech that he and Peggy had discovered. According to Farr, "In his small neat handwriting John drew up a seventeen-page glossary of terms in negro and frontier country speech to help keep the various kinds of dialect consistent."[38]

Prior to publication, when the time came to doublecheck dialect consistency, John's attention to such details stood Peggy in good stead. Surely, he was speaking for himself as well as for Peggy when he later objected strenuously to a Macmillan copyeditor's revisions of key dialect words. Perfecting the regional speech of the different characters required painstaking attention and was a time-consuming activity, and he was obviously furious when he discovered what the copyeditor had done. In his long letter to Lois Cole on February 13, 1936, he pointed out all the mistakes that the Macmillan copyeditor had made. Among many other things the copyeditor had changed such words as "mahseff" and "yo'seff," and other "self" words, to "mahse'f" and "yo'se'f." John explained that whenever possible Peggy wanted to avoid using two apostrophes in one word, and although she accepted this change, she wanted no further changes in the dialect without her approval.[39] This business about where the apostrophes went in words had to come solely from John because he knew how to mechanically express what Peggy wanted. As she explained later, she usually refused to read "any dialect stuff that's like Uncle Remus. And so do most Southerners. I wanted it easily readable, accurate and phonetic. . . . I sweat blood to keep it from being like Uncle Remus."[40] In her effort to record accurately the talk of her black characters, she spent many long afternoons searching the back country for aged blacks reared in slavery so that she could listen to them talk.[41] And neither she nor John wanted a word changed by any Yankee copyeditor.

4

However, dialect was not their only concern. They checked words, expressions, and colloquialisms, and they searched for anachronisms as thoroughly as they could by reading hundreds of old letters, memoirs, and diaries. After *Gone With the Wind* was published, they got furious when a few critics questioned their use of language. For example, soon after the book appeared, Ralph Thompson, a *New York Times* critic wrote that "there are a good many questionable touches in the dialogue—the word *sissy* (implying an effeminate man) is put into the mouths of characters a whole generation too early and such expressions as 'on the make,' 'like a bat out of hell,' 'Gotterdammerung,' . . . sound very strange upon the tongues of Civil War Southerners."[42]

Peggy lashed back with venom:

> I do object to his calling attention to inaccuracies which do not happen to be inaccurate. And it annoys me to think that anyone would think me such a fool as to get myself out on a limb about such matters as the "Gotterdammerung" where I could be sawed off so easily. I only put in three weeks checking up on that small statement. Of course, the opera itself was produced several years after the war but the poems were written in the late Forties or early Fifties, I believe. (I haven't my notes with me and my brain is too addled at present to be absolutely sure.) And after going through all the books in the Library on German folklore and the Wagnerian cycle I found that the phrase "dusk of the Gods" was an ancient

one and, Heaven knows, the legend was an ancient one.

And old time Southerners did travel and practically all of them made the Grand Tour which included Germany. And a few of them in this section did read books, odd though that may seem, and did know music!

And where he rode me about the word "sissy" . . . I picked up that word and the line in which it was used from a letter, dated in 1861, from a boy to his father, explaining why he had run away and joined an outfit in another section. "I just didn't want to join any Zouaves. *I'd have felt like a sissy in those red pants etc.*"[43]

When a British critic for the *Liverpool Daily Post* criticized her for *Gone With the Wind*'s anachronisms and cited her use of iodine as an example, she fired back that it took her about two weeks to run down all her references on iodine and its uses before and during the Civil War.

. . . and I did not, if you will read carefully, ever speak of iodine being used as an antiseptic. Iodine as a drug came into use about 1818, I believe. During the war it was used in the treatment of goiter, taken internally for dysentery and externally for erysipelas, was used on "festers," bruises and wounds. As to whether they were aware of the antiseptic qualities, I cannot say but both Mrs. Gordon and Mrs. Pickett, in writing of those days refer to putting it on wounds, according to the doctors' orders. They were so ignorant of its properties that they painted the wounded every half hour and blistered them badly. "The Medical and Surgical History of the War of the Rebellion" gives its uses in dysentery and stomach complaints and remarks, in passing, that the mortality was quite high in dysentery! Many old ladies with whom I discussed war experiences spoke of iodine. I tried to have four references against every statement of this nature in the book and I have more than four on this one.[44]

While they were editing the manuscript, Peggy worried excessivly about the names of characters and places, something that had not concerned her while she was writing the book. Remembering the stir Frances Newman had caused with her novel, she did not want to make the same mistakes, and she took infinite pains to avoid embarrassing anyone by using names of actual people living in and around Clayton County during the time period of the novel. Of course, it was impossible for her to find any names that had not been borne by someone in Georgia at some time. Therefore, the best she could do was to choose ones that did not appear in records in the counties where the characters lived.[45] "I spent weeks and weeks in county court houses checking the names of my characters against tax books, from 1840 to 1873, against deed books, against militia muster rolls, against Confederate muster rolls, against lists of jurymen, against wills and titles."[46] Yet, despite all her efforts, she still had a couple of problems with names when the book appeared.

Also, she fretted about getting the right-sounding name for each character. She changed Ellen O'Hara's maiden name from D'Antignac to Robillard, and she considered changing Melanie to Melisande or to Permelia but then decided Melanie was best. As she had suggested earlier to Latham, she wanted to replace "Pansy" with a better name; even though Macmillan was satisfied with it, she was not. She explained,

> As to why I chose the name of Scarlett—first, because I came across the name of Katie Scarlett so often in Irish literature and so I made it Gerald's Mother's maiden name. Second, while I of course knew of the Scarlett family on our Georgia Coast, I could find no record of any family named Scarlett in Clayton County between the years 1859 and 1873. . . . The name Scarlett was chosen six months after my book was sold. . . . I submitted nearly a hundred names to my publishers and they chose Scarlett,—I may add it was my choice too.[47]

Other names she considered included Robin, Kells, Storm, and Angel.[48] But she and John knew Katie Scarlett was the right one. When Macmillan agreed and wired back, "Three cheers for Scarlett O'Hara," she and John immediately starting going through every page of the rough copy changing "Pansy" to "Scarlett."

Another name she changed was that of her heroine's home—Fontenoy Hall.[49] For when she changed Pansy to Scarlett, she decided that the Irishness of "Tara" was more in keeping with the Irishness of "Katie Scarlett O'Hara."

5

Around the first of September, Lois Cole requested a photograph of Peggy and a "blurb"—biographical information to be placed along with her author photograph on the inside of the book jacket. John quickly dashed off a blurb, which was edited by Lois and returned for Peggy's approval. In returning the blurb to Lois on October 3, Peggy wrote: "I was so pleased with your nice remarks about John's blurb. I was both enchanted and annoyed at the ease with which he turned it out. And I like the way you all hammered it into shape. I think it sounds swell."

But about the photograph of the author that Lois requested, Peggy explained her difficult circumstances. Because of all the anxiety about getting the manuscript finished and all the long hours researching details, she had broken out in sore boils all over her scalp. In order to treat these infected boils, her physician had to shave round spots on her skull, varying from the size of a silver dollar to that of a penny. Metaphorically, the boils seemed to represent a self-fulfilling prophecy, for Peggy had often exclaimed that writing made her beat on her breast and snatch out her hair.[50]

> I know my face isn't much as faces go but it usually photographs well, my bones catching the high lights very well. Of course, the photographer has a hard job with my scalp looking as though I had just been rescued from the Indians and not a minute too soon, either. And one side of my face and nose is still a little swollen from the infections which I mentioned.... This is just the world's worst time for me to have a picture taken. If I can't get a good profile tomorrow, I'll just give up. It takes hours getting my hair fixed and dried at the beauty parlor and more hours while the poor photographer shoots from all angles (including isosceles) trying to avoid bald spots, Jimmy Durante nose and Marlene D. cheek hollows. All in all, I was six hours at it the other morning, and I cant spare any more six hours.[51]

She asked Lois for Professor Everett's address because she wanted to thank him for his report and the part he played in getting her novel published. As an aside, she told Lois, "He mentioned something about my 'tempo.' Till that moment I had been as unaware of my tempo as I am of my gall bladder, so I was deeply impressed. How ever, when ever I turn an especially lousy few pages over to John, he reads them and says, 'Ha! Some more of your goddamed tempo, eh?'"[52] In her most charming and modest manner, she wrote Professor Everett that she was "dazzled" with his kindness and enthusiasm for her book. "It had never occurred to me that anyone except my husband could possibly find it interesting or entertaining." Unable to ignore his remark about her "tempo," she wrote,

> I nursed your remark in silence until one day when my husband was reading the manuscript which had just been returned. My husband, I should add, used to teach English at the University of Kentucky and has a reverence for the English language which I do not share. He was reading along and suddenly rushed out onto the porch with a double handful of dangling participial clauses and

dubious subjunctives, crying, "In the name of God, what are these?" I said with as much dignity as I could muster that they were tempo and let no dog bark.[53]

Peggy relished all the teasing she got from then on about her tempo. Even Bessie got into the act. One day when the meringue on a lemon pie she had made failed, Bessie said, "I guess something went wrong with my tempo."[54]

6

Meanwhile, John and Peggy continued to struggle over the troublesome first chapter that John had worked on earlier. In a letter of October 30 to Latham, Peggy said that she was still agonizing over the first chapter, particularly the first few pages: "I think they are amateurish, clumsy, and worst of all self conscious. . . . I do not exaggerate when I say that I have written at least forty first chapters in the last two years." As John explained to Medora Perkerson in the 1949 interview, Peggy actually had about sixty or seventy versions of the first chapter, but ended up using what had been the fourth or fifth chapter as her opening scene.[55] John explained that he and Peggy had talked it over and decided, "The book is all about Scarlett. Why not begin with Scarlett?"

And so the book begins with the now-famous description of Scarlett:

Scarlett O'Hara was not beautiful, but men seldom realized it when caught by her charm. . . . In her face were too sharply blended the delicate features of her mother, a Coast aristocrat of French descent, and the heavy ones of her florid Irish father. But it was an arresting face, pointed of chin, square of jaw. Her eyes were pale green without a touch of hazel, starred with bristly black lashes and slightly tilted at the ends. Above them, her thick black brows slanted upward, cutting a startling oblique line in her magnolia-white skin—that skin so prized by Southern women and so carefully guarded with bonnets, veils and mittens against hot Georgia suns. . . .

The green eyes in the carefully sweet face were turbulent, willful, lusty with life, distinctly at variance with her decorous demeanor. Her manners had been imposed upon her by her mother's gentle admonitions and the sterner discipline of her mammy; her eyes were her own.

Since this opening description of Scarlett constitutes a perfect description of Peggy herself as seen through male eyes, it is possible that

John wrote or cowrote these lines with Peggy. In that October 30 letter to Latham, Peggy did say, "I've covered the opening of the story from every possible angle I could think of and in every style and in every way my husband could suggest." Therefore, it is possible that John's suggestions determined the wording of the opening paragraphs as well as other passages in the first chapter that describe Scarlett as the very embodiment of the "Vamp de Luxe" that Peggy herself had been when John first met her. The Tarleton twins even think they are Scarlett's favored suitors just as John had thought he was Peggy's—at first.

Around the time Peggy wrote to Latham about her frustrations with the first chapter, she had a bit of luck in finding the perfect title for the book— in an anthology of English verse, not in a book of Irish poems, as many believed. In January 1937, six months after the novel was published, Michael MacWhite of the Irish Legation in Washington, D.C., wrote Peggy asking her if she got the idea for the title for her book from James Clarence Mangan's poem of the same title in his book *Poems,* published in 1859. Peggy answered that she was familiar with Mangan's poem but had never read his "Gone with the Wind." She added that after her novel appeared many people had asked her if Mangan's poem was the source of her title. "I do not know how I had overlooked this sad and stirring poem," she wrote, "for I knew 'Dark Rosaleen' . . . and others. The truth is I had heard these poems orally and had never had a copy of Mangan's work in my hands."[56]

Actually she got the title from Ernest Dowson's poem "Non Sum Qualis Eram Bonae Sub Regno Cynarae," written to a lost love. The poem had long been one of her favorite pieces and in rereading it one late fall afternoon, she was struck by a haunting line in the third stanza. "I have forgot much, Cynara! gone with the wind. . . ." When she read the phrase "gone with the wind" to John, he agreed that it was the perfect title for a book about a way of life, a tradition, and a kind of people that had been swept away forever. Using the phrase differently from Dowson, she applied it in an almost biblical sense. In verses 15 and 16 of the 103rd Psalm, an Old Testament writer eloquently says: "As for man, his days are as grass: as a flower of the field, so he flourisheth. For the wind, passeth over it and it is gone, and the place thereof shall know it no more."

Peggy sent Lois Cole a list of twenty-two titles that included *Milestones, Ba! Ba! Blacksheep, Jettison, None So Blind, Not in Our Stars,* and *Bugles Sang True.* Next to number seventeen—*Gone With the Wind*— she drew a star and in a penciled note identified Dowson as the source of the phrase and wrote: "I'll agree to any one of these you like, but I like this one the best."[57]

On October 30, 1935, she told Latham that the day before she had received a nice long letter from Lois, who confirmed Scarlett as the heroine's name and spoke of *Tomorrow Is Another Day* as a tentative title. But Sam Tupper, a neighbor of the Marshes who wrote reviews, told her that he had reviewed a book by that title sometime within the previous six or eight months. While she could not find a book by that title listed in the 1935 catalogue at the library, the librarians also assured her that there was such a book, published within the last year. She wrote Latham:

> Maybe we are all wrong and the power of suggestion is working on us. Maybe "Tomorrow and Tomorrow," "There's Always Tomorrow" "Tomorrow Will Be Fair" "Tomorrow Morning" etc. have mixed us up. . . . Also John who is an advertising man, blocked out that title and said that it was awfully long for gracefulness. I hate to seem a chopper and a changer but the more I think of it, the more I incline to "Gone With the Wind." Taken completely away from its context, it has movement, it could either refer to times that are gone like the snows of yesteryear, to the things that passed with the wind of the war or to a person who went with the wind rather than standing against it. What do you think of it?

Latham liked it. Many people agree with Finis Farr, who thought that the novel would have been a success if she had called it simply "A Story." Farr said, "But the extra dimensions of success the book achieved may well be due, more than to any other single factor, to its perfect title."[58]

Lois Cole wrote Peggy on October 31, informing her that Latham was out of town but that she was forwarding Peggy's letter and the original of the entire first chapter in hopes that he would find time to read it and advise her. "I am not at all sure that he will be able to, and, if he can't, I will send it to the man at Columbia who read your whole book and is interested in it." She added, "I know, however, you would rather have Mr. Latham than anybody else." Although Peggy had not asked Lois, who was a little miffed, what she thought of the first chapter or of the title, Lois wrote: "Personally, I like *Gone With the Wind* very much, although I don't think it fits the book as well as *Tomorrow Is Another Day*."[59]

About the blurb Lois wrote, "I am responsible for the paragraph in the blurb which mentioned you and your ancestors. Something has to be said about the author." She was referring to the fact that Peggy had been annoyed with the manner in which Lois had changed the biographical description to read: "The author is descended from people who have loved and fought for Georgia for *two hundred years*." Peggy protested that that would mean that her people came over with Oglethorpe's debtors and bond servants and they did not. "Two hundred years ago is a very definite date in Georgia history," Peggy pointed out. "As a matter of fact, my people straggled into Georgia at different times."[60]

Given the friendship the two women had enjoyed earlier in Atlanta, it appears that Lois would have been Peggy's likely choice for an editor, but Peggy's letters during this period indicate that she did not want Lois to function in any way as her editor and did not want to hear any of Lois's suggestions. It is clear that Peggy preferred dealing directly with Latham, who as vice-president secured manuscripts but no longer edited them. Always more comfortable around men, she probably preferred working with them. And then, too, she was accustomed to working with John. However, Latham traveled and was often unavailable, making it necessary for Lois to carry on Macmillan's communications with the Marshes.

Lois frequently offered her unsolicited advice, as she did here in a postscript to her letter:

> I am still worried about Scarlett. Somebody said it sounds like a Good Housekeeping story, and Rachel Field says it is unwise. . . . If I wasn't so worried about it, I wouldn't mention it. Have you any other thoughts?[61]

The Marshes were more than a little annoyed with Lois's "concern" and with her question, "Have you any other thoughts?" at a time when they were inundated with nothing but nettlesome thoughts about the book, particularly about the first chapter. They decided to ignore her remarks and go on about their business. When Latham's letter of November 4 arrived, they sighed with relief, for he loved the first chapter. He exclaimed, "It is absolutely all right!" In fact, he thought that she had accomplished a great deal and saw nothing "self conscious or amateurish about the first two pages," adding "They are, it seems to me, good writing and essential. I think to pick up intense interest as you do—and I'm sure that begins on page 3— is quite an accomplishment."[62]

Never failing to praise her, Latham wrote what she so desperately needed to know: "Reading this chapter now again stirs in me the emotions your entire book arouses: admiration for your style of writing, and for the excellence of your characterization, and the very human note that predominates in it. I am exceedingly gratified that we are to have the privilege of publishing this novel. I know we are going to do well with it."[63] He instructed her not to give another thought to the first chapter but to go on with the balance of the book.

About the title and the name, he wrote: "I like Scarlett as the name very much. It seems just right. . . . Personally, I also like the title GONE WITH THE WIND—but I don't know how our sales people will like it. I'm leaving that with Lois Cole to investigate with our sales people. . . . It seems to me that it is unusual and intriguing."

He thought her description of getting a photograph undeniably funny, "even though I know the difficulties are anything but funny. You have a way, however, of describing them that takes away from their seriousness."[64] He concluded by telling her with "all honesty" that there had rarely been a novel about the publication of which he had been so excited and to the appearance of which he looked forward more eagerly.[65]

With that kind of editorial support, the Marshes were more determined than ever not to disappoint him. They worked frantically, talking on the phone often during the day. John kept a notepad by his side at work so that he could jot down notes, questions, and ideas. Many times he proofed some sections of the manuscript in his office during the day.[66] Peggy would call him from the courthouse records room or from the library, tearfully asking him for advice or joyfully telling him about some wonderful information she had uncovered. He was so preoccupied with the manuscript that Rhoda did not see how he could continue keeping himself afloat holding down the two jobs. He lost weight and looked tired all the time. He kept a cigarette clamped in his mouth. Instead of eating lunch, he drank Coca-Colas and smoked more cigarettes. Because he worked past midnight every night, he would often oversleep and come to work late in the mornings. His coworkers remembered that around this time he started taking a cab to work instead of the streetcar.[67] But neither Mr. Arkwright nor any of his peers criticized him, for as they said, he had "chips to cash in." They were all quietly supportive, letting their imaginations run free about what the book would be like when it finally appeared.[68] At this point John never talked about it with anyone there except Rhoda, Grace, Mary, and Mr. Arkwright. A kind of business-as-usual attitude existed among the men, and except for the occasional gossip of the secretaries who knew their bosses' business, little talk went on about it.

The two employees closest to him and who knew the most about his business at that time were Rhoda Williams, who was soon to marry Joe Kling, and Grace Alderman. Rhoda was working hard helping him keep up with all of his office business, and Grace was typing all of the manuscript to send to Macmillan. These two women stayed very busy, working overtime for months. Although he did not mean to do so, John made life difficult for them sometimes. He was obsessively careful with the revisions, and he was a perfectionist. Occasionally, he became incensed when either typist inadvertently changed the spelling or the punctuation of a dialect word or a colloquialism. And he was constantly revising. Every morning, John would take the copy he and Peggy had perfected the night before to work with him and give it to Grace, who would hand him the work she had completed the night before. Then John would proof her typed pages. After putting in a full day's work at Georgia Power, Grace did all the typing of the manuscript in the evening at her home on her own typewriter. It was an enormous task for her in more than one way, not only in trying to read all the notes and corrections scribbled all over the pages but also in accommodating all the changes John was constantly making. He kept revising the revisions, the ones that she had already typed. And she was typing carbon copies, which made making corrections even more difficult. Although Rhoda was typing sections too, it got to the point where another typist was needed to help Grace stay caught up.[69] Mary Singleton said Rhoda and Grace were perhaps the happiest, most relieved people of all when the book was finally finished.[70]

7

The pressure during the last weeks before Christmas was enormous. Peggy had become visibly tense and weak. In four weeks, she had lost seventeen pounds.[71] With the shaved spots on her scalp where the boils had been removed, she looked like a small waif. She was also having gynecological problems that would later require surgery. "Ever since I got in that accident in November and got the steering gear in the navel I have been bleeding steadily," she wrote Lois Cole.

> Some times just a little, some times it rises to the hemorrhage point. It has been controlled with shots of petuitrin. However both doctors refused to have anything more to do with me until such a time as I was willing to lie down for two weeks and do nothing. They want to eliminate any possible nervous strain that might be affecting me. During this two weeks they intend to use some new gland stuff antuitrim "S." I think it will do the job. The three shots I've had have worked marvelously. If rest in bed and shots do not work then I'll have to go to the hospital. I do not know whether they will a try curretment first or not . . . I think and hope and believe that if I can just lie still and use these shots and gain back some of my lost seventeen pounds I will be all right in a month or so. I cannot believe I have anything badly out of place among my chittlings because I had them badly out of place more before and know the feeling.[72]

With the combination of physical and emotional ills, she was no longer able to keep up her pace. By November, the work had overpowered her. In a pattern that she had followed all of her adult life when things got too difficult, she got ill, took to her bed, and stayed there until things blew over. In reading the letters that she wrote after the editing process began, one can see that her complaints about her health actually began shortly after the editing sessions started. Sitting long hours at the typewriter or in the library made her back hurt so that she was unable to rest or to sleep. Reading made her eyes weak, and on some days she had to lie in a dark room with a cloth covering her eyes. A growth that arose from holding a pen so much had to be removed from her third finger on her right hand. Then there were those hideous boils on her scalp. With such a wide range of ailments, probably both real and imaginary, she was excused from work. For weeks, she languished while John kept working. All the long, detailed business letters to Macmillan continued to be from him.

Just after Thanksgiving, when Lois started persistently hammering him to give her the manuscript, he asked Mr. Arkwright for some vacation time. On December 16, Lois sent a drawing that was to be used on the jacket design and asked for approval but said that the artist needed the entire manuscript. On December 19, she telegrammed, "Rush all available manuscript."[73] John wired back, "Manuscript sent air mail, more to follow, also letter."[74] With reluctance, he sent some sections that he had not proofed as thoroughly as he would have liked.[75] Now only the last section—part 5—had to be finished. Lois said that Mr. Latham and E. E. (Jim) Hale of the editorial department had come to her separately and both seemed very urgent about it. "I am sure you are working your head off, and I hate to hound you, but do shoot it along." Lois and Jim thought that whatever was finished should be sent immediately and the rest later, although Latham thought it best to wait and get it all at one time.

John worked straight through the Christmas holidays without taking a break until Christmas Day, when Peggy insisted they relax and have friends in. She invited so many people that, she wrote, "some of them had to squat in the hallway."[76] Even though the word about her book was out, and their close friends wanted to celebrate, she still did not feel comfortable talking about the novel until she saw it in print, and she did not talk about it. She lived in fear that something would happen—at the last minute—to cause Macmillan to cancel the contract.

The day after Christmas, John picked up his frantic pace but with the help of a valuable assistant. Miss Margaret Baugh, an intelligent, quiet, sparrowlike woman, began working part-time for him to help finish getting the manuscript out. The Marshes had gotten acquainted with Miss Baugh while she worked in the Atlanta branch office of the Macmillan Company after it had reopened its offices there in 1934. Highly competent and trustworthy, she worked out so well that a year later, he hired her as Peggy's full-time secretary. A loyal friend, Miss Baugh remained with the Marshes, and after their deaths, Stephens Mitchell hired her to continue taking care of the *Gone With the Wind* business. She never married and spent the remainder of her life looking after the book.

Starting at the first of the year, telegrams were flying thick as snowflakes back and forth between New York and Atlanta. On January 7, 1936, Margaret Baugh sent Macmillan a telegram saying, "We are forwarding you about three quarters of Peggy Mitchell's manuscript, the portion she has finished to date."[77] On the eleventh, Lois wired back acknowledging the receipt of the manuscript, saying she would send galleys soon, and asking, "When do you think you'll have the rest finished?" Five days (January 16) later, Margaret Baugh sent more manuscript.[78]

On January 26, 1936, Grace finished all of the typescript except a few sections in part 5, and John stayed up all night proofreading. Peggy slept late, for her physical state had deteriorated to such an extent that she was now spending most of her days in bed with the shades drawn. Her eyes had been strained so badly that her physician ordered her not to read anything, and her back ached so painfully that she could not sit up.

When John arrived at his office around 10:30 the morning of January 28, 1936, the first thing that Rhoda hesitantly handed him was a wire from Lois Cole demanding: "When will the complete manuscript reach us?" Rhoda told others later that John was more exhausted and furious that morning than she had ever seen him.[79]

Toward the middle of the afternoon, when it looked as if they were nearly through correcting all the final typed sheets, he instructed Rhoda, "Go ahead! Send the wire to Macmillan!" At 4:00 P.M., Tuesday, January 29, 1936, she telegrammed Lois: "Completed manuscript will be in mail tomorrow."

8

In unison, they all loudly sighed with relief when Rhoda handed the envelope containing the last of the manuscript to the postal delivery boy. It had taken them nearly five months to do the job. But John and Peggy did not have time to rest or to rejoice in the thought of seeing the book in print or of getting some royalties from it. The day after the last part of the manuscript was mailed, John—not Peggy—entered St. Joseph's Infirmary. His physician had been recommending for the past several months that John have hemorrhoidal surgery, as he had been passing blood for months.

On January 30, 1936, the day he entered the hospital, John wrote Lois a seven-page, double-spaced letter. Exhausted and sick, he wrote nothing about his own condition, but his first line sets the tone for the entire letter:

I hope my telegram and the g d manuscript have reached you long ere this. The Marsh family was in a state of collapse when we finally got it into the mail Wednesday noon and we have just come up for air. Peggy is still sick, hence my performing the job of letter writing to discuss with you one or two matters which she thought shouldn't wait until she was able to sit up to a typewriter.[80]

Politely but coolly, he said how sorry they were that they did not get to see Lois's husband, their old friend Allan Taylor, who had recently been in Atlanta. "Peggy was in no shape to see callers at that time," he explained, going on to say that during the last few months they had alienated the affections of quite a number of people who had been "pestering Peggy," mainly those "in bare acquaintance and some total strangers" who wanted to be around her once they discovered her novel was to be published. About Lois's invitation to Peggy to come to New York after the book came out, John wrote: "*Don't* expect her to come and *don't let the Macmillan Company make any plans on the assumption that she may come.* Of course, your remarks and his [Allan's] may not have been serious enough to justify this comment, may just have been polite expressions of hospitality, but she wanted her position made clear to prevent any future troubles that might grow out of your—and Macmillan's—failure to understand her position."[81]

He went into a lengthy description of all Peggy's ailments, saying rather bluntly:

The reason why she has been in bed the past two weeks is the fact that getting the book delivered to you involved the most serious and the most prolonged strain she has had to undergo in many years. She hasn't yet recovered from the injuries to her back which she received in the automobile accident. . . . Sitting up for hours at a time, day after day, over a period of weeks, typing, editing the MS, handling heavy reference books, etc., was about the worst possible thing she could have done. It was a marvel to me that she held out as long as she did . . . and then her ailments got her down and the doctor ordered her to bed. The doctor thinks she may yet have to have an operation—one which she might have had a couple of months ago except for the book—and her whole campaign now is to get herself rested up and postpone the operation at least until after the proofs are read and the job is finished. It won't help her resting a bit, if she thinks Macmillan is making plans based on her coming to New York when she may not be able to come.

He listed several items that he said Peggy wanted him to mention. She wanted the blurb on the jacket to read "when Appomattox came," not "when Appomattox *fell*"; yes, she did want to read the galley proofs, but not necessarily the page proofs unless she had to; she wanted to know what "end papers" are, as Lois had said she was sending her some to autograph; she wished the dedication page to read "To J.R.M."; she did not have strong feelings about how the sections or parts of the book would be designated but made suggestions; she wanted to know the "extent to which and how a publishing house, like Macmillan, 'reads copy' on a MS such as hers." Then, he asked whether the responsibility for such things as spelling and punctuation rested wholly on the author or whether Macmillan had "folks who go over manuscripts to catch up such disparities."

John had not had time to have the very last part of the manuscript typed because Lois was hounding him for it, and he was apparently worried about sending the original draft of that part, that had so much of his handwriting on it. Although John's intense involvement with the preparation of the manuscript was obvious to all who knew him, in his correspondence with Macmillan he always described himself as a mere secretary and proof-reader, eager that all the credit go to Peggy. Thus he wrote:

> She wishes me to express her regrets that the batch of MS mailed you Wednesday was not in as good shape physically as the stuff sent previously. Much of it was pretty badly marked up and cut up but she hopes it was legible. In her effort to get the complete job to you—and I can make affidavit that she worked like a mule, even if it was late—she had quite a number of chapters at the end of the book typed off before they had been given their final editing, and that editing had to be done on the MS, with the young lady propped up in bed doing part of it and with me acting as her amanuensis on the rest.[82]

The final editing job on some of part 5 had not been completed, but even though he knew he would be in the hospital, he promised Lois they would send those pages within the week. These corrections, he said, would not affect the story but would merely involve final polishing of words, phrases, and punctuation, as had been done with the rest of the book. He wanted to know whether he could edit in red ink the carbon copies they had of part 5 or whether the pages with revisions had to be retyped. "I write a better hand than she does and I'll write in the corrections for her to the extent that I can spare the time to help her on this."[83]

About the dialects, he was adamant about not wanting anyone

to attempt to straighten out any disparities. He explained that there were numerous *intentional* disparities in the dialect, and said,

> It would break her heart if someone ironed out the disparities and made it necessary for her to put them back in again. . . . Peggy's negroes don't all talk the same. Mammy uses a different dialect from Big Sam, for the reason that a house negro talks differently from a field hand. Dilcey also talks differently from Mammy, and Prissy talks differently from all the other house negroes. . . . Her plan in general has been to make negroes talk like negroes, without at the same time putting every single word into dialect and thereby making it difficult to read. . . . But please *don't* try to edit it. No doubt there may be some errors in the dialect which will have to be caught on the proof, but I don't know of anybody who is qualified to do that job but Peggy herself.

This is a modest statement from the man who for years had studied dialect and had kept a glossary of black and southern colloquialisms.

He ended by apologizing for the length of the letter, explaining that its whole purpose was to try to simplify and expedite the completion of this enormous job. He closed, "Peggy is feeling better today, and I hope we may have her well again soon."

On February 3, Lois wrote John that the manuscript had arrived safely and was in the hands of the Macmillan manufacturing department in less than ten minutes, but it presented a number of unexpected problems. Did he know, she asked, that in typed pages, it ran just one hundred pages less than *Anthony Adverse?* "We had not quite expected that!" she announced abruptly. And about Peggy's trip to New York, Lois said Macmillan had merely taken it for granted that any author of a first and successful novel would wish to have some of the fun connected with that success. But the company was not planning anything. "Of course, if we had realized," she added, "that Peggy was endangering her health so seriously and drastically by working on the book we would never have asked to have it finished for spring publication."[84]

After she wrote that letter, Lois sent a memorandum about the dedication page to Mr. Lund in the production department.

Mitchell: GONE WITH THE WIND
With the front matter which I sent you for the dummy of this book was included a dedication page reading To J.R.M. The author notices that this dedication page was omitted from the dummy and wishes to make sure that it be included in the finished book. I am

reassuring her. You will be sure it is not left out, won't you? There would be trouble—that is the lady's husband."[85]

Aware that John was in charge of all of Peggy's business, Lois was beginning to get the notion that he was going to be demanding. She typed his recommendations and sent them to Jim Hale saying that although Alec Blanton did not think the manuscript needed copyediting, the author's husband did.

9

Two days after his operation, John suffered a setback. His kidneys failed to function properly because he had entered the surgery in such a rundown condition from all the work he had been doing for the past year.[86] But as days passed, he recovered his strength. From the hospital on February 7, 1936, John wrote his mother: "I feel that I am well along on the road to recovery now. . . . In spite of my pains and aches and weaknesses, I believe the situation has been worse on Peggy than it has on me and just why that child should love me like she does has always been a mystery to me. I didn't want to be an added burden on her, on top of her other work, so I urged her to not come down here to the hospital oftener than once a day, but she is here several times a day." He and Peggy must have proofed part 5 while he was in the hospital because Peggy sent a telegram to Lois on February 8 saying, "Part V with revision in the mail this afternoon." While he was in the hospital, Peggy received a note from Lois about autographing 750 end pages. When she came to visit that evening, she asked him wearily, "John, what in the hell are end pages?"[87]

Just when Peggy decided to use her maiden name is not known. In all the previous letters to and from Macmillan, she had signed her name as as "Peggy Mitchell Marsh" or "Margaret Mitchell Marsh," and this is how letters were addressed to her. But in this memorandum about the autographed end pages, the name "Margaret Mitchell" is underlined. There is nothing in the Macmillan file now that explains how this decision was reached or whose decision it was.

Even before John returned home to recuperate, while he was still smarting from the last bout he had had with Lois, another message came from her. Having received the completed manuscript, Lois said Macmillan was indeed surprised at the length of the book, which was over four hundred thousand words. They would have to sell the book for three dollars, a high price for those Depression days, instead of $2.50 as they had planned. Unless ten thousand copies were sold, the company would not make a penny. Consequently, they were compelled to ask Peggy to accept a flat 10 percent royalty, with no increase to 15 percent after the sale of ten thousand copies.

Apparently when the Macmillan editors read the original manuscript, which included many versions for many chapters, they could not or did not estimate the actual length of the completed manuscript. Lois said, "The three people who read it here, who are used to reading manuscripts, judged 250-300,000 words, but in the state it was in, of course, it was hard to tell."[88] Lois's letter shocked and disappointed John and Peggy, and they wondered what else Macmillan had in store for them.

On his first day home from the hospital on February 9, 1936, John typed Lois a ten-page, double-spaced letter. Making no mention of his surgery, he wrote, "The old man is still acting as the family typist. Peggy is again up and doing, but sitting up to the typewriter for somewhat lengthy letters is one weary load she won't have to tote as long as I can tote it for her."[89]

Peggy would agree, he said, to the flat 10 percent royalty and wanted that amendment written into the contract as an amendment that did not affect the other provisions of the contract. He wanted a copy sent to her before it was considered final. She wanted to be helpful because she wanted the book to be successful and did not want Macmillan to lose money on her.

This request for reduced royalties would be reversed in May, but the fact that it was made at all put the first strain on the Macmillan-Marsh relationship, a strain that would be further increased in a few weeks.

Certainly Macmillan had given the book a fine send-off in the catalogue and in the *Publishers Weekly* announcement. But, John explained, the publisher's enthusiasm for the book continued to be somewhat mystifying to Peggy, and she did not wish either Macmillan or the book to suffer by reason of the problem Lois had outlined, although "she says she is sure all her Scotch ancestors must be turning over in their graves tonight while this letter is being written." He pointed out:

> She does wish to have it understood, however, that the fix you're in is not of her doing. The Macmillan Company is quite as much to blame for the excessive length of the book as she is. Of course, who's to blame is more or less immaterial, but she has the impression that you may think she added considerable to the MS which you saw last summer. And she didn't. The completed MS is shorter, not longer, than what you read last summer.
>
> If you are now astounded at the length of the book it is only the same feeling Peggy has had about it for several years. For a long time before you ever saw it, she had been saying that it would never be printed unless she found a publisher who was willing to bring it out in two volumes. And she has been in a state of

continuous mystification ever since you bought it, because of Macmillan's insistence that she should do nothing to it but link it together and deliver it to you.[90]

He reminded Lois that Peggy expected at the beginning to be told that it would have to be cut, but from the time Peggy got the Macmillan "reader's report on it and on down until this past week," Macmillan's attitude had been that the manuscript they saw last summer was just right, and they never uttered a word about cutting it. He pointed out: "So, with a puzzled expression on her face, she decided that you all must know a lot more about such matters than she did and she has tried to carry out your wishes." He explained that "surreptitiously, however, she did cut it where she thought that cutting would improve the story. But she never intended to let you know about it. You had impressed her so strongly with the fact that the original you saw last summer was just what you wanted, she was afraid you might want to break the contract if you ever discovered that she had eliminated even one paragraph."

The manuscript they had now, he pointed out, was at least fifty, and perhaps seventy-five or more, typewritten pages shorter than what they had seen the previous summer. And it could and would have been cut even more as she went through it, except for the fact that Macmillan had given her the impression that they did not want it cut. He asked, "Please don't ask her to cut it now. She is plumb wore out on the thing after her labors of the past several months, and I don't believe she is physically or emotionally capable of doing the pick and shovel work" that would be involved in such a cutting and revising job. He wrote:

Here are some of the things which she eliminated from the stuff you saw originally—(1) A chapter more than 30 pages long where Rhett lends Hetty Tarleton some money to buy her mother some horses. Eliminated as wholly extraneous to the story. (2) A long chapter going into detail about what happened after Sherman entered Atlanta. It retarded the action at a time when all interest was concentrated on what was going on at Tara. Essential details were condensed into a few paragraphs and put elsewhere. (3) A 7 or 8 page section in Part V where Mammy finally leaves Scarlett and goes back to Tara. Condensed into 2 or 3 paragraphs. (4) Several pages in which Miss Pitty talks at length about how the Carpetbagger gentleman got her property away from her. Condensed into a few sentences because it seemed to get in the way of the action. (5) Several pages eliminated from the description of the education, etc., of a young lady in the Old South, in the early part of the book, because it seemed to be tediously over-written. (6) Two rather long sections on what happened to various minor characters after the war. These were greatly condensed and sprinkled here and there where items could be brought in conversation, etc.

In addition, numerous paragraphs and pages were eliminated throughout the book, either because they were repetitions, tedious, or obstacles to the movement of the story. On the opposite side, the only stuff which was added in was that which was absolutely necessary in making transitions, bridging gaps and filling in the holes, in order to make a connected story. Almost without exception, these fill-ins were only two or three pages long, and many of them were only two or three paragraphs. The balance was very definitely on the side of shortening the book and not lengthening it.

(My mind was made up not to let this letter run over onto the 10th page, but I seem to have failed. From the length of this and my previous letter, you may get the impression that I wrote Peggy's long novel. Which I didn't. I wish I could write as well as she does. Personally, I am much more enthusiastic about the book, in spite of its length, than she is.)

You may get the impression that she added to the book considerably after you saw it last summer, because of the fact that the book *looks* different now in some places from how it looked last summer. However, this is due, not to the insertion of fresh material in the story, but to revising and rearranging which had to be done for the sake of historical accuracy. . . .

Enough of this junk. Maybe we'll get this job finished some day and then we'll fling a party.[91]

10

On the evening of February 13, just four days after the disappointing news about the reduced royalties, the first set of proofs arrived from Susan Prink, the Macmillan copyeditor. Anxious to see their work in print, John ripped open the package, and he and Peggy sat huddled together reading. When they first saw the corrections that had been made, corrections that erased all the hard work that they had done to achieve the effect they wanted to achieve, Peggy panicked and cried. John cursed, "The sons-of-bitches have wrecked it all!" [92]

The next morning he stayed home from the office and wrote Lois a ten-page typed letter. After his polite preliminary comments, he said, "On *every* matter where she can conscientiously do so Peggy is willing to waive her own personal preferences" but some few things she felt so strongly about she wanted changed. The most important change, one that would require a lot of resetting, was the use of quotation marks on Scarlett's thoughts. All the time and effort he had spent in putting this system of quotations had been erased. Item by item, he listed the copyeditor's mistakes and presented his justification for wanting them corrected.

Although Rhoda's, Grace's, and Margaret Baugh's skills in grammar and punctuation were excellent, they could not help John proofread because only he understood such matters as how the quotation marks were to be used on Scarlett's thoughts and Scarlett's talking to herself. Peggy knew she wanted her book to be lively and easy to read, but her own letters demonstrate that she did not know enough about punctuation to devise the following complicated system that John described in this long letter to Macmillan on February 13, 1936:

> Your editor has struck nearly all of the quotations when Scarlett talks to herself or thinks this and that. Peggy is emphatic in wanting her own style followed on this, and her own style is sometimes quotation marks are used and sometimes they are not. She has deliberately, intentionally made these variations and she wants them followed. There are several good reasons why this should be done—(1) Nearly everything in the book is seen through Scarlett's eyes. She is constantly talking to herself and "thinking" things. Putting her thinking, or a considerable quantity of it, into quotation marks makes the book more lively, makes the reader "hear" Scarlett's conversations with herself, as if she were actually talking. Moreover, it makes her more of an actor. Eliminating the quotation marks, as the editor has done, tends to create the effect on the reader that Scarlett is a thinker, rather than an actor. And Scarlett is *no thinker.* She prattles away to herself throughout the book, and prattling *ought* to be in quotation marks. Eliminating all of the quotation marks tends to make the thing look like a stream-of-consciousness book, and that is definitely something Peggy doesn't want.

Then, he went on to explain four different methods of punctuating Scarlett's thoughts, her talking to herself, and her talking to others. "Peggy's attitude is that the four different methods convey different meaning and feeling. (It may be some of that there tempo your 'reader' said she had, much to her surprise.)"

His message was clear: If the copyeditor could not understand the method, then she should leave the manuscript punctuated and typed as he had sent it. "The foregoing is the most serious matter and the one which will cause the most trouble to straighten out." Another item that distressed him had to do with the fact that the copyeditor had improved Scarlett's grammar.

Scarlett talks colloquially and *thinks* colloquially, which mean she is frequently ungrammatical. Even in the indirect, third person narration of Scarlett's thinking, Peggy has used colloquial language.... Peggy wants it left colloquial. She feels that if the use and non-use of quotation marks is followed, these colloquialisms will seem more natural.... Scarlett's conversations with herself, if Peggy's style is followed, will brighten up page after page. Some of the galley we have looks depressingly like a treatise, whereas you find them to be quite animated, by Scarlet's talking to herself, if you dig into them. You don't need to be told it is much easier to get readers to dig into books which have plenty of conversation, and how hard to get their attention for books that *look* solid and heavy.

The copyeditor had also changed dozens of other things that he wanted put back as he had had them, although he said these changes were not nearly as important as those quotation mark changes were. For instance, he explained that

"Miss Melny" appears on Galley 4 in the negro dialect as 'Mel'ney' and the editor asks if it shouldn't be 'Mel'nie.' The style Peggy wishes used, and which is used later in the book, is 'Melny,' without the apostrophe. Failure to use the apostrophe in this instance is a departure from Peggy's usual practice in dialect and was done for two reasons. First, it helps to collapse the word, as the negroes would say it. Second, it may help inform the average reader as to the correct pronunciation of 'Melanie.' The latter was the deciding reason. Two of Peggy's stenographers spoke most highly of 'Melanie' and gave Peggy a spasm by pronouncing the name, 'Me*lay*ney,' accent on the second syllable. Peggy thought the use the of 'Melny' occasionally might help get over the idea that the accent should be on the first syllable. Usually the negroes say, 'Miss Melly.'[93]

John's letter was delayed in getting to Lois in New York because of a storm, and by the time the letter arrived, the book had already gone to press.

However, Lois answered immediately upon receiving his letter. She wrote on February 15, "The book has been very largely set, but we have called up and stopped the presses." She tartly reminded him that if he had not said in an earlier letter that whoever attempted to "straighten out disparities" was to be guided by Parts II, III, and IV, Macmillan would have never tried to make the book uniform. She explained it was the attempt at uniformity that caused the elimination of the quotation marks from Scarlett's thoughts since, she added, "We had no word that they were to be left as they were. Our editor was following the accustomed usage." Lois went on to say, "However, I agree with you myself about the quotation marks, and although much of the book is set, Miss Prink says they can be inserted."[94]

On February 20, Lois wrote the Marshes again, reassuring them that Susan Prink, the copyeditor, was going over the first proofs and marking all the changes. No charges against Peggy would be made for changes in such things as the dialect and the quotations in Scarlett's thoughts. But Lois warned, "every time you change a comma it means the change of a whole line and each line costs nineteen cents. Of course, you have a fairly big allowance, but also you have a pretty big book and a lot of pages to go over."[95]

Feeling tense, Lois did not know how to react when she received a note from Peggy a day or so later asking for ten dollars for a photograph for the book's jacket. In a message to Miss Hutchinson, the bookkeeper, Lois wrote that she had just received a note from Margaret Mitchell asking, among other things, what her chances were of receiving a check for ten dollars for the photograph. "If we should decide not to send it I suppose she would take it gracefully, but I hope we can for the sake of peace."[96]

In less than two weeks, Lois wrote John saying the manufacturing department wanted all the galley proofs back by March 19 so that they could still publish on May 5. With the feeling that he had finally gotten a stubborn child under control, he finished the job on the evening of March 14 and asked Rhoda to "pack up the proofs so they can go out in tomorrow's 5:00 a.m. mail." A day or so before Peggy had received the balance of the five-hundred-dollar advance and also a check for ten dollars to reimburse her for the photograph.

On Wednesday, March 18, a big package containing end pages arrived at the Marshes' apartment. Horrified to see the thousand sheets waiting for her autograph, Peggy asked John, "How will I ever get all this done?" He shrugged his shoulders, spread out his hands, and shook his head. Then, within minutes, Bessie slapped the following telegram into his hand: "Questions here regarding Scarlett's age at end of book? How old was Ellen when Frank died? How long before Scarlett married Rhett? How old Scarlett when Bonnie born? How old Bonnie at her death? Questions age given as twenty seven seems too young to fit in children. Book being set today but if you rush reply we can change Scarlett's age at very end if necessary."[97] John wired the answer immediately. Just after the printers received his telegram, they locked the forms on *Gone With the Wind* on March 19, 1936.

Because of John's meticulous scrutiny of the manuscript and the proofs, along with the work of Miss Prink, the proofreaders, and the typesetters, *Gone With the Wind* was printed with fewer than a half-dozen typographical errors, no inconsistencies in dialect, and only one minor error in a character's name. That error was pointed out by a fan immediately after the first edition was released. This fan letter intrigued John, who promptly wrote A. J. Putnam, one of the executives at Macmillan, asking if one comparatively minor change could be made in the next printing. "At the bottom of page 596 and the top of page 597, Scarlett addresses Frank Kennedy as 'Frank' for the first time. But she has already called him 'Frank' once before . . . on page 590. Peggy would like to have the correction made on page 590 so that Scarlett at that point would call him 'Mr. Kennedy,' instead of 'Frank.'" John wanted Putman to call this correction to the attention of the publishers of the British edition also. He concluded his letter with, "The item published in Sunday's paper to the effect that you already had orders for 326,000 is too fantastic for belief. Maybe *Gone With the Wind* will prove to be the new industry that will help to pull the nation out of the depression."[98]

This casual remark was not without some foundation in truth, for excitement about Macmillan's forthcoming bestseller permeated the publishing world, revivifying an industry that had suffered during the Depression. Latham's enthusiasm for the novel was infectious among the other editors and the salesmen, and for the first time in years, Alec Blanton, the sales manager at Macmillan, was happily setting up a big promotion to give dealers. However, the struggling Marshes did not know that in the publishing world, the word that Macmillan had a spectacular bestseller was spreading like prairie fire.

Thus Peggy was startled when she started getting requests for articles from magazine editors who had read Macmillan's advance publicity for the book. The first such invitation came from Oscar Graeve, editor of the *Delineator,* a prominent magazine for women. She responded, "As my publication date (June 30) approaches, my knees wilt like boiled custard and it takes all my courage not to take cover in a swamp like a rabbit. All this author business is practically the only thing that has ever happened to me that has thoroughly frightened me."[99]

C H A P T E R **9**

1936

A FANTASTIC DREAM

*The reception the book thus far has gotten not only
exceeds our fondest expectations, but surpasses
anything we might have dreamed of in the wildest
of dreams.*

—John Marsh to his mother, 26 June 1936

1

THINKING THAT THEIR WORK WAS COMPLETED AT LAST, the Marshes believed that all they had to do now was relax and wait for the book to appear. On March 22, John wrote his mother a long letter for the first time in several weeks. "Getting a novel to bed is more, far more, of a job than either of us anticipated when so blithely and innocently the contract was signed last summer.... We finished reading the proofs—without actually putting out both our eyes—a week ago today, so my part of the hard work is over. I hope it is. Since then, I have been staggering out of the fog, trying to restore some semblance of normalness to life, and catching up a few of the loose ends." He added, "I haven't, for example, yet made my income tax return, and whether they will give me the $10,000 fine or the year in the federal, or both, is something I am yet to discover."[1]

Although he felt relatively free that week, the pressure was still on Peggy. Macmillan, he wrote, fired "from one to five telegrams a day" to her, "each demanding an answer." She was still busy autographing the end papers and had about seven hundred of them signed, ready to be pasted into the fronts of the novel. In the event that anyone in his family ran across some friend in the bookselling or book-reviewing business in Delaware, Kentucky, or California, with a personally autographed copy of the book, John jokingly instructed his mother,

> You are to smile knowingly and not let on that you are on the inside of what Marsh-and-Mitchell consider nothing but a dirty Yankee trick. Macmillan is getting these copies autographed so they can present them to "key people" over the country with a sly smile and a wink, telling the recipient how they went to no end of trouble to get the great author to autograph the book "just for you." It's an idea of the Macmillan sales department and part of the special promotion they are putting behind the book. They say it will help to get it introduced and started off right, and perhaps it will, but it makes Peggy feel like all kinds of a fool. And it is quite a chore,

especially when the list came in from the Chicago office and Peggy had to write "To Marie Guttenschlager from Margaret Mitchell," "To Rudy Hippelhausen, etc." and similar unearthly names.[2]

When Peggy first balked about the autographing, Macmillan told her that they used this promotional tactic only with "*very* special books and *very* special authors," but she and John had a strong suspicion that the "very special" aspect of this book was the fact that the publishers had to boost the price on it to three dollars a copy. He wrote, "It's the first $3.00 fiction book Macmillan had brought out in many years, and they insisted that the least Peggy could do was to join in with them in their little deception on the Marie Guttenschlagers of this world, as a part of their heroic efforts to prevent the book from being a complete flop."[3]

The price was something that he and Peggy deplored more than Macmillan or anybody else could. John secretly feared that the length of the novel, which made the high price necessary, might kill the sale of it. But, in spite of that feeling, he got an enormous surge of pleasure after the manuscript had finally been delivered and they received a letter announcing that the thing was so long it would make a book only about one hundred pages shorter than *Anthony Adverse*. That news helped restore his confidence in himself. With characteristic modesty, he told his mother:

Before that news arrived I had been wondering what was wrong with the Old Man Marsh. I had been working on the book steadily since last September every night, all day Saturday, all day Sunday, took my vacation during December and worked practically 24 hours a day on the book, seven days a week,—and the harder I worked the less progress I seemed to make. And I wasn't writing a book, I was just reading it, "Copy-reading" it, straightening out the punctuation and spelling and paragraphing, checking up on the errors, seeing that the style of capitalization was uniform, seeing that babies weren't born too soon after weddings, etc. And I just couldn't seem to get through the job. I'd work myself blue in the face and then out and take another look at the stack of MS and I hadn't even made a dent in it. So I thought it over and decided that the Old Man was slipping. I just couldn't put the stuff on the ball like I used to could. Didn't have the speed of my younger days. Old age was claiming me. Then the cheering news came in that the quantity of the thing was like unto "Anthony Adverse" and my spirits rose again. The job had been tremendously long but we had gotten out a tremendous lot of book.

With eerie prescience, he ended this letter with, "Poor Peggy, I'm afraid, won't be getting back toward a normal life for some time yet. The worst consequence of this book-writing business is still ahead of her." In thinking about all the department stores and booksellers that were already frantically trying to schedule her appearance for autograph parties and book teas, he knew that Peggy would be busier now than ever. Furthermore, the Atlanta office of Macmillan was planning public appearances for her around the state.

John concluded his letter by saying, "Thank heaven, I will escape that. I shall lurk behind a potted plant and be sympathetic but unseen."

2

After lunch on March 20, Peggy sat at her typewriter and began what was now to become her full-time career—writing letters. Instead of writing articles or beginning a new book, she wrote letters—thousands of them. She wrote each one in a tone that was as friendly and informal as if she were sitting in a room chatting with an old friend. Not just to the reviewers but to any stranger who paid her the tiniest compliment or did the smallest favor or asked the most banal question, she wrote lively, conversational, and sometimes very long letters.

Her first public speaking appearance as the author of *Gone With the Wind* occurred the first week in April when she was the guest of honor at the Macon Writers' Club annual breakfast. She made a huge hit with this audience. Later that evening, when she told John about the event, he got so tickled listening to her that he removed his glasses to wipe his eyes. Whenever she saw those glasses come off, she always knew that she had a winning story.[4] Deciding this one was too good to keep, she set it down on paper and sent it to Lois Cole. Perhaps better than anything else extant, Peggy's "Macon letter" gives us an idea of what her contemporaries meant when they all said she had a talent for embellishing ordinary events and for making people laugh. She started out, of course, by denying that the event was a hilarious success.

"Now, about that Macon Writers affair—it was the most dreadful ordeal I ever underwent and untold wealth would not make me repeat it. As to why I didn't tell yall—first place, I didnt know you'd be interested. . . ." She went on to describe how Sue Myrick and others in Macon had pressured her into making this public appearance before her book had even been published:

> I repeated that I hadn't been published, that I loathed meeting strangers, that I had never made a speech and God willing, never

intended to and, moreover that I had glands [her slang for illness]. "You and your goldarned glands," said Sue. "If your glands would hold up under writing such a long book, they will hold up as far as Macon. The UDC [United Daughters of the Confederacy] as well as the Literary ladies are on my neck so get yourself over here." I refused and heard a muffled argument with Aaron. "Appeal to her better nature." "Bah," said Sue. "Try bribery, then." Sue said, "We've got Sherwood Anderson hid out at Aaron's country place and if you'll come, we'll let you associate with him." I said that not even James Branch Cabell would be bribe enough for making a speech. "Try intimidation," said Aaron. "If you don't come," said Sue in a sinister voice, "I will review you in the *Telegraph* and compare you favorably with Ethel M. Dell and Temple Bailey and Aaron will review you in the *News* and compare you with 'Diddie, Dumps and Tots' and moreover he will use the word 'poignant' seven times and the word 'nostalgic' eight times and he will refer to your opus as 'Adequate.'" So I said, "Alright you so-and-sos, I'll come."

It took me from that moment till I got on the train to buy a dress and a hat. I've fallen off to size eleven and there was not an eleven year old dress in town that looked dignified and authorish. Desperate, I finally got a green affair that was unendurably juvenile. I didn't have time to think of what I'd talk about, I thought I'd think of something on the train. But there were people I knew on the train and I didn't get a chance. And Sherwood Anderson met the train and we went to Aaron's house and I never got the chance to think about the speech that night. And Sue let me oversleep till I barely had time to make the luncheon. And when I got to my seat and saw that enormous room jammed with something over two hundred people, I ardently wished I was dead . . . . While the president was introducing me I sat like a newly gigged frog and tried to think of what I would say and I couldn't think of a thing. . . .

When I rose trembling I had a vague memory of how horses "lock" their knee joints when they go to sleep standing up and fearing that I'd fall on the floor, I locked my knee joints and took a good grip on the table and also on some whipped cream on the table cloth. Don't ask me what I said. I haven't much idea. I only know that I hadn't said five words when the crowd began to bellow which so disconcerted me that I couldn't get a word out for a minute. And from then on it was a riot. . . .

She told her audience about the first conversation she had had with Mr. Latham. When he asked what her book was about, she said she answered vaguely, "The South." When he asked if it were like *Tobacco Road* and if it had any degenerates in it, she told him no and explained something about her characters. "Then he said that if Southerners felt that they were maligned by such books as 'Tobacco Road' why didn't they write books to show themselves as they truly were? Editors would just as soon publish books about decent people as Jeeter Lesters—if the decent books were as interesting as the others." She went to explain why she had never submitted the book to anyone except Mr. Latham and only then upon his persistent request.

> I had told him that I didn't think it would sell because there were only four Goddamms in it and only one dirty word . . . and that I didn't think the book would sell because the heroine was in love with another woman's husband for years and they never did anything about it. This is where the UDC's fell on the floor.
>
> After they had been retrieved I had forgotten what I was talking about and plunged into the horrors of galley proofs. I admitted that I could either take subjunctives or leave them, was partial to split infinitives and would not know a dangling participle if it rose up and gave me the Bronx cheer but that Miss Prink was, unfortunately for me, well informed on these subjects and that Macmillan, alas, had a high standard of English. I forget what came next. I had only flashes of consciousness.[5]

Lois cherished this letter. She shared it not only with Allan but also with Latham, Hale, Putnam, and Brett, and then passed it around to others in the building. A month later, she passed it around at a conference held for Macmillan editors, many of whom asked for copies of it. When she and Latham, in a telephone conversation with Peggy, happily told her what a hit her letter had made at the conference and that some people wanted copies of it, Peggy went into what Lois called "a screaming fit."

She even wrote Lois that very day, saying, "I beg, implore, entreat, and supplicate you not to let it out of your hands. Either destroy it or let me have it back. I would have perished if I had known it was going to be read. It is just the kind of personal thing I don't want anybody else to hear, and I wouldn't have written it to you if I had ever thought you would show it to anybody. If any of it ever got back to Macon, garbled as it necessarily would be, I would be gone. I'll never write to you again if you let anybody see it."[6]

Not wanting to upset her any further and afraid Peggy would stop writing her personal letters, Lois apologized. In writing to Charles J.

Trenkle, an editor in the Chicago office who had requested a copy, Lois explained her friend's reaction and said that perhaps later on she would try to copy some of the letter for him—after Peggy "had gotten used to being an author"—but at present she and Latham thought she had better not.[7]

3

The news that *Gone With the Wind* had been selected as the Book-of-the-Month Club adoption for either July, August, or September caused a joyous celebration at Macmillan, for it meant an extra edition of over forty thousand copies for club members. When the final decision was made that the novel would be the club's July selection, Macmillan delayed the trade release date to June 30, rather than May 31.[8] No longer worried about sales, since the financial potential of the book had manifested itself abundantly, George Brett, Sr., president of Macmillan, authorized full-page advertisements in all the major magazines and in all the newspapers in the largest cities. When he instructed Lois that he wanted hundreds of copies of the novel given to reviewers and booksellers, Lois called Peggy asking her to autograph an additional five hundred copies for promotional purposes. All the stops were pulled and plans were set to make *Gone With the Wind*'s debut a stunning event.

While all this excitement was going on in the New York office, momentum for the novel was building in England. Editors at William Collins Sons and also at the London Macmillan Company were reading the proofs of the novel with the same enthusiasm with which their colleagues in the United States had read the manuscript.[9] The managing director of the London office was Harold Macmillan, the future prime minister. Wanting to get an American reader's opinion of the book, he shared his copy with his mother, who had been born and reared in Indiana. Mrs. Macmillan liked what she read and gave her son the thumbs-up sign of approval.[10] By the time the London office cabled the New York office its acceptance, Brett had received a letter from W. A. R. Collins, who thought he had the first option to buy and was eager to close the contract.[11] Although the Marshes never knew about it, Collins's offer was higher than the London Macmillan Company's. However, for business purposes, Brett closed with the London Macmillan instead of Collins—though not before a few unpleasant words were exchanged among him, Collins, and Latham.[12]

By now, all the major film companies were anxiously requesting copies of the novel, and two international publishing bureaus had written Brett wanting the translation rights. When she received a letter from Marion Saunders of New York informing her that she was "handling the Continental rights for Macmillan," Peggy asked Lois, "What in the world are Continental rights—the English edition? This confuses me as I know that Mr. Latham handled that. . . . Does she mean translation? God forbid. How can dialect be translated?" Reading Lois's one-word wire—"Yes!"—Peggy said to John, "Translating dialects! Who'd ever thunk such a thing?"[13] Little did the Marshes know then that *Gone With the Wind* would be translated into twenty-seven languages and produced in at least 185 editions.

While Peggy, muttering and groaning, was still signing a few of the end papers each day, Lois wrote her that the movie agents and the movie companies were pursuing her "with their tongues hanging out." But she advised, "Don't do anything yet—and if anybody writes you direct keep on stalling."[14] She explained that Latham had just decided that he might be able to sell the rights directly to a movie company on the West Coast while he was in Los Angeles in about two weeks.[15]

No one was more determined to get the movie rights to *Gone With the Wind* than Annie Laurie Williams, a big, blond woman from Texas who had become a successful literary agent in New York. She worked for such luminaries as John Steinbeck, F. Scott Fitzgerald, and Thomas Wolfe. In spite of the fact that the only film rights sold for Macmillan books had been the ones that Annie Laurie had sold, Lois described her to Peggy as someone who had made everyone at Macmillan "sick by going around saying that she was their official movie representative when was she not."[16] Lois reported that the agent had "a vicious tongue and isn't the sort of person a publisher can row with. However, it's entirely different for you," she explained, assuring Peggy that she could reject the agent all she wanted.[17]

Consequently, Peggy thought of Annie Laurie as a pushy, obnoxious woman trying to make "a fast buck" instead of viewing her as the astute businesswoman that she was, one who was fully capable of negotiating a profitable film sale for her. If there were any single type of person that both Marshes would grow to despise, it was the kind of person who tried to make easy money off their novel, and in their unenlightened view, agents fell into this category.

Not having any luck working through Lois at Macmillan, Annie Laurie decided on April 25 to call the author herself. Unfortunately, she selected an afternoon when Peggy's paranoia was riding high. Tired and jittery now that her exhilaration from the Macon talk had faded, Peggy was in no mood to deal with the film rights. All the good news had overwhelmed her, and she, never an optimist, suspected that bad reports would surely pop out soon. Her mounting tension manifested itself in insomnia. Unable to eat or to relax, she kept losing weight and complaining of dizziness. In spite of Bessie's and John's warnings to slow down, she accepted every invitation, answered every call, and entertained every visitor. On the day Annie Laurie telephoned, Peggy had been especially besieged with unexpected requests.[18]

Before he left for work that morning, John had instructed her to rest all day because he had tickets for the opera that evening. But one thing after another prohibited her from resting at all. The first interruption came that morning from an unexpected visitor who, after writing a most favorable review of an advance copy of *Gone With the Wind,* wanted to see what the author looked like. "Needless to say, having had no coffee, I looked like Hell," Peggy wrote Lois. "Really she was very nice but I missed my breakfast. And while she was still camped here there came a call from Dot Bates that her mother had broken her hip and her child was into something or other. Would I look after mamma?"[19]

Although her friend's call rescued her from the visitor, she missed lunch and spent the afternoon in the hospital wheeling Dot's mother around for x-rays and "threatening to castrate several nurses." It was supper time before she finally returned home, where she had to listen, incredulously, to Bessie tell her to go rescue an indigent old lady friend, slowly dying of heart failure, from being evicted from her house. "Well, that took till after supper. I had twenty minutes to eat and dress and get to the opery when who should phone but Annie Laurie. Hunger and weariness had taken toll on my good manners." Instead of telling the agent the truth, she said she was ill.

Annie Laurie quickly got to the point, saying that she understood Peggy wanted her to proceed as her agent in the matter of the movies. "Well, I blew up then. It was just the last straw of a day full of straws," Peggy wrote Lois.

> And I said coldly that she was in error. That I had given her no such authority. . . . Well, she backed water quite hastily and said she wanted to come to Atlanta to see me and talk the matter over. By this time, John was doing a fandango to get me away from the phone and Bessie was changing my stockings for me and I saw all chances of a meal disappearing.

By the time they got to the opera, Peggy was so tired and hungry that she sent John out between the first two acts to get her a hamburger. "It wasnt till after midnight that I began to get good and mad about her saying that she understood I wanted her as my agent." Lois wrote back: "I am glad she called when she did, because you might have been too nice to her otherwise." [20]

A day or so later, Peggy was still muddling over the incident. She telephoned Latham, who agreed with her decision not to have an agent and left her with the impression that he was taking care of everything. On the advice of her father, Peggy wrote Annie Laurie a letter saying again that she had not authorized anyone to act as her agent, "either tentatively or temporarily, in handling the movie rights of *Gone With the Wind.*" She reported this letter to Lois, who surely reported it to Latham.[21]

Peggy forgot all about the movie rights after Brett's letter came informing her that her novel had been selected for the July book of the month. She called the Macmillan office to be sure that it was really Brett's signature and not a forgery.[22] She had to tell someone this wonderful news, and since John was in Savannah on business, she went to her father's office. "He was as flabbergasted as I was. Being not only my father, but my severest critic (he says frankly that nothing in the world would induce him to read the book again and that nothing in the world except the fact that I was his child induced him to read it originally) he said it was very strange that a sensible organization should pick this book—an idea in which I heartily concurred."[23]

Knowing that this news was safe to broadcast, she then went around to the *Journal* building and showed Medora the letter from Brett. A couple of Sundays later, Medora ran her first big story in the *Sunday Magazine* on Peggy and the selection of her novel as the book of the month.

4

In late April, Lois reported to the Marshes that she had never seen anything like the money Macmillan was spending on advertisement for *Gone With the Wind.* Macmillan purchased huge advertisements in fourteen newspapers in the nation's five largest cities and bought space in many of the literary weeklies and monthly magazines, including the *Atlantic Monthly, Harper's,* and *Scribner's.* The publisher planned a media blitz for July. In August, advertisements were going to be in all the newspapers of cities that had big bookstores. This kind of investment in the book made Peggy even more uneasy about Macmillan's getting its money back. But John pointed out that publishers generally use an old trick of spending the most money advertising those books that they know are going to sell the best. Not wanting to miss a word printed about the book or about his wife, on the first day in May he engaged the Romeike newsclipping service, which also worked for the Power Company. It was a service that he thought he would use for only a few months but ended up using for sixteen years—the remainder of his life.[24]

When Peggy and John saw the full-page advertisements of *Gone With the Wind* in *Publishers Weekly* and in the *New York World Telegram,* they must have been thrilled, and when they read the reviews, they must have been ecstatic. The *New York World Telegram* stated, "The forthcoming Civil War novel, *Gone With the Wind,* will undoubtedly be leading the best seller lists as soon as it appears." *Publishers Weekly* had a three-page advertisement, but Peggy was so distracted by the picture of her that she did not pay much attention to the advertisement. "My face looks so long and pointed instead of square and I have a loathsome, ratlike, Levantine look. I have become hardened to looking like a cat but never a rat," she wrote Lois.[25] Enclosing a picture of herself that she had taken shortly after she and John married, she told Lois she wanted it used in future publicity material. Sounding unnecessarily frugal, she also wanted that copy back if Lois had a duplicate of it. "I have to pay three bucks every time I get a slick print for an out of town paper.... Yes, I know this picture looks fifteen years younger than I am and furthermore is the most witless looking thing I've ever seen but at least I dont look squinched and mean."[26]

From Arizona, Latham called Peggy saying that he would be in Atlanta Wednesday evening, May 1, to present her with a copy of the first edition of her novel. Not only did he want to see if she had any further corrections to make, but he also wanted to report, in person, all the wonderful news he had about her book. He liked the South and southerners, and the very southern Mrs. Marsh intrigued him with her childlike enthusiasm and her honeyed drawl. He was always so complimentary that Peggy wrote, "It's lucky Mr. Latham doesnt come to town often. My head swells enormously under his words and I spread my tail feathers like a peacock."[27] She often said "what a happy, lucky day" it was for her when Medora invited her to have lunch with Latham.

Although Peggy knew that the Perkersons and many others would love to be entertained at a party for the vice-president of Macmillan, she was determined to have him all to herself.[28] Only John and Bessie knew that he was coming for supper Wednesday evening.

With genuine pleasure, Latham showed the Marshes what the influential syndicated literary critic May Lamberton Becker had written after reading her advance copy: "The Civil War and Sherman's march to the sea crash right through the middle of this book and leave you quite breathless. I meant to save my advance copy for steamer reading; I dipped into it before dinner, and it cost me the rest of the night, and now I can't forget the thing. It is the shortest long novel I have read in a good while."[29] He was certain that when the book was published at the end of June, the critic would write a rave review, but her few favorable introductory words here for her national audience had already helped sales. Latham was also pleased to report on the arrangements Macmillan had made for the sale of her book to the London house.

Although this would have been his opportunity to talk about the movie rights, he did not do so, nor did he suggest that they hire Annie Laurie Williams as an agent. Instead, he left the Marshes with the impression that Macmillan would handle all her film, dramatic, and copyright business. It is difficult to understand Latham's position on this matter, and it is even more difficult to understand why he did not convince the Marshes, as he easily could have, that Annie Laurie had the skill to handle the motion picture rights better than anyone else he knew. Nevertheless, he did not say a word on Annie Laurie's behalf. Because making a movie of the novel was not, by any stretch of the imagination, anything that either Peggy or John could visualize, the movie rights did not really concern them and nothing much was said about them.

The two most exciting bits of news that Latham had to relate that evening as they enjoyed their coffee and pecan pie was that A. J. Putnam had confirmed that full-page advertisements of the novel would appear on July 4 and 5 in the *New York Times,* the *New York Herald Tribune,* and the *Saturday Review of Literature,* that Stephen Vincent Benét was going to review *Gone With the Wind* for the *Saturday Review,* and that Henry Steele Commager would review the book for *Herald Tribune Books.* The news about Benét overshadowed the rest and took Peggy's breath away. Her eyes widened as she turned to John and whispered, "Benét?" She admired him more than she admired any other contemporary writer, and his *John Brown's Body* was her favorite poem. She told Latham about that afternoon in 1928 or 1929 when Allan Taylor arrived with a copy—fresh off the press—of *John Brown's Body*, demanding that she stop work and listen as he read it to her. "When Allan began at the point 'This is Georgia,'" she said her heart sank, and she begged him not to read any more, for Benét had captured "so vividly and so simply everything in the world that I was sweating to catch, done it in such a way I could never hope to do and with a heartbreaking beauty. And just listening to it made me realize my own inadequacies so much that I knew if I heard more I wouldn't be able to write."[30] What in the world, she wondered aloud, would Stephen Vincent Benét have to say about her book?

5

With the anxiety of a candidate waiting for the polls to close, Peggy hunkered down and waited for those reviews. Her tension spilled over into Bessie too. One evening when John came home looking forward to supper, he found his cook upset, babbling about Peggy and all those other "folks" making her so nervous that she had burned two batches of lemon custard and scorched the turnip greens. Although he was just as anxious to see the reviews as Peggy was, he remained outwardly calm and suggested that he take his celebrated little author out to dinner and a movie and let the cook have the night off.[31]

Their situation was getting chaotic. Letters, papers, and telegrams were stacked everywhere, along with those end papers that Peggy loathed signing. Every kind of request and disturbance one could imagine occurred on a routine basis, and the telephone rang continually all day long. But the most annoying problem they had on a day-to-day basis was the increasing number of visitors, generally total strangers, knocking on their ground-level apartment door, which was the second on the right at Four East Seventeenth Street. Their apartment house had no doorman, so when the doorbell rang, either Bessie or Peggy or John answered it. Peggy wrote Latham:

> I am appalled at the inability of the average person to get an interview. Having gotten them myself in taxi cabs, through bars of jails, and in the cabs of locomotives, it would seem like Heaven to me to catch a victim in the home, and have hours with her. People who interview me come and practically spend the day, talk my ear off, go home and write me nice letters telling me how much they enjoyed themselves and finish by saying, "And Mrs. Marsh, will you please write me 5000 words about yourself and your book and its aims? I really didn't get an interview with you while calling on you. . . ." Then I moan "Godalmighty." For it takes me days to write a page and anyway I'm busy and I didn't know I was expected to handle my own publicity. What discoveries one makes when one becomes an author.[32]

It was around this time that John made arrangements with their landlord to lease the first available apartment adjacent to theirs to use as an office for Peggy to hide or to work in.

All of the attention that she was receiving seemed incredible to her and John when her book, except for the advance editions, had not even been published yet. She was getting swamped with requests for appearances, interviews, and for magazine and newspaper articles. A year later, she wrote a friend that the amount of money editors offered her to write was astonishing, "and they don't even want literature of permanent worth. I don't believe if Matthew, Mark, Luke, and John offered to write some more Gospels, they'd be worth the prices that have been offered me."[33] Some people had the nerve to burst into her apartment with manuscripts that they wanted her to proofread. One of the strangest requests came from the editor of a magazine called *The American Hebrew,* who wrote asking her to help combat the secretive forces breeding racial and religious hostility between Christians and Jews. Her standard answer to these kinds of requests was always: "I do not want to ever write anything again, as I dislike writing above all things in the world."[34]

On May 21, Peggy signed the British contract and returned it to

Latham, saying that she was most grateful to him for making such a generous contract possible. "I'd feel even happier about it if I knew you were getting the ten percent!" She went on to tell him that she had read the draft of the story about her that was to appear soon in the Book-of-the-Month Club *Bulletin*, and that she had wired requests for corrections to the editor. Feeling the need to explain her corrections to Latham, she proceeded to do so.[35] First of all, she wanted it clarified exactly when she wrote the novel.

> About striking out "While I was laid up." True I did begin the book while on crutches but unfortunately the idea that I wrote it all "while I was laid up" has spread about and most people, having forgotten that I couldnt walk for several years, have gotten the notion that the book is "some little something I dashed off during a week-end convalescence." This gripes me no little.

Another item that "griped" her even more had to do with the story making her appear as if she were a Civil War survivor. In this regard, she wrote that the lines, "'Even after many years the scars of war....'" had to be eliminated.

Because she had written so realistically about the Civil War, many readers thought that she had actually lived through it and was of great age. That idea always brought out a cloudburst of anger from her, and she felt she needed to set the record straight every chance she got. However, she herself had given the wrong impression about her age when, in her speech to the Macon Writers' Club, she told the story about her mother taking her for a drive on the Jonesboro Road and talking to her about how the world of the people who had lived in the fine plantation homes on that road had blown up under their feet unexpectedly. "In that [Macon] speech I made it plain that it was about 1913 that I made that trip through the Georgia back country with Mother," she explained to Latham. (In telling this story, Peggy always said she was six when it happened. But, if the incident really occurred in 1913, as she claimed, she would have been thirteen.)

> That was in the days before Georgia had good roads—or hardly any roads for that matter. Some of "Sherman's sentinels" were still standing then and also the old foundations of some burned houses. They have long since disappeared with the coming of decent roads and the rebuilding of that section. The Macon reporters who covered the story did not make this plain. The result was that many people who did not know me got the idea that I took that little buggy jaunt in about the year 1867 and wrote me letters under this impression.

Another item she wanted corrected had to do with the manner in which Bessie had been identified. Having southern readers in mind, she wanted Bessie to be identified as her "colored maid" instead of a "colored lady" because the expression in the South had a connotation that she did not wish conveyed. She explained, "As far as I am concerned our Bessie is a lady if there ever was one and I want to go on record as saying so. I know you think this picayunish, but I know Southern reactions."[36] Her concern for the southern reaction dominated her thinking about everything now.

Badgered by such issues as the misstatements in the article in the Book-of-the-Month Club *Bulletin,* Peggy was in a breathless state most of the time. She remained so excited about one thing or another that she could not sleep or even relax. Although she was now plagued with questions about the movie rights, it was the thought of the forthcoming reviews that terrified her. She began complaining about her eyes, about her vision being blurry sometimes. At night, unable to sleep for thinking about what was happening to her, she told John it was all a dream.[37]

6

On May 18, Latham received a memo from Jim Hale regarding the motion picture rights to *Gone With the Wind.* Hale reported that Mr. Costain of Twentieth-Century Fox Films was anxious to make an offer now and wanted to know who was handling the movie rights. Hale wrote: "The plum is ready to be picked, the melon to be sliced, whenever we decide to let it fall in our collective lap." He had spoken with Annie Laurie, who had said that "the figure is going up!" Suggesting that they did not have to accept any offers now, he pointed out that they did need to let the movie people know with whom they should deal. "I repeat," he stated, "that we ought to take the gravy ourselves. The movie people will deal with us as readily as with an agent."[38]

After thinking about it carefully, Latham decided it would be a mistake for them to attempt to sell the motion pictures rights to *Gone With the Wind* themselves. He believed that Annie Laurie might create trouble by claiming that part of the returns were hers because she had talked the book up so much with all of the movie producers. And, too, Latham pointed out to Hale, perhaps she had introduced the book to the very producer who finally took it. He suggested that Hale negotiate the contract through Williams with the understanding that her 10 percent commission would be equally divided between them. He thought this would be a wise arrangement in the end for other considerations as well: it would put the time-consuming responsibility of the contract and all that rather difficult business on her, not them. Latham wanted Hale's decision on this matter immediately: "As this business is getting rather hot.... Miss Williams told me yesterday that offers had been made to her now of $20,000 and $25,000 and that she was sure the ultimate offers would go up to $40,000, $50,000 and she was inclined to think we might even get $60,000."[39]

Right after he wrote that letter to Hale, Latham wrote to Annie Laurie, confidentially explaining what he planned to do and describing how they would divide the commission, but telling her that he had first to persuade Mr. Brett to allow him to represent Peggy in this matter. In the meanwhile, Annie Laurie was—on no authority except Latham's knowledge of her actions—doing everything she could to pave the way for the sale of this book, for which she said her enthusiasm was unlimited.[40]

On May 21, before *Gone With the Wind's* official publication date, Macmillan sent Peggy a check for five thousand dollars; on receipt of that check, the reality of the recent events all began to settle in with the Marshes. On that same day, after he had received Brett's approval, Latham wrote to Peggy that he thought the time had come for them to make some move on the possible motion picture rights. He never mentioned his wanting to engage Annie Laurie to handle the contract. Instead, his letter left the Marshes to infer that Macmillan would handle the motion picture rights and that Peggy would have the final word before any offer was accepted or rejected, although he said Macmillan intended to advise her as to what course was best. In the event of a sale that met with her entire approval, Macmillan would turn over to her whatever sum might be received less a commission of 10 percent. He asked that she sign his letter and return it as a signal of her approval of his arrangements.[41]

Putting the matter to rest, she signed the letter giving Macmillan the right to try to sell the book to the movies and said to Latham, "I feel very relieved about having it in your hands instead of an agents. Thats not disparaging agents but then, I dont know agents and I do know you. Further more I am so impressed with what you did about the English publication that I know you can do far more about movie people than any agent could."[42]

However, she insisted on the movie people giving her some say in approving the final scenario, though she promised not to be "tough-mouthed" about other changes:

> I know that too many things are easy in a novel and difficult, even impossible, to reproduce on the screen. . . . But there are a few changes I wouldn't put up with. I wouldn't put it beyond Hollywood to have General Hood win the Battle of Jonesboro, Scarlett seduce General Sherman and a set of negroes with Harlem accents play the back woods darkies.[43]

Meanwhile, even before he received the signed letter, Latham wrote Annie Laurie on May 26 reminding her that their arrangement was to be a confidential one between her and Macmillan and that all negotiations with the author would be conducted from Macmillan's office.[44] The Marshes had no idea that Latham would, in a sense, go behind their backs in this manner. This incident was the source of the first serious break in the relationship between Macmillan and the Marshes.

To Latham's request that she do some publicity work, Peggy responded that she did not want to do a lecture series as a lecture firm headed by a Mr. Leigh had asked her to do. "What would I lecture about? He [Leigh] suggested the 'Urge to Write,' at which I fell on the sofa and bellowed because I have no urge to write and never had, loathing writing above all things, except perhaps, Wagnerian opera and tap dancing."[45] The only reasons she had agreed to speak to the Librarians Club were because her secretary and friend Margaret Baugh had asked her to do this some months earlier and because she appreciated all the help librarians had given her in doing her research. "And then I had forgot about the matter till I saw it announced in yesterday's paper," she wrote Latham. "Now I am covered with clammy sweat for I can think of no way out at this late date, nor can I think of anything to talk about to librarians except reference books and that seems the dullest of dull subjects. And, librarians, being librarians, I will not even be able to indulge in witticisms of a slightly indelicate nature without having it bruited abroad that I am a trollop."[46]

7

While Macmillan was having its annual sale conference in the last week of May, Lois wrote Peggy that "everyone is atwit about your book. They all say they enjoy selling it more than any other novel we have had and that means a lot. When you buy your Rolls Royce do come North to see us."[47]

When Macmillan sent Peggy several advance copies to give to her family and friends, she gave Rhoda a copy in which she penned a special autograph: "To Rhoda, the right hand of my right arm, With Love, Margaret Mitchell—July 2, 1936."[48] She gave her father and brother each a copy and sent John's mother and each of his brothers and sisters a copy. Within a few days of receiving their books, all of the Marshes, beaming with pride, wrote their warm congratulations. John's youngest brother Gordon and his wife Francesca wrote that the bookstores in Lexington had posters in their showcases that read, "Local man married to author of *Gone With the Wind!*" Francesca also wrote them about an amusing incident involving her mother, Mrs. Renick, an avid reader who adored Peggy and who had snatched the book from her daughter's hand the moment it arrived in the mail. Recalling the incident years later, Francesca smiled and said: "We were all so proud of Peggy and John and of *Gone With the Wind*, and no one was any prouder than my own mother." She went on to explain:

One morning, as she and I were riding the train from Lexington to Richmond, we overheard these two short-haired young women sitting in front of us say how they were "just dying" to get their hands on a copy of *Gone With the Wind.* Mother, a very small woman, perked up when she heard that remark and looked wide-eyed straight at me. Then, much to my surprise, Mother sat up real straight, leaned forward, tapped one of the girls on the shoulder, announcing so loudly that everyone in the train could hear: "*I've already* read *Gone With the Wind,* and it's marvelllllous!" The two young women turned around and stared at mother skeptically and asked: "YOU? How could YOU have read it? The bookstores don't have copies yet!"

Francesca said that her mother, who was not even close to being five feet tall, "sat up even taller, squared her shoulders, pointed her nose at the ceiling, and said in an even louder voice, '*I* have an *advance* copy.' With an incredulous stare, the girls said, 'YOU?' Mother answer proudly, '*I am* the *mother-in-law* of the brother-in-law of the *author!*'"

After learning about this incident, John and Peggy sent Francesca an extra copy to give to her mother. In thanking them for the book, Mrs. Renick wrote a note telling them how Gordon, whom she called Ben, had personally autographed it for her: "To the mother-in-law-of-the-brother-in-law-of-the-author-from-the-son-in-law-Ben-with-love."[49]

With her degree from the University of Pennsylvania School of Social Work and her marriage to a professor of sociology, Frances tended to see sociological aspects in everything, including her sister-in-law's book. She asked Peggy if she were "using Rhett and Scarlett to put over pacifistic propaganda," but an astonished Peggy responded: "I had no notion I was doing it. If it sounds that way, I guess it just happened."[50] She also gave some idea of what two very early reviews were like.

I am very glad that you like Rhett. I liked him but recently my tail feathers have been dragging about him for a man who reviewed the book for the Journal, here, did not like him at all, in fact found him as repellant as Rhett's fellow Atlantans did. And the reviewer called me in person to tell me so. He could look over everything except him deserting Melanie in the wagon, he said.

Also, he thought Rhett the only unconvincing character in the book. Well, I should be grateful for small favors—and large ones—that he didnt find *all* the characters unconvincing.

A Macon reviewer arrived the other day to inform me in no uncertain words that he thought Scarlett was a bitch. To my spirited defense that she was only a normal southern lassie just trying to get along, he said, "Bah!" Then we had a bad wrangle which ended by me saying that it was obvious that he had never realized what normal girls thought, anyway.[51]

Never wanting to appear the least bit "big-headed," she did not mention a word to Frances about all the excitement that was going on around her and the praise that the book had received thus far, not just in the Georgia newspapers but also in those as far away as San Francisco. One of the earliest reviews appeared on May 13 and 14 in the *San Francisco Chronicle,* and the reviewer, Joseph Henry Jackson, was very complimentary, telling his readers, "You won't be far along in the book before you realize that this frank, honest story-telling is impressing you far more than all the fine writing that the more consciously artistic novelists sometimes attempt." Having expected "brickbats," Peggy was thrilled. She wrote Jackson, "It is my first book and I am so new and green at the business of authoring that I don't even know if it is good form for an author to write to a critic. But your column gave me so much pleasure and happiness that I have to write you and say thank you. . . . God knows I'm not like my characters, given to vapors and swooning and 'states' but I was certainly in a 'state.' I have always been able to bear up nobly under bad news but your good news floored me. I suppose because it was so unexpected."[52]

When the *Macon News,* the *Constitution,* and the *Journal* published announcements sparkling with superlatives about the novel, Peggy sighed with relief. She and John had always believed that pleasing the hometown folks was the hardest thing to do, and they had said all along that they were not going to care what the world outside the southern states thought. But as evidence from the outside world began to emerge and to point to the novel's success, they got more and more anxious about seeing the big reviews. They would not feel completely at ease until the New York critics came through in the first week of July.

In thinking about Brett's invitation to go to New York around the publication date, the first of July, Peggy decided she would rather wait until the fall, after she had had a chance to see everyone's reaction to the book. In declining the invitation, she wrote Latham about her inability to withstand the summer heat of New York. "Another draw back is that I'm pretty tired at present . . . for I've been going out too much recently. . . . And

I'd have hated to land in N.Y. looking like a hag and with my eyes hanging out so far you could wipe them off with a broom stick."[53]

But to Frances, she wrote confidentially, "I hate traveling worse than a cat!" She also said that she did not want to be pressed into spending hours autographing in New York bookstores. She had agreed to do it for Davison's book department in Atlanta because she couldn't refuse without looking "very ill mannered and snooty," but the prospect of autographing had taken all of the pleasure and pride out of the publication date for her. She confessed:

> I feel so damned cheap about it that I could bawl. I lie awake at nights trying to figure out polite ways to get out of it. I never would read the book of any author who autographed in book stores. And I never had any respect for an author who'd lend himself to such a cheap scheme. And here I am sucked in, against my will. I'm afraid if I go to N.Y. I'll find myself in a position where I can't refuse, in all courtesy to my hosts or my publishers. So I think I'd better stay at home.[54]

Near the end of May, Lois and Latham were delighted to report to the Marshes that Macmillan was returning to the original contract terms and would pay a royalty of 10 percent on the first twenty-five thousand and 15 percent on all copies sold beyond twenty-five thousand.[55]

Peggy cabled: "Hurrah for Macmillan! Hurrah for Macmillan! Please thank all concerned for kindness and generosity. If you don't stop sending me good news my nervous system will be completely wrecked."[56]

To Brett, she expressed her appreciation and added: "I am continually meeting strangers who tell me in hushed tones that they have it on Gospel authority that my book is so *much* better than *War and Peace, Vanity Fair,* yes, better than all the *Forsythe Saga.* When I track down these rumors I find that they emanate from the Spring Street office [Macmillan's Atlanta office] and from those fine, bare faced liars who work there. Trouble is, how can I live up to their advance publicity?"[57]

8

By June 11, Macmillan had printed ninety-eight thousand copies, of which forty-eight thousand went to the Book-of-the-Month Club, and the printers asked Mr. Putnam if he did not think it would be a good idea to make a duplicate set of electrotypes for *Gone With the Wind* at this point. From all indications, it was clear that they were going to have a really big sale with this book, and if they waited until the plates were worn they would have to reset, and the composition alone would be costly. They wanted to be ready for the demand they felt was coming.[58] This demand would largely be determined by the early reviews, which John and Peggy were eagerly awaiting.

If the reviews were the Marshes' biggest worry, selling motion picture rights was Macmillan's. On June 14, from Bangor, Maine, Latham wired Lois, saying that a wire had been sent to the Marshes—owners of the film rights—notifying them that Macmillan was employing Annie Laurie Williams, who wanted the Marshes' approval of a possible fifty-thousand-dollar cash offer for the movie rights. He wanted Lois to handle the matter as he was going to his vacation home in Onteora Park, New York, that weekend.[59] However, because of all the confusion that occurred later on about Annie Laurie's role as Peggy's agent, it is doubtful that Latham's telegram was ever actually sent to the Marshes.

Annie Laurie had been talking the book up, doing her best to get the film companies competing with each other for the rights. At one point, she had written to Lois that she almost had RKO ready to buy the rights because Katharine Hepburn and RKO's president were all pepped up about the story. However, Pandro Berman, the producer, was afraid that Miss Hepburn would not be sympathetic enough in the part and so vetoed the sale. This was the second time Annie Laurie had had RKO right to the buying point because Hepburn wanted so badly to play Scarlett.

Around the middle of June, the Marshes went to Milledgeville on their annual outing to attend the convention of the Georgia Press Association. The first thing they learned when they arrived at the hotel was that the Press Association was hosting a banquet for Peggy and had arranged for a presentation to honor her. As John wrote later to his mother, Peggy was the belle of the ball, the center of attention at every gathering the entire time they were there.[60] This was Peggy's first real experience as a celebrity, and she loved every minute of it. The Associated Press put out a good story and a good picture of her, which was printed all over the South. "If I were a publicity man for Macmillan, I would expect a raise in salary for getting an advance write-up of the book and picture of the author on the AP. But no publicity man could or did get it done. The AP did it," John said, "because of Peggy and because it knows how popular she is with all the newspaper people."[61] Being treated as royalty by many of the very people who had often teased her earlier about writing a book filled her with pride. No one would ever again tease her about not being a serious writer. Just from the reviews of the advance copies alone, it looked as if she had written not just a book, but a blockbuster of a book.

Left out of the limelight entirely, John had time to savor Peggy's success. In a long letter to his mother on June 26, he reviewed the recent events in a philosophical vein. "It seems that the best way to enjoy the pleasures of being famous is to have your husband or wife, not yourself, achieve greatness. Then you can sit back and revel in the acclaim, while they carry the burdens of it." He wrote that Peggy was kept on the go from morning to night, attempting to handle a steadily rising stack of mail from all parts of the country, getting her first experiences at being interviewed, and "being partied, teaed and receptioned." Describing her as being "worn to a frazzle," he added, "and it seems such a pity, as this ought to be a very happy time for her."

Knowing his mother would enjoy hearing Peggy's voice on the radio broadcast, he told her that the most aggravating burden for the past ten days was writing a radio script for her interview with Medora on the *Journal*'s "Editorial Hour" on July 3. Perhaps because Peggy was too caught up in the whirlwind of activities, she no longer used the word "dream" as a metaphor for her life. Now John did. "But even if she is too tired and rushed and bothered these days to enjoy her fame, I am getting a tremendous kick out of it. The reception the book thus far has gotten not only exceeds our fondest expectations, but surpasses anything we might have dreamed of in the wildest of dreams."[62]

The day he wrote this letter, the book was in its third printing and was said to have had the biggest advance sale of any book in years past. Of course, Macmillan had had other bestsellers: Owen Wister's *Virginian,* Jack London's *Call of the Wild,* and James Lane Allen's *Choir Invisible.*[63] Prior to Peggy's novel, one of the most notable sellers was *Richard Carvel* by the American novelist Winston Churchill. Published in 1899, it sold two hundred thousand copies the first year it was in print. Following it was Richard Llewellyn's *How Green Was My Valley,* one of Macmillan's greatest successes with a sale of 250,000 copies. Astonishing the entire publishing trade, *Gone With the Wind* sold 201,000 copies the first month it was in print.[64]

> All of which makes life a fantastic dream for the two of us (a nightmare perhaps for Peggy). I am enjoying the situation but in a somewhat detached and impersonal way. I haven't yet taken it in that all of these things are happening to the Atlanta Marshes. And the book continues to be, to me, not "the greatest historical novel of modern times," etc., etc., but the same old stack of dirty and scratched up MS that lay around the house for years.

The most gratifying aspect of the whole adventure, he felt, was the reaction of the "home folks, especially the Georgia newspaper people" who made up 90 percent of their friends. In a philosophical mood, he wrote:

There are two things that test the strength of friendships. One is a terrific scandal and the other is a tremendous and sudden success. I believe the latter is a worse test than a scandal. So many people are inclined to be envious, spiteful toward any acquaintance who suddenly leaps into prominence. If something of that kind had happened with Peggy, I wouldn't have been surprised, and it may happen yet. But the attitude displayed by our newspaper friends is proof that Peggy has got the qualities that have won their genuine liking. They seem to be just as happy over her success as I am, which is a lot, and there is a wholeheartedness and sincerity in their expressions of pleasure over the book, in their papers and in person, which is all that anyone might ask.[65]

John pointed out that by the time his mother received his letter, many of the big papers would have published their reviews, and "even if *all* of them should say it was terrible, we nevertheless have gotten enough praise of it already to last us for two or three lifetimes." So far, out of the dozens of reviews that had been exclamatory in their praise, only two had been slightly uncomplimentary: one by Dorothy Canfield Fisher for the *Ladies' Home Journal,* and the other by Henry Siedel Canby in the Book-of-the-Month Club circular. Of Fisher, John wrote that she had displayed her lack of understanding of southern people by saying that Scarlett, Rhett, Melanie, and Ashley were "literary abstractions." He added: "I am pointing that out particularly because it is about the *only* thing that *anybody* has said that wasn't high praise."

About the other reviewer, John wrote: "He [Canby] said Peggy wasn't Dostoievsky, wasn't even Galsworthy, and wasn't Tolstoi. I wouldn't have her if she was anyone of the three, and I thought it rather flattering that he had to pick out three such notables to describe what she wasn't."

He went on to say that the Atlanta papers were "shooting the works in their editions of Sunday." In addition to the radio interview, the *Journal* folks had already had a reception for Peggy and had presented her with a silver vase in token of their pride and affection. "I know I am bragging inexcusably but I don't know anything you can do to stop me."

Stephens and Eugene Mitchell were excessively proud of Peggy and often talked about how thrilled Maybelle would be for her. But what Grandmother Stephens would be saying about the triumph, they all wondered.[66] One uncle who had not been seen or spoken to for many years called Peggy to extend his congratulations and invite her and John to visit him on his farm.[67] When the Atlanta Historical Society had a reception for her on June 28, some of the relatives who had not spoken to Peggy in years showed up.

But more important to John was the fact that nearly every pioneer family in town was represented at that reception. With his habit of close observation, he told Peggy as they were driving home how interesting it was for him to watch the faces of these guests and see the difference between them and the average Atlanta face. "There was a quiet strength about them that was startling—and they all looked a trifle alike!"[68]

John was immensely pleased with everyone's reactions to the book. And nothing intrigued him more than the mail Peggy was receiving from all over the country. Every evening when he came home, he would remove his coat and loosen his tie and head straight for the dining room table to where the day's stack of letters was always spread. "Perhaps we will get very tired of fan mail in time, but now one of the pleasantest parts of the day for me is after supper when I pick up the day's stack and read through them," he wrote his mother, adding, "(I don't have to answer them.)"[69]

9

By the end of June, the Marshes' quiet world had been completely shattered. Based on the reception of advance copies alone, the book had taken on life of its own, a demanding, unrelenting kind of a life that was snatching and pulling Peggy into national prominence. Totally unprepared for the deluge of people pressing against her from all directions, she was physically exhausted. She wanted to be gracious, friendly, and appreciative to everyone who wrote her or spoke to her. But her innate willingness to respond to people was creating a difficult situation for her. She felt as if she were being "gobbled up by clubs and exploited by this and that person."[70]

Then, too, hearing about rumors that were springing up overnight like weeds made her irritable. The "muckhills" (her word for rumors) were about everything from her having a wooden leg, to her having to support an invalid husband, to her having written a final chapter that Macmillan refused to publish, to her having already earned over a million dollars. Instead of merely ignoring them, as John urged her to do, she tried to track them down. For many reasons, John was beginning to have an uneasy feeling that what was happening was not all good for them, and he feared that what they had seen so far was only the tip of the iceberg. Even though he kept assuring her, "All this ballyhoo won't last once the book gets out," he silently braced himself for a gale storm.

When Julia Collier Harris, writer of a weekly column for the *Chatta-nooga Times,* wrote Peggy saying the book would be a tremendous success and suggesting that Peggy save her privacy, energy, and time before the floods of publicity attempted to drown her, Peggy sighed with relief at hearing from someone who understood what was happening to her. She wrote,

I did not realize that being an author meant this sort of thing, autographing in book stores, being invited here and there about the country to speak, to attend summer schools, to address this and that group at luncheon. It all came as a shock to me and not a pleasant shock. I have led, by choice, so quiet and cloistered a life for many years. John likes that sort of life and so do I. Being in the public eye is something neither of us care about but what good does it do to say it? No one believes a word of it or if they do believe it they get indignant. I have been caught up between two equally distasteful positions, that of the girlishly sly creature who keeps protesting her lack of desire for the limelight but who only wants to be urged. And that of a graceless, ungracious, blunt spoken ingrate who refuses to let people do her honor. It has all been very distressing to me.

I'd rather never sell a book than autograph in department stores, other than those of Atlanta. I see no way of escaping those. This is my home town. Everyone has been so kind and helpful that I can never repay them enough. And I *would* seem an eccentric and ungracious person if I refused, here in Atlanta. But it has made me very unhappy.

It is not that I think myself such a wonderful and precious vessel of genius that I do not wish to expose myself to public gaze. It is only that I don't especially like the public gaze and would like to continue my life, which has been a happy one, in its old tenor. And I intend to do it, if there is any way possible.[71]

When the book was officially published for trade release on Monday, June 30, 1936, Peggy said, "All hell broke loose then!" The phone kept ringing and telegrams kept coming. All of her friends at Macmillan sent telegrams of congratulations. In her message, Lois included the news that fifty thousand copies had already been sold. Latham wrote expressing his appreciation of her for letting him have a role in her success, and Brett sent her a further advance of five thousand dollars, giving a her total of $10,500 the day following publication of the novel. That amount did not include the advance for the British edition, for that was yet to come. The check arrived on July 3, the day of her first radio interview and the day before the Marshes' eleventh wedding anniversary. Getting to like money as much as her penny-pinching Grandmother Stephens had, Peggy neatly folded the envelope and put it in her pocket and drove downtown to John's office. Looking frumpish wearing her hornrimmed glasses, white socks, orthopedic shoes, and a loose-fitting, sleeveless, bright green sundress, she strolled past Rhoda, smiling broadly, and dived directly onto John's lap, wrapping her arms around his neck, kissing him loudly all over his face. Watching them through the open door, Rhoda and Mary heard John exclaim: "What the hell's happened now?"[72]

10

"The book continues to be the most engrossing subject of interest and conversation," John wrote his mother on Sunday, July 19, 1936. Without any doubt, he and Peggy were especially pleased with the reception the book was getting in the South.[73] Peggy had been somewhat apprehensive, he explained, "as to the reaction of our Southern die-hards to her frankness over the fact that there were *some* deserters from the Confederate army, etc., but there hasn't been a single unfavorable review in any Southern paper and the almost universal attitude is that Peggy has done the South a service in telling its story in a way that has never been done before." He went on to say,

> That fact and the information Macmillan gives us that orders for two, five, and ten copies are coming in from bookstores in little Southern towns where Macmillan is not accustomed to sell any books at all, pleases Peggy far more than the news you may have seen in the New York papers that the book had gone to the top of the best-seller list in eight out of ten cities the first week it went on sale.

Because they had so many friends in the newspaper business, he said he and Peggy had "discounted the very flattering reviews" the book got from the Atlanta and other Georgia newspapers. "But since the reviews began coming in from other Southern states, we are beginning to believe that the South must really like book." He told his mother that "the prize item" in their collection of newsclippings came from Selma, Alabama, "about as 'deep South' as any place gets to be. It told how everyone in town was reading it, how enthusiastic they all were, said it was the answer to 'Uncle Tom's Cabin' and pictured an old lady reading the book, laying it down with a bang and saying 'I hope every Yankee in the whole world will read that book and BUST.'"[74]

In this same letter, John also described all the "excitement stirred up by the book's success," and he warned his mother:

> If you happened to see the picture of her the AP sent out—the Lillian Gish looking picture— don't let it alarm you. She really doesn't look that bad. Physically, she has stood up under all the

strain in a way that pleases me very well, all things considered. The trouble has been the unremitting excitement, the invasion and upsetting of our placid existence and the need to attempt to adjust herself to her new and unexpected position of prominence in the world. The latter is something that is hard for both of us to grasp. At present, it is not like something happening to us but something we have read about as happening to total strangers.[75]

Throughout recent years, apocryphal accounts have claimed that *Gone With the Wind* was popular only with the masses and that it was ignored or assailed by the important literary critics writing for the most influential newspapers. With the exception of a handful, those first reviews, and nearly all that came out on June 30 and on Sunday, July 5, 1936, gave the novel an excellent rating. Because the placement and length of reviews are often considered as important as what the reviewer has to say, *Gone With the Wind* was considered the most valuable book published in 1936. It received far more attention than any other book published that year. Sunday literary supplements in most of the prominent newspapers gave the novel front-page coverage.

On June 30, two gentlemen, southerners from Mississippi, gave the novel its most glowing welcome to the literary scene. Herschel Brickell, who was a respected veteran reviewer for the *New York Post,* wrote a lengthy review. He began by saying, "I can recall a few books out of the thousands I have read since I began to write a daily column that left me feeling I'd much rather just go on thinking about them, savoring their truth and treasuring the emotional experience that reading them was, than to try to set down my impression of them. This is the case with a novel you will hear much about in the months that are coming. . . ."[76]

The other critic, Edwin Granberry, writing for the *New York Sun,* a paper slanted toward highly educated readers, stated: "The history of criticism is strewn with the wreck of commentators who have spoken out too largely, but we are ready to stand or fall by the assertion that this novel has the strongest claim of any novel on the American scene to be bracketed with the work of the great from abroad—Tolstoi, Hardy, Dickens, and the modern Undset. . . . In its picture of a vast and complex social system in time of war, *Gone With the Wind* is most closely allied to Tolstoi's *War and Peace . . . Gone With the Wind* has a center if ever a novel had it, which in great part accounts for its superb climactic tension."

The *New York Times Book Review* gave the book front-page coverage and J. Donald Adams, its chief staff critic, wrote 1,350 words of sheer praise, concluding with: "This is beyond a doubt one of the most remarkable first novels produced by an American writer. It is also one of the best. In sheer readability, it is surpassed by nothing in American fiction."

In her July 12 *Washington Post* review, Julia Peterkin called the novel "a great book . . . without a dull page." The *New York Herald Tribune* also gave *Gone With the Wind* front-page coverage, and the historian Henry Steele Commager wrote two thousand words of warm approval. He said: "It is dramatic, even melodramatic; it is romantic and occasionally sentimental; it brazenly employs all of the trappings of the old-fashioned Southern romance, but it rises triumphantly over this material and becomes, if not a work of art, a dramatic re-creation of life itself." Ellen Glasgow, author of *Battle Ground*, a fine Civil War novel, described *Gone With the Wind* as "a fearless portrayal, romantic yet not sentimental, of a lost tradition and a way of life." In Los Angeles, Paul Jordon Smith judged it "the most convincing, the most powerful presentation of that tragic period that has ever been put into fiction."

The *Saturday Review of Literature* bore Peggy's picture on its cover and carried Stephen Vincent Benét's full-page review of *Gone With the Wind*. Although the review was a positive one, much to Peggy's relief, John thought Benét "hedged by describing it as 'a good novel rather than a great one.'"[77] Benét wrote many favorable things, such as "Miss Mitchell paints a broad canvas, and an exciting one . . . the book moves swiftly and smoothly," but when Benét compared her book to *Vanity Fair*, Peggy winced. "And there is, to this reviewer, perhaps unjustly, the shadow of another green-eyed girl over Scarlett O'Hara—as Rhett Butler occasionally shows traces both of St. Elmo and Lord Steyne and Melanie's extreme nobility tends to drift into Ameliaishness here and there."[78] But Benét went on to say, "Nevertheless, in *Gone With the Wind*, Miss Mitchell has written a solid and vividly interesting story of war and reconstruction, realistic in detail and told from an original point of view."[79]

Franklin Pierce Adams, in the *Herald Tribune*, gave it his approval when he wrote: "You start that book, and unless you neglect everything else, the first thing you know it's day after tomorrow." Praise came from other influential writers, such as Damon Runyon, author of *Guys and Dolls* and many popular short stories; Alexander Woollcott, known for his sharp tongue, famous wit, and membership in the Algonquin Round Table; and even the amateur columnist Mrs. Franklin Delano Roosevelt.

But not all the critics liked the book. Those antagonists who favored novels calling for social justice had not only negative but downright sarcastic comments to make about *Gone With the Wind*. Part of their dislike for the book stemmed from the fact that the masses loved it. As John wrote years later: "Almost unanimously, they labeled the book as 'purely escapist,' meaning a book to be read for the pleasure of it and not because it would do you good. They said it was lacking in 'philosophical content' and had no 'sociological import.' They complained that the author had no 'social consciousness' and was totally uninterested in 'mass movements.' Those were the serious-minded thirties, remember?"[80]

Demonstrating just how wrong prominent critics can be, Heywood Broun thought it was "a very unimportant book that would soon disappear into oblivion where it belonged." Novelist Evelyn Scott, in *The Nation,* wrote that the book was "sprinkled with clichés and verbal ineptitude ... the author had failed to master the wide significance implicit in her own material."[81] With much snob appeal, Louis Kronenberger, a young aesthete writing for *The New Yorker,* started off his review by saying: "Miss Mitchell proves herself to be a staggeringly gifted storyteller, empowered, as it were, with some secretion in the blood for effortlessly inventing and prolonging excitement." He ended by saying that the book "deserved to be extravagantly praised as a masterpiece of pure escapism. It provides a kind of catharsis, not, to be sure, of pity and terror, but rather of all the false sentiment and heady goo that even the austerest mind somehow accumulates."[82]

In *The New Republic,* Malcolm Cowley wrote a scathing review criticizing *Gone With the Wind* for promoting the "plantation mentality" and called it "an encyclopedia of the plantation legend." He added, "Miss Mitchell writes with splendid recklessness, blundering into big scenes that more experienced novelist would hesitate to handle."[83] But Cowley's editor, Stark Young, a drama critic and novelist who only a couple of years earlier had written the Civil War tale *So Red the Rose,* wrote Peggy an apologetic and laudatory letter, making it clear that he did not share Cowley's opinion.

Appreciating his sensitivity and kindness, she answered:

> About the review ... I sent out and bought it as soon as I got your letter. It was a joy, wasn't it? I had had a cheerless day and that review brought cries of joy from me. A number of friends called during the day and each one read it aloud with joy equal to mine. When they'd read the part about the legend of the old South being "false in part and silly in part and vicious in its general effect on Southern life today" they'd throw themselves on the sofa and laugh till they cried.
>
> I suppose I must lack the exquisite sensitivity an author should have. Otherwise, I should be upset by such criticism. But the truth of the matter is that I would be upset and mortified if the Left Wingers liked the book. I'd have to do so much explaining to family and friends if the aesthetes and radicals of literature liked it. Why should they like it or like the type of mind behind the

writing of it? Everything about the book and the mind are abhorrent to all they believe. One and all they have savaged me and given me great pleasure. However, I wish some of them would actually read the book and review the book I wrote—not the book they imagine I've written or the book they think I should have written. They have reviewed ideas in their own heads—not ideas I wrote.[84]

Those "Left Wingers" Peggy mentioned included the *American Communist* press, who labeled the novel "fascist."

But then admiration for the novel came from influential writers and educators like Dr. William Lyon Phelps, who enjoyed immense popularity as a professor of English at Yale University and who helped shape American literary taste during his day. Phelps declared *Gone With the Wind* his choice for best book of 1936, quite a compliment when the competition is considered. Other books that year, some by popular and seasoned writers, were Walter D. Edmonds's *Drums along the Mohawk,* Pearl S. Buck's *Exile,* Daphne du Maurier's *Jamaica Inn,* Corey Ford's *My Ten Years in a Quandary,* John Gunther's *Inside Europe,* MacKinlay Kantor's *Arouse and Beware,* Granville Hicks's *John Reed,* Dorothea Brande's *Wake Up and Live,* Aldous Huxley's *Eyeless in Gaza,* and John Dos Passos's *Big Money.*[85] But the biggest money-maker in 1936, besides *Gone With the Wind,* was Dale Carnegie's *How to Win Friends and Influence People,* which sold more than 1,300,000 copies.

By the end of September, the total number of copies sold was 526,000. By the end of October, the total had reached seven hundred thousand copies. Six months after publication, in December 1936, one million copies of *Gone With the Wind* had been sold. Those in the publishing business noted that other books had sold more than a million, but no other book had ever sold a million copies in such a short time. For Christmas 1936, every employee at Macmillan got a generous bonus, the first bonus in years. At three dollars a copy, the three million dollars that *Gone With the Wind* brought into bookstores transfused life into dying retail bookstore businesses all over the nation.[86]

The book was not just a literary phenomenon but a social and economic one as well, for it created jobs for people who had been out of work. The book literally helped the nation rise out of the ashes of the 1929 Depression. All over the country, young women began wearing Scarlett O'Hara hairstyles and clothes because the fashion industry began producing dresses, hats, petticoats, underwear, gloves, purses, blouses, and coats in the *Gone With the Wind* style and in colors named "Scarlett Green" and "Melanie Blue." Haberdashers began advertising Rhett Butler's style of hats, trousers, shirts, and jackets.

Interior decorators designed wallpaper, draperies, lamps, and fabrics with Tara and Twelve Oaks pictorial scenes for upholstery materials. Dolls, plates, jewelry, and music boxes, ashtrays, sheet music, pictures, greeting cards, novelties of all kinds were on sale in department stores. Babies, streets, recipes, flowers, restaurants, theaters, pets, and other things were named after the characters in *Gone With the Wind*. Finis Farr described the situation best when he wrote: "A social historian would not have needed to visit decorating establishments to realize the permeating ubiquity of *Gone With the Wind*. He need only have picked up a newspaper and read the advertising columns, for the nation's copywriters, alert as always to whatever occupies the public mind, had recognized, the moment the book appeared, that they could use its characters and title in extolling almost any product or service in the world."[87]

By the second week of July 1936, the *New York Herald Tribune* flatly stated: "*Gone With the Wind* has come to be more than a novel. It is a national event, a proverbial expression of deep instinct, a story that promises to found a kind of legend."[88]

11

When rumors started flying that Peggy had gotten $5 million for the film rights, practically everybody wanted money from her. She grew to revile the telephone and the telegram. She was continually being asked to donate cash for memorials, scholarships, awards, orphans, private schools, indigents, and many other purposes. Only she, John, Stephens, and her father knew about Latham's wire of June 30 stating that the movie rights were being sold for fifty thousand dollars; so she knew the word about the sale got out in Atlanta through the telegraph office. But how did it get out elsewhere? The euphoria she experienced earlier when she received the big check from Brett dissolved into hostility when she was handed a telegram from Annie Laurie. On that same afternoon, Peggy angrily scratched out a letter to Lois Cole. Her words yell off the page: "Feebly I take my typewriter in hand to ask just what the hell Annie Laurie means by jumping on me about rumors that Fox Films had bought the book. At present I am hunting for some one to jump on about all the damn movie rumors which are driving me nuts."

> People are driving me crazy, folks on the relief rolls asking for a hundred because I wont miss it out of my many millions. Friends wondering why in Hell I persist in driving a 1929 model car and wearing four year old cotton dresses and fifty cent stockings and

calling me an old Hetty Green to my face. None of these rumors started from me. . . . Finally they got so bad I had the newspapers here deny the rumors in large print.

The newspapers did print a denial for her, but the rumors still kept dropping like bombs from all directions. She told Lois,

It isn't confined to this section. My ex room mate at Smith (now in N.Y. with United Artists films) wrote me that her book seller had told her that a Macmillan salesman had told him I had refused "forty thousand smackers, and dearie-lamb, that's a heluva lot of smackers to refuse." A friend in Chicago wrote about the same thing, saying that in a round about way they had heard it from someone at Macmillan.[89]

After listing all the other accounts that she had heard as coming from Macmillan salesmen, she wrote, "I believe the book trade gossips back and forth worse than the newspaper people though that hardly seems possible. . . . I just came to the end of everything yesterday and blew up with loud explosions and went to bed and have the tired shakes so bad this a.m. that I can hardly hit the keys."

Before she closed her letter, she exclaimed about the movie stars' roles:

Dear God, Lois. NOT Janet Gaynor! Spare me this last ignominy or else tell Bonnie Annie to hold her up for a million. May I ask which part she intends to play—Belle Watling? Miriam Hopkins has been my choice from the beginning but I knew what I had to say wouldnt matter so I said nothing. She has the voice, the looks, the personality and the sharp look. And I wish that lovely creature (I think her name is Elizabeth Allan) who played David Copperfield's mother could do Melanie. And I wish Charles Boyer didnt have a French accent for he's my choice for Rhett. Next to him, Jack Holt is the only person I can think of.

That day she was especially tense because she was not looking forward to that evening, when she would have the radio interview on the *Journal*'s "Editorial Hour," for which John had prepared the script. She ended her letter by telling Lois, "Tonights my last appearance as Margaret Mitchell unless they come after me with a rope."[90]

Referring to "the unremitting excitement" that had invaded their lives, John wrote his mother, "The result is that neither of us is particularly happy about the situation, when we should be overwhelmingly happy."[91]

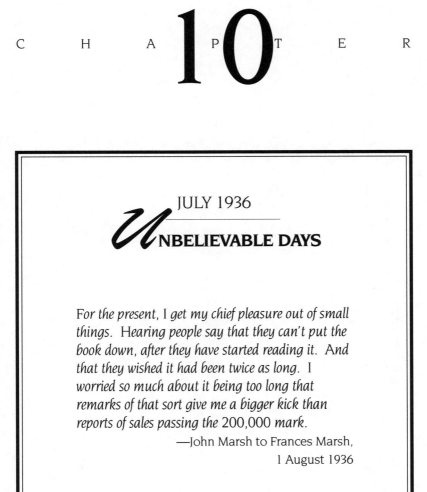

C H A P 10 T E R

JULY 1936

𝒰NBELIEVABLE DAYS

*For the present, I get my chief pleasure out of small
things. Hearing people say that they can't put the
book down, after they have started reading it. And
that they wished it had been twice as long. I
worried so much about it being too long that
remarks of that sort give me a bigger kick than
reports of sales passing the 200,000 mark.*

—John Marsh to Frances Marsh,
1 August 1936

1

_____

ON TUESDAY, JULY 7, 1936, PEGGY WOKE UP exhausted. When John reminded her of the interview that morning with the Associated Press reporters and photographers, she said she did not want any more pictures taken of her. She had lost so much weight that she thought photographs taken at this time made her look old and wizened, "like Margot Asquith."[1] The receptions, the long autographing sessions at Davison's and at Rich's, the interviews, the bags of mail, the national radio broadcast, the steady stream of uninvited visitors wanting autographs, money, answers to trivial and often impertinent questions, the friends dropping in unexpectedly for visits or wanting to entertain her at teas and dinners, the rumors about the money she was making off the movie rights, the telephone ringing continuously—all had created an unreal environment that brought her nearly to a breaking point that morning. Whenever she had not been able to sustain pressure before, John had always been able to cover for her. But now there was nothing he could do, and he felt angry about losing control over their lives.

What contributed to Peggy's bad mood that morning was learning the night before that Bessie, of all people, had written a letter about her and John and had sent it to Medora asking that it be printed in the *Atlanta Journal.* Peggy was furious when she learned about it. Although the letter was well intentioned and lovingly written, it was highly personal. She did not want to hurt Bessie's feelings, but she did not want that letter published. Then, when she discovered that Margaret Baugh had used even less judgment than Bessie in thinking that the letter could be used as publicity and had sent a copy of it to Macmillan without asking for approval, Peggy flew into a rage. The idea of having their privacy invaded by outsiders was bad enough, but for the insiders to do it really stuck in her craw, as southerners would say.

Later that morning, John took care of the matter, for Lois and Medora understood and cooperated with him.[2] While he had Lois on the phone, he also asked that Macmillan not send them any more telegrams because the telegraph company folks downtown had gotten to know Peggy during the past few months and were taking an active interest in all her affairs that passed over the wire.

Thus, instead of the situation quieting down after the book came out, it was becoming progressively worse. Peggy felt as if she were crashing on a speeding roller coaster that would not stop. Concerned about her, John made arrangements for her and Bessie to spend the rest of the week at the cabin near Tallulah Falls, which was less than two hours away from Atlanta. It was a perfect hideaway because fewer than a dozen families, who all worked for the Power Company, lived in the little village near the cabin, and they knew Peggy only as Mrs. John Marsh. The village, named Saw Tooth, had no telephone lines to it at that time and was isolated in the northeastern mountainous tip of the state.[3] Georgia Power had a private line connecting the Terrora Plant with the hydroelectric plant at Tallulah Falls, and all messages to and from the outside world were communicated through this private line.[4] So, for a few days at least, she would not hear a phone ringing. But, the best thing, as she told a friend, was that no one in Saw Tooth "reads anything but the Bible."[5]

By the time John returned home at noon, Peggy was sitting at the kitchen table looking small, forlorn, and tired. The three men from the Associated Press gave her what she described "a brisk work out that lasted three hours."[6] As John placed the suitcases, several mystery books, a little bag of mail, a big bag of groceries, and her typewriter in the back of the car, he told her he hated to see her go but assured her, "Once you are far from the haunts of man, you will feel better."[7]

After settling down in the cabin later that afternoon, she walked up the hill to the power plant where she called John to let him know that she had arrived safely. She was relieved to learn from him that Lois had promised to return Bessie's letter and so had Medora. But that was not all; Lois had also said that Herschel Brickell, the veteran reviewer for the *New York Post*, was coming south in a couple of weeks and wanted to meet her.[8] Inspired by the thought of seeing this New York critic who had praised her work, she wrote Brickell an effusive but sincere letter in which she described herself as a fugitive on the run and her success almost as if it were a misfortune:

I am Margaret Mitchell, of Atlanta, author of *Gone With the Wind,* and I want to thank you so very much for the marvelous review you gave me on June 30. It was my intention to write you the kind of letter that would show you just how much I did appreciate all your kind words. But I'm afraid I can't write that kind of letter tonight.

As you may observe from the postmark, I'm not at home in Atlanta. I'm on the run. I'm sure Scarlett O'Hara never struggled harder to get out of Atlanta or suffered more during her siege of Atlanta than I have suffered during the siege that has been on since publication day. If I had known being an author was like this I'd have thought several times before I let Harold Latham go off with my dog-eared manuscript. I've lost ten pounds in a week, leap when the phones ring and scurry like a rabbit at the sight of a familiar face on the street. The phone has screamed every three minutes for a week and utter strangers collar me in public and ask the most remarkable questions and photographers pop up out of drains. . . .[9]

His planning to visit her was the best news, she told him, that she had gotten since the day she went "on sale." With childlike enthusiasm, she asked him: "Will you really come to see me?" Free-handed with her flattery, she added, "I can't tell you how happy that would make me. It was marvelous enough that you said such things about my book but it will be more marvelous if I could meet you, because—and I must fall back on a trite statement—'I have long been an admirer of yours.'" Always careful to compliment her reviewers on their astuteness, she thanked him for picking up the "parallel between Scarlett and Atlanta," for no one else had "caught it." She appreciated his understanding that even though her story "'bordered on the melodramatic,'" the times of which she wrote "*were* melodramatic." She pointed out that it took a person with a southern background to appreciate just how melodramatic they really were and that she had had to tone down many of the actual events to make them sound believable. She loved his defense of Captain Butler.

I never thought when I wrote him, that there'd be so much argument about whether he was true to life or not. His type was such an ordinary one in those days that I picked him because he was typical of his times. Even his looks. I went through hundreds of old ambro-types and daguerreotypes looking at faces and that type of face leaped out at you. Just as surely as the faces of the pale, sly looking boys with a lock of hair hanging on their foreheads were always referred to with a sigh as "dear cousin Willy. He was killed at Shiloh." (I've often wondered why the boys who looked like that were *always* killed at Shiloh.)

About the matter of Captain Butler, she was caught in a crossfire. The northern critics said he was not true to life; the southerners found him so true that she feared having a lawsuit on her hands despite her protests that she did not model him after any human being she had ever heard of. She asked,

"And how did you know I had a 'memory for what older people had told me?' Because you have that type and had the same things told to you? Good Heavens, I am running on. And I was only going to say 'thank-you.'"

With her voice almost ringing off the page, she offered her hospitality: "I'll give you a party if you want a party or I'll feed you at home and sit and listen to you talk. My cook's a good old fashioned kind, strong on turnip greens and real fried chicken and rolls that melt in your mouth. Personally, I'd rather listen to you talk—and thank you—than give you a party." Her letter made a hit with Brickell. In a short while, Brickell and his wife Norma made a lasting friendship with Peggy and John.

2

Instead of resting the following day, she worked steadily from morning to late evening typing five long letters. All are creatively expressed and give us insight into Peggy's lively personality and her reaction to fame. "I do think it's awful," she wrote George Brett, "when you've sent me a check for five thousand dollars that I haven't had time to buy me a new dress, or have my car overhauled! I didn't know an author's life was like this. Life has been such a nightmare recently that it was all I could do to stay on my feet, much less write letters." With her imagination fired, she explained her "escape" from Atlanta in more dramatic terms and added a bit of fiction: "I've started for the back of beyond in the mountains and stopped here because I was going to sleep at the wheel and afraid I'd kill myself in a ditch. When I reach a place where there aren't any telephones and no newspapers for my picture to be in, I'll stop and write you a letter to tell you just how much I do appreciate the check and all you and Macmillan have done for me." She closed with "Good Heavens! The advertising you've put behind me! With all those ads and the grand publicity the newspapers have given me, Macmillan could have sold Karl Marx up here in these hills!"[10]

She wrote a 225-word letter to Hunt Clement thanking him for his fifteen-word telegram. Then, she composed a thousand-word letter to Gilbert Govan, who had begun his review of *Gone With the Wind* in the July 5 *Chattanooga Times* with what she called "a grand lead." He stated, "One of the things which most Northerners say that they cannot under-stand about Southerners is what they call an obsession with the Civil War. 'We've forgotten about it,' they say, 'why can't you?'"[11] She told him that she, too, had heard northerners say those same words hundreds of times: "And I remembered how I looked at them always in a blank confusion, faced with the fact that I couldn't explain why the war is an 'obsession' with us." She said could not explain then "without taking all night—or writing a book as long as the one I wrote."[12] Then, in her conversational manner of writing, she went on to tell him a story about the night she was having supper with Lois and Allan Taylor:

> I asked him [Allan] what prison his kin folks had been in during the war. And he asked me what prison mine had been in. And I asked what the death rate had been in the prison of his kin. And he wanted to know whether pneumonia or small pox accounted for most of the deaths in the jail where my folks were imprisoned. It seemed an ordinary enough conversation to us and we spoke of it all as though we'd been there. But we came out of it suddenly when Lois looked at us curiously and made the same remark you made in your lead, asked the same question.

One of Peggy's traits that made her so popular was her ability to find something special about an individual and praise that person for it. This trait is strikingly manifested in her letters also. For example, she complimented Govan for recognizing that Gerald O'Hara's security could never be found apart from the land: "No one else picked that up . . . and that depressed me for while I didn't hammer on it I meant it for an undercurrent. And I felt, as I suppose all authors are prone to feel, nine tenths of the time, that I had utterly failed in getting my ideas over." She appreciated his saying that the characters had not been drawn from real life, because "people are picking out Rhett Butlers to such an extent that I may have a law suit on my hands yet for using the grandfathers of certain people who must be nameless. And I have never heard of their darned grandfather. And Melanie has been fitted to a number of people, last of all me."

She was referring to a piece that Harry Sitwell Edwards, one of the local newspapermen, had written in the *Atlanta Journal* on July 7. Edwards wrote, "Inevitably, the true novelist writes herself into her story; a bit here and a bit there, in the characters assembled. And sometimes, one of them may reveal her as a whole. In *Gone With the Wind* . . . the real heroine is Melanie. . . . And Peggy Mitchell is the reincarnation of Melanie." Her response to that idea is found in her letter of July 8 to Govan: "Being a product of the Jazz Age, being one of those short-haired, short-skirted, hard-boiled young women who preachers said would go to hell or be hanged before they were thirty, I am naturally a little embarrassed at finding myself the incarnate spirit of the Old South."

The next person to whom she wrote was Julia Collier Harris, who on July 5 had dedicated "From My Balcony," her long column in the *Chattanooga News,* to *Gone With the Wind.* The columnist had sent Peggy a copy of her column and also a copy of Ralph Thompson's *New York Times* negative review, on which she had penciled, "Shallow and spiteful."

In her reply of approximately 1,180 words, Peggy wrote how happy and pleased her family was about all the nice things Mrs. Harris had written about her. "Though they would die before admitting it, I'm sure they all feel in the old fashioned Southern way—that a lady's name appears in print only when she's born and buried. And I know they had well concealed qualms about seeing my name in print. However, after I took the plunge and was published they rallied to me.... And they were so pleased at your column, not only the nice things you said but the way you said them. So I am saying 'thank you' for the clan as well as myself."[13]

Another letter she wrote while still in the mountains was to Edwin Granberry, who also praised *Gone With the Wind* in his June 30 column in the *New York Evening Sun*. This letter is much like the one she wrote to Brickell except that she discloses a bit more dismay at her sudden fame. After explaining that recent events had made her "incoherent from exhaustion," she went on to thank Granberry for his "kind words about poor Scarlett, for saying that she still keeps your sympathy."[14] While Peggy was writing about Scarlett, it had never occurred to her that such a storm of hard words would descend upon the poor creature's head. "She just seemed to me to be a normal person thrown into abnormal circumstances and doing the best she could, doing what seemed to her the practical thing. The normal human being in a jam thinks, primarily, of saving his own hide, and she valued hide in a thoroughly normal way."

Granberry's compassionate response to Rhett Butler and to Scarlett pleased her no end. One of the first reviewers not only to show sympathy for Scarlett but also to predict the manner in which fans, especially female readers, would adore Rhett Butler, Granberry wrote that "the greatest triumph of the book" was "the creation of the character of Rhett Butler.... He is one of the great lovers in all fiction, and no man ever had his heart more broken than he. Miss Mitchell's objective handling of him rivals Sigrid Undset's way with her Erling. As we remember, we are never—even in his worst moments of torment—led directly into the mind of Rhett Butler; the author is always able to find an action or a speech which reveals the havoc. (Watch for the moment when Butler opens his shirt to show his step-son the scar.)"[15]

Singling out that particular passage, Peggy exclaimed that she did not think anybody would "catch up" with her in that aspect of her book.

> I could live in his mind so thoroughly that I neglected to write about his mind. And I positively got goose bumps when you referred to the incident of Wade Hampton and the scar on Rhett's belly.... And to say he is one of the great lovers of fiction—well, good heavens! If I hadn't been so completely certain my book was

rotten, hadn't thought it rotten for so many years, I would be so conceited about that line that I'd be unbearable!

She ended her letter by telling Granberry how happy he had made her and her family: "My reserved and unenthusiastic father simply purred when he read your review—and why not? I wish there was some way I could tell you how much I appreciated everything you said. I wish I could see you because I talk better than I write and perhaps I could make you understand what your review meant to me. And I hope I do see you sometime."

The next morning, Wednesday, July 9, Peggy wrote one more letter before she and Bessie started back to Atlanta. Perfecting her persona of the suffering servant, she wrote to Stephen Vincent Benét. "I am not in the best condition to write the kind of letter I'd like to write you. . . . I have just made my escape from Atlanta after losing ten pounds since my publication day. . . . My life has been quiet, here-to-fore, quiet by choice and I find all this goings-on very upsetting. So I bolted until things should quiet down." Then she told him how much his work had influenced her, how much it meant to her, and how her heart sank when she heard he was to review her book. "You were my favorite poet; you had written my most loved book. You knew so much and appreciated good writing so much that I fully expected you to blast me at the top of your lungs. I suppose I should have realized that anyone who can write something great can be generous, too."[16]

3

Peggy's letters demonstrate the force of her conversational powers and her feminine magnetism. She presented herself to men as an ill but modest, charming woman who admired and trusted them so much that she was sharing a part of her joy and her sorrow with each one privately. But Peggy wrote letters to all of her admirers and also to her critics, no matter what their age or gender. Indeed, perhaps no other author in the annals of literary history has spent more time and effort in writing letters explaining herself, her illnesses, and her book, or in giving advice to people she had never met than Margaret Mitchell did. Nearly all of the people who wrote her were sincere, and she responded with sincerity.

Most of her letters ran between five hundred and eighteen hundred words, and all are very personal expressions of her appreciation. Sometimes she would answer questions in greater detail, no doubt, than the recipient had expected; and she would also give bits of advice. For example, when two fourteen-year-old girls wrote asking her to write a sequel making Scarlett and Rhett get back together by using the outline they proposed, Peggy encouraged them to practice writing if they wanted to be good authors. "Keep on writing about things with which you are familiar and things you know best and understand best."[17] These were the exact words that John had said to her a decade earlier.

If she were writing to thank someone who had written a good review, she would practically quote the entire review, commenting on and savoring nearly every line. Inviting responses, her letters were so warm, lively, and generous in spirit that the receiver was obligated to write back. Thus she initiated many friendships with people whom she would not have otherwise known, such as the Edwin Granberrys, the Herschel Brickells, and the Clifford Dowdeys.

Whenever anyone questioned her historical facts, she painstakingly responded, often with John's help since he enjoyed nailing down requests like that. For instance, a month after *Time* magazine, in its July 6 issue, published an excellent review of *Gone With the Wind*, the author of the review, K. T. Lowe, sent Peggy a telegram asking about the desecration of the Atlanta City Cemetery by Federal troops. When his telegram arrived on August 3, she was ill and John wired that the answer would be forthcoming. On August 29, she wrote Lowe a long explanation:

> I was, and still am, suffering severe eye strain due to overwork in finishing my book. Even now, I am unable to read or write. This condition has severely hampered me in checking back through my reference works and assembling the authorities for the statement in question. However, with the help of friends, I have been able to get together the data. . . . It never occurred to me that the matter of Federal desecration of Southern cemeteries would ever be questioned. In childhood I heard vivid stories from so many different people who had seen the desecrated cemeteries in Atlanta and other cities. However, I am citing a few authorities.[18]

Then she proceeded to cite four sources and to quote passages from them.

Looking backward, one cannot help wondering why Peggy wasted so much time writing such long letters. She could easily have gotten her secretary Margaret Baugh to type a standard thank-you note to send to fans and reviewers, for doing so would have enabled her to use her time to rest or to write other pieces for publication. Almost all of the important magazines in the nation solicited her to send stories or articles. At one point, John reported to his mother: "One of the big editors wanted to come from New York to Atlanta to talk things over, after he had been given the usual turn-down, and another one insisted that Peggy send them 'just anything.'"[19] She consistently refused such offers, saying, "I am not well enough to do any writing."[20] She never attempted to write anything of that nature, nor did she ever start work on a new book. She said repeatedly, "I hate writing worse than anything in the world and would far rather scrub floors or pick cotton than write."[21]

And yet she spent hours at the typewriter nearly every day for the remainder of her life, expressing herself creatively and vividly in millions of words in her letters. She explained her commitment to letter writing as a matter of moral responsibility: "It is not courtesy to ignore them, certainly not courtesy to send them abrupt letters. . . . They must be answered and answered by me. There are things I have to attend to personally because this happens to be my job, whether I like it or not, and I cannot put it upon anyone else. Nor, as I think it over, can I run away."[22]

However, Edwin Granberry may have come closer to the truth about her letter-writing obsession in his article about her for *Collier's* magazine in March 1937. Commenting on her open, friendly, and gentle writing voice, on her humility and her many references to her debilitating illnesses, he explained that she tried to respond in kind to the "emotional" and the "confessional" tone that many of the letters she received conveyed.[23]

Peggy's letters do indeed have that tone, for many of them touchingly disclose her anxieties and her desperate need to be loved, understood, and accepted. In spite of her phenomenal success, she was never able to dispel her fears of failure and rejection. Her need to be admired was overwhelming. Although she loathed the disadvantages that went along with it, she loved being a celebrity, but her insecurity about herself and her book never waned. She truly meant it when she said time and time again: "Heavens knows I never expected the book to get such good reviews or people to be so kind. The book will never seem like a book to me but just that old dog-eared and dirty bunch of copy paper which took up so much space in our small apartment and seemed with each rewriting to get worse."[24]

4

By mid-afternoon on July 10, Peggy was back in Atlanta reading the special-delivery letters that she and John had just received from Lois Cole. In her letter to John, Lois wrote that Annie Laurie had told her the previous night that she had closed with David Selznick for fifty thousand dollars cash. "She maintains it is the highest price ever paid for a first novel and is sure that none of the companies could have been pushed any higher. Apparently everyone is anxious to get the contract through and signed in a hurry, and, if all goes well, I should have it forwarded to you tomorrow . . . they want to have everything settled by the middle of next week."[25] The enclosed letter Lois wrote to Peggy said about the same thing but added that Selznick was contemplating doing the picture in color and that he wished to take his time in casting the roles in the best possible fashion. Emphasizing that Annie Laurie had made the best possible deal, Lois went on to say, "Annie Laurie says that they tried to get her down and she tried to get them up, but that was the highest that anyone would go, when it came right down to writing a check. She maintains that it is the biggest price ever paid for a first novel." Remembering the scolding she had gotten from Peggy earlier about the Macmillan gossips, Lois assured Peggy that they at Macmillan were not talking about the contract "until it was signed and delivered." The one other thing that Lois mentioned was that Annie Laurie had requested that if they were ever asked what price was paid, they were to say "for something over $50,000, which seems to me," Lois added, "to be stretching the truth—but what of it! Everyone here is very pleased about the sale, and I hope you are, too. I think it is grand."[26]

What not only puzzled but also annoyed the Marshes about the sale of the film rights was the role of Annie Laurie. As the Marshes interpreted their agreement with Macmillan, they thought the publisher was Peggy's agent in regard to selling the film rights. But from Lois's letter, it was clear that Macmillan had retained Annie Laurie Williams to handle the contract for them. From the publisher's angle, hiring a successful, well-established literary agent skilled in handling theater and film contracts was good business. But as Stephens Mitchell later explained to Finis Farr, "It seemed to Margaret that . . . Macmillan had delegated complicated negotiations for which the publishers themselves had accepted a direct responsibility."[27] Now that the Marshes were not so confident that Macmillan was looking after Peggy's interest in the manner that they had believed, they agreed that careful scrutiny of the film contract was imperative before she signed it. Accepting the price was all she had done thus far and was only the start of the contract business. She wanted the contract to be perfectly clear about what she was selling and what she was keeping.

In the meanwhile, Granberry and Brickell, who had made arrangements to lecture at a writers' workshop in Blowing Rock, North Carolina, invited Peggy, on short notice, to join them there. Determined to shield her from the public, they assured her that she would get some rest in this tiny resort town high in the Appalachians. At first, she did not want to go, but John insisted, saying the trip would do her good, and while she was away he could study the contract. His plan was to try to clear up as many of the technical details as possible so that when she returned, all the notes on the changes would be in shape for any item that was of real importance to her.

Arriving in North Carolina on Monday afternoon, July 13, Peggy was greeted by Granberry and Brickell, whom she immediately liked. Although she enjoyed being with them and attended some of the sessions of their workshop, she felt nervous, weak, and anxious, particularly after she received her first letter from John on Wednesday, July 15, announcing the arrival of the contract.

> Sweetheart—By the time this letter reaches you, you may have already seen newspaper announcements that you have sold the movie rights. The movie folks gave out the story in Hollywood last Friday and it was published in New York yesterday. The stories did not state the amount, and Lois says she is doing everything possible to keep the amount from being published.

The Marshes had been concerned about how to release the news that Peggy had sold the movie rights. All of the Atlanta newspapers had been good to her, but John Paschall obviously expected her to give the scoop to the *Journal*. Trying to avoid a conflict, John had asked Lois earlier to release the news about the contract in the afternoon, so all the papers would get the bulletin at the same time. Since that did not happen, John figured that the movie people, "in moviesque fashion decided to bust the story because it was a good story."[28] Because the story had escaped without Macmillan's consent, he asked Peggy not to be angry with Macmillan for putting out their own story for release the next day. He did not see that there was much else they could do. Besides, the publication of the item would not affect her rights in the matter one way or the other. She had agreed to a price only, not to the terms of the contract, he reminded her, and if she did not like the terms, she did not have to accept them.

John told her to think of the publicity about the sale as accomplishing two things: it would relieve their tensions as to which Atlanta paper was going to be scooped on the story, and it would serve to get the first flurry of excitement over and done with at a time when she was away and he could evade direct questions from newspapers by simply saying she was out of town.

The contract, which was about ten pages long and filled with highly technical language, seemed satisfactory to John, except for the fact that it was an outright sale and gave Peggy no right to pass on the final scenario or to have any say at all as to what the film people would do with the book after Peggy signed and accepted their check.[29] In his long talk with Lois earlier that day, he reminded Lois about Peggy's earlier correspondence with Latham concerning two issues: her wanting a voice in what the filmmakers did with her book and her right to approve the final scenario for the movie.

John urged her to stay if she were enjoying herself, and he told her she should not rush back by Sunday or Monday. He thought that one or more letters would have to be exchanged between Atlanta and New York in straightening out points her father would raise about the contract. "My idea, as you may suspect, is to keep you out of town as long as possible. I miss you terribly, but I still think this is a good time for you to be out of Atlanta."

John had received the contract on Monday, July 13, along with a note from Lois saying that it should be sent directly back to her and that she wanted it by Friday of that same week if possible.[30] He replied,

> Please tell Annie Laurie and anyone else who is interested that they should not expect the contract to be signed and delivered back to New York within five minutes or thereabouts after it reaches Atlanta. The Mitchell family just doesn't work that way, as you all may have discovered last summer. With their legal training and legal habits, they wouldn't sign *any* contract without careful consideration and due deliberation. So, in any plans you are making, please allow for at least a reasonable period of time for investigation and study of the contract at this end of the line.

He also ordered Lois to "make it your business to keep a firm hand on the various parties up there and see to it that a leak doesn't occur in New York" regarding the amount Selznick paid for the movie rights.[31]

John explained that Peggy did not want to write the script or go to Hollywood to act as an advisor, or even help select the cast. But she wanted some guarantee in writing that Selznick would not change the novel, its ending, or its characters, their personalities, and dialects. John wanted to have a passage in the contract that obligated Selznick to make a *good* picture, and by "good" he meant one that was true to the novel's historical accuracy. But Annie Laurie told Lois that the movie people no longer allowed authors to put such provisions in their contracts. "Even Dreiser was not allowed such a provision," she explained.[32] The two mediums were so different that it was as impossible for an author to say what should go in a screenplay as it was for a motion picture producer to say what an author should put in a novel. Trying to make the Marshes feel more secure, Annie Laurie said that the Selznick people "were all crazy" about the novel and that she had heard them say they were leaving the ending as it was written because it was "the only logical ending." If anyone could make a great movie of *Gone With the Wind,* Lois told the Marshes, it was Selznick, and she urged them to see what he had done with *David Copperfield.* Fortunately, the Marshes, who had seen the film, agreed. In a letter to his sister Frances around this time, John wrote, "Mr. Selznick made 'David Copperfield' and if he can do as well with this book as he did with that one, we won't complain. His handling of that job was one reason why I was glad to see him get the movie rights to Peggy's book."[33]

On Thursday evening, July 16, Atlanta's drought and heat wave were broken with a terrific thunderstorm. As John sat in his office, he typed another letter to Peggy. His letters during this critical period show his love for her and his desire to take care of her.

> Sweetheart—Please let me urge you not to bother about writing me letters unless there is something urgent you wish to discuss. I don't want you to use up your vacation writing, when you might be resting or playing. To tell the truth, I had no intention when you left of going on any letter-a-day schedule. I have written you yesterday and today because it seemed desirable in order to inform you of important developments.... So, baby, please don't waste time writing unless it's about something important. At this stage of the game, other things are more important than unnecessary letters.[34]

Enclosing clippings from the *Journal* and the *Georgian* and a copy of Macmillan's release, which had reached the papers that morning, he explained that the "who scooped who angle of their problem" seemed to be out of the way now. He told her how he, Stephens, and her father had had a long session about the contract the previous night. The only major problem that they saw with it was the fact that she had no veto over what the movie people might decide to do with the book after they had bought it. "I don't suppose it is logical to suppose that the movies would pay a large sum for the book, and then give you the right to junk *everything* they planned to do with it in your 'uncontrolled discretion.' Since the problem arose, I have been trying to figure out just how a clause might be worded on that point, so as to give due recognition to their rights and at the same time protect yours. Frankly, it's got me stumped, and the Mississippi-accent gentlemen [Brickell and Granberry] might possibly have some suggestions."[35]

Her father was to write a letter setting out the various changes that he thought ought to be made in the contract. If John thought that the changes were appropriate and that she would consent to them, then he would forward the letter to Lois and try to get the changes made before Peggy returned to Atlanta. Giving us some idea of how the Mitchells worked, he added,

> During most of last night's long session, while Steve and your father were arguing heatedly about points which seemed to mean a lot to them, I was balancing your check stubs or reading clippings on your book. If you were here, I imagine you would be doing the same thing—or worse. There are certain things about this contract which are important from a lawyer's viewpoint and

certain others that are important to you as Peggy Mitchell. My idea is that there is no need for you to come back to Atlanta while the "lawyer" stuff is being wrangled over.... But if it doesn't meet with your approval, if you rather I would *not* deal directly with Macmillan without consulting you in advance on each point, just let me know. If the latter course is your preference, you had better wire me or phone me as soon as you get this letter. A wire, "Please submit everything to me before taking up with Macmillan" will be all that is necessary.

The most striking feature about John's management of Peggy's book business is the fact that he always made her feel that she was in complete control. He did all the work, filtered through all the thorny details, and made all the decisions, letting her think that the decisions were hers.

My affectionate and husbandly advice is that you enjoy your vacation and let us bother about these preliminary legal technicalities. You understand, of course, that you will have the final say-so on the whole matter. Nothing that we do will be final until you put your name on the contract, and if you don't like what we have done, you can change it all when you get back to Atlanta.

He closed by telling her that she had "two very sweet letters" waiting for her—one from her Aunt Isabelle and the other from Kate Edwards, relatives she had not heard from in a long time. And he added that there were "many others, too, but these two stand out in my memory.... Have a good time and don't bother about us down here. We're not doing so bad. Lonesome, yes. But I can stand it a while longer."

Even though John had suggested that they not write every day, they did. On Friday, July 17, he typed a note to her on his own personal typewriter and attached it to the business letter regarding the contract that he had dictated earlier to Rhoda.

Darling—I hope you won't feel too harshly over the fact that I have used Rhoda's help in getting the attached letter written. With another session with your father scheduled for tonight and with a mess of things piling up on me here at the office today, the only choice was between dictating the letter or not getting it off to you at all today. And it seemed to me to be too important to be delayed.[36]

Again, he mentioned her fan letters and said how happy he was to find her letter when he got home the night before. He thought she would enjoy Faith Baldwin's letter, which he had enclosed along with the letter he had received from Lois about the contract. (Faith Baldwin—Mrs. Hugh Hamlin Cuthrell—was a writer for the *Pictorial Review*.[37]) Summarizing the situation they faced with the contract, he wrote: "It seems to be a 'take it or leave it' proposition. Apparently the movie folks are going to insist on an outright sale without giving you any privilege of passing on the movie scenario they write from your book."[38]

He added, "I imagine you have the same question in your mind that I have in mine. That is, whether Lois and Annie Laurie have really done their best on this point, whether the movies are as stubborn about this as Lois says they are and whether all of the good movie companies have gone into cahoots and agreed among themselves not to give this privilege to *any* author."

About Lois's question concerning the possibility of Peggy's going to Hollywood as an advisor to Selznick, John said: "I told her that you very definitely did *not* want to go, but that you *might* possibly consider doing it if your presence there might prevent the movie people from mutilating your book and might help in getting them to interpret and cast it properly." Even though the movie people, he thought, would probably pay her for going to Hollywood, he said: "If I were in your fix, I would be willing to go out there at my own expense, if that was the only way I could keep some control and supervision over the type of movie they make from the book." He noted that although the movie contract was mimeographed, a provision had been attached on a typewritten page. This provision gave Selznick an option on Peggy's next book, and John thought Peggy might use this to her advantage. He thought that they might insert a clause in the contract stating that the movies would *not* have an option on her next book unless they did right by her on this one. "Of course, the joke is that you don't intend to write any more books, but the fact that Selznick is sufficiently interested in you to *want* an option on your future production might prove to be a lever through which you could retain some control over what is done in making a movie out of this book."[39]

On Sunday, July 19, while Peggy was still away, John slept until early afternoon, when he heard Bessie coming into the apartment to fix him something to eat. After dressing, while he waited for his breakfast, he sat on the screened porch and smoked a cigarette as he wrote his mother about all the events and how overwhelming everything was to him and Peggy. "That's the trouble," he wrote. "I suppose, it's too overwhelming. My own attitude on the matter is to let things run their course. Later on, maybe I will begin to get happy about it."[40]

5

When she returned on Wednesday, July 22, Peggy looked more like a small, sunburned camper than a lionized author. She found that nothing had changed; Bessie was still grumbling loudly to herself about what a mess everything was in, and the place was littered with letters, telegrams, magazines, and newspapers. The contract lay on the dining room table along with more stacks of mail, magazines, newspapers, and pages of notes in John's handwriting. Pointing to a corner of the living room where there were two tall stacks of *Gone With the Wind* that fans had sent her to be autographed and returned—at her own expense—John said, "Now that kind of business has got to be stopped!"

She was cringing at the sight of those books and the mounds of mail until he laughed and said, "Baby, you're so famous now the post office delivers letters simply addressed to 'Margaret Mitchell, GWTW.' Here's an envelope addressed to 'MM—GWTW—ATLANTA' and here's another with nothing on the envelope but a cartoon drawing of a little man saying 'Goodbye!'"[41] There was even a letter from her idol Stephen Vincent Benét and his wife asking her to come to New York to see them. A few weeks earlier she would have squealed in delight upon receiving such an invitation, but now she just sighed in disbelief. She was awed to learn that in addition to writing wonderful reviews of *Gone With the Wind,* many influential southern writers, such as D. S. Freeman, Stark Young, Thomas Dixon, and Julia Peterkin, sent her personal letters of congratulations. Knowing that she would be delighted to see Julia Peterkin's review and letter, John placed it on top of the stack he handed Peggy to read. The first part of that review, in the *Washington Post,* reads, "It seems to me that *Gone With the Wind* by Margaret Mitchell is the best novel that has ever come out of the South. In fact, I believe it is unsurpassed in the whole of American writing."[42] Macmillan quoted these lines in its early advertisements of the novel.

From another stack of newsclippings he had been saving for her, John read the one about the seven transatlantic liners that sailed from New York the week she was in Blowing Rock. Macmillan salesmen had noticed in the bookshops that many copies of *Gone With the Wind* were stacked up for delivery to passengers on the various steamers. When they asked about the stacks, the booksellers estimated that something in the neighborhood of one thousand copies of *Gone With the Wind* went on the boats that day.[43] Peggy shook her head in disbelief.

Also in the stack of mail were the messages Macmillan had received from Marion Saunders, an agent who handled foreign copyrights, informing them that sets of galleys of *Gone With the Wind* had been distributed to her agents in Sweden, Denmark, Germany, Italy, Holland, Spain, Czecho-slovakia, Hungary, Norway, and France.[44] Shaking her head and rolling her eyes upward, Peggy asked John, "What in the hell will Mammy sound like in Norwegian? I-talian?"[45]

The only disturbing note was from Lois, saying that Macmillan had inquiries from reviewers and from two Catholic magazines, *Commonweal* and *America,* regarding Peggy's use of the name Gerald O'Hara.[46] Peggy had anticipated this trouble. While *Gone With the Wind* was in page proofs, the Roman Catholic Church simultaneously created the Diocese of Savan-nah-Atlanta and appointed to this new diocese a bishop who had the same name as Scarlett O'Hara's rowdy father—Gerald O'Hara. When Peggy read the bishop's name in the newspapers, she was stunned. But by then it was too late to change the character's name, for the book had been printed. It was ironic that His Excellency and her book arrived in Atlanta about the same time. She also worried that her relatives would think that she, a fallen-away Catholic, had deliberately used the name. Because she had taken such infinite pains to avoid using names of real people, this coincidence was, in her mind, a malevolently mystical turn of affairs.

When gossips told her that Bishop O'Hara was embarrassed and offended at having to share his good name with a man who drank, swore, and gambled, she wrote him a long letter apologizing and explaining all that she had done to avoid the very circumstance in which she now found herself. Although she never received a response from him, it appears that he did not take the matter seriously and may have been more amused than offended. Stephens, who handled some legal matters for the diocese, told her that the bishop had been in his office not long after the book came out and was most cordial. "He never mentioned the book and neither did I."[47]

At that time, the names of the characters were just one of her worries. Here she is telling Norma Brickell what those early days of fame were like in the Marshes' apartment:

> Special deliveries wake us at dawn, demanding to know if Scarlett ever got him back, registered letters get us from the supper table demanding the same information. The phone goes on and on, people boldly asking me my age, my royalties, can I get their cook in the movies in "my" film, am I a Catholic? And why haven't I any children? Am I kin to them? They had a cousin named Margaret Mitchell. How can they find the road to Tara? They went to Jonesboro last week end and nobody could tell them how to get there. But so *many* people had told them positively that two of the wings of Tara were still standing. (When I say I made it up, they refuse to believe because they've seen so many people

who've seen Tara and they think I'm pretty ungracious not to direct them there.) And is it true that I was born the last year of the Civil War? Then is that picture they publish a picture of my Granddaughter? Most of the time Bessie answers the phone. I'd as soon pick up a snake as the receiver. But Bessie is not here lots of the time and so I get caught, thinking it's John on the wire or Western Union. It is appalling the barefaced questions people will ask. I thought I had learned most of the peculiarities of mankind while I was a reporter but this is an education. After all, when I was a reporter I only saw criminals, prize fighters, politicians, debutantes and fatigued celebrities. It was seldom that I met the sturdy middle classes. If I could just gain about fifteen pounds I could stand meeting them a bit better.[48]

6

The same day she returned from Blowing Rock, Peggy went to work writing to reviewers while John worked on the film contract. Her letters are vivid in detail and alive with the pleasure of her triumphant entry into the literary world. To Donald Adams, who wrote a favorable review of *Gone With the Wind* for the July 5 issue of the *New York Times Book Review,* she introduced herself boldly, saying "I am a brand new author and your review pleased me so much and made me so happy that I only wish I knew a dozen ways to say 'thank you.'"

Then she proceeded to write nearly two thousand words telling Adams point by point what she liked about his review. She did the same for Julia Peterkin.[49] And to Douglas S. Freeman, she wrote: "I cannot tell you enough how thrilled (yes, I know that is a school girl adjective but I really mean it) I was at having a letter from you! But any Southerner would be thrilled and any Southerner, who had done a little research into the period with which you dealt, would naturally have palpitations. Your *Lee* was the very first thing I purchased with my very first royalty check.[50]

She wrote a charming story to Thomas Dixon, author of *The Traitor: A Story of the Fall of the Invisible Empire.* She told him that she was raised on his books and loved them so much that she plagiarized them when she was a child.

For many years I've had you on my conscience, and I suppose I might as well confess it now. When I was eleven years old I decided that I would dramatize your book *The Traitor*—and dramatize it I did in six acts. I played the part of Steve because none of the little boys in the neighborhood would lower themselves to play a part where they had "to kiss any little ol' girl." The clansmen were recruited from the small-fry of the neighborhood, their ages ranging from five to eight. They were dressed in shirts of their fathers, with the shirt tails bobbed off. I had my troubles with the clansmen as, after Act 2, they went on strike, demanding a ten cent wage instead of a five cent one. Then, too, just as I was about to be hanged, two of the clansmen had to go to the bathroom, necessitating a dreadful stage wait which made the audience scream with delight, but which mortified me intensely. My mother was out of town at the time. On her return, she and my father, a lawyer, gave me a long lecture on infringement of copy-rights. They gave me such a lecture that for years afterward I expected Mr. Thomas Dixon to sue me for a million dollars, and I have had great respect for copy-rights ever since then.[51]

She also wrote letters to other authors, including one to Stark Young, with whom she said she "had fallen in love," and one to Ellen Glasgow for praising her book in the *New York Times*.

By now the book had assumed a life of its own, and in addition to receiving many letters asking about the characters as if they were actual people, she received hundreds of telephone calls from worried people, mainly women, wanting to know whether Scarlett got Rhett back. A few asked unusual questions like why Belle Watling did not have a parrot, because all madams had clever parrots in their parlors. Some fans wanted to know if they were correct in thinking that Rhett had had carnal relations with Melanie, if it were not Melanie he had loved all along, and if that was why he could leave Scarlett the way he did. One young man appeared at the Marshes' apartment one day asking if Rhett Butler was not the father of Melanie's baby.[52] These questions pleased her tremendously because it indicated that her readers thought of the characters as real people. Her standard answer to the Rhett-Scarlett question was:

> I wish I could tell you what happened to them both after the end of the book but I cannot, for I know no more than you do. I wrote my book from back to front. That is, last chapter first and the first chapter last and as I sat down to write it that seemed the logical ending. I do not have a notion of what happened to them and I left them to their ultimate fate. With two such determined characters, it would be hard to predict what would happen to them.[53]

Francesca and Gordon visited them shortly after the book came out and remembered well all the commotion going on in the apartment. Francesca laughingly said she would never forget Bessie's saying, in a tired voice, to one caller after another: "No, ma'am, I don't know if Captain Butler went back to Miss Scarlett. No ma'am, Miss Peggy don't know either. No, Mr. Marsh don't know either. None of us knows what happened to Captain Butler and Miss Scarlett."[54]

When a woman from Alabama wrote a review of *Gone With the Wind* saying how much she liked the black characters, particularly Prissy, Peggy replied: "Prissy was one of my favorite characters. Yes, as you wrote, she was 'aggravating.' She aggravated me unendurably while I was writing her and, when Scarlett slapped her, it was really Margaret Mitchell yielding to her overwhelming urge."[55]

Humorous letters came too and some marriage proposals. The one that amused John the most was written by a Tennessean who owned a poultry farm. This gentleman wrote Peggy a particularly interesting description of himself: "An Emerson-like prose poet, a bachelor, 6 ft., rarely gifted, genuine idealist, greatest lover of fine and useful arts, simplicity and the beautiful, true and just. I have been seeking a REAL lady, rare, talented, original, experienced, wise, bighearted, ambitious, country life experienced; no church member, hypocrite, but Free Thought, Golden Rule, socialist; someone who prizes character, reputation, faithfulness, undying love far above riches. There are no such in my vicinity."[56] Letters like this one went unanswered, as did the negative ones she occasionally received.

Margaret Baugh, who was still working only part-time for them, would come in early in the mornings with the newspapers and the mail. Trying to protect Peggy in every way, John quickly scanned the news and sorted the letters as best as he could before Peggy saw them. He concealed from her the occasional crazily critical or obscene or threatening letters that abnormal minds wrote her, and he instructed Margaret Baugh to do the same and to report all threats and obscenities to the postal inspectors.

7

Getting ready to go on vacation at the end of July, Lois did not want to leave any unfinished business and urged Peggy to get the film contract signed and returned quickly. She even had Macmillan executive Jim Putnam telegram John on July 23, asking: "Is there any difficulty regarding movie contract? Have been expecting signed copies daily." When July 27 rolled around with no word and no contract, Lois told Jim Putnam that she suspected a number of questions would arise now in the "Marsh-Mitchell entourage about the contract."[57] She was right.

On July 27, John mailed his eleven-page, single-spaced letter addressing his major concern that the contract held Peggy liable in so many ways.

Two articles, which he called "the God Almighty clauses," had to be stricken from the contract. One that was completely unacceptable gave the Selznick company permission to do anything it pleased, without limit or restriction, in converting her book into a movie, but made Peggy responsible for any trouble the Selznick company got into as a result of some error they made in changing the book to a movie. The other was about foreign copyrights, which he said were owned by Macmillan, not Peggy.[58]

When Stephens came to visit that evening, the three of them discussed at length the fact that they were not getting far trying to settle details over the telephone or by mail. John suggested that talking face to face would be far more effective and urged Peggy to go with Stephens to New York to attend the meeting Macmillan had arranged with the film people on July 29 and 30 to negotiate the terms of the contract. Peggy dejectedly agreed to go.

When the Brickells' invitation came the next day asking Peggy to take refuge in their home in the quiet woods near Ridgefield, Connecticut, John encouraged her to accept. He said that after she and her brother met with the publisher in New York, Stephens could return to Atlanta and Peggy could go to Connecticut. "I will stay in New York no longer than necessary for me and brother Stephens to clear up this damned moving picture contract," she wrote Norma Brickell. "I do not want to go. I have no clothes and no time to buy any. I have been sick in bed for the last three days and do not feel like tackling a hot trip. But I will lose my mind certainly if this thing isn't settled soon. Just now I don't care which way it is settled."[59]

A short time earlier she would have jumped at the chance to visit with Stephen Vincent Benét and his wife in New York, but now she declined their invitation, saying that she would not go to the city until she was off the bestseller list, and, according to Macmillan, that probably meant after Christmas. She added, "But then publishers are always optimistic." She added that New York would not be as bad as Atlanta, where everyone knew her, but that recent events had made her "timid of crowds and strangers who ask peculiar and very personal questions."[60]

Just before she left for New York, she wrote another letter thanking a woman in Birmingham, Alabama, who described her book as an authentic picture of the South and of southerners. However, she refused the woman's invitation to speak before a club, saying, "I do not think I will be in Birmingham any time in the very near future. I do not think I will go anywhere, except to the mountains, until I am off the best seller list and can be Mrs. John Marsh again instead of Margaret Mitchell."[61]

8

After making Putnam swear her visit to New York would be kept a secret, Peggy boarded the Pullman train late that afternoon with her brother. Early the next morning they arrived in New York and registered at the Grosvenor Hotel, which was in the neighborhood of the Macmillan Company.[62] On the afternoon of July 29, she and her brother met with the Selznick representatives Dorothy Modisett, Katharine (Kay) Brown, and Harriett Flagg, and with the Macmillan officials and their attorneys Richard Brett and Jacqueline Swords, who were from the law firm of Cadwalader, Wickersham, and Taft. Not present were Annie Laurie, Latham, and Lois; they were away on vacation. Peggy would have felt more comfortable had Latham been there, even though all of the people from Selznick's office were friendly. She liked them instantly and called them "Selznickers." She told them that day that she thought they were making a terrible mistake, for no movie could ever be made from the book. But they laughed and heartily disagreed with her.

Stephens could not have avoided feeling intimidated by those officials that day, and his presence in no way improved Peggy's chances of getting the provisions she wanted. In fact, it immediately became clear to him and Peggy that the contract was to remain essentially as it had been presented to her except for a few small concessions. In giving an account of this meeting to Finis Farr, Stephens said that once Peggy signed, she was not to interfere in any way with the making of the film. And at that time, the Selznick people did not invite her to come to Hollywood as an advisor and their offer of fifty thousand dollars was their final offer. After that first session, Peggy, tired and angry, went back to her hotel room and called John. Hating to hear the distress in her voice, he told her to come home without signing anything. But she said that the purpose of the trip was to settle the matter and settle it she was going to do.[63]

Stephens wrote in his memoir:

Margaret wanted to go on and finish the matter. She did not wish to say that Macmillan had not done its best; she saw that no one would offer more.... It is difficult to realize now, but $50,000 was a lot of money then.... So on the following day, July 30, we signed the Selznick contract and Margaret made one last comment. She said that she had sold the motion picture rights because she was worried by a great many things. The sale would get rid of one worry. She did not want another to take its place. She was happy to hear Hollywood did not want her and she was certain she did not want the worries which Hollywood could bring to her. She would not bother them, and they should not bother her. They had the movie rights; she had the $50,000 less commission [10 percent was divided between Macmillan and Annie Laurie Williams]; and we were all happy. With that, she went off to visit friends, and I came home.[64]

But Peggy was not happy. When she arrived in Connecticut around dusk, she found the Brickells' home, Acorn Cottage, lovely, quiet, and cool in its secluded wooded area. Norma had prepared a light supper, and they sat around the table until late talking. Never one to sleep well when away from John, Peggy tossed most of the night, wishing she were home. By early the next morning, she was in an extreme state of anxiety. Before breakfast, quite suddenly, as she was getting dressed, she had a most frightening experience: she went completely blind for a few seconds. The terrified Brickells first called their physician and then called John, who was out of his office at the time. Peggy appeared to be all right a few minutes after the episode and insisted that they not call John again and alarm him unnecessarily. But she wanted to go home at once. After the Brickells took her to their physician, who attributed the episode to months of serious eye strain, they helped her board the train for Atlanta.

Her own physician determined that her sudden blindness was due to hemorrhaging, caused by broken blood vessels. Fortunately, this hemorrhaging had occurred only in the front part of both eyes and did not involve the retina.[65] But it could happen again, he warned, and if it did, the next event could be more serious. He prescribed two weeks of complete rest in a dark room. During her twenty-one-day confinement period, John and Margaret Baugh did all of Peggy's reading and writing for her, and Bessie fended off all visitors and phone calls. In telling his mother about Peggy's condition, John wrote, "So I have become a reader for the great author and a file clerk in addition to ex officio business manager."[66] During her confinement, Peggy learned to dictate letters to the secretary, something she had thought she would never be able to do. In explaining to their close friends what had happened to her, John said he was writing letters "like the sort of letter I write to mother—full of reports on states of health."[67] He wrote Herschel Brickell:

> The first day or two in a darkened room with nothing to do, hour after hour, but twiddle her thumbs was pretty terrible, but after that she began to relax, some of the tightly wound springs inside her mind began to unwind from the steadily increasing tension of the past several months, and since then she has been able to get rest for her body, her mind, and her nerves, as well as her eyes, and I

am convinced the enforced rest is doing her good. . . . She has even let me install a small radio by her bed—the first one ever permitted inside the Marsh home—and she is acquiring an education as to the cowboy ballads and hillbilly songs which seem to divert the American public. And also hearing quite a lot of very dull political speeches, Georgia now being in the midst of a heated primary campaign.[68]

On the evening of August 31, as she lay in her dark room regretting that the book had ever been published, restlessly turning the dial trying to find a station not broadcasting country music, she heard a newspaper commentator say her name. Startled, she sat up in bed, saying: "Good Lord, they're talking about me." She leaned close to radio as she listened to the announcer say that Dr. William Lyon Phelps, at his annual lecture at Pointe Aux Barques, Michigan, had judged *Gone With the Wind* as the best novel of the year and George Santayana's *Last Puritan* as second best. H. L. Mencken's *American Language* was his first choice in his list of general books and Stephen Vincent Benét's *Burning City,* first in the poetry category.[69] To be named first in the company of such excellent writers must have truly overwhelmed Peggy, who, as a freshman at Smith College, had written her brother, "If I can't be first, I'd rather not be anything."

In the evenings, after their supper, John would lie in bed next to her and read letters aloud. Some sweet letters, like the one from Marjorie Kinnan Rawlings, author of *The Yearling,* gave her "goosebumps," and she had John read them over and over. Another one of her favorites was from Hervey Allen, whose famous novel *Anthony Adverse* was knocked out of first place on the *New York Times* bestseller list by *Gone With the Wind.* These letters, and there were so many of them, amazed John as well as Peggy, for he wrote Brickell: "It is one of the unbelievable things of these unbelievable days."

Because the Brickells were concerned about Peggy's health, John wrote Herschel, "You have been extraordinarily thoughtful and understanding throughout this whole situation, and I feel that we have gained a real friend." Writing as if he and Peggy were suffering through a tragedy rather than a literary triumph, he added: "Please don't worry about us. We have been through some pretty tough situations and we have come through them all so far. We have had plenty of experience with adversity and we'll come through."[70] Brickell had warned them to prepare for more assaults on their privacy, for he predicted that sales would continue to soar to 750,000 before dropping down. Doubting that the rush would last, John answered:

In spite of the events that have tumbled one over another in the six weeks that rocked the Marsh world, I still think your estimate of sales of 750,000 copies is extravagant. (Peggy commented that you didn't offer to bet on it.) When I wrote in my previous letter that I had known for years that Peggy had written a good book, I hope I didn't give the impression that I had the faintest inkling of what has happened since June 30. I didn't. My own notion was that the book would have a limited appeal to a select group of readers, and I would have been quite happy if it had sold 5,000. If Peggy were a professional writer, and not an amateur, she could have a steady income for the rest of her life, if we may judge from the rising demand that she go on with the story of Scarlett and Rhett.

When Peggy wrote the ending of the novel she had no intention of ever writing a sequel nor even of giving it a "Lady or Tiger" ending. She merely thought the story ended where it ended. But as years passed, each new generation of readers begged her to tell if Scarlett ever gets Rhett back or vice versa. Very few novelists ever know what it is like to have a throng of readers thinking that their characters are real people. To thousands of *Gone With the Wind* fans Scarlett, Rhett, Melanie, Mammy, Prissy, and the others existed in flesh and blood. The demand for their lives to go on was much like the demand Sir Arthur Conan Doyle experienced when he, tired of his character Sherlock Holmes, "killed" Holmes. Doyle's vast audience stormed the magazine that published the Holmes stories and angrily protested Holmes's death and demanded his resurrection. Like Doyle, Peggy and John were unprepared for the ongoing and lively interest in the lives of her characters, particularly Rhett and Scarlett.

Another surprise was the incredible amount of money the book was earning. It was more money than either of them ever dreamed to have in their lifetimes. Other than permanently securing their future, however, the money did not change their lifestyle. John continued with his job at the Power Company, and they remained very conservative. Although she did buy a full-length dark mink coat and a diamond platinum pin, she still shopped for bargain hats and dresses. The only item John bought for himself was a Rolex watch. Although he always wanted a nice house with a large yard, Peggy never wanted one, nor did she want to travel. The financial rewards of the book did not seem as important to them as the emotional ones, as John pointed out in a letter to Frances.

For the present, I get my chief pleasure out of small things. Hearing people say that they can't put the book down, after they have started reading it. And that they wished it had been twice as long. I worried so much about it being too long that remarks of that sort give me a bigger kick than reports of sales passing the 200,000 mark. And I do get pleasure in telling Cadillac and Lincoln salesmen, "No, we're very well satisfied with the car we've got. Yes, it's a Chevrolet—1929 model." And such small things.[71]

It is interesting to know that their first large purchase, after the big money came in, was an automobile for John's mother. They also paid for the services of a chauffeur to drive Mrs. Marsh wherever and whenever she wished to go for the rest of her life.[72]

After nearly ten days of bed rest in the darkened room, Peggy had done much thinking about how drastically her life had changed and was grateful for her success. One afternoon, while her watchdog Bessie was grocery shopping and Miss Baugh was out on an errand, Peggy slipped the bandages off her eyes and wrote to Latham, greeting him for the first time by his first name: ("Have I called you Harold since you invited me to do so?") At any rate, I call you Harold even though I feel exactly as though I had referred to God Almighty familiarly as 'GA.'" She asked him innocently:

How did you know six months ago that *Gone With the Wind* would be a success? You remember when you were last in Atlanta you told me that just this thing would happen and I laughed, of course, thinking you were just being very kind. I do not see how you anticipated the enormous sales which have been so unexpected and so bewildering to me ... God knows I never expected it to go over at all. A sale of five thousand was the height of my expectations. I know whom to thank for my good fortune, and I do thank you from the bottom of my heart.[73]

However, within a few days, her attitude toward Latham would change. But that day, she was feeling especially good about herself and about him, crediting him as the chief source of her success. When John came home, he asked her what mischief she had been up to that afternoon. As he stood reading through the mail and scolding her for not keeping the bandages on her eyes, she announced that she had a surprise for him. Turning on a phonograph record, she said she had been practicing a "fan" dance for him. She brought out the beautiful, flamingo-colored feather fan with a hand-painted ivory handle that Norma Brickell had given her during her visit with the Brickells. In her decidedly comic manner, she began fandancing, fluttering the fan around her face, tossing her head haughtily, circling and rubbing up against him in a seductive fashion. John teased Peggy later about her fan dance when he described the performance to Gordon, Francesca, Henry, and Mary Hunter, who staged a reunion in Atlanta in early October for the Kentucky-Georgia Tech football game. What was so notable about that dance, John said, was that it was the first time in a long time that Peggy had gone "into one of her acts" and made him laugh.[74] The laughter that once came so easily to them had been conspicuously absent in the last year.

9

In July 1936, George Brett, Sr., retired and his son George Brett, Jr., became the president of Macmillan. It was he who responded later in August to John's letter questioning some of the terms of the movie contract, which had already been signed. In his response, Brett stated emphatically that Macmillan was not and never had been Peggy's agent; Annie Laurie was her agent. Macmillan had acted only as Peggy's "broker" in the negotiation stage and Annie Laurie had substituted for them in that capacity in the later stages. Brett pointed out that Peggy was represented by her own attorney at that meeting in New York on July 30; the Macmillan attorneys were representing the Macmillan firm only and were not there to protect her interests. About John's concern with the foreign copyrights, Brett stunned the Marshes when he informed them that the responsibility of protecting and overseeing the foreign copyrights was not Macmillan's but Peggy's, and therefore he was offering to return the foreign rights to Peggy.[75]

John was furious with Brett's response, and with Stephens's help he drafted another long letter, this one typed on the Mitchell law firm's stationery. The letter, which bore Stephens's signature, included quoted passages from Latham's telegrams and letters proving that Latham had never informed Peggy that Macmillan had hired an agent for her and that Macmillan had employed Annie Laurie without Peggy's knowledge, much less permission.

Unable to shrug this business off, Peggy, disabled by her eye condition, dictated a letter to Latham: "I found this [Brett's letter] most upsetting and distressing. It was especially so, coming as it did when my eyes were in such condition that I could not read or write and I was laid up in bed with my eyes bandaged." She felt she was in a most embarrassing position because the Selznick company had changed its mind about not needing Peggy's assistance and had recently requested through Annie Laurie that Peggy come to Hollywood and assist with the filmmaking. "She is not my agent and has never been. . . . I don't want to have to write her again and tell her she isn't my agent, but then I don't want any unauthorized person seeming to be my agent. As you know I was besieged with requests from people wanting to be my agent, Miss Williams among them. I refused them all and would never have had any agent had you not offered the services of Macmillan. I am so very upset and distressed about it."[76]

Latham answered that he was glad she was still writing him so frankly about things on her mind and that he would be disturbed to think that she did not feel entirely free to do so. However, he did not really respond to Peggy's complaints. Instead, he implied that Peggy was being overly legalistic and petty and was failing to appreciate all of Macmillan's efforts on her behalf. He pointed out that he could not remember Macmillan ever having had to deal with an author through the author's attorney, as it had done with Peggy. He described how everyone at Macmillan was wildly enthusiastic about *Gone With the Wind* and anxious to put the book over and see the author receive recognition. "If I can say so without appearing to brag, I think that we have done a job of publishing for you which could not have been done by any other publisher in America. . . . I cannot express to you the sense of hurt that I saw and felt on the part of my associates when I came in this morning." He closed by saying that it was probably not proper for him to write her in such a personal way. However, he hoped that his "frank" letter would open the way for a resumption of their old cordial relationship.[77]

Disappointed with Latham's reply, the Marshes felt as if he were sidestepping the fact that Macmillan had failed to provide clear information about Annie Laurie's role in the movie deal. John and Peggy did not see that the issue of Annie Laurie's involvement was a rather small point, since she had actually performed a service for both Macmillan and Peggy. They could not let go of the fact that they had been misinformed, and from this point on, John resolved to pay better attention to everything and never to be so trusting again.

False reports about the price Selznick paid for the film contract appeared in gossip columns everywhere. Some said he paid too little; others said he paid too much. Annie Laurie felt hurt, defensive, and caught in the crossfire between the Marshes and Macmillan. After all, she had gotten for them the highest price ever paid for any book, and she could not understand why they were not all happy and appreciative. She wrote Latham telling him that it was not true that Selznick had since been offered three times the amount he paid for the film rights. Just in case Peggy read such false reports, Annie Laurie wanted him to have copies of letters proving that she had gotten the highest price ever paid for a story. She enclosed copies of letters that she had received from various film companies while she had been trying to sell the film rights.[78] She always understood that she was working for the Macmillan Company and not for Margaret Mitchell, and she never made any claims otherwise. All of this furor over Annie Laurie appears to have been a huge, unnecessary misunderstanding that should have been avoided earlier on. Also, it is unfortunate that the Marshes never knew the truth about Annie Laurie's arrangement with Macmillan, for they surely would have been more appreciative and sympathetic toward her.

However, their annoyance about the film business paled beside the copyright issue. In order to protect her copyright to *Gone With the Wind,* Peggy would have to renew the copyright at regular intervals, and by no stretch of his imagination could John see how Peggy could be held responsible for renewing all copyrights according to the various laws governing such matters in all parts of the world.[79] He asked Brett how a housewife living in a little apartment in Atlanta could be expected to know how to keep up with the changing copyright laws all over the world. Entreating Brett, he asked,

> Couldn't we make an agreement that Macmillan will relieve her of the clerical and legal worries involved in this obligation? Peggy is in no position to do this, but Macmillan is. You do such things as a matter of routine. You have your bookkeeping systems to keep track of the time when copyrights should be renewed in this and foreign countries. You have your legal staff who know the intricacies of existing copyright laws and who make it their business to keep up with the revisions of copyright laws in all countries. My understandings from Mr. Stephens Mitchell is that Macmillan has already given its verbal assent on these points, and in view of the fact that Macmillan was Peggy's agent in negotiating the Selznick contract, it seems obvious that these provisions are agreeable to you. But in order to bring this job to a workmanlike conclusion and also to relieve Peggy's mind of the worry of vague responsibilities hanging over her, we would appreciate a statement in writing from the Macmillan Company covering these points.[80]

Jim Putnam, writing for Brett, answered no; their copyright department was not equipped to manage the protection of Peggy's international copyrights. Putnam said Macmillan would do whatever it could to assist the Marshes, but it would not assume the responsibility for protecting her copyrights. The Marshes themselves would have to deal with such matters as Selznick's concern that some other producer could obtain from some foreign country a pirated edition of *Gone With the Wind.* At this point, the already strained Marsh-Macmillan relationship broke.

As a courtesy, Putnam had earlier put John in contact with Marion

Saunders, an agent handling foreign copyrights. After Macmillan conveyed all foreign translation rights to Peggy, including the right to publish the book serially in foreign languages in other countries, but not in the United States, John sent Stephens to New York to work out an agreement with Saunders. Whatever chances the Marshes may have had to return to a relatively simple, quiet life vanished completely in July 1936 when Peggy signed the film and the foreign copyright agreements.

On October 9, 1936, three days past his forty-first birthday, John wrote Putnam:

> Your letter of Oct. 6 has been read with much interest by Mrs. Marsh and myself. You and the Macmillan Company are certainly taking a very generous attitude in your offer to give back to Mrs. Marsh the rights for all foreign translations of her book. Just what we will do with them when we get them, I don't know.[81]

What they—John, Peggy, Stephens, and Margaret Baugh—ended up doing was operating from the Marshes' small apartment a worldwide business specializing in foreign copyrights. Motivated to protect their own interests and self-taught, they became experts in foreign copyright matters.

1936-1937

EAPING THE WHIRLWIND

Did I tell you that I already have a title for Peggy's next book—the story of the young couple who sowed a "Gone With the Wind" and were "Reaping the Whirlwind."

—John Marsh to Frances Marsh,
1 August 1936

1

ALTHOUGH PEGGY WAS FRAZZLED AND EXHAUSTED by all the baggage—
both good and bad—that went along with her sudden explosion of fame,
John initially enjoyed her success, not only because he did not have to carry
the burdens that went along with fame but also because he simply refused
to concern himself with the kinds of petty worries that inflamed Peggy's
emotions.[1] Among these worries were the false and malicious rumors
circulated about them. Just as John and Peggy were unprepared for the
glorious praise and acclaim, so they were also unprepared for the sinister
envy and malice that emerged.

With all the publicity about selling the film rights, rumors about the
Marshes reached a new status. Some rumors made Peggy and John look like
eccentrics or unsophisticated southerners—country bumpkins, yelping in
a goofy fashion about all the money they were either making or not making.
One tale, which even disturbed her publisher, claimed that she was so
countrified that Macmillan had swindled her out of her royalties.[2] Some
rumors were started by women who impersonated her. "I get pretty damned
tired of these people who pass themselves off as me," she fumed to Herschel
Brickell about the dozens of women who were going all over the country
posing as Margaret Mitchell. "If I can just catch one and fry her ears in deep
fat, it will give me great pleasure. . . . I wonder why people do this. God
knows, it's no fun *really* being Margaret Mitchell so what possible fun
could there be in pretending to be Margaret Mitchell?"[3]

Peggy inadvertently started some of the troublesome rumors herself,
although she never admitted that. In all the hundreds of letters that she
wrote, in 1936 alone, not just to family and friends but to complete strangers,
she mentioned her deteriorating health. She wrote about her weight loss,
her disabling eye trouble; she told about having to lie still in a darkened room
with her eyes bandaged for twelve hours a day; she described her general
state of near exhaustion; she refused to make any kind of public appearance
or to accept invitations; she refused interviews; and she refused to write
articles or stories for magazines, always saying that she was too ill. As a

result, many people jumped to the conclusion that something terrible was happening to her. Some even whispered that she, consumed by her sudden success, had gone stark raving mad. It should have been no surprise to her when she heard that she was terminally ill, or the victim of a debilitating disease that had left her a helpless, blind invalid. Yet, when she heard these rumors she said she got angry enough "to buckle on her six-shooter."[4]

"It takes practically nothing to start a rumor, I've found. John and I collect rumors and see who can collect the most in one day," she wrote a friend.

> My yesterday's crop were (1) That I had a wooden leg. (2) That I've had a suite at the Piedmont Hotel for weeks and have been drunk the entire time and throwing my money away. (3) That I am dressing dolls like GWTW characters and selling them for twenty five dollars a doll and making millions. (4) That I have purchased the old General Gilmer home near Clarkesville, Ga. (that's up by Tallulah Falls) and have restored it and the movies will use this place for a background. (5) I am to play Melanie in GWTW.[5]

When his brother came for a brief visit, John told Henry, "The gossips have gotten to be a real pain in the ass because Peggy cannot ignore them." He was referring to her recent outburst about a newsclipping that stated she turned to writing in an attempt to support herself and her husband, a shell-shocked invalid, unable to work regularly and in and out of hospitals for years. Peggy screamed, "I would rather have never written a book, never sold it, never made a cent or had what passes for fame in these parts than have one one-hundredth of such a lie published."[6] When she first heard that story, she immediately thought that the Granberrys or the Brickells had either carelessly or deliberately betrayed her because they were the only ones she had opened up to after the book was published. Although she wanted to track down the source of this lie, John shrugged it off, saying, "Forget about it. I don't give a damn. Besides, the story is old in coming to us and if you demand any retraction you will only stir up more trouble and spread the lie."[7] Peggy silently disagreed and secretly persisted in her course of action.

Without John's knowing, she sent Brickell the clipping and asked that he return it. Growing increasingly suspicious and revealing that her paranoia included even the loyal Margaret Baugh, Peggy announced that she was writing the letter herself: "I didn't trust the secretary. People so dearly love to repeat dirt about people who are on the front page and in twenty four hours the story would be all over Atlanta." Neither Brickell nor

Granberry was to write to the editor of the paper because, she emphasized, John wished to let the matter drop, and his wish was the one to be considered. With an almost pathological antipathy for rumors, she wrote, "I've got to know how wide spread this is and how it all started . . . have you any suggestions as to how such a story could have started?" After reviewing what she had told them about John's illness before they married, their medical debts, and his chronic ulcer problems, she could not see how anyone could say he was "shell shocked." In this letter dated September 10, 1936, she confided to Brickell:

> In these ten days when my eyes were so paralyzed with bella donna that I could see nothing at all, I've been wondering a thousand things. The most distressing one was—could I have some how given you and Edwin such an impression of John? It does not seem possible, but it is a possibility. . . .
>
> The whole affair has put me in a helpless frenzy which hasnt done me much good. . . .

She claimed to have become hardened to whatever people said about her, and except for attacks on her personal integrity, which she would not allow, she planned to take the lies about herself with good grace. But as for her husband and family, it was not their fault that she was "fool enough" to let Latham leave with her manuscript, and she did not want to see her loved ones suffer or be embarrassed in any way. Showing passionate feelings for her husband, she ended her letter by saying:

> If John were any other type in the world, it wouldn't be so bad. But he is such a swell person, a positive genius in his own line, has held down a responsible and delicate job brilliantly for years I just get in a killing rage at the very thought of any one anywhere reflecting on his mental ability. I have become outwardly hardened to what ever people say and write about me, the perverse twistings of my casual words, the out right lies, the stupid rumors, the gossip, malicious and otherwise. After all, I was asking for it when I published a book and it was only right that I take it. And short of any reflection on my personal integrity, I intend to take it with as good a grace as possible, hoping to God that this miserable period will end quickly. But I cannot take with any grace any lies about John or my family.

Ten months later, when Brickell finally found out that the rumor had gotten started by a woman at Blowing Rock, Peggy threatened, "I'm going to crucify that lady if I have to travel all the way to her home town to do it."[8]

Rashes of other outlandish rumors about John broke out regularly. The most popular one had to do with his not being able to handle his wife's fame and her fleeing to Reno to get a divorce. This rumor began to circulate because of the confusion in the public's mind between Peggy and Caroline Miller, another Georgia writer, who had won the Pulitzer Prize in 1934 for her novel *Lamb in His Bosom*. When Miller divorced her husband, the rumor spread that Margaret Mitchell had flown to Reno to get a divorce. "But when will it stop?" Peggy asked Brickell with great frustration in her voice:

> The problem resolves itself around whether I can last till the book stops selling. At first I thought I'd go to Europe till it all blew over. But I realized that I couldn't do that. In the first place I loathe travelling and have no desire to see Europe and would be miserable away from John. In the second place, if I did go away a terrific load would descend upon John and he is already carrying far more of my load than I want him to.[9]

Undisturbed by the gossip, John urged her not to worry about such stupid stories and tried to console her by saying: "This is something that people wanted to believe, but not necessarily with malice. It excites their imaginations because it has an element of drama in it, whereas our quiet and happy devotion is stodgy and dull."[10] When the British newspapers announced that he had died, he was amused and wrote his mother, "Up to now, I have not been able to think of any retort as good as Mark Twain's that the report of his death was greatly exaggerated, but an occasion of this nature calls for something as special as an answer and I am hoping that I can succeed in producing something which will be a credit to myself and family."[11] Then another story started circulating, and this one John took more seriously.

Regularly reporting Kentucky's reaction to the book, Gordon and Francesca, who lived in Lexington, said that bookstores in Maysville, Lexington, Louisville, and Cincinnati, across the Ohio River and a few miles northwest from his hometown of Maysville, could not keep enough copies of *Gone With the Wind* in stock. Practically everyone who was even remotely connected to him or to his family took pride in knowing him or in claiming to know him. Because of his work with the newspapers and his affiliation with the university, many people in Lexington remembered him and took a personal interest in the book. One day he received a disturbing letter from Frances in Wilmington, Delaware, saying that there was a lot of talk about *his* writing the book. Later, when Gordon and

Francesca came to Atlanta in October to attend the University of Kentucky-Georgia Tech football game, they told him that they had heard that rumor too.[12] Francesca remembered how much he hated to hear that news.

In Lexington, the talk stemmed from the remarkable similarities between Belle Watling, *Gone With the Wind*'s queen of the red-light district in Atlanta, and Belle Brezing, the Lexington woman who owned one of the most lavish brothels south of the Mason-Dixon line. Although practically every southern town had its share of madams and "'hor houses," Brezing—like Watling—was no ordinary madam, and she managed no ordinary "house." As the thoroughbred horse-racing capital of the world, Lexington was the host for wealthy visitors, many of whom frequented Brezing's establishment.

John must have cursed himself when he realized how deeply he had slipped in letting Watling resemble Brezing. But a decade earlier, when Peggy was developing the story and she and John were talking about the characters, they were not talking and writing with readers in mind. Peggy had a rich mental storehouse of people from which she could select bits and pieces to create her characters, but she had never been inside a brothel and had never known a real-life madam. When it came to creating an understanding woman who would befriend Rhett Butler when Scarlett spurned his love, it was John who had the perfect model.

After Macmillan accepted the manuscript, John and Peggy believed the book would have only local interest and would sell, at best, a couple of thousand copies to libraries in Georgia and to relatives. Peggy's primary goal in researching Fulton County court records was to make certain she did not use any real Georgian's name, not even for the completely admirable characters like Melanie Wilkes.[13] She even checked with Franklin Garrett, Atlanta's official historian, for the name Watling.[14] But she was not concerned about the Watling character because Lexington, Kentucky, was many miles away from Atlanta, where people had never heard of Belle Brezing or, even if they had, they would not know any details of her life. Besides that, Brezing had been put out of business primarily by the Good Christian Government League in 1917, around the same time John left Lexington, and by the time the book came out, she was a 76-year-old, morphine-addicted recluse. After all that time, John must have thought, who would have heard of her? He never dreamed that anyone would infer that Brezing served as Watling's prototype.[15] Yet people did. The simplest action for him to take was to deny the connection, and that is exactly what he did.

In his intriguing biography of Belle Brezing, a book filled with interesting old photographs, E. I. Thompson says that by the time *Gone With the Wind* appeared on the scene, "Belle Brezing had already reached the status of a local folk legend, and no one could be convinced that Marsh had not furnished his wife with the name and some of the attributes of the character that became Belle Watling in *Gone With the Wind*."[16] The similarities between the two women, as Thompson points out, are just too obvious to pass as mere coincidence.

In *Gone With the Wind,* the description of Watling and her house is an accurate and complete description of Brezing and her house. Both places were large and elegantly furnished and paid for by rich admirers: Watling had the generosity of Rhett Butler, and Brezing had William M. Singerly, a wealthy Philadelphia businessman who came to Lexington each year for the trotting horse meet.[17] Both houses welcomed army officers, and both had black orchestras and a downstairs barroom.[18] Both women delivered engraved invitations to special events.[19] Both women catered to men of means; men who did not have a bankroll to spend had to go to the smaller houses, not Brezing's.[20] Both establishments were operated in a quiet, unobtrusive manner, seldom attracting the attention of police. Just as Belle Watling "presented a prosperous appearance when glimpsed occasionally in her closed carriage driven by an impudent yellow negro,"[21] so, according to Thompson, Belle Brezing rode about Lexington in "the finest phaeton to be had, with a matched team of chestnuts" driven by a liveried black dressed in a black suit and a tall, black hat. Each woman had a child who had been sent away to a boarding school.

Both women had the same first name and both had last names with the same number of syllables and ending in "ing." And both had flame-red hair and similar personality traits. Thompson points out: "Lexington men who had known her 'personally' felt, too, that their Belle was just the kind of good 'ole' whore who would have befriended the likes of Rhett Butler. . . . Her [Brezing's] strength had been in her understanding of the weaknesses in others."[22]

Some people got downright belligerent in asking how John Marsh could deny providing the scene in which Belle Watling approaches Melanie wanting to give her some money for the hospital. Because of the manner in which the money had been earned, Watling's offer is rejected. During the time John was in Lexington, it was commonly known that Belle Brezing offered to contribute to the building of a hospital and that her generosity was rejected for the same reason.

Every time John received letters asking him outright if Brezing was the prototype of Watling, he fired back "No!" But the rumors only escalated with his denial. Months later, when they were still flourishing, he wrote Frances:

Sister, please step on the rumor that I collaborated in Peggy's book, if it shows its ugly head again. It will interest you to know that I am in distinguished company in such rumors, for other stories have credited the book to Peggy's father, her brother, Sinclair Lewis and several other literary celebrities. No, a man who works as hard as I do at my own job doesn't have the time to write 1037 page novels or to collaborate in them. I did help in the mechanics of getting the thing to press—proofreading, checking facts, etc—but that was all.[23]

That was his story, and he stuck to it.

Later, when the *Gone With the Wind* film came out, more talk about the Watling-Brezing similarities spread like wildfire. A Lexington news-paperman, Joe Jordan was fascinated with Brezing and had been collecting information on her for years. He, too, wrote John pointing out the similarities. John telegrammed, "Neither Belle Watling nor any other character in the book was taken from any real person. All are fictional creations and any similarity of names was accidental. My regards to the Leader folks. John Marsh."[24] Jordan said he and the others just figured that the Marshes were afraid of being sued by Brezing.[25]

2

A similar misunderstanding soon cropped up, and this one also involved John. This time the unsettling news came from Washington, D.C., where Harry Slattery, Under Secretary to Secretary of the Interior Harold Le Clare Ickes, was said to be extremely upset about Peggy's use of the name "Slattery" for "a pillaging, house-burning carpetbagger" in *Gone With the Wind*. After sending him a carefully worded apology, Peggy also telephoned him and, in her most charming manner, apologized, saying that she intended no malice toward him or anyone. She explained that she had picked the name Slattery out of a New York telephone directory. Originally she had named the character Satterwhite or something similar and changed it to Slattery, purely by chance, when she decided that Satterwhite was too hard to pronounce. The call ended cordially with his accepting her apologies.

After she received from Slattery a little narrative that his mother had written about growing up in the South, Peggy wrote Slattery again, complimenting his mother's writing, which she said had "a high degree of charm and true literary quality." Then she went on to tell him once more how sorry she was that she had inadvertently offended his mother, him, and his entire family. In her letter, dated October 3, she explained how hard she had worked to avoid using actual names of anyone living in Clayton or Fayette counties, or in Savannah, Charleston, or Atlanta during the period between 1840 and 1873—the time frame of her novel. "I did not wish to embarrass anyone now living or make it appear as though I were writing about their kindred, long dead.... I never knew another writer who bothered about this," she told him.

> But I went to infinite pains, first to choose names that while Southern were not peculiar to Atlanta and its surrounding rural territory. Second, I spent weeks and weeks in county court houses checking the names of my characters against tax books, from 1840 to 1873, against deed books, against militia muster rolls, against Confederate muster rolls, against lists of jurymen, against wills and titles. Wherever I found a duplication of names, even if it were only the surname of one of my characters, I changed the character's name, chose another name and started checking all over again. It was, as you can imagine, a wearisome job. In one instance, the name of "Hilton" was changed about a dozen times, necessitating trip after trip to the Jonesboro court house until I was absolutely certain as far as written legal papers could prove it, that no one by the name of Hilton had lived in Clayton County in the period covered by *Gone With the Wind.*
> So you see why I am so sorry that the matter embarrassed you.

Thinking that she would finish this letter and mail it the next day, she laid it aside. However, the first thing the next morning, Margaret Baugh brought in the mail, which contained a clipping from the *Washington Post,* dated September 29, with headlines reading: "Slattery Drops His Plans to Sue Author of Gone With the Wind—Ickes' Aide Embittered over Use of Name in Novel, Becomes Friend of Miss Mitchell after She Explains 'No Harm Intended.'" Although presumably Peggy was relieved to see this headline, the contents of the article chafed her horribly.

The article stated that Slattery, who was from an old, respected family of Greenville, South Carolina, rice planters, "had been incensed at Miss Mitchell's delineation of a villainous carpetbagger named Slattery," and until he and the author had talked and exchanged letters, he had been thinking about suing her.

Slattery explained in this interview that at first he had concluded that the name had been maliciously and deliberately selected for the "white trash" character because he, as a former conservation commissioner, had been involved in some heated court battles with a Georgia Power Company advertising executive named John Marsh, who he assumed was Margaret Mitchell's husband. The *Washington Post* stated: "Linking the fact that John Marsh, co-author of the book, is an advertising man for the power company with the fact that Slattery had had some sharp encounters with a former promotion man for the same firm, the family concluded that the selection of the name was malicious."[26] The article went on to say, however, that when Slattery learned that "Marsh and his erstwhile power-fight opponent are two different advertising men, although employed by the same utility company," Slattery decided to drop his plans for legal action and he wanted to forget all about the matter. Where he got the wrong idea that there were two John Marshes working for Georgia Power is still a mystery.

Slattery was also quoted as saying: "She still cooks breakfast in her little flat in Atlanta for her husband and he keeps on working at his job, in spite of the fact they suddenly came into a fortune. Atlantans have tried to fete and exploit them—they wrote the book in collaboration over a period of seven years—but they keep their heads and decline all the invitations."

After Peggy read that interview and the letters that referred to it, she picked up her letter to Slattery and typed the following postscript, which is freighted with anger:

P.S. This morning news arrived which upset me so much that I hardly know how to write to you about it. Several letters came to me from strangers, confusing letters, which said that after reading the article in the Washington Post they understood much about *Gone With the Wind* which they had not understood before. They said they had felt that no woman could have written such a book and, after reading in the paper that my husband had collaborated with me in the writing of it, they understood.

I was completely bewildered at this news—bewildered by the very idea that my husband had written any part of *Gone With the Wind*—bewildered about what *had* appeared in the Washington paper. Then a clipping arrived, sent by a friend who knew all about how the book was written and that I alone had written it and then I understood.

I am so upset about this error that I have been unable to do anything but cry ever since I read the clipping. I have given so many years of my life to the writing of this book, injured my eyes, endangered my health and this is my payment—that I did not write it! And I did write it, every word of it. My husband had nothing whatever to do with it. In the first place he is not a Georgian (he was born in Kentucky) and no one but a Georgian with generations of Georgian ancestors could have written it. In the second place, he has a very responsible position and works very hard and he seldom gets time to play golf much less write books.

In fact, he never even read the whole of my manuscript until after the Macmillan Company had bought it. It was not that I didn't want him to read it. It was because the book was not written with the second chapter following the first, and the third following the second. It was written last chapter first and so on until the first chapter was written last—written, in fact several months after the book was sold. My husband could not be expected to catch the continuity of the story when I could only give him scattered chapters to read, which to him, did not connect up.

Not all the financial rewards I may receive can make up to me for this. Moreover it puts me in dreadful light before the world—that I had concealed my husband's work on this book. And he actually had no part in it except helping me with the proof reading when my eyes gave out and my deadline was upon me.

3

This one letter, more than any other, reveals Peggy's terrible insecurity, her great fear that the world would think of her, as she thought of herself, as a fraud. In a voice like that of an angry, frightened child, intensely pleading for someone to believe her, she insisted: "And I did write it, every word of it. My husband had nothing whatever to do with it." The reader can almost see her wet eyes and trembling body.

In one way, her reaction here is understandable, as no one wants the credit that she or he has earned to be snatched away or misdirected. In her day particularly, it was all too easy to negate any achievement any woman attained. However, although her concern about the question of her authorship is easy to understand, it is not easy to understand why this one rumor bothered her more than all the others and caused her to answer in the panicky manner in which she did. All the other rumors made her so angry that she actually perpetuated them herself by talking and writing about them and trying to get to their source. At one point, she even encouraged Medora Field Perkerson to write an article on the rumors circulating about her for the *Sunday Magazine*. But this one rumor frightened her, and she never mentioned it in any of her other extant letters.

In fact, in writing her postscript to Slattery she did not even mention—much less correct—any of the other inaccuracies attributed to him. If she had done so, her argument that John had not coauthored the book would have been far more logical and effective because she could have easily shown that the entire *Washington Post* article was nothing but a mass of misstatements. She could have pointed out that her book had not been sold to the movies for one hundred thousand dollars; that Atlantans had not tried to exploit her and John; that they had not declined all invitations; that many more than two hundred thousand copies of the novel had been sold; that she had never even boiled an egg, much less cooked breakfast, in her life; that there never was and never had been any other Georgia Power advertising executive, or employee, named John Marsh, except her husband; and that it *was* he whom Slattery had encountered in the heated courtroom sessions. Instead, Peggy ignored all those errors and fastened on that one phrase about John's coauthorship. That phrase must have seared her soul deeply for her to deny that he had any part in helping her with the creative process.

In fact, though, the question about her sole authorship began almost immediately after the novel appeared in the marketplace, particularly after a few pages from the original manuscript were exhibited in a showcase in Atlanta's public library. After some people saw John's handwriting all over the pages, speculation about his collaboration migrated around, mainly in the newspaper circles in Georgia and Kentucky and in the Associated Press office in Washington where John had worked. Lois, Latham, Everett, and others at Macmillan, and certainly Rhoda, Grace, and Margaret Baugh— all had seen the original manuscript with its heavily penciled corrections, notes, and revisions in John's typing or handwriting. They knew too, without question, that John had been intimately involved in the writing of the story since its inception. Some of his coworkers remembered the Marshes' taking the typewriter and sections of the manuscript along on John's business trips, and Bessie and Deon remembered the Marshes' long nightly sessions in which they discussed the work in progress. John's family remembered how enthusiastically John and Peggy talked about their work on the novel. In 1935, when Lois told Latham about her friend's manuscript, Lois said to the publisher, "no one has read it except her husband."[27] Peggy herself had explained to Latham when he first took the manuscript that it included so many versions of so many chapters because she had put them there for her husband to read and evaluate.

John's letters to Macmillan alone are eye-opening evidence of his arduous work on the manuscript. Scattered among the papers in the Margaret Mitchell Marsh Collection are many notes in John's handwriting on such items as "Yankee Repeating Rifles in 1864," reference notes on "Plastic Surgery" and on "Reminiscences of an Army Nurse During the Civil War from a book by Adelaide W. Smith." Other notes in his handwriting have to do with music, names of old songs, religious revivals, Bermuda grass in 1848, dogwood as medicine, and the use of iodine. There are also drafts of letters in his handwriting, letters that he composed for Peggy before they were typed and signed by her.

In addition to the chronologies of the characters and their dialects that he started keeping in 1927 were his notes on the reports of the Confederate forces designated as the Army of Tennessee under General Joseph E. Johnston and subsequently under General John B. Hood, who was married to John's great-aunt. Also found on scraps of paper written in his handwriting are lists of the names of Confederate soldiers from Georgia buried in the Confederate Cemetery at Rock Island Arsenal, Illinois. Whereas earlier, she had frequently mentioned John's helping her with the manuscript, now she completely denied it.

But those who knew the Marshes long and well knew about the impenetrable bond between them and had wondered quietly all along about the nature of John's contribution to the novel. Their doubts were not about Peggy's lack of talent or imagination, but about her lack of the kind of discipline required to sustain work on a novel of such breadth and of her ability to polish it as finely as it was polished. They thought she was too madcap and irresponsible to produce a book like that. Besides, her dependence upon John and his loyalty to her were widely known. As a matter of fact, their friends would have been more surprised if he—with his writing and editorial skills—had not helped her.[28] After all, writers—even the best—have editors.

Peggy did not write the *Washington Post* asking for a correction or a retraction, which is what she could have done—or, better still, she could have had John or Stephens do it. If she had handled this situation as she handled every other important one, she would have discussed it with John, and he would have quietly set the record straight with Slattery. A calm, clear, balanced response from him would have been far more effective. The fact that she herself wrote directly to Slattery, and wrote while she was angry, suggests that she did not want John or Margaret Baugh to know what she had written. She must have felt ashamed about denying John's help, but just like Scarlett, she rationalized her actions and begged:

> Mr. Slattery, can you not ask the paper for a retraction of the statement that my husband collaborated with me in the writing of *Gone With the Wind?* Of course, the story has already gone out into the world to rise up and plague me all of my life but a retraction would help some. You see, it is my whole professional reputation which is at stake—my reputation which has been ruined through no fault of my own. I am so distressed about all this that I do not know what to do.[29]

The rumor about her not being the sole author of *Gone With the Wind* was not the only one that sprang up in the fall of 1936, but it was, by far, the one that bothered her the most. Although she must have realized that John's help had illuminated her talent, not diminished it, she obviously feared that any acknowledgment of his assistance would have the latter effect in the eyes of others.

Although it is doubtful that they ever actually discussed it, the Marshes must have known such a rumor would surface. But early in their relationship, they had tacitly accepted the roles each was to play, and neither veered from his and her role. Consistent about remaining in the background, John was no different from any other good editor. He had no egoistic need to claim any of her limelight and never once tried to do so. In fact, he prudently did everything he could do to avoid calling attention to himself.[30] Thus, there was no real reason for Peggy to react as she did when the rumor surfaced publicly in the *Washington Post.* In fact, she should have acknowledged graciously the editorial help that her husband had given her, instead of denying it.

4

Peggy's reaction to this *Washington Post* article may have been exacerbated by a lightning bolt that had struck earlier, in July, when Dr. Thomas H. English of Emory University had written Peggy asking her to donate her manuscript of *Gone With the Wind* to the university. His request shocked her into realizing that she did not even have the original manuscript.[31] She panicked and got hysterical when she realized her "first baby" was gone.[32] After she called Latham to request the return of her manuscript, she became more distressed, for he told her that he was sure that she had it. Then, a day or so later, he wrote apologizing for upsetting her, for he had found the manuscript in the Macmillan vaults and was returning it to her.[33]

Finally, on October 15, 1936, all but three pages of the original manuscript of *Gone With the Wind* was insured at one thousand dollars and shipped to its home in Atlanta.[34] The remaining three pages, which she said Macmillan "inveigled" from her because she was "too exhausted to argue," were kept to exhibit in Macmillan's display booth at the National Book Fair in New York in early November.[35] An article in the *New York Times,* on November 9, 1936, states that many interested people viewed the manuscript display and that "the typed pages have been carefully and liberally corrected in pencil." After these pages were returned to her on December 8, she vowed that as God was her witness not a single page of that manuscript would leave her possession ever again.

In response to all the letters that had flashed back and forth between him and John about the film and the foreign rights, George Brett, on that same day, November 9, issued to all Macmillan officials a memo stating that no change of any kind was to be made in *Gone With the Wind* without first referring the entire matter to his office. Because the publisher had assumed so many "unusual duties" in connection with *Gone With the Wind* beyond those stated in the original contract, Brett stated it was now imperative that an entry be made on the record in all of the departments to which his note was addressed that no change other than the correction of typographical errors be made in the plates, and that no reissue at a different price or in a different format be made without referring to the contract file to make sure that Macmillan complied with all of its obligations.[36] As of this point, the Macmillan-Marsh relationship lost the friendly element that had once characterized it and from this time on remained only perfunctorily cordial.

During this time, John's attitude toward Peggy's success began to change. No longer did he speak or write of it in awe. In fact, anyone reading the letters he wrote during this time would think that the Marshes were dealing with some kind of tragedy. He wrote Frances:

> It occurs to me that Peggy is about as fine an example as I ever encountered of one who has had "fame thrust upon her." She had given up the book as a bad job long before Mr. Latham ever came to town, and I don't think she would have ever turned the MS over to him except for my urging that she do it "on a chance." From that moment until now, events have been sweeping us along, against our will, much as in the case of poor Scarlett and the others in the book. Did I tell you that I already have a title for Peggy's next book—the story of the young couple who sowed a "Gone With the Wind" and were "Reaping the Whirlwind."

In a brooding, philosophical manner, he summarized his feelings:

> Things have happened in such rapid succession that we have both become "anaesthetic" to the situation. We had a long hard training in bad fortune and I think we learned to stand it pretty well, but we have had practically no experience with large scale good fortune, and we find it a real problem to adjust to it. Trying to analyze our state of mind, I think the trouble is that we both were well satisfied with our lives before and we rather resent the new position of prominence we have been thrust into. We were very pleased with each other's company and that of a few friends, we had learned to live inside our income so we had no ambitions for

wealth, our material wants were few and, above all, we had achieved the privacy we both enjoy by getting rid of a lot of boresome acquaintances. Now all of that has changed. We have about as much privacy as the proverbial gold fish. (For an example of what we are up against, I find myself wondering if I should write such things in a letter to you. We have become the objects of public curiosity and must guard our words and our acts, for fear we will find them written up in some newspaper. That thought shouldn't intrude in writing a letter to one's sister, but it does involuntarily as a result of recent events.)

Of course, we'll get used to it. And as I told Mother, my theory is to let matters slide for the present, not try to comprehend the uncomprehensible and wait until later when we will get used to it and begin to enjoy it. Too bad all of this couldn't have happened when we were at the depths of our poverty. . . .

Please don't get the impression that we are downcast and sad over the book's success. We're not, but we are more than a little confused and bewildered by the extraordinary chain of events. And you would be, too, if it ever happened to you.[37]

An example of the kind of invasions of privacy that John wrote about occurred one sweltering September morning when Peggy, dressed in one of her plain, cotton sundresses and flat-heeled shoes, ventured downtown to do some long-delayed shopping. Once in the department store, she found her hopes of avoiding detection dashed as she was immediately surrounded by people wanting to get her autograph. A couple of hours later, tired from standing on her feet for so long and angry because her shopping was still undone, she returned home and went straight to bed, asking Bessie not to disturb her. As she was stretched out on her bed resting and listening to the hum of the fan as it circulated hot air around the darkened room, she suddenly heard an unfamiliar, loud, female voice demanding that Bessie get Margaret Mitchell out of bed. This voice belonged to a woman who had come all the way from Philadelphia, bringing a photographer with her, wanting to be photographed shaking hands with the great author Margaret Mitchell.[38] Bessie, whom John described as being in a class with the best personal secretaries because she had developed "a real talent for firmness accompanied by a smile," managed to get rid of the strangers though it took her a good half-hour to do so. That evening, when Peggy told John about the episode, she said she thought it strange and disappointing to learn that people were for the most part unsympathetic and rude to those they supposedly admired.[39]

Public interest in her never seemed to subside. Atlanta was often flooded with tourists wanting to get a word with and an autograph from Margaret Mitchell. Strangers walked right up to the Marshes' doorstep and rang the doorbell, asking to see the author. When Bessie would tell them that Miss Mitchell was not at home, they would sit in their automobiles for hours in front of the apartment, waiting for her return. Because Peggy usually used the back cellar door, she told Lois that "the tourists have photographed practically every inmate of the Russell Apartments in the happy belief that they have snapped me."[40] In another letter a little later on, she told Jim Putnam, "I will never understand strangers who ... ask Bessie for 'just a peek' at me. I feel that this puts me in the class with an educated pig, a flea circus or a two-headed baby in a jar of alcohol."[41]

5

Then, truly great news came in November 1936 when Peggy and John learned that *Gone With the Wind* was among the nominations for a Pulitzer Prize. However, this thrilling development brought what Peggy considered an effrontery when Sam Doerflinger of the Macmillan Company wrote asking her for her age and for biographical information to give to the Pulitzer Committee. She shot back:

> I'll gladly tell you where I was born. I was born here in Atlanta, Ga. But I am not telling when I was born. I have never felt that a person's age was the concern of anyone except herself and her family. And my feeling on this matter has been considerably strengthened since *Gone With the Wind* was published. The day seldom passes but that seven complete strangers either phone me or call at the door and ask point blank, "Just how old are you?" The newspapers, news services, biographical reviews, etc. have been in a lather about the matter, too. The effect has been to arouse my stubbornness. My age is my own private business and I intend to keep it so—if I can. I am not so old that I am ashamed of my age and I am not so young that I couldn't have written my book and that is all the public needs to know about my age.[42]

Trying to tone down her haughtiness, she closed her letter apologetically: "I am not, of course, finding fault with you for asking me the question, for you are one of the very few with a legitimate reason for seeking the information. But the others, the curiosity seekers, have made me stubborn on this point, and, if my reticence knocks me out of the nominations, then I guess that's just too bad."

The question about her age kept popping up regularly, but she steadfastly refused to give it. On June 25, Brickell wrote her about how amused he was when he picked up the *New International Year Book* for 1936 and turned straight to the fiction survey. He said, "It begins with this marvelous remark: 'The year's sensational success was *Gone With the Wind,* by Margaret Mitchell, a Southern belle before, during, and after the Civil War'!!! All I can say is that for one who has been a belle for so many decades, you are remarkably well preserved."

Peggy replied that the item was not so remarkable as he may have thought. "For a long time the rumor has been afloat that I am far advanced in years and that *Gone With the Wind* was really a verbatim account of what happened to me in my youth."[43] Then she added that the strangest thing she had encountered during the past year was the inability of the public to conceive of creative writing. "People cannot or will not believe that a story and characters can be manufactured from whole cloth. The story must have been the author's life or that of someone the author knew, or it must have been taken from old diaries or letters."[44]

6

With the news about *Gone With the Wind* being nominated for a Pulitzer Prize, more people became interested in meeting the author. However, by late fall, when the nomination was announced, Peggy was in the midst of redecorating the entire apartment in her favorite colors: apple green, moss green, pink, deep coral, and ivory. All of the furniture had been hauled out to be refinished and upholstered, and walls were being replastered, painted, or wallpapered. "I believe I told you once of the excellent word our family used to denote the condition of our house when painters, paperers and upholsterers were ravaging about it—'choss,'" Peggy wrote Brickell in October 1937. "We have been in a state of choss for some time, and the smell of newly painted woodwork was so bad that it gave both of us colds and bronchial coughs and sent us to the Biltmore for a week until the house dried out."[45]

They could well afford the Biltmore, or any place else in the world for that matter. On September 3, 1936, Macmillan had announced that 330,000 copies of *Gone With the Wind* had been printed up to August 30, only two months after publication. Five days later, Macmillan stated that another large printing of the novel was going through, bringing the total up to 370,000.[46] By the end of September, the total was over 525,000 copies, and by the end of October, 700,000. In late September, George Brett sent Peggy a check for $43,500 and in early October, another check for $99,700.[47]

On October 10, many national newspapers carried a statement from the Macmillan Company reporting that "one of the pleasurable troubles connected with the success of Margaret Mitchell's *Gone With the Wind* is the impossibility of making the advertising keep pace with the fast moving sales figures. By the time an advertisement comes out announcing that *Gone With the Wind* is in its 21st printing—525,000 copies, a 22nd printing has started, making 551,000. At the present moment the book is in its 23rd printing, bringing the total to 576,000 copies."[48]

The end of the book's sales was nowhere in sight. Inquiries from one country after another were coming in requesting foreign translation rights. Such reports would surely bring joy to other authors, but not to the Marshes. Peggy wrote to Brickell:

> If the pressure doesn't let up soon, I do not know what will happen to John and me. . . . When you say the book will go to 600,000 I am appalled. That will mean that this present misery will keep up till after Christmas, at least. Things have gotten so bad that I never say anything but "yes" and "no," knowing I'll be quoted and quoted wrongly. You must realize what a burden it is for me to keep my mouth shut and only open it to make completely innocuous remarks. I wasn't cut out to be a celebrity, and as you have probably gathered, I don't like it worth a damn.[49]

Practically every distinguished person who visited Atlanta insisted on meeting Margaret Mitchell and getting her autograph, and according to John, these strangers had their local hosts put every sort of pressure possible—company, family, personal—on him and the Mitchells to get Peggy to see them. In the middle of her redecorating project, Peggy complained in her letters: "Never was there a worse time for visitors. The apartment is bare as a cabin and while I don't give a hoot what people think it does get under my skin to have guests arrive and have no place to sit. I don't see why they can't wait until such a time as is convenient to me—but they don't or won't."[50] However, she was somewhat more tolerant of her literary admirers. Because she would not go to New York, some notable writers and editors came from New York to visit her. Late in November, while the decorators were still renovating the apartment and the upholsterers still had their furniture, Peggy got a bit of pleasure from entertaining some writers and editors in her bare apartment, instead of the Biltmore, where she and John had a suite. This kind of thing, of course, added to the rumors about her eccentricities.

The first guests to visit the Marshes in their newly decorated apartment were Mabel Search, an editor from the *Pictorial Review,* and Faith Baldwin, a novelist who wanted to write an article about Peggy for the *Review.* The Marshes took an instant liking to these two women and, feeling confident that Baldwin would write a favorable piece, Peggy consented to an interview. In her article, Baldwin wrote that on the afternoon of her visit she and Peggy talked about "books, people, dolls, children, houses, and what happens to those to whom Fame comes as an army bearing banners. And we laughed a good deal." Baldwin described the setting: "The living room walls were painted peach color, a very lovely old Persian rug in tones of peach and pastel lay on the floor, and there was a deep rocking chair which I loved and appropriated, and some old carved furniture upholstered in green." She also described John and her perception of his relationship with Peggy:

> And at six o'clock John Marsh, who is not "Margaret Mitchell's husband"—Margaret Mitchell is John Marsh's wife—came in and handed me the evening papers and went off to wash up for dinner. And Bessie was frying chicken in the kitchen and I hoped that in addition there would be turnip greens. And there were.
>
> John Marsh sat at the head of his table. He is tall, blond, and a little stooped. He is young and his hair is thick and graying. He is soft-spoken. He is a person and this is a marriage. It has been a marriage for eleven years, a unity of tastes and complement of personalities, and to see this and to recognize its stability and verity was satisfactory nourishment for my spirit, just as Bessie's fried chicken was satisfactory nourishment for my body.

A few days after Search and Baldwin's visit, Stuart Rose, from the *Ladies' Home Journal,* came to Atlanta, bringing with him Kenneth Littauer of *Collier's.* Both editors politely pressed her to write articles for them. Although she refused just as politely, she and John respected both men and soon became good friends with them. Having lived in the racehorse capital of the world, John found much to talk about with Rose, a distinguished horseman who had served in the calvary, and also with Littauer, who had been awarded a medal of honor during World War I.

The Marshes decided that they might be able to squelch some rumors if Peggy gave a couple of interviews to a few influential writers whom they trusted to write favorably and truthfully about her. So, although Peggy refused to write an article for *Collier's,* she and John liked Littauer so much that she consented to his second request that she permit Edwin Granberry to write an article about her for *Collier's.*

In addition to talking with Granberry and with Baldwin, Peggy agreed to an interview with Lamar Q. Ball, who wrote for the *Atlanta Constitution.* The Marshes had known Ball for years, and Peggy felt comfortable with him. She enjoyed answering his questions about her method of writing, and she candidly told him how difficult it was for her to write. At one point in her interview with Ball, she gave specific information about how she developed Scarlett's flight from Atlanta to Tara.

> This part of the story worried me. I struggled with it in my mind. I prowled around it mentally for a long time, looking at it from all angles and not getting anywhere. I could never write a line of it and never made a try at it, on paper.
>
> I didn't seem able to capture the smell of the cedars; the smell of the swamp; the barnyard odors, and pack them into those chapters. I was in the Ritz Hotel at Atlantic City when it all came to me. I can't explain why. The Ritz is nothing like Tara.
>
> I can only tell you this. I was not even thinking about the story when all this came to me very simply and very clearly how dusty and stifling a red clay road in Georgia looks and feels in September, how the leaves on the trees are dry and there isn't any wind to move them, and how utterly still the deep country woods are. And there is the queerest smell in the swampy bottom lands at twilight. And I suddenly saw how haunted such a section would look the day after a big battle, after two armies had moved on. So I came home and wrote it. . . .
>
> Writing is a hard job for me. I don't have the facility for just dashing along. . . . Those chapters that I wrote as soon as I returned home from Atlantic City are about the only ones in the book that I did not rewrite at least twenty times. As they appear in the book, they are substantially as they were first written. . . .
>
> Persons who have read the book have told me it must be marvelous to be able to sit down and dash off sentences that read so smoothly. I have a hard time convincing them that the sentences I consider the easiest to read in the book are the ones that I labored over and rewrote and rewrote before I was satisfied I had made my meaning clear.[51]

Although she continued to write several hundred words in letters nearly every day, Peggy steadfastly refused all requests from magazine editors. For example, the *Saturday Review of Literature* wanted her to write an article on the sources of *Gone With the Wind* for its Christmas issue,[52] but she refused, and in telling Harold Latham about the author, wrote: "I have been sick again, minus a secretary and everything in creation has come down on me like an avalanche. . . . I am crazy about it and flattered to death. . . . But I just can't do it. . . . At present, I am just not well enough to do any writing."[53] Edwin Balmer of *Redbook* and Graeme Lorimer of the

Saturday Evening Post invited her to write anything she liked for their publications. Lorimer wanted her to do a regular column for fifteen hundred dollars a week. Balmer wrote Peggy that her refusal letter caused more excitement at *Redbook* than any other document ever had, as the staff from all over the building clamored to see her signature.[54]   By the end of November, when she wrote to thank John's mother for sending her a birthday present, she said that she and John had run through all the big-name editors and most of the editors from all the "True Confession type of magazines" too. She added that when she and John got over the "hump of the movie people's invasion," which would end around December 15, they would finally be able "to breathe."[55]   She and John had mercifully been given a little peace and quiet since the Atlanta newspapers, realizing how many people were bedeviling her and John about auditions for the movie, were kind enough to publish pleas to the public not to bother the Marshes, but to bother the Selznick company instead.[56]

Although she had given permission for interviews and articles to only three writers, Granberry, Baldwin, and Ball, that did not keep others from writing about her as if they had had personal interviews with her. When Herschel Brickell wrote in the New York *Evening Post* on October 22 that he would not be at all surprised to see that *Gone With the Wind* had sold a million copies in the United States alone by Christmas 1936, Peggy wrote to thank him and mentioned another article that was not nearly as flattering as his—James T. Street's "*'Gone With the Wind,'* a Woman's Way of Telling the South's True Story" (New York *World-Telegram Week-End Magazine,* 3 October 1936). She told Brickell:

> About the Jimmy Street—John says I am improving. He brought the article and I was all prepared to sit on my head while he read it to me. It was a stupid affair, wasn't it? But I managed to laugh even though I was irritated. What irritated me the most was his bland assumption of an intimacy that never existed.... I only saw Mr. Street three times in my life and the conversations he wrote never existed, except in his own mind. He never even knew I was writing a book. He was too busy telling me about the book he was going to write.[57]

7

When the word got out that Peggy was never going to write a sequel, *Gone With the Wind* fans were distraught. Some would-be novelists wrote asking if she would let them write the sequel. The answer, of course, was always "No!" One of the replies to such a request remains among the materials saved in the Margaret Mitchell Marsh Papers in the Hargrett Library. It is an undated draft of a letter that John wrote for Peggy. Penciled in John's handwriting, the letter reads:

> Dear Miss Hazel:
> You paid my book a number of very fine compliments in your letter. None of them was as fine as your desire to write a sequel to "Gone With the Wind." I regret, however, that I cannot give you my permission to write such a sequel. Scarlett, Rhett and my other characters are solely and exclusively the creations of my own mind. If you or anybody else should attempt to use my characters in a book, they would unavoidably be twisted and changed from their true personalities. It would be impossible to prevent that, as every writers knows, and I would not like to see that happen. Also if you published such a book I would certainly be given some of the credit for it, simply because my name and the names of Scarlett and Rhett are so closely linked up in the public mind. Naturally I would not like to be given credit to which I was not entitled, for work done by somebody else.
> I am not contemplating a sequel to my novel, but if one should ever be written, I feel, very naturally, that I should be the one to do it.

8

In her interview with Lamar Ball, Peggy spoke frankly, entreating him to help her get the public to understand that she wanted to be left alone.

> I know that the public interest in my book is inextricably tied up with its interest in me. There is no separating them, I suppose. I do believe, though, that my private life is my own. After all, I'm not trying to sell my own personality like a moving picture actress or a candidate for public office. I have merely sold the book I've written. I don't like to have women storming into a department store while I am standing there in my petticoat. They actually did this to me. They questioned me like a crowd of hard-hearted district attorneys. They wanted to know the size of my intimate wearing apparel. They screamed at each other about me as if I were an animal in a cage. One of them said, "Ain't she skinny?" Still another said, "I expected her to look more middle-aged at the hips." And I don't like them to comment that I have no lace on my petticoat. If I go down the street with my petticoat hanging a

fraction of an inch below my skirt it becomes a city-wide scandal. If I make no excuses, I hear, "With all this success, she's certainly got the swelled head!" or "She's certainly gotten stuck up!" I want the quiet life I'm accustomed to.[58]

But the quiet life never returned. *Gone With the Wind* continued to have a mysterious appeal to nearly everyone, no matter what age, profession, color, nationality, or sex. It had enormous appeal to old people who had lived through the Civil War and Reconstruction days. Peggy received hundreds of letters from old men and women who, in shaky handwriting, thanked her for writing the book. Sometimes, some of them related memories and family traditions of their own and sent her old diaries and letters. Some asked about being her distant kin. She politely answered each letter, responding to all questions and comments. "There are scores of grandchildren whose voices are rasping and hoarse from reading aloud to them," Peggy wrote to a friend, "and Heaven knows how many indignant grandchildren have told me that they had to sit up all night reading because the old folks wouldn't let them quit till after Scarlett was safe at Tara again."[59] A few of the older people who could read the novel for themselves had to cut the book into five or so parts because their weak wrists could not hold the heavy book.[60]

School-age girls also loved the novel, and grade school children enjoyed it as part of their American history assignments. But then so did millions of others from all walks of life. About her readers Peggy wrote to Brickell on October 9, 1936:

File clerks, elevator operators, sales girls in department stores, telephone operators, stenographers, garage mechanics, clerks in Helpsy-Selfy stores, school teachers—oh, Heavens, I could go on and on!—like it. What is more puzzling, they buy copies. The United Daughters of the Confederacy have endorsed it, the Sons of the Confederate Veterans crashed through with a grand endorsement, too. The debutantes and dowagers read it. Catholic nuns like it. Now, how to explain all this?

I sit down and pull the story apart in my mind and try to figure it all out. Despite its length and many details it is basically just a simple yarn of fairly simple people. There's no fine writing, there's no philosophizing, there is a minimum of description, there are no grandiose thoughts, there are no hidden meanings, no symbolism, nothing sensational—nothing at all that made other best sellers best sellers. Then how to explain its appeal from the five year old to the ninety-five year old? I can't figure it out.[61]

Public and college libraries and bookstores could not keep enough copies on hand. Judges, lawyers, and physicians read it and wrote her the most flattering letters, and psychiatrists found it particularly interesting. Dr. John Favill, president of the Central Neuropsychiatric Association of Minneapolis, in a speech to his colleagues at a professional meeting, discussed the section where Scarlett is talking to Rhett about her guilt feelings over Frank Kennedy's death. In this passage, Rhett makes Scarlett see that she is not really feeling guilty about Frank's death, and he points out: "And if he wasn't dead, you'd still be mean. As I understand it, you are not really sorry for marrying Frank and bullying him and inadvertently causing his death. You are only sorry because you are afraid of going to hell."[62] Dr. Favill used this insight of Rhett's in his discussion of guilt as displacement of selfishness.

Many other psychiatrists wrote Peggy praising her for so clearly delineating psychopathic personalities, particularly in Scarlett O'Hara. Dr. Charles E. Wells, a psychiatrist at Vanderbilt University School of Medicine, wrote a fascinating essay using Scarlett as a model example of the hysterical personality. Dr. Wells states that "Scarlett O'Hara fulfills almost exactly the criteria for the hysterical personality offered by Chadoff and Lyons," who published the classic description of that disorder.[63] Perhaps it was all the attention psychiatrists gave to Scarlett's psychopathic characteristics that made Peggy so angry whenever anyone said that she resembled Scarlett. As time went on, Peggy became very protective of her heroine, as if she never came to grips with Scarlett's iniquities, and she defended her as she does in this letter:

> Personally, I cannot help feeling that Scarlett had good traits. Surely courage is commendable, and she had it. The sense of responsibility for the weak and helpless is a rare trait, and she had this, for she took care of her own even at great cost to herself. She was able to appreciate what was beautiful in her mother, even if she could not emulate her. She loved her Negroes and looked after them. She had perseverance in the face of defeat. Of course those qualities are balanced by her bad qualities.[64]

When an Illinois physician, Dr. Charles E. Mayos, wrote her a letter of warm praise, Peggy replied:

> Nothing could have pleased me more than to have a psychiatrist praise the pattern of Scarlett O'Hara's emotional life. I am one of those people who are disliked by all real psychiatrists. I am a

layman who knows just a little about abnormal psychology. I started out to be a psychiatrist, but, unfortunately, was forced to leave college when my mother died. . . . I realize that I know all the tops of abnormal psychology—and have none of the basic and rudimentary knowledge. It's like knowing geometry and never having known the multiplication tables. Perhaps you can understand, after this explanation, why your words of praise about "The accurate description of human emotions" pleased me so much.[65]

As time passed, Peggy got increasingly defensive about her "poah Scarlett,"[66] whom some called "a first class bitch."[67] When letters came chiding her for making a bad woman the heroine and thus casting a bad light on all southern ladies of days long gone, Peggy pointed out all of Scarlett's good qualities.[68] She also defended Ashley after frequently reading descriptions of him portrayed as a weak, idealistic dreamer and coward. "Ashley was the greatest realist in the book because his eyes, like those of Rhett, were always open," she explained. "He saw things with a cruel clarity, but unlike Rhett, he was not able to do anything about them."[69]

9

Not only did the psychiatrists take a professional interest in the characters but ministers and Catholic priests did also. Some actually spoke homilies from their pulpits about the novel. When a minister from the Peachtree Christian Church in Atlanta preached his sermon on *Gone With the Wind* and sent the author a copy, Peggy told him how much she appreciated his speaking out in defense of Ashley's sense of honor. She thought it was strange that so few people liked Ashley or gave him credit for having a sense of honor and for trying to be true to it. "It has amused me," she wrote, "that generally the very nicest ladies have been most outstanding in their criticism of him."[70] Raymond J. O'Flaherty, a Catholic priest, denounced *Gone With the Wind* in his letter to the editor of the Catholic magazine *America*. The priest wrote that he thought the novel ought to be withheld from young people and that he was surprised that any high-school English teacher would assign the novel to students. Another priest on the staff of the magazine suggested that the novel not be banned but maybe rated "objectionable in parts." In this same January 23 issue of *America,* the Very Reverend Monsignor James H. Murphy from Ellicottville, New York, expressed a different viewpoint. In a letter to the editor, he praised the novel, saying that it was "true to life. It may be sordid in spots; so is life." The monsignor pointed out that "the most beautiful character in the book is Ellen O'Hara," whom he described as an "embodiment of the valiant woman of scripture, a woman whose Catholic life and ideas spread the good odor of sanctity about her and who dies a martyr to charity. After her, for eminence of character," wrote the monsignor, "stands Mammy, that black diamond in the rough, who imbibed her standards of fidelity and learned her rigid code of conduct from her long years with Catholic Ellen O'Hara."

Peggy was absolutely ecstatic when she received a copy of the monsignor's letter to the editor and his letter to her. She answered him immediately, admitting that she often felt so "downhearted" when people criticized her for portraying such a bad woman as Scarlett.

> I had striven to show that Ellen O'Hara was indeed a woman whose children rose up and called her blessed, a woman whose ideals prodded the hardening conscience of Scarlett, even though Scarlett did not obey the prods. I tried to show Melanie as a Christian character so honorable that she could not conceive of dishonor in others. Mammy was as uncompromising about right and wrong as was possible. The stout-hearted matrons who knew about right and wrong refused to tolerate Scarlett. I naturally felt a sense of disappointment that the eyes of many of my readers focused entirely upon the bad woman and paid no heed to the many good women. That is why I thank you.[71]

Other readers, like Robert W. Bingham, publisher of the *Courier-Journal* in Louisville, Kentucky, wrote of Melanie's goodness and beauty, placing Melanie in the same class with his mother. On one of her visits to Saint Joseph's Infirmary, Peggy was told by Sister Mary Loyola, who was in charge of the hospital, that she thought the novel was a moral one because it demonstrated clearly that people have to pay for the wrong they do and that there was nothing in Scarlett's character that would make any young girl want to imitate her.[72]

Neither John nor Peggy could figure out how so many different kinds of people—from all walks of life—saw so many different kinds of meanings in her book. When reviews and articles came out commending her on things that had never entered her mind, she was astonished. When one critic announced that *Gone With the Wind* was a pacifist's novel, a powerful document against war, she wrote:

> Lord! I think. I never intended that! Reviews speak of the symbolism of the characters, placing Melanie as the Old South and Scarlett the New. Lord! I never intended that either. Psychiatrists speak of the "carefully done emotional patterns" and disregard all the history part. "Emotional patterns?" Good Heavens!

Can this be I? People talk and write of the "high moral lesson." I don't see anything very moral in it. I murmur feebly that "it's just a story" and my words are swallowed up while the storm goes over my head about "intangible values," "right and wrong" etc. Well, I still say feebly that it's just a simple story of some people who went up and some who went down, those who could take it and those who couldn't. And when people come along and say that I've done more for the South than anyone since Henry Grady I feel very proud and very humble and wish to God I could take cover like a rabbit.[73]

10

The Marshes celebrated Peggy's thirty-sixth birthday by slipping away for a weekend to Sea Island, their favorite resort on the Georgia coast. John registered them as "Mr. and Mrs. John Munnerlyn," a pseudonym they started using whenever they traveled.[74] The hotel was beautiful and heavenly quiet, and about Sea Island, she wrote, "There is no place in the world so still."[75] They slept late each morning and had hearty breakfasts of hot coffee and fresh fruit, eggs, buttered grits, and bacon served in their room every day. In the afternoons they took leisurely drives "through long avenues of enormous trees with yards of Spanish moss hanging down."[76] John wished that they could stay in that isolated spot for two or three months so that she could get the rest and relaxation she needed. But that was not possible. Just a few hours before they were ready to leave, someone recognized Peggy and shouted to her. She waved back, and then she and John scurried off in the opposite direction, giggling as they made a secret exit from the hotel. Complaining about having to talk to so many people she did not want to talk to, she asked, "Why is it that the attractive people you want to catch are so elusive and the time stealers are with us always?"[77]

Something that truly delighted Peggy around this time was learning that her novel had been put into Braille. When the Atlanta Library for the Blind telephoned her saying the book had arrived, she felt genuinely flattered.[78] And a month later, Lois informed her that a man in California wanted permission to translate the novel into the international language Esperanto.[79]

A couple of weeks after their vacation to Sea Island, John wrote his mother:

> I felt downright encouraged when the *NY Herald Tribune* best-seller box score last Sunday showed that five stores had dropped out on the *GWTW* list—the largest number since July. I

thought it might be the beginning of the end. But next week, Macmillan is breaking forth with a full page ad on the book in the Saturday Evening Post, and that may prolong the excitement and the sales.

The present week has been one of the most strenuous since the book went on sale ... and all the while Steve Mitchell, Peggy's brother and attorney, stands on the sidelines gritting his teeth at me trying to get an interview with me, postponed from night to night for the past three weeks, at which we hope to figure out some way to keep the government from taking all of Peggy's money in income tax.[80]

He told his mother that the Selznick film scouts intended to look for unknown actors in the South, among little theater groups, college dramatic clubs, and junior leagues. Within the next two weeks, director George Cukor and screenwriter Sidney Howard would be in Atlanta.

You can imagine the furor the announcement has created. Everybody who ever wanted to get to Hollywood, and that apparently includes 99% of the total population, is ramping and stamping to get to meet the Selznicks and get auditioned. And in addition to Atlanta, they are planning to carry the search for talent into all the principal Southern cities. My guess is that they will stir up more commotion in the South than at any time since the Civil War. . . .

Selznick really has an honest desire to find new talent for the roles, having become convinced that large numbers of people will refuse to see the movie if Clark Gable does not play "Rhett" and that equally large numbers will stay away if he does (and ditto on the other leading characters). Personally I am doubtful that he will actually find any unknown actors for the parts, but I hand it to him for having designed one of the choicest publicity stunts anybody ever heard of.

It's the toughest situation I have ever been up against but, as Renny says, "It has to be bared." Some day we will sail out of this storm and into peaceful waters again. In the meantime I hope you will bear with us and pull for us as hard as you can. We need it.[81]

11

The British edition produced such excellent reviews that Peggy said they "took her breath away."[82] The Marshes had every reason to believe that the foreign reviews would be just as good. At that time, they were relieved to know that they would soon have the help of Marion Saunders, the literary agent skilled in handling foreign rights whom they had contacted earlier, although they had no idea of the magnitude of problems that would later emerge from her and her services.

As more and more requests for speeches came in, John showed that his sense of humor was still intact when he suggested that Peggy have one of Nathan Bedford Forrest's statements printed on cards to hand out. He was referring to an incident involving an officer to whom General Forrest had refused to grant a furlough on two occasions. When the officer applied the third time, Forrest silently took his pen in hand and wrote, "I tole you twicst godamet know."[83] Peggy explained to Brickell: "So many people want me to make speeches and I refuse as nicely as I know how. Undeterred they write back and insist that I make speeches or 'just come and let us have look at you.' (Oh, nauseous thought! Have I become a freak like the quintuplets or Jo-Jo, the Dogfaced Boy?)"[84]

On the first of December, the Marshes entered into an agreement with Marion Saunders. John wrote Putnam telling him to forward all inquires that Macmillam received from foreign publishers directly to Saunders, and he requested that Putnam send him carbon copies of the letters so that he could keep up with the developments. "Never having had any dealings with a situation of this kind before, I find it interesting to note which countries are inquiring about the book and how many inquiries are coming in from one country or another."[85]

As Christmas approached, many people were buying copies of *Gone With the Wind* to give as presents and an avalanche of requests came for autographs. Wishing for a deus ex machina to whisk them away for a rest, John decided to take more control of their lives and eliminate all unnecessary activities.[86] Autographing was the thing first to go. After looking at Peggy's engagement calendar, he figured out that from nine in the morning until nine at night, every weekday and some weekends, she averaged an appointment every forty minutes. She averaged writing a hundred letters a week and thus far had autographed about thirty-five hundred copies of the book. With a million books in circulation now, he insisted that she refuse to autograph anymore.[87] There was simply no way she could meet the demand for autographs and lead any kind of enjoyable life. He told Peggy and Margaret Baugh that there would be no more unwrapping, autographing, rewrapping, and mailing—at their own expense or at anyone else's—any more books sent to her. He instructed Margaret Baugh to inform the post office not to deliver any more books to the apartment and to tell Macmillan not to send any more books, that

Margaret Mitchell would not sign any more autographs—for anyone, ever.

Thinking of the Christmas sales, Lois was horrified when she heard about this decision and asked if "rubber stamp" autographs would be all right. Just as horrified, Peggy yelled back, "No! Never!" She explained:

> One of the incredible rumors that I've been fighting for months is the one that I have never yet autographed a single book—The Macmillan Company or I have merely used a rubber stamp.... People who had autographed copies got into frenzies when the rumor reached them and rushed to me to know the truth (though why in God's name it should matter, I can't understand). People who were dickering for autographed copies threw up the trade at the news and wrote or wired me to know the truth. Second hand book shops wanted my word of honor that I had honest to God autographed the volume they were trying to sell. I've had to say so often, with what patience I could muster, that I had never used a rubber stamp or a facsimile signature.... Yes, I know all of this sounds incredible but then this last year has been so full of incredibilities....[88]

She told Lois, "When a stranger asks me for an autograph I feel just as if he (or she) had asked me for a pair of my step-ins and it makes me just as sore." Yet, she expressed a concern for the public: "I realize that other people do not feel this way and they do not intend to be insulting and are just being as nice as they know how but my feeling only grows stronger. And this feeling is one of the reasons I never go anywhere except to my office or to the Library. I do not want to hurt people's feelings but, on the other hand, I do not want to get furious forty times a day."[89]

When they could not find Peggy, many people hounded John, her father, Stephens and his wife Carrie Lou, and even Bessie, in attempts to get Peggy's autograph. Peggy complained, "When I make a business appointment with someone they usually turn up staggering under a dozen copies which their friends have wished upon them, in the frank hope that the caller can 'embarrass' me into signing them. And oh, my God the pressure that's brought to bear by charitable organizations wanting an autographed copy for raffling purposes!"[90]

Peggy, most likely, would have made some exceptions to this rule, but not John; he was steadfast enough for both of them. No better example of his determination to stand by his decision to refuse autographs can be found than the Wendell Willkie incident. As the president of the Commonwealth and Southern Corporation and an outspoken opponent of President Roosevelt's New Deal, Willkie scheduled a staff meeting with the presidents of the southern power companies comprising the C & S Corporation. Among those who were to attend that meeting in Charleston, South Carolina, was P. S. Arkwright, president of the Georgia Power Company. Before the meeting, Willkie wrote Arkwright saying how much he enjoyed reading *Gone With the Wind* and requesting that he ask John to get Peggy to autograph his copy, which he had enclosed. Arkwright was to bring the autographed book to the meeting in Charleston. Astonished when John invoked his inviolable rule of no more autographs—for any one, no matter how prominent—Arkwright returned the book to Willkie in its pristine state, and what he and Willkie thought about that is not known.[91]

The last book Peggy autographed may have been the one sent to Mary Louise Nute, John's cousin, in Kentucky. Shortly before Christmas 1936, John wrote her:

> The book has been autographed and is being mailed along with this letter. And where did you get the notion that it wouldn't be a pleasure to autograph *your* book? Peggy is glad to do it for the family and for good friends. It's the great wide world which is about to run her raggetty.
>
> I didn't comply with your request and put my own name in the book. I haven't done that yet in any copy of the book and I don't aim to. It's Peggy's book, and she is the one to do the autographing. She paid me the highest compliment when she put my "JRM" on the dedication page, and that will have to do for me.[92]

Aside from writing a sequel, which they were never going to do no matter how many thousands of requests she got, they could not figure out what to do about the idiotic and unbelievable letters and telephone calls concerning Rhett and Scarlett's reconciliation. "And at the only tea," Peggy wrote Lois, "I've been to (it taught me a lesson. I'll not go to another soon) my sash was torn off, my veil yanked from my hat, punch and refreshments knocked out of my hands as ladies from Iowa and Oklahoma and Seattle screamed the same question at me and poked me with sharp pointed fingernails to emphasize their questions. Good grief. I thought I knew human nature. But this has been a new experience for me."[93]

Why the Marshes did not take stronger actions to ensure their privacy is a mystery. They could have moved to another apartment or had the telephone company give them a new, unlisted number, or had the post office and the telegram and telegraph companies hold all messages and deliver them once a day to Margaret Baugh in the office, rather than to their apartment. One possible answer lies in John's compulsive personality, which required him to be in control, to take care of everything for Peggy. Also, according to his family, he honestly believed at that time that the commotion would not and could not continue. He kept repeating to himself, to Peggy, and to others, "It can't possibly keep up much longer."

On December 4, Peggy received a copy of the beautiful booklet that Macmillan published about *Gone With the Wind.* Containing information about the novel and its author in a question-answer format, this booklet was used by Macmillan as advertisement for the novel and, as such, part of it was printed in periodicals. John proudly sent a copy of it home to his mother for her scrapbook, and Peggy jubilantly telegrammed Lois Cole: "Just seen advertisement in Post. Marvelous! stupendous! colossal! All the grand adjectives. Please tell artist how much I like it. Is it true about a million copies? Good Heavens! Could I have the one millionth copy? Love, Peggy."[94]

In just six months since its publication, *Gone With the Wind* had sold a million copies. Other books had sold that many copies, but not one had sold a million copies in that brief a time. For a Christmas present, Macmillan sent Peggy the millionth copy of her book in which the publisher had designed a special title page that read:

This, the One Millionth Copy of *Gone With the Wind,* is presented to the author Margaret Mitchell with the congratulations and best wishes of her publishers. The Macmillan Company. December 15, 1936.

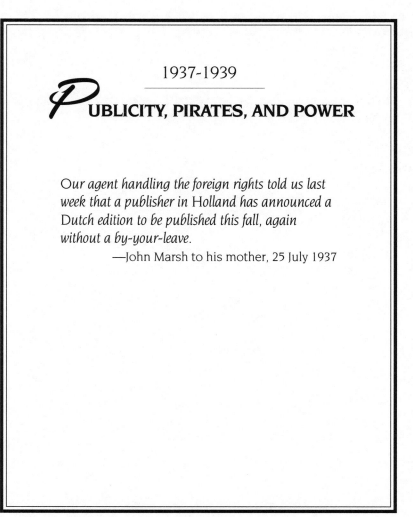

1937-1939

PUBLICITY, PIRATES, AND POWER

Our agent handling the foreign rights told us last week that a publisher in Holland has announced a Dutch edition to be published this fall, again without a by-your-leave.

—John Marsh to his mother, 25 July 1937

1

AFTER RETURNING FROM A HOLIDAY VACATION in Winter Park, Florida, John wrote to his mother in January 1937, thanking her for the Christmas presents she had sent and reporting on their vacation. While they were away, Peggy had gained six pounds, he said, and his only regret was that he could not keep her away six months instead of two weeks.[1] They did not go far enough south to loll on white-sand beaches, as they had planned; in fact, John declared, "We didn't do *anything* exciting, but it was a wonderful vacation just the same." In her letter to Mrs. Marsh, Peggy, who sounded relaxed and happy, added that they stayed in little towns and slept until nine o'clock every morning and ate their first uninterrupted meals in six months.[2] Except for one slip-up in Winter Park, nobody even suspected who Peggy was and so they were "completely carefree and lazy."

In explaining the slip-up, John told how he and Peggy discovered that disclosing their presence to the Granberrys, who lived in Winter Park, turned out to be a big mistake; although Mrs. Granberry kept their secret, Edwin told at least a dozen people—"each one in the strictest confidence, of course." John said, "Edwin is one of those people who are as good as gold and have no guile at all. He was perfectly confident that each of the folks would keep the secret." But after the Marshes learned how many people Edwin had confided in and that he had even given their "alias," they felt uneasy and sniffed a forthcoming banquet, autographs, photos, newspapermen, and the whole routine.

Evidence that their suspicions were correct came around midnight on Christmas Eve, while they were lying in bed talking. A bellboy knocked softly and then slipped a note under the door. The note was from Lida Woods, whom they knew well and who was obviously trying to warn them. The note was an apology for not being able to attend the dinner with them and Hamilton Holt, the president of Rollins College, where Edwin taught and where Lida was secretary to the president. "What dinner? With whom?" Peggy asked John. They knew then that the next step would be actual invitations and personal calls, so they got dressed, packed their bags,

~ 347 ~

and checked out of the hotel early Christmas morning. Sneaking out of hotels before dawn got to be one of their favorite things to do: they got a kick out of outsmarting whoever had schemed against them. "We spent Christmas day riding in the sunshine through the orange groves—the strangest Christmas we have ever spent," John wrote his mother, "but a very happy one because nobody could call us on the telephone—and the rest of our vacation was spent in little hotels in little towns where nobody knew us at all."[3]

For John's and Peggy's Christmas presents in 1936, Mrs. Marsh had made and embroidered each a pair of beautiful, soft, white cotton pajamas, and she made a smock for Peggy. As she had done every year since John had left home, she sent one of her hickory nut cakes. In thanking her, Peggy wrote that since she had gained weight on her vacation, she was not able to button any of her clothes, so the smock was especially appreciated. "The smock is so comfortable and pretty and the deep pockets are wonderful as adjuncts to my filing case. I can shove 'letters to be answered immediately' in one pocket and 'letters to be answered when humanly possible' in another. Also, I can carry pencils, cigarettes and paper clips in them. . . . John always freezes onto the cake and keeps it in his bureau beneath his pajamas and doles me out crumbs at night when we are in bed discussing the events of the day."[4] In his letter, John said to his mother, "Yours and the millionth copy of the book . . . were about the only presents we got, which made each of them doubly appreciated." In thanking her for the pajamas, he asked if she were aware of his "hoarding habit," and then contrasted his and Peggy's personalities:

> When I get pretty things, I save them for weeks, or even longer, just for the pleasure of looking at them, without the new being worn off. So I get a prolonged pleasure of anticipation, in addition to the pleasure of realization. Peggy, poor wight, dives into her new things right away. It's only one of the many basic incompatibilities in our natures which often makes me wonder how we manage to put up with each other, which oddly enough we have been able to do with some success for many years. Maybe, it's because she puts up with my peculiarities, in return for my putting up with hers.[5]

In an earlier letter to his mother, John had described their life in Atlanta as "feverish," and in this letter he wrote that the adjective seemed even more appropriate now than ever. When they arrived home from Winter Park, they could hardly open the door of their apartment because of the mail stacked up and waiting for Peggy. "We had hoped that after the millionth copy was out and Christmas was over, the pressure would slacken. Instead, it's worse than ever before." They had literally fled from the city because of the furor that the first audition crew had created in Atlanta during early December. When Kay Brown and Tony Bundsman, from the Selznick organization, made their first talent-search visit, the Marshes' life was uprooted by throngs of people wanting Peggy to endorse them for one of the roles. Calls, telegrams, and special deliveries flooded the apartment. People camped on the Marshes' doorstep, grabbed her and John as they went out, and pleaded with them for a role in the movie. That one week in December, John told his mother, was the worst week of his life.

Wishing to discourage his mother from visiting them, he wrote tactfully that such an invitation would be the kind children sent to their mothers to come help out in emergencies, such as when babies were being born or when there were serious illnesses. Not wanting to extend that kind of invitation, he said: "This is a situation where nobody can help us but God, and about the only way He could help us would be by raising up some other celebrity to divert the public's attention away from Peggy. We would both love to see you, but under happier circumstances than at present. We could tell the Henrys and Gordons that they could come to see us, if they wouldn't stay but a little while, but we don't want to have you visiting us on any such basis as that." He added that he and Peggy were going to visit her and the family soon if the family promised not to tell "any nearest and dearest friends."

Going to the movies was the Marshes' favorite pastime. While away on vacation they had gone to see Mae West's *Go West, Young Man,* twice. The principal characters are an actress, who is touring around making public appearances, and her press agent. Recommending this movie to his mother, John said, "I told Peggy I got a kick out of it, because the press agent's job of keeping the actress before the public in only the best light reminded me of my job with the Company. It wasn't until a week later that Peggy realized that I was also thinking of my job as 'manager' of the celebrated author, Margaret Mitchell." John urged his mother to see the picture because it would give her an idea, "in a crude Mae Westish fashion, of one of Peggy's worst problems—the fact that her lightest word or her most trivial act is a matter of public curiosity, so that she must always be guarding her words and her acts. Which is a terrible strain on anybody."

Since he was about to enter the hospital for more hemorrhoidal surgery, he asked his mother not to worry if she did not hear from him for a couple of weeks and not to pay any attention to anything she read in the papers. "The condition is not serious. The doctor thought it might help in getting my disorderly digestion back in order, and I am taking time out for it now because I believe it will help me to get through the rest of the Marsh-Mitchell siege.'"[6] Preferring to keep his surgery a private matter and knowing that such a wish was impossible, John jokingly suggested to Peggy that she stand on the street corner and shout as loudly as she could the indelicate nature of his illness. Otherwise, he said it would be all over America that he had beri-beri or leprosy.[7]

2

By February 10, after a two-week stay in the hospital, he was home recuperating with Peggy attentively waiting on him. Although she had an acute aversion to housekeeping, she could have made a career out of nursing. She never wanted anyone making a fuss over her when she was sick, but she enjoyed "fussing," as Deon called it, over others. Back then, patients were not allowed to get out of bed soon after surgery, so she insisted on doing everything for him—bedpan and all, according to Deon. Every morning she helped him bathe and shave, and she brought their meals on trays to the bedroom.[8]

After nearly two weeks at home, during which time he slept most of the day and night, soaking up the rest he badly needed, John began to feel good. Things were unusually quiet that winter. They had no visitors except for Edwin Granberry, who was accompanied by Kenneth Littauer, the editor of *Collier's*. The men came for a brief visit to talk about the article Edwin was writing about Peggy for the magazine. Before Granberry left, John extracted a promise from him to let the Marshes have final approval of his article before he published it.

A couple of weeks later, after Granberry's draft arrived and John read it carefully, he wrote thirteen pages of specific suggestions, giving us an idea of how thoroughly he went about editing.[9] He not only pointed out mistakes in grammar, but he also questioned word choice and rewrote entire long sections. For example, he questioned the word "loitering" and asked, "Why not use *standing*? The railroad men were probably there on business and not just loitering." He did not want Peggy described as "a very young woman" because "Peggy thinks this might cause loud guffaws from friends; who know her real, very advanced age, and also cause disappointment on the part of people who meet her for the first time in the flesh, after having seen only Mr. Asasno's photographic deceptions." (Asasno was a well-known Atlanta photographer at that time who touched up his photographs of Peggy, making her appear younger.) Some entire paragraphs about her charitable acts and gifts he wanted "killed" because they smacked of "commercialization." He stressed, "Also, please don't involve me in any scheme to throw the manuscript away. . . . I wouldn't have done it, and if Peggy had done it, I would have given her a good cow-hiding. (Please don't mention that in your article. Merely change 'they' to 'she.'") He thought that the line about "autographed copies of the first printings" might stir up a commotion about "demands for more autographs from persons owning first editions" and wanted any reference to autographs omitted.

Emphasizing how much he wanted this article to convey the notion to its readers that Peggy needed privacy and quiet, John stressed that she wanted to continue to live in her apartment, in Atlanta, leading the same kind of life she had led before the book was published. So, he added: "Yet if she remains inside her home, a barrage of letters, telegrams, calls by wire, calls in person, pour in upon her from early morning until late at night. There is no secret about her address. Her telephone is listed. Determined to continue her life as she has always lived it, she is not even considering 'refuging' from Atlanta to some secret retreat. Atlanta is her home, it is were she belongs, it is where her husband lives and works, it is where her people have lived since before the city was born. . . ."

Then, oddly enough, he went on to describe how she dedicated herself to answering letters. "She answers all of them herself. She has a secretary—sometimes two, one in the daytime and one at night—but every letter receives Miss Mitchell's personal attention. No form-letter replies are sent." It is difficult to understand why John did not see that such a statement would only encourage more people to write. He was sending out conflicting messages to the public: calls and autographs, no! personal letters, yes! He explained that the majority of the letters she received were so intimate in nature that they could not be answered "with stereotyped politeness," even if she were tempted to let her secretaries handle them. He wrote:

> Miss Mitchell might perhaps ignore them—and thereby gain more time to comply with the requests of the autograph-seekers but having unwittingly been the cause of the desperate tone of some of them, she feels an obligation she cannot evade.
>
> Wives write that the tragedy of Rhett and Scarlett has opened their eyes to similar tragedies under their own roofs and has moved them to correct estrangements from their husbands before it is too late. Husbands write that Rhett's separation from Scarlett after he had loved her so many years has kept them awake at night, fearful that they might also lose beloved wives. Letters come in, hardly legible so shaky are the aged hands that wrote them, asking God's blessing on the young author for picturing so truthfully the war days through which they lived. Other letters, in the painfully precise handwriting of youth, thank Miss Mitchell for having given them their first real understanding of the Old South's gallantry and chivalry that is a part of the heritage of us all. Men

broken by the depression—idealists who could not survive the change and upheaval—pour out their hearts to Miss Mitchell in sympathy for Ashley. . . . Proud wives whose men have been thrown out of work write her letters filled with bitter compassion for Scarlett, for they have learned that no woman knows the degradation she will stoop to until she needs to defend her home and those she loves.

At some point, he realized he was going on too long and told Edwin not to hesitate to cut the passage if it made the article unnecessarily long. He also urged Edwin to give serious thought before publishing the "sort of stuff I have written" and to get Mrs. Granberry's ideas on it, too. He asked:

> Does all this stuff about Peggy's not autographing, not seeing callers, etc., make her seem tough? hard boiled? unfeeling and unappreciative of the honors the public has bestowed on her so generously?
>
> Situations like Peggy's are so foreign to the average person's experience, that it is almost impossible to explain them in personal conversation. And trying to explain them in writing involves a real risk that the explanations won't be understood. Of course, if this explanation does click and if it is published in Colliers, it should *help Peggy tremendously in handling her public problems.* But if you and Mabel don't think it clicks, don't use a line of it. You have a much better outside viewpoint on it than I have.

Granberry incorporated—verbatim—all of John's suggestions, corrections, and even the lengthy section about the letters that John himself wrote. This long article, which appeared in *Collier's* in March 1937, is mostly a repeat of everything that had ever been written about her. The only new line, a puzzling, false statement, is one Granberry himself added: "She is a trained psychologist and knows in a scientific way what alterations sometimes happen in the personalities of those who are caught in a violent upheaval of circumstances."

This article must have given the American public a clear view of Peggy as a harried woman, for the conclusion reads: "She fears that the intense glare of the spotlight beating down upon her, month after month, may eventually drive her into complete seclusion, in the hope of salvaging some remnant of her private life; she fears that she will lose touch with the world she loves because of this seclusion; she fears that people may think her hard and unappreciative and unsociable because of her enforced necessity of refusing. . . ."

As the beautiful February weather brought out the spring flowers, John continued to improve, and the Marshes' preoccupation with illnesses and doctors' visits faded. Even though the commotion about the book had ceased in Atlanta, manifestation of *Gone With the Wind*'s influence on public policies and regulations began to emerge in two ways in early 1937. The first of these had to do with price-maintenance laws. In New York City, department and book stores, trying to outsell one another, ignored the existing price-maintenance laws and started reducing the retail price of the novel, which Macmillan had fixed at three dollars. Some stores were selling the book for less than they had paid the publisher for it. With sales skyrocketing everywhere, stores could not keep enough copies of the novel in stock. Even though Macmillan gave a discount for large orders, it could not sell wholesale at the low price some big department stores, like Macy's, were retailing the novel. Instead of purchasing new books from Macmillan, merchants started buying copies from whoever was selling at the lowest price.

On March 29, 1937, the *New York Herald Tribune*'s lead article in the business section had to do with New York State's newly legalized fair-trade laws.[10] According to the *Tribune* article, which is titled "Macy's Resells 35,940 Copies of Best Seller to Macmillan Co," this action was the first taken under the fair-trade law, and it was the first instance of a retail merchant selling back goods already purchased to the distributor of such merchandise. A long-standing opponent of the price-maintenance laws, Macy's had sold 170,000 copies of *Gone With the Wind* since its publication date. While the price of the novel fluctuated with competition, Macy's had been selling the book for $1.51 a copy. George Brett explained that Macmillan had to act to establish its resale price under the law in order to stop the price wars on the book and added that no other publisher had ever had to act to maintain prices on their books. Other industries, such as drug and cosmetic firms, wanted resale prices maintained, and supported Macmillan's efforts to get the price-protection act passed. In August 1937, President Roosevelt signed into law the much-debated and delayed Tydings-Miller bill, known as the Fair Trade or Price Protection Act. Those who had argued for the bill used *Gone With the Wind* as an important example of the need for such a law, which covered food, drugs, cosmetics, perfumes, tobacco, and many other goods aside from books.[11] But the single product that propelled the act into a law was Margaret Mitchell's *Gone With the Wind.*

The second influence of *Gone With the Wind* on federal regulations resulted from the enormous taxes Peggy had to pay in 1936 and 1937. A revenue law—Code Section 107-C, popularly known as the "Margaret Mitchell Law" because her experience initiated debate on it—was passed by Congress in 1952, three years after Peggy's death. This legislation acknowledged the injustices that authors such as Peggy had endured and called attention to the unfairness some taxpayers experienced when they had to pay huge taxes on the lump sum they received in one year for work that took them several unpaid years to complete.[12]

4

Other than trying to figure out a legal way not to pay huge sums in taxes, the Marshes' major concern in the spring of 1937 had to do with the reports from the foreign editions, which were just now beginning to materialize. In England, by the end of January, the book had sold thirty-eight thousand copies and was in its fifth printing. In early February, Peggy wrote Brickell: "The reviews have begun to come in from South Africa and India and, Herschel, I give you my word, if they'd been written by unreconstructed Rebels they couldn't be better. I get cold chills up and down my back reading the Indian ones." She added: "About the translation rights, everybody except the Chinese and Albanians have put in a bid. We've been working on them for some time and they ought to be closed up within a couple of weeks if we don't hit any more snags. And, good grief, the number of snags we have hit!"[13]

While John took care of the book's business, Peggy continued writing letters, not in the apartment but in her new office. When Eugene Carr, the janitor in their apartment building, informed the Marshes that the apartment adjacent to theirs was available, they rented it as an office for Peggy and Margaret Baugh, who was now working full time for them. Close enough so that Peggy could run home for meals and answer special calls, it was far enough away for her to hide. Because it had no telephone, Bessie screened the calls at home. Every day, while Margaret Baugh got out the mail and worked on bookkeeping matters, Peggy read, took naps on the sofa, or wrote letters.

Editors had stopped asking her to write articles and stories; interviewers had given up trying to reach her; and autographs seekers had almost vanished. Her days were spent quietly doing whatever she wished. Nearly every morning, she visited her father, who was often ailing, and then she spent the rest of her day in her office doing whatever she pleased. Bessie and Margaret Baugh answered all telephone calls during the day and John, at night. He handled all their business. She did not have to talk to anyone but friends and family. Occasionally when she went out to shop or to the library, she said she would get "nabbed, but I do not mind that so much now that I am feeling better. The nabbers are all very kind and polite people, and now that I feel well, they don't bother me as much."[14]

In writing to Brickell in February, she said:

> Things are quieting down a little or if they aren't I don't know about them because I stay at the office till very late and let poor Bessie wrestle things. But I think I'm through with the invasion of editors. They've all come down here and gone away with their minds made up that I'm probably crazy because I won't write short stories or articles for them. When I say with fervor that I wouldn't think of doing anything that would add to the present public interest in me or accept one penny that would run my income into a higher bracket—they just look at me.[15]

By early April, Peggy was in a wonderful frame of mind and health. In none of her other letters throughout her entire life did she ever express the happiness and wellness that she expressed in the letters she wrote in April 1937. "Everything is marvelous here in the country now," she wrote Brickell. She had two sound reasons to be happy: she was confident that a splendid film would be made from her book, and she had heard from numerous sources that she would win the Pulitzer Prize. "I feel perfectly wonderful these days, and have for the last couple of months. As a matter of fact, I am looking for a wildcat so that I can offer the wildcat the first bite before we mix up."[16] Peggy's high spirits at this time come through in her correspondence with Mabel Search about a "wildcat" of her own.

As a result of Faith Baldwin's interview for *Pictorial Review,* Peggy developed a warm friendship with Baldwin and with her editor, Mabel Search. Aware of the Marshes' problems with the nosy Western Union office workers broadcasting all of her telegrams even before she had read them, Mabel sent Peggy a message that she signed "Wish-Wish and Napoleon," the names of her cats. The telegraph operator called Peggy in disbelief, asking, "You don't know anybody in New York named Wish-Wish and Napoleon, do you?" In relating the incident to the editor, Peggy said, "Fortunately, the old Mitchell memory clicked and I said with dignity that of course I knew them—they were old and dear friends. 'Then they sure must be foreigners,' said the operator. 'And does anybody named Old Timer live at your house?'"[17]

Old Timer was a stray cat that Peggy adopted right after John came home the hospital. Describing him as "a tramp and dirty as a stoker," she wrote Mabel that he was "a fine, old striped animal, a great ladies' man, who has been dropping in for a dish of milk every other night." The neighborhood children were not especially nice to cats, and Peggy felt sorry for this one when he appeared on her back door step. Her account here shows how she could spin and weave little scenarios from wisps of everyday occurrences:

> A couple of weeks ago he came calling with all his rear end chewed and mangled and as fine an infection in his equipment as you ever laid eyes on. I put him in the cat hospital and the veterinarians and I labored vainly to save the above mentioned equipment. We saved Old Timer, but, alas, the equipment is gone with the wind. He is at home now being fed on yeast and cod liver oil, for I cannot turn a sick animal out. I fear I will never be able to turn him out for he adores the silk brocade of my rocking chair as it makes such a delightful sound when his claws rip into it. Adopting a cat is a serious matter and apt to change one's life as it means becoming a slave to the creature's insistent desires to get out when he's in and in when he's out. But John and I are rapidly succumbing to his charms. He has the most beautiful stand of whiskers you ever saw.[18]

Since her childhood, Peggy had loved cats, and she fell in love with this one because of his crusty personality. She enjoyed telling anecdotes about Old Timer, and in this letter to Mabel, she wrote: "Poor Old Timer, who has spent his days in coal cellars and garbage cans, had never heard of catnip and he practically lost his mind. I never saw such antics in all my life, and we finally had to put the catnip mice away for fear that in his weakened condition he would have apoplexy." With her earthy sense of humor, she added: "He is doing very nicely but there is still some infection in his twickey. If I put ointment on the twickey he licks it off, or else wipes it off on the brocade chair. John has refused to let me put a diaper on him. John says it is shocking enough for a male creature to be bereft of his dearest possessions without having to suffer the final ignominy of a diaper."

5

The one thing that bothered Peggy during this otherwise pleasant time was the increasing number of reports stating the blacks' objections to Selznick's making a film of *Gone With the Wind*. With great concern, she had followed the course of articles that David Platt wrote for the *Daily Worker,* a newspaper that despised her novel and condemned it every chance it got. However, it was only one of the many African American newspapers and magazines harshly criticizing the novel. The staff at the *Daily Worker* went so far as to write to David Selznick forbidding him to produce the picture and threatening to boycott it, or worse, if he proceeded to make the film.[19] Other individuals and influential African American organizations supported the *Daily Worker*'s stand and vigorously protested the making of the film to the point that Selznick, who was certainly no bigot, worried about it. He wrote Jock Whitney, his friend and chairman of Selznick International's board of directors: "I feel this particularly keenly because it might have repercussions not simply on the picture and not simply upon the company and upon me personally, but on the Jews of America as a whole among the Negro race. . . . I think these are no times in which to offend any race or people. . . . I feel so keenly about what is happening to the Jews of the world that I cannot help but sympathize with the Negroes in their fears, however unjustified they may be, about the material which they regard as insulting or damaging." Selznick emphasized: "I am most anxious to remove any impression (which I am sure is very widespread) that *Gone With the Wind,* this company and I personally are enemies of the Negroes."[20]

Although Selznick did not hire a black technical advisor, as the protestors suggested, he did call a group of influential black reporters to the studio and assured them that he would remove all offensive material and name calling from the script and that they had nothing to worry about as far as the proslavery issue was concerned.[21]

In writing about the issue to Brickell, who had been sending her clippings from New York, Peggy said: "They [the *Daily Worker*] referred to the book as an 'incendiary and negro baiting' book. Personally I do not know where they get such an idea for, as far as I can see, most of the negro characters were people of worth, dignity and rectitude—certainly Mammy and Peter and even the ignorant Sam knew more of decorous behavior and honor than Scarlett did."[22]

6

Except for these and other activities beginning to emerge from the filmmakers, Peggy's life had indeed quieted down remarkably, while John's had not. Because of his unending work schedule, his health was declining, while hers was steadily improving. Since Congress had created the Tennessee Valley Authority in 1933, and had designated as its director David Lilenthal, whom John called a "two-faced-son-of-a-bitch," Georgia Power crackled with tension.[23] John and other Power Company people believed that the underlying purpose of the Tennessee Valley Authority was to put the huge utility monopolies out of business. As the chief of public relations, John had worrisome problems dealing with Roosevelt's propaganda about power companies. He especially despised Lilenthal's utilitarian ethics, saying: "If he would fight fair, I might enjoy the scrap, but his whole philosophy is that the end justifies the means. As his end and aim is the creation of an electric power business over our dead bodies, it is, at the least, annoying when he makes use of unethical and unfair tricks to damage us, while at the same time wearing the mask of a great humanitarian and advancer of the social well-being."[24]

In addition to these pressures at work, John had taken on the exacting job of handling the foreign contracts, which called for endless correspondence and more hard work than he thought was warranted by the small amount of money they brought in. Only two of them, the German and Swedish, had been definitely closed at that time and about a dozen others were in the works. "I think I can see the beginning of the end on that job," he wrote his mother, "but no doubt there will be another tough job arising before that one is definitely cleared. That's the way things have been going for more than a year now, and Peggy and I both yearn for the time when it will all be over. Of course, if she should get the Pulitzer prize, that would merely stir things up again, so it won't hurt our feelings a bit if she doesn't get it."[25]

As summer approached, he made up his mind that he was going to do something about his health and happiness by becoming a golfer again. But every weekend, there was something that had to be done right away. "This week, I've got six urgent jobs that ought to be attended to before Monday," he wrote his mother. "If I work real hard, I may be able to handle three of them. And that's a fair sample of other weekends, and of the reason why I work instead of playing golf." He assured her that life was pleasanter for them than it had been at its worst even though they were "still on a treadmill." In spite of working harder than he had ever done before, he never seemed to get caught up, "with emergency matters demanding immediate attention on an average of three times a week—sometimes on an average of seven days a week—and even getting to see a movie is a rare experience."

7

Toward the end of April 1937, the Marshes received word that Peggy had won the American Booksellers Association Annual Award. Brickell and some of the others had been telling her all along that she would win the Pulitzer, too, but she and John feared that maybe the award committee would believe that someone else should get it because she had already had a lion's share of good fortune. In addition to *Gone With the Wind,* the Pulitzer jury had three other books in 1937 from which to choose: William Faulkner's *Absalom, Absalom!,* John Dos Passos's *Big Money,* and George Santayana's *Last Puritan,* which was high on the bestseller list. Although *Gone With the Wind* was, by far, the most popular book of several decades, the Pulitzer jurors saw something more important in the novel than its commercial success. They chose it, they said, because they viewed it as an important historical romance that was "wholesome, powerful, and fundamentally American."[26]

During the 1930s, as the effects of the Depression spread over the nation, the Pulitzer jurors selected books that reflected a new kind of rugged individualism. "Many persons [in the 1930s] found themselves fighting as bitter a battle for survival as Scarlett O'Hara herself after the Civil War. It was exhilarating to watch Scarlett fight and win; even if she did not always employ the most genteel means, at least she did not lie down and die," explains Edward Wagenknecht in his *Cavalcade of the American Novel.*[27]

Harold Latham came to Atlanta on May 3, ostensibly to visit the reopened Macmillan branch office there. The actual purpose of his visit was to be with Peggy when she received the official word that the Pulitzer Prize Committee at Columbia University had selected *Gone With the Wind* as its 1937 prize-winning novel. Giving Peggy a warm, welcoming hug when he greeted her, Latham said nothing about the award, and Peggy had no idea that she had won. Excited about his visit and stirring about making arrangements for dinner and the evening's entertainment, she had forgotten about their disagreement over Macmillan's handling of the film contract.

On Monday evening, May 3, 1937, she was not at home when the telegram announcing that she had won arrived from Frank D. Fackenthal, the head of the Pulitzer Committee in New York. She was at her father's house on Peachtree Street, where she and John had taken Latham to have dinner with her family before going to Bessie's church to hear the choir sing. On one of his earlier visits, Latham had mentioned his fondness for spirituals, and Bessie, fond of Latham because he lavished such praise on her culinary talents, had arranged a special concert that evening for the editor.

When Lamar Q. Ball, the city editor of the *Atlanta Constitution,* got the Associated Press news flash on the award, he immediately started searching for Peggy. When he found her at her father's home, she agreed to let the photographer take a picture of her, after having refused pictures since September. Dizzy with excitement, she said she did not know what impressed her the most—winning the award or having the city editor leave his desk. Later, she wrote how nervous she got when it came time for them to leave for the choir concert because she did not want "the old bloodhound" Ball to know where they were going. "He would have with great pleasure, shot forty pictures of us and the colored choir and written a hell of a story about where Miss Mitchell went to celebrate winning the Pulitzer Award. . . . I was uneasy all during the singing for fear he was lurking somewhere in the back of the church and I was afraid to pick up the morning paper."[28]

The memorable night that Peggy won the Pulitzer Prize, she sat, trembling with excitement, between John and Latham, in the Little

Friendship Missionary Baptist Church, listening to the choir until one in the morning.[29] With the exception of her father, who did not stay up late at night, all the important people in her life—her husband, her brother and his wife Carrie Lou, Harold Latham, Deon, and Bessie—were present. The packed little church was warm, and to allay the heat, they each were given a paddle-shaped cardboard fan with a picture of a grim-faced Jesus on one side; and on the other side, a grim-faced undertaker and an advertisement for a funeral home. "The choir was marvelous. . . . The whole affair was so sweet, so simple and dignified and in such good taste," she wrote Brickell. "Bessie presided and introduced us all, and we all made little talks. The colored folks were pleased to have us but they didn't slop over us. They just took for granted that naturally Bessie's Madam and Bessie's Madam's publisher wanted to hear them sing and oh, how they sang! One old sister got to shouting and I thought Harold Latham would have a spasm he enjoyed it so much."[30]

The next morning telegrams, telephone calls, friends, family, delivery boys with bouquets of roses, photographers, and reporters stormed the apartment. Peggy agreed to make a statement over the air because she wanted to thank everyone who had helped make her book a success. Because she said she needed his moral support, Latham rode with her and John to the radio station. In the cab on the way, she figured out what she wanted to say, and John wrote it down on the back of a deposit slip that Latham had handed him.[31] In this nationally broadcast program, she read from that slip of paper, saying humbly that she had expected so little of *Gone With the Wind* when Harold Latham took her manuscript with him to New York two years earlier. In her soft southern drawl, she said:

> Since that day I have watched its career with steadily growing amazement, wondering if that book with my name on it could be, in reality, the enormous stack of dusty copy paper which lay around our apartment for so many years. So perhaps you can understand that I was genuinely surprised, and most happy and proud, when the Pulitzer Award Committee gave the prize to *Gone With the Wind*. It is an honor far beyond any I ever expected for my book and I thank you.[32]

Afterward she wrote: "I have sense enough to know that speaking is not my strong point . . . and that is my last radio appearance."[33]

When they returned to the apartment, Bessie handed her a bundle of messages and a beautiful corsage of orchids that George Brett had sent her to wear to the dinner celebration Latham was planning for her that night at the Athletic Club. "I never saw so many or such big, gorgeous ones except perhaps around the neck of a Kentucky Derby winner. Perhaps that's an apt remark for I felt as wild and full of prance as a Derby winner when I wore them out to the party Mr. Latham gave," she thanked Brett. "I still could not convince myself that I had actually won the award but I kept slewing my head sideways and looking at the corsage and telling myself that certainly I wouldn't be wearing those orchids if I hadn't won something."[34] John told his family that Peggy looked positively radiant that day.

The most outspoken critic of Peggy's receipt of the Pulitzer was Heywood Broun, who wrote nastily: "I do not think *Gone With the Wind* is an enduring work of literature, and I not only believe but ardently hope that it will emulate its title in another twelve months." It is not hard to imagine what he must have thought when the novel was placed in a time capsule, along with other contemporary artifacts, and buried fifty feet deep in Flushing Meadows, at the New York World's Fair in 1939.[35]

But hundreds of other literary critics agreed with the *New York Daily News* editorial that stated: "Looking back along the list of Pulitzer Prize novels down the years, we think this is the best novel that has ever won. . . . We've taken *Gone With the Wind* from its regular place in American fiction and parked it alongside Tolstoy's *War and Peace*."[36]

8

By the next weekend, the furor about the Pulitzer had died down, and life in the Marshes' apartment was relatively quiet. On May 7, Peggy wrote John's family: "We were afraid that the Award would serve to stir up public interest in me personally again and were all set for another awful siege. But, fortunately, it worked just the other way, and from the date of the announcement the mail, phone calls and tourists have fallen off sharply. Life is beginning to wear its old face again, and for the first time in months, I have sat down and sewed, and I have been swimming twice."[37] Their friends took seriously her requests for solitude and quiet and no longer made calls on the phone or in person. "None of my friends ever invite me any where," she wistfully wrote Brickell.[38] She spent her days alone, reading and answering letters.

That summer, the Atlanta newspapers made no more mention of her or her book until one day in June, when the papers carried pictures of the four lion cubs in Atlanta's zoo. In honor of the hometown author, the cubs were named Scarlett, Rhett, Ashley, and Melanie. Also, this was the summer of 1937, when "the Communists' hoopla" about *Gone With the Wind* gave them much pleasure. "We were all very thankful that they did not endorse the book," Peggy wrote Herschel Brickell on June 11, "because I could never hold my head up if they had."[39] What she and John found amusing, she said, was that there was "nothing anti-Communist in the whole book, nothing controversial, nothing of a propaganda nature. Yet the Radicals unerringly sensed behind those 1037 pages a Conservative, a Tory die-hard."

Of course, the radicals were right. The Marshes started out in favor of Roosevelt, but as he pushed his New Deal further and further into the South and tried to control Georgia's politics, they got to the point where they loathed him. Peggy called Roosevelt "a traitor to his kind."[40] As a cautious, prudent, solid businessman who had earned his position by hard work, self-discipline, and self-denial, John was set in his ways about certain principles. He was not about to accommodate the new industrial and social programs that Roosevelt wanted to implement. Those programs, he thought, were ruining the country and developing a nation ruled by a bureaucracy, or worse—a dictator. Later, when John heard the news of Roosevelt's death, he told Joe Kling, "The son-of-a-bitch got off without paying for what he did to this country!" Peggy and her friend Edna Daniel, the editor of the Quitman, Georgia, newspaper, had many lively arguments about Roosevelt's policies and about "whether or not the world owes people a living—or, for that matter, owes people anything."[41]

Peggy's political views popped out in many of her letters, such as this one she wrote to Brickell. Calling their friends Willie Snow and Mark Ethridge "Radicals or Liberals" after she read Willie's new book, *Mingled Yarn,* she said:

They are strange bedfellows for such Tory Conservatives as John and me. Willie does not like the paternalism of the cotton mill she wrote about. This dislike is contradictory to her violent espousal of the New Deal, which is, God knows, paternalistic. But Willie does not see her contradiction. She wanted to be completely fair to both sides in her book and to give that old davvle, Capitalism, its due. We wouldn't like to tell Willie this because we don't want to hurt her feelings, but we are finishing the book with a much higher opinion of mill owners than we had before and a far greater approval of paternalism.[42]

A few years later, after reading Henry C. Link's works on American individualism and conservatism, she praised his philosophy of self-reliance and wrote him, saying:

I am old enough to recall the time when little children were taught to recite "Invictus" and to believe in it. But when I grew up it was fashionable for the intellectuals and sophisticates to cry down this poem and its implications and to point the finger of laughing scorn at Kipling's "If." We are in a period now when no man is expected to be the master of his fate and the captain of his soul but as you expressed it, a mere helpless pawn of circumstance. I hope I live long enough to see us come out on the other side of this strange country in which we have been wandering.[43]

Years after his sister's death, Stephens, in an interview with Keith Runyon for the Louisville *Courier-Journal,* denied that Peggy was a conservative but then went on to suggest that she was. He said he thought his sister would not like the Atlanta of the 1970s because things had changed so much since she had known the town. Stephens explained:

The basis of Atlanta, the people who own the town, are descendants of the reconstruction "nobility" that she wrote about, that assembled in the town then. She made a historical misstatement in the book, giving the idea that most of them left town. Most of them didn't leave town. They live in town, they ran the town and they still run it. They call themselves "old families" but the people who are really old families are those who were here sixty years before [Reconstruction], like mine.... Our family was always an extremely reactionary family. And I would say that Margaret was also a reactionary. Now by that, I don't mean a conservative. We are not conservative. She believed that there are certain principles we've always got to go back to. In any era, until the second coming of the Lord, there will be things that are bad. So you'd better go back and look for the things that were good in the past.[44]

As an aristocrat born into a family of wealth and tradition, Peggy was a conservative. Although she would never have admitted it, she was unable to accept the manners of those from different social and economic backgrounds than hers. And the sentiments she expressed in her letters, as well as in her novel, show that she was willing to stand up and fight for traditional values.

9

For the rest of that summer in 1937, the Marshes were busy entertaining out-of-town guests. After Herschel Brickell came for a short visit, John's mother came for a two-week stay. In August, Gordon, Francesca, Henry, and Mary Hunter came to Atlanta to celebrate Henry's promotion to lieutenant colonel. (With his expertise as a chemist, Henry's chief responsibility in the Pentagon was regulating gun powder in ammunition used by the armed services in World War II.) Also, John's cousins Robert, Greta, and Roberta Nute visited them briefly on their way to Florida. One of the main reasons Peggy insisted that she and John live in a small apartment was the convenience of not having room for overnight guests, which she deplored with a passion. She enjoyed having guests for dinner, but not for overnight. John usually rented a furnished apartment in their building, if one was available, and if not, he got rooms at the Biltmore for all their guests.[45]

His family remembered that it was around this time that John had begun to look noticeably thinner and decidedly ill. His smoking habit gave him a rasping cough and shortness of breath, and although Bessie did all she could to fatten him with her good cooking, his old ulcer problems robbed him of his appetite. His coworkers said that he appeared to be tired all the time and that his petit mal seizures were more frequent and of longer duration. Attributing the intermittent, stabbing chest pains he experienced to indigestion, he ignored his symptoms and maintained his hectic schedule. For a brief period he had managed to take a couple of hours off on Wednesday afternoons to go swimming or to play an occasional game of golf with a business partner, but now he no longer felt able to take that time off from work. While he worked, his heart and blood vessels paid the price.

His only form of relaxation was going with Peggy, on weekends, to the movies. Both were wildly fond of the Marx Brothers, and if a Marx Brothers' picture were showing, they would go to see the same movie two or three times. That year they enjoyed *Lost Horizon* and *Captains Courageous* more than any of the other films they viewed. "But," John wrote to his mother, "my baser nature awards the crown to the Marx Brothers' latest, 'A Day at the Races.' I don't know whether you are a Marxian. If not, you may actually dislike them. Many people do, poor wretches. But I hope you are one of us superior folks who can appreciate what true geniuses the Marxes are." While the picture was in Atlanta, he and Peggy saw it three times in one week.[46] But opportunities for such recreational activities were rare for John.

No matter how bad he felt, he never complained. The best description of his stoic attitude is found in one of Peggy's letters to his mother, written in 1933 when Georgia Power was going through its most difficult period with Roosevelt's rural electrification drive through the Tennessee Valley Authority. Because the company's problems went along simultaneously for years with *Gone With the Wind*'s foreign copyright problems, John must have felt as if he were carrying a load of bricks that he could not set down. In this letter describing her husband, Peggy portrays the classic candidate for a heart attack.

The typewriter on which Margaret Mitchell wrote *Gone With the Wind* is now on permanent exhibit in the lobby of the Atlanta-Fulton Public Library, located downtown at Margaret Mitchell Square. About the time of publication, in 1936, the author posed for this picture with a portion of her manuscript. At his wife's request, John Marsh burned most of the manuscript after her death.

When *Gone With the Wind* received the Pulitzer Prize for fiction in 1937, Peggy, decorated with orchid was celebrated at a dinner given by Harold Latham, the editor who delivered her massive manuscript to Macmillan. Newspaper colleague Medora Perkerson completed the trio.

Upon winning the Pulitzer, Peggy agreed to a radio interview with Medora Perkerson.

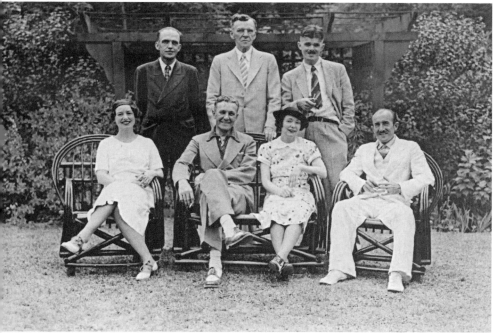

ggy Mitchell basked in the company of other writers, and serving on the faculty at a creative writing seminar Blowing Rock, N.C., gave her such an opportunity. Peggy is seated between longtime friends and colleagues erschel Brickell, veteran New York book reviewer, and novelist Edwin Granberry (far right).

a less formal setting, the Marshes joined literary friends for a retreat. Peggy is in the background at ft, while John gazes at her from a rocking chair, far right.

Before filming began on *Gone With the Wind,* Peggy (shown left) and historian Wilbur Kurtz took a scouting trip for the "Selznickers," as she called them. The author wanted to prove to the filmmakers that most authentic Georgia homesteads lacked white columns.

Peggy's pal, *Macon Telegraph* reporter Susan Myrick, worked as a technical adviser on the picture. Myrick coached cast members such as Fred Crane (left) and George Reeves, who played the Tarleton twins, on southern dialect and customs.

Between takes, *Gone With the Wind* photographers created this on-the-set joke with Olivia De Havilland reviewing the scene in which Peggy described Melanie in childbirth during the siege on Atlanta. When Peggy received a copy of this picture, she wrote to Sue Myrick: "John says that the expression on Miss De Havilland's face is precisely the expression I wore during the time I was writing the book."

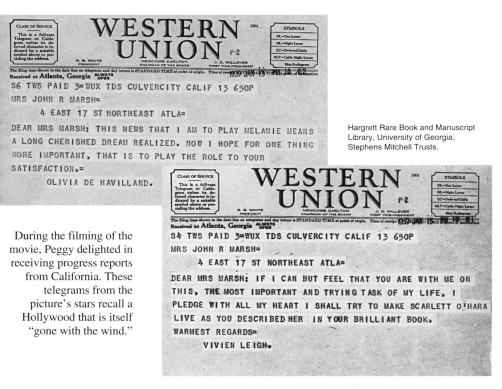

WESTERN UNION

CLASS OF SERVICE
This is a full-rate Telegram or Cablegram unless its deferred character is indicated by a suitable symbol above or preceding the address.

SYMBOLS
DL=Day Letter
NL=Night Letter
LC=Deferred Cable
NLT=Cable Night Letter

R. B. WHITE PRESIDENT
NEWCOMB CARLTON CHAIRMAN OF THE BOARD
J. C. WILLEVER FIRST VICE-PRESIDENT

The filing time shown in the date line on telegrams and day letters is STANDARD TIME at point of origin. Time of receipt 1939 JAN 13 TIME at point of destination
Received at Atlanta, Georgia ALWAYS OPEN

S6 TWS PAID 3=WUX TDS CULVERCITY CALIF 13 650P

MRS JOHN R MARSH=

4 EAST 17 ST NORTHEAST ATLA=

DEAR MRS MARSH: THIS NEWS THAT I AM TO PLAY MELANIE MEANS
A LONG CHERISHED DREAM REALIZED. NOW I HOPE FOR ONE THING
MORE IMPORTANT, THAT IS TO PLAY THE ROLE TO YOUR
SATISFACTION.=

OLIVIA DE HAVILLAND.

During the filming of the movie, Peggy delighted in receiving progress reports from California. These telegrams from the picture's stars recall a Hollywood that is itself "gone with the wind."

WESTERN UNION

CLASS OF SERVICE
This is a full-rate Telegram or Cablegram unless its deferred character is indicated by a suitable symbol above or preceding the address.

SYMBOLS
DL=Day Letter
NL=Night Letter
LC=Deferred Cable
NLT=Cable Night Letter

R. B. WHITE PRESIDENT
NEWCOMB CARLTON CHAIRMAN OF THE BOARD
J. C. WILLEVER FIRST VICE-PRESIDENT

The filing time shown in the date line on telegrams and day letters is STANDARD TIME at point of origin. Time of receipt 1939 JAN 13 TIME
Received at Atlanta, Georgia ALWAYS OPEN

S4 TWS PAID 3=WUX TDS CULVERCITY CALIF 13 650P

MRS JOHN R MARSH=

4 EAST 17 ST NORTHEAST ATLA=

DEAR MRS MARSH: IF I CAN BUT FEEL THAT YOU ARE WITH ME ON
THIS, THE MOST IMPORTANT AND TRYING TASK OF MY LIFE, I
PLEDGE WITH ALL MY HEART I SHALL TRY TO MAKE SCARLETT O'HARA
LIVE AS YOU DESCRIBED HER IN YOUR BRILLIANT BOOK.
WARMEST REGARDS=

VIVIEN LEIGH.

Peggy Mitchell created the characters and the dramatic story of survival against all odds. Vivien Leigh as Scarlett O'Hara and Clark Gable as Rhett Butler helped the movie version of *Gone With the Wind* set a record in garnering thirteen nominations and eight wins on Oscar night.

"She is the most fascinating woman I've ever met," said Clark Gable, after his private meeting with Peggy in the ladies' room of Atlanta's Piedmont Driving Club. And Peggy's reaction upon meeting the screen idol at the Women's Press Club tea: "He's grand, perfectly grand!"

Photograph courtesy of the Herb Bridges Collection.

No one was more baffled than Peggy Mitchell when her tale of the Old South created such frenzied excitement among the general public. It seemed that all of Atlanta turned out for the parade welcoming David O. Selznick and the stars of *Gone With the Wind* to town for the world premiere.

Atlanta went wild when film stars Vivien Leigh, Clark Gable, and Olivia De Havilland arrived for the world premiere of *Gone With the Wind*. But to the actors who played Scarlett, Rhett, and Melanie, Margaret Mitchell was the star they finally got to meet. Here, the author is flanked by those luminaries, as well as film producer David O. Selznick.

On Friday, December 15, 1939, the national spotlight was on Loew's Grand Theater in Atlanta, for the premiere of Margaret Mitchell's lush Civil War epic.

The Marshes experienced a dose of celebrity on the night of the premiere. John chatted with Clark Gable as Gable's movie star bride, Carole Lombard, looked on. Jock Whitney and Olivia de Havilland are at Peggy's right.

Atlanta History Center.

Atlanta History Center.

John toiled over the foreign copyright business of *Gone With the Wind* from the couple's home at Della Manta apartments, 1268 Piedmont Avenue, where they moved in 1939.

Photograph courtesy of Eleanor Marsh Hillers.

The close-knit Marsh family gave Peggy a sense of a loving, extended family. Henry Marsh snapped this picture of a Marsh family reunion in Wilmington, Delaware, about 1940. John is second from left, and Peggy is immediately left of Mother Marsh, who is seated at center.

Atlanta-Fulton Public Library, Margaret Mitchell Collection.

Following World War II, Peggy and her longtime maid, Bessie Jordan, organized care packages for war-torn Europe.

Lounging on the homefront: A rare moment of relaxation for John Marsh, seen with a Czechoslovakian edition of *Gone With the Wind*.

left: It's teatime for Peggy.

Photograph courtesy of Joe Kling.

A rare evening out in the late 1940s is captured at this holiday gathering of Georgia Power advertising staffers. The gang included John's secretary, Rhoda Williams Kling, standing left, with her hand on John's shoulder. Peggy's hand rests on the shoulder of Joe Kling, who worked under John and later became advertising manager himself. The Klings were close friends of the Marshes before, during, and after the publication of *Gone With the Wind*.

Firmly believing that a published picture of the two of them would make it easier for the public to identify them when they were out and about, John and Peggy took great care never to be photographed together. Snapped without their knowledge at a Woman of the Year banquet in 1945, this is a rare image of the couple.

Photograph courtesy of Gordon Renick Marsh.

Throughout her life, Peggy loved cats. Taken only weeks before her tragic death, this is believed to be the last picture of her, at the age of 48.

Peggy Mitchell Marsh was the light of her husband's life. After her death, John spent a great deal of time in the quiet emptiness of the apartment. His sister, Frances, recalled John telling her that he always liked to look at Peggy when she was alive, so why shouldn't he like to look at her — in photographs — once she had gone?

A devoted couple, Peggy and John treasured
their few moments alone together.

People tell me, as they invariably do—"How bland and unruffled your husband is! Nothing ever bothers him. Now *my* husband is so nervous!" I look at John with great admiration because he never makes any parade of his disabilities even in the privacy of home. Yet if any one ever had nerves and a good reason for having them, he is that person. Anything that upsets his routine of food, rest, exercise upsets his food apparatus and that reacts on his nerves to the point that he can't eat. And anything that upsets his nerves, like being mad and having to wait under a strain . . . shoots his nerves. I don't mean the surface nerves that people show when they have the fidgets, jitters, but the deep buried nerves, over which no one has any control, those that control digestion, heart action, kidneys, breathing, sleeping. My job has been to keep things at home going so smoothly that it isn't even obvious that they are going, to make a contrast with the outer world and to make home—and me—a place and a person devoid of "alarms and excursions" and to think of diversions to divert, practical first when he needs it and strength for his weariness when I'm frightened half to death. His job will never be a quiet one, it will always be full of fights, emergencies and surprises, and if we are to continue eating, there's nothing I can do about it. All my energies go to the home end. . . . I do not know why I should burden and worry you, at long distance. . . . You see, there's no one else to whom I can talk, for John as well as I have pride and he, wanting to appear as a normal, healthy mortal, does not wish to talk of his troubles or even have them known.[47]

Peggy's remark "if we are to continue eating" brings up an interesting question. At the time the letter was written, John had to continue working to support them. But once she saw what kind of returns she was getting from *Gone With the Wind,* why did she not urge John to give up his Georgia Power job? By 1937, they had more money than they ever dreamed they would have, and they were investing it wisely and making even more money from royalties. Therefore, John could have resigned in 1937 from the Power Company and spent all of his time taking care of the book's business, and that is what he should have done for his own well-being. However, something about his inherent makeup, perhaps a certain masculine pride, prohibited him from giving up his job and living off his wife's earnings. Mary and Jim Davis said John never spent a penny of "Peggy's money," and perhaps that is why Peggy legally conferred the foreign rights to him and made him her salaried business manager. Still, John never viewed his work as her business manager as a real job. He refused to acknowledge that the book, with a will of its own, demanded the attention of a full-time employee.

Inwardly, John was a deeply conservative man whose underlying Puritan work ethic emerged in a forceful manner with Peggy's signing that contract with Macmillan in August 1935. With unyielding principles about certain things, he clung tenaciously to the notion that no one inappropriately was going to make "a buck" off their book. *Gone With the Wind* had been written when they were poor, during a period when he had struggled to work two jobs just to pay their bills. It had been written for a specific and a loving purpose. That book was theirs—no one else's. And to the end of his life, he relentlessly pursued anyone who tried to take any piece of it away from them. Upon hearing about the multiplicity of complex legal problems *Gone With the Wind* created for the Marshes, many people have wondered why John did not turn the whole matter over to some New York attorneys experienced in copyright law and book publishing. Doing so would have spared the Marshes much anxiety, energy, and time, and may have prolonged John's life.

10

When Brickell wrote in September asking them to go on vacation with him and his wife, Peggy answered that things were "in such a stew," with John and Stephens staying up late every night working on foreign contracts and business matters, that it was impossible for John to get away from the office for any decent length of time. She wrote, "I will admit here and now that I have no intention of going anywhere where I do not have him as a buffer between me and people who want to drag me out to meet their interesting friends."[48]

Indeed, John's life had changed drastically, for in addition to his problems at the Power Company, his work on the book was enmeshing him in a tissue of complex legal problems. The first lawsuit involving the Marshes, and the only easy one, was brought about in February 1937 by Susan Lawrence Davis, an elderly eccentric. She accused Peggy of plagiarizing her book *An Authentic History of the Ku Klux Klan, 1865–1877*, published in 1924 in New York. "You could have knocked me over with a fern frond when the old lady made her claim, for I had never heard of her or her book either until her lawyers wrote," Peggy told a friend.[49] When Brett sent her a copy of Miss Davis's 240-page brief, Peggy spent a bewildering afternoon reading it. "When I finished it," she wrote him, "I figured out that the lady thinks she has an exclusive patent or copyright on everything dealing with the Civil War and Reconstruction and any one who mentions even General Lee is infringing on her book. She also is under the impression that she is the only person who has ever done any research work—therefore anyone who writes about these periods must have copied from her book."[50]

On February 26, 1937, John got a call from Stephens saying that George Brett wanted to know if Peggy had ever seen a copy of Mrs. Davis's book. John answered Brett in a short letter that very day. Not only had she never seen the book, but she had not been able to find a copy in the public library or in any Atlanta store, and none of the history buffs she knew had ever heard of the book. Therefore, he added, Peggy could not have quoted from it or used it for reference purposes in any way. Answering Brett's other question about to whom Macmillan should address correspondence regarding this matter, John told him to write to Stephens:

> From the beginning Mr. Stephens Mitchell and I have attempted to relieve Mrs. Marsh of her many burdens in any way we could. As a result, correspondence relating to business matters has frequently been handled by me and correspondence relating to legal matters has been handled by Mr. Mitchell. However, we are a close-knit family who live within a block of each other and we see each other nearly every day so that one or the other of us may write you at times about matters which ordinarily would be handled by another one of the three of us.

Davis wanted to settle out of court, but Macmillan and the Marshes refused. Peggy said, "We cried, 'Millions for defense but not one cent for tribute.'"[51] Davis sued the Macmillan Company in New York, not Margaret Mitchell in Atlanta, for the grand total of $6.5 billion. Her first charge, that Peggy had dared to bind her book in Confederate gray just as she had done, was patently ridiculous, and it set the tone for all her other charges. She accused Peggy of stealing such items as all the Civil War phrases (like "scalawag" and "carpetbagger") and all the historical events, places, and names of authentic people.[52] "It would seem that these phrases and historic events were the product of her own creation and had never been heard of until she wrote her book in 1924," Peggy told Brickell.[53] Revealing some of the paranoia that she was to experience more and more as time went on, Peggy wrote Lois crustily:

> To tell the truth, I was relieved when the letter announcing her claim arrived. I had been waiting for months for the first racketeer to open fire. It had been a marvel to us all that some chiselers hadn't opened up on me sooner. We didn't know what form it

would take, extortion, attempted blackmail, suits of every kind. It seems the natural thing when a person has got on the front page and made a lot of money. We were glad that the opening gun was a pop gun. It might have been one of those bad affairs where some one alleges that you've run over them and permanently injured them—on a day when you weren't even in your car.[54]

It was such an absurd case that John and Stephens found it amusing, but not Peggy. She wanted it to be tried so that the details would be widely publicized and her reputation cleared. "If the case is non-suited," she wrote Brickell, "no one would ever have known anything about it and several million people would think I bought the old lady off quietly."[55]

On account of this lawsuit, they now had New York attorneys as well as Atlanta attorneys, the former being the eminent firm of Cadwalader, Wickersham, and Taft, 14 Wall Street—"and I suppose," John wrote his mother, "that gives us even more prestige than winning the Pulitzer prize." The suit was declared unsubstantiated and thrown out of court on July 30, 1937. But by that time, the Marshes had initiated two important lawsuits of their own, one of international consequence.

The first litigation the Marshes filed was in July against Billy Rose, a flamboyant showman who, in Fort Worth, Texas, staged a Frontier Fiesta, a song-and-dance show built around four bestsellers, including *Gone With the Wind*. Rose's action was definitely plagiarism because Peggy exclusively owned the dramatization rights. Concerned about what would happen if she permitted Rose's infringement to go unchallenged, John and Steve feared her dramatic rights would be impaired or even lost for good. The fact that Rose was making huge sums of money without having to pay for the right to use the book would only encourage others to do the same. They decided to use Rose as an example to show others that Margaret Mitchell was not going to allow that kind of thing to happen.

For experienced legal advice in this area, John turned to Lewis Titterton, an old friend in New York. The manager of the script division at the National Broadcasting Company, Titterton advised John to talk to Howard Reinheimer, a New York lawyer whose reputation for handling that kind of litigation was widely known and respected.[56] The suit was later settled out of court on March 24, 1938, with Rose sending Peggy a letter of apology and paying her three thousand dollars in damages.

While the Rose lawsuit was going on, Stephens received word from Marion Saunders, Peggy's agent handling foreign rights, that a serial publication of a Danish translation of *Gone With the Wind* had already begun—without a written contract—in *Politiken,* a major newspaper in Copenhagen. Saunders had notified John and Stephens earlier of the offer she had received from *Politiken* and they had approved it, but she had gone ahead and closed the deal without drawing up a written contract. Unfortunately, Saunders viewed such contracts as mere technicalities and did not understand that the Marshes wanted written contracts on each and every sale of foreign rights. Later, she explained to Stephens that written contracts were practically unheard of in sales of foreign serial rights and ordinarily such transactions were handled merely by an exchange of cables. In his brusque manner, Stephens yelled, "No! None of that damn kind of business anymore."

In writing to George Brett a few months later about her legal problems, Peggy said: "I do not believe anyone except John, Stephens, and I can realize what a hellish time we have had over a period of months, and a great part of this hellishness was due to Marion Saunders. We have had to write interminable letters, argue over long distance and in general wear out our nervous systems, trying to get her to do the things she had promised in her contract with me to do."[57]

Stephens's demand for contracts was wise, as he soon discovered in his correspondence with George Brett about this issue. Brett explained that it was necessary for Peggy to have a contract with serial publishers stipulating that a copyright notice be printed in English and in the foreign language in which the newspaper was printed. Unless such a copyright notice accompanied serial publication of the book, pirates would read the story in a foreign newspaper and then simply translate it into another foreign language and publish it, pretending not to know that the story was an original American copyright. Therefore, Brett advised Stephens to get in writing all contracts with foreign periodicals and to make certain that adequate copyright notice be printed in all periodicals serializing *Gone With the Wind*.

Peggy, John, Stephens, and even Eugene Mitchell were shocked to discover that American authors had to do all of this work on their own to protect their American copyrights. Not knowing anything about the intimidating topic of international copyright laws, Eugene and Stephens looked bewilderedly at John, who blanched and said, "Brothers, we are far out in deep, unchartered waters now."[58] The only thing they knew for certain was that if they allowed Denmark to get away without acknowledging the rights and without paying for them, then there would be absolutely nothing to keep other countries from doing the same thing. After conferring with George Brett, they decided to make no sales of foreign serial rights of *Gone With the Wind*, with the exception of the *Politiken* serialization; that sale had already been made before they learned of it, because of the misunderstanding with Marion Saunders.[59] The risk of inviting more piracy was too great to be offset by the sums received for such rights.

And money was not the only issue involved. Far more important, they were shocked to learn, was that the publisher of a pirated edition could change whatever he chose in a book. If a publisher did not like the manner in which American life was presented, he could revise the text to suit himself. Peggy worried that foreigners could change her material in conformity with local prejudice and "thereby present a distorted picture of our country to their readers—with the author of the book made an unwilling party to this deception."[60]

Their determination to protect Peggy's rights and the integrity of her book soon embroiled John in a multiplicity of complicated problems, for the Danish infringement in the spring of 1937 was just the beginning of their myriad troubles with foreign rights.

11

By the first of September 1937, Peggy had signed contracts with Germany, Sweden, Norway, Poland, and Hungary for *Gone With the Wind* to be translated and published by the first of the year. She had also signed a contract with a Danish publisher who would bring out the Danish book edition of the novel after its serial publication in the *Politiken*. France and Italy were the only two large countries where the contracts were not yet completed by that time, and Marion Saunders was working out contracts with publishers in other countries. Peggy received a letter from the Danish publisher, saying that his edition would be out around September 15 and that the name of the novel was *Borte Med Blaesten*—"Blown Away with the Wind."

John wrote his mother about this edition: "We are looking forward to it with interest, to express it mildly, because their book will be *illustrated*. I can't wait to see the Danish conception of what North Georgia looks like." The publisher also explained that his firm was arranging a contest to advertise the book and the grand prize was to be a trip to Georgia to see the *Gone With the Wind* country. "I am thinking of offering a prize to anybody in the family who can pronounce the name of the Polish publisher. On that subject, my child wife came forth with one of her best remarks of recent months. The contract starts off with—'Wydawnictwo J. Przeworskiego, Sienkiewicza 2, Warzawa, Poland (hereinafter called the Publishers)' and Peggy wanted to know why they didn't go ahead and call themselves "the Publishers' in the first place."[61]

John kept track of the translators' names and reported them to his mother, who was keeping a huge scrapbook on the novel. He told his mother that in Germany, the novel titled *Vom Winde Verweht* (translated literally, "by the wind blown away") had been chosen as the book of the month selection, just as it had been in England and the United States. At some point, John must have asked his family not to keep his letters concerning the novel, because his mother wrote asking him if she could place this letter of his about the foreign editions in her scrapbook.

By the end of October 1937, the "legitimate" Danish edition of *Gone With the Wind* with its delightful illustrations, along with its rave reviews, arrived at the Marshes' apartment. By this time, however, John was distracted by another troublesome case of copyright infringement. In July they had heard rumors about a Dutch publisher pirating *Gone With the Wind*. The first mention of this edition is in John's July 25, 1937, letter to his mother: "Our agent handling the foreign rights told us last week that a publisher in Holland has announced a Dutch edition to be published this fall, again without a by-your-leave."[62] A few months later, he and Stephens had entered into negotiations with a legitimate publisher in Holland, but by October they learned that the rumors they had heard were coming true, and that now they also had to deal with a pirate in Holland. This straight-out case of piracy involved John and Stephens in an enormous amount of work, correspondence, expense, and worry. As problems proliferated with the unauthorized Dutch publishers, they realized that they not only needed the help of foreign lawyers, but they also needed the help of the United States government.

The Marshes and the Mitchells had been shocked to discover, in the *Politiken* case, that American authors' works could be pirated from serial publications unless the appropriate copyright notice were placed in the serials, and even that was often ignored by pirates. Now they were horrified to learn that in fact there was no reliable overseas protection of any kind for American literature because the United States had not entered into the treaty known as the international Berne Convention Agreement of 1886.[63]

The Berne Convention, so named because it convened in Berne, Switzerland, was a worldwide agreement among some forty nations to improve the legal protection of copyrights in the literary and artistic fields. At the time of the convention, the United States was still a young country with no well-defined body of literature, and thus it saw no need to enter the agreement.

In fact, United States publishers depended largely upon reprinting—pirating—newly published novels from abroad, particularly from France, Germany, and England. Because there was a national copyright law, American publishers had to pay royalties to American authors, so American publishers actually preferred publishing British and foreign titles and fought against proposals for the United States government to enter into an international agreement even though writers and artists urged their government to do so. Because America was so closely tied to Britain and shared a common language, American publishers relied heavily on reprinting British literature, and authors such as Charles Dickens and Sir Walter Scott were angry with American publishers for "pirating" their works without paying royalties.[64]

Thus, up to the late nineteenth century, the United States was more a consumer than a producer of copyrightable materials and was more concerned with acquiring free access to foreign works than it was with protecting American authors' overseas rights. But as the advocates of the new nationalism accelerated their movement and created a demand for a distinctively American literature, American authors—Mark Twain was one of the most outspoken—clamored for their rights. And, so, the United States worked out treaties with a few individual foreign countries in 1891. But it had no multilateral ties. The treaties it did have were generally unsatisfactory and complex because laws in foreign countries were continually changing. American authors had to count more on the foreign publishers' honesty and integrity than on treaties. Although the Marshes did not know it at the time, that was the reason Marion Saunders saw little need in getting foreign contracts in writing, as Stephens Mitchell and the Marshes wanted her to do. Many foreign publishers ignored contracts, written or verbal ones, and published what they pleased, most often with impunity. For example, John and Peggy received clippings from Italian newspapers in 1937 stating that *Gone With the Wind* was to be published soon; yet the publishers in Italy had never returned the contract that had been sent several months earlier, nor had they sent advance royalty payment.

For the Marshes, problems like this one with publishers began to run rampant all over the world in 1937. In a long letter that John drafted in his own handwriting for Peggy and that was sent to the secretary of state in Washington, D.C., in January 1939, he expressed the shock he and Peggy felt:

> I did not know that book-pirates in foreign countries were waiting to pounce on and steal the books of American authors if they were left unprotected for a minute. I did not know that these pirates could thumb their noses at the American government while they were making away with our books, and that our government was helpless to do anything about it. And I did not even suspect that the ordinary moral standards relating to stealing do not apply to the stealing of books away from their authors. . . . My observation is that the foreign pirates would rather steal American books than those of any other country because they think we are both fools and knaves—fools because we leave the door wide open to them, knaves because they think our government deliberately remains outside the Berne Convention so as not to interfere with pirates *in this country* who steal the books of foreign authors.[65]

The Marshes were shocked to learn that American authors had the responsibility of protecting their own copyrights if they wanted them protected at all—that American publishers could not and did not undertake that time-consuming, complicated, and expensive task for authors. That was the reason George Brett returned Peggy's foreign copyrights to her in June 1936, although the truth is, as Stephens Mitchell later pointed out, the foreign rights were hers all along, and Brett had nothing to give. When John and Peggy realized that the federal government had in no way protected its authors, they felt it was imperative that the United States enter into some kind of agreement with other countries so that American writers would not have to do what they were doing: use their own time, energy, and money to protect their rights. Inexperienced as they were in legislative matters and foreign copyrights, they were not about to let foreign publishers disregard her rights to *Gone With the Wind.* They decided to make Peggy's foreign copyright problems public in order to create public awareness of and interest in America's lack of international copyright laws.

With that united decision, the Marshes and Stephens Mitchell entered a labyrinthian legal suit on December 8, 1937. Headlines in newspapers all over the United States on that date read "U.S. Aid Enlisted in Protection of 'Gone With the Wind.'" For her, there was no hanging back from publicity now. Boldy issuing her public statement to reporters everywhere, Peggy said: "I intend to fight for my rights with every means at my command. I wouldn't mind losing the royalties on the Dutch edition—they are not what matters. The important thing is the many years of hard labor I put into the writing of my book. I can never forget them. . . . I would be a pretty poor sort if I permitted my book to be published, without my permission and in complete disregard of my rights, in Holland or any place else, without putting up a fight to protect it."[66]

At last, the rebel had a legitimate cause to fight for. As she wrote to Willie Snow Ethridge, who had just completed her own novel, "If I lose my case in Holland it will not only affect me personally and cost me thousands of dollars for legal fees, but it will affect every American author."[67]

With their obstinate independence and united insistence on defending principles they held dear, the Marshes made several appeals to the State Department. In August, they filed a lawsuit in Holland against the prominent publishing house of Zuid-Hollandsche Uitgevers Maatschappij Boek-en Handelsdrukkerij—better known as Z.H.U.M. On November 13, Stephens went to Washington, D.C., to discuss the foreign copyright problems with Dr. Wallace McClure, assistant chief of the treaty division in the U.S. State Department. With sympathetic understanding, McClure listened and said that until the United States changed its position on the Berne Convention, he was afraid that what had happened in the Netherlands would repeat itself in Japan and perhaps in a number of other countries. He explained that the United States had virtually given its authors' work away when it entered into an agreement in 1905 with Japan. As incredible as it seems now, this 1905 treaty actually allowed Japanese publishers to publish American authors' books without securing the author's consent and without paying for the author's rights. Supposedly, the pay-off was that the United States could also publish the works of Japanese authors; however, there was no demand for Japanese works in the United States. Thus, the publication of *Gone With the Wind* in Japan could not be considered a piracy case.

An immediate adherence to the Berne Convention was the best possible safeguard for the future, and McClure said that he and Senator Walter F. George (Democrat-Georgia) were doing all that they could toward furthering that end in the Senate. McClure was correct in thinking that Japan would repeat Holland's action, for in only a few weeks, word came that the Japanese were indeed publishing *Gone With the Wind*. A few days after their meeting, McClure wrote Stephens that the matter was of large financial interest not only to his sister but also to her publishers. He suggested that Stephens get the president of Macmillan to use his influence on the two senators from New York to urge their immediate action upon the treaty. McClure added:

> Should you be able to bring about the approval of this treaty, you will be doing your country a real service. Patriotic citizens from Mark Twain to the present day, over a period of many years, have sought to bring about this result. If your sister can achieve it, I suggest that she may be doing a service to her fellows that is at least somewhat comparable to that of producing a masterpiece like *Gone With the Wind*.[68]

On at least three occasions, probably more, John and Peggy went to Washington to appear before the Senate Committee on Foreign Relations. On their first trip in November 1937, she and John met privately with Wallace McClure and other members of the Senate, urging them to ratify the Berne Convention treaty. Despite her, John's, and Stephens's efforts, the Senate did not vote to do so.

12

The long, complex case between the Marshes and the Z.H.U.M. hinged on two factors: one was what the Dutch publishers called Margaret Mitchell's attempt to use a "loophole" in the Berne Convention; and the other, upon which the Dutch pounced with a vengeance, was the fact that U.S. publishers were great pirates themselves. The Dutch were furious that Peggy had inconvenienced them by halting their publication of her book. In a fiery telegram to the U.S. secretary of state, the Dutch blasted Peggy with such statements as the following:

> Mrs. Mitchell, in addition to her great artistic talents also seems to show some likeness to the principal character in her book, the calculating and money grabbing Scarlett. She thought it very marvelous that the Dutch people were anxious to read her book, but she did not like the idea of not securing any monetary profit from it. Therefore she had the whole edition confiscated, as she claimed that the publishing of it was in violation of her author's rights.

The Dutch also pointed out how the United States had chosen to remain outside the international agreement that protected the rights of authors. "Therefore they can steal the artistic treasures of all other countries, but in turn their own can be stolen from them. . . . They now try to escape . . . through a loophole in the Convention."

The "loophole" referred to here was an article in the Berne Convention that stated that authors who were citizens of countries that were not part of the Convention could nevertheless be protected by it if they had their work published simultaneously in a country that was a member of the Convention, as well as in their own country. Canada was a member of the Convention, and the U.S. Macmillan had taken advantage of this "loophole" by contracting with Macmillan of Toronto, a separate entity and not a branch of the New York firm, to publish *Gone With the Wind* in Canada.

However, in May 1936, Macmillan had printed ten thousand advance copies of *Gone With the Wind* in New York, and those copies bore an imprint indicating that publication date—May 1936. These copies were not published because just after that initial printing, Macmillan learned that the Book-of-the-Month Club had chosen *Gone With the Wind* for its July 1936 distribution. At the Club's request, Macmillan withheld publication until June 30, when actual publication for trade release and copyright simultaneously took place in New York and Toronto. The ten thousand copies with the May imprint that had been withheld from circulation were then released to be sold along with the large new simultaneous printing. Thus, by all precedence, *Gone With the Wind* was protected by the Berne Convention although it took years for the courts to decide that. The crux of the lawsuit pivoted on the fact that the Dutch had gotten a copy of the novel with a May imprint and used that copy as evidence of their right to publish the book and of what they called Macmillan's "trick" of maintaining that the book had been simultaneously published in Canada and New York in June 1936.[69]

Thus, it was in 1937 that John began his long, complicated correspondence with Brett, the U.S. State Department, and foreign publishers, lawyers, accountants, and agents all over the world. His voluminous letters and paperwork, spanning the decade of the Dutch piracy case, are an eye-opening and mind-boggling file. Hundreds of his letters demonstrate the close attention he paid to the book's business. He was unwilling to leave any problems in Stephens's or any other lawyer's hands, much less Marion Saunders's, and he even went so far as to counsel Peggy's lawyers as to how to conduct her case.

In July 1939, just two months before Hitler invaded Poland, a Japanese translator sent Peggy a paperbound set of his translation of *Gone With the Wind* and requested that she send him an autographed United States edition. He reported, in excellent English, of the popularity of the book in his country, saying that approximately 150,000 copies had been sold. It had outsold Pearl Buck's *The Good Earth,* and he said that only one book, Katsunori Tami's *Wheat and Soldiers,* had sold more copies than *Gone With the Wind.* Without mentioning the fact that she had not authorized a Japanese edition, Peggy wrote him a friendly letter. Then she sent his letter and a copy of her own to Marion Saunders, who wrote to the Japanese publisher suggesting a contract. The publisher replied politely and indicated his willingness to enter a contract with Peggy, but now that Japan was engaged in war, he said it would be difficult for him to export money from his country. The Marshes were more interested in having the legal contract than they were in having the money if they could not have both. Saunders told them that she had learned that Pearl Buck had also been sent such pleasant letters by the publishers of her book, but no money.

Around this time, they learned that the Chinese also had pirated the novel, but because of the unstable political events in the Orient, the U.S. State Department officials did not think they could take any specific action against either China or Japan. "This is a maddening state of affairs to say the least," Peggy wrote McClure, for all she had received from the Japanese publishers was a "very pretty silk kimono . . . and a Japanese doll nearly three feet high in a red lacquer and glass case about four feet high. If there ever was a white elephant this doll and its case is the elephant." While she was wondering why they had sent it, she received a letter again, this time from the translator, who requested that she have her picture taken standing next to the doll case. They wanted to use her photograph for publicity purposes. "A nation with so much gall certainly should go far," Peggy noted in relating this incident to McClure.[70]

Writing about the decade the Marshes struggled with their overseas problems would require another book as long as *Gone With the Wind,* but such a book deserves to be written because the Marshes made publishing history. Their problems were not resolved until after the end of World War II. Over a period of ten years, they devoted large amounts of their time, energy, and money to protecting their rights in this matter, in the process ensuring protection for all American authors. As fate would have it, however, neither John nor Peggy would live to see the results of their efforts to get the United States to protect its authors' foreign rights. In 1954, after both John's and Peggy's deaths, Stephens Mitchell continued their struggle and submitted to the State Department a detailed narrative of his sister's foreign copyright problems as proof of America's need to enter into an agreement with other nations. The following year, the United States entered such an agreement.[71]

13

While John tackled the perplexing foreign copyright problems, Peggy continued to answer letters and deal with petty kinds of annoying news that the Marshes heard daily. She still had battles over the autograph stories, for some people were selling her autographed books at marked-up prices. She would get furious thinking about how long it had taken her to autograph all those books and about how many of them she had had to mail back to their owners at her own expense. To learn now that some people were making as much as twenty dollars on her signature alone infuriated her. Then there were the incredible stories of women popping up in different parts of the country, pretending to be Margaret Mitchell. "They have signed autographs, given lectures, gotten drunk, picked up gents and done other things not salutary to mention on paper. To date I have been unable to catch a one of them, which is a source of great regret to me."[72]

In 1938, one imposter swindled an American Indian, an interesting, elderly man who had traveled all over the world and had written his memoirs going all the way back to frontier fighting days. Peggy wrote: "I think I now have a chance to nail one of these imposters, and by doing so scare off the others. Indians are government wards and I am hoping the government will take a hand in this case." She had called and also written the State Department about the matter. "If I could just get one of these women behind bars it might make a few others think twice before they said they were me and picked up gentlemen on trains."[73]

One day, she received a newspaper clipping stating that an Italian professor on a lecture tour in the States met "a great editor in New York who introduced him to Margaret Mitchell, a quiet, inconspicuous little woman" who had written *Gone With the Wind.* None of the Macmillan editors had any idea of how the story originated, and Peggy never discovered who the imposter was.[74] Another clipping from Dublin, Ireland, reported that she spent Christmas in County Meath, where a party was held for her at a Dublin hotel. Peggy wrote: "Ireland is one country I wouldn't mind seeing. So, it was nice of this lady to see it for me."[75]

One swindler masquerading as Margaret Mitchell insisted that a high-fashion Los Angeles department store present her a private fashion showing after the store closed in the evening and walked away afterwards with seventeen hundred dollars worth of clothes charged to Margaret Mitchell. Many other imposters autographed copies of *Gone With the Wind* in bookstores across the country. When Kenneth Roberts, author of *Northwest Passage,* read about these Mitchell frauds autographing books, he wrote Peggy telling her not to worry, that the same thing had happened to him and it only sold more books. But unlike Roberts, Peggy was unable to shrug this kind of thing off. These imposters became so numerous and the idea of them bothered Peggy so much that John hired the Pinkerton detective service to find them. He retained the service for years.

Peggy also became upset about the reports that several families in the Jonesboro section were passing off their plantation homes as the real Tara. These families were making money off the northern tourists who desired to visit the places mentioned in the novel. She would get into her automobile and drive around for hours, "in cognito" as she put it, trying to locate these "liars of the first water."[76]

Instead of ignoring the stories that came to her by the grapevine, Peggy seemed compelled to collect them. The truth is she enjoyed gossip, as she once revealed in a letter to Stark Young, also a southerner: "Northerners always wonder how Southerners manage to know so much about other Southerners whom they have never met and probably never will meet. For my part, I pity Northerners. Evidently, the grapevine does not work in the North, and I think people above the Mason and Dixon line miss many choice bits because they must depend on such crude devices as the radio and the newspapers for their information."[77]

She caviled over minutiae, wasting extraordinary amounts of time and energy in trying to track the source of rumors, and yet more time and energy in responding to them and then again in repeating them in her conversations and letters.

A few of these stories were humorous, such as the one about the northern organization "The Society for the Dissemination of Correct Information about the Civil War," which, she said, had been sending all over the country volumes of mimeographed material "about what a horrible and unladylike person I am and how utterly false is the picture I presented in my book. This outfit never had the courage to send me any copies, but they had been circulating them sub rosa." Eventually she was sent a copy and, much to her surprise and dismay, she learned, among other things, that she had been referred to as "the Atlanta midget."[78] Although Peggy pouted over this epithet, John threw his head back roaring with laughter every time he told one of their friends about it.[79]

After receiving much weird mail, she commented to him that insane people had beautiful, clear handwriting and showed him such handwriting in a letter from a British fan, who had a fetish for lady's underwear; this fan had written asking her to write a novel about lingerie! Another abnormal mind requested from Peggy the fifteen thousand dollars he said he needed to finish his epic poem and included passages of complete gibberish as examples of his work. Many more people wrote begging for money or help with their manuscripts.[80]

The book continued to bring them varied and interesting experiences. One day, Peggy received a letter from Germany addressed to Captain Rhett Butler. As John laboriously translated it, it became apparent that the lady was upbraiding Butler, telling him it was his own fault that he had made a mess of his life. She wrote that he got just what he deserved, and she wished she could take him by the shoulders and shake him through and through ("durch und durch"). At the end of her letter, she revealed that she was writing more in sorrow than in anger and bade him a farewell full of compassion. The fact that the letter came from a convent in Germany really intrigued them. In relating this incident to his mother, John added that a mother superior of a Catholic institution in the South, "a lady with the appearance and regal manner of a medieval abbess, is one of Captain Butler's most outspoken admirers."[81]

14

Although *Gone With the Wind* was off the bestseller list by March 1938, it continued to create new and harder problems for John. Earlier Peggy had written to John's mother explaining why he had not written her recently; she said Stephens and John had been working with a batch of papers about the French translation rights, which had to be attended to immediately and gotten in the earliest mail. She realized that John was working too hard and that he was not feeling well, but she did not know what to do about it.

> For nearly every night for two years John has worked on business matters arising out of *Gone With the Wind*. For a year it involved the correcting of typescript and the reading of proof. For the last year it has been the handling of contracts and an endless fight to

keep people from exploiting me for their own ends. We never get a chance to go anywhere or see anyone and, instead of work slacking, it seems to get heavier. I feel very depressed about this, as I had hoped that all work and worry would be over by this summer so that John could get some rest and relaxation. As it now stands I do not think we will even get much of a vacation this year. But I suppose it cannot keep up forever, even if it appears at present that it will.[82]

Indeed, John's work on the book had gotten heavier while his job at Georgia Power continued to demand great energy. The effects of holding down two difficult jobs steadily for almost three years were physically manifesting themselves as he began to look much older than his forty-three years. The most obvious change in his appearance was his hair. Although it was still thick, it had all turned white. Peggy worried about him constantly and did her best to persuade him to stop smoking. She knew that now it was her turn to see to it that he got away for a while to rest. So, after much insistence on her part, they set out in the spring of 1938 on a three-week vacation, drifting about small Florida towns. No one knew them or recognized them, and so no one asked for autographs or photographs.[83] At each of their stops, they visited friends, stayed in small hotels, and dined in the best restaurants. When they returned home, she wrote Brickell that she had gained weight and was up to 120 pounds. "I have to unzip all my dresses to breathe. I am breaking ground for my third chin and I never felt better in my life. . . . I am as hefty as a hog at killing time."[84] Actually she had gained twelve pounds, too much for her small frame.

John, too, felt much better, telling his mother, "My weight is now up to 156 pounds stripped, which is nine pounds above my previous normal and the most I have weighed since I got out of the army. It's very encouraging as I have been trying unsuccessfully to put on weight for many years."[85] The extra pounds were due in part to the fact that he had tried to cut out smoking. He boasted, "Just before I went back to the office I had gone twelve days with no cigarettes at all. Then I broke over, but not too badly." Once back to the routine of Georgia Power and the foreign copyrights, he resumed smoking, unable to kick the habit when under stress.

For their vacation, John brought along two books, *Northwest Passage* and *Of Mice and Men,* but the papers in his briefcase got most of his attention. While he worked, Peggy read his books and whatever else was available in the hotel lending libraries where they stayed. She still liked popular fiction that she could read "in gulps."[86] After reading *Appointment in Samarra, Butterfield 8, The Postman Always Rings Twice, Serenade,* and *Imperial City,* "and dozens of others," she complained in a letter to her friend Brickell on April 14 that she was having "a bad case of emotional indigestion."[87] She thought if she had stretched out the reading over a long period, she would not have felt as depressed about the novels as she did. But reading one right after the other, she felt that their "impact was too strong" for her and explained to her friend:

> I hope you will understand that my emotional indigestion did not arise from any sense of shock or disapproval at the goings-on of these characters. What depressed and bothered me was the tiredness of everyone concerned. These characters did not leap gaily in and out of strange beds as did the characters of the jazz age, nor did they commit murder, forgery, etc. with passion, enthusiasm or regret. They did all these things—for what reason I cannot say. Certainly, they got no pleasure from any of their sins, nor did they have any sense of remorse. We came home slowly, visiting our friends in the small towns of Georgia and Florida, and I looked upon my friends and their friends with new eyes. . . .
>
> For I could see that the old morals persist and the old ways of looking at sin and such have not changed. Remorse for ill-doing is as strong as ever and social pressure toward ill-doing as strong as it was a hundred years ago. There is a vitality and enthusiasm for life in both its good and bad aspects in these small town people.[88]

Thinking about the contrast between the modern fiction she had been reading and the real lives of average people, she was seized with a strong desire to write a story about a girl who went wrong and certainly did regret it. This idea occurred, she said to Brickell, because she did not find in any of the stories she had read "the perfectly normal feminine reaction of fear of consequences, of loss of reputation, of social disapproval or of that good old-fashioned Puritan institution, conscience." She thought that her desire to write such a book put her back into the Victorian period but added, as an afterthought, that *Gone With the Wind* was "probably as Victorian a novel as ever written."[89] This was the only time that she ever mentioned wanting to write another book.

Since their return from Florida, she wrote, "Life has almost reverted to its pre-War Between the States status—the phone does not ring, the tourists come no more, the mail has dropped off. . . . I only hope the movie does not cause a recrudescence."[90] With the return of her "quiet and normal and very happy" life, Peggy was back into her old habit of reading a book or two a day.[91] Writing fewer letters and those mostly to her friends, she often mentioned the books she was reading. The one novel that she and John named as their favorite book of 1938 was *The Yearling*. This was a book, she said, that did not fit into any category and she supposed that fact would "annoy people who like to paste labels on literature. Books like this are just what they are and we can only be grateful that they come to us."[92]

Because her book had been criticized for lacking social consciousness, she wondered when she finished reading *The Yearling* what might have happened to such a simple story if it had been written by "a writer bitten with 'social consciousness' and 'have-and-have-nots' feeling. Can't you see what an underprivileged child Jody would have been? And what wouldn't a socially conscious writer have done with those gorgeous bewhiskered Forrester boys? That scene where the boys get up early and, stark naked, tune up and have a 'hoe down' is something I will cherish." Then she concluded this letter to Brickell by saying: "To everyone who, as a child, has run wild in the woods it must bring back a thousand memories, even as it did for me. My memory for smells is very strong and this book brought back smells years old so strongly."

She kept up with other writers of less importance than Rawlings. To Helen Dowdey, another writer friend who worried about lying fallow and asked if Peggy had ever had a compulsion to write during the last two years, Peggy answered: "I am in favor of bigger and better fallowing.... The exact opposite has been my problem. I loathe writing and will go to any lengths to keep from writing. Having a definite antipathy for putting words on paper, the only reason I ever wrote any was because I had nothing to do at that particular time and, having started something, was goaded on by the Puritanical adage that one should finish what one had begun. John's large shoe placed on the metaphorical seat of the pants of my soul accelerated some of my efforts." Because Helen and Clifford Dowdey were going on a vacation soon, Peggy added, "It would be grand if you could go West with nothing on your minds except your hair."[93]

After she and John attended a tea for Willie Snow Ethridge, whose new novel *Mingled Yarn* Macmillan had published in the spring in 1938, she got a good dose of what it meant to be out of the limelight. The wife of Mark Ethridge, editor of the Louisville *Courier-Journal,* Willie was a native of Macon, Georgia. Now that the spotlight had finally been removed from her, she wrote her friend Brickell, "Everything is in a stew, as we do not have bushels of authors in this section as you do in New York. ... I cannot tell you of my heartfelt pleasure that it was Willie and not me who was having to undergo all of this. She has unbounded energy and enjoys bushels of teas and parties and she is never at a loss for 'a few words' and she makes those words very charming ones. This is a gift—and one I do not possess."[94]

13

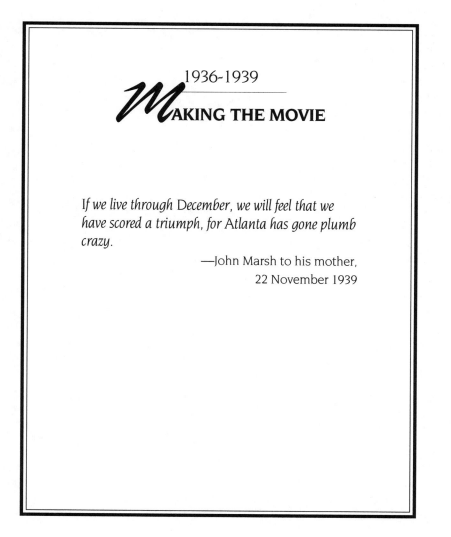

1936-1939

MAKING THE MOVIE

If we live through December, we will feel that we have scored a triumph, for Atlanta has gone plumb crazy.

—John Marsh to his mother,
22 November 1939

1

DURING THE YEARS WHEN JOHN AND PEGGY WERE CAUGHT UP in the aftermath of the publication of *Gone With the Wind* as a book, Peggy's masterpiece was being born as a movie. While John was becoming entangled in complex copyright issues and Peggy was answering letters and reading reviews about the book, dealing with rumors and lawsuits related to the book, and winning awards for her great novel, they were also affected by the excitements and irritations involved in the creation of *Gone With the Wind* as a film. It took David Selznick four years to make his most famous film—from 1936, when the book was first published, through 1939, when it premiered in Atlanta. During these four years, while John and Peggy were "reaping the whirlwind" of her book's publication, Selznick was creating a whirlwind of his own.

The initial publicity about the movie generated a kind of turmoil that—at first—was fun for Peggy. Because she had said loudly, clearly, and repeatedly that she was having nothing to do with making the film, writing the script, or selecting the cast, she believed that the monkey, so to speak, was off her back and onto that of the filmmakers. So she looked forward to enjoying the excitement from a distance, without suffering the personal intrusions that had deluged her after the publication of the book. She liked all of the "Selznickers" that she had met at the July 1936 meeting in New York and thought they were exciting and smart. She particularly admired Kay Brown, the attractive young woman who worked for Selznick in his New York office and who had convinced him to buy the film rights to *Gone With the Wind.*

In her first letter to Kay in October 1936, Peggy revealed that her hopes for an armchair view of the movie-making process were already dashed. She wrote, "Life has been awful since I sold the movie rights. I am deluged with letters demanding that I do not put Clark Gable in as Rhett. Strangers telephone me or grab me on the street, insisting that Katherine Hepburn will never do. It does me no good to point out sarcastically that it is Mr. Selznick and not I who is producing this picture."[1]

But the Marshes' real nightmare did not begin until late fall, 1936, when Selznick launched publicity on his nationwide search for an entire cast of new faces. It was then that Peggy told her brother-in-law Henry and others that she was up to her "rump with folks wanting to get in the movie."[2] Several years later, she recited a long list of interruptions that she endured after Selznick began his search, complaining to the producer on January 30, 1939: "My life has been bedlam . . . very largely because of thousands of people who thought I was producing *Gone With the Wind* single-handed in my back yard and who believed that I, and I alone, could give them parts in it." She was not exaggerating. Many people did call her asking for minor parts in the picture or offering to sell their grandparents' furnishings to be used in the film, and hordes of people bedeviled not only her and John but also her father, brother, and sister-in-law about getting personal letters of introduction so that they could go onto the lot and watch the filmmaking. For awhile, it was not unusual for the Marshes to open the door of their apartment in the mornings to find hoop-skirted, would-be Scarletts, Melanies, and Mammys, begging to see Miss Mitchell.[3] They often got late-night telephone calls from people who had been arguing about the cast and "probably drinking about it too since dinnertime," Peggy wrote Kay. "John is patience itself and soothes indignant ladies who just can't bear Mr. Gable's dimples. He tells them that Mr. Selznick would dearly love to have a letter from them on the subject."[4]

The nation of *Gone With the Wind* fans took a personal interest in casting the roles for the major characters. When a Hollywood reporter announced that it was a cinch the roles of Scarlett and Rhett would be played by Norma Shearer and Clark Gable, Peggy warned Kay that Gable was not popular in the South as he was in other sections of the country. Southerners thought he was a fine actor, "in the tough and hardboiled roles, yes, but in other roles, no." He did not look or act southern and, she wrote, "he in no way conforms to their notion of a Low-Country Carolinian. In looks and in conduct Basil Rathbone has been the first choice in this section, with Frederic March and Ronald Coleman running second and third."[5] About Norma Shearer, Peggy wrote that southerners thought she was a wonderful actress, but would be "sadly miscast in the part of Scarlett. . . . She has too much dignity and not enough fire for the part."[6]

No different from everyone else, John's family also speculated about a cast. In answering a letter from his sister, John said:

> You are engaging in what appears to a popular game. But, as a friend, please don't urge Clark Gable. A great many people have picked him for Rhett, but he is persona non grata to the Marsh-Mitchell family. In our opinion, his he-man stuff is synthetic. He

just doesn't ring the bell. I liked him a lot, years ago, when he first appeared in a picture which I think was called *Night Nurse*. His socking of ladies on the chin in that picture stirred me greatly, but I have never liked him since. He was good as a tough guy but he has never gotten over with us in parts where the force and violence are more subtle.

Then he added, "But I suppose it would be difficult for any movie actor to please us in any part, because the people in the book are so much like real people to us."[7]

Contrary to the opinion of southerners, the national favorite for Rhett Butler was Clark Gable, who was without question the greatest sex image and the biggest film star in the entire world.[8] But Gable, at that time, was under contract to MGM, who would only loan him to Selznick for 50 percent of the net proceeds for the next seven years. Chary of paying such a price, Selznick considered Gary Cooper, the other great sex symbol of the age, who was under contract to Sam Goldwyn. Although Goldwyn refused to negotiate a deal, by then it did not matter what the producers thought because the public demanded that Gable play Rhett. Uncertain about his ability to meet the public's expectations of Rhett Butler, Gable did not even want the part. He later said, "Rhett was simply too big an order."[9] Merian Cooper, a member of the Selznick International Pictures board of directors and an old friend of Selznick's, said flatly: "We couldn't make the picture and satisfy the public without Gable."[10] It took almost two years of debate and anguish before Selznick finally announced that Gable would play the role.

A creative genius with manic energy and a passion for excellence, Selznick loved making movies. The confluence of his reverence for the past and his love for classics had been manifested at MGM, where he made splendid films from three long novels—*David Copperfield, A Tale of Two Cities,* and *Anna Karenina.*[11] He knew what hard work it was to turn big books into good films. Wanting to capitalize on the public's consuming interest in what he was about to do with its favorite book, he pleaded, and he got Kay to plead, with Peggy to let him use her manuscript, or parts of it, for promotional purposes. She adamantly refused, claiming she had burned it. So he milked the talent search gimmick for as long as he could— nearly two years.

In the fall of 1936, when he instructed Kay to start the casting campaign for unknown actors, he warned her, "*Copperfield* and *Tom Sawyer* have been child's play by comparison. You had better get yourself prepared accordingly."[12] But Kay was not prepared for the gale force the *Gone With the Wind* fans exerted on her and everyone involved in the production. She was shocked when one thousand hopefuls showed up for the first audition.

The most frightening experience in her life came one evening when a crazed man waved a pistol at her saying, "I want to play Rhett Butler." She told him that she would see to it and dashed out and called the police.[13]

While Kay, Charles Morrison, and Oscar Serlin combed little theaters and high school and college drama classes all over the country searching for talent, Selznick selected a team of experts to help him pull his extravagant endeavor together.[14] By the end of October 1936, he announced that George Cukor would direct the film. Having just directed Greta Garbo in MGM's *Camille,* Cukor had a reputation for being the ideal director for female actors.

When it came to getting a screenplay writer, Selznick asked Merian Cooper to help him get Sidney Howard, the Pulitzer Prize-winning playwright. Formerly from Macon and Athens, Georgia, Cooper had read *Gone With the Wind* and thought it was "the most supreme book written on courage in the English language."[15] With his enthusiasm for the story, Cooper easily convinced his friend Howard, with whom he had flown during World War I, to adapt the novel for the screen. In a news release, Selznick described Howard as "the best constructionist around right now" and said he would be paid $22,500 for the script.[16] With a reputation for producing work of the highest quality in a narrow time frame, Howard could set the rules by which he would work. Much to Selznick's consternation, he refused to work in Hollywood, where he knew Selznick, who had an obsessive compulsion to control every aspect of whatever film he was making, would be looking over his shoulder and distracting him.[17] Howard worked either in his home in New York City or in his farmhouse in Massachusetts.

The Marshes were delighted to learn that the book had fallen into the hands of a writer with such an impeccable reputation, for that meant the script would be good.

In his first letter to Peggy on November 25, 1936, Howard told her how sincerely he admired her novel and that he liked the idea of making it into a picture, adding, "as who would not." Planning to go to Atlanta with George Cukor and Kay Brown around the first of December 1938, he looked forward to meeting her and asked if she would help him if he felt obliged to write any additional dialogue for the Negro characters. "Those are the best written darkies, I do believe, in all literature," he wrote. "They are the only ones I have ever read which seem to come through uncolored by white patronising."[18] He also asked if she would read his first layout of material and tell him what she thought of the script, and he hoped that she would continue to read the script as it developed.

The Marshes had no intention of becoming involved with the script. In response to Howard's letter, Peggy reiterated:

When I sold the book to the Selznick Company, I made it very plain that I would have nothing whatsoever to do with the picture, nothing on backgrounds, costumes, continuity. They offered me money to go to Hollywood to write additional dialogue, etc. and I refused. I sold the book on that understanding. Not more than a week ago, I wrote Miss Katharine Brown . . . and asked her if you were familiar with my attitude and she wired me that you were. But now your letter arrives and I realize that they have not told you. . . . [19]

She told Howard that she knew no more about writing scripts than she did about writing "Sanscrit grammar," and besides, she did not have time to read a script, much less help write one. "I never dreamed writing a book meant losing all privacy, leisure and chance to rest. Since July 1, I've averaged an engagement every forty minutes from nine in the morning till long after midnight. And, between those engagements, I've had to handle an enormous mail and try to see my family," she wrote.

It is true that a film script is a radically different literary form than a novel, and it is also true that by this time Peggy was tired and longed for peace, privacy, and rest. She had already proven her mettle, so to speak; now let Selznick prove his. Furthermore, at this point John had no time or energy to help her, as he had done when she had written her novel. But perhaps the best explanation for Peggy's refusal to help Howard lies in the very protectiveness she felt about the book. Just as she had been obsessed with the southern reaction to *Gone With the Wind* and had consistently and thoroughly supported every bit of historical information included in her novel, so she was concerned with the southern reaction to the movie. She believed that if she even glanced over the script, she would be held responsible for every small item in the film that incensed or even annoyed southerners. And not for "worlds or money" would she offend a single southerner; they had been too kind to her and her book.[20]

So, as protective as they were of the book, Peggy and John must have decided that it would be in her best interest if she refused—publicly, repeatedly, and consistently—to have anything to do with the film treatment of her novel.

Furthermore, having been "deviled by the press and the public," she stated outright she did not care who played what roles or where the film was made. She joked privately among her friends that Groucho Marx or Donald Duck could play Rhett Butler for all she cared.[21] But to Howard, she said: "To be quite frank, I have all the confidence in you and Mr. Cukor and Mr. Selznick so why should I rush about issuing statements to the press on matters that are none of my business."[22]

Peggy repeated to Howard what she had written Kay Brown: that she would only be too happy to help the visiting film crew meet research workers and local historians who knew what really went on in the South during the period of the novel. She offered to drive the crew from Dalton to Milledgeville, show them the entrenchments and the old houses, and introduce them to people in each town along the way. But that was all she was going to do. "I just can't," she said emphatically. "I'm too nearly crazy now with the load I'm carrying." She closed by saying, "Speaking of Civil War monuments—you should see our Southern ones. I believe they were put out by the same company that put out the Northern ones. They are twice as ugly and three times as duck-legged!"[23]

A gentle man who valued his own privacy, Howard understood her position and told her so. The Selznick company had said nothing to him about her attitude toward helping with the film. He explained that he wrote her as he did only because he wanted to assure her that all possible measures were being taken to get her approval or criticism before the picture got to the irrevocable stage. On two earlier occasions when he had worked with novels by Sinclair Lewis, he had submitted his script to the novelist, and he simply wanted to extend that courtesy to her. "But I understand all too well how you feel," he wrote. "I should not dream of going near a play of mine after it has opened. . . . I take you at your word and shall not trouble you."[24]

2

Kay Brown and Sidney Howard were gracious in accepting Peggy's reasons for not participating in the filmmaking, but the overly enthusiastic ace publicity manager Russell Birdwell, whom Selznick had appointed to ignite a tremendous publicity campaign, was not. When Birdwell sent Peggy, at her request, the story he had prepared to release to the national wire services, she became incensed. The release stated that Kay Brown was going to Atlanta, where Margaret Mitchell was to help her select the cream of the crop of the young girls auditioning for the role of Scarlett, and that Margaret Mitchell hoped it would be a southern actress. The other misstatement claimed that Sidney Howard was also coming to Atlanta to make certain that his screenplay satisfied the author of the novel and that Margaret Mitchell was going to have a huge party for the film people.

Thoroughly upset after reading that release, Peggy steamed downtown to the Georgia Power building to show John what "that so-and-so" had done.[25] John rolled up his sleeves and wrote drafts of two telegrams for Peggy to send. (Both drafts are in his handwriting but written in her first-person voice; he wrote as if he were she.[26]) One telegram is to Kay Brown, saying that if the Selznick publicity department did not state Peggy's position correctly, she would leave Atlanta and not come back until the search for actors had been completed. The other telegram, which went directly to Birdwell, stated,

> My contract specifically provides that I have nothing to do with the movie and I have stated personally and by letter to various Selznick people that I will have nothing to do with talent search, casting, adaptation of story or filming but apparently I must repeat this to each new member of the organization I come in contact with. When Miss Brown and others come to Atlanta I will feed them fried chicken, show them Stone Mountain and introduce them to anybody they want to meet. But all parts of the film job are on their hands and not on mine. Am releasing story to Atlanta afternoon papers today after deleting references to me and Mr. Birdwell please make the same corrections in any releases you give out. On this and any future stories I want no references made to me except as author of book.[27]

Apparently, Birdwell ignored the Marshes' telegram and released the information just as he had originally written it. John angrily wrote him again, telling Birdwell that he had better be cocksure of his facts before he released any more news, or Peggy would refuse even to meet Cukor and Howard if she were misrepresented again.[28] He stated unequivocally that if a story went out making it appear that she were giving a tea for the Selznick representatives, she would recall her invitations and cancel the tea. She was giving a party, but it was for her friends in the press who had been so kind to her. It was the only way in which she could show her appreciation. "And it's *their* party and in *their* honor." It would be nice if Mr. Cukor, Mr. Howard, and Miss Brown could attend, he said, because they could meet people who might be of some assistance to them and because Peggy wanted to be hospitable to them and to make their visit to Atlanta pleasant. In an earlier letter to John's mother, Peggy had written that it was a party she was looking forward to giving, for she wanted to thank the press, both of Atlanta and neighboring cities, the reference librarians, the booksellers, the book reviewers—all the people who had been so kind to her and done so much for her. "I'm using the movie folks as an excuse to give the party so I can thank everyone at one time. For people have certainly been good to me."[29]

3

For several days before the film people arrived in Atlanta in December 1936, newspapers throughout the South made pleas to the public not to bother the Marshes or Eugene or Stephens Mitchell, or any of their relatives. Such pleas did seem to deter the local people, but not those from out of state. When Kay Brown, Tony Bundsman, and Harriet Flagg arrived in early December, the city went into a frenzy. All the newspapers emphasized that the film crew's search was limited and that they were hoping to find possible screen test candidates for the four principal characters: Scarlett, Rhett, Melanie, and Ashley. On December 2 the *Georgian* quoted Kay Brown as saying: "We won't be able to consider any character parts, though if there is a possible Aunt Pittypat around we would be delighted to find her. We would also be delighted if we could find twins to play the parts of the Tarleton boys. But we won't be able to consider any of the numerous 'mammies' that have been recommended nor any babies." When the audition crew arrived in Atlanta, they were overwhelmed with Atlanta's enthusiasm for the movie. Later that evening, after her terribly long day, Kay warned her boss, "Sherman's march through Georgia will be nothing compared with Selznick's."[30]

Kay and her two-man crew auditioned five hundred candidates that first day. Exhausted from the day's work, she wired Selznick that evening: "We are in Atlanta, barricaded in our rooms. The belles turned out in droves. For the most part they are all healthy mothers who should have stayed at home; the rich debutantes are all offering to pay us to play Scarlett, and all the mammys in the South want to play Mammy. I feel like Moses in the Wilderness. . . . I need a drink and Georgia is a dry state."[31]

If Kay was exhausted after the audition, so were the Marshes. Their apartment was stormed for days by strangers wanting an audition. They were besieged by an unbelievable number of people who had no experience in the theater or in films but who thought that all they needed was Margaret Mitchell's approval to land a part in the film. Distressed and frustrated, Peggy wrote Sidney Howard: "The populace of six states descended on me, demanding that I endorse each and every one of them for the role of Scarlett, etc. The phone went every minute and wires and special deliveries deviled me and shoals of people camped on the doorstep and clutched me if I went out."[32]

The search for actresses in the South turned up only three girls. The most prominent one was Alicia Rhett, a fair-skinned, golden-haired, slender beauty whom Cukor found in Charleston, South Carolina, in a rehearsal of *Lady Windermere's Fan*. At first, he thought perhaps she could play Melanie, but he ended up giving her the role of India Wilkes, Ashley's sister, because many of the crew remarked how much she resembled Leslie Howard, who played Ashley. The other two actresses were Mary Anderson and Marcella Martin; both played minor parts.

In April, George Cukor, Hobart Erwin, John Darrow, and Kay Brown returned to Atlanta to search for an actress to play Scarlett. The Marshes gave a cocktail party for them and invited 250 guests. For many Atlantans, the excitement of the filmmakers' return overshadowed the fact that Hitler had just ripped apart Czechoslovakia and was headed toward Poland while Britain and France looked helplessly on.

4

No one was more persistent or obnoxious in her efforts to play Scarlett than Betty Timmons, the beautiful daughter of a man whose brother married one of Peggy's aunts—Aline Mitchell Timmons. Although Peggy was not kin to her and had never even seen the girl, Betty Timmons went to New York introducing herself as Margaret Mitchell's niece and broadcasting around that Margaret Mitchell herself had not only picked her out for the part but had also modeled the character of Scarlett on her. Newspaper reporters from New York, San Francisco, and elsewhere called Peggy to ask if the girl's story were true.[33] Because the press gave her some attention, Timmons managed to get an audition from the Selznick Company.

Her audition turned out poorly, and the Selznick organization, sick of the girl's hounding them for another tryout, dubbed her "Honey Chile." Undeterred by the bad publicity and the embarrassment she was causing her family, Timmons pursued her course by following George Cukor to Atlanta in April. Failing to find him, she did learn that he was leaving by train that evening for New Orleans and she was determined to go with him. Her wild chase at the railroad station made the front page of the *Atlanta Constitution,* which carried the headline "Socialite, with O'Hara Dash, Races Madly to See Cukor."[34] Peggy thought the escapade was hilarious and wrote Kay, in New York, and others about it.

But for some reason, maybe because he was exhausted, John found nothing amusing about Betty Timmons's antics. In fact, it prompted him to write what he himself described as "an unpardonably long letter" to his sister Katharine Bowden and Anne, her daughter, who lived in California. His purpose was to convince his niece, who was pursuing a film career, not to mention to a soul that she was related to Margaret Mitchell. Wanting Anne and her mother to avoid any kind of embarrassment and publicity, he told her about "Honey Chile's" absurd pursuit for the role of Scarlett, and he entreated her to avoid, at all costs, giving even the slightest appearance that she was another "niece of Margaret Mitchell." His single-spaced letter is nine pages and includes approximately six thousand words on the agony Peggy had experienced since the publication of her book. Writing his frustrations down in such detail must have been some kind of a catharsis for John. He asked his sister to destroy his letter after reading it.

In introducing his reason for writing such a long letter, John wrote his sister:

> You may think I am exaggerating but I am not. One writer summed up the situation better than I could when he said that probably no American in private life, except Lindbergh, had ever been called upon to face so blinding a glare of publicity, so avid a public curiosity, so passionate a determination to pry, as Peggy has. . . . The truly great ladies of the literary world, such as Willa Cather and Ellen Glasgow and Julia Peterkin and others, do not have their private lives smeared over the pages of newspapers. They stand upon their accomplishments, not on their "hobbies," and I am proud that Peggy feels this way. Her friends understand this. . . . They have discovered from bitter experience that some careless remark, such as "Peggy is so fond of her brother's two little boys," gets into the New York gossip columns in twenty-four hours as "Peggy is so fond of *her* two little boys."[35]

Nearly everything Peggy said was distorted in a newspaper somewhere, particularly whenever she spoke with people in high places who tried to cut through red tape for an actress friend. One such call came from Mrs. Ogden Reid, the owner of the *Herald Tribune,* who ostensibly called Peggy about attending a meeting of distinguished women in New York. In the course of their brief conversation, Mrs. Reid asked Peggy what she thought about Katharine Hepburn. Peggy replied that she thought the actress "looked pretty in hoopskirts," and that she had enjoyed her performance in *Little Women.*[36] That was all. The next day, the news went out from New York that Mrs. Reid had heard Margaret Mitchell say that she wanted Katharine Hepburn to play Scarlett. Tied up for hours making denials, Peggy issued the following statement to the Associated Press: "I never expressed a preference and I never will. If Mrs. Reid understood me to say I felt a strong preference for Miss Hepburn in the role, I owe her and Miss Hepburn an apology." Privately, Peggy said to friends, "I could not help resenting Mrs. Reid's action for I had given her no cause for making such a statement. I made notes of my conversation with her and there were two witnesses to my statement."[37]

The Atlanta newspapers during this period are full of examples of the press's interest in Mitchell minutiae. For example, on December 14, 1936, Peggy got a parking ticket for the first time in her life. She had not parked illegally, but rather than take the time to argue the case, which she believed would cause headlines, she had Stephens go down to the courthouse and pay the three-dollar fine. Despite her efforts, however, news of Peggy's traffic ticket was published in the newspapers and broadcast over the radio.

Newspapers carried stories about the kinds of gifts the Marshes sent as wedding presents. Sometimes, casual remarks Peggy had made to supposedly good friends were spread all over town or printed in the newspapers, "with the result," John wrote his mother, "that she now keeps her mouth shut or talks in platitudes except when she is with very dear and trusted friends . . . she is being forced into two-facedness, into talking one way before her 'dear public' and being herself only when in the presence of the family or friends who can be relied upon."[38]

John was rightfully frustrated, for he was losing all control over their lives. No one annoyed him more than the clerks in the Atlanta Western Union office, who got positively euphoric every time Peggy received or sent a telegram. They repeated publicly every word that went across the wire from or to her. Without her knowledge, much less permission, they even reported her telegrams to the newspapers, including her telegram from Leslie Howard. When Howard wired Peggy on January 13, 1939, the telegraph operator, instead of calling Peggy first, called the *Atlanta Constitution* notifying the city editor that Miss Mitchell had received a wire from the British actor. The editor showed Peggy the courtesy of calling her. "I feebly told the newspaper editor that yours was a personal wire, but little good that did," Peggy wrote Howard. "Now I am not sorry that it was published for everyone thought it amusing and charming. I suppose you know that from the beginning you have been the choice of this section for the part of Ashley. Here in the South a sigh of relief went up when the announcement about you was made. . . . I look forward to the time when I can see you as Ashley Wilkes."[39] Peggy was not exaggerating when she wrote Howard, "I have little privacy these days and whether I like it or not, almost everything that happens to me becomes public property."

5

When she visited the Marshes for the first time in December 1936, Kay Brown emphasized Selznick's determination to maintain the authenticity of the dialects and of every other aspect of the novel. When she returned in late 1938, she repeated Selznick's urgent, sincere request that Peggy please come to California, as a well-paid advisor, to oversee the filming and to act as a historical consultant. Even though Peggy cared about the film as much as Selznick did and was surely more curious than anyone else about the filmmaking process, she refused the offer. "I don't mind being obliging and I am hopeful that the picture will be accurate as to the background, costumes, etc., but I can't and won't take on the responsibilities of serving as an adviser and we might as well understand each other on that point before we go any further."[40] It was around this time that she and John seriously started thinking about whom they could recommend to go to Hollywood on her behalf.

Meanwhile, she sympathetically answered many questions for the "Selznickers," for as John pointed out to her and to his family, the kinds of things Selznick's research department asked proved the dedication the producer had to achieving authenticity in details.[41] The Marshes were eager to assist in this important matter. Above all else, they did not want history distorted, for, as Peggy told Selznick, "Southerners get indignant when our history is portrayed improperly."[42] The diligent research department, managed by the highly competent Lillian Deighton, was having a difficult time finding visual information on Atlanta during the period of the novel because so much of Atlanta's past had been destroyed in the 1864 fire. They desperately needed old pictures, photographs, and other tangible evidence of the period.[43] Some of Deighton's questions were forwarded to Peggy through Assistant Director Eric Stacy:

How many house servants at Tara? How many people would be seen at prayer and the nature of the group? What type of orchestra played at Belle Watling's establishment? Trio? Quartet? What instruments? Were there sheep on lawns of some of the big houses? What type of music would they play? How many people attended the barbecue at Twelve Oaks? Proportion of adults and children? Proportion of old and young? Were colored children and white children playing together? How many slaves would be seen at one time at Tara? How many men in artillery Battalion. Did the convicts working at Scarlett's mill wear uniforms or rags? Could a hospital in Atlanta during wartime be located in a church? Was the symbol of the Red Cross used on ambulances in the Civil War?[44]

Peggy answered every question as thoroughly as she could. For instance, she wrote that she did not believe the Red Cross insignia was in use in the South at that time, and about the sheep on the lawns, she answered no. "It was hard to grow grass, except Bermuda grass, and people were very proud of their lawns. They did not even want chickens to scratch there. The sheep would have been in the sheep pasture, perhaps next to the cow pasture, but not a part of the cow pasture as sheep cut the grass so much shorter than cows. On some plantations the sheep were rotated through several pastures in order to give the grass time to grow again."

She explained that black and white children did play together. "It was the custom then for each white child to be given a colored child as a 'play child' and the children were inseparable. (As the 'play children' of the little girls grew up they became maids to their mistresses. Many of the 'play children' of the boys, when they grew up, went off to the War with their masters.) White children frequently went into tantrums if their 'play children' could not accompany them to fetes such as the barbecue."

The wardrobe department had its own problems with research and wanted to know such things as, "Was Mammy's headkerchief tied with knots showing or knots tucked under?" Truly impressed with this question, Peggy rooted around in her files for hours searching for some old photographs of women wearing such kerchiefs but was unable to find any. Disgusted, she told John, "Hell if I know, and I'm not going out on a limb over a head rag."[45]

Whenever Sidney Howard asked her questions about such details as blockaders' stores, names of ladies' charitable societies, refugee centers, signs on churches calling for iron, cast iron balconies in prewar Atlanta, crops, and medical treatments, Peggy went out of her way to answer. What she did not know, she researched thoroughly. Her letters answering these questions are interesting and informative and prove her in-depth knowledge of the Civil War period and the vast amount of oral history she had collected. About the iron balconies, she said that she had never heard of them nor seen any pictures of them. She explained that that type of architectural decoration was found in the coast section, 250 miles away around Savannah, and that it had reached its glory in New Orleans. She pointed out that "most of the iron in Atlanta had been donated for munition purposes long before Gettysburg because the pinch of the blockade was felt before the summer of 1863."[46]

None of the old people with whom she had talked remembered a single iron balcony in Atlanta during the war period. "Nor did any of them recall any signs on churches calling for iron or, for that matter, calling for anything. The churches did not ever have such signs upon them. Any appeals of this type would have appeared in the Atlanta papers," she explained. Because of the serious paper shortage, she doubted if there would have been any handbills bearing such appeals, and as best she could determine, General Beauregard's last appeal for old iron came some time shortly before March 27, 1862, when the general asked for church bells. The original appeal she found in the Beauregard Collection of the Confederate Memorial Museum in Richmond, Virginia.

I do not know about the general response to this appeal. I only know that the Methodist Protestant Church in Atlanta, of which my great-grandfather was a minister, gave their bell in 1862.

The memories of old timers agree with what I had heard

about there being no charitable centers for refugees. The best help I can give you on this matter is as follows. Adjoining the railroad tracks and the depot was the city park. It would be in this park that refugees who came by train would pause. Here they would wait with their baggage until friends and relatives came in their carriages to get them . . . or until some kind-hearted citizen offered them shelter, or they would sit until they started the weary tramp around the town to find what already overcrowded boarding houses could take them in.

About the blockaders' stores—blockade goods was sold in several ways. Many storekeepers went to Wilmington [North Carolina] and bought goods on the docks at auction and shipped them back to Atlanta to their stores. Others had large warehouses in Atlanta. They had their agents in Wilmington ship the goods to the warehouses and they held auctions in these warehouses. . . . Men engaged in blockading cotton to England had offices here in Atlanta for the purpose of purchasing cotton from the rural districts around the city. These establishments—wholesale, retail and cotton offices—would probably have borne no other signs than the names of the proprietors . . . the stores usually announced the arrival of new blockade goods by advertisement in the newspapers, although I have seen a handbill which ran vaguely like this, "Blank & Blank beg to announce that they have just received a consignment of goods through the blockade—tooth-brushes, ladies' merinos, fine tarlatans, etc." I am still hunting for one of these ads so I can send you a photostat.

She provided Howard with names of all the ladies' charitable societies and explained that those organizations corresponded to the ladies' canteen workers during World War I in that they met all troop trains with such items as baskets of food and socks. These volunteers also assisted the doctors in getting the wounded off the trains and into hospitals and even took some convalescents into their own homes. And she said the closest thing that she could find to a refugee center was the "Calico House," where all garments, packages, bandages, and food for soldiers and their needs were assembled.[47]

6

As swarms of people continued to seek roles in the film, swarms of others insisted that the actors in the leading roles be southerners, with southern looks, manners, actions, and accents. For a while, during the time the cast for the movie was still being selected, chain letters circulated around the South asking that southern accents be used in the film. Peggy wrote Herschel Brickell this amusing evaluation of southern accents.

> The political races are on and the air thick with campaign speeches. Yesterday, Mr. Roosevelt invaded Georgia to try to swing the senatorial election from the Conservative Democrats. I listened to the speaking and I hope sincerely that the Selznick company was not listening. The reason is this—many Southern newspapers have been running campaigns urging Mr. Selznick to use real Southern accents in *GWTW*. They've raved about the beauty of Southern voices, the accuracy of pronunciation and enunciation; they've threatened to boycott the movie if the Southern accent isn't right. Yesterday, after listening to a vast number of Southern accents, I thought how bewildered Mr. Selznick would be. I don't believe Southerners realize how they sound. Those on the air yesterday were not illiterate country folk—they were college graduates and the flower and chivalry of our dear Southland—and they said: "Sarroldy" for Saturday, "yestiddy" for yesterday, "neye-eeece" for nice, "guh-munt" for government, "intehdooce" for introduce, "instuhment" for instrument, and "puhzuhve" for preserve.
>
> If the bewildered Mr. Selznick made his puppets speak like this the South, suh, would secede and declare that we had all been insulted.[48]

So many people had expressed their wish to Selznick that he not have his actors use "imitation" southern accents that he became sensitive to this request. He insisted that his staff be sensitive too. In fun, some of them started practicing such expressions as "Good mawning!" or "G' mawning!" or "I heah yo' all down thar," or "I've never bean in Georgia befor'." Even Cukor started talking southern, and by the time filming began, he pronounced all words containing "R's" just as any Georgian would.[49]

While Kay was testing the Wisconsin-born Ona Munson in the studio for the role of Belle Watling, she telephoned Peggy asking her if Belle's accent would have been different from Scarlett's and Melanie's and in what way. Peggy tried to explain that the accent did vary "as it always does between the educated and the illiterate," that "the voices would be flat and slightly nasal," and that "they generally changed e's and i's—calling a pen 'a pin,' men 'min' and accenting such words as settlement and government on the last syllable, 'settlemint' and 'governmint.'" Kay got confused listening to her and asked if there were any southerners in New York who could sit in on an audition for Belle and help out with the accent. Peggy recommended Elinor Hillyer or Norma and Herschel Brickell. In telling Brickell what she had done, she said:

> Knowing the movie people and their ways, I would not be at all surprised if they had dispatched Rolls Royces with couriers and outriders to Ridgefield last night to kidnap you and Norma.... My modest and old fashioned family have become accustomed to anything in the last year and a half and, like the queen in "Alice in Wonderland" get up every morning ready to believe six impossible things before breakfast.[50]

Even her father was convulsed at the idea of someone telephoning from New York to discover how the madame of a Confederate bordello talked.[51]

Early on, a possible solution to the problem of ensuring southern authenticity had been suggested by W. T. Anderson, the editor and publisher of the *Macon Telegraph*. Anderson wrote that Sue Myrick, one of his writers, had told him about how Peggy had refused to go to Hollywood to see that her book was correctly filmed. He suggested: "If you don't think of anything better I should like to see Sue Myrick deputized to supervise. She has studied stage business, knows Southern dialect, has a Southern background and understands the characters and the qualities every foot of the way. I think you would do the best job, and think Sue would do the second best job. She'd fight to keep the picture off the rocks."[52]

A tall, plain-looking, blond-haired woman, Sue Myrick sparkled with genuine enthusiasm for people and for life. Witty, intelligent, and popular, she had never married and lived all of her life in Macon, where she wrote for the newspaper. Although she was forty-five years old in 1938, she looked and acted much younger, and she and Peggy had the same sense of mischief and fun.[53] Peggy had this to say about her: "Unfortunately, she is full of dialect stories about Negroes and Crackers. She inspires John and me to similar stories. After an hour of this we are unable to talk grammatically in normal social intercourse. For days after Sue has been here we sound like a group of Erskine Caldwell's characters having a reunion with the characters of Joe Chandler Harris."[54]

After talking it over, John and Peggy decided that Anderson's idea was a good one, especially since Sue would surely share with them all the "graveyard secret stuff" about the filmmaking that a stranger would never share. So Peggy replied to Anderson, "I will certainly beat the drum for her." But for some reason, she said nothing about the matter to Kay Brown until two months later after she met Sue again, in Macon, at the funeral of their mutual friend Aaron Bernd. It was at that time that Peggy became convinced that Sue could be trusted and would indeed be the ideal person to go to Hollywood. The next day, February 14, 1937, Peggy wrote a long letter to Kay praising Sue's qualifications and wisely omitting the part about Sue's study of "stage business" for fear that might destroy her chances of being selected. Peggy concluded her letter by saying, "Now, Katharine, please don't think you've got to consider her seriously just because I suggested her or just because she's a friend of mine. If the idea doesn't seem good to you, just tell me so. It won't bother me and Sue will never know that I've written to you so there'll be no skin off anyone's nose."[55]

The other person Peggy recommended as a possible advisor for the film was the well-known Atlanta architect, writer, and painter Wilbur Kurtz, originally from Indiana. As a young man he had talked with Civil War veterans and walked over the battlefields with them, and he knew the Atlanta campaign like the back of his hand. Peggy said, "He knows where every battery stood and where every mule got its ears shot off."[56] In recommending him to Kay on March 8, 1937, Peggy explained that Kurtz was one of the greatest authorities on the Civil War in that section and "had mapped out the position of the troops. He has a fine collection of early Atlanta pictures . . . if you wanted an honest to God expert on the War part of the picture you couldn't do better than kidnap Mr. Kurtz and take him to Hollywood."[57]

Kurtz really wanted to go to Hollywood, and he even campaigned for the job by writing to the president of the Atlanta Chamber of Commerce. Early in 1938, he was hired as the historian for the film, and his wife, Annie Laurie Fuller Kurtz, was also hired as an authority on rural Georgia accent. They went to Hollywood for three weeks in late January. Although he thought the movie people would ignore him, Kurtz found just the opposite to be true. They were pleased to have his assistance and respected him. Not long after he reached Culver City, Kurtz assured the Marshes that Selznick's desire for authenticity was genuine and described one of his first conversations with the producer:

> Mr. Selznick asked me, "What did Atlanta look like in 1862?" "Well," I said, "it had a population of something like ten thousand in 1860. It had a city hall of some architectural pretensions." The question I was answering was this: In what manner did Atlanta differ from any other Western town? He was thinking about the same kind of movie sets that are used in Wild West things. "A city hall of architectural pretensions. Three churches with tall spires pointing heavenward. Gaslight street illumination. Three-story buildings. And a car shed built

to accommodate the four railroads of Atlanta. A huge structure. . . ." "You say that's the car shed that is mentioned in the
novel?" "Yes sir." "Well, I thought it was one of those little
butterfly sheds that you see at railroad stations today." "No," I
said, "it was one hundred feet by three hundred feet long. It had
four railroad tracks running through it." He slammed his fist on
the table and said, "We'll build it."[58]

No one in Culver City, Kurtz said, had the faintest idea of what
Margaret Mitchell's reference to the car shed meant; they thought it was a
mere plank depot. But years earlier Kurtz had found the original plans of
this huge structure, designed by Edward A. Vincent, in an old trunk on
Washington Street in Atlanta. This car shed, built in 1854 and burned by
General Sherman's orders in November 1864, was the best known of
Atlanta's wartime landmarks.[59]

Peggy confessed she was "simply hopping with excitement" to hear all
about what was going on with the script, the sets, and the casting.[60] But she
complained to Kay that she only got news from Kurtz on his return visits
to Atlanta, when she could pick at him for information. "Wilbur is a close-
mouthed individual and would not even tell anything interesting over the
telephone . . . cautious Wilbur does not even trust the telephone operators."[61]
She pleaded sweetly with Kay to give her news about the casting of even
minor characters. "I'd love to know about them, and I would not spread
the news."[62]

The laconic Kurtz gave Peggy all the more reason for wanting the more
communicative Sue to hurry out to California. However, Sue was not hired
until nearly a year later. About her departure for Hollywood on January 5,
1939, Peggy wrote Kay: "John and I went out to the airport to tell her goodbye, thinking she might be a little lonely. Good Heavens, half of Macon was
there and the staffs of the two Macon papers. The airport restaurant was so
jammed with them that other travelers could get nothing to eat. I asked who
was getting out the *Macon Telegraph* that night and they replied that it
was in the hands of the office boy, the antique colored porter and Mr. W. T.
Anderson, owner and publisher."[63]

Although it took her nearly a year and a half, Peggy managed to place
three of her own friends in Hollywood on the *Gone With the Wind* set
when the film production began on January 26, 1939. The third person was
a former Atlantan, Marian Dabney, who was in charge of the women's
costumes in the wardrobe department. But only Sue Myrick was Margaret
Mitchell's eyes and ears.[64]

7

The first of Sue Myrick's newsy and entertaining letters arrived on January 11, 1939, and it did not disappoint the Marshes, who were anxious to get "all the inside dope." Sue wrote:

> Gosh, but I wish you were here so I could talk for ten hours. There ain't strength in my fingers to write all I'd like to say. And to your ears alone can I say the following. I have not written it to a soul and the studio is so secretive about it all I'm almost afraid to write it to y'all. But I have seen the gal who is to do Scarlett. I am even yet afraid to say her name aloud. Will Price and I speak of her in hushed tones as "That Woman" or "Miss X" and we have spent several mornings with her talking Southern just for her stage-taught ears. She is charming, very beautiful, black hair and magnolia petal skin and in the movie test I have seen, she moved me greatly. They did the paddock scene, for a test, and it is marvelous business the way she makes you cry when she is "making Ashley." I understand she is not signed but far as I can tell from George [Cukor] et al, she is the gal.[65]

By this time, the suspense about Scarlett's role was becoming intolerable for the public as other roles were being filled. Thomas Mitchell had been hired for Gerald O'Hara, and Butterfly McQueen, for Prissy. Warner Brothers released Olivia de Havilland to play Melanie. Hattie McDaniel, who had enjoyed reading *Gone With the Wind,* was delighted to have the role of Mammy. Although Leslie Howard thought he was too old to play Ashley, Selznick plied him with money and an offer to co-produce and act in *Intermezzo* once they finished *Gone With the Wind.*[66] On August 26, 1938, Selznick had announced that Clark Gable would play Rhett. But no Scarlett was in sight.

When somehow the word had gotten out that Margaret Mitchell had said a southern girl should play Scarlett, Atlanta's collective head had nodded yes and another giant commotion had broken out. The Atlanta Women's Press Club had announced that it wholeheartedly agreed with "Miss Mitchell's statement," and, as if they had any say in selecting the cast, had issued with pompous authority the following endorsement: "With a long background of Southern ancestry, her forebears among the distinguished Georgians in the Southern army, it is fitting that the South should see one of its favorite daughters, Miriam Hopkins, on the screen as Scarlett, the Georgia heroine of a Georgia story."[67]

It seems as though everyone had a favorite actress to play Scarlett.

Cukor wanted Katharine Hepburn, who coveted the part so badly that she was angry with RKO for not buying it for her. But Selznick imagined a much more "feminine, seductive, and younger woman," who was "shrewd but not bright . . . with the kind of beauty and sex appeal that would make Rhett Butler's twelve-year pursuit of her convincing to moviegoers."[68] Hepburn was not the only star who wanted the part. Keen competition came from Margaret Sullavan, Bette Davis, Miriam Hopkins, Paulette Goddard, Claudette Colbert, Libby Holman, Jean Harlow, Joan Crawford, Tallulah Bankhead, Dorothy Jordan, Loretta Young, Jean Arthur, and Joan Bennett.[69] At one time, Selznick thought that his best possibilities for the role of Scarlett were Jean Arthur, Loretta Young, Katharine Hepburn, and Paulette Goddard. But he really did not want any of them. He wanted a fresh face, one that movie audiences would not associate with other roles. He believed that his failure to find a new girl would be the great failure of his career.[70] As it turned out, he found that "fresh face" himself.

8

In England, confined to her bed with an ankle injury from a skiing accident, Vivien Leigh read the British edition of *Gone With the Wind* in December 1936. The 23-year-old beauty was so forcibly taken with Scarlett O'Hara and saw so many similarities between herself and the character that it seemed to her as if Margaret Mitchell created Scarlett with her in mind. With identical Irish-French ancestral backgrounds, they even looked alike. She set her heart on playing that role and began planning a way to capture Selznick's heart.

Her agent, John Gliddon, reminded her that she was under contract with Alexander Korda, who said he could not see the American public accepting her playing the role of a scheming, spoiled southern flirt.[71] Nevertheless, Korda agreed to say something to Selznick about it and to call attention to her role in *Fire over England,* which was to open in New York in March 1937. When Kay Brown, in New York, saw *Fire over England,* she instantly saw Scarlett in Vivien Leigh and excitedly wired Selznick about the actress. But he responded: "I have no enthusiasm for Vivien Leigh. Maybe I will have, but as yet have never even seen photographs of her."[72]

Selznick saw Vivien Leigh for the first time on the *Gone With the Wind* set, on the night he shot the stunning recreation of the burning of Confederate munitions in the Atlanta train yards. The meeting had been arranged by his brother, Myron Selznick, who was the American agent for Laurence Olivier. At that time, Leigh and Olivier were involved in a passionate love affair despite the fact that both were married to other people.

Around 11 P.M. on December 10, 1938, after the conflagration had been filmed and the flames were dying down, Selznick and Cukor, thrilled by the entire operation that they had manufactured, worked their way down from their thirty-foot observation tower. Myron, waiting with Leigh and Olivier, called out to his brother telling him he wanted to introduce him to Scarlett O'Hara. It was very cold that night, and Vivien Leigh was wearing a full-length dark mink coat and a dark hat that framed her beautiful face. The light from the dying flames illuminated her fair complexion and green eyes and highlighted the darkness of her long hair. Stepping forward as she extended her hand, she let her coat fall open, showing her beige silk dress, which emphasized her fragile slimness. With a lilt of laughter in her voice, she said, "Good evening Mr. Selznick."[73] After they stood in the chilly night talking for several minutes, Selznick took her by the arm and walked with her off the set toward his car.[74]

The next day, Selznick wrote his wife: "The fire sequence was one of the greatest thrills I have had out of making pictures, first because of the scene itself, and second because of the frightening but exciting knowledge that *Gone With the Wind* is finally in work. . . . Myron rolled in just exactly too late, arriving about a minute and half after the last building had fallen and after the shots were completed. With him were Olivier and Vivien Leigh. Shhhhh: She's the Scarlett dark horse, and looks damned good. Not for anybody's ears but your own: It's narrowed down to Paulette [Goddard], Jean Arthur, Joan Bennett, and Vivien Leigh."

Selznick later said, "When my brother introduced her to me, the dying flames were lighting up her face . . . I took one look and knew that she was right—at least as far as her appearance went . . . and right as far as my conception of how Scarlett O'Hara looked. . . . I'll never recover from that first look."[75]

As a veteran publicity man himself, John thought Selznick's two-year search for Scarlett and the other lead roles was "the best damn publicity stunt" he had ever seen.[76] With the final casting announcement of Vivien Leigh as Scarlett came the end of a nationwide search that involved fourteen hundred prospects, ninety screen tests, more than 142,000 feet of black-and-white film, and thirteen thousand feet of technicolor film—and all at a total cost of ninety-two thousand dollars.[77]

9

Around 9:00 P.M. on January 13, 1939, Peggy received a call from the Western Union clerk telling her that a long wire was on the way from David Selznick and that portions of it would arrive at fifteen-minute intervals. Wanting to avoid delay in delivery, Peggy and John hopped in their car and drove downtown to the Western Union office. In writing to Selznick the next day, she said:

> Three sheets telling about Miss Leigh had arrived by the time we reached the office; I knew our morning paper was going to press and of course I wanted the home town papers to have the break on this story, so I left John at the Western Union office to wait for the remainder and I went to the *Constitution* office. By good luck, they had a photograph of Miss Leigh and they tore out part of the front page, put her picture in, and began setting your wire. At intervals the rest of the wire came in. It was all very exciting and reminded John and me of our own newspaper days.

Peggy added that if she could judge from the reactions of the newspapermen she saw that night, the choice of Miss Leigh was an excellent one and so was the announcement of Olivia de Havilland. "For a bad five minutes it looked as if a picture of Miss de Havilland in a scanty bathing suit was going to appear in the morning paper, bearing the caption 'Here Is Melanie, a True Daughter of the South.' That picture was the only view of her the file clerk could find at first. I made loud lamentations at this, especially when the editor said, 'We can explain that Sherman's men had gotten away with the rest of her clothes.' Finally we found the sweet picture with the old fashioned bangs." She concluded, "I know that you must feel a great sense of relief this morning—a relief far greater than mine."[78]

That same night at the *Constitution* building, while Peggy was waiting for the story to be set up in type, John arrived waving a telegram and calling across the city room to her that she had a wire from Vivien Leigh. The city editor heard him, ran over and snatched the telegram out of John's hands, and dashed into the composing room with it. Peggy did not get to see it until two hours later.[79]

At first, many southerners did not like the idea of Vivien Leigh playing Scarlett. They were not looking forward to hearing some more of the "bogus Southern talk" that they had heard so often on the stage and screen. In the *Atlanta Journal* on January 20, 1939, Frank Daniel reported that the Dickinson Chapter of the United Daughters of the Confederacy celebrated General Robert E. Lee's birthday on January 19 by "deploring Vivien Leigh, and announcing the chapter's secession from Selznick International because that studio had chosen an English actress to play the Southern heroine of *Gone With the Wind*. . . . The Ocala Daughter, in a resolution, protested vigorously 'against any other than a native-born southern woman playing the part,' and added, 'we resolve to withhold our patronage if otherwise cast.'"[80] The ladies' objections broke into a national story.

Peggy was right when she told Sue Myrick, "It sometimes seems to me that *Gone With the Wind* is not my book any longer; it is something about which the citizens are sensitive and sore at real and fancied slights and discriminations and are ready to fight at the drop of a hairpin."[81]

Drawing from some of his own public relations tactics, John suggested that the Selznick company try to deflect some of the negative publicity about the English actors by having its own publicity department focus on all the good work that was being done by the southerners Sue Myrick and Wilbur and Annie Laurie Kurtz. John said, "Selznick needs to emphasize all that he is doing to make the film authentic. That'll get some heat off him." So Peggy conveyed that advice in a letter to Kay on January 21, 1939, adding, "Your publicity department has done nothing with them [Myrick and Kurtz] in the way of dramatizing them and showing just what good assistants Mr. Selznick has."

The intense interest the southerners had in *Gone With the Wind* may be difficult for some readers to understand. But in the 1930s, the United States population still divided itself up into Yankees and southerners. In a letter to Helen and Clifford Dowdey in 1938, Peggy wrote that when she read the title of an article the couple had written, "Are We Still Fighting the War?" she laughed aloud. In this letter, she gives us an excellent account of a southerner's view.

Ever since Roosevelt's Barnesville speech Senator George [Georgia's senator] and his supporters have been on the air. I have heard so many yells of "states' rights" and "Northern oppression" and "sinister centralization of power" and so many bands playing "Dixie" that I have wondered whether this was 1938 or 1861. I feel that if I look out of the window I will see the Confederate troops, headed by General John B. Gordon, marching toward Washington. When I read Heywood Broun's sneering remarks about Senator George "arousing sectionalism" and his other remarks about some Southerners acting as if Appomattox had never occurred I wondered whether he was just plain dumb. His ideas, and those of a number of Northern commentators of pinkish tinge, seem to be that Appomattox settled beautifully and peacefully and justly all the problems, economic and social, for which the South was fighting. Their idea seems to be that might made right in 1865. Common sense should show that many of the problems that sent us to war have never been settled, and the same injustices persist—tariff, freight rates, et cetera. As far as I can see, Appomattox didn't settle anything. We just got licked.[82]

The southerners' situation was, in some places, she thought, much worse than it had been then, and the same kind of problems were still raising their heads. That, she said, is what annoyed "Mr. Broun and his playmates. After all, when a section has been held in economic slavery for over seventy years that section should have the delicacy of feeling not to squawk."[83]

She had been reading Jonathan Daniels's book *A Southerner Discovers the South,* and she recommended that the Dowdeys read the section where Daniels compares "the South with Carthage and remarks that the Romans, after all, were politer than the Northern conquerors, for after they had sown Carthage with salt they never rode through it on railroad trains and made snooty remarks about the degeneracy of people who liked to live in such poor circumstances."[84]

10

As the lively search continued for actors for the minor roles, thousands of people clamored for even a bit part in the movie. Even Mrs. Eleanor Roosevelt got involved in the talent search when she wrote a letter to Kay Brown recommending her maid Lizzie McDuffie for the part of Mammy. A native Georgian, McDuffie was given a screen test, but the role went to Hattie McDaniel, who won an Academy Award for her performance.

Curious about the casting of supporting roles, Peggy wrote Kay: "Your item about the possible Prissy whetted my interest. I have been especially interested in who would play this little varmint, possibly because this is the only part I myself would like to play. For this reason, whoever plays Prissy will be up against a dreadful handicap as far as I am concerned, for I will watch their actions with a jealous eye."[85] She had confessed earlier that the only character that did not come out of her head was Prissy, who was based on an indolent young black servant Peggy had known.[86] The role went to Thelma "Butterfly" McQueen, to whom it brought instant fame. At first, McQueen was turned down for the part because, she was told, she was too old, fat, and dignified. (In the novel, Prissy is a skinny twelve-year-old when she is brought to Tara.) Although she did not like playing the charming but lazy, dim-witted slave, who is described in the novel as "a simple-minded wench," she thought the role her best and later said, "It paid well. I went through a full semester at U.C.L.A. on one day's pay."[87]

By the end of January 1939, the excitement about Vivien Leigh and the other British stars had subsided. Peggy assured Kay that the Selznick company need not worry now about the picture being boycotted, at least not in the South. After all, she aked, if southerners did not see the picture, how would they be in a position to criticize it?[88]

In January, Sue Myrick started writing her "Straight from Hollywood" columns, which appeared in the *Macon Telegraph* for six months (January 12 through July 13, 1939). She wrote more than two dozen articles about the filming of *Gone With the Wind* for the *Georgian*.[89] In these light narratives, she told how hard she and Wilbur Kurtz worked to keep Hollywood from making "Miss Mitchell's South a 'South That Never Was.'" But in her confidential letters to Peggy and John, she offered much more interesting accounts of the goings-on, such as Olivier's being banned from the set so he would not distract Leigh from her work, and Leigh getting so cranky that Selznick had to let her go spend weekends with Olivier. She told how starry-eyed she was about being introduced to Clark Gable, who was nicknamed "Dutch." She said the palm of Gable's hand was moist when she first shook hands with him. "He had a look of a man with so much red blood— so hot as it were—he couldn't help a little perspiration." She thought his hair was too long, his eyes very blue, and his lashes beautiful. "He wore a tan coat over a canary-yellow silk sports shirt, a tie of raspberry and yellow stripes and gray trousers and looked fresh washed."[90] She talked about how good natured and sweet Gable was and how everybody liked him.

Although she never wrote about Selznick's demanding personality in any of her newspaper articles, Sue told the Marshes about the time he insisted that Scarlett's hair hang down about her shoulders, and Hazel Rogers, the hairdresser, got so angry she threatened to quit if she had to make "Scarlett look like a floozy." Sue wrote, "She would have, too if I had not told George I thought the hair-do was terrible and not of the period and that Mammy and Ellen would have killed Scarlett before they'd have let her go out like that. So George made David change the hair dress and Hazel withdrew her resignation." One day in early April, Sue wrote Peggy that Walter Plunkett wanted her to know that he was doing his "damndest to have the costumes" as Peggy wished them, but that Selznick, determined to make the picture a sex affair between Rhett and Scarlett, demanded that Scarlett looked pretty no matter what.[91]

Always obliging about passing titillating gossip on to the Marshes, she wrote that Leslie Howard was "a tireless Ladies' man" whose current mistress was a pretty redheaded English girl, Violette Cunningham, whom he introduced as his "secretary" so that Selznick could not complain about her following Howard to the set every day.[92] About the makeup artist Monty Westmore, Sue wrote:

> He swears with every breath and knows all the stars and tells their worst points. Like all the other folks out here, he hates the guts out

of the actors and actresses and adores talking about their private lives and washing their very dirty linen for us while we roll on the floor with laughter. He told the other day about going to Mae West's apt to take measurements to make some wigs for her when he worked at Paramount. Mae's bed, he told us, is wide enough for six men to sleep in—then without a change of countenance he added 'no doubt six men had slept in it' and con'd the tale. . . . I'll tell you more that he told if I ever get back to Georgia.[93]

Sue's opinion of Russell Birdwell, Selznick's publicity man, who had irritated Peggy two years earlier, delighted the Marshes. Sue wrote, "Well, Birdwell is the revolving bastard if there ever was one. (The Revolving Bastard, in case you don't know, is a bastard any way you turn him.)" Referring to a draft of her newspaper column about the filming, she explained, "He kept my copy four days and edited the hell out of it."[94]

However, Sue liked all the stars and all the film crew. Laura Hope Crews, who played Aunt Pittypat to perfection, was one of her favorite people, and she adored 73-year-old Harry Davenport, who played Dr. Meade. He made all kinds of fun of the movies and of Selznick too and kept Sue giggling whenever she was around him. She told the Marshes: "He sounds just like a Confederate Decoration Day orator when he talks."[95] But Gable refused to talk "So'thern" and that was that. Although Leslie Howard picked up pronunciations of words quickly, he was not consistent in his usage. Olivia de Havilland had lots of trouble learning certain sounds in Georgia speech. Sue had her practice saying, "I can't afford a four-door Ford," and "I can't dance in fancy pants."[96]

Sue had much to say about Vivien Leigh's beauty and intelligence. In her diary, she recorded other, even more personal impressions, such as this one on March 3, 1939: "Vivien is a bawdy little thing and hot as a fire cracker and lovely to look at. Can't understand why Larrie Olivier when she could have anybody."[97] George Cukor agreed. Impressed with her, he thought Vivien fit Margaret Mitchell's description of Scarlett perfectly. "She was Rabelaisian, this exquisite creature, and told outrageous jokes in that sweet little voice."[98]

12

For all her blustering bravado about not wanting anything to do with the filmmaking, Peggy plied the Kurtzes, Myrick, and Brown for information about it. At one point Wilbur Kurtz's wife, Annie Laurie, casually mentioned something in a letter that, Peggy said, "turned my few remaining hairs white." She wrote a long letter to Sue on February 10, grousing:

She spoke of the bazaar scene with Scarlett and Rhett dancing together, and mentioned that Scarlett had on a bonnet and veil. In the name of God, what was she doing with a hat on at an evening party where everybody else was bareheaded and wearing low-cut gowns? My temperature jumped seven points at the news. I cannot imagine even Scarlett showing such poor taste.[99]

Five days later, the thought of that bonnet and veil were still festering in her mind, and she wrote Sue again: "The more I look at the picture of the bonnet and the veil that Scarlett was wearing at the bazaar the worse it gets. I suppose this must be one of the things that comes under the head of 'pictorial.'" And then a few days later, she wrote about it again, pleading with Sue, "If they do re-shoot the bazaar, I hope you get the bonnet off Miss Leigh."[100]

With great disdain, Sue replied, "The fools paid John Frederics of NY a hundred bucks for that bonnet and they are bound she'll wear it."[101]

Peggy's temperature soared again when she heard about Selznick's putting columns on Tara, making it and Twelve Oaks far too elegant to be historically authentic. North Georgia houses during the prewar period were not white-columned mansions. Over and over, she explained that the South was not a land of white-columned plantations surrounded by thousands of slaves humming and hoeing cotton as the plantation owners, dressed in white suits and broad-brimmed hats, sat on the porches watching and sipping mint juleps. She mused:

> When I think of the healthy, hardy, country and somewhat crude civilization I depicted and then of the elegance that is to be presented, I cannot help yelping with laughter. God forbid that Scarlett's Reconstruction house should be a poem of good taste. That would throw out of balance the whole characterization of the woman. Hurrah for George [Cukor] and Mr. Platt [designer for interiors] for standing up for a bad-taste house. Hobe Erwin [interior decorator] had some swell ideas on that house and we had a hot correspondence on wallpaper and many other details, including a perfectly ghastly gas lamp fixture which stood at the bottom of the stairs (my own idea), a large brass nymph, discreetly draped and bearing aloft the gas fixture.[102]

The Tara she had described in her book was a square house, built of whitewashed brick and set far back from the road, with an avenue of cedars leading up to it. It was built on a hill a quarter-mile from the river. Peggy had made certain that no such actual house existed, and said she located her

Tara on a road that she found on one of General Sherman's maps of 1864. "This road no longer exists and it has fallen to pieces and I had to travel it on foot."[103] She shuddered to think what Hollywood was going to do with her beloved Tara. A few days later, she read in the *Constitution* that the State Commission was building a replica of Tara to house the Georgia exhibits at the World's Fair. She was pleased and excited but also fearful that the commission would build a southern colonial house of the Greek Revival type, such as those in Milledgeville. On February 16, she wrote to Jere Moore, a member of the World's Fair Commission, thanking him and telling him her concerns. She pleaded with him not to call the house "Tara" if it were not a typical Clayton County house—"ugly and sprawling but comfortable looking." She explained: "This section of Georgia was so much newer than Middle Georgia and it was cruder, architecturally speaking. I wrote about hardy, hearty country people, whose civilization was only a few years away from the Indians."[104]

In closing, she added, "'Tara' was very definitely not a white-columned mansion. I am mortally afraid the movies will depict it as a combination of the Grand Central Station, the old Capitol at Milledgeville, and the Natchez houses of 'So Red the Rose.' I fear they will have columns not only on the front of 'Tara' but on the sides and back as well, and probably on the smokehouse too. But I can't do anything about that." Tara was real and dear to Peggy because in her mind it was the old Fitzgerald farm place, and she was sensitive to what others did to it. But despite Selznick's insistence on historical accuracy, he refused to have Tara look like a rustic farmhouse.

This was the only disagreement he and Kurtz had during the entire project. They finally compromised about Tara; instead of round columns on three sides, Selznick agreed to square columns, and in the front only. But Selznick refused to tone down Twelve Oaks, even though Kurtz told him and the production designer William Cameron Menzies, who had a genius for technicolor and composition, that such a house would not be found in Clayton County.[105]

13

In March, Peggy received a letter stating that Smith College, her alma mater, wished to bestow on her an honorary master of arts degree. Thrilled by the honor, she promised to attend the ceremony on June 12 in Northampton if no one asked her to make any speeches. "I have never been a speechmaker, I have made no speeches at all since July, 1936, and I do not accept invitations even to 'say a few words.'"[106]

As early as February 1938, organizations and individuals, convinced that the world premiere of *Gone With the Wind* would be in Atlanta, had started hounding Peggy and John for seats. "I really dread the months ahead until the picture has actually been produced," Peggy had written. "With interest already so high, this coming year may even be harder on us than 1936 was."[107]

By April 1939, John and Peggy had had about as much as they could stand hearing about the filmmaking business, the copyright pirates, and the mounting requests for seats at the premiere. He decided that they needed to get away for a few days. Although they preferred traveling in their own car, Peggy was too nervous to drive, so John made arrangements for them to go by train to the Gulf Coast, where they had never been before. On the day of their departure, a dozen interruptions at John's office, everything from a sudden downpour of rain to a traffic jam on their way to the station made them fear that they would miss their train. Away only a week, they returned to Atlanta because the weather turned so cold. Nevertheless, after the trip, Peggy felt much better. What they enjoyed the most, John wrote his mother,

> was the blessed relief of never hearing the telephone ring except two or three times when we asked the hotel to wake up us up in the morning, and of spending days at a time just being lazy.... We decided some time ago that we must learn how to mix rest periods into our work here in Atlanta, but we haven't succeeded at it, and it is only when we sever physical connection with our problems and get out of town that we can enjoy a real let-down from the never ending pressure of things that *must* be attended immediately. That is why our vacation journeys to places where we know nobody and nobody knows us mean so much to us these days.[108]

In this letter he did not mention anything about the movie, but he said that their collection of foreign editions had increased with the recent arrival of the Latvian translation. "Steve Mitchell says their language is nearer to Sanscrit than any modern language, so we are not likely to read it. Peggy's name on the jacket is 'Margreta Micela.'" He added, "I think I told you that the book had also been published in Japanese—without Peggy's permission. She had a letter a few days ago from the translator saying he was mailing her a copy. That also will be interesting, but not to read."

14

The Marshes loved getting glossy still pictures from Selznick, who was generous about sending them often. On February 15, Peggy wrote Sue: "The picture of Melanie in labor, with *Gone With the Wind* clutched to her and Scarlett anxiously cooling her brow, was wonderful. John says that the expression on Miss de Havilland's face is precisely the expression I wore during the time I was writing the book."[109]

During the filmmaking, keen attention was given to the actors' southern accents, and after each take the director would look at Sue and ask, "Okay for Dixie?"[110] Clark Gable and Leslie Howard were, according to Sue, the "worst offenders." Vivien Leigh and the other actors picked up the accent quickly. After awhile, Sue thought things got ridiculous when she received a memo from Selznick saying: "It is probably superfluous for me to remind you that the Yankee officer in the jail scene is not to be coached on Southern accent."[111] When she related this to the Marshes, Peggy responded: "John begs me to ask you not to lose the memorandum. . . . He says that he and I will believe such a thing but no one else will without documentary proof. We laughed about that all day too."[112]

The Marshes also laughed about another Selznick memorandum saying he understood that Miss Mitchell very strenuously objected to having blacks in the background singing. "He is utterly wrong about this," Peggy wrote Sue, "and I am so glad that you set him right by stating that I did not want the field hands to suddenly burst into song on the front lawn of Tara."

> John, not I, was the one who made this objection, but he spoke my ideas. He told George Cukor that everyone here was sick to nausea at seeing the combined Tuskegee and Fisk Jubilee Choirs bounce out at the most inopportune times and in the most inopportune places and sing loud enough to split the eardrums. And even more wearying than the choral effects are the inevitable wavings in the air of several hundred pairs of hands with [their] shadows leaping on walls.

She thought this kind of thing was appropriate in "Porgy but pretty awful in other shows where it had no place. I feared greatly that three hundred massed Negro singers might be standing on Miss Pittypat's lawns waving their arms and singing 'Swing low, sweet chariot, Comin' for to carry me home' when Rhett drives up with the wagon." As an afterthought she added, "By the way, speaking of musical scores—I hope they keep the music soft."[113]

Although the film crew was working under intense pressure long hours every day, they were a good-natured group with a sense of humor. The Marshes enjoyed reading about the pranks pulled on the actors to keep them from not taking themselves too seriously. One time, the cameramen hid percussive caps under boards that were to be nailed down; when the caps exploded, the grips yelled, "The Yankees are coming!" On April Fool's Day, when they were to shoot the scene at Aunt Pittypat's house where Rhett carries the sick Melanie downstairs to put her into the wagon for their flight to Tara, the laugh was on Clark Gable. When the star went to lift the small Olivia de Havilland in his arms, he was shocked because he could barely move her. Batting her eyelashes demurely as she looked up at him, Olivia asked, "Am I heavy?" Gable was dumbfounded until the crew started giggling, and he realized he had been tricked. When Olivia stood up, the several thirty-pound weights that had been hidden in the blanket wrapped around her dropped to the floor.[114]

15

It is ironic that the Golden Age of Hollywood (1931-40) coincided with a national economic depression. During this period many elaborate, expensive period films, or "costume epics," attracted a populace eager to escape from the Great Depression into such fantasy worlds as that of *Gone With the Wind.* Certainly, no one seeing Selznick's sets would have suspected the country was burdened as it was. Referring to Selznick's friend and business partner, Sue exclaimed: "May God have mercy on the soul of Jock Whitney and his money for I swear these fools are spending enough to make ten movies." She described the lavish castle the filmmakers had built for Twelve Oaks and the throng of extras they paid to decorate the lawn, the hall, and the piazza for the set. "There were 250 extras at the outdoor shots we made in Busch Gardens in Pasadena (incidentally the barbecue setting looked like the palace at Versailles) not including the twenty colored waiters and the cooks, the ten maid servants and five Mammys and ten little nigger chillun and fifteen white chillun! And that ten acre field of the Anheuser Busch gardens was stinkin with people and horses and tables and benches. And I bet Queen Mary hasn't as much royal silver [as] the Wilkeses had at that barbecue."

Knowing how the Marshes felt about such excesses, she went on to say,

You'd have died laughing if you could have seen my face when I went to inspect a plate they brought to show in a close up for Scarlett. I must have looked some of my disgust. On the plate was a bone about the size you'd feed a mastiff or a St. Bernard with a bit of meat clinging, a serving of potatoes that would have been enough for the Knights of the Round Table and a huge slice of cake—about the size of which you'd serve guests. I persuaded the prop man to remove the bone, put on a slice of meat, take off half the other stuff and then walked off the set and frowed up. I can't decide whether to bust into a sort of wild insane laugh about it all or to walk off the lot.[115]

Sue was "sticking it out" because she knew she was "stopping lots of mistakes and gross errors so the few score I can't stop I'll just try not to think about."

16

On February 15, the day director George Cukor walked off the set, Sue gave the Marshes the inside scoop. She explained that the problem resulted from the script, or lack of script. In May 1938 screenwriter Sidney Howard, weary of Selznick and the job, had left for New York. Selznick then hired a variety of other writers to work on the script—or rather, to write what he told them to write. Sue said that when Cukor compared the new version of the script to Howard's, "He groaned and tried to change some parts back to the Howard script. And Peggy, I swear on my word of honor that we often get a scene (say about 2 and half pages script) at five in the afternoon that we are to shoot tomorrow morning. . . . And how can George study scenes and plan out action when he doesn't know what he is to shoot some days until he comes on the set at 8 o'clock?" She went on to describe how Cukor told Selznick that he would quit if the script were not improved and that he wanted the Howard script back. "David told George he was a director— not an author and he (David) was the producer and the judge of what is good script (or words to that effect) and George said he was director and a damn good one and he would not let his name go out over a lousy picture [and] if they did not go back to the Howard script (he was willing to have them cut it down shorter) he, George, was through. And bull-headed David said 'O K get out!'"[116]

After Clark Gable's good friend Victor Fleming took Cukor's place, Sue wrote the Marshes, "Fleming seems a bright chap though he is a sour puss if I ever met one."[117] Although she grew to like and respect him too, Cukor remained her favorite.

The problems with the script continued as they all worked fourteen and eighteen hours a day. The arduous schedule made Fleming ill, and on May 2 he collapsed on the set. Sam Wood took over for a few days while Fleming recovered.

The script had been a problem from the start because Selznick was so enamored with the book that he wanted to use everything in it "just as Miss Mitchell had written it." On January 24, 1939, just two days before the principal filming began, he wrote Peggy asking for help with an important scene introducing Melanie at the barbecue. He asked if she would write dialogue for that scene because he wanted to bring "Melanie to life with the graciousness and sweetness and charm which we hope this character will possess."[118] In a long letter, Peggy answered "No . . . I can see your problem clearly. I am very sorry that I cannot help you with this problem."[119]

As late as May 1938, after Sidney Howard and Selznick had written several drafts, the script was far too long to film. The major problem with editing was Selznick's desire to keep everything in. He insisted on using Peggy's dialogue whenever possible.[120] Whenever her dialogue was cut out, he would put it back in. At this point, Howard left for New York. Then Selznick asked Hal Kern, his supervising film editor, to tell him how he thought it should be cut. After Kern's attempt, he got F. Scott Fitzgerald to work on a few scenes for a couple of weeks in January 1939. Having no patience with Selznick's insistence that only Mitchell's dialogue be used, Fitzgerald told Selznick that the script had too much of her dialogue in it already and pointed out, among other things, how the actor's expressions took the place of dialogue. When Peggy learned that F. Scott Fitzgerald was working on the script, she wrote: "If anyone had told me ten or more years ago that he would be working on a book of mine I would have been stricken speechless with pellagra or hardening of the arteries or something."[121]

Sue had explained that screenplays are written much the way chefs make soup. "The chef gets an idea from a soup he ate. He spends days making a stock that is just right. He tastes, adds seasonings, tastes again, adds again. Then he adds more things to it until he has the finest soup in the universe. Whereupon, he calls in other chefs and they all stand around and pee in it! And this, the treasonable ones of us seem to agree is what happened about GWTW."[122] It was little gems like this one that prompted Peggy to tell Sue what a great joy her letters brought her and John. "I know you'll have a crown in Heaven. . . . Your last one, which announced that Sidney Howard was back on the script, kept us laughing all day."[123]

But for Sidney Howard the script was no laughing matter. For two weeks in April, Howard was brought back for five hundred dollars a day, and he found the job as difficult as ever. "I have been working very hard and very long hours," he wrote his wife Polly on April 8.

> My job was to lay out the end and put it back in shape for shooting. Selznick is the same. He is obdurately refusing to cut the story or to condense and combine. . . . My difficulty in breaking away is

not going to be leaving the script unfinished because I can finish it easily and may even get it OKed. The jam I see ahead is the hypersensitive state of everything connected with the picture. I have never been placed in quite this position of having everybody come to me to take their trouble to David because I am the only person around who doesn't upset him. And he feels that and calls me in to listen to all manner of problems with which, as writer, I have nothing whatever to do. And I want to get home.[124]

Several days later, he described to his wife what he called "a miasma of fatigue" engulfing his environment. About Fleming, who had already collapsed from exhaustion on the set once, Howard wrote: "Fleming takes four shots of something a day to keep going and another shot or so to fix him so he can sleep after the day's stimulants. Selznick is bent double with permanent, and I should think, chronic indigestion. Half the staff look, talk and behave as though they were on the verge of breakdowns. When I have anything to say I have to phrase it with exaggerated clarity. I can stay on here almost indefinitely at $500.00 a day. Nothing would please Selznick more in spite of the fact that I persuaded him to let me go this Wednesday."[125]

Before Howard left, he told Sue the script was finished, adding that no doubt Selznick would rewrite it and would probably call him back from New York in a few weeks to rewrite it again. However, that was the last time Howard worked on the script. He did not live to see the film. He died in August 1939 in a tractor accident on his farm near Tryingham, Massachusetts.

Although their names are not listed in the screenplay credit, more than a dozen other gifted writers, including John Van Druten, Ben Hecht, Barbara "Bobby" Keon, Oliver H. P. Garrett, Charles MacArthur, Donald Odgen Stewart, John Lee Mahin, Val Lewton, Jo Swerling, Winston Miller, Edwin Justus Mayer, and F. Scott Fitzgerald contributed to the script. It is impossible to distinguish the work of each writer, and only Sidney Howard's name appears as the writer of the screenplay.

17

On June 27, 1939, five months and one day after the filming of *Gone With the Wind* began, it ended—except for some final shooting with bit players. It was completely finished on November 11, with 160,000 feet of film printed out of the 449,512 feet shot. The total cost was more than that of any other film in the history of Hollywood movie making— $4,085,790. Selznick's wife, Irene, described the film as "the longest running emergency on record."[126]

When Annie Laurie Kurtz returned to Atlanta, she brought Peggy a gift from one of the young women in the wardrobe department. Thinking that Miss Mitchell would like to have a memento of the film, the studio worker, after being told that Peggy had a predilection for little pillows, made her one by sewing together scraps of Scarlett's costumes.[127] Peggy was moved by the girl's thoughtfulness and kept the pillow in her rocking chair by the window in the living room.

By August, the news had come that the premiere of the movie would be held in Atlanta and also that Macmillan was getting ready to put out a paperbound edition of the book on the market coincidentally with the showing of the movie. Macmillan expected to sell two or three thousand copies. John wrote his mother that Atlanta was as excited about the premiere "as if America was about to be discovered again or the San Francisco earthquake was about to take place or something else of equal magnitude." He wrote that if it were possible to show the picture at the Georgia Tech stadium, he was confident it would be filled to its thirty-thousand-seat capacity.

> We spend our time telling people that we have ab-so-lute-ly nothing to do with the premiere, because we don't intend to stand the grief of placating all the folks who won't be able to get in, but a considerable part of the troubles are bound to roost on our doorstep anyhow. Tasmania or Tibet are the places where we would like to be for a month before and a month after the premiere, but the old sense of duty, the thing that has already caused us so many of the past troubles, will hold us here, I suppose, and I hope we live through it.[128]

Another thing that temporarily disrupted their lives was their move into the Della Manta apartments at 1268 Piedmont Avenue, apartment 3. For a long time they had needed more space, particularly, as John said to his mother, "ever since Peggy's book made it necessary for me to work here at home nearly seven nights a week and all week-ends and holidays." This new home gave him the extra room he needed for an office, and it also gave them a sort of separation between their living and working quarters. He wrote, "That's pretty important after years of trying to live in a clutter of papers, file cases, typewriters, and other mess." This apartment looked out on the woods north of Piedmont Park, Atlanta's biggest park, about eight or ten blocks from where they were living and "Over thataway," John said. "And so for the first time in our married lives we will be out from under the eyes of neighbors and can parade around in our bvd's at any hour of the day or night we please."[129]

All of the letters John wrote to his mother in 1939 reveal that he was under a tremendous strain. While Peggy fastened on all the minutiae about the filmmaking, John struggled with the foreign copyright problems and his work at the Power Company. On September 1, 1939, the day World War II began when Germany overran Poland, all he had to write was,

> I suppose I should be saying appropriate things about the war, but I am sorry to say that I haven't been able to get excited about it. This is partly because I have felt for a long time that a war was inevitable, that unless God struck Hitler down we mortals would have to pitch in and do it. But the principal cause of my disinterest is a phenomenon Peggy and I have noticed many times before and which we call "making molehills out of mountains." We have taken such a battering, emotionally and otherwise, it is difficult for us to get worked up about anything.[130]

Several weeks prior to the premiere, Peggy's physician told her that she needed surgery immediately to remove the abdominal adhesions that were causing her irregular vaginal bleeding and cramps. Having no other choice, she postponed the operation until after the premiere. Then, as if she did not have enough problems, a freak accident occurred while she was attending a luncheon given by the book buyer at Rich's department store. The purpose of the luncheon was to honor three southern novelists—Julia Peterkin, Marjorie Kinnan Rawlings, and Margaret Mitchell—all Pulitzer Prize winners. Among the distinguished guests were the president of Macmillan, George Brett, Jr., his sales manager, Alec Blanton, their wives, and Lois Cole and Allan Taylor. Peggy was the guest of honor, and just as she was about to sit down at the table, someone pulled back her chair, causing her to fall. This incident was not reported in the newspapers because the luncheon was not open to the press. Although she managed to joke about the mishap and made it through the luncheon, she was in terrible pain by the time she got home. The fall had seriously injured her spine.[131] Feeling helpless and discouraged when he saw her in such pain that evening, John decided to take her to Sea Island to rest so that she could build her strength for the premiere and for the surgery she was facing.

She was just one of life's casualties. Too many things were stacked against her for her to get well, John wrote his mother pessimistically, "even with my fighting folks off of her." In this letter on November 22, 1939, he announced, "If we live through December, we will feel that we have scored a triumph, for Atlanta has gone plumb crazy."[132] The theater where the picture was to be shown had only two thousand seats, "whereas several times that number are determined to see the film on its first night. That has been one of the principal causes of our trouble. By telephone, telegraph, letter, and personal pleading, we have been importuned to get seats for friends, relatives, and total strangers."

He also told her that the big social event was the Junior League Charity Ball to be given the night before the premiere. Clark Gable, Vivien Leigh, and all the other stars were to attend. However, he did not mention that Peggy refused to attend the affair being given in her honor. Although Peggy maintained a friendly attitude toward members of the League and never openly displayed any petty resentment, she remembered all too well how the Junior League had rejected her. Now it was her turn to reject them.

18

Always an observer, John liked to stand back and watch people, and the line of people waiting to buy tickets to the movie fascinated him. A couple of times during the days before the premiere, he walked around to where the line had formed and followed it completely around the four sides of a large city block and down the next block. He wrote his mother, "It's interesting to see the expression of relief on their faces when they actually get the tickets in their hands."[133]

Peggy had declined George Brett's and Macmillan's invitation to give her a grand party the night of the premiere. In a six-page letter, she described the hundreds of other invitations she had refused, and the one she accepted. Having joined only one organization, the Atlanta Women's Press Club, because the members were all active newspaper women and old friends of hers, she was only going to attend the club's small, informal party. No gaudy Hollywood affair with spotlights, champagne, and ballyhoo for her. All of her family, the managing editors of the three papers, the mayor and the governor, Selznick, Kay Brown, and any members of the cast who wished to attend were invited. She asked, "Cannot you and any others of the Macmillan folks who come to Atlanta be the guests of the Press Club party?" Assuming her modest southern lady persona, Peggy wrote:

> I accepted it . . . partly because of old friendships, partly because of my obligations to the members of the club, but chiefly because of the nature of the party they were planning—one that would be simple, unpretentious and in good taste. . . . If they had been planning a Hollywoodish kind of party I would not have accepted, even for my oldest and dearest friends.

About Atlanta's feelings, she said:

I do not believe that you or anyone outside of Georgia can realize how strongly Atlanta feels about this whole situation. In your letter, you referred to the premiere as "Selznick's show." I don't believe Atlanta people feel that way about it all. Mr. Selznick will put on the show, of course, but the premiere will be *Atlanta's* night, not Selznick's. Long ago, I gave up thinking of *Gone With the Wind* as my book; it's Atlanta's, in the view of Atlantans; the movie is Atlanta's film; and the premiere will be an Atlanta event, not merely the showing of a motion picture. From the way things are shaping up, my guess is that it will be one of the biggest events in Atlanta's modern history.[134]

19

Scheduled for Friday, December 15, the premiere caused a tidal wave of excitement that was without precedent for premieres. In speaking with Selznick over the telephone in early December, John advised him to be prepared for the worst—for "'a kindness and hospitality' that could kill and a city for which the premiere would be 'the major event of modern times.'"[135]

The celebration began on Wednesday, December 13, as the stars and celebrities started arriving by plane and train. There was a motorcade from the airport to the Georgian Terrace. Howard Dietz and Howard Strickling, publicists from MGM, arrived first to help Selznick's publicity man, Russell Birdwell, convert Atlanta into one huge, live advertisement for *Gone With the Wind.* Atlanta's own Evelyn Keyes, who played Scarlett's sister Suellen, was already in town visiting with her family. Ann Rutherford, who played Scarlett's sweet youngest sister, was the first actor to arrive in the city. Then came Laura Hope Crews, "Aunt Pittypat," in an appropriate state of palpitations because the train in which she was riding had been in a slight accident. On that same day (Wednesday) arrived David Selznick and his wife Irene Mayer, Vivien Leigh and her companion Laurence Olivier, Olivia de Havilland, Ona Munson (Belle Watling), and Alicia Rhett (India Wilkes). Also with Selznick's party were a number of the film's supporting actors and some celebrities, including Claudette Colbert, who was not in the movie but was an enormously popular star at that time. They were followed by Jock Whitney, Merian Cooper, and other Selznick International and MGM executives, their families, staffs, and crews. All the while, politicians and dignitaries kept pouring into the city. The very last ones to appear were Clark Gable and his wife Carole Lombard. They arrived at 3:30 P.M. in a specially chartered plane that had the words "MGM's *Gone With the Wind*" printed on its sides, much to Selznick's disappointment.

Leslie Howard and Hattie McDaniel were the only two major actors who did not come to Atlanta for the event. Howard, who had returned to his home in England after the war started, sent a telegram apologizing to Peggy for his absence. The great star who played Mammy, Hattie McDaniel, simply chose not to visit the segregated city, where she could not stay in the same hotel nor eat at the same table with the white actors. Sadly enough, none of the other black actors had been invited.[136] Also absent was Victor Fleming, who said that he was attending the funeral of his old friend Douglas Fairbanks, Sr., even though rumors had it that Fleming was in fact angry with Selznick for saying in a news release that five directors worked under the producer's direction on the film.[137]

Since they were late in arriving, Gable and Lombard were rushed directly from the airport to the starting point of the motorcade nearby, where the other stars had been kept out of sight until Gable's arrival. Watching for the thirty convertibles carrying the stars and the celebrities, people were standing six deep at the curb for the full nine miles from the airport in Hapeville to Five Points downtown. One source estimated the crowd as over 650,000. In 1939, the population of Atlanta was three hundred thousand, and it more than doubled for this event. The crowd followed the motorcade, which ended in front of the Georgian Terrace at the corner of Peachtree Street and Ponce de Leon Avenue, less than a mile from the business district. Welcoming the guests were Mayor William B. Hartsfield; Governor E. D. Rivers; the city councilmen; Kay Kyser, the orchestra leader whose band played for the Junior League Charity Ball that Thursday night; and the four surviving Confederate veterans of the Battle of Atlanta. Noticeably absent were Margaret Mitchell and her husband John Marsh.

All the celebrities were gracious but curious, asking, "When can we meet Margaret Mitchell?"[138] Later that night, David Selznick, his wife Irene, Olivia de Havilland, Vivien Leigh, and Laurence Olivier did meet Peggy and John in a private visit at the Marshes' apartment. All the film people were as thrilled to meet Peggy as she was to meet them. They all mentioned her modesty and her generosity. One of the little-known but thoughtful things that Peggy and John did was to have azaleas placed in the hotel rooms of every visiting guest. Peggy also sent a telegram to Hattie McDaniel telling her how sorry she was that "Mammy" was not there for the premiere.

Peggy was afraid to leave the apartment because so many people had descended upon her, pleading for tickets to the premiere or, if not that, for invitations to meet the stars. As strange as it may seem, she simply was not given that many tickets; the few she had she doled out carefully to the family first and then to those closest to her and John, like Margaret Baugh and Rhoda Kling. Newspapers reported that sixty thousand people wanted tickets at ten dollars each, but the theater could seat only 2,051, so people were frantic to get tickets through Peggy. She was actually afraid to go into Rich's department store to shop for a dress to wear to the premiere; John went instead and selected an outfit for her, finally finding her right size, a nine junior, in the teen department.

All the Atlanta newspapers reduced the European war front news to secondary status because of the premiere and carried articles similar to the one in the *Constitution* on December 17, 1939, about Peggy's premiere gown. The dress had a tight-fitting bodice with rows of tiny pleats leading to a sweetheart neckline, and a bouffant skirt made of layers of blush pink tulle over a slip of pale pink crepe. John also bought her a pair of long white kid gloves, a white velvet evening purse, and a lovely, long, white velvet, princess-style evening coat that was threaded with gold and silver and buttoned from the neckline to the waistline with covered buttons. He asked the clerk to find him a narrow, satin pink ribbon for Peggy's hair and a pair of silver slippers, size four. For the final item, he purchased a large diamond, which he had fastened into a platinum pin, the only jewelry that he had ever heard Peggy say she wanted.

The night before the premiere thousands of fans crammed tightly at the intersection of Peachtree Street and Ponce de Leon Avenue, straining to see the celebrities assembled on the platform in front of the Georgian Terrace. Dressed in a ten-gallon hat and a jimswinger coat, Lambdin Kay, the manager of Atlanta's first radio station, WSB, announced the names of the guests for this program, which was nationally broadcast.

In the front-row seats on the platform were Atlanta's popular Mayor William B. Hartsfield and the governors of Georgia, Florida, Alabama, South Carolina, and Tennessee. Limousines had delivered the movie stars to a side entrance of the hotel on Ponce de Leon Avenue so they could enter the lobby and walk onto the platform to be introduced one at a time. The supporting actors were introduced first, and by the time Olivia de Havilland came out, and then Vivien Leigh, the crowd had reached a pitch of excitement; when they saw Leigh they gave her a resounding, authentic rebel yell, screeching as high and hard as they could. And when Clark Gable appeared, it became obvious that he was their favorite. A newspaper reporter stated that when Clark Gable appeared in the "December dusk, the thousands, who had waited so cheerfully while they stamped their feet in the penetrating cold, broke into a roar of adulation." Barely heard over applause, Gable spoke into the microphone, saying he wanted to pay tribute to Margaret Mitchell for writing the book that had brought them all together. He added that he hoped to have the honor of meeting her while he was in Atlanta. No doubt, he and the others expected to meet the author that very night at the Junior League Charity Ball. They did not know that Peggy had declined her invitation to the ball.

After a thunderous applause for all the stars, Mayor Hartsfield said, "Words can't express the pride I feel in Atlanta and her people." After the brief speeches were made, the celebrities went to their suites to rest, eat dinner, and change into evening clothes. Meanwhile, the parade moved slowly down to the Atlanta Municipal Auditorium, site of the Junior League ball. The front of the auditorium was covered with Confederate colors and flags, and one huge United States flag was draped above the marquee. The auditorium was made to look like the Confederate bazaar in the book and the film. Reminding Atlantans of their city's rise from the destruction heaped upon it by the Civil War was a fifteen-foot representation of Atlanta's seal with its phoenix and motto, "Atlanta Resurgens." Six thousand guests dressed in formal attire or Confederate costumes attended this ball. The smooth music from Kay Kyser's orchestra inside the auditorium swelled the air and mingled with the crowd's applause outside as each movie star stepped out of a limousine.

Gable and Lombard went with Mayor and Mrs. Hartsfield and the four of them occupied a box together. Accidentally left behind at the hotel, Olivia de Havilland arrived dramatically with a police escort just about the time the master of ceremonies, Major Clark Howell, editor and publisher of the *Atlanta Constitution,* was about call her name. Instead of taking the time to go around to the box entrance in the back of the building, de Havilland, escorted by Edmund Miller, the night auditor at the star's hotel, and Jack Malcolm, a police officer, hurriedly walked directly to the box where she was to sit with Vivien Leigh and Laurence Olivier. The police officer lifted de Havilland up to Olivier, who in turn lifted her effortlessly over the railing and into the box, delighting the audience, which cheered happily and loudly.

First on the program was a performance by the black choir from the Ebenezer Baptist Church, and then there was a parade of the debutantes in antebellum costumes. As the master of ceremonies introduced the celebrities, ceiling spotlights beamed on them, and each one stood up to receive recognition. Not one of the actresses was dressed in a period costume; they all must have figured that Atlantans wanted some Hollywoodish glamour, and so it was glamour that they put forth, with their lavish gowns that outlined their beautiful figures.

Although Peggy's brother and his wife attended the ball, Peggy and John stayed away. What the Marshes did or thought that night is not known, but on the afternoon of the premiere, Peggy and John attended the Atlanta Women's Press Club tea party, held at the Piedmont Driving Club, just across the street from the Marshes' new apartment. In addition to all the members of the Press Club, the actors, the screen executives, the Macmillan executives, and the mayor and governor were also invited. Peggy wore a tailored black dress that set off her shapely figure, and a black felt hat that had a large, stiff, black velvet bow on top. When John saw her dressed, he thought she looked exceptionally pretty and teased, "Godalmighty, you look like you got on rabbit ears!"[139]

Looking as if they were doing nothing more than going to visit a neighbor, John and Peggy held hands as they strolled across the street to the Piedmont Driving Club to the party honoring her. A national magazine photographer, waiting outside on the steps, did not recognize Peggy but realized that she was going to the party. He asked her to help him get inside so that he could snap a photograph of Margaret Mitchell. Peggy winked at John, turned to the photographer, and said, "Why I am Margaret Mitchell. Go ahead and get your picture now." The disbelieving man replied, "Yeah, lady, thanks a lot." Peggy shrugged her shoulders and she and John walked ahead. The photographer finally made his way into the front hall of the club and created a commotion with the men in charge. They were about to throw him out when he discovered that the lady with whom he had just spoken really was Margaret Mitchell. He clenched his jaw and cursed himself as Peggy beamed smilingly at him. Feeling sorry for him, she broke away from the crowd and allowed him to take some pictures of her.[140]

In a few seconds, Clark Gable appeared and drew her aside into a nearby ladies' room, where he locked the door so that they could talk privately. They were together for about ten or fifteen minutes. When he reappeared, he was obviously taken by the old Mitchell charm, for he kept repeating afterwards, "She is the most fascinating woman I've ever met." And Peggy told reporters, "He's grand, perfectly grand!"

20

As Harold Martin, a columnist writing for the Atlanta *Georgian* on December 16, 1939, stated: "Nowhere in the world, was a picture shown to an audience more spiritually suited to receive it. It was not the glitter and the fanfare that made it great. Nor the array of visiting dignitaries. . . . It was the spirit which gripped the crowd." That spirit was evident everywhere in the city. The three days before the premiere were unofficial holidays filled with parades, bands, fancy dress balls, dances, speeches, costume contests, and box lunches in the parks. But December 14, the day of the big *Gone With the Wind* parade featuring all the movie stars, was declared by the governor of Georgia an official state holiday—"Premiere Day." The Atlanta newspapers carried front-page stories about the premiere, not about the war front, for those three days. The city was filled with hundreds of people dressed in salvaged Civil War clothes proudly walking the streets day and night. A lamplighting ceremony took place at 10:15 A.M. at the corner of Whitehall and Alabama streets, where the single lamppost that had withstood Sherman's siege was lit in commemoration of the Confederate dead. Selznick's publicity people had done their job superbly well: they had placed Confederate flags and huge posters of the stars in all the storefront windows, and had built in front of the Loew's Grand Theater a facade of Twelve Oaks. Placed high in the center front, between the fourth and fifth stories of the Loew's, was an enormous oval picture of Scarlett looking up adoringly at Rhett.

On the night of the premiere, a crowd of nearly eighteen thousand gathered in front of the Loew's Grand Theater, and two thousand were seated inside. When Gable stepped up to the microphone, he grinned and told the crowd, "Tonight I am here just as a spectator. This is Margaret Mitchell's night." Then Peggy stepped out of Selznick's limousine and spoke a brief greeting into the microphone while John stood in the dark behind her. She simply thanked everyone and hurried toward the theater. No one paid any attention to John following her until Julian Boehm, who was the announcer for the evening, recognized him and pulled him back, asking him, "Aren't you proud of your wife, John?" Smiling, John replied grandly, "I was proud of her even before she wrote a book."[141]

When the Marshes entered the packed theater, the audience gave Peggy a rousing standing ovation. As the lights faded out, the curtain rose, and the music filled the air, Peggy became so overwhelmed by emotion, she began to cry. With his own heart pounding so loudly that he thought people around him could hear, John reached into his back pocket and handed her his handkerchief. Tears streamed down her face as she watched her name appear in huge letters on the screen: "Margaret Mitchell's *Story of the South.*" Then in a grand, rolling movement came that beautiful title—*Gone With the Wind*—in letters so huge that each word momentarily filled the entire frame of the screen. The words were spelled out in front of beautiful, carefully selected southern scenes. The audience went wild, cheering, screaming Rebel yells, jumping out of their seats, stamping their feet, laughing, and clapping uproarishly. Peggy turned to John, shook her head in disbelief, and he nodded in disbelief too. She reached for his hand and held it tightly throughout the entire picture.[142]

After the film was over and the lights in the theater were turned on, the audience cheered wildly and applauded for several minutes. All that Julian Boehm, the announcer on the stage, said before he turned the program over to the mayor was, "God bless our little Peggy Marsh." With those words, the audience began stamping its feet and applauding. Boehm turned the microphone over to Mayor Hartsfield, who kept waving his arms trying to get the crowd silent, as he called for Selznick and the stars to come to the stage. Then, according to Harold Martin, "the place tightened up till you could hear the breathing and he asked Margaret Mitchell to come down."

As Gable and Leigh escorted her to the stage, the applause that went up was clearly for Peggy alone. She never looked more beautiful or radiant than she did that night as she walked energetically up the steps, exuding youth and confidence. Julian Boehm reached out his hand to grasp Peggy's while with his other hand, he handed her a corsage of pink camellias. Martin wrote, "Her face was white and her eyes were big, and you could tell she was under a strain almost unbearable." But her voice, he said, was steady as she began to speak softly and slowly into the microphone. The theater fell silent as she spoke:

> Friends, and I know that more than three fourths of you here tonight are friends of mine, I want to say just this. Nobody needs to be told the value of friendship and consideration, shown to one in adversity. But from my heart I tell you that its value can be greater to one who has experienced the incredible success that I have. To all of you here—and to many who aren't, to the man at the grocery, the boys at the filling station, the folks on the newspapers—I want to say, thanks for your kindness. Of this picture, I feel that the only expression adequate for use is that one made trite by usage many times. We have just come together through a great emotional experience. I know it was to me. And I know I'm not the only one whose eyes have been wet tonight.
>
> I want now to say a word about the man who made this picture. All of you, I know, heard the jokes about the search for Scarlett—"I'll see the picture when Shirley Temple gets old enough to play the role," and all that sort of comment. But I want to pay my tribute to David O. Selznick, for his stubbornness and determination in getting the Scarlett he wanted. He wanted a perfect cast, and to my mind, he got it. You've all been most kind to me. Now, please that the picture's here at last, be kind to my Scarlett.[143]

After making this simple speech, Peggy, looking so small standing next to Gable, fell silent. She stared out into the crowd as if she wanted to savor the moment. Then, she lifted her arm and waved her hand over her head to the audience. When the audience saw her wave, the percussion of the applause was deafening.[144]

1940-1945

*P*ATRIOTIC VOLUNTEER

Within just a few weeks, one phase of the world's history has definitely ended and another has begun. Everybody is an old timer now who can say "I remember when people thought Hitler was a joke." Times have changed, almost overnight, and I hope that all of us, and our country, can survive the change.

—John Marsh to his mother, 17 June 1940

1
_____

ON SUNDAY AFTERNOON, December 17, with help from the manager of the Loew's Grand Theater, the Marshes slipped through the back door of the theater to see *Gone With the Wind* for the second time. They liked it even better than they had the first time because they were able to view it more objectively. They thought Vivien Leigh was "devastatingly beautiful" and "magnificent" as Scarlett, and they were delighted with the performances of Clark Gable and all the other actors.[1] Leslie Howard was not quite as strong an Ashley as Peggy had imagined and Prissy not quite as young, but they made their characters come alive nonetheless.[2] Although they did not like the rolling prologue's description of the South as "A Land of Cavaliers and Cotton," they figured it was useless to protest that Peggy never intended to write about cavaliers and that all of her characters, "except the Virginia Wilkeses, were of sturdy yeoman stock."[3] She believed that southerners could write about the antebellum South as it really was—"with few slaveholders, yeomen farmers, rambling, comfortable houses just fifty years away from log cabins, until Gabriel blows his horn—and everyone would go on believing in the Hollywood version."[4]

The opening scene in the film they thought was "a little stagy," but they were pleased with the treatment of the southern accent. None of the actors used "y'all" when speaking to one person and none spoke, Peggy said, as if he had "a mouth full of hot buttered okra."[5] Sue Myrick had, indeed, done miraculous work. The Marshes said nothing negative publicly or privately to their families about the film except that they regretted the profusion of white columns Selznick put on all the Georgia plantation homes. "North Georgia homes were plantation plain. . . . North Georgia wasn't all white columns and singing darkies and magnolias. . . . But people believe what they like to believe and the mythical Old South has too strong a hold on their imaginations to be altered by the mere reading of a 1,037 page book," she bemoaned in a letter to a friend.[6]

Seeing the movie quietly for the second time gave John and Peggy the opportunity to notice many things that they missed entirely at the first showing, as he explained to his mother:

> That first night we not only had our own strains and tensions from
> being in an unbelievable situation, but we picked up some of Mr.
> Gable's tensions. He was so anxious for the thing to be a success,
> and we couldn't keep our minds on the picture for wanting to tell
> him, "There, there, Captain Butler!" If that sounds funny, try to
> imagine yourself sitting next to a man who had staked his career,
> almost, on that one role, while the film was having its premiere
> before the audience whose good opinion mattered most to the
> world. It was not a kindly thing to seat him next to us, or us next
> to him. And when it was over, we were truly happy we could tell
> him, honestly, that we like his work.[7]

In this same letter to his mother, who had not yet seen the film, John
said that she would be impressed with the fact that Selznick had succeeded
in making it southern. "It isn't North Georgia, and there are some gauche
Hollywoodisms, especially in making the homes too ornate, but the
southern atmosphere is there. . . . I don't intend to write a review of the film,
and what I have written is for the family *only,* but I must say one thing. Be
sure to watch Mammy. She does a fine job."

2

On Monday morning, December 18, as John was doing all the cleanup
jobs that had to be done after the premiere and Peggy was downtown
making preparations for their vacation, their apartment building caught fire
at about eleven o'clock. The fire started in the basement directly beneath
their glassed-in porch, where John was dictating a letter to Margaret Baugh.
The flames only missed getting into their apartment by inches and were
close enough to blister the paint on the baseboards of the porch. When John
and Margaret saw the sudden bales of smoke outside the window, the first
things he said he, Margaret, and Bessie carried out were his files, not
Peggy's fur coat. "If I had lost the four-year record of my work as Peggy's
business manager, it would have been catastrophic."[8] As it turned out,
smoke and water damaged some of their things in a storage bin in the
basement, but nothing important was ruined.

Badly in need of a real rest, they left Atlanta the next day. Knowing
how the Western Union office broadcast all of his and Peggy's telegrams,
John did not send his mother a Christmas greeting or any information about
where he and Peggy could be reached, so their exact destination is not
known. However, his family and those closest to the Marshes at Georgia

Power knew that the cabin in the woods near Tallulah Falls was their secret hiding place, and with all of the newsreels and newspaper pictures of Peggy at that time, it is likely they would have been afraid to go anywhere else. About those newsreels, John told his family in early January 1940 that MGM planned to present Peggy with a film of all the material their newsreel cameramen had shot during the premiere, between two and three thousand feet of it. The newsreel that had been shown in the theaters ran only about two hundred feet.[9]

Before he left town, he had sent his mother dozens of copies of newspapers containing articles and pictures of the week's events. While on his vacation, he wrote her a long letter on December 20, describing the highlight of the premiere.

> Atlanta's wonderful ovation to her when we entered the theater and at the end of the performance was so heartwarming . . . her speech hit just the right note apparently, for everybody praised it . . . the audience really went wild. What pleased us most was not the acclaim itself, but the proof it gave that the hard work we have done has borne fruit. Instead of making enemies, she has apparently grown in public respect by her determination to remain herself in spite of the book's success (and "remaining" in that sort of situation is about the toughest job in the world—not because *you* want to be different but because the public is determined that you shall be different.) When we finally got home from the theatre, about 1 o'clock in the morning, we were so happy that it was all over and that milestone had finally been passed, we did something practically unprecedented in our modern lives. We went to two, not one, so-called after-the-premiere "breakfasts" and didn't get to bed until 6 a.m.

Later, when the picture was in its fifth week in Atlanta and still playing to sold-out houses, John noted that he had never been past the theater when there was not a line of people at the ticket window. The booksellers told him that film lovers were buying the newly published, 69-cent premiere paperback edition of the book as quickly as the volumes were placed on the bookstore shelves.[10]

3

On Saturday, January 13, 1940, Peggy entered Piedmont Hospital for surgery to remove abdominal adhesions; it was surgery that she had been putting off for nearly a year—until after the premiere. Her surgery went well, but while she was on her way to recovery, John came down with a severe case of the flu that he could not seem to shake. After three weeks of running a persistent but low temperature and feeling so ill that he could not keep up with his work, he entered St. Joseph's Infirmary. Tests showed that he had high blood pressure. Living on a treadmill that spit out one deadline after another, plus plenty of nicotine, spelled coronary heart disease.[11]

Although his fever vanished after he rested a week in the hospital, his vitality and strength did not return. Peggy told his mother, "I think rest will do wonders for him, and I wish so fervently he could have a long one."[12] Knowing how intensely driven John was, his physician, Dr. W. C. Waters, urged him to cut back on his fifty-to-sixty cigarettes a day and to play some golf. He was convinced that John's present problems were largely due to physical exhaustion and emotional strain. He reminded him that two years earlier he had warned him to cut back on his smoking and his work because his body was pointing out in more than one way that it was being pushed too hard. This time, Dr. Waters told him and Peggy outright that if John did not take radical steps to slow down, the consequences would be dire.[13]

John's thinness, listlessness, and the depression that showed through his pale blue eyes as they both listened to the doctor made Peggy weep. She knew now for certain that he could not continue his late-night and weekend work on the foreign copyright business and keep up with his daytime job, too. As she explained to his mother, for four years he had worked all day at the Power Company and most of the nights and weekends at home. They seldom had time to go to the movies or have friends in because "visitors at night mean that we have to start our work after they leave, and frequently John works till four o'clock."[14] Drastic changes had to be made in their lives. After Dr. Waters left, Peggy sat on the edge of John's bed and told him she wanted him to resign from Georgia Power so that he could concentrate solely on his *Gone With the Wind* business. Taking care of the foreign copyrights was clearly a full-time job that only he could do, but others could do his work at the Power Company.

A few days later, in explaining his situation to his mother, John wrote:

The story is briefly this—For four years I have been working day and night, almost literally seven days a week. It hasn't broken me yet, but the doctors say it is certain to break me if I keep it up much longer. So I am taking the only step open to me. I can't quit my "M. Mitchell job." So, I am quitting the one I can quit. I will still have a full-size job; I merely won't be trying to do two men's work, won't be breaking my back trying to do the impossible, will have enough to keep me busy but with sometime left over for recreation and diversion and for getting my health built up again. And for seeing my folks, too![15]

He and Peggy had always kept thinking that his "M. Mitchell job" would end. "Always we think that if we can get over the top of the hill we are climbing, our troubles will be over and always there are more hills beyond."[16] He did not now need Dr. Waters to tell him that he was on a timetable of destruction; his chest pains told him eloquently enough. For the first time ever, he admitted to his mother that he was seriously sick: "In the past several months, I have been getting pretty discouraged about the never-endingness of the 'M.M.' job, but it was the mysterious temperature of recent weeks that finally brought things to a head. . . . Any rate, I reached the state of mind where I was ready to quit, resign, give up my job entirely, anything to get a little rest."[17]

Then, he went on to say that Mr. Arkwright, who "took a fair and generous view," refused to let him resign and, instead, offered him a year's leave of absence. John accepted this offer only on the condition that he would not be on the payroll. Feeling as if he had imposed enough on the company, he wrote:

> Home work has interfered with my Company work for some time and has taken time and energy which my regular job would normally have gotten. So I wouldn't have felt right about taking such a long vacation on pay. I am happy enough to know that the job is there waiting for me when I am in shape to go back to it, for my thoughts about resigning were not because of any desire to cut loose entirely. I felt definitely nervous about the possibility of having no job, and it was quite a relief when Mr. Arkwright offered me the leave of absence."[18]

Oddly enough, John never considered his work on the book as a real job; he always viewed it as just a way of helping Peggy. In his mind, his real job was at Georgia Power, and his identity was so intricately tied into his work there that he found it painful to let it go.

4

Peggy had John as buffer between her and the world, but John had no such protection. As the months rolled into years and the book's business increased instead of diminishing, he had a pervasive feeling of hopelessness and helplessness. Although he always seemed calm—everyone spoke of his calmness—he was in a constant state of vigilance, always challenged by the fear that he was going to lose all control of their lives.

His illness in early 1940 was precipitated by a run-in he had with George Brett that began a few months before the film was released. The trouble started when Brett asked Peggy to make concessions on her royalties. He felt as if he were taking a huge risk publishing the 69-cent paperback and also a two-dollar hardback, especially since Selznick had refused to let him use movie stills, which he believed would enhance the book and make it more marketable. Therefore Brett asked that she agree to a 50 percent cut in her royalty. John thought that Brett's request unfairly violated Peggy's contract, and he was only willing to trade on any proposition that would be to the advantage of both parties—Macmillan and Mitchell.[19] If Brett wanted to deviate from the contract and ask Peggy to make concessions in order to help him out with his gamble, then Brett should make concessions too, and should offer to make them. John scolded the publisher: "It is not right for you to put me in the embarrassing position of having to ask for them each time."[20]

Several very frank and angry letters shot back and forth between them. In his last letter to Brett, John explained, "The whole thing is a matter of principle with me, a point of honor, in fact." He pointed out that he had no idea if Macmillan were going to sell ten million copies or one hundred thousand, but he had serious doubts that any really big volume could be sold. After all, the book had been on sale for a long time. So, he stressed, the amount of money involved, either way, was not enough to quarrel about. "But the principle is," he thundered. "And it becomes a point of honor. . . . Briefly and bluntly, your proposition is the sort that a grown person might offer to a child, according to my way of looking at it. . . . If my sacrifice makes it possible for you to make big profits, then you placed yourself under an obligation to reward me for my sacrifice." Brett had said that if the venture proved successful, they would reinstate Peggy's usual royalties as stated in the original contract. But John pointed out that a return to "the straight royalties is not a reward. Unless there is something extra, no reward has been paid. You have gotten the benefit of my sacrifice without compensating me for it."[21] And that, in John's mind, was grossly unfair.

His position seemed so simple that he could not see why Brett did not understand it. After all, he pointed out, he had never asked Brett to increase the royalties when the novel turned out to be such a phenomenal success. Nevertheless, he said he would accept Brett's terms because he believed that failure to have the two-dollar edition or some other edition on the market soon would create an embarrassing situation and, while he would not be to blame for it, he would be involved in it. "I am too weary these days to get into any embarrassing situation which I can avoid, so if you insist . . . I agree to it."[22]

Fortunately, the situation eventually reached an amicable solution. When Brett received the final cost reports, he was pleased to find that his original figures were slightly inaccurate. He sent the Marshes a sample of the new edition, which he called "a gorgeous thing," and said these new costs indicated that Peggy could continue to receive her usual 15 percent royalty. He was "mighty happy" that costs had worked out so as to make this scale economically possible. By March, a very happy Brett told the Marshes that Macmillan had only about three hundred thousand copies left out of the 1,050,000 copies they had printed. He and Alec Blanton, his business manager, were betting that they would sell them and more of what he called "your remarkable novel. What a history it is writing in the annals of American publishing."[23]

5

Since *Gone With the Wind* had become such a phenomenal commercial success, a few literary critics began panning it on the obvious assumption that literary and commercial value were mutually exclusive. Loathing that kind of superficial logic, John wondered aloud if such critics realized that Shakespeare, Tolstoy, and Dickens were both commercial and literary successes. He and Peggy were delighted when a woman in North Carolina sent them a review of the movie that criticized such critics. In her column, "Scarlett Materializes," for the February 18, 1940, edition of the *Raleigh News,* Nell Battle Lewis began:

> The high brow critics make me laugh. It is not comme il faut, you know, to consider *Gone With the Wind* a very good piece of literary work. It's really not so much of a book, it seems—except in the minds of several million readers with whose low-brow opinion no real critic could agree. But, regardless of such an estimate, Scarlett is not going down in literature any more than in life. Hear me turn prophet: Scarlett is going to survive the high brow critics. For as long as life is a challenge which men must have courage to meet, the fighting O'Hara who wouldn't say die is going to live.[24]

In her letter thanking Lewis, Peggy provides insight into a reaction exhibited by the moviegoers. She mentioned how especially interested she was in what the reviewer had written about the lack of applause when the Confederate battle flag was shown flying over the acres of wounded

Confederate soldiers at the car shed. At the premiere in Atlanta, Peggy explained, there was a great deal of applause early in the picture, and later on, when "Scarlett shot the Yankee deserter on the stair the tense audience practically yelled. But during the scene you mentioned there was a deathly stillness, just as you noted in the Raleigh theatre." She, John, and some others had talked about the audience's reaction to that same scene. "One man summed it up this way—'Have you ever felt like applauding in a Confederate Cemetery on Memorial Day? No, you haven't; you feel something too deep for applause.' I think he was on the right track. Had the Confederate flag been shown for the same length of time over a crowd of charging soldiers or even going down a dusty road in retreat, I think audiences would have yelled themselves hoarse."[25]

6

As spring rolled into summer 1940, the world news was unsettling. Things changed almost overnight when France surrendered to Germany in June, placing England in serious danger. As increasingly tragic events unfolded daily, it became clear that the United States was going to have to enter the conflict. On the same June day when the Germans invaded Holland, the Marshes started their automobile trip to Wilmington, Delaware, to attend John's family reunion. "For our peace of mind, it was fortunate that we could not and did not listen to the radios. Reading the papers was bad enough. It's no fun having a ringside seat for that spectacle, the collapse of Europe," John wrote his mother. "Within just a few weeks, one phase of the world's history has definitely ended and another has begun. Everybody is an old timer now who can say 'I remember when people thought Hitler was a joke.' Times have changed, almost overnight, and I hope that all of us, and our country, can survive the change."[26]

Remembering the fervent patriotism the boys of her generation had felt at the start of World War I, Peggy resented the attitude held by many of the young men in Atlanta now that it looked as if the United States was headed into a second world war. One such young man wrote her that he and his college classmates felt as if they were being deprived, "cruelly cut away," from a good and secure future in a safe world. He complained that he and his friends found it hard to look ahead to any kind of decent world for themselves, that they cried out for security. He wrote, "We have yearned for it more than any other blessing. And we have been constantly warned that, of all things, security was the one we were least likely to find."[27]

The youth's comments stirred Peggy's fervor. She wrote him a long letter that she never mailed, perhaps because she believed it to be too harsh. Many years later, her brother Stephens found it among the papers John had left him. Nowhere else does Peggy so spiritedly define her values and philosophy as she does in this letter. Shrugging philosophically, she wrote: "I arise to ask, in a loud, hoarse voice, 'Who the hell ever promised you and your generation security? And, most important of all, why should any youth want security?'" What bothered her about some of young people was that, to the best of her knowledge, they were the first younger generation she had ever heard about "who not only yearned for security, but confidently expected it as their lawful right and were bitter and disgruntled when it was not handed to them on a silver platter." She pointed out:

> There is something very frightening about the young people of a nation crying out to be secure. Youth has been, in the past, thrusting and willing and able to take chances. If the youth of today wants to be safe and secure and leave to the older people the tough job of fighting and taking the hazards, then we are all in a bad way.

Peggy described the anecdotes of her ancestors, who had been in the gold rush of 1849, the Revolutionary War, the War of 1812, and the Seminole Wars. "I do not recall a single instance where any of these old timers ever expected security or even thought they might attain it. In fact ... if you had discussed the matter with them, they would have been as angry as if you had accused them of the rankest cowardice." Looking back to the Revolutionary War era, to "the 1812 time," and to the time when "Andy Jackson wrecked the banks," she observed that the youth of these generations "expected nothing except the opportunity to work like hell and not get anywhere."

> As for what young people faced in the South after Appomattox, not even half of the horrors have been told. There was no money, no opportunity, and hardly as much hope as the Belgians under Hitler now have. I personally knew that generation very well. They were a tough and hardbitten lot; they knew there was no safety anywhere in the world; I doubt if it ever occurred to them that they merited security; they knew that the race was not to the swift nor the battle to the strong; they knew they could break their backs working and give their lives to rebuild their section and yet in the end lose everything, even their lives. But the ones I knew certainly enjoyed scrapping, and they rebuilt our section with no more security than their own guts to build on it.

Referring to her mother's generation, who married during the panic of the 1890s and brought up their children in the successive panics of 1907 and 1914, she said her mother "would have laughed if you had talked about security for youth." As for her own generation, "if someone had been silly enough to talk to us about security or to tell us that we merited it, we would not have been silly enough to believe them. Furthermore, we would have been furious because doubts would have been cast upon our courage and our capabilities. I recall the worst insult which could be flung at my generation was, 'Oh, so you want it safe.'" Asserting that her generation had fought against safety, she added: "Even the girls who came from sheltered homes wanted to get out and take their chances, and most of them did. The ones who didn't were looked upon as weaklings." Her generation saw the Victorian age crash about their feet, "and, far from feeling disgruntled or bitter that life was not going to be what we expected, we were pleased to death, for here was something new, a land without landmarks, a country to be pioneered—spiritually, at least."

Peggy blamed the new generation's demand for security on the New Deal, which told young people "they were God's chosen creatures, that the world not only owes them a living but a good living and an awfully good time. Granted that your generation has been told this, why on earth have you believed it?"

Peggy concluded this long letter by saying that people of her generation rarely express the feelings she had expressed, for "the young persons we are talking to will not comprehend what we are saying or having comprehended, will say indignantly that we are Tories standing in the way of the more abundant life. But these are things we think."

> Probably by now you have forgotten what you wrote in your letter and will wonder at the length of my reply to one small item you wrote, but I had it in mind and I like you, so I had to write it. Come to see John and me when you are in Atlanta next. We will make a large pot of coffee and talk till dawn if you like.[28]

7

The Marsh family reunion at Henry's home in Wilmington, a gathering that brought all of John's siblings, their spouses, and their children together with their mother, was a happy occasion. It was the first time since the publication of *Gone With the Wind* that they had all gotten together. The children always enjoyed John, whom they called "Uncle Mouse" because he amused them by making mouse puppets out of his handkerchiefs. As for Peggy, the children were enthralled with her dramatic ghost stories, her mischief, and the attention she lavished upon them. Her little nieces and nephews adored her. Instead of talking to the adults, she would sit on the floor and play jacks or romp with them in the yard. They jabbed at each other, arguing about who would have her on a team and who would sit next to her at the table. One afternoon while Peggy was playing baseball in the front yard of Henry's home with her young nephews, Renny, Craig, and Sandy, a reporter tried to take photographs. As she hid from view, he interviewed the little boys. When he asked what impressed them the most about their famous aunt, they answered in unison, "Her size! She's no bigger than we are."[29]

Now that John was no longer working at the Power Company, he and Peggy had more time for vacations. Several months after the family reunion, on October 25, 1940, the Marshes set out on another long automobile trip with Peggy driving all the way in their new green four-door Ford. First they went to Chattanooga, then followed the valley up through Tennessee and Virginia all the way to Maryland to the battlefield of Sharpsburg, where Peggy saw, for the second time, the place where her grandfather, Russell Mitchell, had been wounded. From that point, they turned back into Virginia, where they spent three days in Richmond visiting with the Clifford Dowdeys.

Always impressed with other authors, Peggy did not realize that she sounded no different from the thousands of fans who wanted to meet her when she asked the Dowdeys to please make arrangements for her to meet Douglas Southall Freeman, James Branch Cabell, and Cabell's aunt, Ellen Glasgow. Not willing to wait for Dowdey's intercession, she went ahead and telephoned Glasgow's house the next morning, asking the nurse who answered if she could please visit Miss Glasgow for five or ten minutes that day. Her wish came true when later that afternoon she was admitted into the bedroom of the aged author, who was suffering from a heart condition.

Later, in thanking Glasgow for the visit, which lasted over an hour, Peggy said: "My husband hopes that if we make another visit to Richmond he may have the pleasure of meeting you. . . . John has long admired you, not only for your books but for the way you have carried success and public acclaim—not just a brief grassfire flare of notoriety but solid success that grew from year to year, which was based on true worth of character and back-breaking work. It is no small feat to carry success with dignity that has no stuffiness and with graciousness that has no condescension."[30] When Glasgow was awarded the Pulitzer Prize for *In This Our Life* the following year, Peggy sent her a telegram of congratulations. On May 27, 1942, Glasgow wrote back, "I have a charming recollection of your flitting in and spending an hour by my bedside."[31]

The high point of their stay in Richmond came when Douglas Southall

Freeman, author of a biography of Robert E. Lee, invited the Marshes to Sunday dinner. When they arrived at the Freemans' home, they were pleasantly surprised to learn that the other guests were Mr. and Mrs. James Branch Cabell and Dr. and Mrs. John Bell Williams. Mrs. Williams was Rebecca Yancey Williams, the author of *The Vanishing Virginian,* and Dr. Freeman had written the introduction to her book.

The best part of their trip for Peggy was that dinner party, but for John it was seeing the Shenandoah Valley for the first time and thinking about one of his great-uncles, Samuel Kercheval, who had written a history of the Shenandoah a hundred years earlier.[32] He and Peggy drove a hundred miles out of their way to visit Kercheval's grave in the Hite family burial grounds in Long Meadows. He wrote his mother about the scene: "It is really beautiful. I don't believe I have ever seen any place more beautiful unless perhaps it is Kentucky. And the comparison is an apt one, for the valley is a bluegrass section and in many ways is similar to Kentucky, not only in appearance but in the people and in the type of prosperous agricultural civilization. Everywhere I went in that section I was surprised to note how many of the names were Kentucky names, and I imagine that Kentucky people are closer kin to the valley people than to the people in Richmond or the tidewater."[33]

In giving his mother a handsome account of his visits to the towns and counties where his ancestors had lived, he laughingly wrote, "When I am narrating some interesting event to Peggy, she says, 'Now, tell it like a woman,' meaning give the details, not just the broad facts . . . but fill in the small items that together create the picture and enable the listener to participate in the event."[34]

This trip exhilarated Peggy; she felt more relaxed than she had felt in years. When she returned home, she found no huge stack of mail piled on the dining room table; no long list of telephone messages; no newspapers carrying pictures or articles about her; and no significant news about the book. Margaret Baugh's messages were all about their foreign business, and all of those were for John. On the afternoon of their arrival home, Peggy wrote her friend Brickell about her vacation and described how quiet things were.

> I think the war, of course, had something to do with the cessation of public interest in me, and the election naturally diverted attention. However, Atlanta has become such an enthusiastic literary center that I have spent most of my time during the past six months (when I wasn't making bandages at the Red Cross) galloping about meeting authors. . . . It's fun getting back into circulation again after so long. I had not realized how much I

missed normal life and parties and seeing friends and meeting attractive strangers. It must be good for both of us, for John had gained fifteen pounds and I am bursting the seams of all my clothes. I never felt better in my life and do not care how fat I get.[35]

8

On October 6, 1940, John turned forty-five. Peggy gave him a quiet birthday party at home with a few friends. Her gifts to him were "two pairs of alleged silk pajamas of gaudy hues" and a birthday cake. As John remarked later, "Before I passed forty, nobody could have paid me to wear a red necktie. Now I like them as bright as I can find and preferably red. Passing forty seemed to release me from the compulsion to be dignified which had tightly gripped me during my twenties and thirties."[36]

In late November 1940, the Marshes took another long train ride. This time John took Peggy home to Kentucky for her first visit. Although his mother had moved away years earlier to Wilmington, Delaware, to be near Henry and help him rear his child Mary, she went to Kentucky to meet them along with Gordon and Francesca, who lived in Lexington, Kentucky. Also, Miss Anna Frank and her brother George, who owned the retail clothing store downtown where John had worked as a teenager and who had meant so much to him while he was growing up, were still in Maysville, as were many other old friends and neighbors. The freezing rain that had fallen steadily all day and the night before suddenly stopped just as their train pulled into the Maysville station.

Seeing his hometown for the first time in twenty years and the crowd that had gathered at the station to greet them deeply stirred John's emotions. He was also totally unprepared for the warm homecoming he and Peggy received when they arrived at the old homestead of Miss Anna Frank and her brother George on East Second Street, where they were to spend the night. Peggy exclaimed that it looked as if all of Mason County, not just Maysville, turned out to see them. The visitors kept coming until nearly midnight. Early the next morning, John slipped out of the house while everyone else was asleep and walked over to Forest Avenue to see the house where he had grown up and the house next door where his grandmother, aunt, and uncle Bob had lived. He ended his solitary tour of the little town in Traxel's Confectionery on Main Street, where the men had already gathered for their morning coffee and exchange of news, just as they had done when he was boy. Nothing had changed, except him, he thought.

In an interview for the *Daily Independent,* the newspaper that grew out of the one John's father had edited and published years earlier, Peggy looked pretty as she sat in Traxel's wrapped in her new, full-length, dark mink coat. As a growing crowd gathered around her listening, she told the reporter, "I feel that I know every house on Forest Avenue. For fifteen years John and the Marsh family have talked about Maysville and Kentucky." Making everyone laugh, she boasted: "Just to prove to you how well I know the townspeople and their business, recently when Mother Marsh wanted to know the maiden name of a married friend in Maysville, I was the only Marsh who remembered the name."[37] Yet, moments later, when she was asked to address the similarities between Belle Watling and Belle Brezing, who had just recently died in Lexington, Peggy replied that the name "Belle" was common and that there "were a number of ladies of that profession in Atlanta." She refused to comment any further on the issue.

The next day they crossed the Ohio River and went to Cincinnati, Ohio, to visit John's relatives the Charles Nutes, who lived there in the Kennedy Heights section. On the third day they went to Lexington on a little one-car train that was heated by a coal stove. Peggy wrote,

> We stopped at every wide place in the road and at some of the stops both old friends of John's and perfect strangers came aboard. The telegraph operators up and down the line had been gossiping with the Maysville operator and they spread the news. After hanging over the back platform for three and a half hours, I did not know whether I felt more like a fugitive from justice or Mrs. Roosevelt. At one stop, just as the train was pulling out, a girl dashed frantically out of a house and jumped on the platform, crying breathlessly, "Is Clark Gable really darling?" I assumed as rapturous an expression as I could under the circumstances and said, "He's simply divine. Get off the train before you break your neck." She said, hoping for the worst, "Is it true he's in love with his wife?" I assumed an expression of complete dejection and said, "My dear, I never saw a more devoted couple." "Oh, my God," said the young lady, and fell off backwards. It didn't hurt her, and she waved good-bye from a pile of frost-covered rocks.[38]

In Lexington the next afternoon, the reporters asked about Belle Brezing's resemblance to Belle Watling. Peggy insisted that she had never heard of Belle Brezing until after her book had been published.[39] And that was all she or John, who did his best to avoid reporters, would say. That evening, they were the guests of honor at an informal gathering at the University of Kentucky's student center. The following day, she and John toured the campus with Dr. L. L. Dantzler, head of the English program, who introduced them to the journalism and the English departments. In her charming manner, she spoke modestly to the students and professors about the difficulties of being a writer. Later that evening, they, along with Gordon and Francesca, had dinner with Dr. Frank MacVey, the president of the university, and some other state and local dignitaries.

As soon as they got back to Atlanta, they discovered that Metro-Goldwyn-Mayer, in its efforts to pull off a "second premiere," was trying, John said, "to steal Peggy's stage dramatization rights." Two weeks of wrangling and letter writing ensued before John had the matter straightened out.[40]

About this same time, David Selznick asked for permission to produce a Broadway musical version of *Gone With the Wind*. They were hard pressed to turn him down because Selznick was one of the few people they admired and respected. He had consistently tried to be fair with them, and they knew he would do a superb job with whatever he chose to do, but they were horrified by his casual remark about a nationwide talent search for new faces and voices. John wrote Kay Brown that they did not feel like making the trade on the basis Selznick proposed. He explained:

> What you said about a talent search wasn't the only reason for the rejection of the offer but it was one reason, and I am going to make one more effort to explain our position. Apparently we did not succeed in doing that before, judging by your statement that you understood Peggy's objection was only to a talent search in Atlanta.
>
> No amount of money would ever induce Peggy to go through another experience like the one she was subjected to by the talent search for the movie. It was a fine buildup for the movie, it got publicity for the movie which you might not have gotten other-wise, but it was hell on earth for Peggy. I doubt that Mr. Selznick has ever gotten the faintest conception of what it did to Peggy.
>
> Your idea that Peggy might escape a similar experience simply by not having a talent search *in Atlanta* disregards the fact that the United States mail and the telegraph and telephone lines are still operating. Even if there were no publicity about the search in Atlanta at all, Peggy would still have to deal with a swarm of pitifully unqualified humans demanding her assistance in obtaining roles in the show.
>
> It is the fact that a talent search stirs up the pitifully unquali-fied—and is intended to do so—that makes it offensive and distasteful and a burden to her. . . . It also uses up innumerable hours of time, and time is the only working capital of an author, by still further postponing the time when she can begin writing again, as she ardently wishes to do.[41]

John's reference to Peggy's desire to write is intriguing. Only once, in her letter to Herschel Brickell of May 3, 1938, did Peggy ever express any desire to write another novel, but here, and also in a later letter to Dr. Dandy about Peggy's back surgery, John indicates that Peggy was enthusiastic about getting back to her writing. There is no evidence that Peggy wrote anything—except letters—after *Gone With the Wind,* but it is quite possible that when her and John's life returned to relative normalcy during World War II, they discussed ideas for a next novel. John's remarks during this period strongly suggest this possibility, but in addition to her active involvement in the war effort, Peggy was too ill herself, and too busy attending her dying father, to carry out any ideas she and John may have discussed.

As the war heated up, John continued to receive news of foreign piracies. At the end of March 1940, Marion Saunders informed him that a Bulgarian publisher had translated *Gone With the Wind* from the French and was publishing an unauthorized edition in three weeks. After Saunders, following John's instructions, demanded the publisher sign a contract, print the United States's Macmillan copyright notice in all future editions, and pay a royalty, John received a letter from him. The publisher asked to be excused from paying royalties, saying that it was not the custom of famous American writers to charge the Bulgarians for translations.[42] The war interrupted John's correspondence with the publisher. Finally, in 1945, the publisher reported eight thousand copies sold before he had to flee the country. He stated that he had deposited the advance payment in a bank in Sofia, but no royalty money was ever received by the Marshes.[43]

Pirates in Chile and Cuba were more difficult to deal with. After writing Peggy that he would not pay or acknowledge her rights, the Chilean publisher, for some unexplained reason, did a sudden about-face, signed a contract, and sent one hundred dollars in royalties to Macmillan.[44] The Cuban publisher did not sign a contract and paid no royalties. In July, John attempted to extract a contract from a Greek publisher of a newspaper in Athens, which had started serializing *Gone With the Wind* without permission. Not long after the Russians took over Estonia, a publisher in that tiny country was translating the novel. "I never thought when I finished the last galley proof of my book and sent it off to the press that I would be skirmishing in so many foreign countries," Peggy wrote Dr. Wallace McClure in the State Department.[45]

When they received news that the Japanese were pirating the movie *Gone With the Wind,* the Marshes were relieved, thinking that problem belonged to Selznick. Peggy wrote McClure that she would like to see a

Japanese version. "If they placed it back in the sixties, the Japanese Confederates would doubtless be marching forth to defend Atlanta in Samurai armor and Scarlett would be dashing about in a 'ricksha instead of a buggy."[46]

McClure wrote regularly to the Marshes to share what little news he was able to obtain. Generally his letters brought only more reports of pirates in other places. From 1937 through 1939, he had the Marshes come to Washington several times to meet with various congressmen who were working on the copyright agreement. International copyright had long been one of McClure's assignments in the State Department. After he had sent them some paragraphs on copyright infringement in the early days of Ireland's history, Peggy wrote him: "It was fascinating reading and I found it interesting to see how laws began. I think the King of ancient Tara must have been a just man and I wish, like you, that I could meet with similar justice in Holland. . . . Before we have finished my difficulties in the Netherlands my brother and my husband will have become the leading Southern authorities on international copyright. Both of them find this subject very interesting and they study any material they can find upon it."[47]

As World War II progressed, John was unable to communicate with the foreign publishers and seldom heard from Marion Saunders. So there was little for him to do with the book's business. For the first time in his adult life, he rested during his one-year sabbatical from Georgia Power. In addition to his leisurely travels with Peggy, he did a lot of reading. He wrote to his mother about reading *The Late George Apley,* a book that Peggy recommended to him, and said he knew the Apleys well. He thought it was remarkable to see how closely that Boston family resembled southern families, including the Mitchells and the Marshes, in viewpoints and traditions. "I suppose there is a fundamental similarity among all folks raised up in a certain tradition that goes back to England . . . and is deep-rooted in American life, both Southern and Northern."[48]

He especially enjoyed Marjorie Kinnan Rawling's *When the Whip-poorwill,* a collection of short stories, which he recommended to his mother. "Some are very funny and some very moving," and he liked everything about the book except the title, which he thought was "lousy."[49] The more works by Rawlings he read, the more she amazed him. He thought that there was something genuinely American in her stories and that she often displayed "some of Mark Twain's better qualities." He regarded her as one of the superior writers of his time.[50]

Not easily impressed with writers or celebrities, or anyone else for that matter, John was taken with Rawlings. When he and Peggy went to Florida for Christmas in 1941, the highlight of the trip, for him, was meeting Rawlings and having her take them on an all-day tour through the Cross

Creek "scrub country," the scene of *The Yearling*. They had never before seen anything like that area, where the soil was covered with a tangle of scrub oak, scrub pine, and saw palmetto, and the soil made up almost entirely of sea shells. Except for a few rutted roads, the whole section was as primitive as when it was created, and during the several hours they were in the scrub, they saw only two automobiles and four or five people. It was not the kind of place they would have gone alone, but they felt safe with Rawlings, who knew the section well.[51]

When lunchtime came they were surprised when the author went out in her side yard and chopped down a tree from which she served them a hearts-of-palm salad. She told them that it was something "nobody ever ate except the richest people in the Waldorf or the Ritz and the poorest crackers in the Florida scrub."[52] Rawlings introduced them to the people upon whom she based the characters in her book, like old Martha and a number of her brood, and Norton Baskin, whom Marjorie married. She showed them Jody's homeplace in *The Yearling*. The actual home of a family she had met a decade earlier on a hunting trip, the house had been abandoned for years and had fallen into ruin, but MGM, making a movie of her novel, had restored it, using worn and weathered timber gathered from other old houses and split-rail fences collected from the surrounding area. "When we rolled up to it, we recognized it immediately from Marjorie's description in the book. From the faithfulness of the restoration, it appeared that MGM did not plan to turn the book either into moonlight and honey suckle romance or another 'Tobacco Road' but were trying to show the Baxters for what they were, a self-respecting, prideful family, even though they did happen to live in primitive surroundings."

In discussing her copyright problems with the Marshes, Rawlings did not express much disturbance about the Dutch, who had also pirated *The Yearling*. Although she did not pursue her foreign copyrights as aggressively as the Marshes did theirs, she did have the excellent assistance of a Florida senator, Claude Pepper, who was a member of the Senate's International Copyright Agreement Committee. Ironically, the Dutch publishers ended up sending Rawlings a check for one hundred dollars but until 1947, they sent nothing to Peggy.

"Everytime I think that the two best selling American novels of recent years have been pirated by one of the smallest countries in the world I get mad all over again," Peggy wrote Dr. McClure. "Of course, the passage of the treaty will not help *The Yearling* or *Gone With the Wind* either now, but I will feel proud indeed if I have had even a small part in helping to get protection abroad for other authors coming out after me."[53]

10

By 1941, Eugene Mitchell had multiple health problems, including kidney stones, kidney infections, and prostate disease. While enduring a nearly fatal bout of uremic poisoning in 1940, he converted to Catholicism, something that his wife had wanted desperately for him to do years earlier. However, his conversion did nothing to sanctify his temperament. The older he got, the more irascible he became, driving all his servants away and demanding more and more of Peggy's time.

Francesca remembered some of the exasperating things he did that annoyed Peggy, such as insisting on eating sardines from the can, and then, much to Peggy's dismay, turning the empty can up to his mouth and drinking the oil.[54] Although he staged some remarkable comebacks, after 1941 he was never well enough to return to his office or to his home on Peachtree Street. Until his death in 1944, he remained in St. Joseph's Infirmary, which was operated by the Catholic Sisters of Charity. Peggy visited him there at least twice every day and had a frustrating time finding nurses to look after him. By 1943, he had gotten to the point where he was a difficult and helpless invalid. Because of the war, male hospital orderlies were not readily available, and the blacks whom he had always depended upon to care for him had all gotten better jobs in factories or had joined the armed services. Unable to stay with him every day, all day, she wrote Mrs. Marsh that her problems were complicated by her father's lack of comprehension of the changed labor markets. "It is difficult for him to understand how desperate is our struggle to keep three colored orderlies a day for him." Even though she was paying good wages, she could not keep the workers because "when Father is feeling well he spends a good deal of time happily quarrelling with his attendants, so that they either quit or are on the verge of quitting."[55] Oftentimes he would get so cranky and belligerent that Peggy would find his nurse-aides in tears.

"Even at death's door, Father is just as easy to handle as a wildcat in his prime," she wrote Mother Marsh. "He does not like hospitals, to put it mildly, and resents the ministrations of nurses. He dozes all day and is awake all night bothering the orderlies on the night shift who expect to sleep most of the night. Two months ago he reached the point where he would not even take an aspirin unless I administered it. And I suspect this was done only to harass the nurses and put the doctors in their places."[56]

11

When his year's leave of absence was up, John went back to his office at Georgia Power, where his workload had tripled. Peggy wrote: "War, defense work and matrimony have made vast inroads on John's staff, while at the same time his work has gotten heavier. . . . It's almost impossible to get replacements for John's type of work."[57] After the man who edited *Snap Shots,* the company magazine that was circulated over the nation to other companies and customers, went off to officers' training camp, Mary Singleton asked John if she could have the job. At that time, women had not been given such positions, but John hired her on the spot. Mary Singleton not only got out a good publication, but she also became a close friend of both Marshes.

In addition to the manpower shortage, work at the Power Company was made more difficult by the fact that in 1941 Georgia suffered from the worst drought it had had in years. As a result of the low water levels in its dams, Georgia Power faced the most severe power shortage it had ever experienced. John had to go before the public requesting that everybody cut down on the use of electricity. The power companies, like the railroads, already had tremendous loads thrown on them by the war, and the drought made things far worse. Peggy wrote: "Life on the civilian front is toughening up—at least as far as our family and friends are concerned. I am not talking about the gas and tire and sugar shortages, for they should not bother anyone in their right mind. The civilian problem at present is that so many men have gone into the service the few men who are left behind have to do six men's work."[58]

In the evenings, John, along with Angus Perkerson, Frank Daniel, Joe Kling, Ralph McGill, and other friends, was actively involved in the civilian defense programs. He served as a sector warden, and Peggy worked right along with him as an air warden for the Piedmont Park section. In fact, the war crisis brought out the best in Peggy, who became the quintessential volunteer. She organized paper, scrap, and salvage drives; and she worked several hours every weekday as a member of the Red Cross, making surgical dressings and packing boxes of food to ship overseas. Able to attract huge crowds, she sold more war bonds and saving stamps than anyone else in Georgia. She wrote Lois Cole:

> If anyone had told me a year ago that I'd be gallumphing about the countryside making speeches and selling bonds, I would have fallen on my rear screaming with laughter and kicking my heels. But, oddly enough war brings out the best and the worst in one (take your choice, dearie) and that's what I've been doing. The other day Rich's department store busted loose with a full-page ad announcing that I'd be selling bonds in their booth and would not give autographs. By now I'm convinced that no one ever reads anything right. Shoals of people decided I was going to auto-

graph, and so we had quite a crowd—$212,000 in four hours. Many mothers brought their two-year-olds to buy their first ten cent stamp, and held the babies up to the counter to lick the stamps I was holding. Abjured to "Now lick, sugar," they enthusiastically and obediently licked me on my cheeks. Several infants reached delightedly for the stamps and swallowed them. I was kept busy running my hands into infants throats and retrieving stamps. One little boy licked, and pasted the stamp on my hand. God knows how many children I kissed. I had started in high-heeled slippers, but seeing that it was not a sit-down job, telephoned Margaret Baugh to bring my oldest and largest pair of shoes. This she did, arriving with all the celerity of the marine corps, but by that time the crowd was so thick I couldn't change. Fifty or sixty comfortable matrons were loafing about determined to see whether I was going to pull off my shoes then and there.[59]

Her old-fashioned pride in the South and her patriotism were of the highest rank. She wrote George Brett that enlistments were higher in the South than in any other part of the United States, and that the South appeared less frenzied but more unified. She said there was a "calm and resigned determination as if everyone thought a war inevitable and intended to do their share.... I suppose the Southern people still have the memories of what it feels like to be defeated and they don't aim to be defeated again."[60]

12

In June 1941, Lieutenant Commander E. John Long invited Peggy to the navy shipyards in Kearny, New Jersey, to christen a new cruiser, the U.S.S. *Atlanta.* This invitation thrilled her more than perhaps any other she had ever received. She accepted immediately. Her excitement and anxiety is evident in the letter she wrote the commander on June 23, 1941, giving him the biographical information he requested. In this amazing eight-page, single-spaced letter full of trivial questions, she "talked" the poor man's ear off. This letter demonstrates better than anything else available how Peggy focused on insignificant details, and it give us a good idea of the kinds of worrisome questions she must have inflicted on John regularly.

She began by explaining that since she had spent her entire life in an inland city and had never had any intentions of launching a ship, she needed much information. Using her old technique of drawing a man into her confidence, she wrote, "Some of my questions may seem ingenuous, so I hope that you will keep this part of my letter confidential."[61] No one recorded the commander's reaction to her letter, but the poor man must have been dumbfounded when he read it. She asked him everything from what she should wear for the occasion to how many changes of clothes she should bring. After telling him how small she was, she asked that if the navy had any intention of presenting her with flowers, would he please see to it that the flowers were small ones? She wrote a long paragraph about the bouquet and her concern about where she was going to put it when the time came for the launching. She wanted to have both hands free to "take a good two-handed swing with the bottle."

She needed his advice about the best technique of "smashing bottles on battleships," because she did not want to miss or fail to break the bottle. She worried about flying glass and asked if the bottle had any kind of covering to protect her. "Does the champagne usually spray on the sponsor as well as the battleship, so that I can expect to christen a dress as well as the U.S.S. *Atlanta?* And will you please ask the proper person to see that the platform is constructed with consideration for my size, so that my smallness will not prevent me from getting a proper swing?"

She wanted directions to the shipyard and wondered who was going to escort her and, if no one was, how she was to present herself in Kearny. She wanted him to tell her what sort of gift she should make to the ship she was to christen, and if bringing gifts was customary. She was thinking of bringing some after-dinner coffee cups that the Atlanta Historical Society had had made by Wedgwood in England, and went on for three paragraphs describing these cups. She worried that they might be too "small and delicate" for navy officers and asked him to please tell her if these cups were appropriate.

After several postponements, the launching date was finally set for September 6, 1941. Because of business complications, John could not accompany her to New York on September 4. Upon her arrival the next morning at her suite at the Waldorf-Astoria Hotel, she was greeted by the Macmillan publicity officials and the New York press corps. In the *Constitution* the next day, she was described as "dauntless, composed, and scintillating" in her interview, which lasted an hour.

When asked about the status of *Gone With the Wind,* she answered: "Well, there is still a lot of business connected with the book. It is published in nineteen foreign countries including Canada and England and that means working under nineteen different copyright laws, nineteen different financial setups, nineteen different sets of unwritten customs. It all takes a great deal of time."

One reporter asked her if she had an agent. "A foreign agent, but I have no American agent. My husband is my business manager. My father and brother are lawyers." When asked why she had filed suit against the Dutch for copyright infringement, she replied bluntly: "So that

American books would be safe anywhere."

Many other questions about the film, the talent search, and the premiere were asked also. Finally, someone asked her whether, if she wrote another book, it would be about the South. "Sugar," she answered, "I don't know anything else." As they were leaving, the newsmen were laughing, for she had charmed them all. The next day, the launching was a tremendous success, and Peggy hit the battleship with her first swing.

13

In December 1942, two thousand soldiers were camped in Piedmont Park, right across the street from the Marshes' apartment. When the Red Cross set up a canteen for an army show in the park, Peggy joined the other Red Cross ladies serving the soldiers' meals and mending uniforms and gloves. "I went down there yesterday," she wrote a friend, "all dressed up in white uniform and veil, and spent the day changing chevrons, sewing on buttons and stitching up rips in soldiers' pants. I do not mean to criticize the army, but there must be something wrong with soldier's pants because the seams always bust out at the same place—and a most strategic place it is."[62] In describing to John's mother just how active the Atlanta Marshes were in civilian defense, Peggy wrote on October 6, 1942, that during the first daytime air raid practice, "I galloped forth, in helmet and armband, to assist in patrolling this block. . . . I had a fine time stopping traffic on Piedmont Avenue and urging people to take cover in buildings. After I had galloped a long block, I was so winded that I couldn't speak. Fortunately, people were very cooperative and when I jerked my thumb they left their automobiles."[63]

Because she was so famous, Peggy cut across the bureaucratic red tape to do special favors for soldiers. For instance, when one young man was forbidden to take his guitar, named "Betsy," overseas with him, Peggy got permission to send it in a special shipment. The soldier wrote back thanking her and saying that Betsy was going through Italy with him. When she learned that certain managers of the marine post exchanges in the South Pacific refused to stock snuff and chewing tobacco for the southern soldiers, she shipped abundant supplies straight through to the marines on those islands. To many others, she sent individual gifts, like tobacco and pipes. With Bessie's help, she sent a continuous flow of food packages, clothing, and medicine to war victims abroad. She served in every possible way that any private citizen can serve its country during a war.

She was an active Red Cross volunteer. She did not work regularly at the Red Cross canteen in the Habersham DAR house on Fifteenth Street, close to Piedmont Park, as other writers have stated; she did her regular Red

Cross work in the sewing unit on West Peachtree across from the Biltmore Hotel, where she operated an electric cutter, like those used in factories, cutting a dozen surgical dressings at a time. On the occasions when she worked at the Red Cross canteen, she made many friends among the soldiers, who later wrote letters to her. She answered every letter, hundreds of them. She corresponded with so many soldiers overseas that Bill Mauldin, the Pulitzer Prize-winning soldier-cartoonist, drew a cartoon of a tired, dirty combat "Soldier Somewhere in Italy," licking his pencil as he wrote a letter to "Dear, Dear Miss Mitchell." This cartoon appeared in newspapers all over the nation in May 1945.

When Peggy first saw the cartoon in the *Constitution,* she laughingly wrote,

> Dear, Dear, Sergeant Mauldin . . . I am so flattered by that drawing. . . . It has done me a great deal of good here in Atlanta, for it has raised my stock with the small fry to extravagant heights. I have been out ringing door bells for the Seventh Bond Drive and have met any number of children. I cannot tell you how respectful they are to me because my name appeared in your cartoon, and they believe I really did get such a letter. . . . Your cartoons are so wonderful and so astringent. They have made many people safe at home realize what war is like. Your soldiers are so real that we feel cold with them and hungry and feet-itchy, too, and unillusioned. Thanks for mentioning me in the same breath with them.[64]

Yet when Al Capp, creator of the popular cartoon "Li'l Abner," used the names of *Gone With the Wind* characters in his cartoons without asking her permission, she had John zap him with legal papers. Not only did Capp have to apologize publicly to her, but he also had to transfer to Peggy the copyrights of those cartoons bearing her characters' names. People like Al Capp, Billy Rose, Sam Goldywn of MGM, and others, whom Peggy identified as "slick Nawthum gempmum," had no idea of how far she and John would go to protect their copyrights. But they soon found out. The older the Marshes got, the more of like mind and character they became. Together they doggedly pursued their course of holding on to what belonged to them, regardless of the cost in worry, energy, time, and money.

14

On rather short notice, Peggy was invited back to the navy shipyard to attend the ceremony, on December 24, commissioning the *Atlanta* to wartime service. Because Christmas Eve was an inconvenient time for her to leave town, John urged her not to go.[65] But she told him that at the risk of sounding sentimental, she felt "that the *Atlanta* should not put out to sea without someone from this town present to say 'good luck.'"[66] As the sponsor of the ship, she felt she had to go, but would be back home by 4:00 P.M. on Christmas day. Even though this was a rushed trip, she had a marvelous time. After the luncheon aboard the *Atlanta,* the captain arranged for her to shake hands with all the sailors who had lined up on deck to greet her. For this occasion she wore her Red Cross uniform because John told her she looked beautiful in it. But to the officers, she said, "All my clothes (both dresses) were at the dry cleaners." Always conscious of outward signs, she wore that uniform proudly because she said it "seemed to fox everybody, especially the New York reporters."[67] The ceremonies were so "impressive and solemn" that she considered this experience one of the major highlights of her career.

Later, she wrote the ship's captain, S. P. Jenkins: "Even in peace times, I would have felt a natural sense of pride at being a sponsor of so fine a ship. Now, in time of war, that pride is increased a hundredfold, and with it is mingled a sense of faith in the ships and men of our Navy, and the *Atlanta* especially."[68] She asked him if each ship had a seamen's fund of some type, for she wanted to contribute something to the *Atlanta* if such a fund existed.

The following November, Peggy was deeply saddened to learn that the *Atlanta* had been sunk off Guadalcanal and all its men lost at sea. Remembering the faces of those young men with whom she had eaten lunch and shaken hands at the launching ceremony, she wrote, "I felt sick at my stomach."[69] After her initial reaction of shock, she demonstrated one of her finest traits: her ability to act in a courageous manner in time of need. Although she had been suffering back pain for months and had just been diagnosed in early November at Johns Hopkins as having a ruptured disc requiring surgery, she refused to have the surgery until after she had carried out her plan. She rallied her Red Cross ladies around her and immediately launched a campaign to raise $35 million in bonds to replace the *Atlanta*. In spite of her back problem, which was aggravated from helping her father turn in his bed, Peggy worked harder than anyone else at raising that money. With evangelical zeal, she put in long hours every day.

In late January, John wrote his mother about Peggy's crusade, saying that she was "headed for a real adventure" in her upcoming trip to Blue Ridge, Georgia, in the heart of the Georgia mountains, to make a speech. "Peggy had turned down many an invitation to make speeches before large and distinguished audiences," he explained, "but she accepted this one because it came from a man whose son was wounded in the last battle of our *Atlanta* cruiser."[70] Little Blue Ridge wanted to join in Atlanta's campaign for a new cruiser and invited her to start its fundraiser. The only way to get to that small, isolated spot was by a rickety little train that took several hours to travel a hundred miles. Riding on such a train would not be good for her back, but she felt it was her duty to go.

The newspapers started carrying pictures of her again as she worked at these fundraisers. One of the outdoor bond sales took place in February at Five Points on the coldest day that Atlanta had ever seen. "The wind screamed down all five of the streets to explode in a hurricane around our table," she wrote Ensign S. A. Martin on March 18, 1943. "We had Navy and Marine guards present and their main job was holding bonds and certificates down on the table. Every time a thousand dollar bond was purchased the Navy boys fired a cannon and before the day was over I was so deaf that when I got home I yelled things like 'Please pass the biscuits' at the top of my voice."

She told the young sailor that it was the only time in her memory that she had seen all types of people united behind one movement. For the most part throughout the two-month campaign, she stayed in a corner of the lobby of the Citizens and Southern Bank on Marietta Street, making out certificates for purchasers of bonds, so she said she had a front-row seat throughout the campaign. "There were newsboys who came in every day to buy ten-cent stamps and men in overalls and girls from behind the counters buying a bond a week. There were stout matrons in mink and heads of enormous businesses who bought a million dollars at a time, and housewives in bungalow aprons with money from their sons in the Army in Africa. I knew we'd get thirty-five million but I never dreamed we'd manage nearly sixty-five million. So now we'll have two destroyers to run interference for the new cruiser."

In only two months, she and the Red Cross Ladies had raised nearly $65 million. Busy doing this significant work, she was truly happy, and there is no question that she was the sole reason so much money was raised in such short time. In her honor, a big victory celebration was held in the Civil Auditorium. The visiting naval dignitaries, who were there to receive Atlanta's check, included the Secretary of the Navy Frank Knox, Vice Admiral William Alexander Glassford, Jr., and Rear Admiral George Dominic Murray. "There were so many high ranking Navy people present and so much gold braid that I gave up trying to figure out their rank and just called everybody Admiral, which seemed to please everybody."[71] Mayor Hartsfield read Secretary Knox's letter announcing that Margaret Mitchell was the sponsor of the new *Atlanta*.

With such rousing success as a fund raiser, Peggy was asked by the Red Cross if she would travel around the United States as one of the Red Cross national speakers and sell war bonds. Although she truly wanted to accept this offer, she had to decline. She had overexerted herself during the campaign, and her back pain had become too severe for such travel. Indeed, she had reached the point where she had to get medical help. In mid-March 1943, John took her back to Johns Hopkins University Hospital in Baltimore, where he had taken her several months earlier upon the advice of their family physician, Dr. Waters. One of the most eminent neurosurgeons in the world, Dr. Walter Dandy, examined Peggy and told her and John that removal of a ruptured invertebral disc was the only solution for Peggy's back pain. With confidence, Dandy predicted that in two weeks after the surgery she would "get up and do the rhumba."[72]

Highly optimistic and confident herself, Peggy had the surgery on March 26, 1943, for the removal of a concealed invertebral disc. However, Peggy remained in excruciating pain long after the operation and she never fully recovered her strength or her mobility. Yet, several days after the operation, Dr. Dandy reported it successful despite the fact that his patient was unable to walk, dress herself, or take care of her personal needs by the time he had said she would. The physician implied that Peggy's problems, perhaps, were imaginary or psychogenic.[73] Well into the third week after the surgery, she still had not improved. In fact, her condition had grown worse. She could barely move for the constant pain. After remaining at her bedside for over two weeks, John had to return to Atlanta without her to take care of business. He worried about leaving her at the hospital, but there was no way she could have withstood the seven-hundred-mile train ride home. Also, she needed to be near the physician who had done the surgery. In their daily telephone conversations, she often cried, telling John she wanted to go home and that the hospital was a nightmare to her. Although he was reluctant under the circumstances to have her so far away from her physician, he brought her home on April 19. Severely disabled, she was unable to either stand up or sit down except for short periods. Her left foot, leg, hip, and her neck and shoulders were the most painful areas.

Seeing that John was worrying too much about her, she optimistically assured him that she would fully recover in time and good naturedly started answering her letters from servicemen. To the Marshes' friend Leodel Coleman, a former editor from Statesboro, Georgia, who was serving as a war correspondent overseas, she wrote: "The doctors pried open my spine and took pressure off a big nerve, and I hope eventually I will be able to wear the silliest and highest heeled slippers of any white girl in Fulton County.

Of course during these past years I have gotten so in the habit of running around the house barefoot as a yard dog that John is probably going to have to rope and tie me and back me into shoes blindfolded."[74]

To Clifford and Helen Dowdey, too, she demonstrated that she still had her sense of humor: "I got home the day before yesterday and stood the trip very well. I've been able to sit up half the day, strapped up in a brace which improves my figure below the waist but does nothing for me above, as thirty pounds below the waist have been displaced to the north. John says with the addition of a few medals I'd be a dead ringer for General Goering."[75]

16

As days passed, it became evident that the surgery had placed her in worse shape than ever. Gravely concerned about Peggy's future, angry and disappointed with the hospital and the surgeon, John went after Dr. Dandy with all the protective instincts of a pit bull. On May 18, seven weeks after the surgery, he typed a six-page, single-spaced letter to Dr. Frank L. Ostenasek, head of Neurological Surgery at Johns Hopkins, explaining Peggy's condition in detail, asking for advice, and requesting a technical statement about the operation so that he could have Peggy examined by another physician.[76]

After several exchanges of long letters between John and Dr. Dandy, the surgeon offered to come to Atlanta to examine Peggy, without charge except for his expenses. Because he perceived that the surgeon still believed Peggy's problems were "nerves," John answered, "We would hesitate to take you away from your patients. . . . Especially as we might spend your visit in a wrangle about 'nerves,' which would be definitely bad for Mrs. Marsh. I won't waste time arguing our difference of opinion on the subject of 'nerves' but I believe I should correct one wrong impression which you apparently have, as indicated by your statement that she should 'divert her mind' by becoming interested in her literary work again."[77]

John explained that Peggy had not been "moping and holding her hands" during her lengthy convalescence; she had been busy with her large correspondence, getting new dresses fitted, and other personal matters.

One job has been trying to get a satisfactory brace made. The one which your expert fitted (?) her with is now being worn with great comfort and satisfaction by a colored friend who is a foot taller and forty pounds heavier than Mrs. Marsh. She needs no more prodding to be "interested in her literary work" than you do in your surgery, for writing is her trade even as neuro-surgery is yours. When she is able, she will certainly write again, but her disabilities are an effective obstacle to that now. Books are not written while authors recline on sofas and dictate to secretaries. Hack work might be turned out that way but not good books. There is a technique to writing just as you have your operating room technique. It consists of perspiration in quarts and the application of the seat of the pants to the seat of a hard typewriter chair for months and years. As I have tried to make clear in my previous letters, it is the seat of Mrs. Marsh's pants which is the painful problem.[78]

As several more weeks passed, Peggy showed only slight improvement. By now, Dr. Dandy himself was more than a little concerned. He offered to remove the second disc from her spine, saying he was convinced that was the source of her persistent problem. He wanted her to return to Baltimore for an examination. John wrote that Peggy would not go back to Johns Hopkins for any purpose at any time because her memories of that place were most unpleasant ones. He composed a seven-page, single-spaced letter, which read in part:

> The trouble was not the pain she suffered—she expected that—but an apparent agreement at Johns Hopkins that she was a neurotic and therefore anything she said was to be discounted or disbelieved. As you remarked in one of your letters, "We felt in the beginning that several of her complaints were of nervous origin." Her pains were assumed to be imaginary and she was treated on that basis. Anything she said about being in pain was used against her, to support the diagnosis of neurosis, instead of her symptoms being observed and studied to find out what they might really mean. (I was with her during the greater part of her stay in Baltimore and I myself observed this attitude toward her. . . .) She had come to you for relief from bona fide pain and disability. She approached the operation with confidence and hope because of her belief in you as the greatest man in your line. On the night before the operation she talked a great deal about how much happier her life was going to be when you had freed her from the handicap she had endured for many years. I am sure you gave the operation the best you've got but, after the operation, she began having the experiences which have made Johns Hopkins an unhappy memory for her.
>
> She is an adult and a highly intelligent one but she found herself being treated like a bothersome child. She was at first mystified and then intensely embarrassed by the attitude toward

her. . . . She wondered if you all did not consider her crazy or a liar when she was even refused simple relief for discomforts—a hot water bottle or an enema for the bad abdominal colic which plagued her, an ice pack or hot water bottle for her painful neck, a dose of soda for a stomach cramp.

After several experiences at finding that almost anything she said was misinterpreted, she became hesitant about saying anything when she was in pain and, in fact, began to worry whether she had really turned neurotic. In her efforts to cooperate, she walked when she was told to walk, even though it caused her extreme pain. She was ordered to sit up for several hours at a stretch and she did it—and almost fainted from the pain and the strain. (I have never seen her faint in the nearly twenty-five years I have known her, and I have seen her in situations that knocked out 200-pound men.) When she made further efforts to explain things, she was met with as little comprehension as if she had been talking in a foreign language. She got through the experience somehow.

John wrote that he was convinced that the trouble arose "from the fact that my wife is not only Mrs. John Marsh but 'Margaret Mitchell.'"

Because she once wrote a book that sold four million copies, I believe it was assumed in advance at Hopkins that she *must* be "temperamental." She was not judged on the basis of herself but on a preconceived notion that if she was "Margaret Mitchell" she must be nervous, queer, neurotic. Certainly, you must have personal knowledge of this sort of thing. Because you are the top man in your line, don't you find that strangers have preconceived notions about "The Great Dr. Dandy" which are very different from the real Walter Dandy?[79]

His letters explaining Peggy's pain are as detailed and precise as the most meticulous physician's medical records are, and he was aware that they were. "If you sometimes wonder why I know such intimate details and can see progress from week to week," he wrote Dr. Dandy, "it is because since her accident [the automobile accident in 1934] I have been massaging Mrs. Marsh's back. It gives her some relief when pain and muscular spasms are present." He went on to say,

For a full month after she returned from Johns Hopkins I could not rub her at all from the back of her head to her toes—the slightest pressure was too painful. Then, for another month, the only massage I could give was little more than "going through the motions." During the past month or so I have been able to increase the pressure gradually, though not yet up to full strength. By avoiding the too painful areas and handling others gently, I have been able to give her some relief. This is my best evidence of her gradual but very slow progress from widespread, general pain and soreness involving the entire lower half of her body and her upper back, at the time she left the hospital, to a localized area of pain now, especially in her lower back, left hip, left leg, and left foot.[80]

Ten weeks after the surgery, Peggy still could not sit on a hard chair at all and could not undertake any activity where the circumstances did not allow her to leave and lie down immediately if the pain became too great. In closing this long letter to the physician, John wrote,

The noise or sensation which she describes as "grinding, grating and slipping" in her back is present almost always when she walks. She did not have this sensation before the operation, except when she did sitting-up exercises. Her neck vertebrae remain sore and also her old shoulder injury. As the wide area of soreness gradually diminished from her entire back, I discovered a heretofore silent vertebra which is now almost as painful as the lumbar ones. It is slightly above where the lowest ribs hitch to the spine. She can bend very little . . . and still needs help with her left shoe and stocking.

In addition to all these problems since the surgery, John pointed out, she also had bloating and digestive problems. Before the surgery, she had had a hearty appetite and no digestive troubles at all. John reminded Dandy that when Peggy came to him for the operation in March 1943 she was in her best physical condition of several years. If she returned for another operation, it would only be after a prolonged siege of severe pain. He felt that with all her capacity for endurance, she would be less able to stand another such siege. As the days passed, she grew a little stronger, or perhaps just more accustomed to the chronic pain. Some days she was much more mobile and comfortable than she was on other days, for no discernible reason.

All during that spring and summer, she wore a lightweight rubber-and-steel brace under her loose-fitting housedresses. The brace was none too comfortable in the Georgia heat, but she believed that it supported her back. If she had realized how long it would take her get well and be strong again, she said she would not have had the operation, particularly at that time, when her father's health was failing.[81] He was not well enough to be left alone unattended, but he was not sick enough to stop quarreling with his attendants, who were always on the verge of quitting, so she was continually called upon at all hours to soothe an attendant's ego. On July 27, 1943, she wrote to Dr. Dandy, who kept insisting that she return to him for a second surgery. She told him plainly, "The last four months have been the most painful of my life. . . . I have been so bewildered by the oddness of my experiences at Johns Hopkins and the misunderstandings occurring there that mental shrinking is added to physical disinclination."

Truly perplexed and concerned, Dr. Dandy continued to write her and insisted upon seeing her again. In fact, he came to Atlanta in early December 1943 to examine Peggy. At that time her X rays showed so clearly that the second disc was indeed the source of her problem that he urged her not to waste any more time.[82] He wrote early in January 1944, suggesting that they go ahead and schedule her surgery, but the Marshes did not answer his letter. By this time, they were preoccupied with Eugene Mitchell, who was seriously ill. Then, on April 29, Dr. Dandy wrote again, asking her or John to send him a note about her condition and saying, "I do so want to see you well." Margaret Baugh sent him a brief note in May at Peggy's request. Tired of hospitals and illnesses, Peggy ignored Dr. Dandy's notes. Persistent in his efforts to get the Marshes to reply, the physician wrote again on September 26. Thinking that his letter had miscarried, he sent her another on December 7, 1944, almost pleading with her to tell him how she was, saying he hoped that she would return for the second operation. Apparently neither she nor John ever answered. Dr. Dandy died of a coronary occlusion on April 19, 1946, at Johns Hopkins Hospital.

Peggy never recovered from that first surgery and never had the second operation. She consulted with some Atlanta physicians, who were able to help her regain some measure of her former mobility, but she was never well enough to participate fully or regularly in social engagements or public work after this time.

17

As the war continued, *Gone With the Wind*'s foreign copyright problems became murkier because communications with foreign publishers were nearly impossible. As far as John could tell from the reports he had received, nearly every European country had its own translated edition of the book. Yet he was receiving only sketchy reports from Marion Saunders. At that point, he had their international accounting firm—Peat, Marwick, Mitchell, and Company—investigate Marion Saunders's records. It was through this audit that they learned Saunders had stolen several thousand dollars of the royalties paid to Peggy by foreign publishers.[83] They got rid of her as their agent but did nothing about prosecuting her, fearing involvement in unpleasant publicity. The problems with Saunders created a nightmare for John. Trying to find an honest agent with knowledge of international copyright laws while writing to publishers all over the world during wartime was the most frustrating activity he had ever had to perform.

The Marshes kept encouraging Wallace McClure to pursue the international copyright treaty. On May 12, 1943, Peggy wrote him that although it was too late for such a treaty to help her now, she and John remained interested in it because it would help all future American authors. After telling him about her slow recovery, she wrote: "As yet I have had no company and see no one except John and my secretary."[84]

By the end of May, she could walk about the apartment fairly well and could climb the stairs a few times, but she had not ventured out. They had no visitors anymore except Medora, who stopped by occasionally, and if Bessie or Deon had not been there, she would have been left alone in the apartment after John went to work.[85]

Because her friendship with Brickell and Granberry had fallen away over time, she corresponded mainly with John's family and with Leodel Coleman, their war correspondent friend from Statesboro, Georgia. In one of her frequent letters to him composed while she was in a reflective mood, she wrote:

> In a way, it's been an interesting experience, for this is the first time since *Gone With the Wind* was published, in 1936, that I've had time to just sit. My friends have mercifully let me alone and the general public has done likewise, so the phone rings but seldom and letters from strangers are few. I do miss not being able to do work at the Red Cross or on bonds and I felt very peculiar when an alert went off the other night and the town blacked out and John grabbed his warden's helmet and galloped out, leaving me here alone. I felt I should be galloping out too, if for no other reasons than to harry first aiders and stretcher squads. Still, I think it's doing me good physically and mentally just to sit and have a little time to think without the phone and door bell ringing all the time. However, as I do not see anyone, I have no news of interest to pass along to you.[86]

With gas rations as scarce as they were, she saved as many as she could by riding the buses whenever she went downtown shopping. Her first real visitor in more than three months was Susan Myrick, who came up from

Macon to see her. Peggy had been saving her meat ration points to buy a ham for some special occasion and decided that this was it. Showing what changes the war had brought to everyone, Sue, more impressed with the ham than anything else, declared she could no longer doubt the Marshes' affection, for she knew exactly how many ration points that ham had cost.[87]

In another letter to Coleman, Peggy urged him to write about everything he observed so the "homefolks will know what a war is really like."[88] The need was great, she explained, for good writing to bridge that almost unbridgeable gulf between soldiers and the civilians at home. Thinking about the past, she mused that such a gulf did not exist in "our Confederate war," nor would it exist in England after the war either. But in the United States, where the fighting was so far away, it was different. She and John had had many conversations about the disappointments of soldiers in the last war when they returned and found how little the civilians understood about war and about the terrible things it did to soldiers. So she urged the correspondent "to write in such a way that the true sensations of men who have fought will be made as vivid to us as they can possibly be made. So, when you write things remember this gulf and try to bridge it."[89]

In July, when the Georgia Press Association met in Atlanta on the hottest day of the year, Peggy had her first real outing and her first opportunity in months to see many of her friends. She was not well enough to attend any of the meetings with John, but she did go to the reception Governor and Mrs. Arnall gave for the editors at the Governor's Mansion. Although the mansion, built on a hill, had wide rooms and tall windows, it was suffocatingly hot and jammed full of editors. She wore a new white silk suit with a man-tailored jacket that hid her back brace and her "treasured three-year-old pair of nylon stockings." Nylon stockings were, as she remarked, "scarce as frog's hair in those days," and women were painting their legs with tanning lotions. At the reception, she observed: "Nearly all the female guests were stockingless and had their legs painted varying shades of tan. These leg lotions are guaranteed to be moisture-proof but the girls ought to get their money back, for you never saw such streaked and spotted and mottled legs in your life. At any rate, they were cooler than me."[90]

That outing was pleasant, although the main topic of discussion was the problem of getting volunteer part-time workers to harvest the crops. Planting was no problem at this time, but harvesting was, and in some small towns everything closed up two afternoons a week and the inhabitants, from bankers to butlers, volunteered to help with the crops. Prisoners of war were sent to south Georgia where they were used to harvest crops, especially the bumper crop of peanuts that year. Peggy noted in a letter, "The presence of prisoners in Georgia is something that is hard for me to believe."[91]

With regard to the serious labor shortage, she sent her friend a clipping from the *Constitution* about Ralph McGill and the *Constitution* cotton pickers, writing,

> There isn't a person in this state who will not brag that they picked cotton when they were a child, and could manage a hundred pounds by the time they were seven. Even people who have never been off hard pavement tell outrageous lies like this. So all the people on the Constitution who have been big-mouthed were sent out to pick cotton and prove whether they could do it. John had lunch with Ralph McGill yesterday and Ralph was so sore he didn't know whether to sit down or stand up. In fact, it nearly killed the Constitution staff members.[92]

Although Peggy sometimes found the energy to spend days at the Red Cross, she was not always able to be very active in Red Cross work. So, she found other ways to contribute. She did many generous and thoughtful things for young women in the Florence Crittendon Home for unmarried mothers. Not only did she encourage them to go on with their lives, but she also paid for them to have permanents, manicures, new clothes, and shoes when they went out to look for jobs. She also started a fund at Grady Hospital for such things as medicine, crutches, braces, corsets, and wheelchairs for poor patients. She saw to it that there was always car fare for their families to visit the hospital. Devoted to the children at the Formalt Mission, she made sure that they had clothes and toys and whatever else they may have needed. Then she got involved in helping prisoners.

After the Red Cross asked her to thank the inmates in the Atlanta federal penitentiary for their contributions to the war effort, she became interested in the plight of the prisoners there. Many of them, she learned, were volunteers in the malaria experiments and regular contributors to the Red Cross, as well as bond buyers and supporters of the Welfare Club. On January 7, 1942, in the prison auditorium, twenty-four hundred inmates assembled to receive Peggy's thanks for their gift of $1,225.50 to the Red Cross. When she finished her brief talk, the audience gave her a standing ovation. Back home that afternoon, she told John she wanted to do something for the prisoners, but could not figure out what. In talking about it, they came up with the idea of sponsoring a creative writing contest for the prison's publication, the *Atlantan.*

In explaining her idea to the warden, she said she wanted to involve as many people as possible in the contest. Although she hated to dictate how the money she was donating should be awarded, she asked that not just the most polished writers be selected as winners. She wanted those men whose mechanical writing skills were not so good but whose ideas were uniquely expressed to be winners also. This annual writing contest was a tremendous success. Years later, G. M. Kobernate, the associate warden, said that he could not speak from a literary point of view, but from the standpoint of personality improvement and constructive mental exercise, the project was invaluable.[93]

In addition to the cash prizes, she sent five copies of *Gone With the Wind*, with five personal notes, to the award-winning writers. She did not autograph the books but wrote the notes so that they could be pasted on the flyleaves if desired. Through the years Peggy received many sincere letters from prisoners thanking her for giving them "something to think about . . . something to break the mental sluggard out of almost any man." One wrote, "You have carved a deep niche of admiration for yourself in the hearts of all the men who participated as well as the officials of the institution."[94] Because of this pleasant experience, she was impressed with many of the prisoners and with the remarkably humane manner in which the Atlanta federal prison was managed. She was outspoken about wanting Georgia's entire penal system managed as well as the federal one was. She got angry whenever news reports went out about the brutalities of Georgia's wardens and guards in some of the isolated prison camps. It is ironic, in view of how her own life ended, that in this same letter, she wrote so sympathetically, "Some of these men were only doing a year for reckless and drunken driving."

18

In August 1943, Jock Whitney and David Selznick, whose health had been wrecked because of the energy he had put into his filmmaking, decided to dissolve Selznick International Pictures. After dividing the profits from *Gone With the Wind* and *Rebecca*, they each had nearly $4 million. In 1943, Whitney bought Selznick's share of *Gone With the Wind* for four hundred thousand dollars and subsequently sold it to Metro-Goldwyn-Mayer.[95] When he did this, he and Selznick sent Peggy a check for fifty thousand dollars in appreciation of her courtesy and helpfulness. Because this gift was unsolicited and unexpected, the Marshes thought it was remarkable. They greatly appreciated it, for it was the only instance of someone giving freely to them rather than taking or trying to take away. In writing her appreciation, Peggy said:

> I came home from a long day at the Red Cross, too tired to take my shoes off, and . . . found your letter and the very generous check. . . . I had to read it twice before it made any sense and then

it almost made me cry. You two and I and hundreds of others have been associated in the most phenomenally successful event in motion picture or theatrical history. I have seen the picture five and a half times now and have examined it from many angles—musical scores, costumes, bit players, etc., and I like it better each time. And each time the film reaches out and takes my hand to lead me down paths that seem ever new, for I forget in watching that I was the author of the book and am able to view the film with fresh eyes. At the Grand Theatre here in Atlanta, they play the theme music from Gone With the Wind when the last performances of the night are over. Frequently John and I and many other Atlantans remain in our seats to listen to it. . . . I never hear this music without feeling the strange mixture of emotions that I experienced on that night nearly three years ago when I sat in the same theatre and saw the film for the first time. I doubt if I could describe those emotions, but they did not include fear that it would not be a great picture. Years before I had seen your picture David Copperfield and I realized that here was a producer of . . . integrity who was breaking all the Hollywood rules by producing the book the author wrote . . . adding to it his own color, firing it with his own imagination, heightening effects with his own genius. So on the night of the premiere, I knew before the film began to roll that it would be a great picture and before many minutes had passed I knew it was even greater than I could have expected. I have always thought myself fortunate that Selznick International produced GWTW.[96]

19

As time passed, Peggy no longer got fan mail, but still received a few crank letters. No matter how often John begged her to ignore them, telling her, "You don't get anything out of kicking a skunk except a very bad smell," she persisted in wasting time answering such letters, which she filed under "Curioso." A good example of her obsession with minutiae is a "Curioso" from a woman who described herself as a "clairaudient and clairvoyant—strongly psychic . . . and not one of Margaret Mitchell's fans."[97] Nevertheless, this lunatic claimed that *Gone With the Wind* was a little like her own story. Whether Peggy knew it or not, Peggy was evidently so psychic that her work was practically done through "automatic writing," and the trouble with her eyes stemmed from departed spirits inhabiting them and enabling her to write the book she wrote. "Godalmighty!" Peggy exclaimed. She set about writing this woman a long letter that began, "I am afraid you have been misinformed, for there is nothing at all the matter with my eyes, and so there cannot be any 'departed spirits' bothering me. . . . I am the least 'psychic' of any living human being and, far from having written *Gone With the Wind* through 'automatic writing,' I labored over it for ten years. . . . I doubt if any 'departed spirits' would possess that much energy. Someone has evidently given you misinformation about me and my writing."[98]

Although John found amusing many of the trivial things that incensed Peggy, he found nothing amusing about a woman who impersonated her and charged accounts in department stores all over the country. He hired the Pinkerton National Detective Service to help him locate the imposter. Reports about this woman described her as being "very fond of men," and the Marshes found the stories about her sexual behavior embarrassing. John wanted to put her out of business as quickly as he could. He also had this detective service track down a falsehood about Peggy's writing part of the novel in the Albert's French Restaurant on University Place and Eleventh Street in Greenwich Village. Later he was even more disturbed when another such rumor cropped up about her writing the novel at Brickell's Acorn Cottage in Connecticut.

20

In February 1944, John and Peggy went to Washington, D.C., to visit his mother and his sister Frances, and then on to Camden, New Jersey, for the official launching of the new *Atlanta,* one of two destroyers that had been built with the money Georgia raised and had been unofficially launched a few months earlier in Charleston.[99] John worried whether a person with a bad back could launch a ship without fresh injury to herself, but Peggy assured him that she could.

During the first half-hour of their arrival, John was thinking more about Peggy than about the ship. But then his attention shifted to where a group had formed into a tight knot on the launching platform. Watching intently, he stayed down on the ground until a minute or two before the ship was launched. He had always been thrilled to see the moment when big power plants were put into action for the first time, and now he was fascinated with watching the workmen getting things ready for this event. He knew it was a job that had to be done exactly right or it could be a terrible failure. When he saw that the preliminary signals were being given, he climbed the steps to the platform for a better view.

He wrote his mother,

Less than a minute later, the final signal was given, the ship slowly at first began to move, Peggy swung the champagne bottle with a mighty smash—and I was no longer calm. It is an experience that takes aholt of you clear down to your toes. Whether you are, or wish to be, calm on such an occasion, you can't be calm. I had never realized before what a "climactic" event a launching is. It is an ordinary piece of land construction turning into a sea animal, it is the culmination of the work of many men for many months, more stirring than the dedication of any land building could be, and it is the final crucial test of engineering and physical labor that built the ship. The wives of the company officials who had lunch with us said that they always said their prayers before the launching of any big ship, that no matter how many others they had launched successfully they could never feel certain that *this* one wouldn't turn over when she hit the water or suffer some other catastrophe. . . . But "our" ship moved off like a lady and everything went just right.[100]

In a letter to her friend Leodel Coleman, Peggy wrote,

I think if I swung a champagne bottle at a ship every day of my life the queer excitement would never diminish. There is a feeling that cannot be put into words when the first small shiver of tons of steel is felt. Then when she begins to slide slowly and picks up speed like a greyhound and finally hits the water with a crash and a splash it is impossible not to be torn between Rebel yells and tears. I wasn't the only one who felt that way. The captain of the other *Atlanta,* Sam Jenkins, who was badly wounded in that fight when his ship was lost, was standing near me at this launching. My naval aide, DeSales Harrison, formerly an Atlanta Coca-Cola official, was beside me, too, and I discovered that I was not the only one whose face was wet, and it was not from splattering champagne.[101]

After the launching the shipbuilding company took the Atlanta party to the company cafeteria for lunch. There Mr. Campbell, the president of the company, presented Peggy with a gold pin in the shape of a "V," which bore in colored enamel several signal flags that spelled out "U.S.S. Atlanta." Proud of that pin, she wore it on her coat lapel.[102]

21

Her father had taken a bad turn for the worse on May 15, 1944, and was being kept alive with intravenous solutions. He was so weak he could barely speak, but he made it clear that he wanted Peggy to stay close to him. She and Carrie Lou, Stephens's wife, took turns sitting with him. Peggy wrote a friend, "I have seen my father in almost as bad condition before and seen him pull through, and so he may get over this particular sinking spell. However, I do not know if I would want him to, bad though that may sound. He has been ill five years and has had no pleasure from life and very little comfort either."[103]

Eugene Mitchell died quietly in the early morning hours of June 17, 1944. No member of his family was present. Even with all the preparation for this event that Peggy had had throughout his long illness, she was shocked. "This was the first death in which I have been so closely involved in my adult years," John wrote his mother, "and it taught me things I didn't know before—about myself, I mean. Even when you know something like that is for the best, it is a shaking experience."[104] In his characteristic manner of doing whatever needed to be done, John made all the arrangements for the funeral. "Steve and Peggy were glad to be relieved of the load," he wrote his mother, "but just how I lived through that day myself I scarcely know. On top of all the many details that needed handling, Bessie was sick and I had my first experience with shopping with ration points, and the weather was just about as hot as it ever gets to be down here, glaring, dazzling heat without a breath of wind before 11 o'clock at night. As one who had never before had anything to do with funerals except as a 'guest,' I learned a new admiration for the people in families who have carried this same load before."[105]

22

The Marshes traced the progress that was being made in the Pacific in the summer of 1944. In July, they were heartened by the news that U.S. troops had landed on Guam, though the casualty lists were high. Peggy wrote Leodel: "Those of us at home who have friends or relatives in the thick of the fight rejoice when advances and victories are reported and do our best not to get sick at our stomachs as we wait for news of those we know. I know you'll know what I mean when I say that, while the home front is proud of the way the services are fighting, we cannot be wildly happy, knowing what a price has to be paid for each advance."[106]

As the end of the war grew nearer, the book's foreign business grew more complicated. *Gone With the Wind* was enormously popular in Europe, where it was admired for its antitotalitarian views. The Communists and the Nazis hated it and attacked it every way they could, but banning it, of course, made it all the more desirable. Bob Considine, writing in the *New York Journal American* on March 25, 1944, reported that copies of *"Gone With the Wind* were bootlegged in France for $60.00 and almost that figure in Holland, Norway, and Belgium. Persons have been shot for possessing it. Orders have gone out from Germany to seize all copies. The people of the occupied lands see in *Gone With the Wind* proof positive that a nation's armies can be defeated and its land ravaged by superior forces and yet remain spiritually unconquered—its traditions and pride intact. To these people the book has a message much deeper and keener than the now historic love life of the book's principal figures."[107]

The French newspaper *France Soir* wanted to serialize *Gone With the Wind* because the French considered the novel an anticommunist book. Although the Marshes were in favor of helping the French, they never wanted any serializations, sequels, or comic strips made from the book. Since they did not want the French to think they were refusing because of lack of interest, they asked George Brett to refuse for them.

As soon as the war was over, John was inundated with mail and telegrams from foreign countries. Marion Saunders had left things in a mess. As he looked into the abyss of international copyrights, he reeled back in dismay.

1945-1952

REALITY OF DARK DREAMS

I have known all along that Peggy had an enormous public following but what has happened has exceeded my expectations many, many times. I have been extraordinarily fortunate in having such a person for my wife.
        —John Marsh to his mother, 26 August 1949

1

IMMEDIATELY AFTER THE WAR ENDED, a number of European publishers and agents who had survived the siege began reporting to the Marshes and sending them copies of the foreign editions. Their correspondence was especially complicated and time-consuming at first because translating the letters was difficult. Margaret Baugh could read the French letters, John, the German, and Steve, the Italian and Spanish. For all the other languages, John had to turn to people working in banks and import businesses, returned missionaries, refugees, and war brides. When the word went out that the Marshes desperately needed translators, calls came from people like Dr. Goodrich White, president of Emory University, who gave Peggy the address of a missionary who could read Chinese. Even an excited child called saying he and his mama could read Bulgarian.[1]

Gone With the Wind sales had soared in occupied countries, where it was banned by the Nazis and sold on the black market. The first bulk of letters came from France, Germany, Czechoslovakia, Italy, and Bulgaria. Then a publisher in Hungary wrote that the Hungarian translation of *Gone With the Wind* had sold nearly sixty thousand copies. The Marshes found it hard to believe that many copies were sold in such a small country, but the publisher explained that his edition had set a record for any translation of a "foreign" book in his country.[2]

The foreign reviews, the book jackets, and the pictures fascinated John and Peggy. When they received a copy of the pirated Chinese edition, they laughed at how the publisher had altered Peggy's photograph, making her eyes tilt upward, giving her a more Oriental look. In addition, he gave her the virtues that the Chinese consider attractive in a woman, describing her as "modest, pure, and benevolent."[3] Peggy wrote, "Also, they have credited me with another highly thought of Chinese characteristic—that I am a perfect housekeeper."[4]

In all the translations there were glossaries for such words as "barbeque, brunswick stew, toddy, and sassy."[5] John could never get used to seeing blacks say, "Ach, Gott!" instead of "Gawdlmighty" in the German edition.[6]

The novel was fiercely attacked in Communist-dominated countries. Although the Communist press called the novel a waste of time and paper and said that people ought to be ashamed of themselves for idling away their valuable time, the book was enormously popular. John wrote his mother,

> It is described as almost treasonable because it makes heroes of people who fought a war in defense of their native land and not because of their loyalty to "The United States." One reviewer quotes the passage where Ashley writes to Melanie, telling her that after being in the war for a while, he now knows what he is fighting for . . . he says he is willing to keep on fighting, not in defense of slavery, or for the Confederate States, but simply because of his love for his own home and his desire to protect it. The Yugo-slav writer says this is a terrible view point for anybody to have. People ought to do things for the honor and glory of "The State" and not because of their love for some piece of land. As you know, the struggle in Yugoslavia is between the Communist conquerors and the small farmers who are still resisting them. If GWTW can encourage them in their struggle, it is serving a finer purpose than we ever dreamed of when it was in the making.[7]

In addition to many requests for a sequel, they had also received offers for new translations in the Slovak language of Czechoslovakia, the Slovene language in Yugoslavia, and the Hebrew language in Israel. "The latter, if it is actually published, is an edition which we will regard as a prize item in our collection," John told his mother. "Naturally, all business arrangements are in a tangle now, but some of the complications are being straightened out. We even have hope of getting revenge on the publisher in Holland who pirated her book. Although the prospects of collecting any money from him are not good, we will get considerable pleasure out of forcing the pirating publisher to settle, if it can be done."[8]

The foreign editions had given the book prestige and a widespread audience, and the Marshes believed that someday they might actually make a great deal of money out of them. But at that time all they had gotten was a good education, partly because of the restrictions on payments from various European countries to the United States, and partly because some of the foreign publishers did not aim to pay. John said, "They seem to regard it as an imposition if a 'foreigner' attempts to collect the royalties they have agreed to pay."[9]

The *Gone With the Wind* movie, which had not been shown in the United States for two or three years, was beginning to get its first showing in several of the European countries. It was the first movie ever shown at the famous opera house in Paris. In England, all during the bombings, fires, and last-ditch defenses, it had a continuous run for five years at London's Leicester Square.[10] During those blitz days, Londoners identified with the Battle of Atlanta and Scarlett's struggle to survive. As the hundreds of letters Peggy received demonstrated, Scarlett was more to the victims in war-torn countries than a mere romantic heroine. Trying to analyze the book's success, John wrote his mother, "Each country suffering the hardships of an invading army seems to identify itself with the South, and take courage from Peggy's story of how the South survived its hard experience. I suppose that is the explanation of the popularity we never expected for the book in the foreign countries."[11]

In 1945, poignant letters came in daily like this one from a German who wrote, "From the 'Tara' we have lost, I escaped with Goethe's poems and your beloved book. You have written what we are living and your view of the past has described our disaster just exactly as though you had lived through it."[12] A German Jewess wrote, "What I want to tell you is that you helped to keep me alive. Thoughts of you and your exceptional book made my life bearable." Hundreds of requests for financial help came in, like the following from an Hungarian woman: "Like her [Scarlett], I have no job and no money.... Perhaps you will be able to help me. There is no earthly reason why you should of course. Except that you wrote 'Scarlett.'" From a Chinese student came a request for two suits of clothes and some ginseng for his father. Because the housing shortage was so bad, some people asked her to help them find a place to stay.[13] At one point, Peggy told Medora, "I don't believe anybody in the world is afraid of me. People ask me to do anything and everything, from writing a history paper for a 12-year-old son to collaborating on a novel for which I am promised 10 percent of the proceeds."[14]

While John took care of all the business matters, Peggy took care of the personal ones. Like many other concerned Americans, she sent packages of food and clothing to England and Europe all during the war. She continued doing so until her death, whereupon John continued until his death. Thereafter Stephens continued the practice for years, though on a much smaller scale.[15] During that postwar time of shortages, Peggy had to spend extra time shopping. John wrote, "Buying food requires a personal expedition so that one can keep on good terms with the grocer. Peggy says that she has found that cajolery and flattery are not nearly as effective as being sympathetic with the grocer and butcher. She sympathizes with them when they are sorry that they have nothing to sell, and occasionally they do find something for her to buy."[16]

After VE Day, she sent to each liberated country three boxes of gifts—one to her publisher, another to the translator, and another to the agent who handled the rights. In addition, she started sending boxes all over Europe, trying to respond to every request she received. Whenever she could, she fulfilled specific requests like the one from the Chinese student. It was almost as if she had some moral responsibility to answer each request. She shopped for the items herself and did all the packaging and wrapping on the dining room table in the apartment. Bessie never helped except, perhaps, in storing the cans and boxes in the pantry when Peggy brought them home from the grocery.[17] Into each package, she always placed a few toys and candy for children, saying, "I remember my disappointment as a child when a parcel would be opened, and there would be nothing in it for me."[18] On good days, when her back was not hurting too badly, Peggy carried the parcels down the steps of the apartment, loaded them into the car, and took them to the post office herself. Margaret Baugh, who filled out the customs declarations, said that mailing boxes to some countries required as many as four forms, and that as the years passed sending the parcels amounted to a huge expense: "The volume of packages grew without our realizing it."[19] Peggy's generosity during these years is truly remarkable.

2

Nearly all of the hot, dry summer and fall of 1945, Peggy was often sick, suffering from allergies and arthritis. She had developed the kind of allergies that break out on the skin, itch, and burn. She not only felt but also looked bad—bloated and blotchy. In June, she was stricken with bursitis in both shoulders and had to wear her right arm in a sling for several weeks. She felt as if she were falling apart. Some mornings she was so stiff and sore she could hardly get out of bed. Her eyesight had deteriorated so badly that she had to wear thick eyeglasses in order to see anything. She rarely left the apartment except to go to the post office, or to Rich's department store to buy more goods to send abroad; and every Thursday she went to the grocery store on Tenth Street, and then to Dr. Waters's office for B-1 vitamin shots, which she said relieved her arthritic back pain.[20]

Convinced that vitamins would help her, she took handfuls of them daily. "But they haven't helped much so far," John wrote his sister. "Recently she has been taking a course of the fertility vitamin—E. I am told that doctors are using that now for neuritis. ... I was surprised when Peggy told me that lettuce was one of the principal sources of this fertility vitamin. I could not associate lettuce with any idea of fertility, but Peggy set me right when she asked, 'What are rabbits?'"[21]

Although she was only forty-five years old, she looked much older. Like many other pretty women, she loathed losing her beauty and vitality, but she did nothing to improve her appearance. People who had not seen her in a long time were surprised by the frumpish way she looked. Because of her inability to be active, she weighed a blimpish 135 pounds. Making no attempt to style her hair, which was graying and thinning, she wore it too long for her age and parted on the left, held back with a tortoise-shell barrette. Because of the back brace that she had been using since her surgery, she wore loose-fitting, sleeveless cotton sundresses year-round. In cold weather, she wore an oversized brown wool cardigan over them. Except for special occasions when she dressed up, she always wore white socks and flat-heeled brown leather shoes that laced.

Although her appearance had changed remarkably, her personality had not. She was still as funny as ever when she wanted to be, and "sprightly and gay when she felt well," wrote Margaret Baugh. "There was a great deal of laughter around MM. She used to call me 'Miss Alice B. Toklas.' The thing that made that even funnier was that she didn't care at all for Gertude Stein's writing."[22]

But Peggy still focused on petty details and rumors. Although her name was rarely mentioned by the media anymore, whenever she discovered an occasional misstatement in the press or on the radio, she would spend hours talking on the phone or writing letters trying to correct it. When a reporter named Paul Jeral wrote that Margaret Mitchell had leukemia, she sent George Brett a copy of the letter she wrote Jeral, saying, "I hope it may draw from him the source of his information and then I can land on the source like a duck on a June bug and stop this rumor before it spreads too far. Sometimes I've had luck in nipping these affairs in the bud."[23]

And as if Brett had nothing else to do but watch for rumors about her, she asked him to communicate matters of this type to her if any arose in the future.

> I have had a great many rumors to contend with in the last four years and I sometimes wonder whether all authors are so plagued and embarrassed. I have had, according to legend, a broken back from which I would never recover, incurable blindess . . . a wooden leg, three children, a divorce from John, and a pregnancy—twins at that. . . . I am at a loss to understand why the public appears to want me to be in a doomed condition. Far from being doomed at present, I am twenty pounds heavier than I have ever been in my life and most embarrassingly fat. As I can take no exercise until the end of June, I suppose I will have to trundle my avoirdupois about for a while longer—and doubtless take to wearing Mother Hubbards, as I can find nothing which will fit me.

She still continued to write long letters demonstrating her mastery of relating anecedotes and her sense of humor. When two U.S.S. *Atlanta* seamen with whom she had been corresponding for a couple of years sent her a beautiful bouquet of summer flowers, she rewarded them with a delightful story. She told them about the recent drought, which had been so severe that the "farmers were all desperate" and everyone was worried that food was going to be short the next year. She wrote, "Everyone was perspirey and irritable, but we aren't ever going to complain of the heat any more—for this reason." She went on to explain that as she was going to the Red Cross with a friend, she mentioned a little item she had read in the newspaper about how the farming community of Millen, Georgia, losing all their crops for lack of rain, got together to pray for rain. Her friend said to her that she wished people wouldn't do things like that or else wished the newspapers wouldn't print such stories.

"Just think how silly such conduct makes us appear to Northern people," she said. "I feel right mortified that Southern people should act that way." I replied that I did not care what Northern people thought. And I had barely said these words when, with no warning, the heaviest rain I ever saw fell upon us. By the time the bus got to the Red Cross the water in the streets was above our ankles. It rained all day all over the state and in Southern Georgia most of the chicken coops were carried away and they do say that the rabbits were climbing trees to keep from being drowned. It slacked up around six o'clock, and the night issue of the Constitution carried a story that the Millen people were going to church the next morning in a body to thank the Lord for the rain. About a half hour after the Millen folks thanked the Lord, it began to hail and the hailstones were bigger than lemons. I was trying to get to the Red Cross again and fearing that my skull would be fractured at any minute, and it rained and hailed all day. As our old colored janitor said, "It don't do no good to trifle with the Lord, 'cause if you akse him for somethin' He likely to sen' mo' than you can handle." As you know, shoes are not too plentiful and no one likes to ruin their shoes by getting them wet. And all over town I heard people saying that somebody ought to take steps about the Millen people and make them stop praying, or else we'd all be stomp barefooted. I was wet and cold so much those two days that I don't think I'll ever complain about the heat again.[24]

Well into autumn, as their overseas business was becoming heavier and more complicated, John came down with a high fever, just as he had done in 1940. That time, though, the fever disappeared after he rested a week in the hospital. This time it did not disappear. After four weeks of malaise and fever, he wrote his sister Frances:

I enjoy being lazy when I have sufficient excuse to satisfy my conscience. We must have had some Puritan ancestors, for it is my nature to feel that I must always be busy and even in my recreation I must feel there is some practical benefit in it, that it does me good to play golf et cetera. But when the compulsions of conscience have been removed by an official order to rest, I don't know anybody who can be any lazier than I can or enjoy it more. I have even been working cross-word puzzles, which are a symbol of luxury and laziness to me and something I never do except when I am laid up sick.[25]

By the end of October, he felt a little better even though he continued to run a temperature. He was able to do almost a regular day's work without running the temperature up or being afflicted with the heavy sweating characteristic of undulant fever. His condition was more of a handicap than a disability, he assured his mother, telling her there was nothing for her to worry about. His physician figured that John, who took his lunch downtown every day, had gotten infected by drinking some impure milk somewhere. (In those days, Atlanta did not have a law requiring that all milk be pasteurized.) He told his mother, who had fallen and injured her hand, that Peggy, too, continued to have severe pain whenever she tried to use her right wrist, hand, and arm.[26]

As the end of the year approached, *Gone With the Wind* business continued to provide the ailing John with more work than he had the energy to do, and he hired another secretary to help him and Margaret Baugh. Tired as they all were with translating the accounts, they still got excited when they received word from a publisher in Denmark saying that he expected sales to pass one hundred thousand copies by the end of the year. Norway had also checked in with a report of sales of about forty thousand. But not all the news was good. One of the returned American soldiers with whom Peggy had been corresponding during the war wrote her that he had seen an edition in Flemish while he was in Antwerp. Because she had not authorized any edition in Flemish, she had another piracy case on her hands. The good news was that the Dutch piracy case showed signs of being cleared up.[27] "This foreign stuff keeps us busy," Peggy wrote a friend.[28]

Back to his old grind of working on the book's business at night and on weekends, John was still running a temperature in December. He fibbed to his mother when he wrote that his condition was no longer serious. In a letter to Lois Cole written shortly before Christmas, Peggy pessimistically acknowledged: "Neither John nor I have done very well in the last six months. He is always so fatigued it frightens me, but there is nothing much to do about it except 'supportive' treatment. Perhaps by spring this new drug, streptomycin, will be out of the experimental class and we can try it. As for me, my inability to use my right arm throws too much extra work on John and Margaret. We never seem to get caught up on our work."[29]

As the holiday approached, the Marshes abruptly decided to go to Sea Island to rest. To them, the stretch of coast from Savannah southward to Brunswick was the most beautiful, most peaceful place in the world. Their paradisiacal retreat was Sea Island, a tiny, droplet-shaped piece of land across the marsh off the tip of the larger, historic St. Simon's Island. Although the resorts had boats to rent for fishing, horses for riding, and tennis courts, swimming pools, and golf courses, John and Peggy found simply driving down the long, sandy roads under the huge, moss-covered live oak trees a most tranquilizing experience. "Up at the end of St. Simon's Island," she wrote a friend, "there is a stillness of marsh water and trees like the day after creation, and this stillness never fails to have a very soothing effect on this weary and harassed pair."[30]

The millionaire manufacturer Howard Coffin had developed Sea Island and built the beautiful Cloister Hotel there in the late 1920s, and the Marshes frequently spent long weekends resting there in the early 1940s. Their only objection to staying at the luxurious hotel was that it did not face the sea or the marshes. They preferred the Cloister apartments in the River House, which was built close to the hotel but right on the edge of a beautiful river that ran through the Marshes of Glynn.[31]

Ordinarily, Peggy drove them to the islands, but with her right shoulder and arm inflamed with arthritis, she could not drive this trip. So, on Christmas Eve 1945, they boarded the train to Jesup, a little railroad junction town in southeast Georgia, on the Atlanta-Birmingham and Coast Railroad line. At Jesup, they had to change trains to go to Brunswick, about forty-five miles away. A still waterway—the Marshes of Glynn—lay between Brunswick and St. Simon's, and a station wagon from the Cloister Hotel would meet them at the Brunswick train station and transport them the five or six miles across the bridge to Sea Island.

Their train pulled into Jesup during a driving, cold rainstorm. It was Christmas Eve, late in the evening, and no porters were in sight to help John with their luggage. They had no umbrellas or raincoats, just their overcoats.

John handed Peggy the newspaper he had been reading and told her to cover her head and run ahead to the shelter. As he struggled in the blinding rain carrying their two suitcases and his briefcase, he felt a sudden, stabbing tightening in his chest and neck. For a moment, he could not breathe or move. His hat, overcoat, and feet got soaking wet. When he finally made it into the depot, he dropped the bags and sat down. Peggy knew something was terribly wrong, but he assured her that he was all right. Once the train to Brunswick pulled into sight, John had to carry the bags again in the pouring rain. Wet and cold, he became chilled and ashen. He said nothing about the smothering sensation or the chills as they rode silently on to Brunswick. Noticing his labored breathing, Peggy became seriously alarmed.[32]

By the time they finally got registered and settled into their apartment, John was so sick he stumbled onto the bed. Within seconds, he suffered a massive heart attack. Terrified that he was going to die, she got hysterical as she rang for help. Adding to her terror was the shocking news that the hotel had no doctor—that the island, in fact, the desk clerk apologetically told her, had no doctor. Her helplessness loomed large in her mind as she thought about all those years that John had been taking care of everything for her. He always knew what to do and he did it. And now when he needed her so desperately, she was helpless. Forcing herself to become calm, she listened to the desk clerk say that the best he could do was to have the station wagon driver take them to the hospital in Brunswick.

Somehow the driver, the desk clerk, and Peggy managed to move John, near death, into the station wagon, and they arrived at the hospital in the late-night hours. With John crumpled in the back seat of the car waiting with the driver, Peggy raced up the steps into the hospital, where she found the anteroom bare. The doctors and nurses, even the orderlies, off on their Christmas Day vacation, were nowhere in sight. In pure terror and anger, Peggy stood in the silent, dimly lit corridor and screamed with all her might for help.[33]

John's condition was gravely complicated by the delay in his receiving medical attention, and it was astonishing that he survived at all.[34] He was so sick that it was three weeks before he could even be moved to Piedmont Hospital in Atlanta. All during the time he lay in the Brunswick hospital, Peggy rarely left his bedside for more than a few minutes. Because the war was on, the shipyards had gobbled up all of the available labor and the hospital was having a hard time retaining even a minimum staff of competent people after the Christmas holiday.[35] Thus Peggy did not feel safe leaving him unattended for a moment and refused to do so.

When Margaret Baugh and Stephens arrived on Christmas evening, she told them, "Go back to Atlanta. Look after things for us. I can't think about anything but John. I've got to get him well." Henry Marsh left for Brunswick shortly after Peggy called on Christmas morning, tearfully telling him the news. Gordon and Frances followed the next day. All of John's brothers and sisters feared the worst, for they remembered how their father had died suddenly after running a fever for a long time when he was about John's age.

Francesca recalled later that for someone who had been in the crippling condition Peggy had endured for two years, she responded to the ordeal with remarkable strength. She refused to let the orderlies do anything for John that she could do herself. She took her meals in his room, slept on a cot placed next to his bed, dressed and washed in his hospital bathroom. She asked questions about his medications and got furious with the staff when she thought they were not moving as quickly as they should. Although John could not talk to her, she talked to him, read to him, and told him little funny stories. And throughout each day, she frequently caressed his face as she whispered into his ear that she loved him. Francesca said that Peggy was truly heroic and that it was very moving to see them together in that sad setting.[36]

As soon as they heard the news, Angus and Medora rushed to the Brunswick hospital. When Medora wanted to know what she could do to help, Peggy asked her to go to the Cloister apartment and get her padded silk bag containing her last two pairs of nylon stockings, scarce commodities during the war. Medora recalled that as Peggy was washing a pair of these stockings several days later, one of them slipped from her hand and slid down the drain of the hospital lavatory, hopelessly snagged in the pipe. When that happened, Peggy uttered a deep groan from the back of her throat and let go of the other stocking. Dropping to her knees, she bowed her head, crying profusely as she sat on the floor. John was not progressing as well as she had hoped, and she must have felt as if he was slipping from her hands as easily as her stocking had slipped, and there was nothing she could do about it. Until that moment when the floodgates broke open, she had held up courageously throughout the ordeal.[37]

4

Two months later, Peggy had John back in Atlanta and in Piedmont Hospital, where he was slowly edging his way back from death's door. In responding to Lois Cole's telegram, Peggy explained:

> You know that I am the least optimistic of people. So when I say that I am happy at his good progress and have hope for a decent life for him if he is very careful—then you know that he is doing

very well.... He was in pretty bad shape when his heart gave out. During the attack his lungs had filled with fluid and, fearing pneumonia, he was given penicillin. He has had no whiff of fever since then, which proves that he did not have undulant fever, for penicillin availeth naught with that disease.[38]

Although the Atlanta heart specialist whom Peggy selected came highly recommended, he was not communicative and she did not like him. Upon dismissing John from the hospital, the physician left brief written instructions to John to the effect that, once home, he should get up and about, walk up and down the three flights of stairs to his apartment, go on automobile rides, and return to work in April. Trying to proceed accordingly on the first day he got home, John nearly fainted without doing anything more vigorous than sitting up at the table to eat breakfast and standing up to shave. Angry with the physician's lack of response when she tried to explain John's worsening condition, she dismissed him and called in Dr. W. C. Waters. Having had a serious heart attack himself, Dr. Waters was much more understanding and conservative.

In a long, undated, typed letter to John's mother in the early spring of 1946, Peggy wrote about the hectic time she had had since returning from Brunswick.

There was a month or six weeks' foreign stuff back up waiting for me, all of it of No 1 importance.... There were several new contracts ... and our contracts are something that have to be seen to be believed. Most authors never even look at what they sign and become terrorized when publishers and agents say coldly, "This is our standard contract." When possible I try to knock the teeth out of anyone who tells me to sign a "standard" contract, for I know they are knaves or fools or both. So our contracts are pretty troublesome.... Food shortages keep me shopping half the day; the usual stupidities of people who do not care a hoot if they disturb John by crashing into the house ... and the foreign stuff keeps rolling along.

She added that when she realized that she had a bed patient on her hands, she did her best to slow down.

Unfortunately, it was like throwing on the brakes when you are doing a hundred and ten, and it took some time to get us slowed. Regardless of the pressures from outside, John comes first and when he is not having a good day, everything stands still.... I think these weeks of enforced quiet have done all of us good. Right now I can consider with equanimity my long delayed action in the matter of a piracy in Belgium, when six months ago I would have had the American Embassy in Brussels, lawyers, auditors and possibly the U.S. Marines on the job.[39]

Stephens, Margaret Baugh, Henry Marsh, Bessie, and Deon—all noted that for as long as any of them could remember, the Marsh household had centered on Peggy's needs, but now it centered on John's. They noticed too that Peggy seemed stronger and was determined to do what John had always done for her. His incapacity forced her to grow up at last. Their roles reversed, she became his protector.

With the European sales reports pouring in, she was fierce about getting her royalties from publishers who appeared not to want to pay her. Her motivation stemmed from her desire that John not have to worry about being unable to work again. Although he talked about a complete recovery and about going back to Georgia Power, she knew that his future was bleak. The doctors in Brunswick had told her that he had only a year or two at the most to live.[40]

Anyone looking at the tremendous volume of paperwork that John Marsh alone handled—the letters, the contracts, and the transactions with accountants, lawyers, agents, and publishers in countries all over the world, from 1936 until 1945—in addition to his work at Georgia Power, can imagine what chronic stress he endured and why his heart gave out. According to Margaret Baugh's bookkeeping, 1,250,000 copies of the foreign translations had been sold by the spring of 1946, and that was only counting the authorized editions. "God knows how many unauthorized copies are out there!" Peggy snorted sourly. "Let's crack down on the bastards!"

The first week in May, Macmillan announced that 3,713,272 copies of the American edition of *Gone With the Wind* had thus far been sold.[41] With that kind of achievement, Peggy had secured her immortality.

5

As his convalescence dragged on, John became depressed and was often unable to sleep. For several months, he could not even sit up in bed for very long without becoming exhausted. His craving for nicotine was agonizing; his helplessness and inactivity were frustrating and dull. He could not shut his mind off. Worried about Peggy, Steve, and Margaret Baugh carrying the full load, he felt useless. "I knew that I *must* get back on the job," he later wrote a friend. "Peggy needed me, the Power Company needed me. I had stayed in bed as long as I could, and no damned heart was going to keep me in bed any longer. That period was the worst one." But then he went on to say, "Eventually I stopped struggling, and I immediately began getting better."[42]

As the months passed, John's condition slowly improved. By spring-time, he wrote that the bad news was that weakness and weariness overtook him after the slightest exertion. But the good news was that he had not smoked a cigarette since December 24, and his senses of smell, taste, and hearing were keener than they had ever been. When he gradually became able to sit up for longer periods, he started writing to his family and to a few close friends. These letters are beautifully expressed personal records of his determination to recover, and they are noticeably devoid of any mention of *Gone With the Wind* business. By acknowledging his destructive "workaholic" habits, he deliberately learned to practice mind control and relaxation techniques to make himself stronger. In the beginning of his recovery, he spent much of his time thinking and talking to Peggy about his childhood and in writing about it. In a nostalgic mood, he wrote a letter to his cousin Mary Louise Nute on October 7, 1946:

> It is odd how these old recollections are colored by a person's emotions. Some of the houses and families I remember vividly and others very indistinctly, and nearly always it is because of some liking or disliking. . . . I have sharp and clear recollections of the store on the corner of Commerce and Second Streets which was run by the two old men with squeaky voices. They sold candy out of a barrel, five pieces for a penny, and when I got a penny I would go over there and buy some. One time when Mother sent me there to get some groceries, I took one of her pennies and bought some candy and told her the storekeeper had short-changed me. At the time it didn't bother me but a few years later when I entered the religious phase it weighed on my mind heavily as a Sin.

Until his heart attack, John had always been what he called a "natural born sleeper," and Peggy had been the sleepless one. Now, except for short naps, he hardly slept at all. In the spring of 1946, he wrote Frances:

> I have been compelled to learn some of the tricks by which a person gets off to sleep when he isn't extremely tired. Among ideas suggested by Peggy was a plan by which a person can slow down his mind from going buckity-buckity and thus making sleep impossible. It was to wander in one's thoughts down some old

familiar street or road, trying to recall each house and all other details of the landscape. I've found it not only helpful in getting off to sleep but interesting as well. In these past weeks I have in reverie wandered over Maysville and Lexington more than at any time since I moved away from Kentucky. After a person has worked at it a while, it is remarkable how vividly the old scenes come back.[43]

With the wrenching nostalgia that only a person who has had a close brush with death can feel, he wrote his sister how much he loved his family, and the place, and the period of history into which he had been born.

I doubt that many children have, in addition to their devoted parents, the care of a Grandmother, an Aunty, and an Uncle Bob living just Over Home, plus a kind and wise Grandfather long enough for us older children to know him. . . . We grew up at a time when the world was not only at peace but could truly believe that there would never be any more wars. It is hard to imagine a greater contrast than that which exists between those days and the present. In our days, we needed to worry about nothing beyond what happened up and down Forest Avenue, but the children of today face a really frightening world. . . . I suppose it is natural for a person who has passed fifty to look back on his own childhood as a time of romance and to view the coming generation with alarm.[44]

In October 1946, extra stresses were placed on the Marsh household when Deon had surgery. She had been such a help to John and Peggy, and they had gained new appreciation of her from the way she had risen to the situation during John's illness. While Deon was away, Bessie, though not in good health herself, came in her place, bringing Deon's little daughter, Jimmie Lee, to help her. "It was like manna from Heaven when she arrived and said she was going to work," John wrote his mother.

I suppose that in time Jimmie Lee will inherit us. We were not consulted when Bessie sent Deon to work in her place three years ago. Neither were we consulted when Bessie decided to come back to us during Deon's illness. I suppose when they get ready, they will turn us over to Jimmie Lee and we will know nothing about it until it has been done. . . . I don't know how we could have gotten through this trouble without our colored friends.[45]

6

Shortly before Christmas 1946, when it looked as if neither she nor John was ever going to be able to climb the stairs in their apartment building easily, Peggy started looking for a house to buy in their general neighborhood. She found one small house nearby that suited her perfectly, but refused to pay sixty-five thousand dollars for a house that she claimed was worth no more than thirty thousand.

As John got better, she postponed her search for a house. On February 14, 1947, she wrote to Helen Dowdey: "I don't go anywhere except to the grocery store and seldom see anyone except Medora Perkerson and frequently Sam Tupper [their neighbor]. Sam says he does not come to see us for love of us but because of the free moving pictures we are showing." They had always loved going to the movies, and so once John was able to sit up for long periods, Peggy rented a 16-millimeter movie projector and sent the janitor to town every day to get them films. They especially liked old films, such as the old Chaplins. Peggy wrote: "Machine guns rattle every night here or the roar of the motors of 1918 Curtis jennys deafen the neighbors or the tom-toms of 'South of Pago Pago' wake the echoes."[46]

The first evening they got the projector, they worked for about two hours trying to get the thing to work. They used "everything including a pickle fork, a jelly spoon, egg beater, a carved backscratcher, an after-dinner coffee spoon engraved 'Chicago World's Fair 1893,' a piece of Jensen silver sent to Peggy by one of her admirers in Denmark," John wrote his mother. "Both of us, being subnormal in health, would work a while and then stretch out on the divan and pant. Finally around midnight, I had an inspiration. Maybe a coat-hanger, a plain ordinary coat-hanger would do the trick, and strangely enough it did. It is things like this which provide my triumph these days, and I much prefer them to the other type of triumphs."[47]

After informing them that alchohol relaxes the blood vessels and is good for heart complaints when used moderately, Dr. Waters prescribed a little alcoholic drink in the evenings. Around four o'clock every afternoon, Peggy would go across the street to the Piedmont Driving Club with a mason jar in a paper sack and bring it back full of champagne cocktails. They would sip their drinks and eat their supper as they conversed or watched a movie.[48] Not optimistic about his future, Peggy told Helen: "I can't predict how well he will get or when he will recover. . . . I don't know if he will go back to work or when. We have not even discussed the matter. All our energies have been bent, first, to seeing that he stayed alive at all, next, that he was happy and occupied, and, last, that he improved."[49]

Part of John's weariness and frustrations with the book's business came from his having to keep an eye on Macmillan as well as the foreign publishers. He thought that some of Macmillan's acts were unconscionable. In early 1947, after Margaret Baugh, who was doing the bookkeeping, pointed out a minor problem with royalties from Macmillan, John politely explained the miscalculations to George Brett. The mistake was one that had been made before, but not deliberately either time. After apologizing and saying the adjustment would be made immediately, Brett went on too long when he referred to an old rumor about Peggy's leaping at the opening bid of fifty thousand dollars when Selznick had been prepared to pay her $250,000. That rumor had always annoyed Peggy because it made her look like a sucker or a yokel who did not realize the value of her work until later and then began complaining about the fifty-thousand-dollar payment.

In a hazardous burst of energy, John angrily wrote Brett saying that the remarks about the contract were, "at their mildest, slurring."

> Peggy was offered $50,000 for her motion picture rights in 1936 and she accepted this price . . . she has never been dissatisfied and she has never complained, either publicly or privately. But everybody else seems to complain for her. Everybody else seems to think she ought to be dissatisfied and unhappy about the $50,000. It all carries the suggestion that she would wish to welsh out of a trade which she had made, and we don't like it. Now you have joined your voice in that chorus.

He angrily reminded Brett that their dissatisfaction with the motion picture contract did not arise from the amount of money involved, "but from the way Macmillan put a blindfold over Peggy's eyes and tied her hands behind her back and delivered her over to Selznick." He bitterly recounted the old complaint that the publisher had misled Peggy and him into believing that Macmillan was her agent, when in fact "Macmillan's representatives had acted solely to protect Macmillan's interests, versus Selznick and versus Peggy."[50] All the negative emotions generated by reading and answering Brett's letter robbed John of his strength. He realized then that he would never get any healthier if he continued to deal with such matters. He decided to push all *Gone With the Wind* business away forever. After receiving that letter, Brett had little else to say to the Marshes.

In a melancholy mood on the eve of his twenty-second wedding anniversary, John thought about how the years had passed so quickly, how they had all "run together in one mass." He wrote to his mother:

The endlessness of the labor that had to be done after Peggy's book hit the jackpot left no time for meditation and recollection; it was a desperate drive to try to keep abreast of the many problems that rose up faster than we could knock them down. However, it was an experience that very few people ever have, and if it did contribute toward breaking down my body it did build up my mental assets. I doubt if there is anybody in the United States who knows as much about international copyright matters as Peggy and I, and Margaret Baugh and Stephens Mitchell. We had some highly expensive and famous New York lawyers employed for a considerable time but eventually we fired them because we had to tell them what to do whenever trouble arose. Of course there is no "profit" in all this knowledge. If some other author asked me to handle his foreign copyright problems, I would shoot him on sight, but there is some satisfaction in knowing that we know some thing which people in general don't know.

No other person in the history of literature ever identified his spouse's success with the sorrow that John Marsh eventually did: "Peggy and I get satisfaction out of the knowledge that she has come through the fire without the catastrophes which are so often the fate of people who acquire sudden fame.... We have won our battles but we had to pay a big price. From here on out I aim to make our health and happiness our principal goal, and I hope my good resolutions will not waver when I have regained enough strength to get back in the harness again."[51]

When John made up his mind not to let his illness disfigure his life more than it should, he began to enjoy his confinement, not merely endure it. Once he decided to let Margaret Baugh handle the book's business almost entirely, he began to get well. When his mother asked him in 1947 if his trouble stemmed from the fact he smoked so many cigarettes, he answered: "Perhaps.... For a long time it was believed that it was brought on by too much hard work and worry."[52] He believed his recovery was due to his new-found philosophy, best expressed by William James: "Be willing to have it so. Acceptance of what has happened is the first step in overcoming the consequences of any misfortune."[53]

Later, speaking as a five-year survivor, he advised Edna Daniel, a friend who had just had her first heart attack: "You do not whip heart trouble in an American way. You do it in an Oriental way. You go to Mr. Gandhi's India and imitate his passive resistance. You go to the Hebrews and learn to say 'Thy will be done.' You go to the Chinese and by analogy apply the lesson of their proverb 'When rape is inevitable, relax and enjoy yourself.'"[54] He told Edna, "Think of it this way, if you had a broken leg, it would have been put into splints or otherwise immobilized until it had repaired itself. You can't immobilize a heart, not in this world, but you can 'take the weight off it' to some extent. That is why you are being encouraged, by drugs and otherwise, to lead a placid life."

John never mentioned reading books about relaxation therapy; apparently, he figured out on his own how to focus his mind to rid his body of tension. He believed strongly in the human body's regenerative powers. Attempting to upgrade his friend's spirits, he urged her to relax so that her body could heal itself:

> The mind can soar when the body is being its most placid. Often it does. Do you remember how it floated and sailed, up into the clouds and beyond, when you lay on your back under a tree on a hot summer day and you about the age of fifteen? The most complete relaxation a person ever feels in his whole lifetime, when the smell of the clover and the fragrance of the honeysuckle and the warm touch of the breeze have dulled the senses and the mind goes travelling higher and higher into lands we may never see again. You must have memories like that, so you know for yourself that having the body dulled or unstimulated does not retard the mind. Often it gives it a richness it has at no other time.
>
> Maybe you are not yet willing to let yourself be lazy.... The habits are not easily changed. You could be resenting what you *can't* do and letting that hold you back from what you *can* do. And that might be why your mind seems dull.
>
> What I can offer you out of my own heartbreak is—*Use what you have got.* Enjoy it. Don't let the things you can't do prevent you from doing, and enjoying the things you can do.... Now the situation is—you have everything mental you ever had, plus the broadening and deepening of a great experience.

8

At the beginning of his long confinement, when he could not sit up, Peggy read to him from the works of the novelist Angela Thirkell. They enjoyed her books so much that Peggy sent her packages and letters in appreciation, and they developed a friendship with her through correspondence. When he got strong enough to sit in a chair and read for himself, John read Dickens, Carlyle, Williams, James, Emerson, and the works of other philosophers. He became interested in birds, trees, and flowers. Their roles completely reversed now, Peggy brought him armfuls of books on ornithology and horticulture to study.

The little boy whom she hired to assist him gathered leaves, branches, and flowers from the park for him to examine and identify. He became knowledgeable about trees and birds. His and Peggy's observations of nature were a highly interesting pastime; they especially enjoyed bird watching. To Margaret Cate, their friend the postmistress at Sea Island, he wrote: "The birds have been merely a part of my 'discovering' of my surroundings, noticing things which have been right here before my eyes all of these years but which I have been too busy to notice, finding trees and flowers right outside my window which I never knew were there, and learning by keeping my eyes open that the bird population of our neighborhood is much more varied than I ever knew."[55]

Peggy placed bird feeders at all the windows to attract as many birds as she could from Piedmont Park. And when the birds were having trouble picking up the raisins John fed them, she threaded the raisins on a string for them. He was amused when she decided to remove the feeder in the bathroom window because it made her nervous to have the mockingbirds watch her from their perch on the windowsill a few feet away. She said they gave her a look as if *she* were intruding. John wrote his sister Frances:

Ever since I have known Peggy, she has wanted to have her breakfast alone and undisturbed. That suits me because I have never regarded breakfast as a social occasion, and we never eat breakfast together if we can avoid it. However, Peggy now permits the birds to disturb and interrupt her breakfast and apparently enjoys it. She eats her breakfast from a tray on the porch and one of the favorite feeding places is the window sill near where she sits. Before Peggy eats her own breakfast, she puts out fresh feed for the birds. If she doesn't, she says that the mockers and the cardinals curse at her if they arrive and find no feed waiting for them. Peggy will call to me half a dozen times while she is eating to tell me about new stunts the birds are doing. I never thought anybody or anything would be able to come into her life to this extent.[56]

Continuing to let Margaret Baugh look after the book's business, he went on writing long, thoughtful letters on his observations and philosophy, not ever mentioning *Gone With the Wind* again. To Mary Hunter, Henry's wife, who had written him a full account of his mother's condition after a fall, John wrote: "We men have a habit of writing and talking in generalities but you ladies get down to concrete facts. I have often noticed that difference between my stuff and Peggy's, and I will give you three guesses as to which one of us can tell the story better."[57]

And yet his letters are more full of observations than Peggy's, which contain more ancedotes. For example, one day he observed a flight of migratory birds of some kind in the park across the street. They never came close enough for him to identify them, but they were visible for all of one morning. He guessed that there must have been a thousand of them and they reminded him most of a flock of blackbirds. He wrote to his mother,

> You know how they swarm down on a field which a farmer has just sowed with wheat, go after the wheat and the insects as if their lives depended upon it, then swarm up into the air when something frightens them. They whirl and swoop in an organized battalion and then down to the ground again. The passing automobiles kept them flying up into the air and then diving down again. When they would first take off up the side of one of the little hills in the park and over its crest, they looked like water flowing over a dam.[58]

9

Not until more than a year after his heart attack did John walk down the thirty steps to the ground floor of their apartment house and step foot outside. "My first trip outdoors was yesterday, May Day," he wrote his mother on May 2, 1947.

> It seems that important events in my life have a way of occurring on anniversaries. My heart attack was on Christmas Eve, I had my bad setback on Lincoln's Birthday, and I am out of doors again on May Day. As you may remember, Peggy and I originally planned to be married on Valentine's Day and ended up getting married on the Fourth of July. I suppose that I will die on Whitsuntide or Michaelmas Eve or Septuagesima Sunday and rise from the dead on Resurrection Day.

Once he was finally able to go for a walk down Walker Terrace and South Prado in the summer of 1947, Peggy bought him a little aluminum seat that folded up. She or Margaret Baugh or Deon would take him walking once a day, and if he got tired, which he often did, he could rest on the chair. After he got seated, the little chair was reasonably comfortable. But sitting down or getting up was tricky because it tipped easily. Thus he told his mother, "There is an element of adventure in my outings as well as exercise."[59]

After her tomcat Old Timer vanished, Peggy adopted a kitten and named him Count Dracula, not because he looked like a vampire but because of his ability to fly through the air and climb up the side of perpendicular surfaces. After observing him leaping distances several times his own length, with all four legs outstretched, Peggy told John she suspected that the Count's mother had been friendly with a flying squirrel. Count Dracula did not waste time slowly pulling himself up to the windowsill—he just ran up the back of their best and tallest upholstered chair, much to Peggy's dismay. And even though the kitten chased all the birds away, John wrote this vivid description:

> I have become very fond of him and the principal reason is that he is a healthy extrovert. I would not say he is highly intelligent, but he is completely lacking in the introspective, moody, self-conscious, withdrawn, inferiority-complex characteristics which I have observed in so many other people's pets. The effect of modern civilization on so many dogs and cats is to make them neurotic and even psychotic. This kitten apparently never heard of such things; all that interests him is a romp, a fight, things to eat and not being bothered when he is asleep. He is a rowdy element in our sedate household. He frightens the birds which we have laboriously attracted to our window sills. He attacks the potted plants to which I have given so much care and attention. He sleeps all day and wants to play all night and in general he does what he pleases whether it pleases us or not. But the simple fact of his disorderly nature makes life very appealing in a family which has been compelled to be orderly, and perhaps he will set us an example and aid us in breaking some of our chains.[60]

Not as tolerant as John of the kitten's antics, Peggy gave the rowdy Count Dracula away. In no time at all, Mrs. West, one of their neighbors and something of a cat collector, brought to the Marshes' back door one afternoon a little stray calico kitten that she had rescued from a sewer. She thought that a pet might be good company for John. After listening to Mrs. West's funny description of the animal's behavior, John accepted the gift and named the kitten Maud. In talking to Mrs. West's husband, John told a risqué story about a woman named Maud who worked in a house of ill repute, saying he thought "Maud" was a funny name for such a woman. The kitten turned out to be a wonderful companion for John. She entertained him with her playfulness and curled up next to him in bed, where she took long naps. Peggy adored this kitten and mentioned her in letters. After a picture of Peggy cradling Maud in her arms appeared on the cover of the *Sunday Magazine* on December 14, 1947, along with a little history of the kitten's name, the Victorianly discreet Miss Baugh told the not-so-Victorian Mr. Marsh that she thought it was far more appropriate to explain to the *Journal* that "our Maud, the cat, was named after Tennyson's Maud, rather than that other Maud."[61]

10

Although there were still many problems extracting royalties from other countries, particularly Romania and Germany, many European publishers were now paying royalties. The best news in early 1947 came from Fruin telling them that the Dutch lawsuit against the pirate Z.H.U.M. was finally coming to a successful close. The Dutch publisher had paid Fruin a certain sum in royalties; had printed in the Dutch newspapers a statement confirming the copyright; and promised to insert the United States copyright in every future volume he printed.[62] Because of Wallace McClure's valuable assistance in this case, Peggy sent him a copy of the *World Trade Law Journal* in which Edward V. Saher discussed the Z.H.U.M.-Mitchell case. She said the article was not as complete as she would have liked it to be, but at least it presented *Gone With the Wind*'s problems with its foreign copyrights.[63]

In August 1947, John had another heart attack and had to be hospitalized again for two weeks. His condition worsened when he learned that his eighty-year-old mother had fallen again and broken her hip. Always generous to his mother, he wrote to her from his hospital bed offering to hire a secretary for her so that she could continue writing to her children and friends and have assistance in taking care of her business.

The new tests that John had undergone showed that the damage to his heart was far more serious than they had earlier believed. "This was not news to me, as I had always thought him in pretty bad shape and had treated him accordingly with very excellent results," Peggy wrote on September 4, 1947, to Helen Dowdey. "The doctor said John must not ever go back to his job at the Power Company, or any similar job where deadlines had to be met and where John would have to keep working regardless of how tired he was. . . . We had been expecting this news and it did not bother us. I was very happy and relieved, for I would never had had an easy moment if he had gone back part time, as we sometimes thought he might."

In many ways, Peggy made remarkable strides during John's illness. With the help of Stephens and Margaret Baugh, she accomplished much. "Miss Baugh and I have certainly had a hot time this year. I never dreamed I'd learn as much about such business matters as international banking."[64] About her achievements, she proudly told Helen: "I think Miss Baugh and I have done wonders, for I am casting modesty to the four winds when speaking to you. We've cooked up more foreign contracts and got more money out of places where nobody expected to get money than seems possible. But I will be happy when John can do some of the foreign stuff and let me hold down the domestic line. The doctor said it would be very good for him to do this work if he could. Really, the work seems to get heavier and heavier as time goes on instead of getting lighter."[65]

John did not want to resign from Georgia Power. To him, that was a sign of the end. But after he received the results of yet another electrocardiogram, he decided that there was no point in delaying the decision any longer. In September, he wrote his mother, "I have finally crossed my Rubicon and have handed in my resignation." Knowing how ill she was and how much she worried about him, he assured her:

> I'm not bad off at all, only feeble. I don't want you to think my condition has taken a bad turn, which it has not, or to think I am in any pitiful or depressed situation. I am really enjoying my situation. As to mental "shape," I am really enjoying this new experience of being a man of leisure. My situation is that I am doing all right except that I have such a small amount of strength. I must lie down and rest several times a day, the doctor has prescribed a drink of whiskey in the late afternoon, and then there is another medicine I take now and then, namely a Hershey bar. I don't have any pain or discomfort of any kind, except that it is annoying to tire so quickly.[66]

In this same letter he described how his attitude toward his illness had changed. Referring to Ralph Waldo Emerson's essays, which he had read in high school and reread in recent years, he said that the two essays that impressed him the most were "Compensation" and "Self-Reliance."

> As you recall, his thesis in "Compensation" is that for every action, there is an equal and opposite reaction, and that this principle laid down by Mr. Newton applied to human affairs as well as physical matters. In unpleasant experiences there is quite often something of interest and something of value, and often something which is quite pleasant. In this particular experience I have found many interesting and pleasant and quite valuable things, and I have no doubt that I will find many others as time goes on. It is not what I would have chosen, but I have already learned a lot of things from it which I did not know before and it might be that I will, by reason of this experience, round out my life in a

pleasanter and more valuable way than I could have done by continuing the never ending drive of my old job.

Then, he closed this letter with this observation:

Among the interesting experiences I would not otherwise have had is our cat. Even though she is shut up here in our apartment with old people, never even touching her feet to the ground or the outside world, she finds life endlessly interesting—a fly buzzing on the ceiling, a piece of string on the floor, the mystery of her own reflection in the mirror, my slippers or Peggy's stocking, a dancing pattern of sunlight on the wall when the leaves on the trees outside are blowing. She is never lacking in something to interest and entertain her, and I know that I am smarter than a cat.

John developed new insights about himself, learned new ways to cope. He continued to grow intellectually by exploring new ideas in philosophy that helped him to live better. His letters and his advice to his friend who had suffered a heart attack show that he believed that if negative emotions had made him sick, positive ones could make him at least reasonably well. Although Peggy learned some practical things about taking care of their business, she essentially remained the same high-strung, dynamic person, bogged down in minutiae and her concern about her fading public image.

In May 1948, when John had recovered enough to travel, he and Peggy went to Augusta for a week and planned to go on to Sea Island for another week. But about the time they were getting ready to leave Augusta, she developed one of her skin allergies and had to go to the Augusta city hospital for emergency treatment. With the medication and the condition, she felt so bad that they returned home. Occasional flareups of hives troubled her nearly all that summer.

Toward the end of 1948, their social life in Atlanta had picked up again slightly, and occasionally they went to dinner and concerts with a few close friends. But Peggy's correspondence had slackened so that she received and wrote few letters. She was finally and completely out of that glaring, limelighted fishbowl that she had complained about for the past decade. With the foreign business coming under control now and managed well by Margaret Baugh, and with John getting stronger every day, she should have been happy. But she was not. She did not adapt to her quiet life, her confinement, and her illnesses as well as John had adapted to his. Although he tried to help her by listening to her and sympathizing with her, she could not seem to pull herself up out of her mental slump.

John's philosophy of treating another person's pain is beautifully explained in a letter he wrote to his family in 1949: "If a person is in pain, it does not matter whether it comes from a broken leg or from cracker crumbs in the bed. Maybe there's nothing you can do about the broken leg, but you can brush out the cracker crumbs, and if the sum total of the pain is reduced the sick person is better off."[67] So he continued trying his best to brush those metaphorically painful "cracker crumbs" from his wife's bed, but without much success.

Stephens, too, noticed the odd changes in his sister's behavior, appearance, and attitudes and recorded them in his memoir. Although he did not realize it, she was undergoing her most serious bout with depression. One of the strangest things she did in May 1949 was to have their telephone number removed from the directory.[68] Much to Stephens's bewilderment, she got an unlisted number. After all those years of having the number listed and complaining incessantly about the number of calls interrupting her, Stephens could not figure out her reason for getting an unlisted number now when she received so few calls. In his memoir he wrote: "People called me and asked, indignantly, why Margaret had done this, or they tried to get her number from me. All of this was wearing on Margaret. She was tired, she was nervous, she was irritable. I had never known her to be like that in all her life. The worry told on her, and she began to look older and a strained look came into her face."[69]

On November 21, 1948, she wrote her will in her big, scrawling longhand and called three of her Red Cross coworkers—Mary Young Grayson, Kathryn Polhill Mason, and Ethel Blankenship—to witness the will. After they left, she phoned Stephens to come over and read what she had written and discuss some business with her and John. A decade earlier, at the peak of success, she had had Stephens draw up a will for her. Now she told him she wanted that one replaced with this new one.

In this new will, one quarter of her estate was to go to Stephens, three-quarters to John. She left five hundred dollars to Bessie and two hundred to Deon, and she wanted the house they occupied on 446 Ripley Street to be given to them. The first call on her estate was to pay the sum of an annuity that she had been buying for her secretary Margaret Eugenia Baugh, and in addition, she wanted Margaret Baugh to receive five thousand dollars. She left a modest amount to all of her nieces and nephews on her and John's side of the family, and also to her three godchildren, Mitchell Gibson, Turmay Taylor and Josephine Guidici. To Stephens's two sons, Joseph and Eugene, she also left her share of the old Nesbit farm on the Chattahoochee River. She wanted one thousand dollars to go to the Atlanta Historical Society and one thousand to the library at Fayetteville, Georgia. She made a list of furniture and silver belonging to her family and wanted Stephens to have them if he wanted them. She wanted all *Gone With the Wind* rights of all kinds—domestic and foreign—to go to John, and she left him all her papers and written matter of all kinds, as well as all her household furnishings and personal belongings. She stipulated that if her executors found that the proportion of the residue of her estate to be given to John was less than two hundred thousand dollars, she wanted them to abate all legacies—except Bessie's, Deon's, and Margaret Baugh's—equally until such a sum was realized.

She and Stephens went over some business files together and discussed what should be done if she died before Stephens and if John were incapacitated, unable to carry out her wishes. Although she wrote nothing in her new will about destroying her papers and manuscripts, she apparently discussed this wish, for Stephens later told Finis Farr that "She wanted her manuscripts and notes destroyed."[70] As they talked late into the night, she asked him about his law practice, concerned that her business had taken so much of his time. Even though she paid him well for her work, she hated that it had interrupted his own career. He told her his practice was gradually growing. When she, who had hoped to make him rich, asked him why he felt compelled to put what she had paid him for doing her work into the firm's account, he said he had done so because that was the only fair way. He told her, "I have never taken any pride in the work I did for you, nor in the money I made from it. I have taken pride in my specialty—real estate law—and that's the thing on which I want to base my reputation." And he proudly told her that he had even completed a 776-page book, *Real Property under the Code of Georgia and the Georgia Decision,* which he hoped would be the definitive authority in its field.[71]

After awhile, their serious discussion about what would happen to her property after her death turned to religion. Stephens, who had remained a devout Catholic, wrote the essence of their conversation in his memoir. He wrote that when he asked her if she were turning back toward the religion of their youth, she made this intriguing remark: "That's something I don't want to talk about. I'm just going to say one thing about it. When you make a bargain with the devil, you had better stick to your bargain. I may have made one, but whenever I give my word on something, or whenever I take a course of action, I am not going to try to crawl out of that course of action because I may have made a mistake in starting it. It is not the fair thing to do."[72]

11

After the unseasonably warm, springlike weather during December and January, which had caused the camellias to bloom all over Atlanta, winter finally arrived on the morning of January 31. When John got out of bed and looked out the window, he saw that the trees and wires were covered with ice. During the night the electric lights had flickered occasionally, indicating that the big power lines leading into the city were breaking, or otherwise in trouble, but it was not until about nine o'clock that morning that the lights finally went out and stayed out. The apartment was heated by electrical radiators, so the only heat they had was what was left in the house from the night before. Peggy stayed in bed the rest of the morning hidden under blankets while John wrote a long letter to his mother about his first big outing—a dinner for the presentation of awards to Atlanta's Women of the Year.[73] After describing the awards, John wrote: "I think that I was just about the *Mister Man of the Year.* . . . Practically everybody there came up to speak to me, including many I did not know, and my hand tingled from the numerous handshakes. The next day, I was very tired, of course, but otherwise suffered no ill effects so I believe I have toughened enough to stand a lot of things which I could not stand even a few months ago."

John also included an interesting description of the big new building into which the *Atlanta Journal* had just moved.

The Journal building doesn't have any murals, but we old-timers who worked in the crude, cracked and dirty quarters of the old building find it hard to adjust ourselves to the brightly lighted, spacious, clean and sound-proofed quarters of the new building. I can't help wondering whether they can get out as good a newspaper in the new building as they did in the old. The old one was dirty, dark, crowded, with trash on the floor and big rats dashing from one trash heap to the other as soon as the working people had begun to clear out in the afternoons. The typewriters had to be coaxed to make them work and more often than not the desk drawers wouldn't open. It offered very little to make the reporters' work easier. One result was the development of individuality and personality. I keep wondering whether the folks will be overawed by the new building, whether its many comforts and conveniences will discourage them from working things out for themselves, whether its clean and quiet atmosphere will make the reporters tame. It's certain they weren't tame in the old building, but they got out a mighty good newspaper and many of them achieved fame in other fields—Don Marquis, Grantland Rice, Jacques Futrelle, Lawrence Stallings, Ward Morehouse, Ward Green, Margaret Mitchell and several others.

He closed nostalgically: "Such thoughts have brought back recollections of the Maysville Daily Bulletin, which certainly was crowded, cluttered and dirty enough to produce genius, if my theory is correct."

12

In early January 1949, Peggy received a letter from Red Upshaw's stepmother saying that Red had died in a fall from a fifth-floor window in a hotel room he had been sharing with three other men. The police suspected suicide. He left a nineteen-year-old son and he had had three other wives, all of whom divorced him. He also had some sisters and brothers. An alcoholic who had been in and out of mental institutions for years, he had led a tragic life. Years later, when Lois Cole asked Margaret Baugh, "Did Peggy really keep a gun by her pillow always until Red died?" Baugh replied: "Steve says he doesn't know. All I know is there was a pistol on her bedside table for years. She never explained why. Once when I asked whether she could shoot it, she said of course, her mother had taught her or had seen to it that she learned to shoot. In January 1949 Red's stepmother wrote that he had died. I didn't notice at first, but a while afterward I realized that the pistol was no longer there, and it never reappeared."[74]

On March 22, 1949, John wrote his mother: "Peggy continues not very well but I am glad to say that she is somewhat better." In his opinion, her trouble was due to allergies and stemmed from her experience in Augusta a year previously. He pointed out that at that time, a vitamin that she had been given as a medicine brought on "a gigantic and colossal" allergic reaction. He thought that this experience had made Peggy more susceptible to allergic reactions for some time afterward. "At any rate," he wrote, "she is showing improvement. . . . She has had a lot of pains and aches and other troubles in recent years, and I hope we can get her where she can get a little more pleasure out of life."[75]

John understood how hard it was for Peggy to keep her emotions on an even keel. He knew that she was experiencing a letdown now that the *Gone With the Wind* business had shifted down. Too, his illness had placed such a terrific strain on her. Thinking that she needed a change of scene, he suggested that they visit his mother in Delaware. In June 1949, they went to Wilmington and then to New York. Once in the big city, she went unnoticed. There was no fanfare, no press corp hungry for an interview, no admiring fans clamoring for autographs, no Macmillan reception. When they returned to Atlanta, she sank deeper into her depression. John suggested that she make plans for them to go to Sea Island, but she never got around to doing it.[76]

She became increasingly nervous, and the least little thing would send her into a fury. Instead of being pleased that the Dutch case was finally over and that she received her royalties and rights, she blasted the New York law firm of Cadwaller, Wickersham, and Taft for cheating her in the final settlement by giving too much money to Fruin. After all, she said, Stephens and John had done most of the work. After she returned from New York, she blasted Granville Hicks for mentioning in a speech that Macmillan had bought *Gone With the Wind* after reading only one chapter. His speech was reported in the newspapers and the newsclipping service sent her a copy. She fired off a letter to Hicks condemning him for misleading young writers by making them think that writing "is a very easy type of work . . . it is the hardest work in the world and one serves a longer apprenticeship than at any other in the world." She fibbed, "I have so many writers and would-be writers on my neck, and practically none of them want to do any work because they believe erroneous statements that I wrote a bestseller with no previous experience and sold it on the strength of one chapter."[77]

On the heels of that little episode came another from the *Reader's Digest,* which carried a harmless little joke about Ashley Wilkes being killed at Gettysburg fourteen months before baby Beau was born. It was a takeoff on the old rumor about Rhett and Melanie having an affair. When Peggy saw it, she became enraged and acted as if some member of her family had been maligned and another called a bastard. Neither John, Stephens, nor Margaret Baugh could make her understand how ridiculous it was for her to get steamed up over such an absurd joke. As if she had lost her mental stability, she pursued the magazine's editors, who were bewildered by her complaint. She even wrote to Harold Latham, offering him her generic excuse—that she was "ill from fatigue, over work and indignation" and that she wanted "reparation" from *Reader's Digest.*[78] Using a chillingly prophetic simile, she fumed to Latham:

> What they did to me was so inexcusable and reprehensible that I do not intend to take it lying down. They appeared to have no comprehension of any damage they had done me, nor did they appear to care. In fact they have acted like a hit-and-run driver that had damaged an innocent pedestrian, and have been trying to get away from the scene as fast as possible.[79]

13

That summer of 1949 was one of the hottest in years, and the Marshes' apartment had no air conditioning. Peggy always withstood the hot weather better than John. She once told Herschel Brickell that the hotter the weather, the better she liked it. "I must be like Georgia cotton—need red dirt and hot, dry weather."[80] But that sultry evening of August 11, she complained about the heaviness of the air, for the humidity was as high as the temperature, far up into the nineties. They decided to cool off by going to the nearby Peachtree Arts Theatre to see *A Canterbury Tale*. This theater, torn down years ago, was located at the northeast corner of Thirteenth and Peachtree streets, not far from their first apartment on Crescent Avenue nor from her father's lovely home where she had grown up.

Peggy drove them the ten blocks or so and parked their car across the street from the theater. As was her custom since John's heart attack, she got out and walked around the front of the car to help him out. It was exactly 8:20 P.M. as they started across Peachtree Street. Walking a little in front of him, holding John's arm tightly, she looked both ways and said the last words she was ever to say to him. "It looks all right now." When they reached the center of the street, both saw a car come careening down Peachtree at a high speed and veer toward them. After a moment's hesitation, John ran forward, thinking that Peggy was starting to run forward too. But then suddenly for some reason she turned and ran back in the direction from which they had come and directly in front of the speeding automobile. She was knocked to the pavement and dragged fifteen feet.

John ran over to her and knelt down. When he looked at her face, he saw she was unconscious. "My poor, poor Baby," he groaned as he gently gathered her up in his arms. As he lightly brushed her hair back from her face, he stared at an ominous, narrow, steady stream of blood flowing from her right ear. Pressing his cheek next to hers, he whispered, "Hold on, Baby, hold on. I'm going to get you some help." He asked a bystander who had stepped up close to him to call an ambulance and to get the license number of the car. As a crowd huddled around staring at them, he drew Peggy's lifeless body even closer to him to shield her from the gawking onlookers, who had no idea who this man and injured woman were. It took the ambulance twelve minutes to arrive. John rode with Peggy, holding her hand all the way to the hospital.[81]

Remarkably able to remain calm and to think clearly in a crisis, he asked the ambulance driver to take them to Grady Memorial Hospital rather than to Piedmont Hospital, where they ordinarily would have gone. John knew that Grady, a big charity hospital in the center of the city, was better prepared to deal with emergencies and accident victims.[82]

The young intern in the ambulance that night happened to be the son of one of the Marshes' friends. He was Dr. Edwin Paine Lochridge, the son of Lethea Turman, one of Peggy's Washington Seminary classmates.[83] The young physician knew when he saw her that she was badly injured. She was brought into Grady Hospital shortly before 9:00 P.M. and placed in Room 302 under an oxygen tent and given blood transfusions. Dr. George

Bowman, an Atlanta brain specialist, was summoned to her bedside. Doctors W. C. Waters, Charles Dowman, and Exum Walker remained in constant attendance throughout the night. The next day the three of them took their meals in her room to keep her under constant observation. A half-dozen other physicians visited and consulted with each other. They determined that she had suffered a basal skull fracture, as well as injury to her internal organs and her left leg. One bad symptom was her high temperature.

Stephens, Carrie Lou, Medora, and Angus were the first to come to Grady Hospital that Thursday night. Then Julius of the Piedmont Driving Club, who brought the Marshes their dinners on Sunday and Thursday nights, came in tears and brought Bessie with him. As the word got out, more and more people came to the hospital. Some of the Mitchell family members, trying to offer John encouragement, recalled how Grandpa Russell Crawford Mitchell was run over by Atlanta's first streetcar. Although he lost consciousness, he fully recovered.

At 1:00 A.M. on Friday, Dr. Waters insisted that John leave and spend the rest of the night in the physician's own home rather than in the Marshes' apartment. Before leaving the hospital, John went back into Peggy's room to see her one more time. She did not recognize him or say anything. Looking old, crumpled, and filled with despair, he sat in the chair staring at her. No one knew better than he what a spunky little fighter his wife was, but he feared this was one battle she would not win.

When the newsboys got out on the street corners screaming "Extra! Extra! Margaret Mitchell in coma! Struck down by drunk taxi cab driver!" and the radio reports went out that the author of *Gone With the Wind* was lying with a high fever and in a deep coma from devastating blows to her head, the whole world gasped and listened. Years later many people recalled exactly where they were and what they were doing when they heard the news.

So many calls and telegrams poured into Grady that a special room had to be arranged to receive messages and flowers. Special lines had to be installed to take care of the calls that jammed the hospital switchboard. Medora Perkerson, Augusta Edwards, and Rhoda Kling organized volunteers into four-hour shifts so that the messages that came from all over the world could be answered. President Harry S. Truman wired his concern and good wishes. Eugene Talmadge, the governor of Georgia, state and church dignitaries, Clark Gable, Vivien Leigh—people from all walks of life called expressing their concern. Some people waited in front of the hospital. A news reporter clamored to talk to John and asked him Peggy's age. Knowing how sensitive she was to that question, he shaved off a few years in hopes that if she survived she would laughingly commend him for "fooling the nosey son-of-bitch."[84]

The messages and the names of the callers were all written down in the hope that if Peggy lived she would know the kind of support she had received. One of the most touching messages came from the Atlanta federal prison, where inmates volunteered to donate their blood to help her.

On August 13, Peggy showed the faintest sign of improvement, or what some thought of as improvement, when she was given a drink of water. She murmured in a delirious manner, "hurt all over," and asked that the tube be removed from her arm. Sister Mary Cornile, sister superior and director of St. Joseph's Infirmary, brought the few remaining drops of water she had saved from Lourdes, the miracle-working spring where Bernadette, the young French girl, claimed the Virgin Mary appeared to her.

On the morning of August 16, Peggy showed no sign of improvement, and the physicians were prepared, as a last resort, to do brain surgery on her early that afternoon. Around eleven o'clock, Carrie Lou, Stephens's wife, told John that she would sit with Peggy while he went home to eat lunch and rest awhile. In his memoir, Stephens recorded that as noon approached on that dread day, he walked from his law office, where he had taken care of some business for John, down Edgewood Avenue and on to Grady Hospital. When he went into the press room, he instantly knew something was wrong. Someone asked him Peggy's full name. As Stephens answered, Frank Daniel, the Marshes' old friend from the *Journal,* stood up, reached for Stephens's hand, and said, "Steve, I'm terribly sorry, but she's gone." When Stephens turned away to hurry upstairs to find Dr. Waters, he heard Frank speaking into the telephone to William Key in the newsroom at the *Journal.* "Margaret Mitchell is dead. Time of death, 11:59 A.M. Margaret Mitchell is dead. Repeating time of death, 11:59 A.M."[85]

Just a few weeks earlier, she and John, on one of their daily afternoon drives, had visited Daniel and Key and others in the *Journal*'s new building. The city editor had teased her about coming back to work for him. In writing about that moment when they all heard the news, Key wrote: "Margaret Mitchell's death was a news event of worldwide importance, but the *Journal*'s people did not react to it as Hollywood might conventionally have pictured it—with confusion, excitement, shouting, and running about. There was, for at least a minute, only this dull and empty and meaningful silence."[86]

Many people knew about her death before John did. He was home dictating a letter to his family to Margaret Baugh. Bessie was preparing his and Baugh's lunch when the telephone rang. She answered the phone in the kitchen. It was Dr. Waters telling her that Peggy had just died moments earlier, that he and Stephens were on their way over to tell John, and that he wanted her to make certain all the radios were turned off and that no calls were given to John. He did not want him to hear the news from anyone except him and Stephens. Bravely, Bessie held back the tears and went about serving lunch as if nothing had happened. She recalled later how hard it was to look at John. "I was trying to get a good meal down Mr. Marsh before he saw Dr. Waters and Mr. Stephens. When they came and broke the news to him, I didn't hear so much as a whimper once."[87]

Flags were flown at half-mast in Georgia as messages of sympathy came from all over the world. President Truman wired: "The nation to which she brought international fame through a creative work of lasting merit shares the sorrow which has come to you with such sudden and tragic force. Great as an artist who gave the world an eternal book, the author of *Gone With the Wind* will also be remembered as a great soul who exemplified in her all too brief span of years the highest ideals of American womanhood."

John granted the physician's request for an autopsy, which revealed that only Peggy's indomitable spirit had kept her alive after the accident. Concerned about how to handle politely the crowd wanting to attend the funeral, he and Stephens began making arrangements for a private service at Spring Hill Chapel Funeral Home the next day. They decided the best thing to do would be to issue admittance tickets to family and friends and explain to others that they could not possibly include all those Peggy would have wanted. John had three hundred engraved invitations printed in a last-minute rush and hand delivered by friends. Joe Kling recalled that scorching hot afternoon that he and a few others spent running all over the city delivering those invitations.

Neither Peggy nor John cared for any organized religion, but for years they had admired Dean Raimundo de Ovies, the rector emeritus of St. Phillips Protestant Episcopal Cathedral. John asked Stephens to get Dean de Ovies to conduct the service, saying he wanted no eulogy and no digression from the simple rites of the "Service for the Dead" from *The Book of Common Prayer.* For the music, John selected Bach's "Come Sweet Death," Schumann's "At Evening," Handel's "Largo," and "Crossing the Bar."

Instead of flowers, he asked that contributions be sent to Grady Hospital, where someone had already started collecting for a Margaret Mitchell Memorial Pavilion there. But flowers came in abundance. The only ones that he personally accepted were a massive blanket of white roses sent by the prisoners, who had grown the roses in their garden at the Atlanta federal prison, and another blanket of red roses and white carnations, a gift from the organized florists in the city. These blankets covered the casket. The florists also sent the two white orchids that were pinned to Peggy's short-sleeved, blue silk dress. When he saw those orchids, John remembered how she had happily pranced around their living room wearing the huge white orchids George Brett had sent her the day she won the Pulitzer Prize. He remembered how she dazzled him with her smiling look as she joked about Brett: "He doesn't know I'm not the orchid type!"

In honor of Margaret Mitchell, Governor Talmadge proclaimed that all state employees "pause for three minutes as a tribute of respect to this noted Georgian at the ten o'clock hour of her funeral." Mayor Hartsfield asked that all activity in Atlanta be momentarily suspended as the hour of the funeral struck. In the chapel, just before the service began on that gloomy, overcast August 18, the organist played "The Strife Is Over" from an Episcopal hymnal. The service began promptly and lasted only nine minutes. At the conclusion of the rites, the clergyman prayed: "Let she who brought the past into the present carry the glory of the present into the future." Under a leaden sky, the cavalcade of mourners began their journey to the old Oakland Cemetery. As the hearse approached Peachtree and Fifth streets, the sun, as if by some divine command, suddenly broke through the clouds as Margaret Mitchell crossed for the last time her beloved Peachtree, the street that she had made so famous and where she had lived, loved, and died.

All along the way to the cemetery, the streets were lined with people standing quietly, many with handkerchiefs held to their eyes. In the red-brick-bordered cemetery, shady with huge magnolia trees, John walked steadily from the car to the gravesite. His brothers Henry and Gordon were on either side of him. Stephens, Carrie Lou, their two sons, Bessie, and Deon were close behind. His friends drew a tight semicircle around him. His eyes dry, his face and body heavy with grief, he sat to the left of Dean de Ovies. After the brief service, he refused to leave and sat watching the two khaki-clad workmen lower the casket into the ground and cover it with the red dirt.

All afternoon and late into the evening on the following days, people who were not present at the funeral made pilgrimages to the cemetery lot to pay tribute. The cemetery office said it was besieged with calls for several days.

In his journal the day after the funeral, Stephens recorded:

The long train of automobiles went to Oakland Cemetery. It is the old city cemetery, set up in 1854. Across the valley loom the great buildings of the new city and the sun bounces back from the ranks of their windows to the country town graveyard near their midst. They buried her there beside her father and her mother and her little brother who died in babyhood. There was a grave space left for John. The flowers were banked high. I forgot to tell the caretakers to give the flowers to the crowd. I did it the next day. There was a crowd there for two or three days. She had said something to her people and they had answered. And when I looked across at the city riding high in the sunlight on the long ridge, crowded with towers, I broke and cried.[88]

14

John's heart had taken a terrible jolt. Many people wondered how and whether he would survive the senseless and shocking tragedy of Peggy's death. He, no doubt, wondered too; for immediately after the funeral, he started setting his house in final order. He wrote a new will and signed it on August 24, 1949. He left all of *Gone With the Wind*'s rights of all kinds—publication, copyrights, radio, television, dramatic, and opera rights and all and any others that might come into being—and all royalties to Stephens Mitchell or to Stephens's two sons should Stephens die before John.

He willed all of Peggy's great collection of *Gone With the Wind* awards and mementos of her literary career to the Atlanta Public Library. His own collection of editions of the novel and his personal collection of pictures of Peggy went to his mother. He also stated that he wanted all of his personal possessions, including furniture and other effects, to go to his mother. He bequeathed one-half of his estate to be divided among his mother and his brothers and sisters; the other half he wanted to go to Stephens Mitchell. He asked that one thousand dollars from his estate be given to Bessie Jordan and Deon Ward, and five hundred to Eugene Carr, the janitor at the Della Manta apartments. To Margaret Baugh he gave $2,500, and to each of his nieces and nephews he gave one hundred dollars. He wanted ten thousand dollars to be given to Grady Memorial Hospital, and a thousand dollars each to the Good Samaritan Clinic, Saint Joseph's Infirmary, and the Georgia Baptist Hospital—all in Atlanta. He willed one thousand dollars to the Margaret Mitchell library at Fayetteville, Georgia.

On the afternoon of August 26, John wrote his mother and family for the first time since before the fatal accident:

I wish you to know something which has been comforting to me. Peggy was probably never in pain. The newspapers referred to partly conscious intervals but I believe she was never nearer to consciousness than a person who has been under anesthesia and is beginning to come out. . . . Peggy made automatic responses sometimes when the doctor spoke to her, such as moving a hand or foot, and she babbled some words now and then but I believe we can say that she did not suffer or have pain. In fact it was quite probable that she never knew anything after the first instant when the automobile struck her.

Our hopes were based on the fact that she was internally injured and that bodily functioning—her heart, breathing, blood pressure, et cetera—went along in a most functioning way. Our hope was that her body might keep going until it had healed the brain injury. After she was gone, the autopsy showed that the marvel was that she stayed alive as a long as she did, the brain damage was very severe. The doctors say that the chances are that she could never have recovered fully. I could not wish that she had survived if it was only for years of invalidism. . . .

You may have seen in the newspapers, the driver of the automobile has been indicted for involuntary manslaughter which carries a penalty of one to three years if he is convicted. Involuntary manslaughter is when a person kills somebody without premeditation and malice aforethought while engaged in an unlawful act that carries the risk of killing somebody. I suppose that about describes what happened. It was the high speed at which the automobile was being driven that caused Peggy's death. We were crossing Peachtree at Thirteenth Street. There is a wide curve in Peachtree that ends at Twelfth Street. Because of the curve we did not see the automobile and the driver did not see us until he had reached the head of the curve at Twelfth Street. The block between Twelfth and Thirteenth is a short one. We were about in the middle of the street. In one of those split second decisions I decided that the safe course was to go forward. Peggy apparently decided the safe course was to run back to the curbing we had just left. I do not think she made a wrong decision. I believe she would have gotten back to the curb safely except for one thing, the speed of the car. Because of the speed the driver could not get the car under control. It swerved further and further to the left and finally went into a skid. That pulled it in the direction Peggy was going until it finally caught up with her.

Her face was not cut up and torn nor was her body. She had some bad bruises here and there on her body, of course, but her face was not even dirty when we picked her up. In fact, none of the injuries were extreme except the head injuries.

I hope these details are not too unpleasant, but I thought you would wish to have a first hand account from me. If that part is bad I can also give a first hand account of the amazing and touching outflow of love and affection for her that has come from every class and type of people and from all parts of the world. I have known all along that Peggy had an enormous public following but what has happened has exceeded my expectations many, many times. I have been extraordinarily fortunate in having such a person for my wife.

15

On the morning after the funeral, as he sadly looked around the bedroom at Peggy's personal items, John suddenly wondered what had happened to the clothes she had worn the night of the accident. After calling Frank Wilson, the administrator at Grady Hospital, he and Stephens went to the hospital and picked up the package containing the remnants of her garments. It contained her dress and slip. Both had been cut up while she was being undressed in the emergency room but neither showed much damage from the accident itself. When he returned home, he handed the package to Bessie saying, "I brought her shoes home the night of the accident. Would you please get them?" Together they walked slowly downstairs to the basement where he watched as Bessie placed the package into the roaring fire of the furnace.[89]

Then John began going through all their files and separating letters and papers he wanted destroyed.[90] This task was so arduous and painful that it took him nearly two years to complete it. Although he even asked his family to destroy all the letters he and Peggy had written to them, fortunately they did not. And they sorely regretted destroying the few they did.[91]

As he gradually sorted out a pile of papers, he would burn it himself in a wire basket in the backyard of his Della Manta apartment. According to Margaret Baugh, the first papers he burned, with the exception of those few pages he had chosen to save, were the entire original manuscript pages of *Gone With the Wind*. Baugh thought that he also burned "'Ropa Carmagin," the novelette Peggy had written before she and John married, because neither she nor anyone else ever saw it again.[92] After he had burned so much precious material, including many letters, he became distraught. Baugh wrote, "This was such a distressing experience that he turned over to me the destroying of the correspondence. After we had burned a lot of letters, we found that some of them would have been useful in carrying on. So the burning stopped (to my relief, for it was distressing for me too). Then, after John's death, Steve had the responsibility, and he had me burn the remaining manuscript [the thirty-page fragment of the jazz age novel] and some more letters."

In describing the outpouring of sympathy he had received, John wrote his mother in September that he had left Margaret Baugh with the job of writing and mailing two thousand thank-you cards.

> But before the cards were put into the mail, my cautiousness got the better of me and I felt impelled to look at the addressed envelopes to see if I noticed any errors. . . . In the course of this, I read some of the letters. They are a remarkable collection. I have mentioned already that many of them came from people who never knew Peggy but there was an unbelievable number from people we did know in some degree and in some manner. Like peeling an onion, you take off a layer, then there is another layer underneath it, and then others. Every phase and aspect of our lives had its representation.[93]

In October 1951, John received a request from David Mearns asking if Peggy's papers could be placed in the Rare Books and Manuscripts Division of the Library of Congress. Although he wrote nothing about what he had already done with the papers, he explained that he would rather have them there than any place else:

> But they are not being turned over to anybody and will not be turned over to anybody. Peggy did not wish her private papers to fall into the hands of strangers. She felt very strongly about this. She put on me the duty of destroying them if she were to die without having done it herself. . . . She talked to me numerous times about not wanting strangers or members of her family, other than me, going through her files. Part of this was her nature and part of it was a belief that an author should stand before the public on the basis of her published work. She believed that attempting to go behind the published work, digging into an author's private papers, led to wrong conclusions more often than to right ones. . . . I have tried to carry out her wishes and I will continue to do so.[94]

Around this time John's sister Frances traveled to Atlanta and stayed with John for a month. Later, she wrote that she would never forget sitting with him in the quiet and dark emptiness of the apartment. He always wanted to look at photographs of Peggy, saying that he had liked to look at her when she was alive, so why shouldn't he like to look at pictures of her now? From a large box of photographs, he picked out his favorites—the one in profile with her smiling up at Red Upshaw, another of her as a girl reporter sitting in the engineer's cabin of a locomotive, and another of her in a white velvet coat entering the theater on the night of the premiere. Frances wrote, "Then he said, 'I liked to listen to her talk when she was alive so why shouldn't I like to listen to her now.' And he put on the record made at the premiere of *Gone With the Wind* when she made her little speech, thanking the audience for liking her 'poah Scahlett.'"[95]

After Frances's visit, Katharine Bowden, John's oldest sister, came from California for a month, and after she left, Francesca and Gordon came from Lexington to stay with him. They were all afraid to leave him alone. "We all knew he was living on borrowed time," Frances wrote.[96] For the first time in his life, John admitted to them that he was afraid to stay alone. The Marshes' neighbor Sam Tupper said that John would often ask him to spend the night because he could not bear to be alone in the apartment.[97]

16

Peggy's death aroused national concern about safety regulations and laws governing drunken drivers. Editorials in newspapers all over the country called for stricter guidelines in granting and withdrawing drivers' licenses. Atlanta launched an intensive examination into the records and the qualifications of taxi drivers and formed a traffic safety board named the "Margaret Mitchell Safety Council," which later became known as the "Georgia Safety Council."

During the fall of 1949, John had the burden of appearing as a witness during the trial of Hugh Gravitt—the man who had killed Peggy. The county officials were kind to John, who was terribly frail, and they provided a place in one of the rooms for him to lie down and rest whenever he felt the need to do so. Reliving the tragedy was a horrible experience for him.

After he looked into John Marsh's face and saw those grieving eyes, Superior Court Judge Walter C. Hendrix refused to permit the state to introduce photographs of Peggy's body lying crumpled in the street because they were too gruesome. John testified on the stand, "I am afraid I'll see the rest of my life the vision of my wife and the car running together." He explained to the court that Peggy chose the crossing near the theater and looked to see if the way was clear because he could not walk fast. "Peggy said, 'It looks all right now,' and we walked into the street." Then, in a low, hoarse voice, John said he saw the speeding car bear down on his wife and strike her as she tried to get back to the curb. He repeated, "I am afraid I'll see that vision the rest of my life. If he was going less than fifty miles an hour I am very badly mistaken. The paths of the two were going smack together every instant. The curve of this man's car reached after every step she took."[98]

In writing to his mother about the trial, he said:

My appearance on the witness stand was not as much of a strain as the oration to the jury on the following day by Gravitt's lawyer. He employed every kind of demagogy. . . . He told the jury "How many of you have ever driven 40 miles per hour? How many of you have ever driven your automobile after drinking a bottle of beer? If you have, you are just as guilty as this poor boy and you cannot vote him guilty." He twisted the statements which I made and other witnesses had made and tried to create the impression that Peggy had run in front of Gravitt's car, and therefore, was more to blame than he was. . . . I was confident the jury was influenced by the defense argument and I was not too certain that they would find the man guilty. It was really hard to take, having to sit there and listen to the lawyer make a speech like that without being able to do anything about it. My only satisfaction was that I helped to convict the man, I believe. I think my testimony registered with the jury and I believe I helped to keep the heat on, simply by being present in the courtroom. If I had not been present, even if I had been kept away by serious illness, the defense lawyer probably could have built up more sympathy for Gravitt. So I have all along regarded my presence at the trial as something that I owed Peggy, regardless of how much of a strain it might be, and when we got the guilty verdict I felt that we had saved her from having a smear put on her by the defense lawyer. . . . In the courtroom was the first time I had ever seen Gravitt. He is a wormy individual, thin, sharp featured, scrawny, a washed out blond. He had been well coached by his lawyer and did not give out with any grins, as he did in that picture of him made while he was in jail. He was very quiet and sober and when he was on the witness stand he talked in such a weak voice you could barely hear him. The defense pictured him as a poor hard working boy who had his living to make and who had been persecuted and abused by the newspapers ever since the accident.[99]

The truth was that the 29-year-old Gravitt, a poor boy who came from the tiny town of Cumming, Georgia, to Atlanta, where he had gotten a job driving a taxi cab, had a police record for reckless driving. He had been charged with twenty-two traffic offenses, eight of which were dismissed or suspended. The two policemen who took him into custody after his car hit Peggy that night testified that "Gravitt was thick-tongued, and his eyes did not focus. Perhaps the man was not drunk, but he had certainly been drinking."[100]

The Atlanta newspapers reported that no case in recent years, not even a sensational murder trial, had inflamed the public more than Gravitt's trial. Gravitt was convicted of involuntary manslaughter and was sentenced to serve one year to eighteen months in prison.

17

During the summer of 1950, John purchased something that he had always wanted—a house. It was on Walker Terrace, just a few doors from his Della Manta apartment on Piedmont, and its principal attraction was that it permitted him to live and carry on his business on the ground floor and to enjoy a beautiful wooded backyard. From the outside, this house looks small, but inside it widens out into a spacious dwelling of the kind southerners built before 1918. It has large rooms, high ceilings, tall windows, and beautiful floors of rare old longleaf pine. For his bedroom, he chose the room that overlooked the backyard, which was actually a little forest filled with birds, chipmunks, and squirrels.

He had the entire house painted and cleaned and the terrace apartment remodeled so that Bessie and her husband, Charlie Jordan, could move in with him. About the time he got ready to move, Maud, the cat, disappeared, much to his disappointment. Her disappearance made the front page in the Atlanta papers, and many people searched for her, particularly after John offered a generous reward for her return. Even though there were rumors of cats answering to Maud's description being seen around the neighborhood, Maud remained lost. When offers of kittens of every species poured in, John's response was, "No. I don't want just any cat. I want that cat."[101]

In September, Henry came to Atlanta for a few days and then took John back to Wilmington with him to visit with their mother. That was the last time John ever saw his mother. She died of a heart condition in December 1950, when she was eighty-four years old, and was buried next to her husband's grave in the cemetery in Maysville, Kentucky. Unable to watch another loved one placed in the cold earth, John did not attend the funeral. He was grateful that his mother went as quickly as she did, for he did not want her to have to endure senility or invalidism.

Once settled in his new house, John organized one room as his office, and each day he worked on *Gone With the Wind* business with the assistance of Margaret Baugh and another lady, Miss Norris, whom he hired to help Margaret. Regularly, John declined offers to write sequels and to make stage plays and musical dramas, and he administered to the overcrowded world market for translated editions. He continued Peggy's attempt to stamp out rumors, and he scrupulously edited line by line a long article that

Robert Ruark wrote about Peggy for *McCall's* magazine. He continued to sponsor Peggy's writing contest for the prisoners in the federal prison, and he contributed to many charities in Peggy's name. He was even considering letting someone, perhaps Medora, who had asked him, write a biography of Peggy. Even though he knew Peggy never wanted a biography, he realized that someone would eventually write one, and he wanted control over what was written so that the record of her life would be correct.

He lived quietly, taking care of his business and visiting with a few close friends. On Sundays and Thursdays, the nights that Bessie had off, he dined at the Toddle House or the Piedmont Driving Club or at friends' homes. Rhoda and Joe Kling often invited him to their lovely home on the Chattahoochee River. He saw Sue Myrick and Edna Daniel whenever they came to town, and he often went with Mary Singleton, Beth Cooper Powers, and Margaret Baugh to the movies and the opera. His brothers and sisters, who visited him frequently, said he was a different man after Peggy's death. His own words were, "The sparkle has gone out of my life."[102]

From the first anniversary of Peggy's death well on into the fall, John was in a melancholy mood. On November 27, 1950, John wrote his friend Sue Myrick, whose health was failing:

> The advantages of a sudden death have grown on me in these years when I have had much time for meditation. Some people can stand life with a ball and chain on their leg, just as some birds can survive a broken wing and some animals can endure life in a circus cage. But it is not the life I would wished. . . . When I knew how badly Peggy had been damaged, I was glad she went fast.

The Atlanta opera season began the first week in May in 1952. On Thursday, the opening night, John escorted Sue Myrick to the performance of *La Traviata.* On Saturday, May 3, he attended the performance of *Aida* with Mrs. Calvin Prescott, an old friend of his and Peggy's. After the opera, he and Mrs. Prescott went to the opera party dinner at the Piedmont Driving Club. The next afternoon, Augusta and Lee Edwards invited him to their home on Woodward Way to see their garden, where the deep purple and bronze iris named "Margaret Mitchell" was in full bloom. He told them, "If people are going to name things for Peggy, I'm glad they name such beautiful things." He stayed with them about an hour. Then his chauffeur, Henry Ed Hyrams, drove him downtown, where he had supper alone in a restaurant on Luckie Street. Then he went home and to bed.

When Bessie and Charlie returned from Sunday evening church service, Bessie went to see if John needed anything. She said he was sitting up in bed reading. He told her he was feeling all right and sent her to bed.

Later, she explained, "My room is right under his, and I could always hear when he was stirring around. I heard him get quiet, like he was asleep. Then he woke up for his midnight snack. I heard him walking around. Then I heard him go to bed. So I went to bed myself."

Around 1:00 A.M., Bessie woke up startled by the sound of the buzzer that John kept by his bedside. She ran straight to his room where she found him lying in bed in terrible pain, gasping, unable to breathe. She called the doctor and then got a glass of water for him to take a pill. "I don't think he ever got the pill in his mouth. I held the glass for him to drink. He lay back, and I saw his breath coming shorter and shorter. I knew he was leaving. In two or three minutes he went away to join Miss Peggy in heaven. Mr. Marsh loved and cherished Miss Peggy. He saw to it that she had the best of care. He left nothing undone that was in human power."[103] After his death, the autopsy showed evidence of many heart attacks.[104]

18

In writing John's obituary for the *Atlanta Journal* on May 5, 1952, John and Peggy's long-time friend Frank Daniel stated: "Few but Mr. Marsh's most intimate friends realized the extent of the support and detailed attention he provided for the writing of *Gone With the Wind.* Mr. Marsh always emphasized that the inspiration and talent for the novel was his wife's alone, and insisted that his part was chiefly mechanical. The sympathy and encouragement, the advice and literary taste that he contributed were no doubt invaluable—as the dedication acknowledges."

Nearly three years earlier, on August 17, 1949, Daniel had written a poignant article for the *Journal* about Peggy's death, titled "Simplicity, Loyalty, and Love Produced *Gone With the Wind.*" Daniel wrote:

> Only one person in the whole world could ever have written Gone With the Wind. And it might never have come into being but for the encouragement provided by the man to whom the novel is dedicated. "To J. R. M." This shortest and simplest of dedications prefaces the book. If it had been as flowery as the inscription which precedes the Sonnets of Shakespeare it could no more clearly have conveyed the completeness of the bond between Margaret Munnerlyn Mitchell and John Robert Marsh. . . . This is not to imply that *Gone With the Wind* is not wholly Margaret Mitchell's novel. But Margaret Mitchell was Mrs. John R. Marsh. . . . He was there, with calm judgment, quiet admiration, whole souled devotion.

I *have forgot much, Cynara! gone with the wind,*
Flung roses, roses riotously with the throng,
Dancing, to put thy pale, lost lilies out of mind;
But I was desolate and sick of an old passion,
Yea, all the time, because the dance was long:
I *have been faithful to thee, Cynara! in my fashion.*

—Ernest Dowson

NOTES

Abbreviations

AHB	*Atlanta Historical Bulletin*
AHC	Atlanta History Center Library Archives
EU	Emory University, The Robert W. Woodruff Library-Special Collections
FM	Francesca Marsh
FMZ	Frances Marsh Zane
GB	George Brett, Jr.
GWTW	*Gone With the Wind*
HB	Herschel Brickell
HM	Henry Marsh
HSL	Harold S. Latham
JK	Joseph Kling
JRM	John Robert Marsh
LDC	Lois Dwight Cole
MB	Margaret Baugh
MFP	Medora Field Perkerson

MM	Margaret Mitchell
MMD	Mary Marsh Davis
MMMP	Margaret Mitchell Marsh Papers
MS	Mary Singleton
NYPL	New York Public Library, Rare Books and Manuscripts Division, Margaret Mitchell File 1935-1962
SM	Stephens Mitchell
SMP	Stephens Mitchell Papers
UGa.	University of Georgia Libraries, Hargrett Rare Book and Manuscript Library
UK	University of Kentucky, Margaret I. King Library, Division of Special Collections and Archives

Preface

1. Finis Farr's *Margaret Mitchell of Atlanta* (Morrow, 1965) was authorized by Mitchell's only sibling, Stephens Mitchell, an Atlanta attorney. Anxious to protect his sister's privacy after her and John's death, Stephens saw to it that Farr was assisted by Margaret Baugh, the Marshes' long-time, loyal secretary whom Stephens hired after the Marshes' deaths to oversee the management of *Gone With the Wind*. Consequently, Farr's book contains valuable but highly selected material, is admiring in tone, and presents an accurate but narrow account of the some of the major events in Mitchell's life. Farr makes no attempt to flesh out Marsh or Mitchell. He hints at but does not explain the vital role that Marsh played in her life and work. He does not imbue her with the charm and vitality those who knew her remember. Nor does he explore any of her intriguing frailties; he shrouds her in a glorious mist that obscures the woman behind the legend. The other biography is Anne Edwards's *Road to Tara* (Ticknor & Fields, 1983). **2.** Anne Edwards's *Road to Tara* is a popularized biography that makes for good reading but contains some errors that, taken together, portray Margaret Mitchell and John Marsh in a manner in which neither of them existed. Darden Pyron's *Southern Daughter* (Oxford University Press, 1991) perpetuates some of Edwards's errors. **3.** Photocopies of two of John's letters to his mother are in the Frances Marsh Zane collection. Darden Pyron had access to this collection and in his biography, *Southern Daughter,* he quotes passages from these two letters. **4.** Other biographers have had access to the Zanes' letters, but because of the insight the letters provide into the Marsh-Mitchell relationship, I have quoted more extensively from them.

Chapter 1
A Man of Character

Note: The epigraph is taken from a letter John wrote to his mother, spring 1945, a few months after he had suffered a major heart attack on Christmas Day 1944. William E. Mitchell was the president of the Georgia Power Company from 15 May 1945 to 18 Feb. 1947. John's college sweetheart was Kitty Mitchell from Bowling Green, Kentucky.

1. Interview with MS. **2.** UGa. MB's Notes, 4. After Peggy started working at the *Journal* and while she was still married to but separated from Red Upshaw, she and John dated steadily. At John's encouragement, she started writing a novel about youths in the 1920s. This was the manuscript they worked on together before they married. The heroine was Pansy Hamilton, a spirited teenager, from whom Scarlett O'Hara later emerged. This manuscript, along with all of Peggy's childhood stories, was of great sentimental value to John. Baugh wrote, "This fragment was still in the house, along with the childhood stories after John's death. As a matter of fact, I think he had already destroyed this novel of the 20's, along with the manuscript of GWTW (and maybe Ropa Carmagin). But his fragment of thirty pages still remained, as it was Steve who had me destroy it." About the completed novel "'Ropa Carmagin," Baugh wrote to Finis Farr: "No one ever again read it is correct, but as you say on pages 173 & 174, Mr. Latham and Lois had already read it. Margaret or John one had already destroyed Ropa. I didn't do it. I don't remember when it was removed from the file cabinet. At any rate, I never saw it again, and no one else did either." **3.** MFP, "The Mystery of Margaret Mitchell," *Atlanta Journal Magazine.* The date is missing, but this article had to have been published fairly soon after John's death in 1952, after the codicil to his will was made known. **4.** Interview with FM, whose information came from the three people: John's housekeeper, his janitor, and Margaret Baugh, his secretary, who telephoned Henry Marsh describing this event and her concern about John's health. After Baugh's call, Henry Marsh left for Atlanta to be with John. **5.** Andrew Sparks, "Why Were Margaret Mitchell's Letters Burned?" *Atlanta Journal and Constitution,* 5 Oct. 1952, 8. **6.** UGa. MB's Notes. Also, MFP, "The Mystery of Margaret Mitchell," *Atlanta Journal Magazine,* 1955. Also, interview with FM. **7.** UGa. MB's Notes, 5. **8.** MMD. MM's letter to HM, n.d., Tuesday a.m. [May or June 1926]. **9.** UGa. MM to Dr. Thomas H. English, 11 July 1936. **10.** UGa. MM to Katharine Brown, 10 Dec. 1937. **11.** Finis Farr, *Margaret Mitchell of Atlanta* (New York: Morrow, 1965), 225-26. **12.** Fulton County

Courthouse, Atlanta, GA. In 1948, Peggy had about three hundred thousand dollars in cash and securities. After making some modest bequests in her will to Bessie and Deon, and to her nieces, nephews, and friends, she left three-quarters of her estate to John and one quarter to Stephens Mitchell. She left all domestic and foreign rights to *Gone With the Wind* to John. **13.** Andrew Sparks, "Why Margaret Mitchell's Papers Are Now 'Gone With the Wind,'" *Atlanta Journal and Constitution,* 5 Oct. 1952, 7. Also, UGa. SM's Memoir. Box Number 114. Folder 14.9. The Mitchell's Peachtree mansion was also torn down in late August 1952 because Stephens said he and his sister wanted it torn down: "We didn't want anyone else to live in it and we didn't want it to deteriorate to a third-rate boarding house. I insisted that it be torn down and that was in the contract when I sold it." Quoted from "It's What She Wanted—Wrecking Crew Takes Over Margaret Mitchell's Home," *Atlanta Constitution,* 26 Aug. 1952. **14.** Ralph McGill, "Little Woman, Big Book: The Mysterious Margaret Mitchell," in *"Gone With the Wind" as Book and Film.* Ed. Richard Harwell (Columbia: University of South Carolina Press, 1983), 76. **15.** Fulton County Courthouse, Atlanta, GA. **16.** John's codicil states: "So I am saving these original *Gone With the Wind* papers for use in proving, if the need arises, that Peggy and no one else was the author of her novel." Fulton County Courthouse, Atlanta, GA. **17.** Codicil to JRM's will. **18.** From one of FM's newsclippings titled "Part of Priceless *GWTW* Manuscript in Vault: Remains of Literary Treasure May Never Be Taken from Cache," by Davenport Steward. No date or name of newspaper but probably from the *Atlanta Journal* in early summer 1952. Picture above article of the Mitchell's home on Peachtree with caption that reads, "Margaret Mitchell Home to Be Torn Down This Summer, Author Wanted House, Close Personal Effects Destroyed." The house was torn down in late August 1952. This article states: "Miss Margaret Baugh, secretary to both Miss Mitchell and Mr. Marsh, confirmed Mr. Mitchell's belief that a few pages of the manuscript are in the vault of the Citizens and Southern National Bank.... Mr. Mitchell said he had not examined the contents of the safety deposit box where Mr. Marsh placed samples of Miss Mitchell's writing in a sealed enveloped. He added that he had no intention of ever breaking the seal on the envelope unless requested to do so by tax authorities.... Miss Mitchell had a passion for leaving nothing in the way of close personal possessions behind her, her brother implied. Even the family home 1401 Peachtree St., N.E., now occupied by Mr. Mitchell will never pass to the hands of strangers. 'I'm going to tear it down and sell the lot this summer.'" **19.** Sparks, "Why Were Margaret Mitchell's Letters Burned?" 9. **20.** Codicil to JRM's will. **21.** UGa. SM's Memoir. Box Number 114. Stephens's papers consist of his letters, memoirs, notes, genealogies, notes to Margaret Baugh, the Marshes' secretary, and notes to Finis Farr, whom he authorized to write the first biography of his sister. Stephens's memoir is beautifully written and informative, but it is not a complete narrative. At least, what is in the Hargrett Library is not complete. It appears to be something that he worked on intermittently and unfortunately never completed. The pages are not all numbered and some pages that have consecutive numbers have a few pages missing. Thus, some information gleaned from his writings cannot be assigned page numbers in these notes. Whenever page numbers are available, I have given them. For the sake of clarity, I have also referred to this piece of writing as his "Memoir" throughout my notes, though he did not give it that title. **22.** A magnificent bulk of it—well over fifty thousand items, ten thousand carbon copies of her letters alone and several hundreds of his—is in UGa. **23.** Many ridiculous rumors were bandied about. Because of the novel's historical background, some said her father, an attorney who had a passion for Georgia genealogy and Atlanta history, or her brother, who was also a history enthusiast, had written it. A few said she took the novel from her Grandmother Stephens's journal. **24.** UGa. SM's Memoir. 6. Also, Stephens wrote several pages explaining exactly what his sister and JRM wanted. SM's Accession No. 303, Box No. 114, Folder Heading 14:9—seven typed pages about rumors, MM and JRM's wills. **25.** MMD. JRM to his family, 3 April 1937. **26.** Interview with MS. Also, JK's letter to the author, 16 Sept. 1991. **27.** Interview with MS. Also, JK's letter to the author, 16 Sept. 1991. **28.** UGa. MM to HB, 8 Dec. 1936. **29.** Harwell, *"Gone With the Wind" as Book and Film,* 76. **30.** MMD. JRM to his mother, November the Last, 1921. Also, from an *Atlanta Journal Magazine* article about Margaret Mitchell; date is missing from this newsclipping. Also, a letter dated May 28, 1993, to the author from Thomas Weesner. Weesner gives the Rabbit Hole's formal name, its exact location, and the names of its owners—Florence

Merritt and Gaby Bridewell. **31.** Interview with FM. Francesca was married to John Marsh's brother Ben Gordon Marsh, who was only two years younger than John. Ben Gordon and Francesca married two years after John and Peggy married, and they often visited the Atlanta Marshes. The couples were friends as well as relatives. John, in his customary reportorial manner, told both his brothers about his first meeting with Peggy. Shortly after their marriage in 1927, Ben Gordon and Francesca visited the Atlanta Marshes who, at that time, were happily talking about their work on Peggy's book; later they would clam up about the book. A long-time friend of John's, sports editor O. B. Keeler wrote the biography of Bobby Jones. **32.** MMD. JRM to his mother, 19 Dec. 1921. **33.** Interview with MMD. John reported this evening to HM. **34.** Interview with FM. MM's contemporaries spoke of her storytelling talent and her ability to make others laugh. **35.** UGa. MB's Notes, 3. **36.** Interview with MS. Also, FM pointed out how much MM resembled Scarlett in appearance. **37.** Interview with FM. **38.** MM to Allen Edee, 13 Sept. 1919. Jane Bonner Peacock, *Dynamo Going to Waste: Letters to Allen Edee, 1919-1921* (Atlanta: Peachtree Publishers, 1985), 31. **39.** Peacock, 81. MM to Allen Edee, 26 March 1920. **40.** John wrote about his courtship with Ruth Gimbel in his letters to his mother. **41.** FMZ. JRM to FMZ, 20 Jan. 1922. **42.** MMD. JRM to his mother, 29 Aug. 1921. **43.** Interview with MMD. **44.** Richard Harwell, ed., *Margaret Mitchell's "Gone With the Wind" Letters, 1936-1949* (New York: Collier, 1976), xxxii. **45.** FMZ's Papers. **46.** UGa. MFP's Narrative. 2. **47.** Interview with FM. **48.** Interview with MS. Also found in UGa., MFP's Narrative. 2. **49.** MMD. JRM to his mother, 26 Sept. 1921. **50.** Interview with JK. **51.** MMD. JRM to his mother, November the Last, 1921. **52.** MMD. JRM to his mother, November the Last, 1921. **53.** MMD. JRM to HM, 28 Dec. 1921. **54.** MMD. JRM to HM, 28 Dec. 1921. **55.** MMD. The first mention of this job offer is in JRM's letter to his mother of 22 June 1921, and the last in his letter of November the Last, 1921.

Chapter 2
Opposites Attract

1. Interview with MS. **2.** JK's letter to the author, 15 Aug. 1990. **3.** Interview with JK. **4.** Edmund Davis's letter to the author, 3 Oct. 1991. **5.** Interview with MS. Also UGa., MM's letters. **6.** Interview with JK. **7.** Interview with JK. **8.** Joe Kling remembered the time John fired an employee for alcoholism and absenteeism, and then rehired him before the man had a chance to clean out his desk. Joe said John felt sorry for the fellow and his family and tried to get him help. **9.** Interviews with JK, FM, and MS. **10.** Interview with FM. **11.** UGa. SM's Memoir. 65. **12.** EU. Harvey Smith's note attached to MM's letter. 24 May 1933. **13.** MMD. JRM to his mother, 18 Sept. 1921. **14.** UGa. Cukor's comment is taken from a letter Susan Myrick wrote the Marshes shortly after she arrived in Hollywood in January 1939 to serve as an arbiter of southern dialect, manners, and dress. This letter and other of Myrick's letters to the Marshes are on file in the Hargrett Library. **15.** AHC. Stephens Mitchell, "Margaret Mitchell and Her People," AHB 9, no. 34. 6. **16.** UGa. SM's "History of the Fitzgerald Family." 5. **17.** UGa. SM's "History of the Mitchell Family." 36-37. **18.** UGA. Eugene Mitchell's obituary in 1944, in all the Atlanta newspapers, mentions his earning the highest marks ever made at the time he graduated. **19.** UGa. SM's "History of the Mitchell Family." 37. **20.** UGa. SM's "History of the Mitchell Family." 37. **21.** AHC. Stephens Mitchell, "Margaret Mitchell and Her People." 13. **22.** UGa. SM's Memoir. 19. **23.** UGa. SM's Memoir. 15. **24.** UGa. SM's Memoir. 15. **25.** UGa. SM's Memoir. 15-16. **26.** UGa. MM to Joseph Henry Jackson, 1 June 1936. **27.** Finis Farr, Margaret Mitchell of Atlanta (New York: Morrow, 1965), 18. **28.** UGa. SM's Memoir. 39-40. **29.** UGa. SM's Memoir. 39. **30.** UGa. SM's Memoir. 45-46. **31.** UGa. SM's "History of the Mitchell Family." 39. Russell Mitchell's second wife was Clara Neal Robinson, by whom he had two daughters— Clara Neal and Lillian. **32.** UGa. SM's Memoir. 41-42. **33.** UGa. SM's Memoir. 41. **34.** Eugene Mitchell was born in 1866 and Maybelle Stephens Mitchell was born in 1872; neither had any first-hand knowledge of the war but both remembered the chaotic period that followed it and talked about it often. **35.** UGa. MM to Julia Collier Harris, 28 April 1936. **36.** UGa. MM to Julia Collier Harris, 28 April 1936. **37.** UGa. SM's Memoir. 15. **38.** Farr, 14. **39.** UGa. SM's Memoir. 22. **40.** AHC. Stephens Mitchell, "Margaret Mitchell and Her People." 13. **41.** Letter provided by

Jane Dieckmann, 3 May 1993. **42.** UGa. SM's Memoir. 23. **43.** UGa. SM's Memoir. 27. **44.** UGa. SM's Memoir. 27. **45.** UGa. Maybelle to MM, n.d. **46.** UGa. SM's Memoir. 25. **47.** UGa. MM to Henry Steele Commager, 10 July 1936. **48.** UGa. MM to Henry Steele Commager, 10 July 1936. **49.** Darden Pyron, Southern Daughter (New York: Oxford University Press, 1991), 450. **50.** EU. Harvey Smith's note attached to MM's letter. 21 April 1933. **51.** UGa. SMP. Note. Also Farr, 19. **52.** UGa. MM to Joseph Henry Jackson, 1 June 1936. **53.** Evidence of Maybelle's frequent absences are found in Eugene Mitchell's letters to her, but her illnesses are not identified. **54.** UGa. SM's Memoir. 65. **55.** UGa. SM's Memoir. 32. Mary Johnston's novels were *The Long Roll* and *Cease Firing*; the latter was the book that Peggy said was the "best documented novel ever written" about the war, and she consulted it for certain facts about the campaign from the Tennessee line to Atlanta. MM to Paul Jordon Smith, 27 May 1936. **56.** UGa. SM's Memoir. 31. **57.** UGa. Several of these copybooks are in the Hargrett Library, and a couple of others are in the AHC. **58.** UGa. SM's Memoir. 71. **59.** UGa. SM's Memoir. 66. **60.** UGa. SMP. **61.** UGa. SM's Memoir. 66. **62.** Farr, 34. **63.** UGa. SMP. **64.** Farr, 40. **65.** UGa. In his papers, Eugene Mitchell makes no mention of such injustices. **66.** UGa. SM's "History of the Mitchell Family." **67.** UGa. Eugene Mitchell to Maybelle Mitchell, July 1901. **68.** EU. MM to Harvey Smith, 15 March 1933. **69.** AHC. Stephens Mitchell, "Margaret Mitchell and Her People." 14. **70.** Farr, 22. **71.** UGa. SM's Memoir. 66. Greek Revival architecture spread all over Georgia around this period, the early 1900s, and it reached its peak just before the boll weevil's coming ruined the cotton industry and ended this architectural style as completely as the Civil War had ended the other. **72.** UGa. SM's Memoir. 66-67. **73.** UGa. SM's Memoir. 71. **74.** Interview with JK. Washington Seminary was a wealthy citizen's converted residence located near Peachtree Station in an area of elegant homes; it was not a building designed from the beginning to be a school. **75.** Interview with JK. **76.** Farr, 38. **77.** Jane Bonner Peacock, *Dynamo Going to Waste* (Atlanta: Peachtree Publishers, 1985), 13-19. **78.** Peacock, 18. **79.** UGa. MFP File. "Twenty-fifth Anniversary of *Gone With the Wind*," Atlanta Journal and Constitution, 16 May 1954. **80.** Farr, 46. **81.** UGa. MMMP. Wanting to use the simile of wheat and buckwheat in her novel, Mitchell, while working on *Gone With the Wind*, wrote to Dr. Stuckey, an agriculture specialist. She asked him if the story her relatives told her were true. In his reply he explained that the seed of buckwheat ripens while the main stem of the plant is still green; consequently, buckwheat plants, blown over, will come nearer rising again because the stem growth has not ceased. The habit of all growing plants is to stretch up toward the sun. Straw of wheat ripens or becomes dry with the ripening of the grain. A dry wheat straw, once blown down, will not be able to rise because growth processes have ceased. Hence, her "buckwheat people" simile applied to those who were strong, flexible, resilient, and resourceful.   **82.** John's maternal grandfather's people were Kennans (sometimes spelled Kennon). Richard Kennan, a wealthy gentleman, was the first Kennan to come to America from England sometime prior to 1670. He settled about five miles below Petersburg, on the James River in Virginia. He and three of his friends, Francis Eppe, Joseph Royall, and George Archar, became joint grantees of a patent for 2,827 acres of land in Henrico County, Virginia, and the Virginia Land Registry Records show that between this period and 1761 there are grants of land to various members of the Kennan family to the extent of more than fifty thousand acres. Richard Kennan was a merchant and an agent for a firm in Glasgow, Scotland, doing business in America; in this connection, he made many trips to Scotland and England. He imported glazed brick and built the first brick house in his locality. He married Elizabeth Warsham and they had four children.   **83.** Thomas Berry was born in July 1733 at Berry Plains in King George County, Virginia. In 1757, he married Frances Anne Kendall (born 1737 or 1738, died 1818). They had ten children whom they raised at Berry Plains. Later they and their children moved to Kentucky. In his old age, Captain Thomas Berry returned to Virginia, where he died 18 Dec. 1818. (The names of his children are found in the Register of the Kentucky State Historical Society, 22, no. 65, pp. 196-98.) In addition to genealogical information Jim Davis provided, I obtained other information from UK.   **84.** Lewis Collins and Richard H. Collins, *History of Kentucky* (Frankfort, KY: Historical Society, 1966), 2: 545-93.   **85.** UK. Also Jim Davis's history of the Marsh family.   **86.** Mason County Museum. Maysville was established as a town in 1787 by the legislature of Virginia. Until Kentucky became a state in 1792, all of the region known as Kentucky County was owned by Virginia. **87.** Mason County Museum. Maysville, KY. **88.** UK. Maysville Daily Bulletin, Sunday, 30 Dec. 1904. **89.** Sara Jane Kennan was born in 1832 and died in 1915. Robert Toup was born in 1825 and died in 1902. **90.** Marsh family interview. **91.** MMD. JRM to his mother, 18 Jan. 1949. **92.** UK. Newsclipping from Maysville Daily Bulletin, 30 Dec. 1904, provided information about John's father and funeral service. **93.** Katharine Kennan Marsh Bowden was born 21 Aug. 1890, and died 2 Oct. 1981. Henry Neal Marsh was born 6 May 1893, and died 4 Dec. 1969. Ben Gordon Marsh was born 20 Oct. 1897, and died 2 May 1954. Frances Maitland Marsh Zane was born 23 Jan. 1901 and died 3 March 1986. **94.** Interview with FM. **95.** AHC. FMZ's interview for Anne Edwards's Road to Tara. **96.** AHC. FMZ's interview for Anne Edwards's Road to Tara. Interview with FM. Katharine Marsh, John's oldest sister, sketched a picture of their mother doing the puppet shows for the children. **97.** MMD. JRM to Miss Anna Frank, 13 Dec. 1950. JRM to Edna Daniel, 22 Dec. 1950. **98.** MMD. JRM to Miss Anna Frank, 13 Dec. 1950. JRM to Edna Daniel, 22 Dec. 1950. Information about the school and factory came from the curator at the Mason County Museum in Maysville, Kentucky. **99.** Interview with MMD. **100.** AHC. FMZ's interview for Anne Edwards's Road to Tara. **101.** Interview with FM. **102.** Interview with FM. **103.** Interview with FM.

Chapter 3
Reasonable Ambitions

1. UK. History of the University of Kentucky. **2.** MMD. MMD's letter to the author, 31 May 1990. Letter quotes from a tape recording her father, Henry Marsh, made about his and John's college days. **3.** Interview with MMD. Henry Marsh was born in Maysville, Kentucky, 6 May 1893. After earning a bachelor of science degree from the University of Kentucky, he started with the Hercules Powder Company as a chemist at the Experiment Station, then at Kenvil, NJ, in 1917. In 1930 he was named assistant to the director of operations, Explosives Department, and by 1939 he had become manager of the smokeless powder division. In August 1946, he assumed the managership of both the smokeless powder and the sporting powder divisions, which were then merged. He served as a lieutenant colonel in the Ordnance Reserves in World War II and as a consultant to the National Defense Council. He has six United States patents and one British patent in the propellant field to his credit. He was divorced from his first wife, Mary Frances Moore, by whom he had one child, Mary Otwell Marsh Davis. His second wife was Mary Genevieve Hunter, by whom he had three children, Eleanor, Jane, and Henry, Jr. **4.** MMD. JRM's college letters to his mother frequently mentioned Kitty during this period. **5.** John took a course named "Pre-Shakespearean and Shakespearean Drama, an intensive study of the native English element in Shakespeare," and followed it by a study of Shakespeare's works. **6.** Telephone interview with Don Edwards, writer for the Lexington *Herald Leader.* **7.** E. I. "Buddy" Thompson, *Madame Belle Brezing* (Lexington, KY: Buggy Whip Press, 1983), 87. **8.** Interview with FM. **9.** Interview with FM. **10.** MMD. From a Lexington *Leader* newsclipping that John's mother had saved. **11.** MMD. From Mr. H. Giovannoli, editor and manager of the Lexington *Leader,* who wrote John on 28 May 1918. The editor's letter is among Mary Marsh's papers. **12.** MMD. JRM to his mother, 9 March 1919. According to Thomas Weesner (letter to the author, 28 May 1993), Mrs. Fannie Prim was the widow of S. C. Prim, and her boarding house was on West Peachtree Street between Kimball Street (now Ponce de Leon Avenue) and Third Street. Mr. Weesner also informs me that the 1924 city directory lists John R. Marsh, copyreader for the *Journal,* as living at 45 Peachtree Place, between Cypress Street and Columbia Avenue, which was the home of Mrs. Beulah Gault, widow of J. T. Gault. I am also indebted to Mr. Weesner for the information on John's Langdon Court apartment in chapter 5. **13.** Interview with FM. **14.** MMD. Questionnaire for Georgia Power Company, Advertising Department. **15.** MMD. JRM to his mother, 21 May 1920. **16.** MMD. JRM to his mother, 21 May 1920. **17.** MMD. JRM to HM, 22 May 1920. **18.** MMD. JRM to HM, 22 May 1920. **19.** Interview with FM. **20.** AHC. William S. Howland, "Peggy Mitchell, Newspaperman," *AHB* 9, no. 34. 50. **21.** AHC. Howland, *AHB* 53. **22.** MMD. JRM to HM, 22 May 1920. **23.** UGa. MMMP. Newsclippings. **24.** Finis Farr, *Margaret Mitchell of*

Atlanta (New York: Morrow, 1965), 50. **25.** EU. Harvey Smith's note attached to MM's letter. March or April 1933. **26.** Accounts of her relationship with her family are found in Mitchell's early letters and are also found in Stephens Mitchell's memoirs. In Finis Farr's authorized biography there is mention of the disputes between her and her grandmother and between her and her father. **27.** Jane Bonner Peacock, *Dynamo Going to Waste* (Atlanta: Peachtree Publishers, 1985), 31-32. MM to Allen Edee, 13 Sept. 1919. **28.** UGa. SM's Memoir. **29.** Interview with MMD. **30.** Jane Bonner Peacock, *Dynamo Going to Waste* (Atlanta: Peachtree Publishers, 1985), 29. MM to Allen Edee, 21 July 1919. **31.** Peacock, 97. MM to Allen Edee, n.d., 12 o'clock Wednesday p.m. [summer 1920]. 32. Farr, 55. **33.** Peacock, 83. MM to Allen Edee, 26 March 1920. **34.** Peacock, 64. MM to Allen Edee, 4 March 1920. **35.** Peacock, 75. MM to Allen Edee, 26 March 1920. **36.** Peacock, 114. MM to Allen Edee, circa May 1921. **37.** Peacock, 35-36. **38.** Peacock, 104. MM to Allen Edee, Sunday afternoon, 31 July 1920. **39.** Peacock, 69. MM to Allen Edee, 13 March 1920. **40.** Interview with FM and Deon Rutledge. **41.** Peacock, 49-51. MM to Allen Edee, 18 Nov. 1919. **42.** Farr, 53. **43.** UGa. MM to Mrs. Alix Gress Sellers, 4 June 1947. **44.** After Peggy left Northampton in 1919, the year Edee graduated and took a job in New York, she wrote him until December 1921, when he returned to the Midwest to manage his father's clothing store. Once he left New York, he broke off his correspondence with her. He married in 1922 and, apparently, never made any effort to write or speak to her again. These letters have been gathered and edited by Jane B. Peacock in *A Dynamo Going to Waste*. **45.** Peacock, 75. MM to Allen Edee, 26 March 1920. **46.** Peacock, 101. MM to Allen Edee, 31 July 1920. **47.** Peacock, 74. MM to Allen Edee, 13 March 1920. **48.** Peacock, 74. MM to Allen Edee, 13 March 1920. **49.** Peacock, 125. MM to Allen Edee, 21 Aug. 1921. **50.** Peacock, 132. **51.** FMZ. MM to FMZ, n.d., Monday morning [late spring 1926]. **52.** Peacock, 88. MM to Courtenay Ross, n.d. (attached to MM's letter to Allen Edee dated 26 March 1920). **53.** Peacock, 55. MM to Allen Edee, 1 Dec. 1919. **54.** Peacock, 54-55. MM to Allen Edee, 1 Dec. 1919. **55.** Peacock, 76. MM to Allen Edee, 26 March 1920. **56.** Peacock, 77. MM to Allen Edee, 26 March 1920. **57.** Peacock, 55. MM to Allen Edee, 1 Dec. 1919. **58.** Peacock, 87. MM to Courtenay Ross, n.d. (attached to MM's letter to Allen Edee dated 26 March 1920). **59.** Peacock, 86. MM to Courtenay Ross, n.d. (attached to MM's letter to Allen Edee dated 26 March 1920). **60.** Peacock, 86. MM to Courtenay Ross, n.d. (attached to MM's letter to Allen Edee dated 26 March 1920). **61.** Charles E. Wells, "The Hysterical Personality and the Feminine Character: A Study of Scarlett O'Hara," in *"Gone With the Wind" as Book and Film.* Ed. Richard Harwell. (Columbia: University of South Carolina Press, 1983), 118. **62.** FMZ. MM to FMZ, n.d. [1926 or 1927]. **63.** Peacock, 117. MM to Allen Edee, Monday, 1 or 2 Aug. 1921. **64.** AHS. *Road to Tara* file. **65.** Farr, 56. **66.** AHC. Stephens Mitchell, "Margaret Mitchell and Her People," *AHB* 9, no. 34. 22-23. **67.** Peacock, 100. MM to Allen Edee, 31 July 1920. **68.** Peacock, 128-29. MM to Allen Edee, 21 Dec. 1921. **69.** Peacock, 128-29. MM to Allen Edee, 21 Dec. 1921. **70.** Peacock, 125. MM to Allen Edee, 21 Aug. 1921. **71.** Peacock, 104. MM to Allen Edee, 1 Aug. 1920.

Chapter 4
A Bizarre Courtship

1. FMZ. JRM to FMZ, 20 Jan. 1922. **2.** *GWTW*, 818. **3.** FMZ. MM to FMZ, n.d., Monday a.m. [Feb. or March 1925]. **4.** FMZ. MM to FMZ, n.d., Monday morning [late spring 1926]. **5.** UGa. Anne Equen, "Margaret Mitchell's Story for Annual Once Rejected," *Atlanta Constitution*, 11 Dec. 1939. Interview with JK. **6.** UGa. SM's Memoir. Box 114. Folder Heading 14:9. **7.** UGa. MFP. "Was Margaret Mitchell Writing Another Book?" *Atlanta Journal Magazine*, 18 Dec. 1949. **8.** Interview with FM. **9.** UGa. SM's Memoir. 71-72. **10.** *The Youth's Companion* was for many years the mainstay of a New Hampshire part-time farmer, teacher, and poet—Robert Frost. *Saint Nicholas* published poems by one of Peggy's contemporaries, Edna St. Vincent Millay, in 1908 and 1909. It is not known whether Peggy submitted any of her material to the popular magazine, which published some of its readers' contributions monthly. During the 1890s through the 1920s, this magazine inspired more than one young American who later became a famous writer. **11.** UGa. MM to Donald Adams, 9 July 1936. **12.** Finis Farr, *Margaret Mitchell of Atlanta* (New

York: Morrow, 1965), 77. **13.** Interview with FM. **14.** UGa. SM's Memoir. **15.** FMZ. JRM to FMZ, 20 Jan. 1922. **16.** Jane Bonner Peacock, *A Dynamo Going to Waste* (Atlanta: Peachtree Publishers, 1985), 74. MM to Allen Edee, 13 March 1920. Also, JRM to his mother, 15 Oct. 1924. **17.** Interview with FM. **18.** FMZ. MM to FMZ, n.d., Monday morning [late spring 1926]. **19.** FMZ. JRM to FMZ, 20 Jan. 1922. **20.** *American Heritage Dictionary, Second College Edition*, 1985. **21.** *GWTW*, 175-76. **22.** UGa. MM to Julia Collier Harris, 8 July 1936. **23.** Farr, 53. **24.** Farr, 54. **25.** Farr, 54. Also, in UGa. SMP; in *Atlanta Journal* feature article in UGa.; and in Peacock, 112. **26.** Farr, 54. **27.** FMZ. MM to FMZ, n.d. [late 1925 or early 1926]. **28.** John and Henry Marsh took care of their mother all of their adult lives, and they also took care of Frances until she married. Information about Upshaw from UGa.; from Farr, 56; and from interviews with FM and MS. **29.** *GWTW*, 940. **30.** UGa. SMP. Also Farr, 56. **31.** Interview with FM. **32.** Farr, 56. **33.** FMZ's Papers. **34.** Peacock, 54. MM to Allen Edee, 1 Dec. 1919. **35.** Interview with FM. **36.** *GWTW*, 1016. **37.** FMZ. JRM to FMZ, 27 March 1922. **38.** FMZ. MM to FMZ, n.d. [spring 1926]. **39.** AHS. FMZ's interview with Anne Edwards. **40.** FMZ's Papers. **41.** MMD. JRM to his family, 9 May 1924. **42.** MMD. JRM to his mother, 30 July 1922. **43.** Farr, 56. **44.** Peacock, 117. MM to Allen Edee, 1 or 2 Aug. 1921. **45.** Augusta Dearborn's interview with Anne Edwards, AHC. **46.** Interview with FM. **47.** JK to the author, n.d., Palm Sunday Eve [1989]. **48.** Darden Pyron in *Southern Daughter* (New York: Oxford University Press, 1991) claims that Peggy patterned Rhett after her mother Maybelle. **49.** *GWTW*, 1022. **50.** *GWTW*, 843. **51.** *GWTW*, 844. **52.** *GWTW*, 846. **53.** *GWTW*, 1016. **54.** *GWTW*, 928-29. **55.** FMZ. JRM to FMZ, 11 Aug. 1922. **56.** MMD. JRM to his mother, 6 Sept. 1922. **57.** Farr, 56. **58.** MMD. JRM to his mother, 6 Sept. 1922. **59.** Interview with FM. **60.** MMD. JRM to his mother, 6 Sept. 1922. **61.** Interview with FM. **62.** Interview with FM. MM said this to FM in 1927; however, she told others too. She never even tried to keep her "mistake" a secret; it was well known among their circle at the Georgia Power Company, according to Mary Singleton. **63.** Peacock, 136. **64.** MMD. JRM to his mother, 6 Sept. 1922. **65.** MMD. JRM to his mother, 6 Sept. 1922.

Chapter 5
Love Regained

1. Interview with MS. **2.** UGa. SMP. Also, interview with MS. **3.** Finis Farr, *Margaret Mitchell of Atlanta* (New York: Morrow, 1965), 57. **4.** UGa. SMP. Also, interview with MS. **5.** FMZ. JRM to FMZ, 30 July 1923. **6.** This gun belonged to John. It was the one given to him when he went with the federal agents into the Georgia mountains to hunt bootleggers. Interview with FM. **7.** Farr, 55. **8.** Interviews with JK and MS. JK's letter to the author, 8 Nov. 1988, speaks of Peggy looking up to John and turning to him for advice. MS and others remembered how his colleagues at Georgia Power used to tease John about his supporting Peggy before they married. **9.** Nearly all of the information about the newspapers was provided by JK. **10.** FMZ. JRM to FMZ, 27 March 1922. **11.** Interview with MS. **12.** AHC. William S. Howland, "Peggy Mitchell, Newspaperman," *AHB* 9, no. 34. 47. **13.** Michael Schudson, *Discovering the News: A Social History of American Newspapers*, (New York: Basic, 1978), 98-99. **14.** Interview with MS. **15.** Farr, 58-59. **16.** AHC. Howland, *AHB*, 48. **17.** UGa. MM to Mrs. Julia Collier Harris, 28 April 1936. **18.** AHC. Howland, *AHB*. 54. Hedley B. Wilcox was the business manager at the *Journal* when Peggy worked there. **19.** AHC. Howland, *AHB*, 55. **20.** AHC. Howland, *AHB*, 62. **21.** Farr, 65-66. **22.** AHC. Howland, *AHB*, 61. **23.** AHC. Howland, *AHB*, 62-63. **24.** Farr, 59-60. **25.** The weaknesses in Peggy's first article are also pointed out in Howland, *AHB*, 56-57. **26.** Blacks in Atlanta who did voodoo magic were called "conger niggers." Omie was an elderly black woman who lived in John's hometown. John and his family admired her. **27.** Interviews with MS and JK. **28.** Interviews with JK and MS. Also in Farr, 69-70. **29.** MFP, "When Margaret Mitchell Was a Girl Reporter," in *"Gone With the Wind" as Book and Film.* Ed. Richard Harwell (Columbia: University of South Carolina Press, 1983), 39. **30.** Farr, 70. **31.** Peggy's articles are in a scrapbook in UGa. **32.** Farr, 70. **33.** Interview with FM. **34.** UGa. Mitchell scrapbook. Note in JRM's handwriting on "Camping Out on $7 a Week," Peggy Mitchell, *Atlanta Journal*, 8 July 1923. **35.** Interview with JK. **36.** AHC. Howland, *AHB*, 64. Also Farr, 69. **37.** AHC. Howland,

AHB, 53. **38.** AHC. Howland, *AHB*, 49. **39.** AHC. Howland, *AHB*, 54. **40.** AHC. Howland, *AHB*, 49. **41.** Interview with JK. **42.** AHC. Howland, *AHB*, 49. **43.** AHC. Howland, *AHB,* 50. **44.** AHC. Howland, *AHB*, 54. **45.** Letter from Thomas Weesner to the author, 28 May 1993. **46.** UGa. MM to Norma and Herschel Brickell, 4 Sept. 1938. **47.** MMD. JRM to his mother, 11 June 1923. **48.** FMZ. JRM to FMZ, 30 July 1923. **49.** Interview with MMD. **50.** Peggy filed for divorce 14 Nov. 1923. She testified before two juries, once on 17 July 1924, and another time on 16 Oct. 1924. Her divorce was granted 16 Oct. 1924. Records are in Atlanta's Fulton County Courthouse. **51.** FMZ. JRM to FMZ, 30 July 1923. **52.** *GWTW*, 819. **53.** Farr, 163. **54.** Interview with FM. **55.** MMD. JRM to his family, 9 May 1924. **56.** MMD. JRM to his mother, 21 May 1924. **57.** Interview with FM. **58.** Later to be named the Georgia Power Company. **59.** MMD. JRM to his mother, 7 Sept. 1924. **60.** Interview with FM. **61.** MMD. MM to Mother Marsh, 14 Feb. 1925. **62.** UGa. Nearly all of Peggy's articles are preserved in her scrapbook. **63.** FMZ. MM to FMZ, n.d., Monday [Feb. 1925]. **64.** FMZ. MM to FMZ, n.d., Monday [Feb. 1925]. **65.** FMZ. MM to FMZ, n.d., Monday [Feb. 1925]. **66.** FMZ. MM to FMZ, n.d., Monday [Feb. 1925]. **67.** FMZ. MM to FMZ, n.d., Monday [Feb. 1925]. **68.** FMZ. MM to FMZ, n.d., Monday [Feb. 1925]. **69.** MMD. MM to Mother Marsh, 14 Feb. 1925. **70.** FMZ. MM to FMZ, n.d., Wednesday 3 p.m. [Feb. or March 1925]. **71.** FMZ. MM to FMZ, Thursday, 11 March 1925. **72.** MMD. MM to HM, n.d., Sunday morning [March 1925]. **73.** FMZ. MM to FMZ, Saturday, 7 March 1925. **74.** MMD. MM to HM, n.d., Thursday afternoon [Feb. or March 1925]. **75.** FMZ. MM to FMZ, Saturday, 7 March 1925. **76.** FMZ. MM to FMZ, n.d., Wednesday 3 p.m. [Feb. or March 1925]. **77.** FMZ. MM to FMZ, Friday, 26 Feb. 1925. **78.** FMZ. MM to FMZ, Thursday, 11 March 1925. **79.** FMZ. MM to FMZ, Thursday, 11 March 1925. **80.** FMZ. MM to FMZ, 26 Feb. 1925. **81.** FMZ. MM to FMZ, n.d., Monday a.m. [Feb. or March 1925]. **82.** FMZ. MM to FMZ, Thursday, 11 March 1925. **83.** FMZ. MM to FMZ, n.d. [Feb. or March 1925]. **84.** FMZ. MM to FMZ, Thursday, 11 March 1925. **85.** FMZ. MM to FMZ, Thursday, 11 March 1925. **86.** FMZ. MM to FMZ, Thursday, 11 March 1925. **87.** MMD. MM to HM, n.d., Thursday afternoon [Feb. or March 1925]. **88.** FMZ. MM to FMZ, n.d. [Feb. or March 1925]. **89.** MMD. MM to HM, n.d., Thursday afternoon [Feb. or March 1925]. **90.** FMZ. MM to FMZ, n.d., Monday a.m. [Feb. or March 1925]. **91.** Farr, 70. **92.** Interview with JK. **93.** The medical term for these seizures is "absent seizures." Interview with FM. Peggy reported this incident, not long after it happened, to Henry and Ben Gordon Marsh, who had gone to Atlanta to see how John was recovering. In those days, epilepsy was a dreaded, mysterious disease, which unfortunately and falsely was associated with insanity by some people. The brothers never told their mother and sisters that John had a mild form of this condition. For a long time, this secret was well kept in the family. It was not until years later when John himself, explaining to Frances why he refused to drive an automobile and disliked traveling alone, told her the truth. But his mother never knew, and fortunately, he never had an attack while in her presence. **94.** Darden Pyron in *Southern Daughter* (New York: Oxford University Press, 1991) incorrectly leads his readers to think that John suffered from narcolepsy, a condition characterized by sudden and uncontrollable attacks of deep sleep. **95.** Interviews with JK and MS. **96.** FMZ. MM to FMZ, Saturday, 28 Aug. 1926. **97.** UGa. MFP File. **98.** Interview with JK.

Chapter 6
A Writer in Progress

1. Interview with JK; a letter from Thomas Weesner, 28 May 1993. Weesner explains, "From an early period there was a cluster of small houses along the bend in the road, and just about the present Tenth Street crossing there was a wagon yard, a blacksmith shop, and several small wooden stores. This settlement became a stopping place for wagons from north Georgia. A rough lot lived along the crescent and right after the Civil War, when the suburbs of Atlanta were infested by criminals, the area became a 'hang-out' for robbers. The road was very narrow and crooked, and it became a common saying that it took a mighty tight squeeze to get through with one's life. Thus arose the name of 'Tight Squeeze' for the neighborhood." **2.** Interview with JK; telephone interviews with Mary Rose Taylor and with Tommy Jones of the Georgia Trust for Historic

Preservation. **3.** UGa. MFP's Narrative. 11. **4.** Interviews with JK and FM; also found in UGa. MB's Notes. **5.** Male reporters were paid only thirty-five dollars a week. **6.** FMZ. MM to FMZ, n.d. [late 1925 or early 1926]. **7.** FMZ. MM to FMZ, n.d., Monday Mrg. [late spring 1926]. **8.** MMD. MM to HM, n.d. [early 1927]. **9.** MMD. MM to HM, n.d., Tuesday a.m. [May or June 1926]. **10.** Interview with FM. **11.** MMD. MM to Mother Marsh, 26 June 1933. **12.** FMZ. MM to FMZ, n.d. [late 1925 or early 1926]. **13.** UGa. MFP's Narrative. 12. **14.** MMD. MM to Mother Marsh, n.d., Monday [fall 1925]. **15.** UGa. MB's Notes. **16.** MMD. MM to Mother Marsh, n.d., Monday [fall 1925]. **17.** UGa. MFP's Narrative. 11-12. **18.** Interview with JK, who said Allan Taylor's "crush" on Peggy used to annoy her but amused John and their friends. **19.** UGa. MM to Stephen Vincent Benét, 9 July 1936. **20.** UGa. MM to Stephen Vincent Benét, 9 July 1936. **21.** UGa. John's limerick and pun are in MMMP. **22.** UGa. MB's Notes. 6. **23.** EU. MM to Harvey Smith, 15 March 1933. **24.** MMD. MM to HM, n.d. [early 1926]. **25.** Interview with MMD and FM. **26.** MMD. MM to HM, n.d., Sunday night. **27.** See Darden Pyron, *Southern Daughter* (New York: Oxford University Press, 1991). **28.** Edmund Davis's telephone conversation with and letter to the author, 3 Oct. 1991. **29.** EU. Harvey Smith's note attached to MM's letter. March or April 1933. **30.** Interview with JK. **31.** EU. Harvey Smith's note attached to MM's letter. March or April 1933. **32.** Anne Edwards, *Road to Tara* (New York: Dell, 1983), 265 and throughout the text. **33.** Interview with JK. **34.** FMZ. MM to FMZ, n.d., Saturday, Jan the something [1926]. **35.** MMD. MM to HM, n.d. [early 1926]. **36.** AHC. Peggy Mitchell, "Georgia Generals: For the Stone Mountain Memorial." *AHB* 9, no. 34. 66-99. **37.** MMD. MM to Mother Marsh, n.d., Tuesday afternoon [early 1926]. **38.** MMD. MM to Mother Marsh, n.d., Tuesday afternoon [early 1926]. **39.** MMD. MM to Mother Marsh, n.d., Tuesday afternoon [early 1926]. **40.** MMD. MM to Mother Marsh, n.d., Tuesday afternoon [early 1926]. **41.** MMD. MM to Mother Marsh, n.d., Tuesday afternoon [early 1926]. **42.** MMD. MM to HM, n.d., Bennet 14 ems 8pt sun mag [early 1926]. **43.** Interview with JK. **44.** MMD. JRM to his mother, 7 Jan. 1926. **45.** MMD. MM to HM, n.d., Sunday night [1925]. **46.** Wade H. Wright, *The History of Georgia Power, 1855-1957* (Atlanta: Georgia Power Company, 1957), 221. **47.** MMD. JRM to his mother, 7 Jan. 1926. **48.** Interview with FM. **49.** Peggy's scrapbook in the Hargrett Library contains her articles. Information about Peggy's dislike for her job came from interviews with JK and MS. **50.** Interview with FM. **51.** Interview with FM. **52.** FMZ. MM to FMZ, n.d., Saturday, Jan the something [1926]. **53.** FMZ. MM to FMZ, n.d., Saturday, Jan the something [1926]. **54.** *GWTW*, 246. **55.** Pyron in *Southern Daughter* (185) takes Peggy's remark about John's needing "more sleep than any white boy I know" out of context. Without quoting any of the information that Peggy gives Frances about John's schedule and without mentioning anything about John's circumstances at work, where he was virtually holding down the workload of three men—as Peggy says and Joe Kling verifies—Pyron gives his readers a false impression of John, wrongly stating that John was narcoleptic. As everyone who ever knew him knew, John suffered from petit mal seizures, not narcolepsy. The petit mal seizures did not interfere with his work, and everyone who knew John Marsh said he was an extremely hard-working man. A person suffering from narcolepsy could not have accomplished all that John Marsh accomplished. **56.** Jane Bonner Peacock, *Dynamo Going to Waste* (Atlanta: Peachtree Publishers, 1985), 129. MM to Allen Edee, Dec. 1921. **57.** MMD. MM to HM, n.d. [spring 1926]. **58.** FMZ. MM to FMZ, n.d., Monday morning [late spring 1926]. **59.** FMZ. MM to FMZ, n.d., Monday morning [late spring 1926]. **60.** Interview with FM for Peggy's frequent expression of ill health. **61.** FMZ. MM to FMZ, Saturday, 28 Aug. 1926. **62.** MMD. MM to Mother Marsh, n.d., Monday [early 1926]. **63.** FMZ. MM to FMZ, Saturday, 28 Aug. 1926. **64.** UGa. MM to Clifford Dowdey, 29 July 1937. **65.** Interviews with JK and with MS. **66.** John's boosting Peggy's confidence and his anger about her lack of it was common knowledge among family and close friends. **67.** MFP's interview with John Marsh, "Was Margaret Mitchell Writing Another Book?" *Atlanta Journal*, 18 Dec. 1949. Interviews with John's family and coworkers. **68.** FMZ. MM to FMZ, n.d. [late 1925 or early 1926]. Darden Pyron in his *Southern Daughter* quotes several passages from this five-page, double-spaced letter but he noticeably omits Peggy's comments about John's role in getting her this work and in helping her write it. He also assigns different dates to the passages he quotes. Pyron quotes two passages from one page of this letter and documents the passages as coming from two different letters. One passage that he quotes on page 211 of his book he documents as coming from a letter he dates "April to June 1926." On page 212 of his book, he quotes from the same page of the same letter and documents it as coming from a letter dated "March to April 1925." **69.** MMD. MM to Mother Marsh, n.d., Monday [early 1926]. **70.** Interview with FM. **71.** MMD. MM to Mother Marsh, n.d., Monday [early 1926]. **72.** FMZ. FMZ's Narrative. 16. This narrative is a personal account of Frances's recollections of various events. **73.** Interview with FM. **74.** FMZ. MM to FMZ, n.d., Monday morning [late spring 1926]. **75.** AHC. William S. Howland, "Margaret Mitchell: Newspaperman," *AHB*, 9, no. 34. 55. **76.** FMZ. MM to FMZ, n.d., Monday morning [late spring 1926]. **77.** Peacock, 84. MM to Allen Edee, 26 March 1920. **78.** MMD. MM to HM, n.d., Tuesday a.m. [May or June 1926]. **79.** MMD. MM to HM, n.d, Tuesday a.m. [May or June 1926]. **80.** FMZ. MM to FMZ, 28 Aug. 1926. **81.** Interview with MMD. **82.** FMZ. MM to FMZ, n.d., Friday [Oct. 1928]. **83.** FMZ. MM to FMZ, 23 Aug. 1926. **84.** FMZ. MM to FMZ, n.d., Friday [Oct. 1928]. **85.** FMZ. MM to FMZ, n.d., Friday [Oct. 1928]. **86.** FMZ. MM to FMZ, n.d., Monday morning [late spring 1926]. **87.** FMZ. MM to FMZ, n.d., Monday morning [latespring 1926]. **88.** FMZ. MM to FMZ, n.d., Monday morning [late spring 1926]. **89.** FMZ. MM to FMZ, Saturday, 28 Aug. 1926. **90.** Peacock, 104. MM to Allen Edee, 31 July 1920. **91.** JRM's interview with the Lexington *Herald Leader* on 23 Oct. 1936. **92.** MMD. JRM to his mother, Sunday, 1 Aug. 1926. **93.** MMD. JRM to his mother, Sunday, 1 Aug. 1926. **94.** FMZ's Narrative. 7. JRM to FMZ, n.d. [1926]. **95.** FMZ. JRM to FMZ, 16 Oct. 1926. **96.** FMZ. JRM to FMZ, Sunday, 1 Aug. 1926. **97.** FMZ. MM to FMZ, n.d., Saturday, Jan the something [1926]. **98.** Interview with FM. Francesca and Ben Gordon Marsh, as newlyweds themselves, visited John and Peggy in their Crescent Avenue apartment in the spring of 1928, shortly after Peggy started work on the novel. John described to Henry this evening when he removed the cast. **99.** MMD. JRM to his family, 15 Oct. 1924. **100.** Finis Farr, in *Margaret Mitchell of Atlanta* (New York: Morrow, 1965), 76, states that MB read both of these manuscripts before destroying them at John's and Stephens's instruction. Interview with FM. **101.** According to MB, who read this manuscript, it was later destroyed in the fire that burned all the Marshes' other papers and most of the *Gone With the Wind* manuscript. **102.** Peggy finished "'Ropa Carmagin" in the form of a novella and submitted it to the Macmillan Company when she submitted the *Gone With the Wind* manuscript. The Macmillan executive Harold Latham read and praised it but rejected it because of its length. Latham gave it to his assistant editor, Lois Cole, who also praised it, saying, "It sent an authentic chill up the spine." Farr, 77, 103. John destroyed this manuscript in the fire. Also, interview with FM. **103.** Interview with FM. Sometime during that fall of 1926, John's mother and Henry's little daughter Mary made their first visit to Atlanta to see John and Peggy; they heard talk about Peggy's book, which at that time was a Jazz Age adventure story about a teenage girl. Then John's brothers, Henry and Ben Gordon, came to visit in 1927. By spring 1928, when Ben Gordon brought his bride Francesca to see the Atlanta Marshes, Peggy had written many chapters of what was later to become known as *Gone With the Wind*. In those early days, John and Peggy talked enthusiastically about their writing project. John always boasted to his family about Peggy's work. There was no secrecy about what they were doing. The secrecy that shrouded all that Peggy wrote came about much later. **104.** UGa. MM's scrapbook. **105.** Interview with FM. Francesca remembered precisely the talk about Mrs. Benning because of the analogy that John made between his mother and Mrs. Benning. When she and Ben Gordon visited John and Peggy in 1927, she said the couple was "enthralled and engrossed in the novel—and we were too!" **106.** Interview with FM. Francesca said Peggy appreciated that typewriter in the same manner another woman would appreciate being given "a full length mink coat!" **107.** Interview with FM. **108.** JRM's interview with MFP, *Atlanta Journal Magazine*, 18 Dec. 1949. **109.** Peggy often said she wrote in this manner. This fact was well known among family and friends. **110.** Interview with JK. **111.** EU. Harvey Smith's note attached to MM's letter. 23 July 1927. **112.** Pyron, in *Southern Daughter* (289ff), makes several incorrect statements concerning John's involvement in Peggy's writing of *Gone With the Wind*. Here is one example: he refers to a letter John wrote in 1931, in which John mentions his and Peggy's visiting scenes that he says are "of big events in the Civil War and in Peggy's novel." Pyron incorrectly states, "This reference is John Marsh's *first* recorded notice of his wife's novel. In all of his detailed correspondence to his sister and mother throughout the twenties he had never mentioned it before. This supports the impression that only now was Mitchell sharing her writing, even with her husband" (290). And Pyron says that "she [Peggy] *dragged* John off to nearby points of Chattanooga, Chickamauga, and Lookout Mountain" (italics mine).

Chapter 7
In the Wake of a Masterpiece

1. Finis Farr, *Margaret Mitchell of Atlanta* (New York: Morrow, 1965), 79. **2.** UGa. Bessie Jordan's "My Dear Employer, Miss Peggy." *Atlanta Journal and Constitution Magazine,* 12 Aug. 1951. **3.** Farr, 82. **4.** Interviews with FM and MMD. **5.** Farr, 87. **6.** UGa. MM to John Macleay, Liverpool, England, 23 Nov. 1936. **7.** Farr, 84. Stephens's essay appeared in 1927 in the *Bulletin,* a journal published by the Atlanta Historical Society, an organization that Eugene Mitchell helped to establish the previous year. **8.** Farr, 84. **9.** MMD. JRM to his mother, 6 May 1927. **10.** Interview with JK. **11.** Interview with JK. **12.** Interview with JK. **13.** UGa. MM to Clifford Dowdey, 29 July 1937. **14.** This is an example of the kind of important information that only Stephens Mitchell could provide when John and Peggy did not. Stephens talked to Finis Farr about Peggy's reaction to Boyd's novel. See Farr, 83. Also, Peggy mentioned her reaction to Boyd's novel in her letter to Clifford Dowdey, 29 July 1937. **15.** UGa. MM to Clifford Dowdey, 29 July 1937. **16.** UGa. MM to Clifford Dowdey, 29 July 1937. **17.** MMD. JRM to HM, 4 Aug. 1927. **18.** MMD. JRM to HM, 4 Aug. 1927. **19.** FMZ. MM to FMZ, n.d., Friday [Oct. 1928]. **20.** Interview with MS. **21.** Farr, 82. **22.** Farr, 82. **23.** FMZ. MM to FMZ, n.d., Friday [Oct. 1928]. **24.** Interviews with FM and MS. **25.** UGa. MM to Harriet Ross Colquitt, 7 Aug. 1936. **26.** Kitty and her young son were to spend only one day in Atlanta before continuing their train journey, but the child became ill and had to be hospitalized; he and Kitty stayed for nearly a month. **27.** FMZ. MM to FMZ, n.d., Friday [Oct. 1928]. **28.** FMZ. MM to FMZ, n.d., Friday [Oct. 1928]. **29.** FMZ. MM to FMZ, n.d., Friday [Oct. 1928]. **30.** FMZ. MM to FMZ, n.d., Friday [Oct. 1928]. **31.** FMZ. MM to FMZ, n.d., Friday [Oct. 1928]. Renick Marsh was born 4 Feb. 1929. **32.** FMZ. MM to FMZ, n.d., Friday [Oct. 1928]. **33.** FMZ. MM to FMZ, n.d., Friday [Oct. 1928]. **34.** Interview with JK. **35.** Interview with Deon Rutledge. **36.** Interview with Deon Rutledge. **37.** Interview with JK. **38.** Electric Railway Journal 74, no. 6. 348. **39.** MMD. JRM to his mother, Sept. 1931. **40.** Richard Harwell, *White Columns in Hollywood* (Macon, GA: Mercer University Press, 1982), 3. **41.** NYPL. MM to HSL, 9 July 1935. **42.** FMZ. JRM to FMZ, 20 Sept. 1931. **43.** Interview with MS. **44.** Interview with JK. **45.** FMZ. JRM to FMZ, 20 Sept. 1931. **46.** FMZ. JRM to FMZ, 20 Sept. 1931. **47.** MMD. JRM to his mother, 16 June 1934. **48.** MMD. MM to Mother Marsh, 19 June 1934. **49.** Interview with JK. **50.** Interview with JK. **51.** MFP, "Was Margaret Mitchell Writing Another Book?" (interview with John Marsh), *Atlanta Journal Magazine,* 18 Dec. 1949. **52.** Interview with FM. **53.** MMD. JRM to his mother, 2 Dec. 1932. **54.** Interview with MMD, who visited in this apartment as she was growing up. **55.** Peggy often spoke sympathetically about Scarlett. For examples, see MM to Astride K. Hansen, 27 Jan. 1937 (UGa.), and FMZ's narrative for "My poor Scarlett." **56.** Interview with FM. **57.** Interview with Edmund Davis. **58.** Interview with MS. **59.** Richard Harwell, ed., *"Gone With the Wind" as Book and Film* (Columbia: University of South Carolina Press, 1983), 58-59. **60.** Harwell, *"Gone With the Wind" as Book and Film,* 58-59. **61.** Harwell, *"Gone With the Wind" as Book and Film,* 58. **62.** Lois Cole's brother was a president of Amherst College and also an ambassador to Chile. Farr, 81. **63.** Harwell, *"Gone With the Wind" as Book and Film,* 57. **64.** Harwell, *"Gone With the Wind" as Book and Film,* 57. **65.** Interview with JK. **66.** Interview with JK. **67.** Interview with JK. **68.** Harwell, *"Gone With the Wind" as Book and Film,* 57. **69.** Harwell, *"Gone With the Wind" as Book and Film,* 57. **70.** Harwell, *"Gone With the Wind" as Book and Film,* 57. **71.** MMD. JRM to his mother, 15 July 1934. **72.** MMD. MM to Mother Marsh, 19 June 1934. **73.** MMD. JRM to his mother, 16 June 1934. Francesca said that she and the others knew that John and Peggy took the typewriter and sections of the manuscript, as well as some of John's business matters, with them on some of their trips home to family gatherings. John and Peggy, she said, worked on the manuscript during their leisure. She also said that is the reason why the family asked about the book regularly for so many years. They all saw evidence of the book, but they did not know much about it except that it was a Civil War novel. **74.** UGa. MM to Alexander L. May, Berlin, Germany, 18 Nov. 1938. **75.** UGa. MM to Alexander L. May, Berlin, Germany, 18 Nov. 1938. **76.** UGa. MM to Donald Adams, 6 July 1936. **77.** UGa. MM to Donald Adams, 6 July 1936. **78.** UGa. MM to Donald Adams, 6 July 1936. **79.** UGa. MM to Donald Adams, 6 July 1936. **80.** MMD. JRM to HM and MMD, 29 Sept. 1934. **81.** Wade H. Wright, *History of Georgia Power, 1855-1957* (Atlanta: Georgia Power Company, 1957), 181. In the early 1900s the expanding Georgia Power Company started building five dams and five lakes on the Tugalo, the Tallulah, and the Chattooga rivers to provide water for new hydroelectric plants. After nearly two decades, when the project was finally completed and the construction workers gone, the company refurbished some of the workmen's cabins and converted the dwellings into summer retreats for its executives. The company also maintained little company villages for its employees at each plant. In 1925, after the Terrora development was completed near Tallulah Falls, the president of Georgia Power, P. S. Arkwright, gave one such cabin to John to use for entertaining editors and others in the line of business and also to use for his personal business. **82.** MMD. JRM to HM and Mary Hunter, 29 Sept. 1934. **83.** MMD. JRM to his mother, 20 Jan. 1935. **84.** Peggy gave Caroline Miller's *Lamb in His Bosom* to John for Christmas 1933. **85.** Harwell, *"Gone With the Wind" as Book and Film*, 58. **86.** UGa. Harold Latham, "How I Found *Gone With the Wind,"* *Atlanta Journal Magazine*, n.d. 20- 22. **87.** Harwell, *"Gone With the Wind" as Book and Film*, 58. **88.** Latham, 81. **89.** Harwell, *"Gone With the Wind" as Book and Film*, 59. **90.** JRM's interview with MFP, *Atlanta Journal Magazine*, 18 Dec. 1949. **91.** JRM's interview with MFP, *Atlanta Journal Magazine*, 18 Dec. 1949. **92.** MMD. MM to Mother Marsh, 17 April 1936. **93.** Latham, 22. **94.** Latham, 20. **95.** Latham, 22. **96.** Latham, 81. **97.** Farr, 94. **98.** Latham, 22. **99.** Farr, 95. **100.** NYPL. MM to HSL, 16 April 1935. **101.** NYPL. MM to HSL, 16 April 1935. **102.** NYPL. MM to HSL, 16 April 1935. **103.** Interview with FM. **104.** NYPL. MM to HSL, 16 April 1935. **105.** Harwell, *"Gone With the Wind" as Book and Film*, 59. **106.** NYPL. MM to HSL, 9 July 1935. **107.** NYPL. HSL to MM, 15 July 1935. **108.** NYPL. HSL to MM, 15 July 1935. **109.** NYPL. MM to HSL, 17 July 1935. **110.** A writer from Como, Mississippi, Stark Young was for over twenty years an editor for the *New Republic* magazine and also for *Theater Arts*. He translated several of Anton Chekhov's plays and edited *A Southern Treasury of Art and Literature*. He is best known for his Civil War novel *So Red the Rose*, published in 1934. He died in 1963 at the age of eighty-two. After *Gone With the Wind* came out in 1936, *So Red the Rose* faded quickly into oblivion. **111.** Farr, 101-2. **112.** NYPL. HSL's memorandum, 15 July 1935. **113.** NYPL. HSL to MM, 17 July 1935. **114.** Harwell, *"Gone With the Wind" as Book and Film*, 59-60. **115.** NYPL. MM to HSL, 27 July 1935. **116.** NYPL. MM to HSL, 27 July 1935. **117.** NYPL. MM to HSL, 27 July 1935. **118.** NYPL. MM to HSL, 27 July 1935. **119.** NYPL. MM to HSL, 27 July 1935. **120.** NYPL. MM to HSL, 27 July 1935. **121.** NYPL. MM to HSL, 27 July 1935. **122.** NYPL. HSL to MM, 30 July 1935. **123.** NYPL. HSL to MM, 30 July 1935. **124.** NYPL. MM to HSL, 27 July 1935.

Chapter 8
Midwife to a Novel

1. Interview with MS. **2.** NYPL. MM to HSL, 1 Aug. 1935. **3.** NYPL. MM to HSL, 1 Aug. 1935. **4.** NYPL. MM to HSL, 1 Aug. 1935. **5.** NYPL. MM to HSL, 1 Aug. 1935. **6.** NYPL. LDC to MM, 5 Aug. 1935. **7.** NYPL. MM's telegram to HSL, 6 Aug. 1935. **8.** NYPL. MM's telegram to HSL, 6 Aug. 1935. **9.** NYPL. HSL to MM, 13 Aug. 1935. **10.** Interview with FM. **11.** This check arrived 21 Aug. 1936. Personal interview with JK, whose wife Rhoda Williams was in John's office at the time Peggy called and heard what John said. **12.** *Georgia Power Citizen*, "John and Peggy, Rhett and Scarlett," May 1984. 4. Interviews with JK and MS. **13.** NYPL. MM to HSL, 3 Sept. 1935. **14.** *Georgia Power Citizen*, "John and Peggy, Rhett and Scarlett," May 1984. 3. **15.** NYPL. MM to HSL, 3 Sept. 1935. **16.** NYPL. MM to HSL, 3 Sept. 1935. **17.** NYPL. MM to HSL, 3 Sept. 1935. **18.** UGa. MM to Captain Achmed Abdullah, 14 April 1937. **19.** UGa. MM to Captain Achmed Abdullah, 14 April 1937. **20.** UGa. MM to Captain Achmed Abdullah,

14 April 1937. **21.** Peggy often said and wrote in letters to friends that she wanted southerners to like her book and to find it correct. **22.** UGa. MM to Sara Helena Wilson, 3 Nov. 1936. **23.** Finis Farr, *Margaret Mitchell of Atlanta* (New York: Morrow, 1965), 104. **24.** UGa. MM to Sara Helena Wilson, 3 Nov. 1936. **25.** UGa. MM to Captain Achmed Abdullah, 14 April 1937. **26.** UGa. MM to Henry Steele Commager, 10 July 1936. **27.** Interview with Deon Rutledge. **28.** In answering a request from Alexander L. May, from Berlin, Germany, Peggy wrote, on 22 July 1938, the titles and authors of seventeen history books she used in writing her novel. **29.** UGa. MM to Paul Jordan-Smith, 27 May 1936. **30.** UGa. MM to Douglas S. Freeman, 13 Oct. 1936. **31.** NYPL. LDC to MM, 4 March 1936. **32.** NYPL. MM to LDC, n.d., [1936]. **33.** NYPL. JRM to LDC, 6 Feb. 1936. **34.** Interview with JK. **35.** Interviews with MS and JK. **36.** Interview with MS. **37.** Interview with FM. **38.** Farr, 109. **39.** NYPL. JRM to LDC, 13 Feb. 1936. **40.** UGa. MM to Donald Adams, 9 July 1936. **41.** UGa. MM to Donald Adams, 9 July 1936. **42.** Ralph Thompson, in his review of *Gone With the Wind* for the *New York Times*, 30 June 1936, wrote this positive comment also. "The historical background is the chief virtue of the book, and it is the story of the time rather than the unconvincing and somewhat absurd plot that gives Miss Mitchell's work whatever importance may be attached to it. How accurate this history is is for the expert to tell, but no reader can come away without a sense of the tragedy that overcame the planting families in 1865 and without a better understanding of the background of present-day Southern life." **43.** UGa. MM to Julia Collier Harris, 8 July 1936. **44.** UGa. MM to John McLeay, 23 Nov. 1936. **45.** UGa. MM to Frances Scarlett Beach, 19 Oct. 1936. **46.** UGa. MM to Harry S. Slattery, 3 Oct. 1936. **47.** UGa. MM to Frances Scarlett Beach, 19 Nov. 1936. **48.** Farr, 105. **49.** Farr, 108. Irish Brigades helped Maurice de Saxe defeat the Duke of Cumberland in 1745 in a Belgian village named Fontenoy. Legend has it that Tara in County Meath, Ireland, was the seat of ancient kings. **50.** UGa. MM to Stark Young, 29 Sept. 1936. **51.** NYPL. MM to LDC, Sunday, 3 Oct. 1935. **52.** NYPL. MM to LDC, Sunday, 3 Oct. 1935. **53.** Farr, 115. **54.** Farr, 115. **55.** JRM's interview with MFP, *Atlanta Journal Magazine*, 18 Dec. 1949. **56.** UGa. MM to Michael McWhite, 27 Jan. 1937. **57.** Richard Harwell, ed., *"Gone With the Wind" as Book and Film* (Columbia: University of South Carolina Press, 1983), 60. **58.** Farr, 108. **59.** NYPL. MM to LDC, 31 Oct. 1935. **60.** NYPL. MM to HSL, 30 Oct. 1935. **61.** NYPL. LDC to MM, 7 Nov. 1935. Rachel Field, an American author published by Macmillan, is best known for her books for children. *Hitty, Her First One Hundred Years* (1929) won her a Newberry medal in 1930. *Calico Bush* (1931), a story of a French servant girl in Maine, is considered her best work. **62.** NYPL. HSL to MM, 11 Nov. 1935. **63.** NYPL. HSL to MM, 4 Nov. 1935. **64.** NYPL. HSL to MM, 4 Nov. 1935. **65.** NYPL. HSL to MM, 4 Nov. 1935. **66.** Interview with JK. **67.** Interview with JK. **68.** Interview with JK. **69.** Interview with MS. **70.** Interview with MS. **71.** Interview with FM. **72.** NYPL. MM to LDC, 18 March 1936. **73.** NYPL. LDC's telegram to JRM, 19 Dec. 1935. **74.** NYPL. JRM's telegram to LDC, 19 Dec. 1935. **75.** NYPL. JRM's telegram to LDC, 19 Dec. 1935. **76.** Farr, 111. **77.** NYPL. MB to LDC, 7 Jan. 1936. **78.** NYPL. MB to LDC, 16 Jan. 1936. **79.** Interview with MS. **80.** NYPL. JRM to LDC, 30 Jan. 1936. **81.** NYPL. JRM to LDC, 31 Jan. 1936. **82.** NYPL. JRM to LDC, 31 Jan. 1936. **83.** NYPL. JRM to LDC, 31 Jan. 1936. **84.** NYPL. LDC to JRM, 3 Feb. 1936. **85.** NYPL. LDC to JRM, 3 Feb. 1936. **86.** MMD. JRM to his mother, 7 Feb. 1936. **87.** Interview with MS. **88.** NYPL. LDC to JRM, 13 Feb. 1936. **89.** NYPL. JRM to LDC, 9 Feb. 1936. **90.** NYPL. JRM to LDC, 9 Feb. 1936. **91.** NYPL. JRM to LDC, 9 Feb. 1936. **92.** Interview with FM. JRM told this to HM in explaining the agony that went into getting the manuscript ready for publication. **93.** NYPL. JRM to LDC, 13 Feb. 1936. **94.** NYPL. LDC to JRM, 15 Feb. 1936. **95.** NYPL. LDC to MM, 20 Feb. 1936. **96.** UGa. LDC to Miss Hutchinson, 9 March 1936. **97.** NYPL. LDC's telegram to JRM, 19 March 1936. **98.** NYPL. JRM to Mr. Putnam, June 1936. **99.** Farr, 126.

Chapter 9
A Fantastic Dream

1. MMD. JRM to his mother, 22 March 1936. **2.** John's mother lived with Henry Marsh and his family in Wilmington, Delaware, where Frances and Rollin Zane also lived. His oldest sister

Katharine Marsh Bowden and her family lived in California. Ben Gordon and Francesca lived in Clays Ferry, Kentucky. **3.** MMD. JRM to his mother, 22 March 1936. **4.** Interview with FM. **5.** Although Lois Cole's letter to Charles J. Trenkle (Macmillan Company, 2459 Prairie Ave., Chicago, IL, 10 June 1936), referring to Peggy's Macon letter, is in the Macmillan File, NYPL, Peggy's famous Macon letter is in UGa. Lois Cole sent Peggy's Macon letter to Stephens Mitchell on 10 Dec. 1964 so that he could include it in Farr's biography. It is now in UGa. **6.** NYPL. LDC to Charles J. Trenkle, Macmillan Company, Chicago, IL, 21 June and 26 June 1936. Lois quotes Peggy's letter. **7.** NYPL. LDC to Charles Trenkle, Macmillan Company, Chicago, IL, 10 June 1936. **8.** NYPL. A. J. Putnam to HSL, 15 April 1936. **9.** The London Macmillan Company was an old and highly respectable publishing house founded by the brothers David and Alexander Macmillan, who built the firm in 1843, from a bookstore they had purchased in Cambridge. Although closely connected with the parent firm, the American Macmillan was a separate business started in 1896 by George Brett, Sr. Although it had grown successfully and had published such bestsellers as *Richard Carvel*, *The Virginian*, *The Call of the Wild*, and *The Choir Invisible*, it was experiencing in 1936 the economic depression from which the entire nation was suffering. **10.** Finis Farr, *Margaret Mitchell of Atlanta* (New York: Morrow, 1965), 120. **11.** NYPL. Collins's cable to HSL, 6 May 1936. **12.** Collins's letters expressing his offers and his disappointment in not being able to acquire *GWTW*, as well as his letters regarding the misunderstanding that he had with Latham are in NYPL. **13.** Interview with MMD. **14.** NYPL. LDC to MM, 9 April 1936. **15.** NYPL. LDC to MM, 9 April 1936. **16.** NYPL. LDC to MM, 29 April 1936. **17.** NYPL. LDC to MM, 29 April 1936. **18.** NYPL. MM to LDC, 27 April 1936. **19.** NYPL. MM to LDC, 27 April 1936. **20.** NYPL. LDC to MM, 29 April 1936. **21.** NYPL. MM to LDC, 5 May 1936. **22.** NYPL. MM to LDC, 27 April 1936. **23.** NYPL. MM to LDC, 27 April 1936. **24.** NYPL. MM to LDC, 14 May 1936. **25.** NYPL. MM to LDC, 27 April 1936. **26.** NYPL. MM to LDC, 27 April 1936. **27.** NYPL. MM to LDC, 5 May 1936. **28.** NYPL. MM to LDC, 5 May 1936. **29.** Farr, 122. **30.** UGa. MM to Stephen Vincent Benét, 9 July 1936. **31.** MMD. JRM to his mother, 26 June 1936. **32.** NYPL. MM to HSL, 21 May 1936. **33.** UGa. MM to HB, 8 Feb. 1937. **34.** Farr, 127. **35.** NYPL. MM to HSL, 21 May 1936. **36.** NYPL. MM to HSL, 21 May 1936. **37.** Interview with MMD. **38.** NYPL. E. E. Hale to HSL, 18 May 1936. **39.** NYPL. HSL to E. E. Hale, 19 May 1936. **40.** NYPL. HSL to A. L. Williams, 19 May 1936. **41.** NYPL. HSL to MM, 21 May 1936. **42.** NYPL. MM to HSL, 25 May 1936. **43.** NYPL. MM to HSL, 25 May 1936. **44.** NYPL. HSL to A. L. Williams, 26 May 1936. **45.** NYPL. MM to HSL, 25 May 1936. **46.** NYPL. MM to HSL, 25 May 1936. **47.** NYPL. LDC to MM, 28 May 1936. **48.** Interview with JK. **49.** Interview with FM. **50.** FMZ. MM to FMZ, 27 May 1936. **51.** FMZ. MM to FMZ, 27 May 1936. **52.** UGa. MM to Joseph Henry Jackson, 1 June 1936. **53.** UGa. MM to HSL, 1 June 1936. **54.** FMZ. MM to FMZ, n.d. [June 1936]. **55.** NYPL. LDC to MM, 28 May 1936. **56.** NYPL. MM to LDC, 29 May 1936. **57.** NYPL. MM to GB, 6 June 1936. **58.** NYPL. Notes. **59.** NYPL. HSL to LDC, 14 June 1936. **60.** MMD. JRM to his mother, 26 June 1936. **61.** MMD. JRM to his mother, 26 June 1936. **62.** MMD. JRM to his mother, 26 June 1936. **63.** Farr, 124. **64.** NYPL. "What is believed to be a record in recent years has been established by Margaret Mitchell's *Gone With the Wind*. Although it has been published only one month printings already total 201,000 copies." Memo in *Book News*, 23 July 1936. **65.** MMD. JRM to his mother, 26 June 1936. **66.** MMD. JRM to FMZ, 1 Aug. 1936. **67.** MMD. JRM to FMZ, 1 Aug. 1936. **68.** UGa. MM to Clark Howell, 28 June 1936. **69.** MMD. JRM to his mother, 26 June 1936. **70.** UGa. MM to Julia Collier Harris, 29 June 1936. **71.** UGa. MM to Julia Collier Harris, 29 June 1936. **72.** Interview with MS. **73.** MMD. JRM to his mother, 19 July 1936. **74.** MMD. JRM to this mother, 19 July 1936. **75.** MMD. JRM to his mother, 19 July 1936. **76.** Herschel Brickell, "The Best Friend GWTW Ever Had," in *"Gone With the Wind" as Book and Film*. Ed. Richard Harwell (Columbia: University of South Carolina Press, 1983), 25. **77.** AHC. John R. Marsh, "Margaret Mitchell and the Wide, Wide World," *AHB* 9, no. 34. 35. **78.** In William Makepeace Thackeray's *Vanity Fair* 1847-1848), Amelia Sedley is a kind, gentle girl; Lord Steyne is the brutal, cynical man of the world; and Becky Sharp is the cunning, selfish, and cynical, but never bitter, heroine whom readers enjoyed seeing defeat less admirable characters. St. Elmo is in Augusta Evans's popular novel *St. Elmo* (1896). Another famous character named Amelia is the virtuous, devoted heroine in Henry Fielding's novel *Amelia* (1751). **79.** Julia Peterkin, Book of the Month Review, in *"Gone With the Wind" as Book and Film*. Ed. Richard Harwell (Columbia: University of South Carolina Press, 1983), 21. **80.** AHC. Marsh, *AHB*, 36. **81.** AHC. Marsh, *AHB*, 37. **82.** AHC. Marsh, *AHB*, 37. **83.** AHC. Marsh, *AHB*, 36. **84.** UGa. MM to Stark Young, 29 Sept. 1936. **85.** Farr, 141. **86.** AHC. Marsh, *AHB*, 34. **87.** Farr, 132. **88.** Farr, 140. **89.** NYPL. MM to LDC, 3 July 1936. **90.** NYPL. MM to LDC, 3 July 1936. **91.** MMD. JRM to his mother, 19 July 1936.

Chapter 10
Unbelievable Days

1. UGa. MM to HB, 8 July 1936. **2.** NYPL. Lois Cole's memorandum to Hutchinson, Blanton, Brett, Putnam, Beaty, 7 July 1936. "I have just had a call from John Marsh in Atlanta telling me that a copy of a letter which their cook, Bessie, wrote to the Atlanta Journal about Peggy and himself is being forwarded by Miss Baugh to someone in this office with a suggestion that it be used for publicity. He asked that we do not use this letter in any way. Of course he does not mind our reading it here, but he asks that it neither be used for publicity nor given to the salesmen to use. His point of view is quite understandable. I have promised him that the letter will not be used in any way. Will whoever receives this copy from Miss Baugh, please give it to me so that I may return it to Mr. Marsh?" **3.** Interview with JK. **4.** Interview with JK. Also MMD. JRM to HM, 29 Sept. 1934. **5.** UGa. MM to HB, 7 July 1936. **6.** UGa. MM to HB, 7 July 1936. **7.** Interview with MS. JRM instructed her to make the arrangements for the cabin to be cleaned and ready for MM when she arrived. He always had another employee, named Mr. Machine, the supervisor of the Tallulah plant, look after Peggy whenever she went there alone with Bessie. **8.** MMD. JRM to his mother, 17 July 1936. **9.** UGa. MM to HB, 7 July 1936. **10.** UGa. MM to GB, 8 July 1936. **11.** UGa. The reviews of *Gone With the Wind* are in the Hargrett Library. John's mother also kept a scrapbook of the reviews. **12.** UGa. MM to Gilbert Govan, 8 July 1936. **13.** UGa. MM to Julia Collier Harris, 8 July 1936. **14.** UGa. MM to Edwin Granberry, 8 July 1936. **15.** Edwin Granberry, "The Private Life of Margaret Mitchell," in *"Gone With the Wind" as Book and Film*. Ed. Richard Harwell (Columbia: University of South Carolina Press, 1983), 46. **16.** UGa. MM to Stephen Vincent Benét, 9 July 1936. **17.** UGa. This passage is quoted from only a draft of a letter. **18.** UGa. MM to K. T. Lowe, Time magazine, New York, 29 Aug. 1936. **19.** MMD. JRM to his mother, 26 Sept. 1936. **20.** NYPL. MM to HSL, 13 Oct. 1936. **21.** UGa. MM to Kate Duncan Smith, 24 July 1936. **22.** UGa. MM to HB, 17 Jan. 1937. **23.** Harwell, *"Gone With the Wind" as Book and Film*, 50. **24.** UGa. MM to Gilbert Govan, 8 July 1936. **25.** NYPL. LDC to JRM, 8 July 1936. **26.** NYPL. LDC to MM, 8 July 1936. **27.** Finis Farr, *Margaret Mitchell of Atlanta* (New York: Morrow, 1965), 145. **28.** UGa. JRM to MM, 15 July 1936. **29.** UGa. JRM to MM, 15 July 1936. **30.** NYPL. LDC to JRM, 11 July 1936. **31.** NYPL. JRM to LDC, 13 July 1936. **32.** NYPL. LDC to JRM, 15 July 1936. **33.** MMD. JRM to FMZ, 1 Aug. 1936. **34.** UGa. JRM to MM, 15 July 1936. **35.** UGa. JRM to MM, 15 July 1936. **36.** UGa. JRM's letter to MM, 17 July 1936. These three letters that John wrote to Peggy while she was at Blowing Rock in July 1936 are among the ones that Anne Edwards misquotes in her *Road to Tara* (New York: Dell Publishing Company, 1986), 230-32, and thus gives the wrong impression of the Marshes' relationship. **37.** UGa. Faith Baldwin, "The Woman Who Wrote *Gone With the Wind:* An Exclusive and Authentic Interview," *Pictorial Review* 38, no. 8 (March 1937), 4, 69-70, 72. **38.** UGa. JRM's letter to MM, 17 July 1936. **39.** UGa. JRM's letter to MM, 17 July 1936. **40.** MMD. JRM to his mother, 19 July 1936. **41.** Interview with FM. **42.** Julia Peterkin's review of GWTW appeared in the 12 July 1936 issue of the *Washington Post*. **43.** NYPL. Memorandum, 15 July 1936. **44.** NYPL. Marion Saunders to Macmillan, 16 July 1936. **45.** Interview with FM. During this time and thereafter, John and Peggy would occasionally telephone different members of the family, usually on Sunday evenings, to fill them in on the news. This bit about the dialects spoken in the foreign languages was a joke among those in the Marshes' circle for a while. **46.** NYPL. LDC to SM, 17 July 1936. **47.** NYPL. SM to LDC, 21 July 1936. **48.** UGa. MM to HB, 18 Sept. 1936. **49.** UGa. MM to Julia Peterkin, 26 July 1936. **50.** UGa. MM to Douglas S. Freeman, 13 Oct. 1936. **51.** UGa. MM to Thomas Dixon, 15 Aug. 1936. **52.** Farr, 142. **53.** UGa. MM to Mrs. E. L. Sullivan, 18 Aug. 1936. **54.** Interview with FM. **55.** UGa. MM to Sara Helena Wilson, 13 Nov. 1936. **56.** Farr, 159. **57.** NYPL. LDC to Jim Putnam, 27 July 1936. **58.** NYPL. JRM to Macmillan, 27 July 1936. **59.** UGa. MM to Norma Brickell, 27 July 1936. 60. UGa. MM to Stephen Vincent Benét, 23 July 1936. **61.** UGa. MM to Kate Duncan Smith, 24 July 1936. **62.** UGa. MM to HB, 9 Oct. 1936. **63.** Farr, 147. **64.** UGa. SM's Memoir. **65.** UGa. JRM to HB, 14 Aug. 1936. **66.** MMD. JRM to his mother, 12 Aug. 1936. **67.** UGa. JRM to HB, 14 Aug. 1936. **68.** UGa. JRM to HB, 14 Aug. 1936. **69.** UGa. MM to Dr. William Lyon Phelps, 23 Sept. 1936. **70.** UGa. JRM to HB, 14 Aug. 1936. **71.** MMD. JRM to FMZ, 1 Aug. 1936. **72.** Interview with FM. Also found in JRM's letter to his mother. **73.** UGa. MM to HSL, 13 Aug. 1936. **74.** Interview with FM. **75.** NYPL. SM to GB, 21 Sept. 1936. Stephens quotes Brett's letter in his own. **76.** NYPL. MM to HSL, 23 Sept. 1936. **77.** NYPL. HSL to MM, 6 Oct. 1936. **78.** NYPL. Annie Laurie's letters prove that Paramount, Metro-Goldwyn-Mayer, Universal, Columbia and Major Productions were never interested in buying *Gone With the Wind,* and RKO would not buy the story for Katharine Hepburn no matter how much Hepburn insisted on having the role of Scarlett O'Hara. Annie Laurie explained: "They felt she might not be sympathetic in the part and also that the production would be too expensive." She sent Latham the letters she had received from Mr. Costain at Twentieth-Century Fox and from Doris Warner Leroy of Warner Brothers. T. B. Costain thought that the story was not worth as much to him as Latham wanted to get for it and withdrew his offer. At the start, Macmillan had asked for one hundred thousand dollars. The daughter of one of the Warner brothers and wife of Mervin Leroy, who directed *Anthony Adverse,* Doris Warner Leroy wrote that she was terribly disappointed in the asking price for *Gone With the Wind* and found it impossible to do business at that figure. She also pointed out that *Anthony Adverse* had sold for forty thousand dollars and that she was still interested if the price came down. **79.** UGa. JRM to GB, 6 Oct. 1936. **80.** UGa. JRM to GB, 6 Oct. 1936. **81.** NYPL. JRM to Jim Putnam, 9 Oct. 1936.

Chapter 11
Reaping the Whirlwind

1. MMD. JRM to his mother, 26 June 1936. **2.** NYPL. Jim Putnam to MM, 22 April 1937. Also, NYPL. MM to Miss Hutchinson, 5 Feb. 1937. **3.** UGa. MM to HB, 6 July 1937. **4.** Interview with FM. **5.** UGa. MM to LDC, 5 March 1937. **6.** UGa. MM to HB, 10 Sept. 1936. **7.** UGa. MM to HB, 10 Sept. 1936. **8.** UGa. MM to HB, 7 July 1936. **9.** UGa. MM to HB, 17 Jan. 1937. **10.** FMZ's Narrative. 16-17. Narrative quotes JRM's letter to his sister. **11.** FMZ's Narrative. 16-17. Narrative quotes JRM's letter to his sister. **12.** MMD. JRM to his mother, 26 Sept. 1936. Interview with FM. **13.** UGa. MM to Harry S. Slattery, 3 Oct. 1936. **14.** AHC. MMMP. **15.** Interview with FM. **16.** E. I. "Buddy" Thompson, *Madame Belle Brezing* (Lexington, KY: Buggy Whip Press, 1983), 1. **17.** William M. Singerly owned the *Philadelphia Record,* a newspaper, and owned the street railway system in Philadelphia. In addition, he owned a large brick yard, lumber yard and planing mill, knitting mill, paper mill, gleaning and binder factory, theaters, commercial buildings, and over a thousand houses he had built and rented. He was the president of two banks. He owned Record Farm in Montgomery County, Pennsylvania, and several hundred acres on which he raised Holstein cattle and high-grade sheep. He loved horses, particularly trotting horses. Many charitable organizations benefited from his generosity. A Democrat, he lost his bid for governorship of the state. In early 1898, the financial empire he had built collapsed, and he died in February 1898. Notables from all over the nation sent expressions of sympathy to his family. Presidents Arthur, Cleveland, Harrison, and McKinley, many governors, senators, and other dignitaries sent messages of condolence (Thompson, 88-89). **18.** Thompson, 179. **19.** Thompson, 4. **20.** Thompson, 85. **21.** GWTW, 649-50. **22.** Thompson, 1. **23.** MMD. JRM to his family, 3 April 1937. **24.** Thompson, 2. **25.** Thompson, 2. **26.** *Washington Post,* 29 Sept. 1936. **27.** Richard Harwell, ed., *"Gone With the Wind" as Book and Film,* (Columbia: University of South Carolina Press, 1983), 58. **28.** Interview with MS. **29.** UGa. MM to Harry Slattery, 3 Oct. 1936. **30.** Interview with JK. **31.** UGa. MM to Dr. Thomas H. English, 11 July 1936. **32.** UGa. MM to Dr. Thomas H. English, 11 July 1936. **33.** NYPL. HSL to MM,

15 Oct. 1936. **34.** NYPL. Order form to insure and return MS to MM. 15 Oct. 1936. **35.** UGa. MM to HB, 8 Dec. 1936. **36.** NYPL. GB memo to department heads, 15 Oct. 1936. **37.** FMZ. JRM to FMZ, 1 Aug. 1936. **38.** MMD. JRM to his mother, 26 Sept. 1936. **39.** MMD. JRM to his mother, 26 Sept. 1936. **40.** NYPL. MM to LDC, 23 April 1937. **41.** NYPL. MM to Jim Putnam, 22 April 1937. **42.** UGa. MM to Sam Doerflinger, Thanksgiving Day, 1936. **43.** UGa. MM to HB, 28 June 1937. **44.** UGa. MM to HB, 28 June 1937. **45.** UGa. MM to HB, 20 Oct. 1937. **46.** AHC. John R. Marsh, "Margaret Mitchell and the Wide, Wide World," *AHB* 9, no. 34. 34. **47.** Finis Farr, *Margaret Mitchell of Atlanta* (New York: Morrow, 1965), 161. **48.** NYPL. News Release, 10 Oct. 1936. **49.** UGa. MM to HB, 9 Oct. 1936. **50.** UGa. MM to HB, 13 Nov. 1936. **51.** *Atlanta Constitution*, 9 Nov. 1936. **52.** NYPL. HSL to MM, 7 Oct. 1936. **53.** NYPL. MM to HSL, 13 Oct. 1936. **54.** Farr, 168-69. **55.** MMD. MM to Mother Marsh, 29 Nov. 1936. **56.** MMD. MM to Mother Marsh, 29 Nov. 1936. **57.** UGa. MM to HB, 22 Oct. 1936. **58.** Farr, 162. **59.** UGa. MM to HB, 9 Oct. 1936. **60.** UGa. MM to John Macleay, *Liverpool Daily Post*, Liverpool, England, 23 Nov. 1936. **61.** UGa. MM to HB, 9 Oct. 1936. **62.** *GWTW*, 820. Also Farr, 162-63. **63.** Charles E. Wells, "The Hysterical Personality and the Feminine Character: A Study of Scarlett O'Hara." *Comprehensive Psychiatry* 17 (1976): 353-59. Also in Harwell, "*Gone With the Wind as Book and Film*," 114-23. **64.** UGa. MM to Astride K. Hansen, 27 Jan. 1937. **65.** UGa. MM to Dr. Charles E. Mayos, 22 Aug. 1936. **66.** FMZ's Narrative. **67.** Ronald Haver, *David O. Selznick's "Gone With the Wind"* (New York: Bonanza, 1986), iv. **68.** UGa. MM to R. W. Bingham, 23 Feb. 1937. **69.** UGa. MM to Jackson P. Dick, Jr., 16 Feb. 1937. **70.** UGa. MM to Rev. R. W. Burns, 14 June 1937. **71.** UGa. MM to Very Rev. Mons. Jas. H. Murphy, 4 March 1937. **72.** UGa. MM to Very Rev. Mons. Jas. H. Murphy, 4 March 1937. **73.** UGa. MM to HB, 9 Oct. 1936. **74.** Munnerlyn was Peggy's middle name and the name of her ancestors on her paternal grandmother's side of the family. **75.** UGa. MM to HB, 13 Nov. 1936. **76.** UGa. MM to HB, 13 Nov. 1936. **77.** UGa. MM to HB, 13 Nov. 1936. **78.** UGa. MM to Georgia D. Trader, 18 Nov. 1936. **79.** NYPL. Memorandum from LDC to MM, 7 Dec. 1936. **80.** MMD. JRM to his mother, 25 Nov. 1936. **81.** MMD. JRM to his mother, 25 Nov. 1936. Renny is Renny Marsh, Ben Gordon and Francesca's son. **82.** UGa. MM to HB, 22 Oct. 1936. **83.** UGa. MM to HB, 22 Oct. 1936. **84.** UGa. MM to HB, 22 Oct. 1936. **85.** NYPL. JRM to Jim Putnam, Dec. 1936. **86.** Interview with FM. **87.** Farr, 173. **88.** NYPL. MM to LDC, 5 March 1937. **89.** NYPL. MM to LDC, 5 March 1937. **90.** NYPL. MM to LDC, 5 March 1937. **91.** Interview with JK. **92.** JRM to Mary Louise Nute, 14 Dec. 1936. **93.** Farr, 175. **94.** NYPL. MM to LDC, 4 Dec. 1936.

Chapter 12
Publicity, Pirates, and Power

1. MMD. JRM to his mother, 17 Jan. 1937. **2.** MMD. MM to Mother Marsh, 14 Jan. 1937. **3.** MMD. JRM to his mother, 17 Jan. 1937. **4.** MMD. MM to Mother Marsh, 14 Jan. 1937. **5.** MMD. JRM to his mother, 17 Jan. 1937. **6.** MMD. JRM to his mother, 17 Jan. 1937. **7.** UGa. MM to Mabel Search, 2 April 1937. **8.** Interview with Deon Rutledge. **9.** UGa. Granberry's draft and John's thirteen pages of notes are in MMMP. **10.** This law is the Feld Crawford Trade Act 1935, Laws of New York, Chapter 976. **11.** NYPL. *New York Herald Tribune*, 29 March 1937. **12.** Finis Farr, *Margaret Mitchell of Atlanta* (New York: Morrow, 1965), 232-33. UGa. MB's Notes. **13.** UGa. MM to HB, 22 Feb. 1937. **14.** UGa. MM to HB, 8 April 1937. **15.** UGa. MM to HB, 18 Feb. 1937. **16.** UGa. MM to HB, 8 April 1937. **17.** UGa. MM to Mabel Search, 4 March 1937. **18.** UGa. MM to Mabel Search, 23 Feb. 1937. **19.** In the *New York Daily Worker*, 29 Oct. 1936, David Platt wrote: "The film must be stopped. The Klan must not ride again. Send your protest to Selznick International Pictures, Hollywood, to make sure that it doesn't." **20.** Ronald Haver, *David O. Selznick's "Gone With the Wind"* (New York: Bonanza, 1986), 17. **21.** Haver, 17. **22.** UGa. MM to HB, 8 April 1937. **23.** Interview with MS. **24.** MMD. JRM to his mother, 6 May 1938. From May 1936 to the time JRM wrote this letter in May 1938, the Georgia Power Company and seventeen other southern power companies had been involved in a lawsuit against the TVA in the United States District Court for the Eastern District of Tennessee. Basing their case on broad constitutional grounds, the power companies tried to enjoin the TVA from the generation, distribution, and sale of electric power in the areas the companies served. The District Court denied the injunction, and the power companies subsequently appealed to the United State Supreme Court, which affirmed the judgment of the lower court in January 1939. As a result of the Supreme Court's decision, several companies serving the same areas as TVA went under, having had no alternative but to sell their electric properties to the TVA. But Georgia Power held its own grounds because, prior to the Court's decision, it had made some peaceful adjustments with the North Georgia Electric Membership Corporation, a rural electric cooperative fostered by the TVA. **25.** MMD. JRM to his mother, 24 April 1937. **26.** W. J. Stuckey, *The Pulitzer Prize Novels: A Critical Backward Look* (Norman: University of Oklahoma Press, 1966), 107. **27.** Edward Wagenknecht, *Cavalcade of the American Novel* (New York, 1952), 424-26. **28.** UGa. MM to HB, 9 May 1937. **29.** MMD. MM to Dear Family, 21 June 1937. **30.** UGa. MM to HB, 9 May 1937. **31.** Interview with FM. **32.** UGa. MM to President Nicholas Murray Butler, Columbia University, 8 May 1937. **33.** UGa. MM to Hendrick Willem Van Loon, 5 May 1937. **34.** NYPL. MM to GB, 10 May 1937. **35.** Farr, 189. That capsule also contained magazines, newspapers, a World Almanac, newsreels of Franklin D. Roosevelt, a Miami fashion show, copies of the Lord's Prayer in 300 languages, and a variety of timely articles, including a telephone, a can opener, a lady's hat, a wristwatch, a package of cigarettes, and a slide rule. The capsule is not to be opened until 6939. **36.** Farr, 178. **37.** MMD. MM to "Dear Family," 21 June 1937. **38.** UGa. MM to HB, 6 July 1937. **39.** UGa. MM to HB, 11 June 1937. **40.** Interview with JK. **41.** UGa. MM's letters to Edna Daniel. **42.** UGa. MM to HB, 25 May 1938. **43.** UGa. MM to Dr. Henry C. Link, 23 July 1941. **44.** Keith Runyon, "Mr. Mitchell Remembers Margaret," in *"Gone With the Wind" as Book and Film*. Ed. Richard Harwell (Columbia: University of South Carolina Press, 1983), 76-82. **45.** Interview with FM. **46.** MMD. JRM to his mother, 25 July 1937. **47.** MMD. MM to Mother Marsh, 26 June 1933. **48.** UGa. MM to HB, 9 Sept. 1937. **49.** UGa. MM to Louie Morris, 24 May 1937. **50.** NYPL. MM to GB, 2 March 1937. **51.** UGa. MM to HB, 28 May 1937. **52.** UGa. MM to Louis Davent Bolton, 22 July 1937. **53.** UGa. MM to HB, 28 May 1937. **54.** UGa. MM to LDC, 5 March 1937. **55.** UGa. MM to HB, 28 May 1937. **56.** UGa. Howard E. Reinheimer to Mitchell & Mitchell, Esqs., 28 July 1937. **57.** UGa. MM to GB, 24 Sept. 1937. **58.** An expression John used in discussing with Henry his and Peggy's first round of foreign copyright problems. Interview with MMD. **59.** NYPL. SM to GB, 23 April 1937. **60.** UGa. MM to Joseph Henry Jackson, 15 Feb. 1938. **61.** MMD. JRM to his mother, 2 Sept. 1937. **62.** MMD. JRM to his mother, 25 July 1937. **63.** The background of this case had to do with the United States not seeing fit to join the international Berne Convention for the Protection of Literary and Artistic Works. In the late nineteenth century, a group of authors and artists started a movement securing an international union of nations that would protect authors' rights. This movement resulted in what became known as the Berne Convention, because the countries convened at Berne (Bern), Switzerland, on 9 September 1886. The union was important because it was the first worldwide, multilateral copyright treaty in history and required a country entering into the agreement to give foreign authors the same kind of protection it gave its own authors. Only fourteen countries in 1886 chose to join the union; America and the Soviet Union did not choose to join. Because it was not a member, America could without risk of penalty have foreign books translated and published. But that also meant that American books were free in other countries; American authors were not protected in other countries. Mark Twain was only one author who suffered bitterly from having his works pirated. In order to be protected, American authors' works had to be published simultaneously in the States and in some other country that was a member of the Berne Convention. As a result, many Americans were able to have their books published in Canada, which was a member. Nevertheless, publishers in many other countries were continuing the publication of American books without paying authors' rights because they wanted to force America to join the Berne Convention. **64.** Merle Curti, Richard H. Shryock, Thomas C. Cochran, and Fred H. Harrington, *An American History* (New York: Harper & Brothers, 1950), 408-10. **65.** UGa. JRM to Dr. Wallace McClure, Jan. 1939. **66.** MMD. Newsclippings, 8 Dec. 1937, attached to JRM's letter to his mother, 9 Dec. 1937. **67.** UGa. MM to Willie Snow Ethridge, 10 March 1938. **68.** UGa. Dr. Wallace McClure to SM, 16 Nov. 1937. **69.** UGa. Box Number 156.

Folder Heading 156.1. Residentiebode, The Hague, June 1, 1939. **70.** UGa. MM to Dr. Wallace McClure, 9 Oct. 1939. **71.** Farr, 234. **72.** UGa. MM to HB, 25 May 1938. **73.** UGa. MM to HB, 25 May 1938. **74.** Farr, 189. **75.** UGa. MM to HB, 25 May 1938. **76.** UGa. MM to Charles Smith, 12 June 1937. **77.** UGa. MM to Stark Young, 21 July 1938. **78.** UGa. MM to Katharine Brown, 16 Mar. 1938. **79.** Interview with MS. **80.** Farr, 193. **81.** MMD. JRM to his mother, 29 May 1938. **82.** MMD. MM to Mother and Katharine, 21 June 1937. **83.** UGa. MM to HB, 14 April 1938. **84.** UGa. MM to HB, 14 April 1938. **85.** MMD. JRM to his mother, 29 May 1938. **86.** UGa. MM to HB, 3 May 1938. **87.** UGa. MM to HB, 14 April 1938. **88.** UGa. MM to HB, 14 April 1938. **89.** UGa. MM to HB, 14 April 1938. **90.** UGa. MM to HB, 6 May 1938. **91.** UGa. MM to HB, 25 May 1938. **92.** UGa. MM to HB, 25 May 1938. **93.** UGa. MM to Helen Dowdey, 16 Sept. 1938. **94.** UGa. MM to HB, 16 May 1938.

Chapter 13
Making the Movie

1. UGa. MM to Katharine Brown, 6 Oct. 1936. **2.** Interview with MS. **3.** Interview with FM. **4.** UGa. MM to Katharine Brown, 13 July 1938. **5.** UGa. MM to Katharine Brown, 13 July 1938. **6.** UGa. MM to Katharine Brown, 13 July 1938. **7.** FMZ. JRM to FMZ, 1 Aug. 1936. **8.** Ronald Haver, *David O. Selznick's "Gone With the Wind"* (New York: Bonanza, 1986), 9. **9.** Haver, 9. **10.** Haver, 11. **11.** Haver, 28. **12.** Haver, 4. **13.** Judy Cameron and Paul J. Christman, *The Art of "Gone with the Wind": The Making of a Legend* (New York: Prentice Hall, 1989), 37. **14.** Haver, 4. **15.** Haver, 4. **16.** Cameron, 35. **17.** Cameron, 35. **18.** UGa. MM to Sidney Howard, 21 Nov. 1936. **19.** UGa. MM to Sidney Howard, 21 Nov. 1936. **20.** UGa. MM to Sidney Howard, 21 Nov. 1936. **21.** Interview with FM. **22.** UGa. MM to Sidney Howard, 21 Nov. 1936. **23.** UGa. MM to Sidney Howard, 21 Nov. 1936. **24.** UGa. Sidney Howard to MM, 1 Dec. 1936. **25.** Interview with MS. **26.** UGa. Both drafts are in MMMP. **27.** UGa. MM to Russell Birdwell, 21 Nov. 1936. This letter is signed by Peggy but a draft of the letter shows that John wrote it for her, as he wrote many other letters for her. **28.** UGa. MM to Russell Birdwell, 5 Dec. 1936. Also signed by Peggy, but draft in John's handwriting. **29.** MMD. MM to Mother Marsh, 29 Nov. 1936. **30.** Cameron, 225. **31.** Haver, 5. **32.** UGa. MM to Sidney Howard, 4 Jan. 1937. **33.** JRM to Anne Bowden, n.d. [probably around early April 1937]. **34.** UGa. *Atlanta Constitution*, 7 April 1937. **35.** FMZ. JRM to FMZ, n.d. The first two pages of this letter are missing, but the date is probably April 1937. **36.** Finis Farr, *Margaret Mitchell of Atlanta* (New York: Morrow, 1965), 184-85. **37.** Farr, 185. **38.** MMD. JRM to his mother, 17 Jan. 1937. **39.** UGa. MM to Leslie Howard, 30 Jan. 1939. **40.** Richard Harwell, *White Columns in Hollywood* (Macon, GA: Mercer University Press, 1982), 10-11. UGa. MM to Wilbur Kurtz, 16 Dec. 1938. **41.** Interview with FM. **42.** Haver, 15. **43.** Haver, 15. **44.** Harwell, *White Columns in Hollywood*, 9-10. **45.** Harwell, *White Columns in Hollywood*, 10. **46.** UGa. MM to Sidney Howard, 8 Oct. 1937. **47.** UGa. MM to Sidney Howard, 11 Oct. 1937. **48.** UGa. MM to HB, 12 Aug. 1938. **49.** Harwell, *White Columns in Hollywood*, 74. **50.** UGa. MM to HB, 4 Nov. 1937. **51.** Farr, 187. **52.** Harwell, *White Columns in Hollywood*, 2. **53.** Harwell, *White Columns in Hollywood*, 13. **54.** UGa. MM to HB, 12 Aug. 1938. **55.** Harwell, *White Columns in Hollywood*, 5. **56.** UGa. MM to HB, 14 April 1938. **57.** UGa. MM to Katharine Brown, 8 March 1937. **58.** AHS. Wilbur G. Kurtz Papers. Also, Cameron, 114. **59.** Harwell, *White Columns in Hollywood*, 167. **60.** UGa. MM to Katharine Brown, 16 March 1938. **61.** UGa. MM to Katharine Brown, 16 March 1938. **62.** UGa. MM to Katharine Brown, 16 March 1938. **63.** Harwell, *White Columns in Hollywood*, 8. **64.** Cameron, 73. **65.** Harwell, *White Columns in Hollywood*, 14. **66.** Cameron, 56-62. **67.** Farr, 170-71. **68.** Haver, 4. **69.** Haver, 4. **70.** Haver, 17. **71.** Alexander Walker, *Vivien: The Life of Vivien Leigh* (New York: Weidenfeld & Nicholson, 1987), 84-86. **72.** Walker, 86. **73.** Walker, 113. **74.** AHC. Wilbur Kurtz's Journal entry for 10 Dec. 1938. Also, Cameron, 64. **75.** Haver, 24. **76.** MMD. JRM to his mother, 31 Jan. 1939. John made his comment about Selznick's publicity stunt to his family and to his colleagues at work in publicity. **77.** Cameron, 37. **78.** UGa. MM to David O. Selznick, 14 Jan. 1939. **79.** UGa. MM to Vivien Leigh, 30 Jan. 1939. **80.** UGa. MM to David O. Selznick, 30 Jan. 1939. **81.** UGa. MM to Susan Myrick, 10 Feb. 1939. **82.** UGa. MM to Helen and Clifford Dowdey, 22 Aug. 1938. **83.** UGa. MM to Helen and Clifford Dowdey, 22 Aug. 1938. **84.** UGa. MM to Helen and Clifford Dowdey, 22 Aug. 1938. **85.** UGa. MM to Katharine Brown, 13 Aug. 1937. **86.** UGa. MM to Dr. Mark Allen Patton, 11 July 1936. **87.** Harwell, *White Columns in Hollywood*, 88. **88.** UGa. MM to Katharine Brown, 31 Jan. 1939. **89.** Susan Myrick was born in Baldwin County, Georgia, 20 Feb. 1893; she died on 4 Sept. 1978 in Macon and was buried in Milledgeville, Georgia. **90.** Harwell, *White Columns in Hollywood*, 87. **91.** Harwell, *White Columns in Hollywood*, 126, 166. **92.** Harwell, *White Columns in Hollywood*, 128. **93.** Harwell, *White Columns in Hollywood*, 129. **94.** Harwell, *White Columns in Hollywood*, 20. **95.** Harwell, *White Columns in Hollywood*, 50. **96.** Harwell, *White Columns in Hollywood*, 88. **97.** Harwell, *White Columns in Hollywood*, 126. **98.** Walker, *Vivien: The Life of Vivien Leigh*, 114. **99.** UGa. MM to Susan Myrick, 10 Feb. 1939. Also Harwell, *White Columns in Hollywood*, 166-67. **100.** Harwell, *White Columns in Hollywood*, 167. **101.** Harwell, *White Columns in Hollywood*, 167. **102.** UGa. MM to Susan Myrick, 10 Feb. 1939. **103.** UGa. MM to Harry E. Ransford, 4 Jan 1937. **104.** UGa. MM to Jere Moore, 16 Feb. 1939. **105.** Cameron, 121. **106.** UGa. MM to Annetta I. Clark, Smith College, 4 March 1939. **107.** UGa. MM to Annetta I. Clark, Smith College, 4 March 1939. **108.** MMD. JRM to his mother, 16 April 1939. **109.** Harwell, *White Columns in Hollywood*, 90. **110.** Harwell, *White Columns in Hollywood*, 88. **111.** UGa. Susan Myrick to MM, 9 April 1939. **112.** UGa. MM to Susan Myrick, 17 April 1939. **113.** UGa. MM to Susan Myrick, 17 April 1939. **114.** Harwell, *White Columns in Hollywood*, 105-6. **115.** Harwell, *White Columns in Hollywood*, 166. **116.** Harwell, *White Columns in Hollywood*, 127. **117.** Harwell, *White Columns in Hollywood*, 128. **118.** UGa. David O. Selznick to MM, 24 Jan. 1939. **119.** UGa. MM to David O. Selznick, 30 Jan. 1939. **120.** Haver, 11-12. **121.** UGa. MM to Susan Myrick, 10 Feb. 1939. **122.** Harwell, *White Columns in Hollywood*, 14. **123.** Harwell, *White Columns in Hollywood*, 239. MM to Susan Myrick, 17 April 1939. **124.** Harwell, *White Columns in Hollywood*, 240. **125.** Harwell, *White Columns in Hollywood*, 240. **126.** Cameron, 210. **127.** Farr, 195. **128.** MMD. JRM to his mother, 4 Aug. 1939. **129.** MMD. JRM to his mother, 4 Aug. 1939. **130.** MMD. JRM to his mother, 5 Sept. 1939. **131.** Farr, 3. **132.** MMD. JRM to his mother, 22 Nov. 1939. **133.** MMD. JRM to his mother, 22 Nov. 1939. **134.** UGa. MM to GB, 12 May 1939. **135.** Cameron, 225. **136.** Cameron, 229. **137.** Cameron, 229. **138.** Farr, 2. **139.** Interview with FM. Peggy described this scene to John's family. Also Farr, 8. **140.** *Atlanta Journal Magazine*, 18 Dec. 1949. Thinking that this incident was truly funny, Peggy related it to John's family and to friends. **141.** Harold Martin, "Atlanta's Most Brilliant Event," *Atlanta Georgian*, 16 Dec. 1939. *"Gone With the Wind" as Book and Film.* Ed. Richard Harwell (Columbia: University of South Carolina Press, 1983), 149. **142.** Interview with FM and MS. **143.** Harwell, *"Gone With the Wind" as Book and Film*, 149. **144.** Interview with MS.

Chapter 14
Patriotic Volunteer

1. MMD. JRM to his mother, 15 Jan. 1940. **2.** MMD. JRM to his mother, 15 Jan. 1940. **3.** UGa. MM to Virginius Dabney, 23 July 1942. **4.** UGa. MM to Virginius Dabney, 23 July 1942. **5.** UGa. MM to Virginius Dabney, 23 July 1942. **6.** UGa. MM to Virginius Dabney, 23 July 1942. **7.** MMD. JRM to his mother, 15 Jan. 1940. **8.** MMD. JRM to his mother, 20 Dec. 1939. **9.** MMD. JRM to his mother, 15 Jan. 1940. **10.** MMD. JRM to his mother, 15 Jan. 1940. **11.** MMD. MM to Mother Marsh, 28 March 1940. **12.** MMD. MM to Mother Marsh, 28 March 1940. **13.** MMD. JRM to his mother, 29 March 1940. **14.** MMD. MM to "Dear Family," 22 March 1940. **15.** MMD. JRM to his mother, 29 March, 1940. **16.** MMD. JRM to his mother, 29 March 1940. **17.** MMD. JRM to his mother, 29 March 1940. **18.** MMD. JRM to his mother, 29 March 1940. **19.** UGa. JRM to GB, 28 Aug. 1939. **20.** UGa. JRM to GB, 28 Aug. 1939. **21.** UGa. JRM to GB, 7 Nov. 1939. **22.** UGa. JRM to GB, 7 Nov. 1939. **23.** UGa. GB to MM, 27 March, 1940. **24.** Nell Battle, "Scarlett Materializes," *Raleigh News,* 18 Feb. 1940. *"Gone With the Wind" as Book and Film.* Ed. Richard Harwell (Columbia: University of South Carolina Press, 1983), 170-74. **25.** UGa. MM to Nell Battle Lewis, 15 March 1940. **26.** MMD. JRM to his family, "Dear Folks," 17 June 1940. **27.** Finis Farr, *Margaret Mitchell of Atlanta* (New York: Morrow, 1965), 204. **28.** Farr, 204-7. **29.** FMZ's Papers; Interview with Henry Marsh's daughter, Jane Dieckmann, 3 May 1993.

30. UGa. MM to Ellen Glasgow, 11 Nov. 1940. **31.** UGa. MM to Ellen Glasgow, 11 Nov. 1940. **32.** MMD. JRM to his mother, 17 Nov. 1940. **33.** MMD. JRM to his mother, 17 Nov. 1940. **34.** MMD. JRM to his mother, 15 Oct. 1940. **35.** UGa. MM to HB, 11 Nov. 1940. **36.** MMD. JRM to his mother, 11 May 1944. **37.** "Margaret Mitchell Visits Here," *Daily Independent* (Maysville, Kentucky), 17 Nov. 1940. **38.** Farr, 203-4. **39.** *"Gone With the Wind* Author, Husband Are Visitors in City," Lexington, Kentucky, *Herald*, 29 Nov. 1940. **40.** MMD. JRM to his mother, 4 Feb. 1941. **41.** Farr, 209-10. **42.** UGa. MM to Wallace McClure, 8 Aug. 1940. **43.** UGa. Main Library, Government Files. Stephens Mitchell's statement to a Joint Subcommittee of the Committee on Foreign Relations and the Judiciary Committee of the Senate with Respect to the Universal Copyright Convention and to S. 2559. **44.** UGa. Main Library, Government Files. Also UGa. JRM to GB, 24 June 1940. **45.** UGa. MM to Wallace McClure, 16 Aug. 1940. **46.** UGa. MM to Wallace McClure, 8 Aug. 1940. **47.** UGa. MM to Wallace McClure, 22 July 1939. **48.** MMD. JRM to his mother, 17 June 1940. **49.** MMD. JRM to his mother, 17 June 1940. **50.** MMD. JRM to his mother, 17 June 1940. **51.** MMD. JRM to his mother, 4 Feb. 1943. **52.** MMD. JRM to his mother, 4 Feb. 1943. **53.** UGa. MM to Wallace McClure, 27 Sept. 1941. **54.** Interview with FM. **55.** MMD. MM to Mother Marsh, 27 July 1943. **56.** MMD. MM to Mother Marsh, 27 July 1943. Also Farr, 211. **57.** UGa. MM to Leodel Coleman, 23 Aug. 1943. **58.** UGa. MM to Leodel Coleman, 23 Aug. 1943. **59.** Farr, 213. **60.** UGa. MM to GB, 9 June 1941. **61.** UGa. MM to Lieutenant Commander E. John Long, 23 June 1941. **62.** UGa. MM to Leodel Coleman, 15 Dec. 1942. **63.** MMD. MM to Mother Marsh, 6 Oct. 1942. **64.** UGa. MM to Sgt. Bill Mauldin, 14 May 1945. **65.** MMD. JRM to his mother, 19 Dec. 1941. **66.** UGa. MM to Lt. K. H. Kalmback, USNR, 7 March 1941. **67.** UGa. MM to Lt. K. H. Kalmback, USNR, 7 March 1941. **68.** UGa. MM to Captain and Mrs. S. P. Jenkins, 26 Dec. 1941. **69.** UGa. MM to Leodel Coleman, 27 April 1943. **70.** MMD. JRM to his mother, 23 Jan. 1943. **71.** UGa. MM to Ensign S. A. Martin, 18 March 1943. **72.** UGa. MM to Clifford Dowdey, 13 May 1943. **73.** UGa. JRM to Dr. Frank J. Ostenasek, 18 May 1943. **74.** UGa. MM to Leodel Coleman, 27 April 1943. **75.** UGa. MM to Clifford and Helen Dowdey, 21 April 1943. **76.** UGa. JRM to Dr. Frank L. Ostenasek, 18 May 1943. **77.** UGa. JRM to Dr. Dandy, 8 June 1943. **78.** UGa. JRM to Dr. Dandy, 8 June 1943. **79.** UGa. JRM to Dr. Dandy, 16 July 1943. **80.** UGa. JRM to Dr. Dandy 16 July 1943. **81.** MMD. MM to Mother Marsh, 27 July 1943. **82.** UGa. Dr. Walter Dandy to MM, 17 Jan. 1944. **83.** UGa. MM to Wallace McClure, 13 Dec. 1943. **84.** UGa. MM to Wallace McClure, 12 May 1943. **85.** MMD. JRM to his mother, 21 Oct. 1943. **86.** UGa. MM to Leodel Coleman, 31 May 1943. **87.** UGa. MM to Leodel Coleman, 31 May 1943. **88.** UGa. MM to Leodel Coleman, 31 May 1943. **89.** UGa. MM to Leodel Coleman, 31 May 1943. **90.** UGa. MM to Leodel Coleman, 20 July 1943. **91.** UGa. MM to Leodel Coleman, 11 Sept. 1943. **92.** UGa. MM to Leodel Coleman, 11 Sept. 1943. **93.** UGa. G. M. Kobernat, Associate Warden, Atlanta Federal Penitentiary, 13 Nov. 1950. **94.** Notes on prisoners' letters are in UGa. **95.** Ronald Haver, *David O. Selznick's "Gone With the Wind"* (New York: Bonanza, 1986), 79. **96.** Haver, 79. **97.** UGa. Jessica M. Silsby to MM, 30 Oct. 1943. **98.** UGa. MM to Jessica M. Silsby, 3 Nov. 1943. **99.** UGa. One cruiser was named for the Marine Sergeant Clyde Thomason and the other for Lieutenant Julian Jordon who died at Pearl Harbor. **100.** MMD. JRM to his mother, 4 March 1944. **101.** UGa. MM to Leodel Coleman, 24 Feb. 1944. **102.** MMD. MM to Mother Marsh, 23 Feb. 1944. **103.** UGa. MM to Leodel Coleman, 17 May 1944. **104.** MMD. JRM to his mother, 24 June 1944. **105.** MMD. JRM to his mother, 24 June 1944. **106.** UGa. MM to Leodel Coleman, 8 Aug. 1944. **107.** UGa. Article in newspaper file.

Chapter 15
Reality of the Dark Dreams

1. FMZ. JRM to FMZ, 24 Sept. 1945. Also *Atlanta Journal Magazine*, 14 Dec. 1947. 7. **2.** FMZ. JRM to FMZ, 24 Sept. 1945. Also *Atlanta Journal Magazine*, 14 Dec. 1947. 7. **3.** *Atlanta Journal Magazine*, 14 Dec. 1947. 6. **4.** UGa. MM to Dr. W. B. Burke, 14 May 1947. **5.** UGa. MM to Dr. W. B. Burke, 14 May 1947. **6.** FMZ's Narrative. **7.** FMZ's Narrative. **8.** FMZ. JRM to FMZ, 24 Sept. 1945. **9.** FMZ. JRM to FMZ, 24 Sept. 1945. **10.** UGa. *Atlanta Journal*, 17 Aug. 1949. **11.** FMZ. JRM to FMZ, 5 Dec. 1945. **12.** *Atlanta Journal Magazine*, 14 Dec. 1947. 6. **13.** FMZ's

Narrative. **14.** *Atlanta Journal Magazine*, 14 Dec. 1947. **15.** UGa. MB's Notes, 4. **16.** FMZ's Narrative. **17.** UGa. MB's Notes, 18-A. **18.** Finis Farr, *Margaret Mitchell of Atlanta* (New York: Morrow, 1965), 219. **19.** Farr, 219. **20.** MMD. JRM to his mother, 1 April 1947. **21.** FMZ's Narrative. **22.** UGa. MB's Notes, 17, 24. **23.** UGa. MM to GB, 8 April 1940. **24.** UGa. MM to Seamen J. Ed Manget and Mackie McCrorey, 21 July 1945. **25.** FMZ. JRM to FMZ, 24 Sept. 1945. **26.** MMD. JRM to his mother, 23 Oct. 1945. **27.** MMD. JRM to his mother, 5 Dec. 1945. **28.** Farr, 216. **29.** Farr, 216. **30.** UGa. MM to Mr. and Mrs. Alfred Lunt, 11 Nov. 1941. **31.** UGa. MM to Mr. and Mrs. Alfred Lunt, 11 Nov. 1941. **32.** Interview with FM. **33.** Interview with FM. **34.** UGa. MM to LDC, 8 March 1945. Drs. Greer and Towson were John's physicians in Brunswick. **35.** UGa. JRM to Edna Daniel, 15 Nov. 1950. **36.** Interview with FM. **37.** Interview with FM. UGa. MFP's Narrative. 38. Medora related this incident to Henry and Ben Gordon Marsh. This incident is incorrectly described and incorrectly documented in Anne Edwards's *Road to Tara* (New York: Dell Publishing Company, 1986), 316. **38.** Farr, 217. **39.** MMD. MM to Mother Marsh and family, n.d. [spring 1946]. **40.** Interview with FM. **41.** UGa. MB's Notes. **42.** UGa. JRM to Edna Daniel, 15 Nov. 1950. **43.** FMZ. JRM to FMZ, 23 April 1946. For the Maysville history buffs, here are John's questions: "What was on the corner of Second and Market Streets, directly south of Mr. Jimmy Wood's drug store? Going out Lexington Street toward the Flemingsburg Pike, was there anything but trees and farm land between the John Hall place and Watkins Pond? The house across the street from us where the Slacks lived was later bought by a countryman whose name was Bramble, I think. He had two buxom daughters, Hazel and May, I believe, and a son. Somebody lived in the house between the Slacks and Brambles. I feel like I ought to know the answer to this one but it just won't seem to come back to me." **44.** FMZ. JRM to FMZ, 23 April 1946. **45.** MMD. JRM to his mother, 7 Oct. 1946. **46.** UGa. MM to Helen Dowdey, 14 Feb. 1947. **47.** MMD. JRM to his mother, 3 July 1947. **48.** UGa. JRM to Edna Daniel, 19 Feb. 1951. **49.** UGa. MM to Helen Dowdey, 14 Feb. 1947. **50.** UGa. JRM to GB, 23 Nov. 1947. **51.** MMD. JRM to his mother, 3 July 1947. **52.** MMD. JRM to his mother, 11 Sept. 1947. **53.** UGa. JRM to Edna Daniel, 22 Dec. 1950. **54.** UGa. JRM to Edna Daniel, 15 Nov. 1950. **55.** UGa. JRM to Margaret Cate, 30 May 1947. **56.** FMZ's Narrative. **57.** MMD. JRM to Mary Hunter Marsh, 16 Oct. 1946. This is a note attached to his letter to his mother. **58.** MMD. JRM to his mother, 26 March 1947. **59.** MMD. JRM to his mother, 3 July 1947. **60.** MMD. JRM to his mother, 30 May 1947. **61.** UGa. MB's Notes. **62.** UGa. MM to Wallace McClure, 7 Jan. 1949. **63.** UGa. MM to Wallace McClure, 7 Jan. 1949. **64.** UGa. MM to Mrs. Ira Henry, 29 April 1947. **65.** UGa. MM to Helen Dowdey, 4 Sept. 1947. **66.** MMD. JRM to his mother, 11 Sept. 1947. **67.** MMD. JRM to his family, 12 May 1949. **68.** MMD. JRM to his family, 12 May 1949. **69.** Farr, 220. Also SM's Memoir. **70.** Farr, 226. **71.** Farr, 226. **72.** Farr, 226-27. **73.** MMD. JRM to his mother, 31 Jan. 1949. **74.** UGa. MB's Answers to LDC's Questions Re Farr Biography. **75.** MMD. JRM to his mother, 22 March 1949. **76.** Interview with FM. **77.** UGa. MM to Granville Hicks, 7 Feb. 1949. **78.** NYPL. MM to HSL, 2 July 1949. **79.** NYPL. MM to HSL, 12 July 1949. **80.** UGa. MM to HB, 1 Aug. 1939. 81. UGa. Onlookers at the scene of the accident gave the account of the scene to the Marsh brothers. The details of the accident, the subsequent events, and the funeral were reported in John's conversations with brothers and in a letter to his family. They were also reported in newspaper accounts and in the court records of the trial that convicted the drunken, off-duty taxi operator. All of John's notes on the funeral arrangements are in the Margaret Mitchell Marsh Papers. **82.** Interview with JK. **83.** Farr, 228. **84.** UGa. JRM's notes on final accident. Interview with FM. **85.** Farr, 228. **86.** Farr, 229. **87.** UGa. Final Accident File. Also, interview with FM. **88.** Farr, 229-30. **89.** UGa. JRM's penciled note titled "P.'s Last Illness," 27 Aug. 1949. 90. Mrs. Frank W. Troost, daughter of Katharine Marsh Bowden, John Marsh's oldest sister, wrote to me on 18 Nov. 1987: "My mother destroyed almost all of her letters before she died. Peggy and John had a thing about that and had asked her to destroy their letters." **91.** UGa. MB's Notes, 4. **92.** UGa. MB's Notes. **93.** MMD. JRM to his mother, 19 Sept. 1949. **94.** UGa. JRM to Bob, 18 Oct. 1951. **95.** FMZ's Narrative. **96.** FMZ's Narrative. **97.** Interview with Sam Tupper. **98.** UGa. *Atlanta Constitution*, 23 Nov. 1949. **99.** MMD. JRM to his mother, 22 Nov. 1949. **100.** UGa. Newsclipping. **101.** MMD. Newsclipping from scrapbook. **102.** FMZ's Narrative. **103.** UGa. *Atlanta Journal*, 6 May 1952. **104.** UGa. MB's Notes.

INDEX

A

Acorn Cottage. *See* Brickell, Herschel
African Americans. *See* blacks
Alderman, Grace (typist of GWTW book)
    xiv, 217, 230–231, 233
Allen, Hervey 304
American Booksellers Association 358
Anderson, Mary 392
Anderson, Sherwood 250
Anderson, W.T. 400
Anthony Adverse (Allen) 248, 304, 538
l'Apache dance 76
Arkwright, P.S. 182, 221, 230, 343, 435
Asasno 350
Atlanta 53, 54, 57–58, 99, 185, 351, 396–
    398, 401–402, 425, 508
    GWTW film enthusiasm 340, 383, 391–
    393, 419–428
Atlanta Constitution 54, 55, 76, 95, 271, 359,
    393, 412, 424, 425, 452, 480
Atlanta Federal Prison 465–466, 506, 507
Atlanta Historical Society 168, 268, 452, 499
Atlanta Journal xiii, 27, 39, 54, 75, 76, 78,
    94, 96, 97, 99, 101, 102–103, 104, 109,
    130, 142, 143, 151, 158, 163, 186, 191,
    194, 255, 263, 264, 267, 268, 277, 281,
    285, 291, 293, 406, 496, 501, 506, 517
    See also Mitchell, Margaret: journalism
    career
Atlanta Municipal Auditorium 58, 425
Atlanta Public Library 7, 509
Atlanta Women's Press Club 403, 421, 425–
    426
An Authentic History of the Ku Klux Klan,
    1865–1877 (Davis, S.) 366

B

Baldwin, Faith 330–331, 355
Ball, Lamar Q. 331–332, 333, 334, 359
Bates, Dorothy "Dot" 58, 87, 254
Baugh, Margaret 3–4, 232-233, 262, 281,
    300, 310, 314, 341, 343, 354, 423, 432,
    462, 483, 490, 491, 494, 496–497, 499,
    506, 509, 511, 512, 515, 516, 523
Benét, Stephen Vincent 133, 171, 257, 287,
    296, 301, 304
Berne Convention Agreement of 1886 371,
    372, 375, 377
Birdwell, Russell 390–391, 410, 422
blacks 57, 205–206, 356–357, 388, 396, 414,
    423, 425, 449, 488
Blanton, Alec 420, 437

Boehm, Julian 244, 427–428
boll weevil 57, 94, 99
Book-of-the-Month Club 252, 255, 259
Borglum, Gutzon 104, 138
Bowden, Katharine. *See* Marsh, Katharine
Boyd, James 170
Branch, Harlee 95, 104
Brett, George P. Jr. 307, 326, 353, 360–361,
    369, 373, 420, 436, 437, 471, 479, 490,
    508
Brett, George P. Sr. 252, 307, 508
Brezing, Belle 49, 83, 144, 317–319, 444
Brickell, Herschel 272, 282–283, 290, 301,
    303, 304, 306, 314–315, 333, 358, 363,
    366, 463, 468
Broun, Heywood 361, 407
Brown, Katharine "Kay" 5, 302, 385, 387,
    388, 390–393, 395, 404, 421
    GWTW film 349, 385, 387, 388, 400
    relationship with Margaret Mitchell 386,
    391
"buckwheat people" 13, 37, 526
Bundsman, Tony 349, 392
Butler, Rhett (fictional character) 25, 83–85,
    283, 286, 318, 336, 385, 386, 403

C

Cabell, James Branch 441, 442
Cadwalader, Wickersham, and Taft 302,
    368, 503
Caldwell, Erskine 400
Capp, Al 454
Carr, Eugene 3, 354, 509
Catholic Church 337. *See also* Mitchell,
    Margaret: religion
Cease Firing (Johnston) 31, 170, 219
Civil War 30, 31, 37, 38, 138–139, 161, 167–
    168, 170–171, 178, 259, 366–367, 397–
    398, 427, 441
    southern obsession with 284, 407
    See also Mitchell, Margaret: Civil War
Cleckley, Dr. Hervey 107
Coffin Award 168
Cohen, Major John S. 194–195
Cole, Lois Dwight 213, 232
    friendship with Margaret Mitchell 229, 285
    GWTW involvement 190–192, 195–196,
    202, 208, 251, 253, 281, 291–292,
    295, 302, 342, 420, 537
Coleman, Leodel 457, 463–464, 469
Commager, Henry Steele 219, 257, 273

H

J

James, William 491
Johnston, Mary 31, 170, 219
Jordan, Bessie xiv, 359, 360, 488, 499, 506, 508, 515, 516
  after Margaret Mitchell's death 3, 499
  cook and housekeeper 151, 180, 203, 282, 284, 295
  Gone with the Wind business 257, 260, 281, 300
Journal. See Atlanta Journal and Mitchell, Margaret: journalism career
Junior League
  charity ball before premiere 77, 421, 423, 425
  rejects Margaret Mitchell 75–77

K

Keeler, O.B. 9, 101
Kennedy, Frank (fictional character) 203, 208, 244, 336
Kercheval, John 38
Kern, Hal 417
Keyes, Evelyn
  cast as Suellen O'Hara 422
Keyser, Kay 425
Kling, Joe xiii, 74, 83, 101, 183, 507, 516
Kling, Rhoda Williams xiii, 230, 262, 424, 505, 516
Korda, Alexander 404
Ku Klux Klan 13, 200, 207, 539
Kurtz, Annie Laurie Fuller 401, 407, 410, 419
Kurtz, Wilbur 401–402

L

Latham, Harold 503
  editorial role 208, 256–257
  reactions to manuscript 198–199, 203–205, 206–207, 229–230
  relationship with Margaret Mitchell 208, 251, 306
  role in GWTW film rights 260–262, 266, 302
  visits Atlanta 195–199, 256–257, 359, 360
lawsuits 366–369, 371, 373, 374–375, 496
Leigh, Vivien
  cast as Scarlett O'Hara 404–405, 406, 410, 422, 423, 431
Lewis, Sinclair 390
Lexington Leader 11, 15, 48–49, 50, 53, 319
Lilenthal, David 357

Littauer, Kenneth 331, 350
Loew's Grand Theater 427, 431
Lombard, Carole 422, 423, 425
Lorimer, Graeme 332
Louisville Courier-Journal 338, 363, 382

M

Macmillan Publishing Company
  film rights 260–262, 266, 289–290, 307–309
  GWTW book 267, 275, 276–277
  London Macmillan 252, 536
  price wars 353
  publicity 255–256, 266, 291, 340, 344, 537
  relationship with Marshes 238, 262, 309, 326, 436–437, 490
  scouts South 195–196
  Toronto Macmillan 375
  See also Latham, Harold *and* Cole, Lois
Macon Telegraph
  "Straight from Hollywood" columns 400, 402, 409
Mammy (fictional character) 26, 206, 338, 357, 397, 432
Margaret Mitchell Law. *See* GWTW book: influence on public policies and regulations
Margaret Mitchell Library 509
Margaret Mitchell Memorial Pavillion 507
Margaret Mitchell Safety Council. *See* Georgia Safety Council
Marsh family 43, 179, 188–189, 439–441, 443, 532. *See also* Round Robin letters
Marsh, Ben Gordon (John's brother) ix, 22, 40, 41, 43, 175–179, 262, 263, 484, 508, 513
Marsh, Frances (John's sister) 40–41, 43, 62, 88–89, 151, 177, 263
  relationship with John 12, 51, 53, 75, 78, 86, 95
  relationship with Margaret Mitchell 62
  visiting Atlanta 75, 80–81, 111, 154, 484, 512–513
Marsh, Francesca Renick (John's sister-in-law) ix–xi, 83, 175–178, 262–263, 363, 484, 513, 525
Marsh, Henry (John's brother) 40, 41, 43, 47, 527
  helps support mother and Frances 75, 78, 171–172, 529
  relationship with John Marsh 47, 81
  relationship with Margaret xii, 135
  visits Atlanta 120, 363–364, 484, 508, 527
  work 364

ABOUT THE AUTHOR

In 1985, Marianne Walker was asked to give a talk on *Gone With the Wind* for the Kentucky Humanities Council. She had never read the novel and had very little interest in it, but when she learned that John Marsh, the husband of author Margaret Mitchell, was from nearby Maysville, Kentucky, she decided to look further into the subject, hoping to find some new information to spice up her presentation.

Walker's search led her all over Kentucky, then much of the rest of the country. Beginning with Marsh's 83-year-old sister-in-law, Francesca Renick Marsh, she interviewed many people who were close to the couple and found newspaper clippings, photographs, telegrams, and, most importantly, 200 never-before-published letters from Mitchell and Marsh to their family and friends. The result of this research is this book.

Marianne Walker has also written for the New York Times Book Review and the Louisville Courier-Journal. She is a professor of English and philosophy at the University of Kentucky/Henderson Community College, where she has taught for seventeen years. A graduate of St. Mary's Dominican College in New Orleans, she received her M.A. from the University of Evansville in Indiana in 1976.